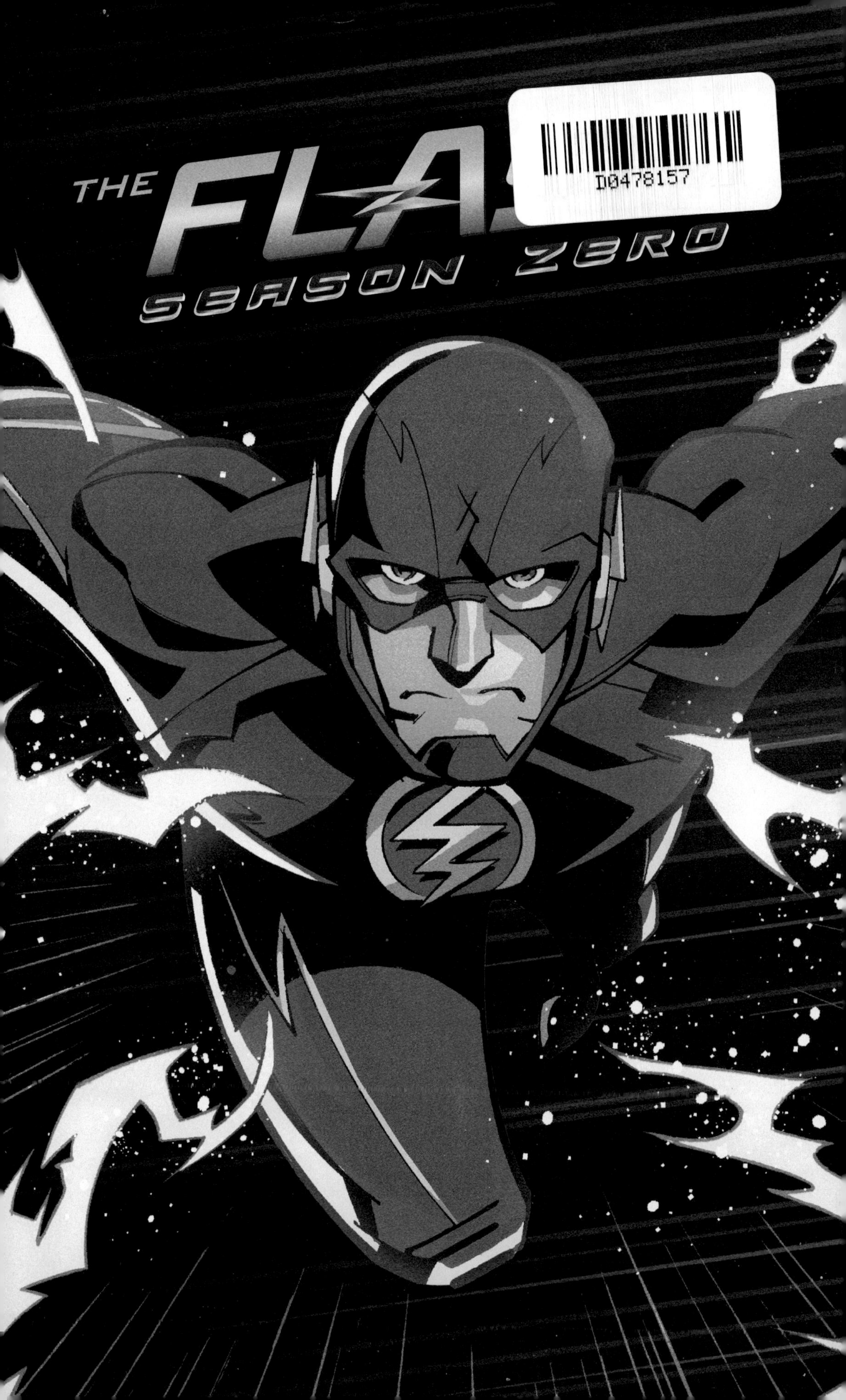
THE
SEASON ZERO

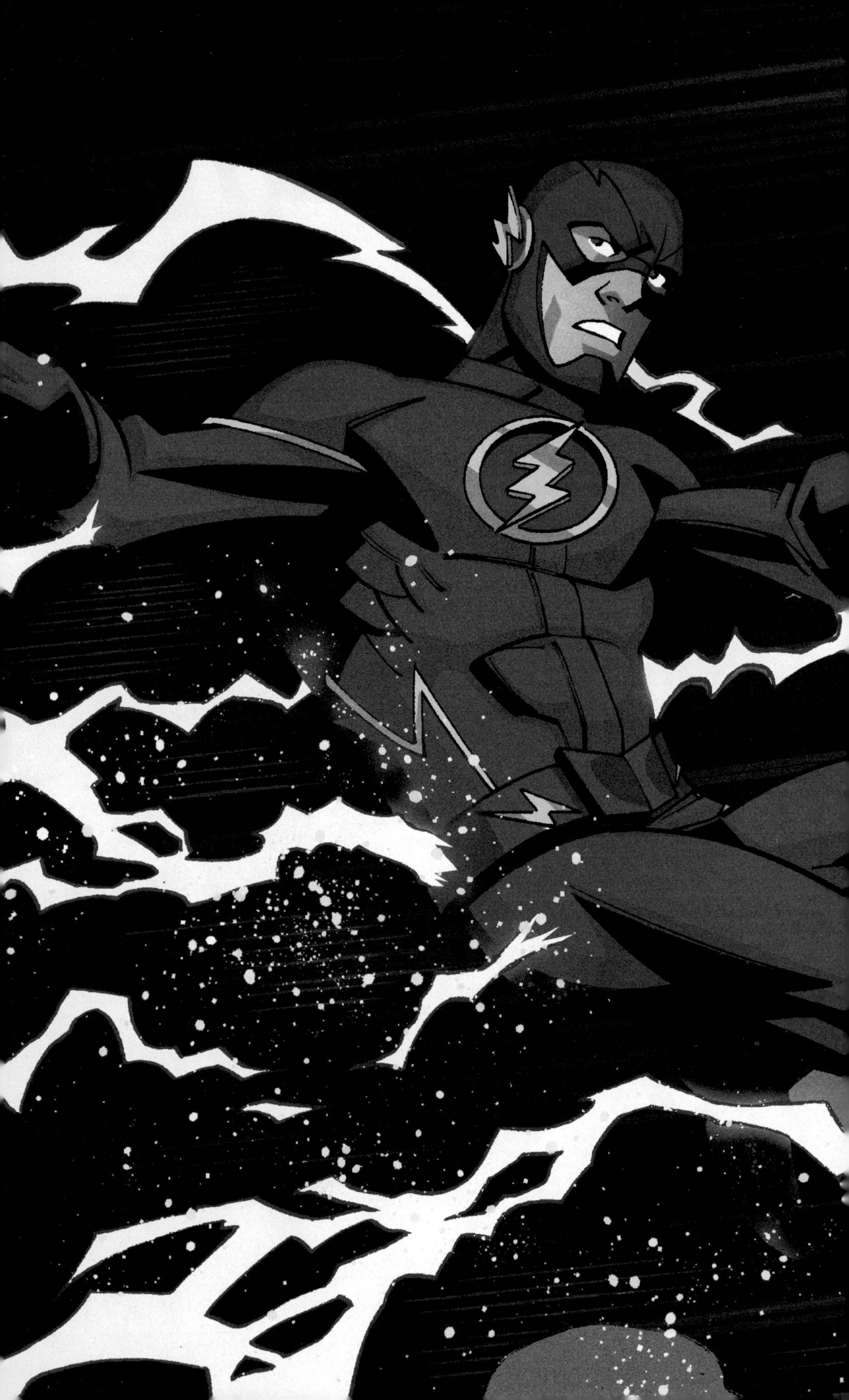

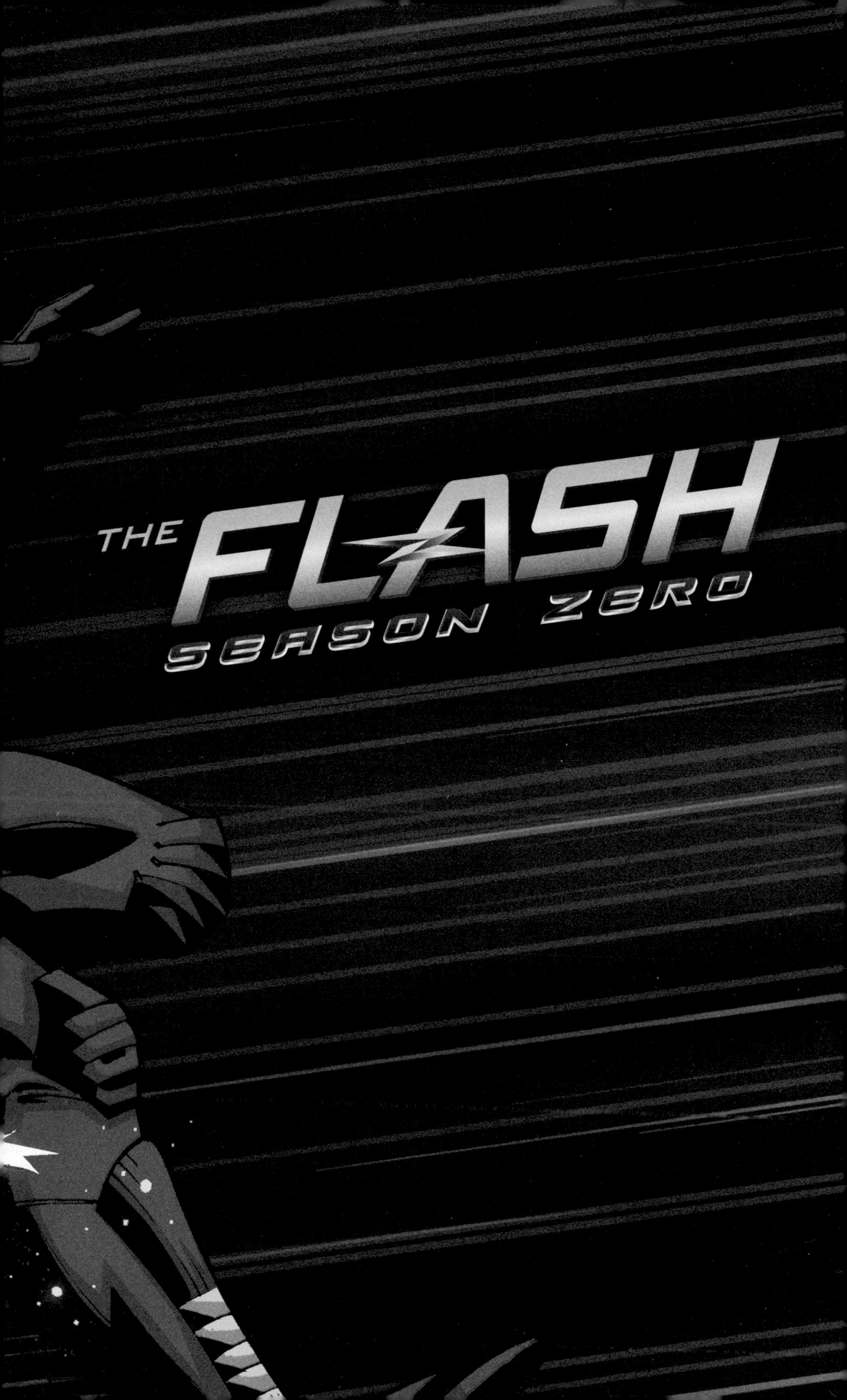
THE FLASH
SEASON ZERO

ALEX ANTONE Editor – Original Series
BRITTANY HOLZHERR Assistant Editor – Original Series
ROBIN WILDMAN Editor
JEB WOODARD Group Editor – Collected Editions
SARABETH KETT Publication Design

BOB HARRAS Senior VP – Editor-in-Chief, DC Comics

DIANE NELSON President
DAN DIDIO and JIM LEE Co-Publishers
GEOFF JOHNS Chief Creative Officer
AMIT DESAI Senior VP – Marketing & Global Franchise Management
NAIRI GARDINER Senior VP – Finance
SAM ADES VP – Digital Marketing
BOBBIE CHASE VP – Talent Development
MARK CHIARELLO Senior VP – Art, Design & Collected Editions
JOHN CUNNINGHAM VP – Content Strategy
ANNE DEPIES VP – Strategy Planning & Reporting
DON FALLETTI VP – Manufacturing Operations
LAWRENCE GANEM VP – Editorial Administration & Talent Relations
ALISON GILL Senior VP – Manufacturing & Operations
HANK KANALZ Senior VP – Editorial Strategy & Administration
JAY KOGAN VP – Legal Affairs
DEREK MADDALENA Senior VP – Sales & Business Development
DAN MIRON VP – Sales Planning & Trade Development
NICK NAPOLITANO VP – Manufacturing Administration
CAROL ROEDER VP – Marketing
EDDIE SCANNELL VP – Mass Account & Digital Sales
SUSAN SHEPPARD VP – Business Affairs
COURTNEY SIMMONS Senior VP – Publicity & Communications
JIM (SKI) SOKOLOWSKI VP – Comic Book Specialty & Newsstand Sales

THE FLASH: SEASON ZERO

DC Comics, 4000 Warner Blvd., Burbank, CA 91522
A Warner Bros. Entertainment Company.
Printed by RR Donnelley, Owensville, MO, USA. 7/31/15. First Printing.

ISBN: 978-1-4012-5771-2

Library of Congress Cataloging-in-Publication Data

Kreisberg, Andrew, 1971- author.
The Flash season zero / Andrew Kreisberg, writer ; Phil Hester and
Marcus To, artists.
    pages cm
  ISBN 978-1-4012-5771-2 (paperback)
1. Graphic novels. I. Hester, Phil, 1966- illustrator. II. To, Marcus,
illustrator. III. Flash (Television program) IV. Title.
  PN6728.F478K74 2015
  741.5'973—dc23
                                    2015012139

FREAK SHOW p.7
Story: **Andrew Kreisberg**
Script: **Brooke Eikmeier & Katherine Walczak**
Pencils: **Phil Hester**
Inks: **Eric Gapstur**

SMOAK SIGNALS p.87
Story: **Andrew Kreisberg & Marc Guggenheim**
Script: **Andrew Kreisberg**
Art: **Marcus To**

KING SHARK p.107
Story: **Andrew Kreisberg**
Script: **Kai Yu Wu & Lauren Certo**
Pencils: **Phil Hester**
& Eric Gaspur (p. 157-166)
Inks: **Eric Gapstur**

BLACK STAR p.187
Script & Pencils: **Phil Hester**
Inks: **Eric Gapstur**

DAY IN THE LIFE p.197
Script: **Ben Sokolowski**
Art: **Marcus To**

ICE AND FIRE p.207
Script: **Andrew Kreisberg & Lauren Certo**
Pencils: **Phil Hester**
Inks: **Eric Gapstur**

MELTING POINT p.227
Script: **Sterling Gates**
Art: **Ibrahim Moustafa**

Colors: **Kelsey & Nick Filardi**
Letters: **Deron Bennett**

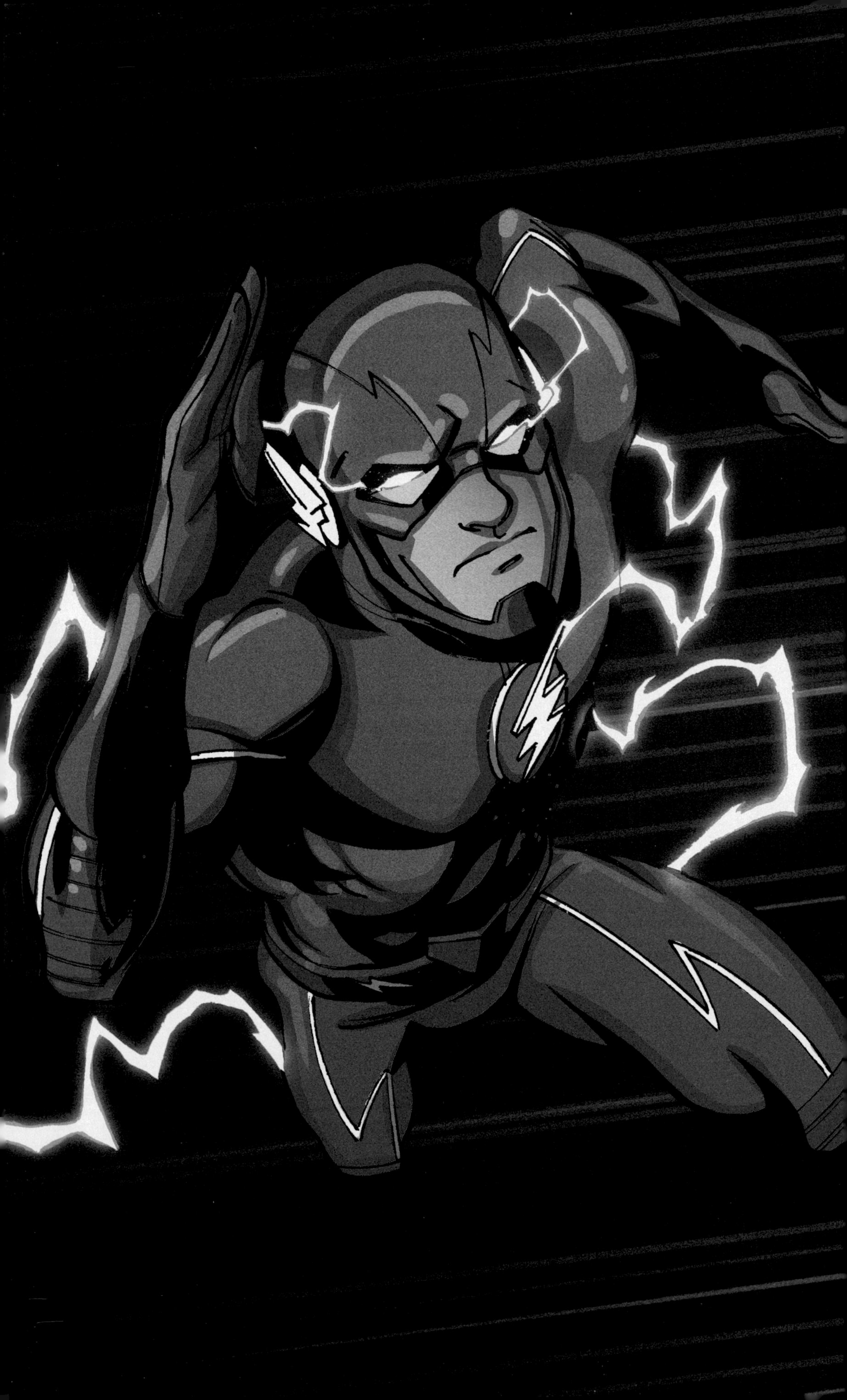

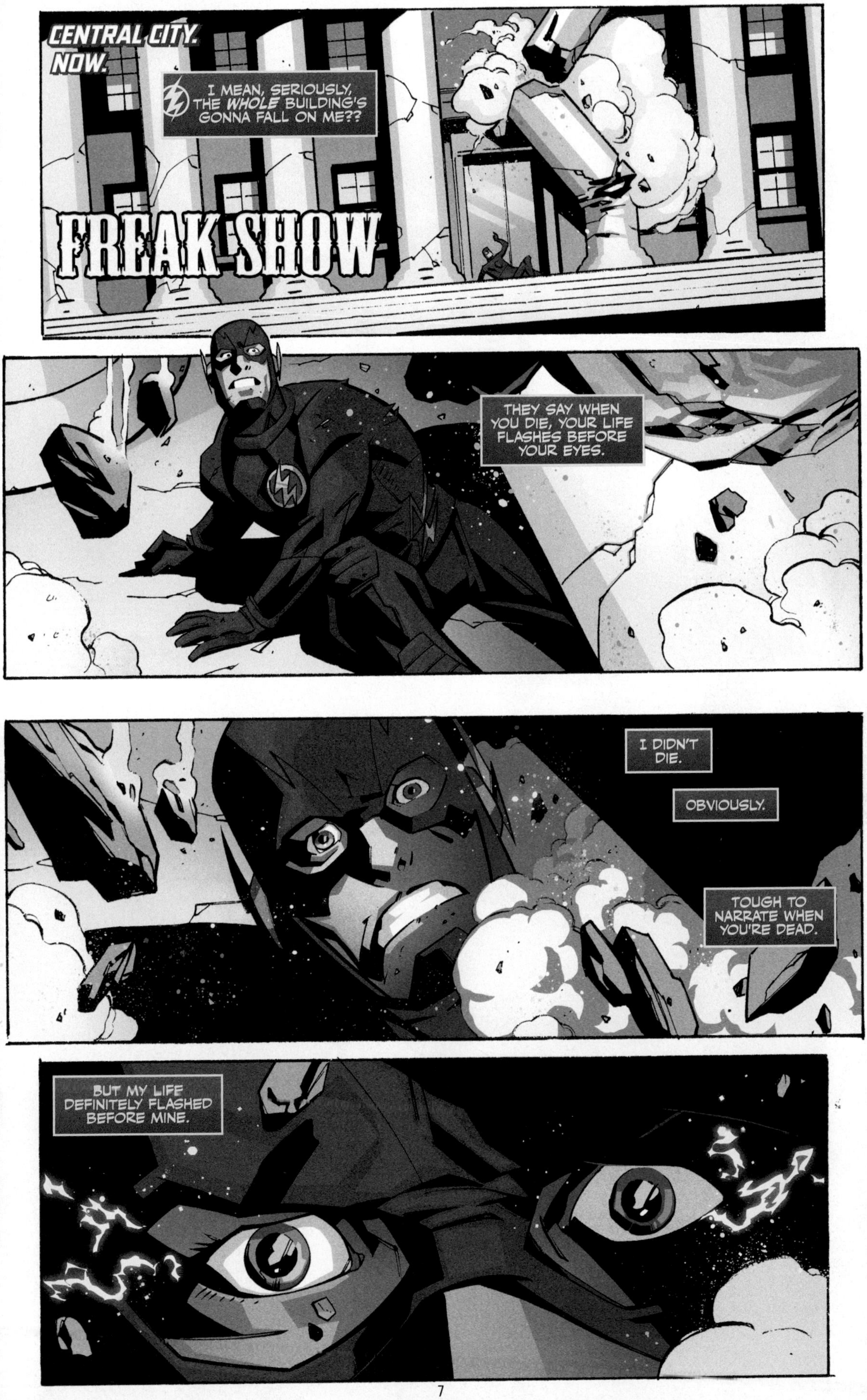
CENTRAL CITY. NOW.
I MEAN, SERIOUSLY, THE WHOLE BUILDING'S GONNA FALL ON ME??
FREAK SHOW
THEY SAY WHEN YOU DIE, YOUR LIFE FLASHES BEFORE YOUR EYES.
I DIDN'T DIE.
OBVIOUSLY.
TOUGH TO NARRATE WHEN YOU'RE DEAD.
BUT MY LIFE DEFINITELY FLASHED BEFORE MINE.

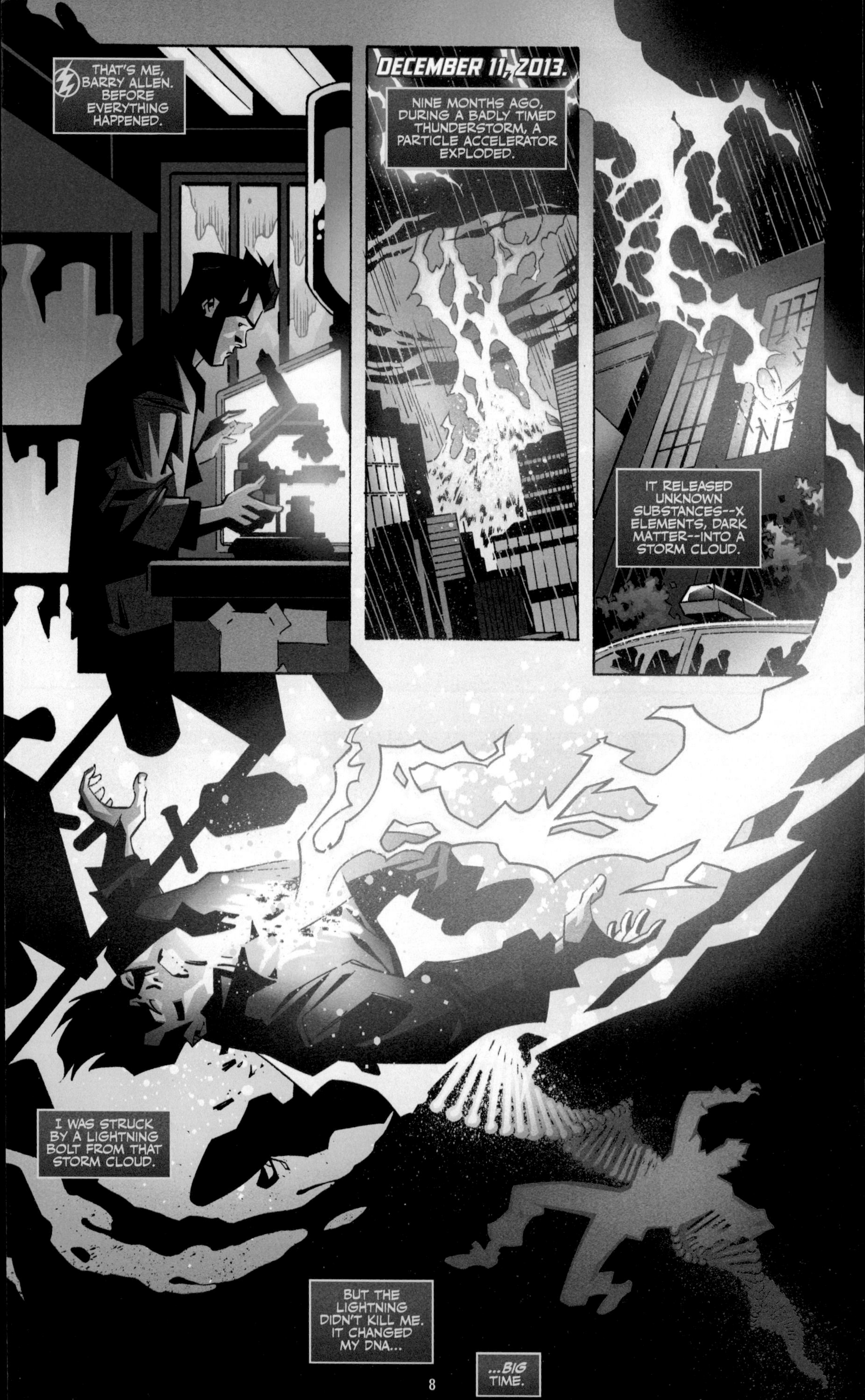
THAT'S ME, BARRY ALLEN. BEFORE EVERYTHING HAPPENED.
DECEMBER 11, 2013.
NINE MONTHS AGO, DURING A BADLY TIMED THUNDERSTORM, A PARTICLE ACCELERATOR EXPLODED.
IT RELEASED UNKNOWN SUBSTANCES--X ELEMENTS, DARK MATTER--INTO A STORM CLOUD.
I WAS STRUCK BY A LIGHTNING BOLT FROM THAT STORM CLOUD.
BUT THE LIGHTNING DIDN'T KILL ME. IT CHANGED MY DNA...
...BIG TIME.

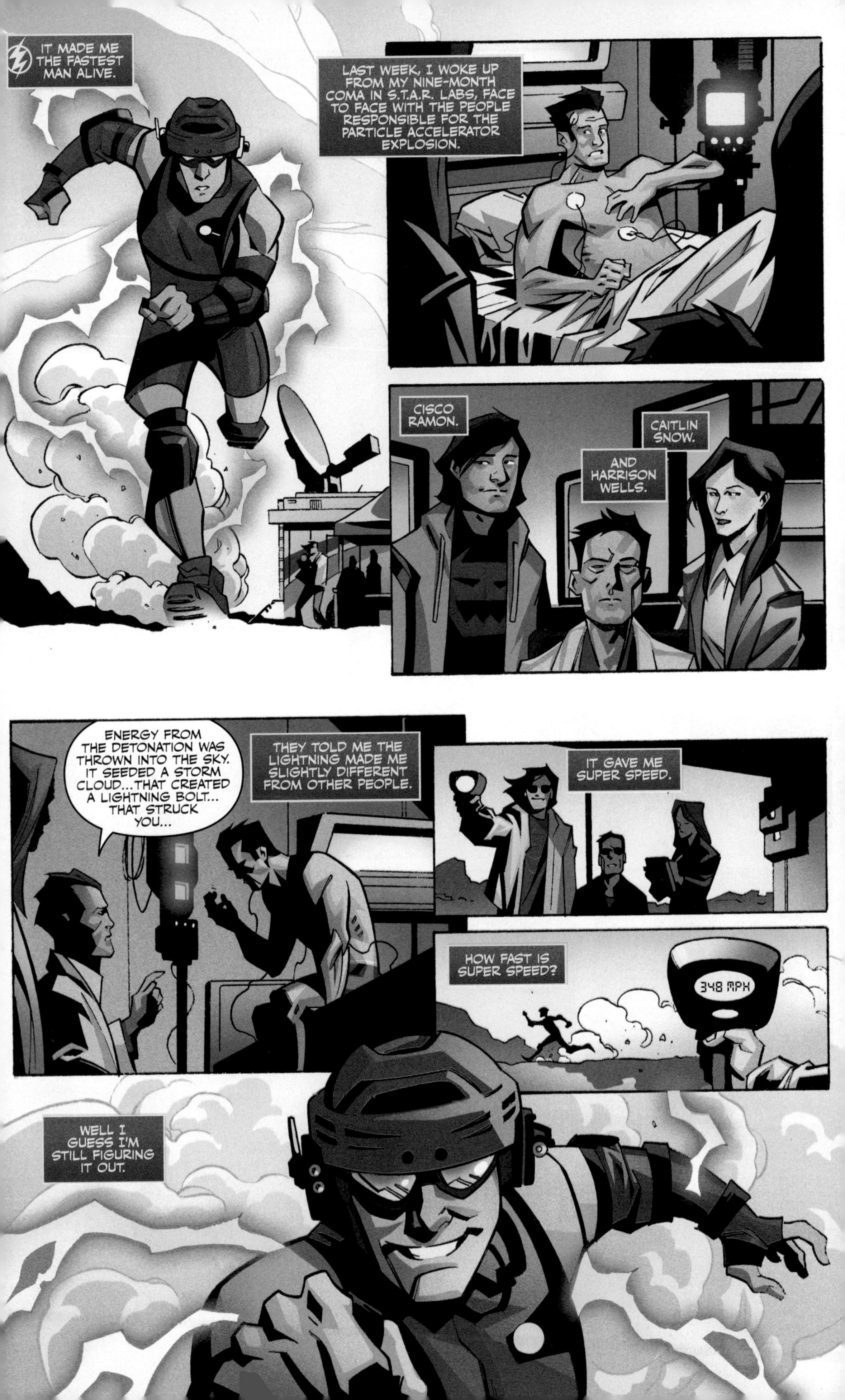
IT MADE ME THE FASTEST MAN ALIVE.
LAST WEEK, I WOKE UP FROM MY NINE-MONTH COMA IN S.T.A.R. LABS, FACE TO FACE WITH THE PEOPLE RESPONSIBLE FOR THE PARTICLE ACCELERATOR EXPLOSION.
CISCO RAMON.
CAITLIN SNOW.
AND HARRISON WELLS.
ENERGY FROM THE DETONATION WAS THROWN INTO THE SKY. IT SEEDED A STORM CLOUD...THAT CREATED A LIGHTNING BOLT... THAT STRUCK YOU...
THEY TOLD ME THE LIGHTNING MADE ME SLIGHTLY DIFFERENT FROM OTHER PEOPLE.
IT GAVE ME SUPER SPEED.
HOW FAST IS SUPER SPEED?
348 MPH
WELL I GUESS I'M STILL FIGURING IT OUT.

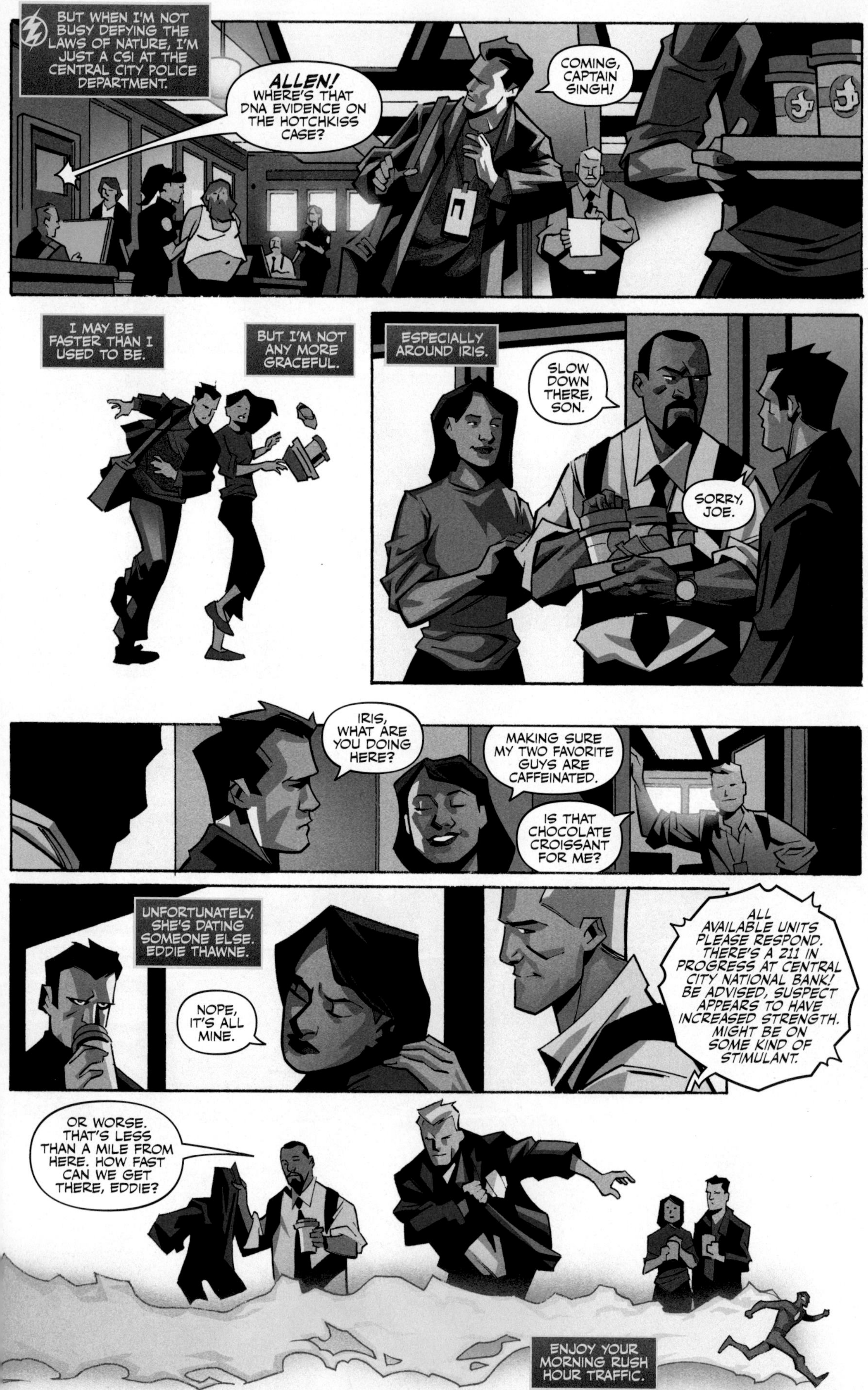
BUT WHEN I'M NOT BUSY DEFYING THE LAWS OF NATURE, I'M JUST A CSI AT THE CENTRAL CITY POLICE DEPARTMENT.
ALLEN! WHERE'S THAT DNA EVIDENCE ON THE HOTCHKISS CASE?
COMING, CAPTAIN SINGH!
I MAY BE FASTER THAN I USED TO BE.
BUT I'M NOT ANY MORE GRACEFUL.
ESPECIALLY AROUND IRIS.
SLOW DOWN THERE, SON.
SORRY, JOE.
IRIS, WHAT ARE YOU DOING HERE?
MAKING SURE MY TWO FAVORITE GUYS ARE CAFFEINATED.
IS THAT CHOCOLATE CROISSANT FOR ME?
UNFORTUNATELY, SHE'S DATING SOMEONE ELSE. EDDIE THAWNE.
NOPE, IT'S ALL MINE.
ALL AVAILABLE UNITS PLEASE RESPOND. THERE'S A 211 IN PROGRESS AT CENTRAL CITY NATIONAL BANK! BE ADVISED, SUSPECT APPEARS TO HAVE INCREASED STRENGTH. MIGHT BE ON SOME KIND OF STIMULANT.
OR WORSE. THAT'S LESS THAN A MILE FROM HERE. HOW FAST CAN WE GET THERE, EDDIE?
ENJOY YOUR MORNING RUSH HOUR TRAFFIC.

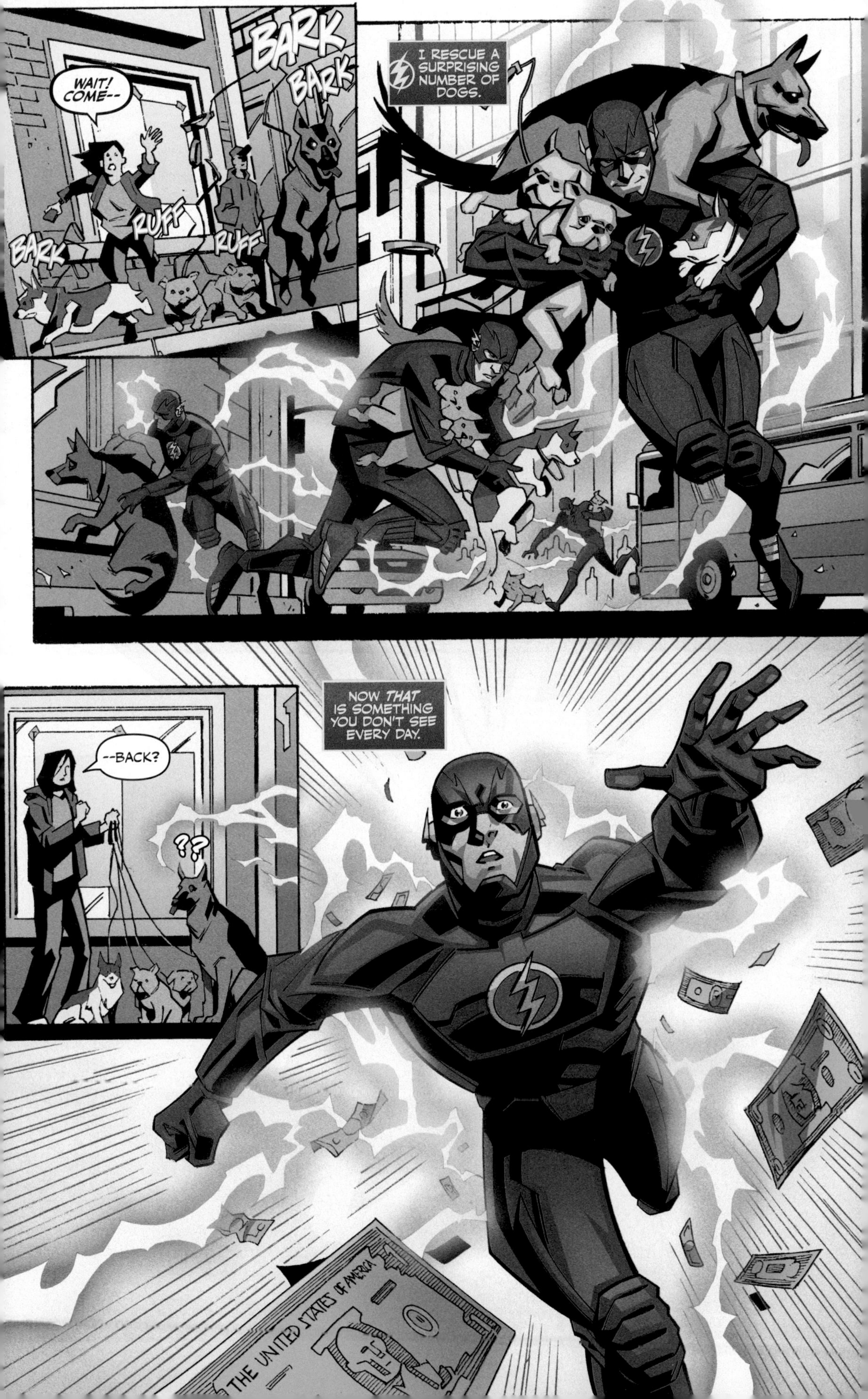
WAIT! COME--
BARK
BARK
BARK
RUFF
RUFF
I RESCUE A SURPRISING NUMBER OF DOGS.
--BACK?
??
NOW THAT IS SOMETHING YOU DON'T SEE EVERY DAY.
THE UNITED STATES OF AMERICA

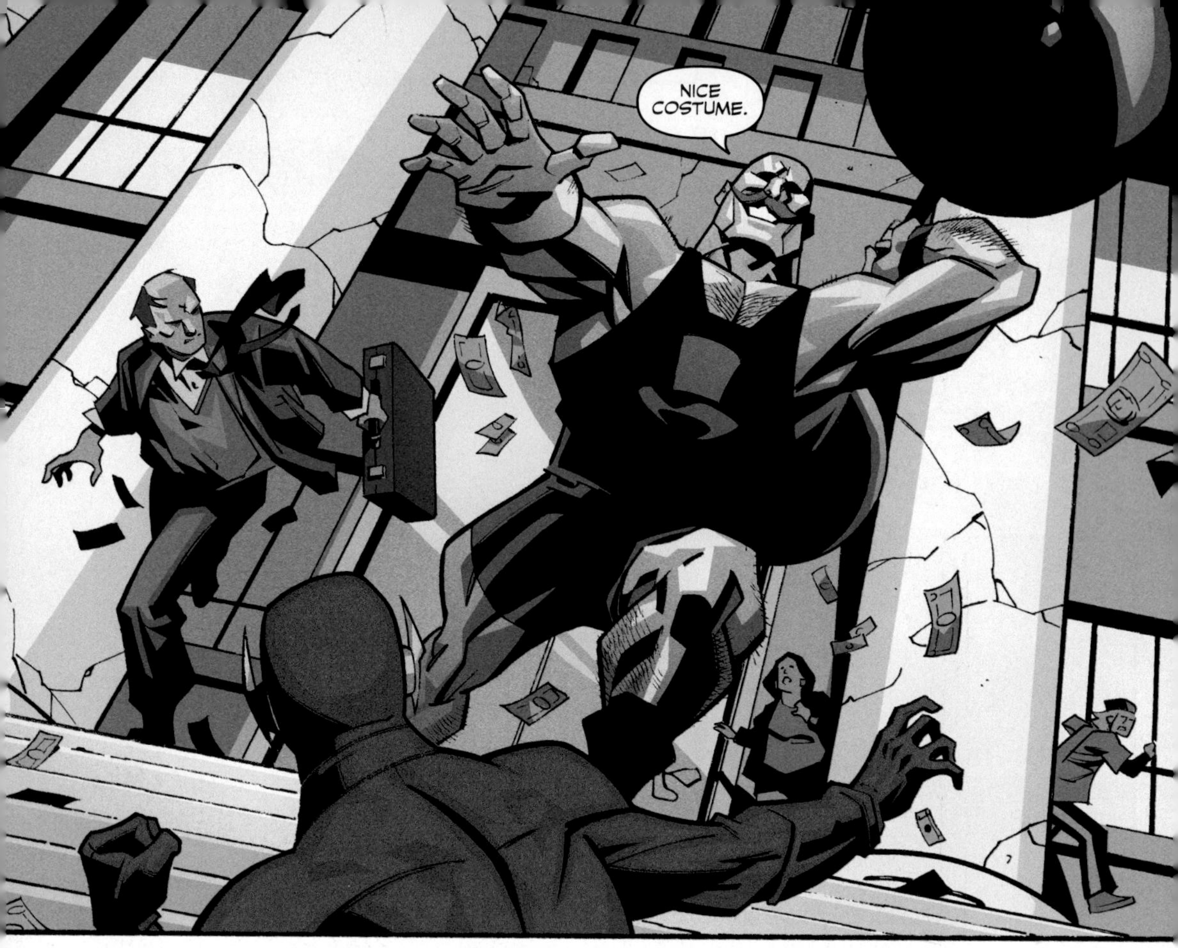
NICE COSTUME.

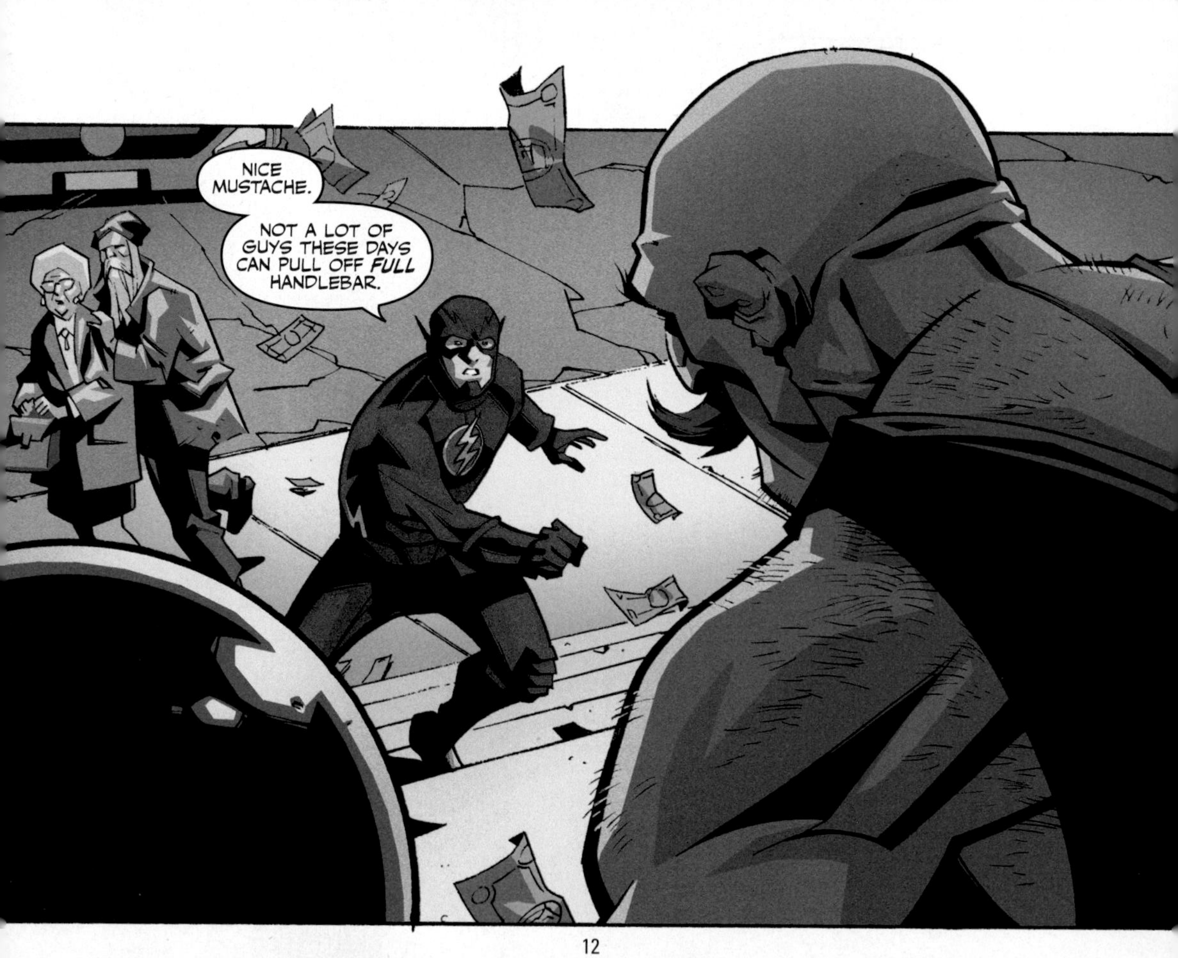
NICE MUSTACHE.
NOT A LOT OF GUYS THESE DAYS CAN PULL OFF *FULL* HANDLEBAR.

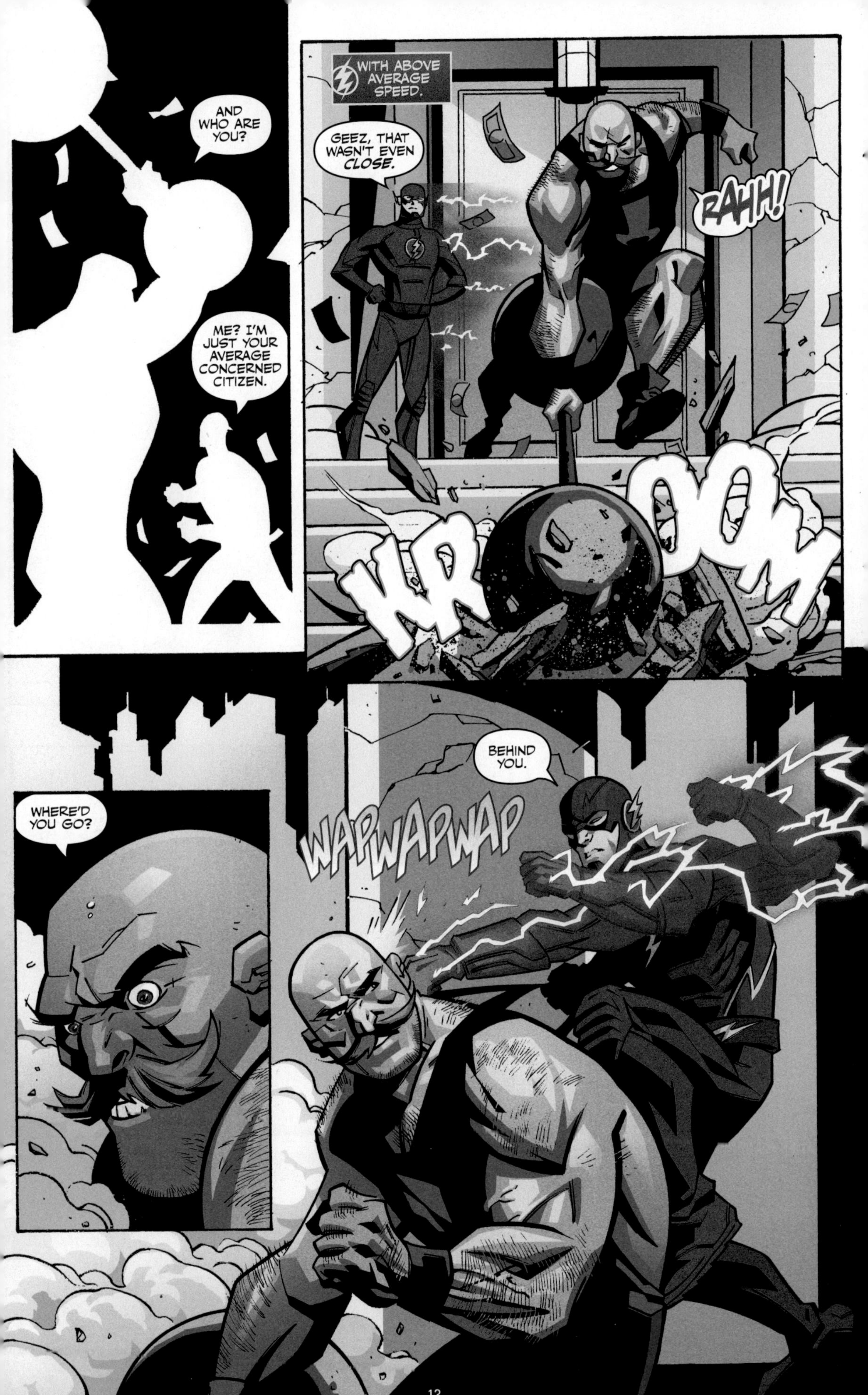

AND WHO ARE YOU?
ME? I'M JUST YOUR AVERAGE CONCERNED CITIZEN.
WITH ABOVE AVERAGE SPEED.
GEEZ, THAT WASN'T EVEN CLOSE.
RAHH!
KRDOOM
WHERE'D YOU GO?
BEHIND YOU.
WAPWAPWAP

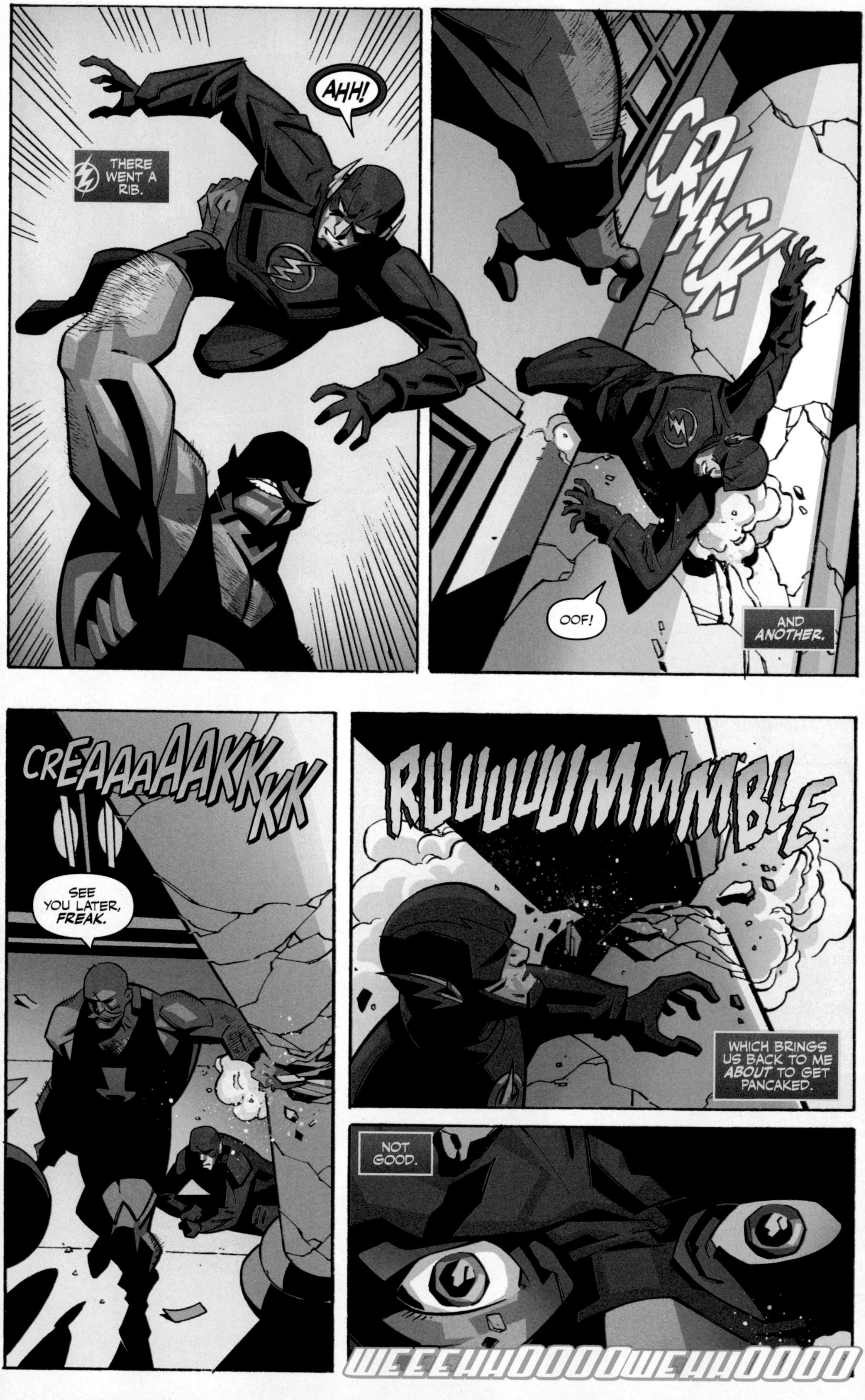
AHH!
THERE WENT A RIB.
CRACK
OOF!
AND ANOTHER.
CREAAAAAKKKK
SEE YOU LATER, FREAK.
RUUUUUMMMBLE
WHICH BRINGS US BACK TO ME ABOUT TO GET PANCAKED.
NOT GOOD.
WEEEHHOOOOOWEHHOOOO

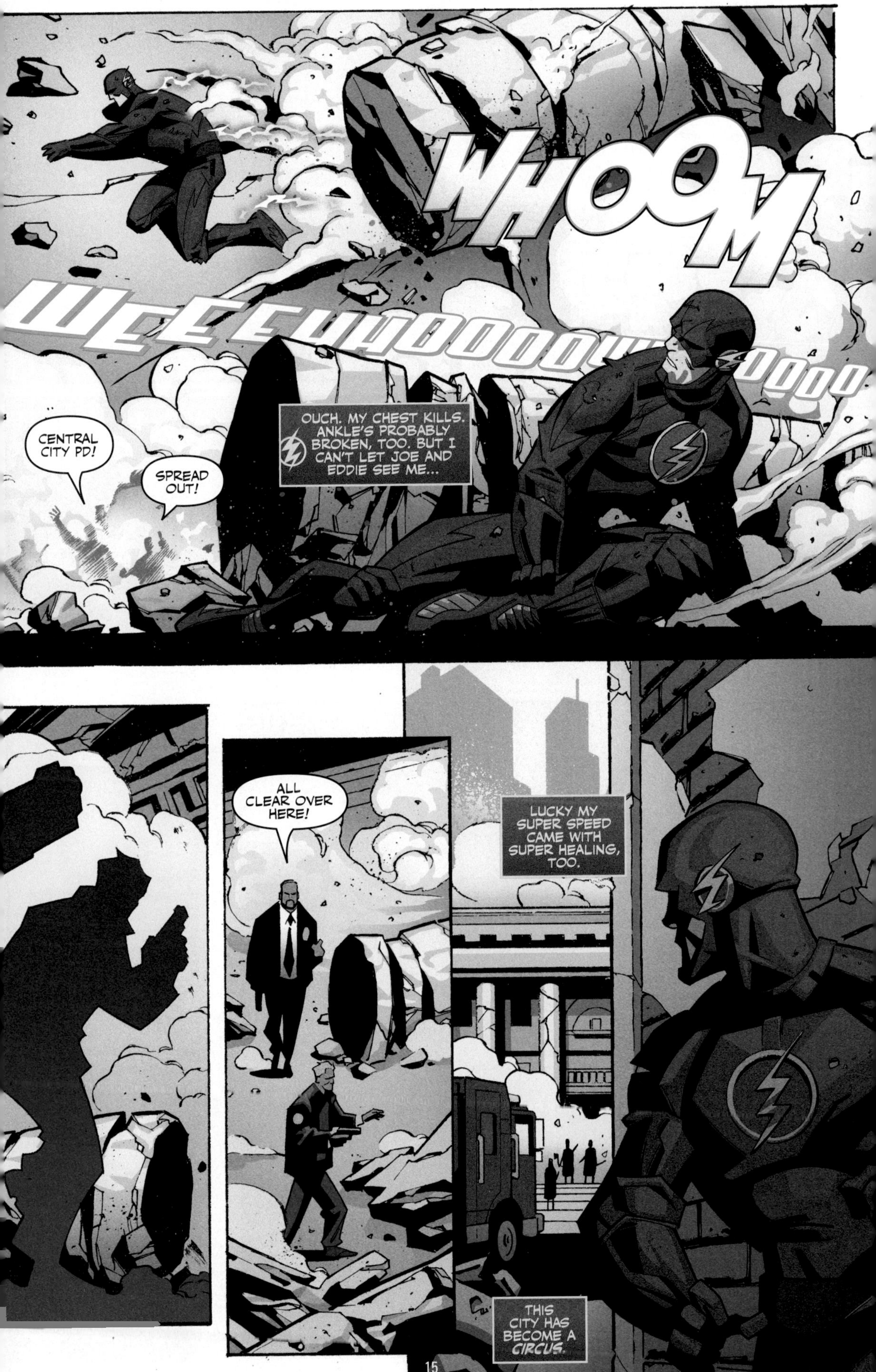
WHOOM
CENTRAL CITY PD!
SPREAD OUT!
OUCH. MY CHEST KILLS. ANKLE'S PROBABLY BROKEN, TOO. BUT I CAN'T LET JOE AND EDDIE SEE ME...
ALL CLEAR OVER HERE!
LUCKY MY SUPER SPEED CAME WITH SUPER HEALING, TOO.
THIS CITY HAS BECOME A *CIRCUS*.

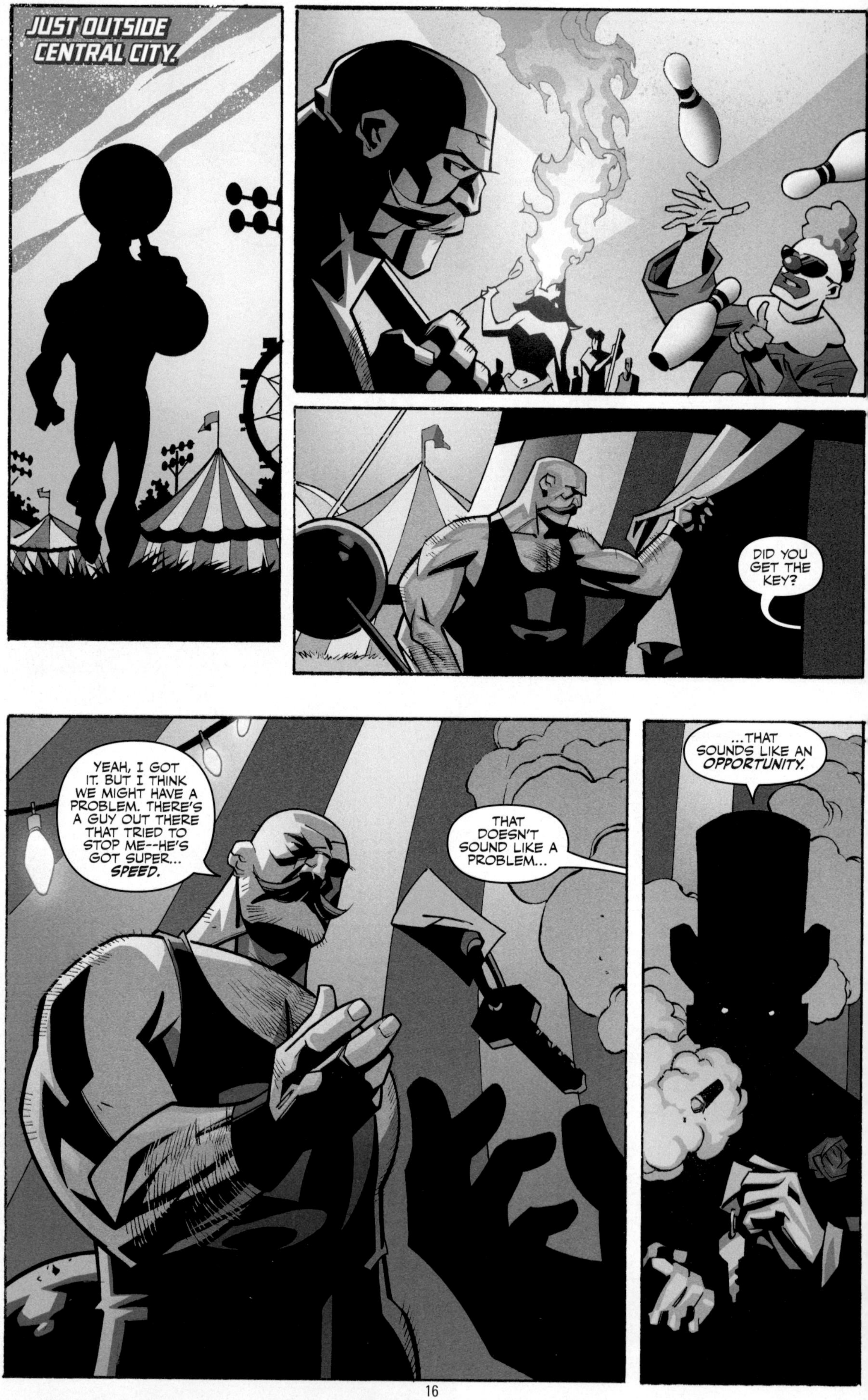
JUST OUTSIDE CENTRAL CITY.
DID YOU GET THE KEY?
YEAH, I GOT IT. BUT I THINK WE MIGHT HAVE A PROBLEM. THERE'S A GUY OUT THERE THAT TRIED TO STOP ME--HE'S GOT SUPER... *SPEED.*
THAT DOESN'T SOUND LIKE A PROBLEM...
...THAT SOUNDS LIKE AN *OPPORTUNITY.*

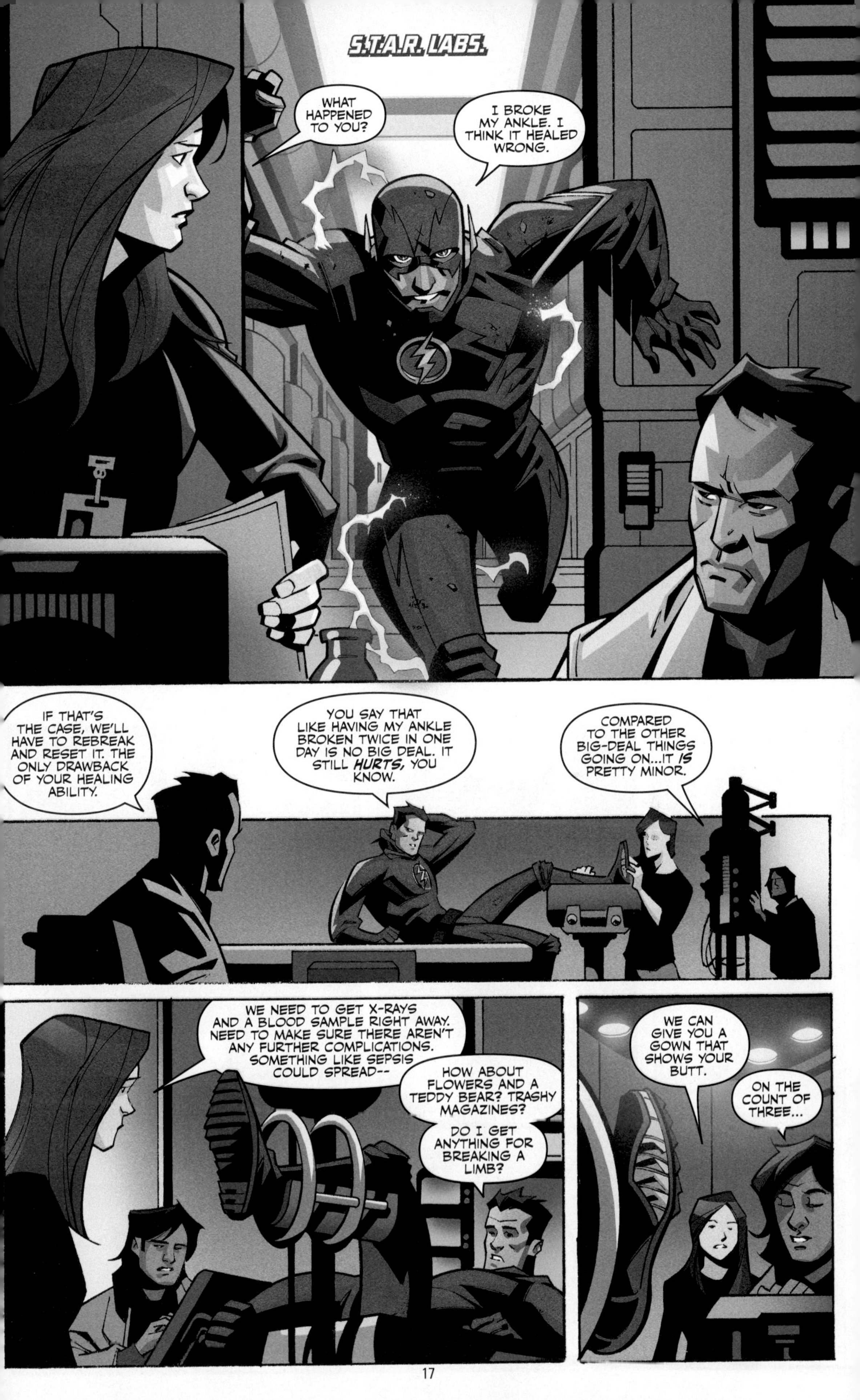
S.T.A.R. LABS.
WHAT HAPPENED TO YOU?
I BROKE MY ANKLE. I THINK IT HEALED WRONG.
IF THAT'S THE CASE, WE'LL HAVE TO REBREAK AND RESET IT. THE ONLY DRAWBACK OF YOUR HEALING ABILITY.
YOU SAY THAT LIKE HAVING MY ANKLE BROKEN TWICE IN ONE DAY IS NO BIG DEAL. IT STILL *HURTS,* YOU KNOW.
COMPARED TO THE OTHER BIG-DEAL THINGS GOING ON...IT *IS* PRETTY MINOR.
WE NEED TO GET X-RAYS AND A BLOOD SAMPLE RIGHT AWAY. NEED TO MAKE SURE THERE AREN'T ANY FURTHER COMPLICATIONS. SOMETHING LIKE SEPSIS COULD SPREAD--
HOW ABOUT FLOWERS AND A TEDDY BEAR? TRASHY MAGAZINES?
DO I GET ANYTHING FOR BREAKING A LIMB?
WE CAN GIVE YOU A GOWN THAT SHOWS YOUR BUTT.
ON THE COUNT OF THREE...

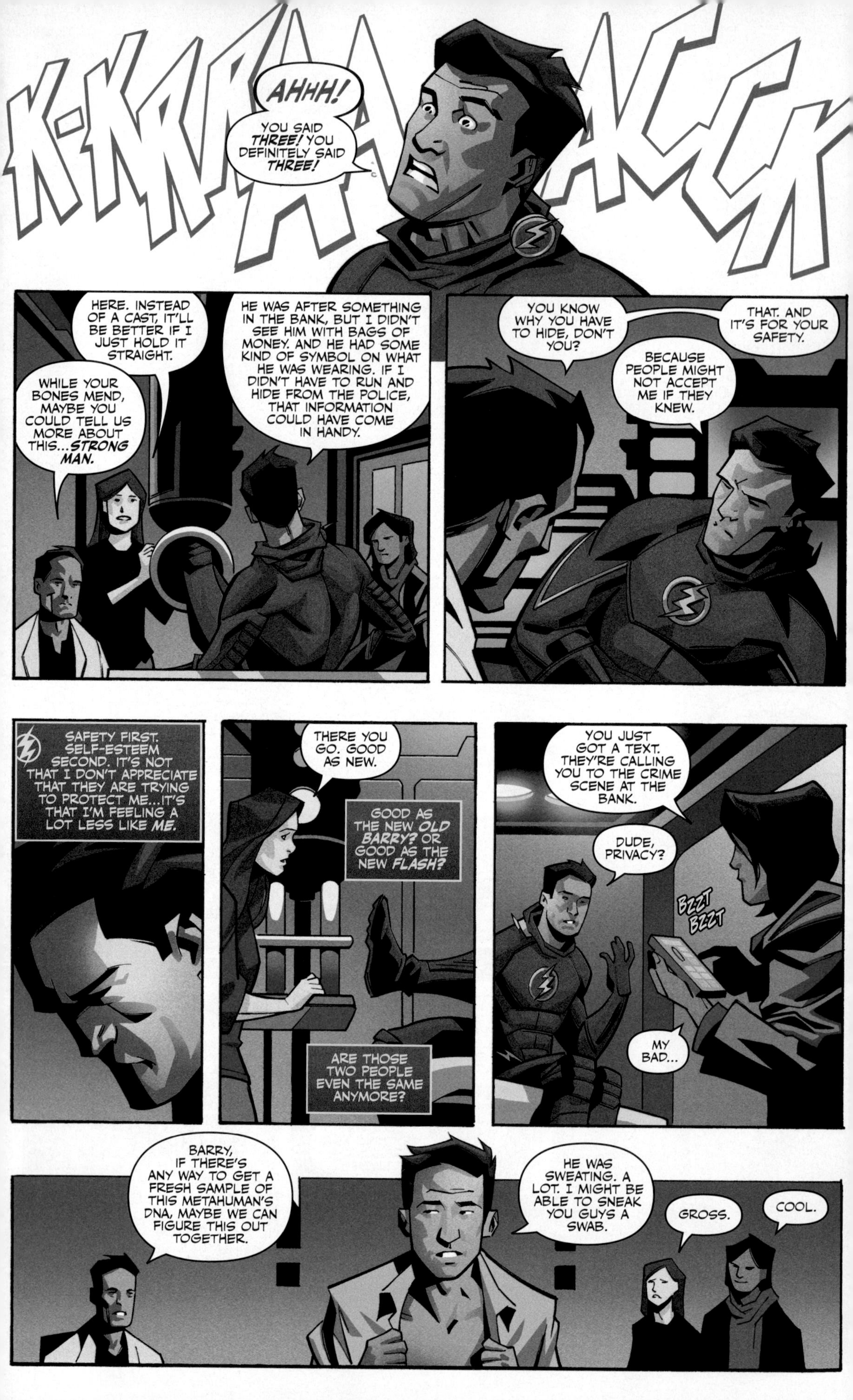
K-KRRAAACCK
AHHH!
YOU SAID *THREE!* YOU DEFINITELY SAID *THREE!*
HERE. INSTEAD OF A CAST, IT'LL BE BETTER IF I JUST HOLD IT STRAIGHT.
WHILE YOUR BONES MEND, MAYBE YOU COULD TELL US MORE ABOUT THIS...*STRONG MAN.*
HE WAS AFTER SOMETHING IN THE BANK, BUT I DIDN'T SEE HIM WITH BAGS OF MONEY. AND HE HAD SOME KIND OF SYMBOL ON WHAT HE WAS WEARING. IF I DIDN'T HAVE TO RUN AND HIDE FROM THE POLICE, THAT INFORMATION COULD HAVE COME IN HANDY.
YOU KNOW WHY YOU HAVE TO HIDE, DON'T YOU?
THAT. AND IT'S FOR YOUR SAFETY.
BECAUSE PEOPLE MIGHT NOT ACCEPT ME IF THEY KNEW.
SAFETY FIRST. SELF-ESTEEM SECOND. IT'S NOT THAT I DON'T APPRECIATE THAT THEY ARE TRYING TO PROTECT ME...IT'S THAT I'M FEELING A LOT LESS LIKE *ME.*
THERE YOU GO. GOOD AS NEW.
GOOD AS THE NEW *OLD BARRY?* OR GOOD AS THE NEW *FLASH?*
ARE THOSE TWO PEOPLE EVEN THE SAME ANYMORE?
YOU JUST GOT A TEXT. THEY'RE CALLING YOU TO THE CRIME SCENE AT THE BANK.
DUDE, PRIVACY?
BZZT BZZT
MY BAD...
BARRY, IF THERE'S ANY WAY TO GET A FRESH SAMPLE OF THIS METAHUMAN'S DNA, MAYBE WE CAN FIGURE THIS OUT TOGETHER.
HE WAS SWEATING. A LOT. I MIGHT BE ABLE TO SNEAK YOU GUYS A SWAB.
GROSS.
COOL.

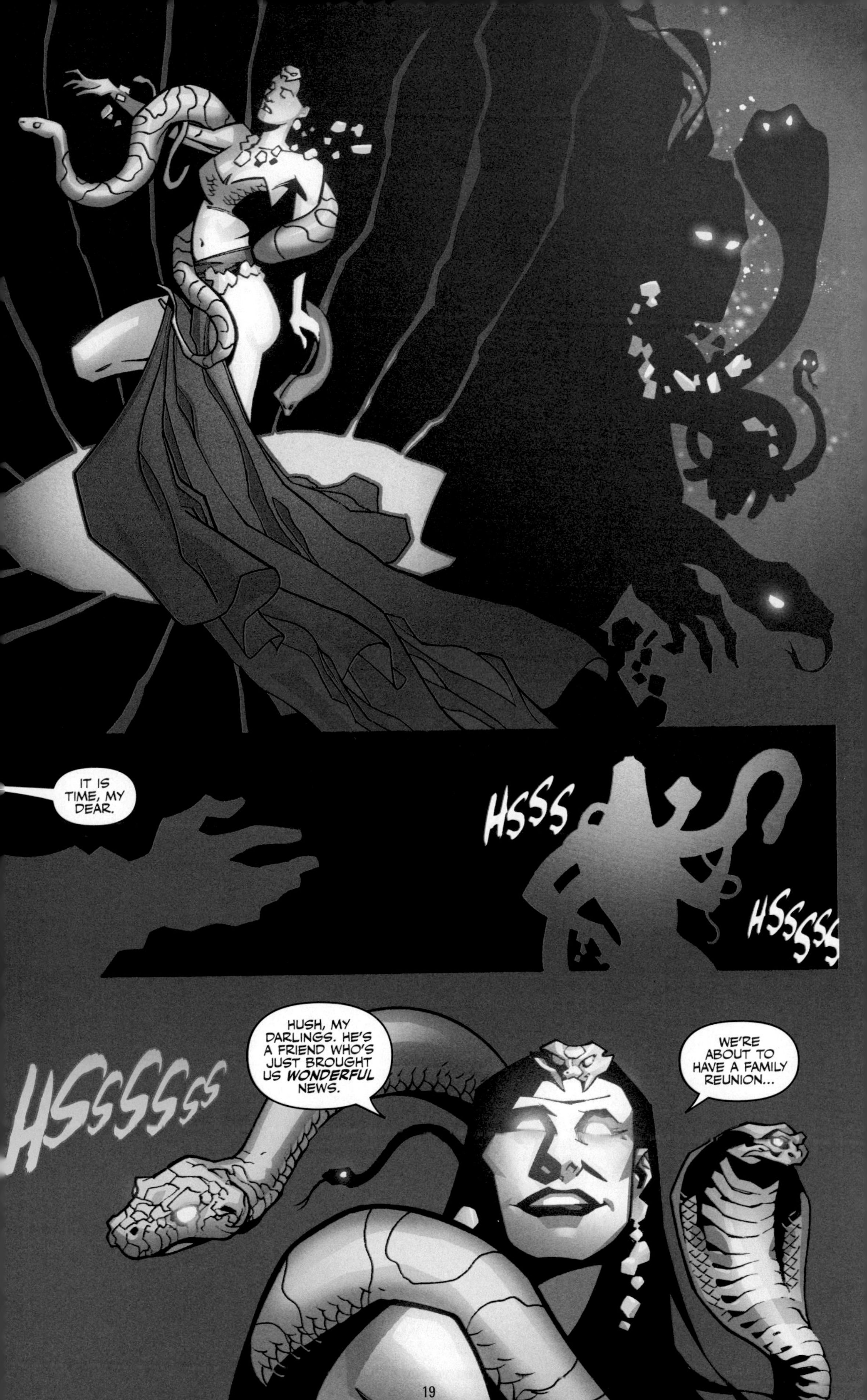
IT IS TIME, MY DEAR.
HSSS
HSSSSS
HSSSSSSS
HUSH, MY DARLINGS. HE'S A FRIEND WHO'S JUST BROUGHT US *WONDERFUL* NEWS.
WE'RE ABOUT TO HAVE A FAMILY REUNION...

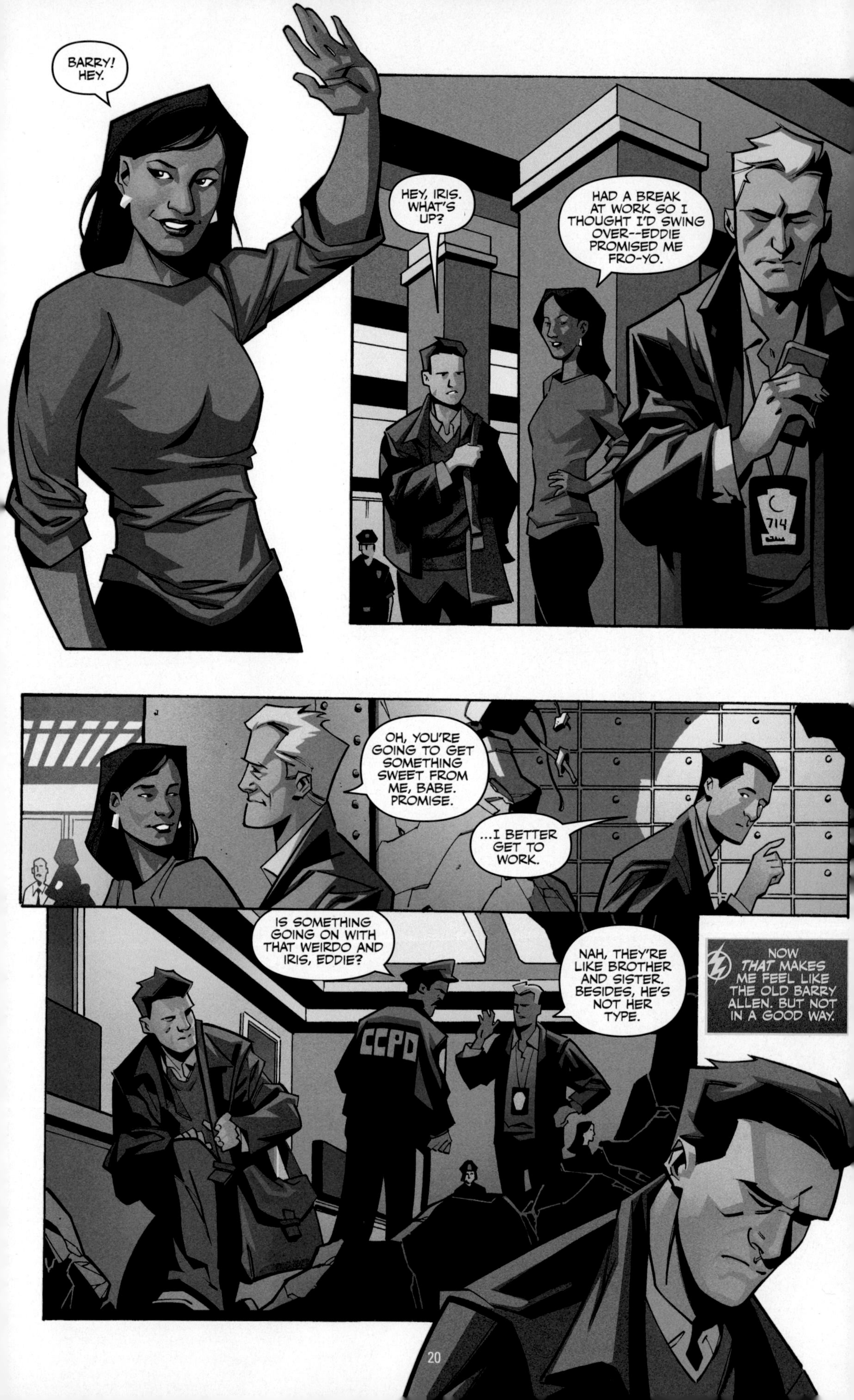
BARRY! HEY.
HEY, IRIS. WHAT'S UP?
HAD A BREAK AT WORK SO I THOUGHT I'D SWING OVER--EDDIE PROMISED ME FRO-YO.
714
OH, YOU'RE GOING TO GET SOMETHING SWEET FROM ME, BABE. PROMISE.
...I BETTER GET TO WORK.
IS SOMETHING GOING ON WITH THAT WEIRDO AND IRIS, EDDIE?
NAH, THEY'RE LIKE BROTHER AND SISTER. BESIDES, HE'S NOT HER TYPE.
CCPD
NOW THAT MAKES ME FEEL LIKE THE OLD BARRY ALLEN. BUT NOT IN A GOOD WAY.

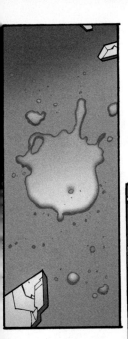

MAYBE IF YOU ISOLATE THE CHANGES IN HIS DNA--YOU CAN MIX UP SOME MUSCLE-BUFFING THERAPY FOR ME. WOULDN'T HURT, RIGHT?

I LIKE THAT YOU'RE ON THE SKINNIER SIDE.

I MEAN... IT DOESN'T MATTER WHAT I LIKE. SO...SURE. WHATEVER YOU WANT.

HEY, BARRY, I NEED YOU TO GET SOME FINGERPRINTS OVER HERE!

THE OLD BARRY WOULD THINK THIS WAS ALL WEIRD...

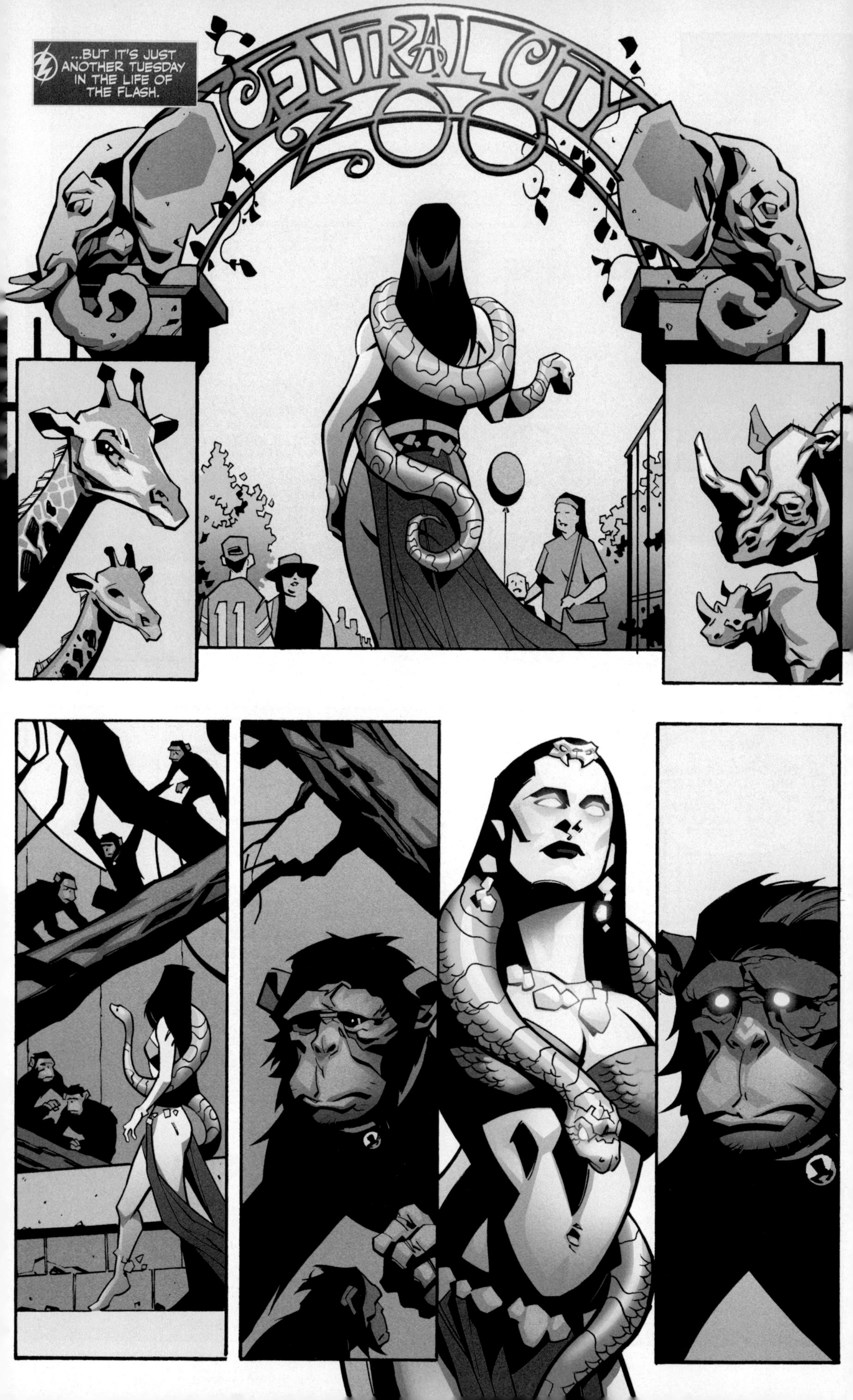

...BUT IT'S JUST ANOTHER TUESDAY IN THE LIFE OF THE FLASH.
CENTRAL CITY ZOO

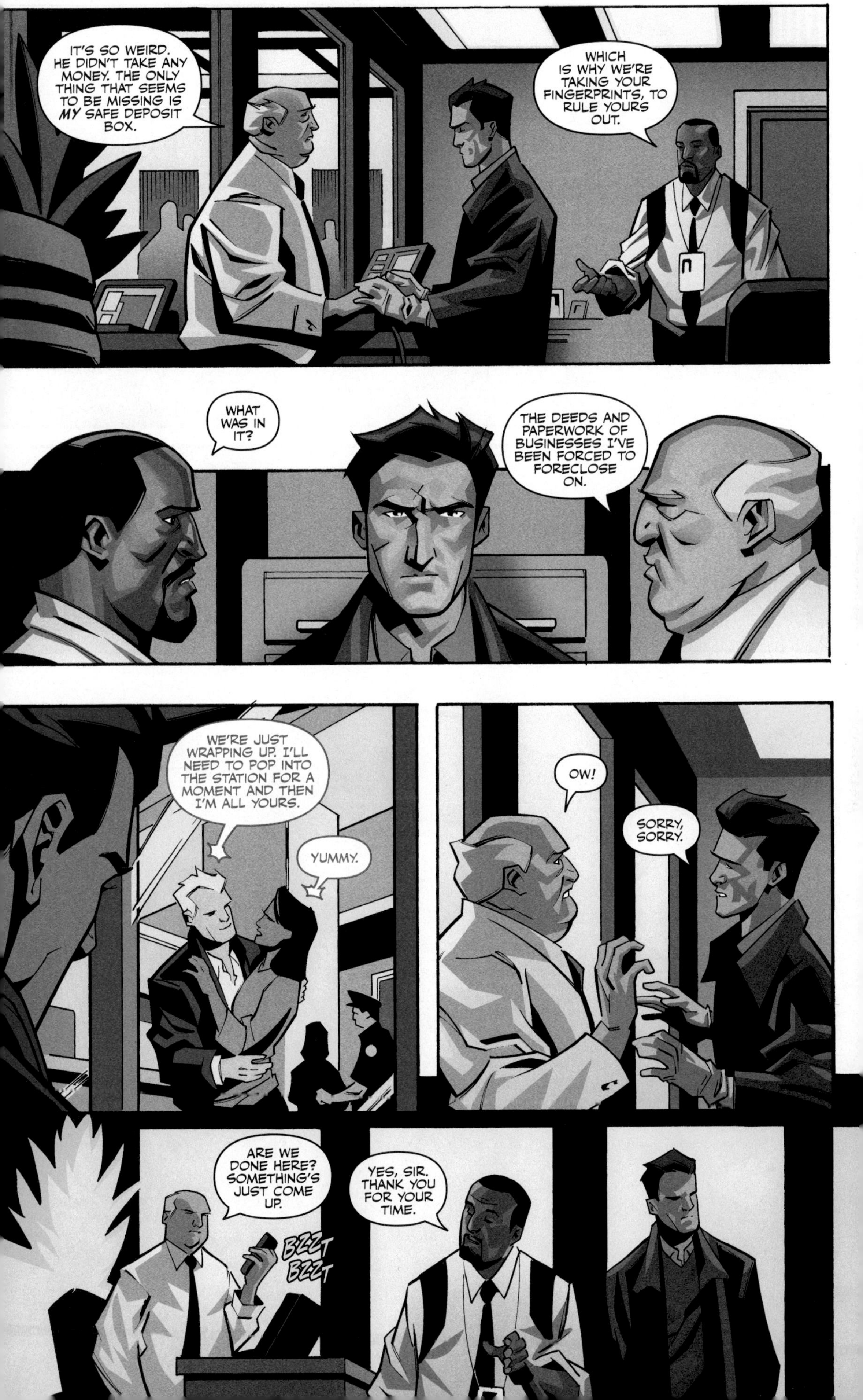
IT'S SO WEIRD. HE DIDN'T TAKE ANY MONEY. THE ONLY THING THAT SEEMS TO BE MISSING IS *MY* SAFE DEPOSIT BOX.
WHICH IS WHY WE'RE TAKING YOUR FINGERPRINTS, TO RULE YOURS OUT.
WHAT WAS IN IT?
THE DEEDS AND PAPERWORK OF BUSINESSES I'VE BEEN FORCED TO FORECLOSE ON.
WE'RE JUST WRAPPING UP. I'LL NEED TO POP INTO THE STATION FOR A MOMENT AND THEN I'M ALL YOURS.
YUMMY.
OW!
SORRY, SORRY.
ARE WE DONE HERE? SOMETHING'S JUST COME UP.
BZZZT
BZZZT
YES, SIR. THANK YOU FOR YOUR TIME.

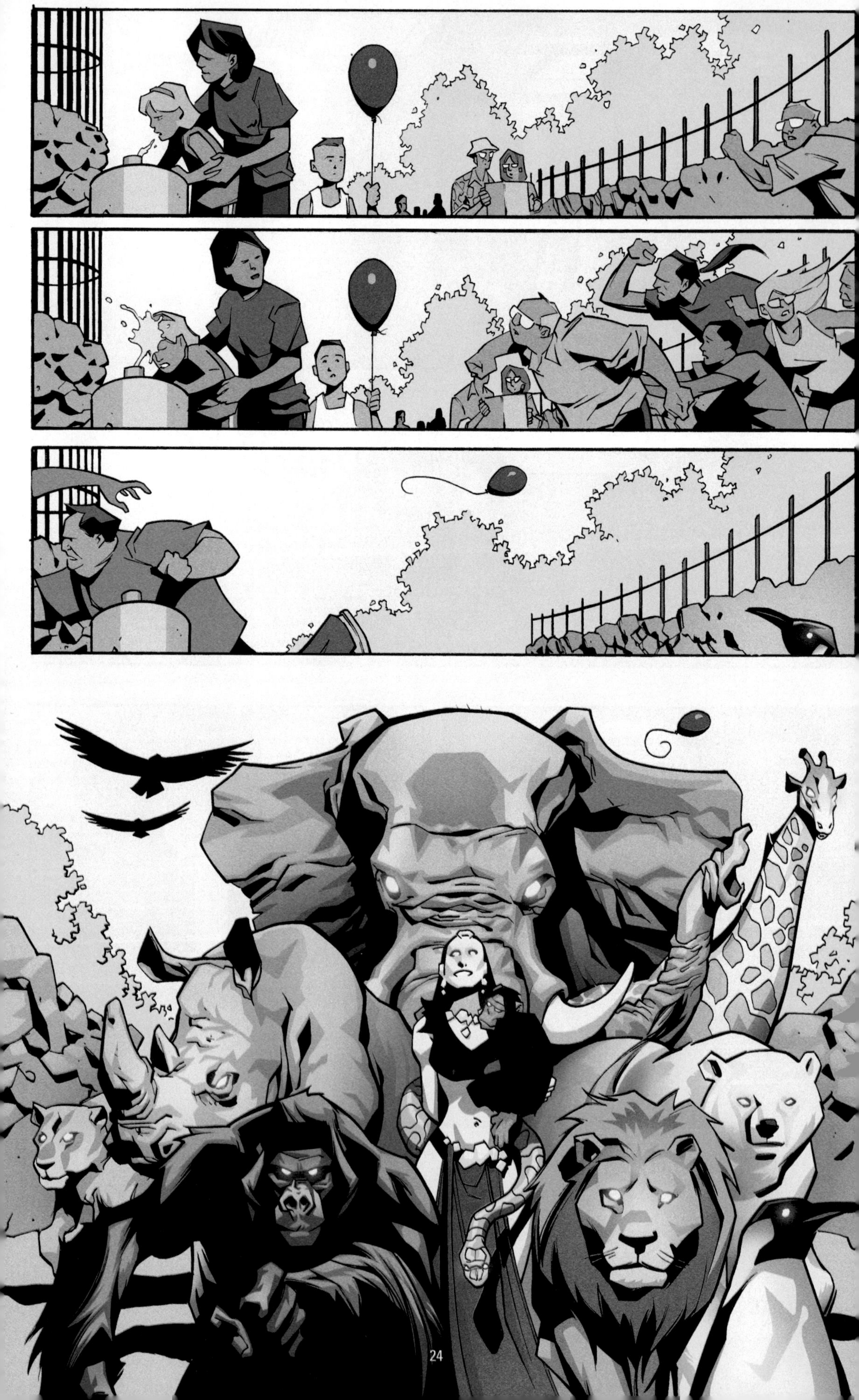

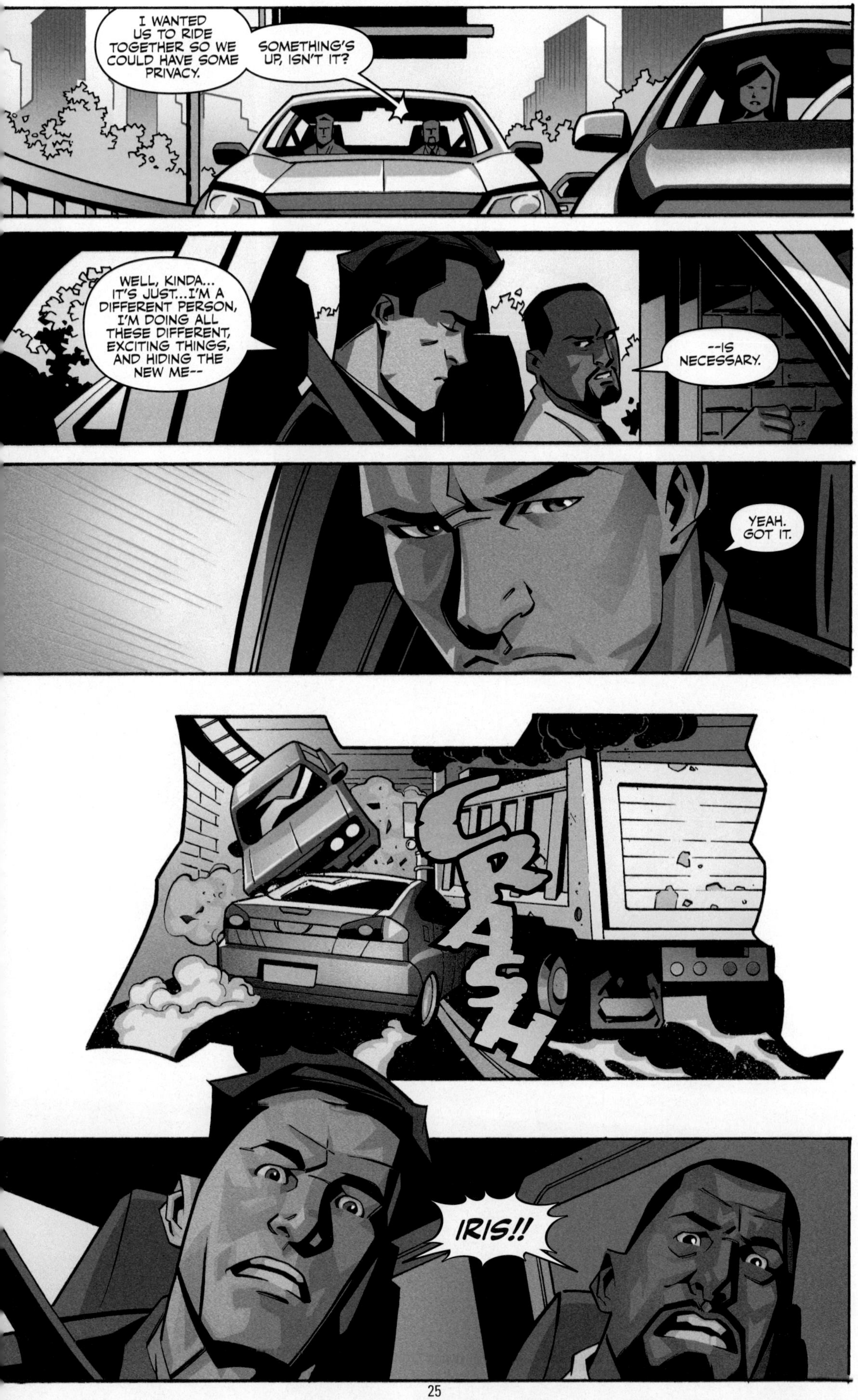
I WANTED US TO RIDE TOGETHER SO WE COULD HAVE SOME PRIVACY.
SOMETHING'S UP, ISN'T IT?
WELL, KINDA... IT'S JUST...I'M A DIFFERENT PERSON, I'M DOING ALL THESE DIFFERENT, EXCITING THINGS, AND HIDING THE NEW ME--
--IS NECESSARY.
YEAH. GOT IT.
CRASH
IRIS!!

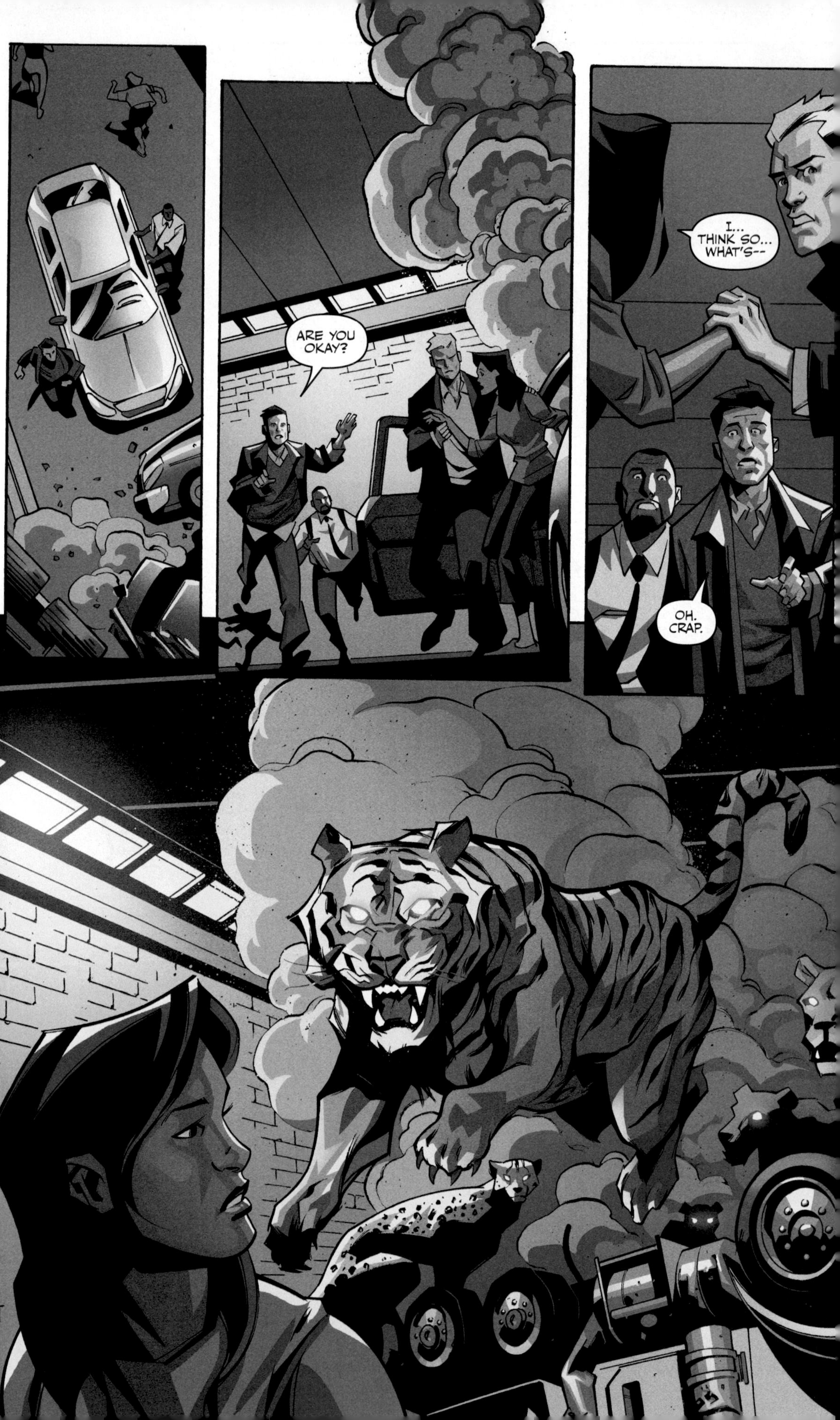
ARE YOU OKAY?
I... THINK SO... WHAT'S--
OH. CRAP.

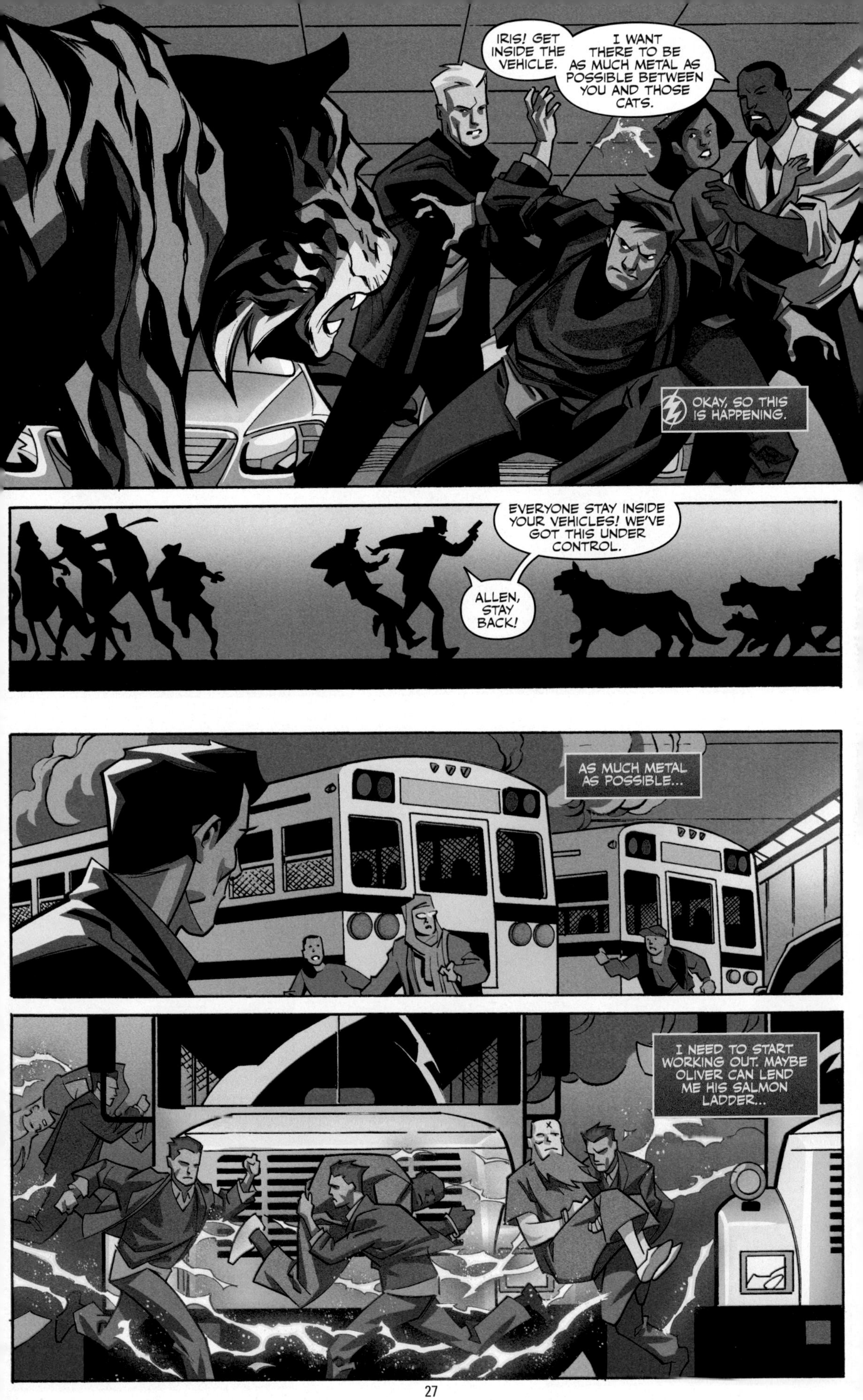
IRIS! GET INSIDE THE VEHICLE.
I WANT THERE TO BE AS MUCH METAL AS POSSIBLE BETWEEN YOU AND THOSE CATS.
OKAY, SO THIS IS HAPPENING.
EVERYONE STAY INSIDE YOUR VEHICLES! WE'VE GOT THIS UNDER CONTROL.
ALLEN, STAY BACK!
AS MUCH METAL AS POSSIBLE...
I NEED TO START WORKING OUT. MAYBE OLIVER CAN LEND ME HIS SALMON LADDER...

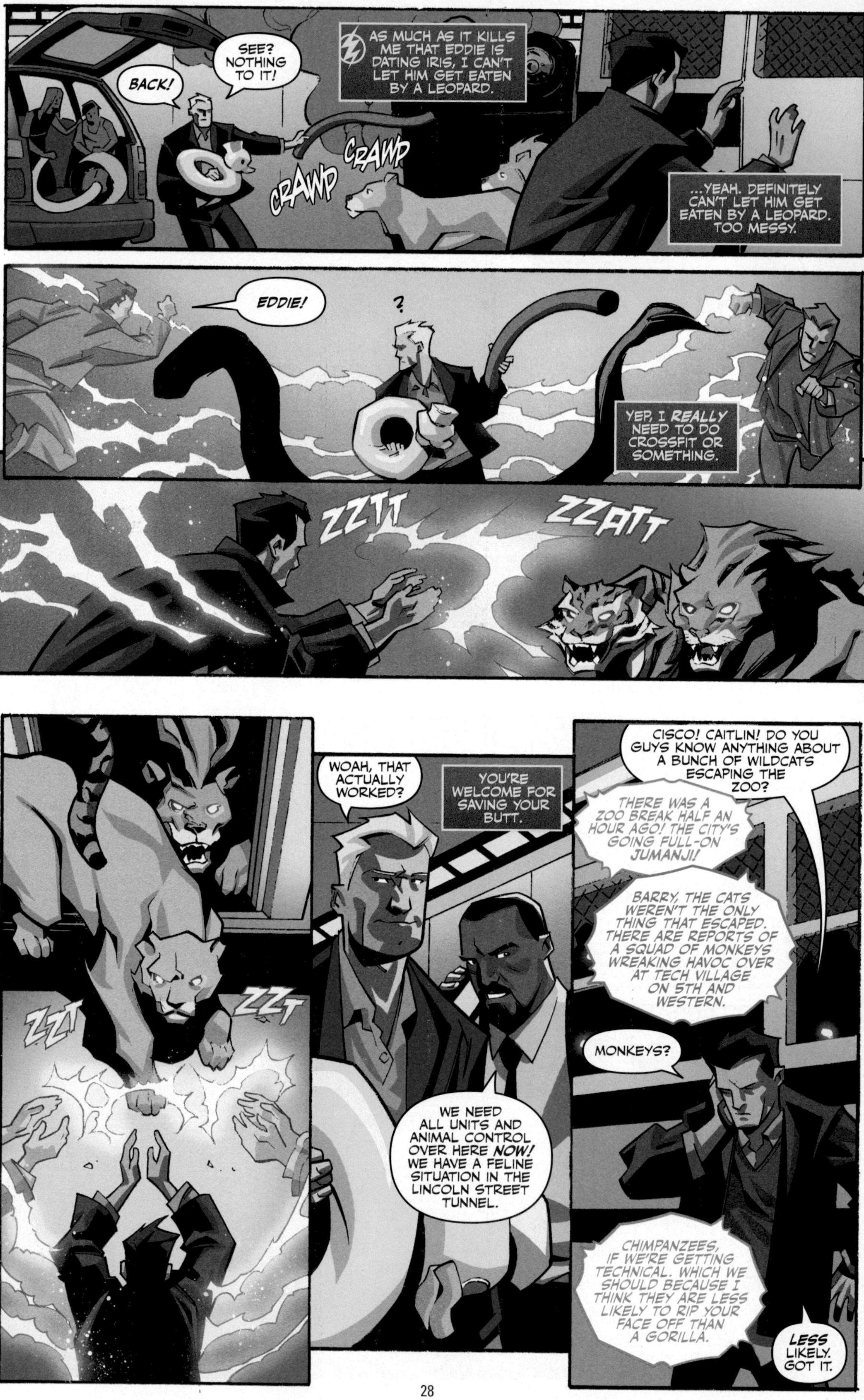

BACK!
SEE? NOTHING TO IT!
AS MUCH AS IT KILLS ME THAT EDDIE IS DATING IRIS, I CAN'T LET HIM GET EATEN BY A LEOPARD.
CRAWP
CRAWP
...YEAH. DEFINITELY CAN'T LET HIM GET EATEN BY A LEOPARD. TOO MESSY.
EDDIE!
?
YEP, I REALLY NEED TO DO CROSSFIT OR SOMETHING.
ZZTT
ZZATT
ZZT
ZZT
WOAH, THAT ACTUALLY WORKED?
YOU'RE WELCOME FOR SAVING YOUR BUTT.
WE NEED ALL UNITS AND ANIMAL CONTROL OVER HERE NOW! WE HAVE A FELINE SITUATION IN THE LINCOLN STREET TUNNEL.
CISCO! CAITLIN! DO YOU GUYS KNOW ANYTHING ABOUT A BUNCH OF WILDCATS ESCAPING THE ZOO?
THERE WAS A ZOO BREAK HALF AN HOUR AGO! THE CITY'S GOING FULL-ON JUMANJI!
BARRY, THE CATS WEREN'T THE ONLY THING THAT ESCAPED. THERE ARE REPORTS OF A SQUAD OF MONKEYS WREAKING HAVOC OVER AT TECH VILLAGE ON 5TH AND WESTERN.
MONKEYS?
CHIMPANZEES, IF WE'RE GETTING TECHNICAL. WHICH WE SHOULD BECAUSE I THINK THEY ARE LESS LIKELY TO RIP YOUR FACE OFF THAN A GORILLA.
LESS LIKELY. GOT IT.

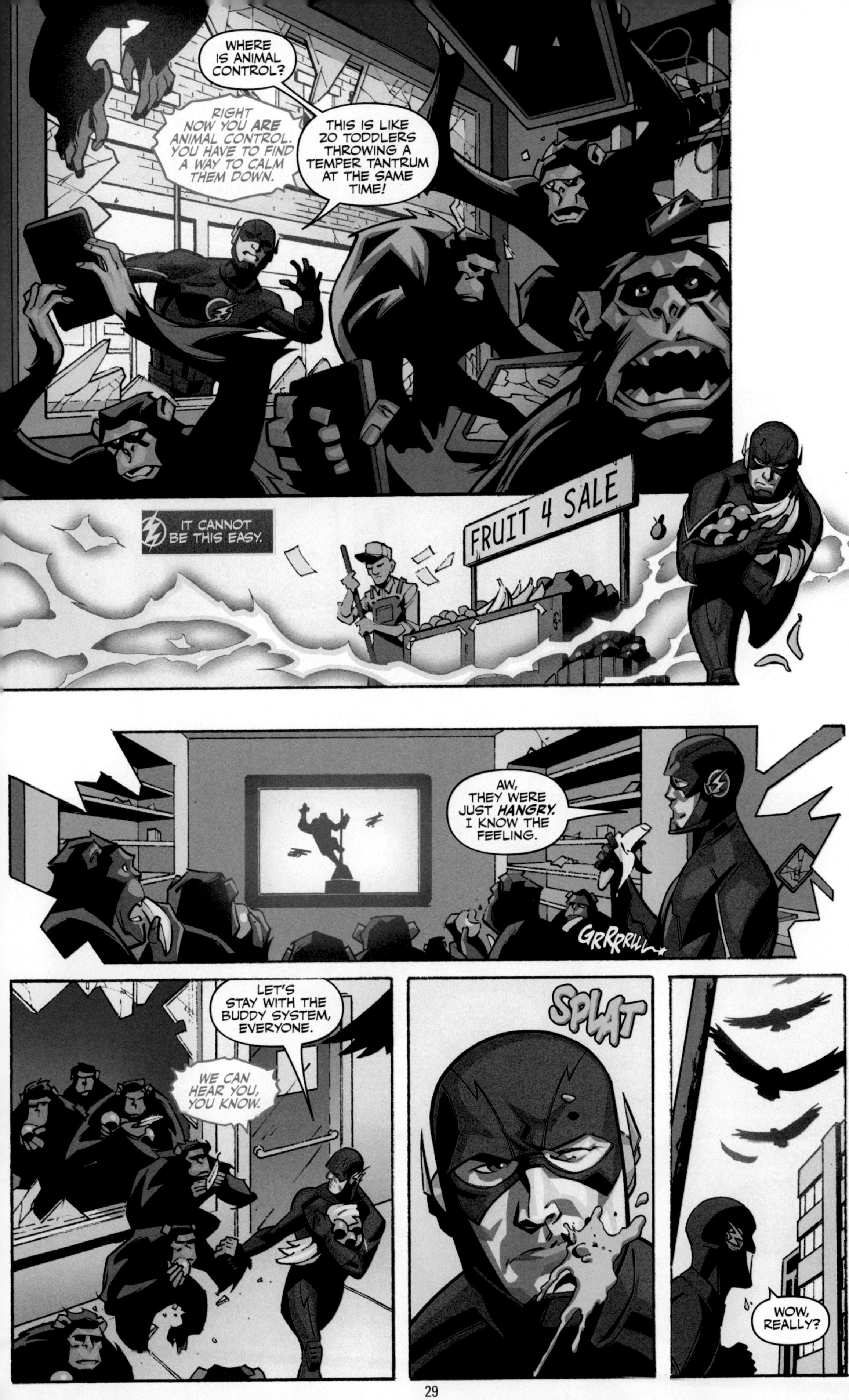
WHERE IS ANIMAL CONTROL?
RIGHT NOW YOU ARE ANIMAL CONTROL. YOU HAVE TO FIND A WAY TO CALM THEM DOWN.
THIS IS LIKE 20 TODDLERS THROWING A TEMPER TANTRUM AT THE SAME TIME!
IT CANNOT BE THIS EASY.
FRUIT 4 SALE
AW, THEY WERE JUST HANGRY. I KNOW THE FEELING.
GRRRRLL
LET'S STAY WITH THE BUDDY SYSTEM, EVERYONE.
WE CAN HEAR YOU, YOU KNOW.
SPLAT
WOW, REALLY?

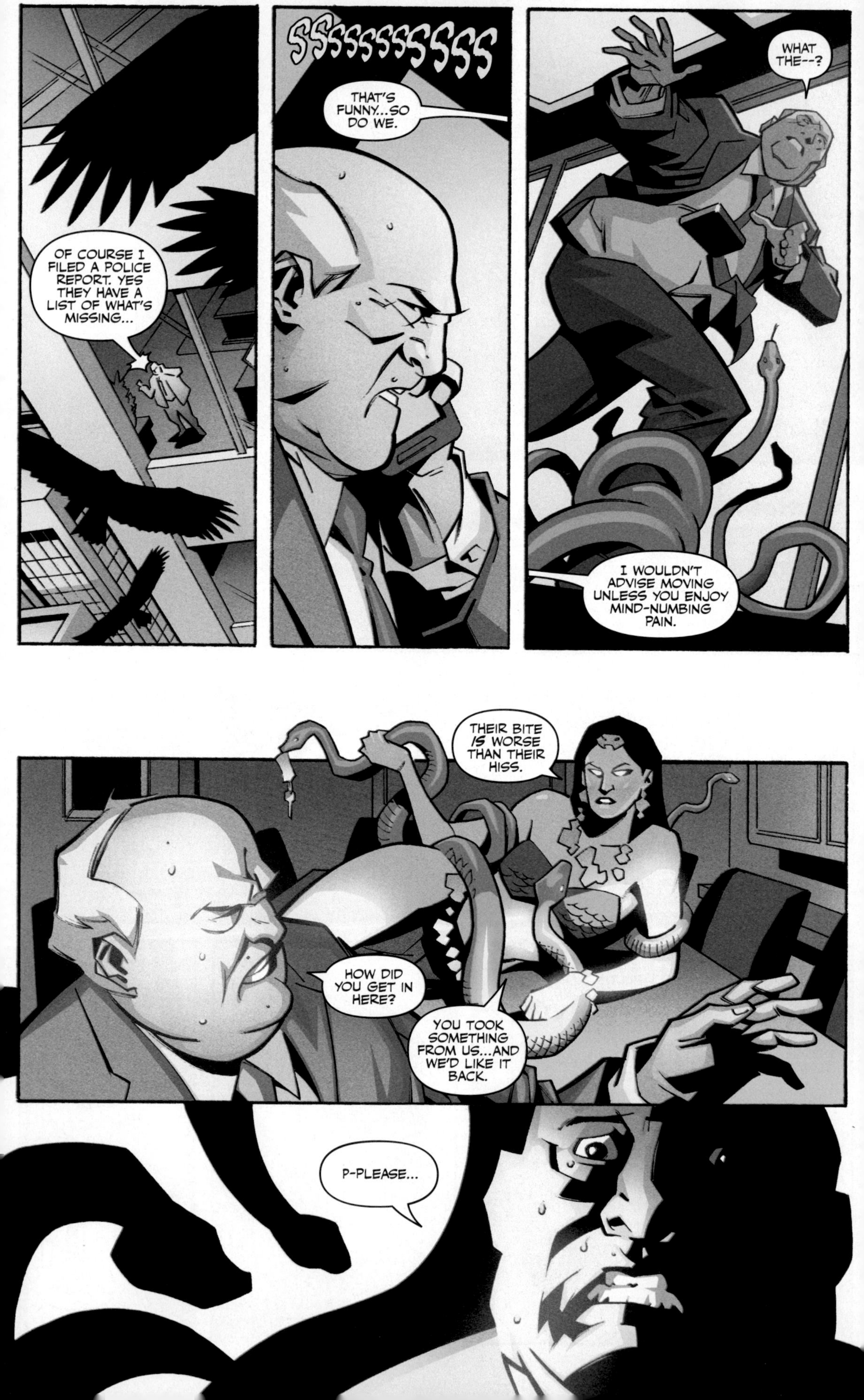
OF COURSE I FILED A POLICE REPORT. YES THEY HAVE A LIST OF WHAT'S MISSING...
SSSSSSSSSSSS
THAT'S FUNNY...SO DO WE.
WHAT THE--?
I WOULDN'T ADVISE MOVING UNLESS YOU ENJOY MIND-NUMBING PAIN.
THEIR BITE *IS* WORSE THAN THEIR HISS.
HOW DID YOU GET IN HERE?
YOU TOOK SOMETHING FROM US...AND WE'D LIKE IT BACK.
P-PLEASE...

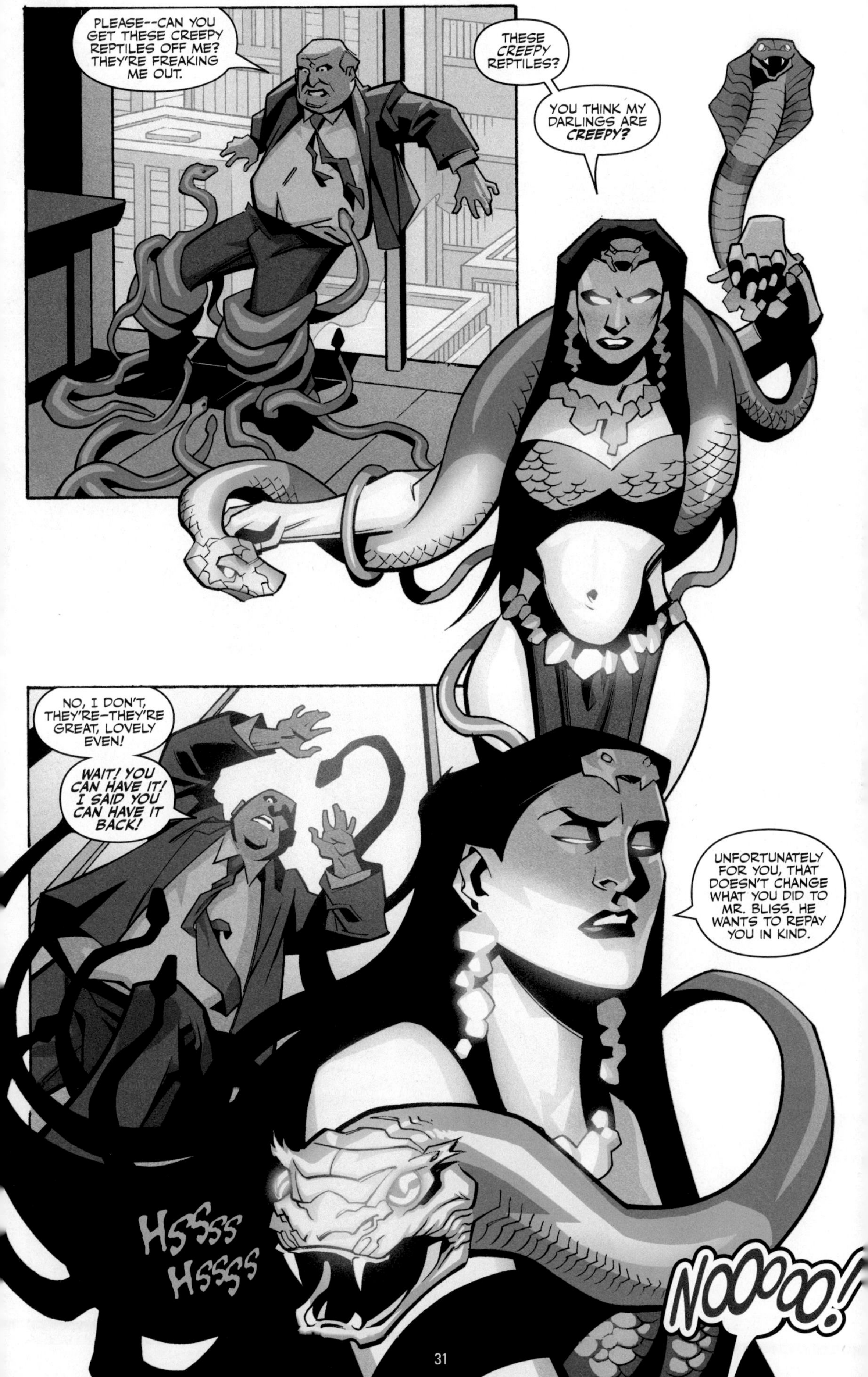
PLEASE--CAN YOU GET THESE CREEPY REPTILES OFF ME? THEY'RE FREAKING ME OUT.
THESE *CREEPY* REPTILES?
YOU THINK MY DARLINGS ARE *CREEPY?*
NO, I DON'T, THEY'RE--THEY'RE GREAT, LOVELY EVEN!
WAIT! YOU CAN HAVE IT! I SAID YOU CAN HAVE IT BACK!
UNFORTUNATELY FOR YOU, THAT DOESN'T CHANGE WHAT YOU DID TO MR. BLISS. HE WANTS TO REPAY YOU IN KIND.
HSSSS HSSSS
NOOOOO!

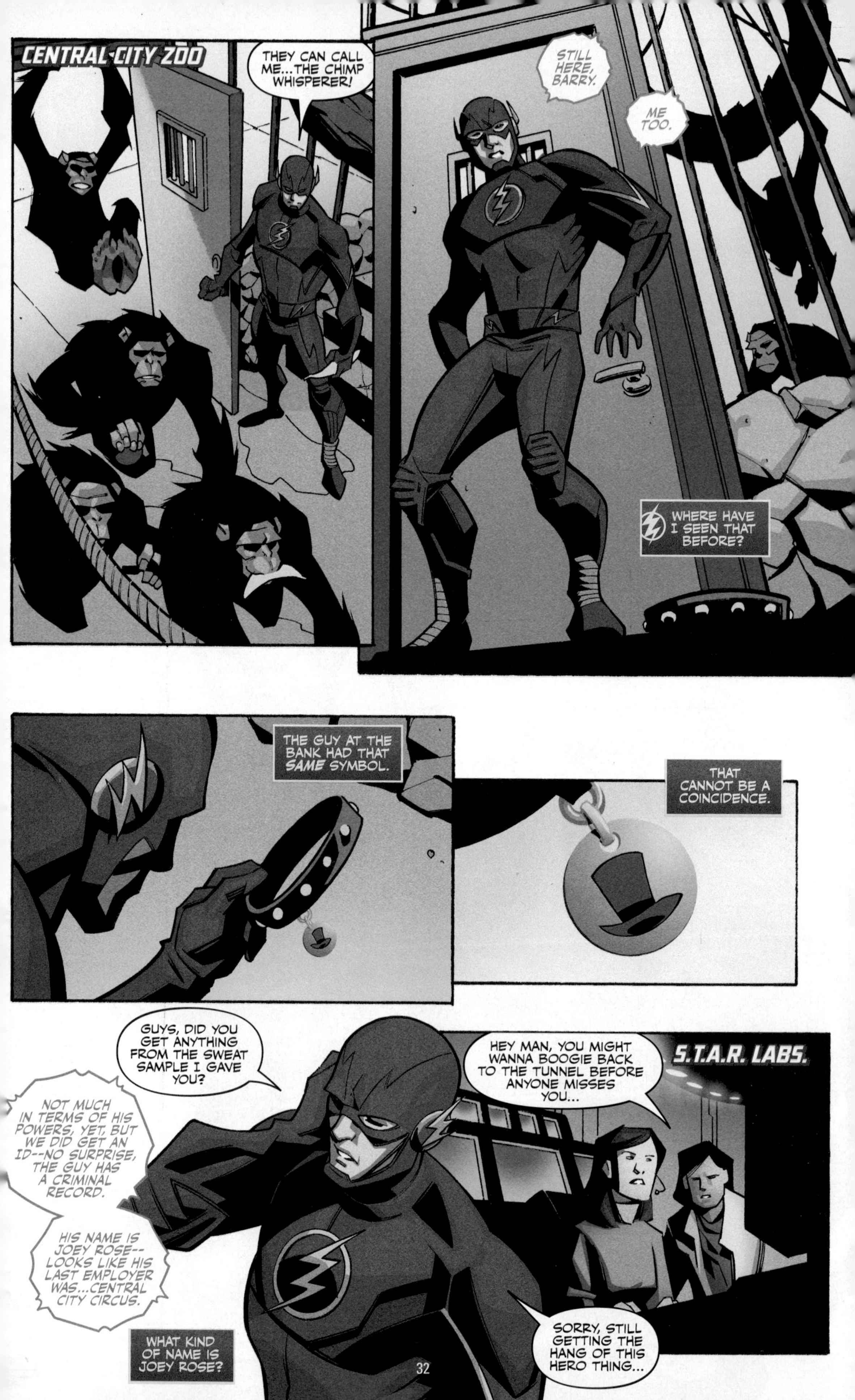

CENTRAL CITY ZOO
THEY CAN CALL ME...THE CHIMP WHISPERER!
STILL HERE, BARRY.
ME TOO.
WHERE HAVE I SEEN THAT BEFORE?
THE GUY AT THE BANK HAD THAT SAME SYMBOL.
THAT CANNOT BE A COINCIDENCE.
S.T.A.R. LABS.
GUYS, DID YOU GET ANYTHING FROM THE SWEAT SAMPLE I GAVE YOU?
HEY MAN, YOU MIGHT WANNA BOOGIE BACK TO THE TUNNEL BEFORE ANYONE MISSES YOU...
NOT MUCH IN TERMS OF HIS POWERS, YET, BUT WE DID GET AN ID--NO SURPRISE, THE GUY HAS A CRIMINAL RECORD.
HIS NAME IS JOEY ROSE-- LOOKS LIKE HIS LAST EMPLOYER WAS...CENTRAL CITY CIRCUS.
WHAT KIND OF NAME IS JOEY ROSE?
SORRY, STILL GETTING THE HANG OF THIS HERO THING...

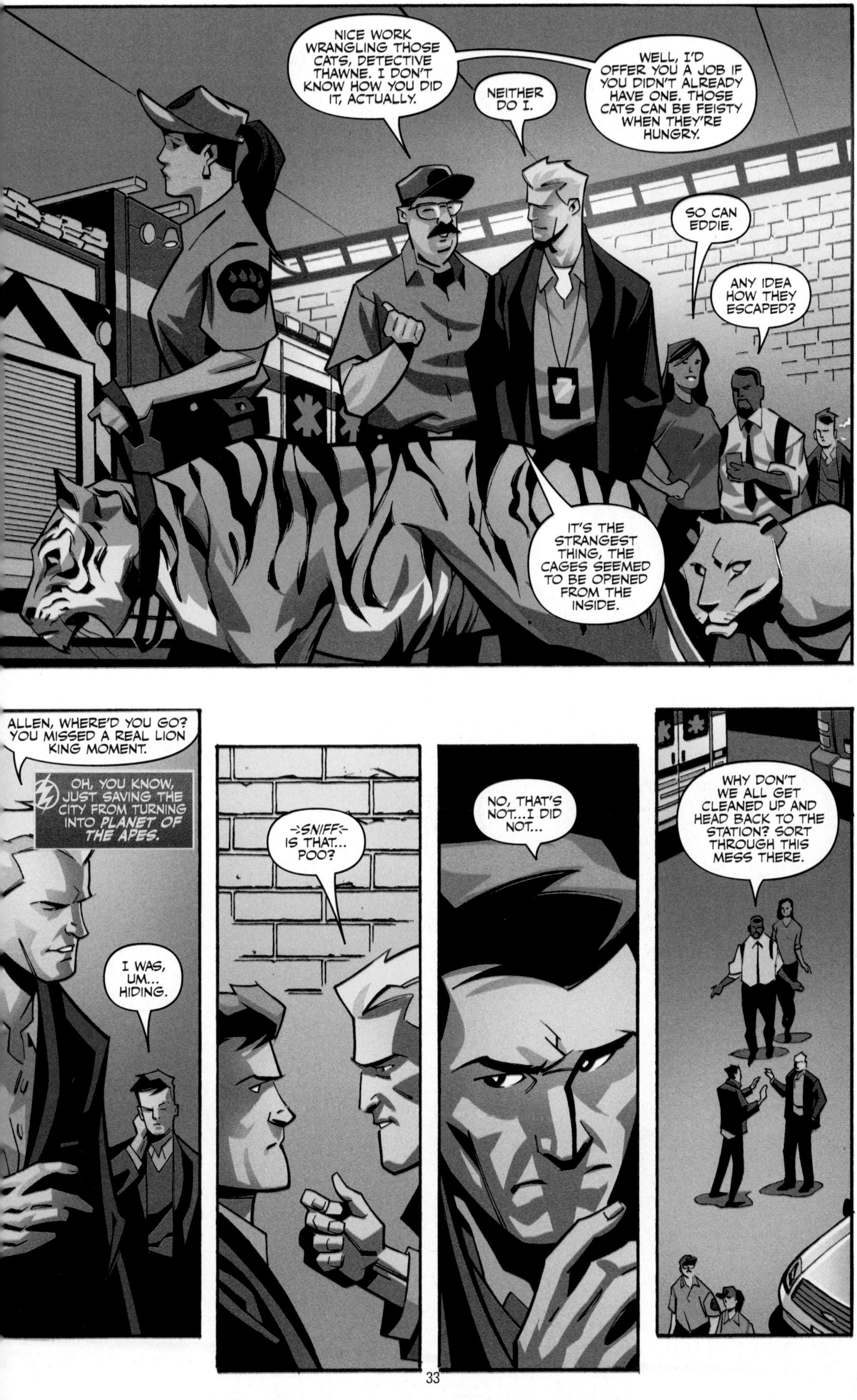
NICE WORK WRANGLING THOSE CATS, DETECTIVE THAWNE. I DON'T KNOW HOW YOU DID IT, ACTUALLY.
NEITHER DO I.
WELL, I'D OFFER YOU A JOB IF YOU DIDN'T ALREADY HAVE ONE. THOSE CATS CAN BE FEISTY WHEN THEY'RE HUNGRY.
SO CAN EDDIE.
ANY IDEA HOW THEY ESCAPED?
IT'S THE STRANGEST THING, THE CAGES SEEMED TO BE OPENED FROM THE INSIDE.
ALLEN, WHERE'D YOU GO? YOU MISSED A REAL LION KING MOMENT.
OH, YOU KNOW, JUST SAVING THE CITY FROM TURNING INTO PLANET OF THE APES.
I WAS, UM... HIDING.
-SNIFF- IS THAT... POO?
NO, THAT'S NOT...I DID NOT...
WHY DON'T WE ALL GET CLEANED UP AND HEAD BACK TO THE STATION? SORT THROUGH THIS MESS THERE.

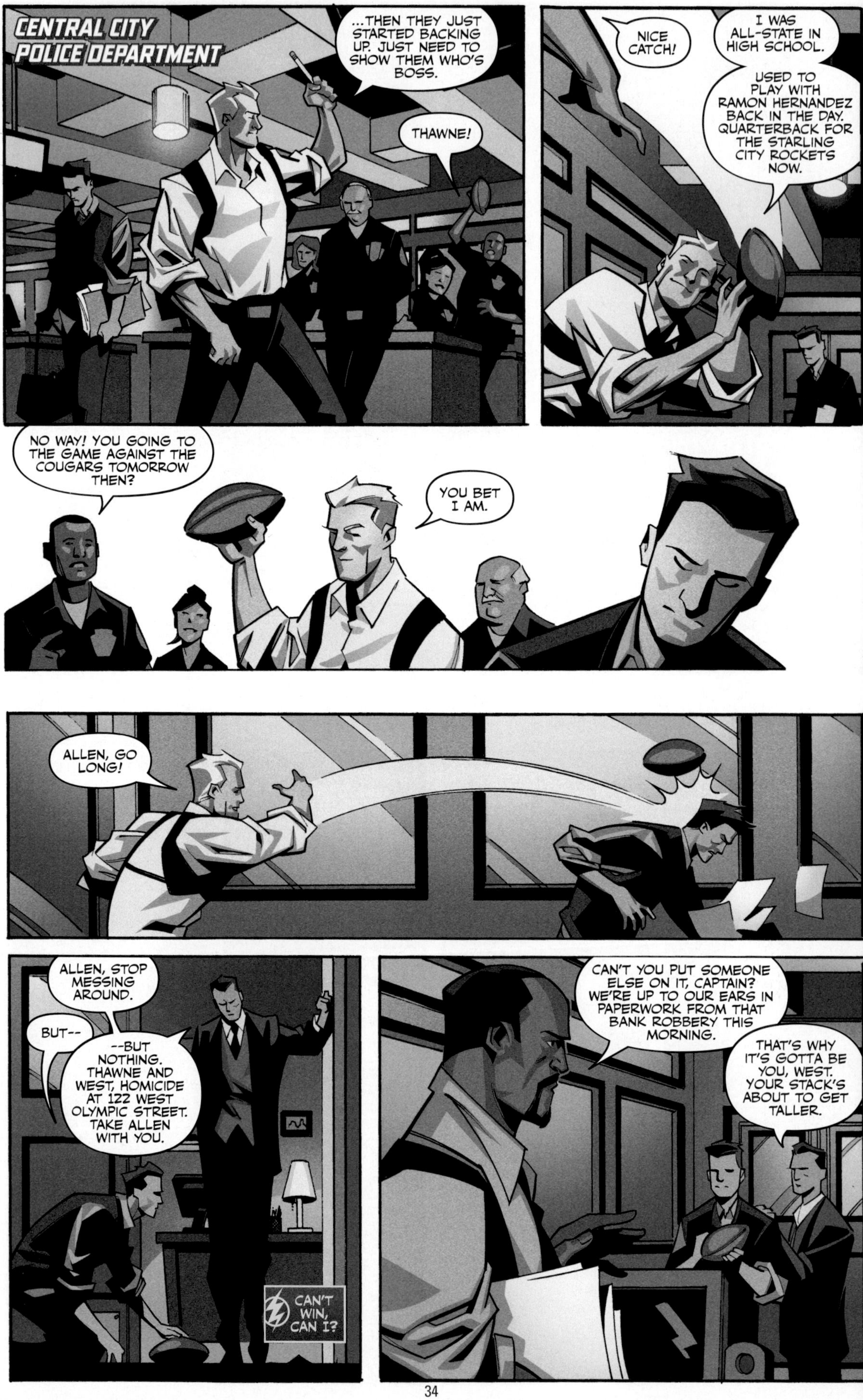
CENTRAL CITY POLICE DEPARTMENT
...THEN THEY JUST STARTED BACKING UP. JUST NEED TO SHOW THEM WHO'S BOSS.
THAWNE!
NICE CATCH!
I WAS ALL-STATE IN HIGH SCHOOL.
USED TO PLAY WITH RAMON HERNANDEZ BACK IN THE DAY. QUARTERBACK FOR THE STARLING CITY ROCKETS NOW.
NO WAY! YOU GOING TO THE GAME AGAINST THE COUGARS TOMORROW THEN?
YOU BET I AM.
ALLEN, GO LONG!
ALLEN, STOP MESSING AROUND.
BUT--
--BUT NOTHING. THAWNE AND WEST, HOMICIDE AT 122 WEST OLYMPIC STREET. TAKE ALLEN WITH YOU.
CAN'T WIN, CAN I?
CAN'T YOU PUT SOMEONE ELSE ON IT, CAPTAIN? WE'RE UP TO OUR EARS IN PAPERWORK FROM THAT BANK ROBBERY THIS MORNING.
THAT'S WHY IT'S GOTTA BE YOU, WEST. YOUR STACK'S ABOUT TO GET TALLER.

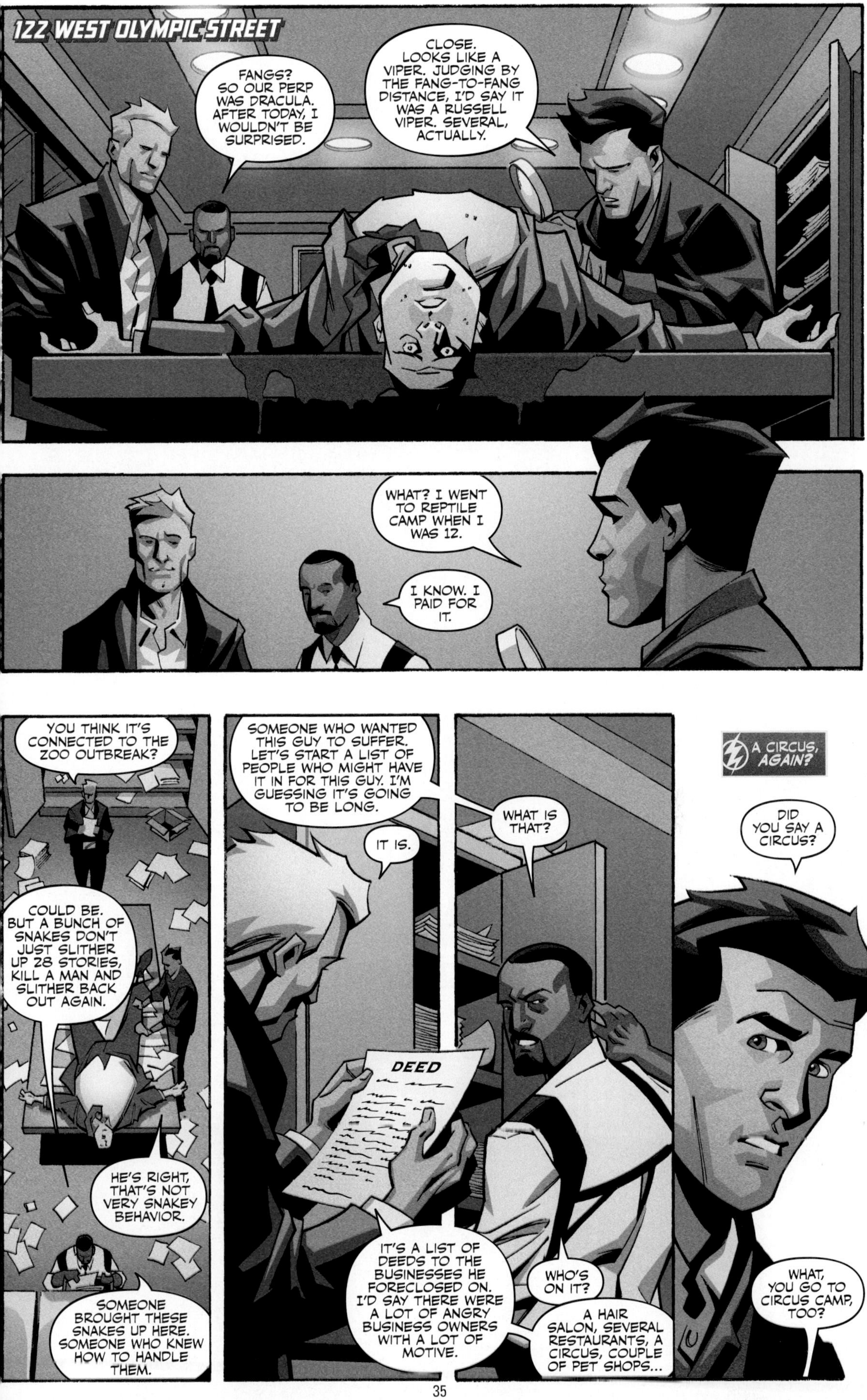

122 WEST OLYMPIC STREET
FANGS? SO OUR PERP WAS DRACULA. AFTER TODAY, I WOULDN'T BE SURPRISED.
CLOSE. LOOKS LIKE A VIPER. JUDGING BY THE FANG-TO-FANG DISTANCE, I'D SAY IT WAS A RUSSELL VIPER. SEVERAL, ACTUALLY.
WHAT? I WENT TO REPTILE CAMP WHEN I WAS 12.
I KNOW. I PAID FOR IT.
YOU THINK IT'S CONNECTED TO THE ZOO OUTBREAK?
COULD BE. BUT A BUNCH OF SNAKES DON'T JUST SLITHER UP 28 STORIES, KILL A MAN AND SLITHER BACK OUT AGAIN.
HE'S RIGHT, THAT'S NOT VERY SNAKEY BEHAVIOR.
SOMEONE BROUGHT THESE SNAKES UP HERE. SOMEONE WHO KNEW HOW TO HANDLE THEM.
SOMEONE WHO WANTED THIS GUY TO SUFFER. LET'S START A LIST OF PEOPLE WHO MIGHT HAVE IT IN FOR THIS GUY. I'M GUESSING IT'S GOING TO BE LONG.
IT IS.
WHAT IS THAT?
DEED
IT'S A LIST OF DEEDS TO THE BUSINESSES HE FORECLOSED ON. I'D SAY THERE WERE A LOT OF ANGRY BUSINESS OWNERS WITH A LOT OF MOTIVE.
WHO'S ON IT?
A HAIR SALON, SEVERAL RESTAURANTS, A CIRCUS, COUPLE OF PET SHOPS...
A CIRCUS, AGAIN?
DID YOU SAY A CIRCUS?
WHAT, YOU GO TO CIRCUS CAMP, TOO?

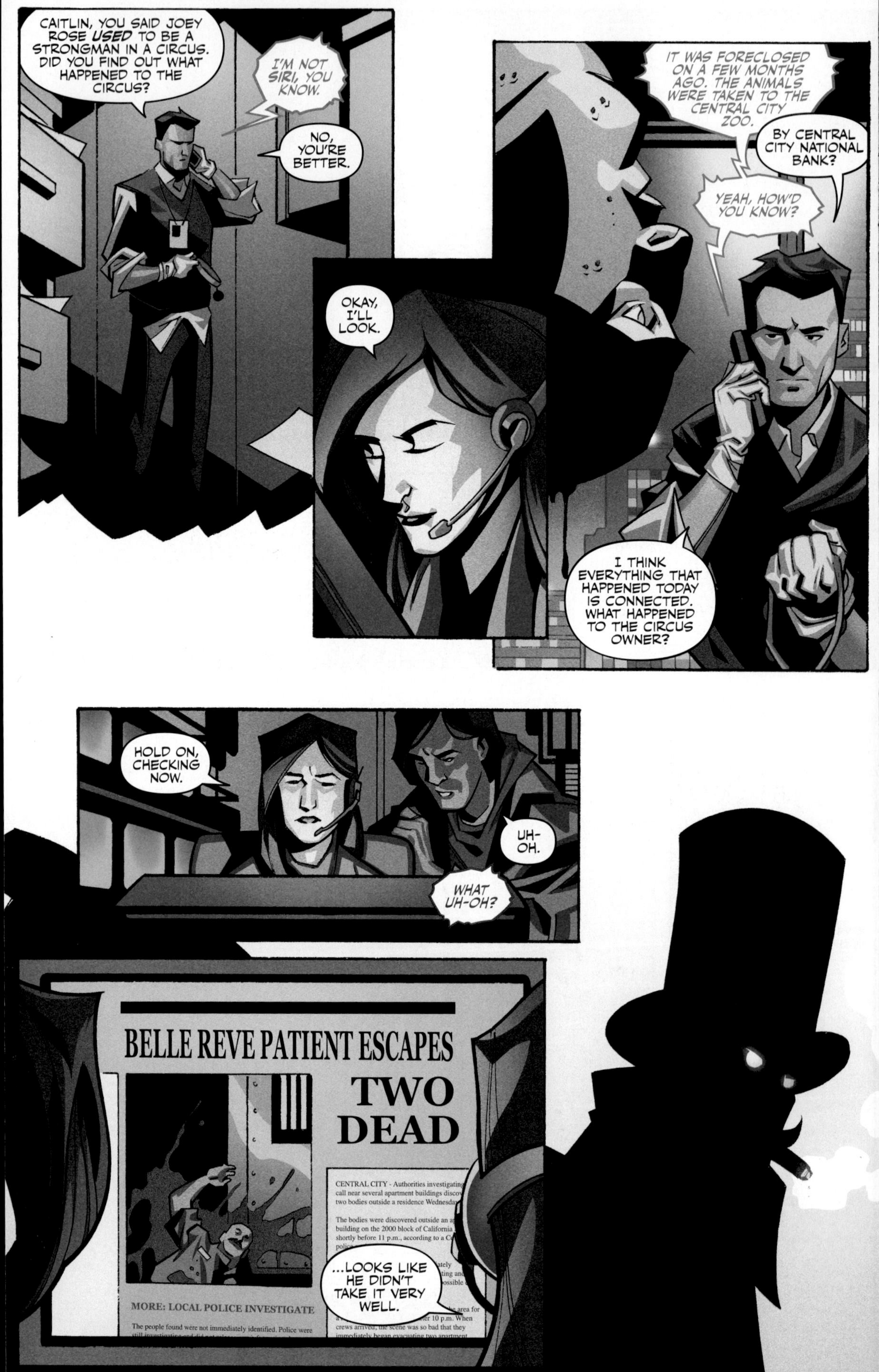
CAITLIN, YOU SAID JOEY ROSE *USED* TO BE A STRONGMAN IN A CIRCUS. DID YOU FIND OUT WHAT HAPPENED TO THE CIRCUS?
I'M NOT SIRI, YOU KNOW.
NO, YOU'RE BETTER.
OKAY, I'LL LOOK.
IT WAS FORECLOSED ON A FEW MONTHS AGO. THE ANIMALS WERE TAKEN TO THE CENTRAL CITY ZOO.
BY CENTRAL CITY NATIONAL BANK?
YEAH, HOW'D YOU KNOW?
I THINK EVERYTHING THAT HAPPENED TODAY IS CONNECTED. WHAT HAPPENED TO THE CIRCUS OWNER?
HOLD ON, CHECKING NOW.
UH-OH.
WHAT UH-OH?
BELLE REVE PATIENT ESCAPES
TWO DEAD
MORE: LOCAL POLICE INVESTIGATE
The people found were not immediately identified. Police were
...LOOKS LIKE HE DIDN'T TAKE IT VERY WELL.

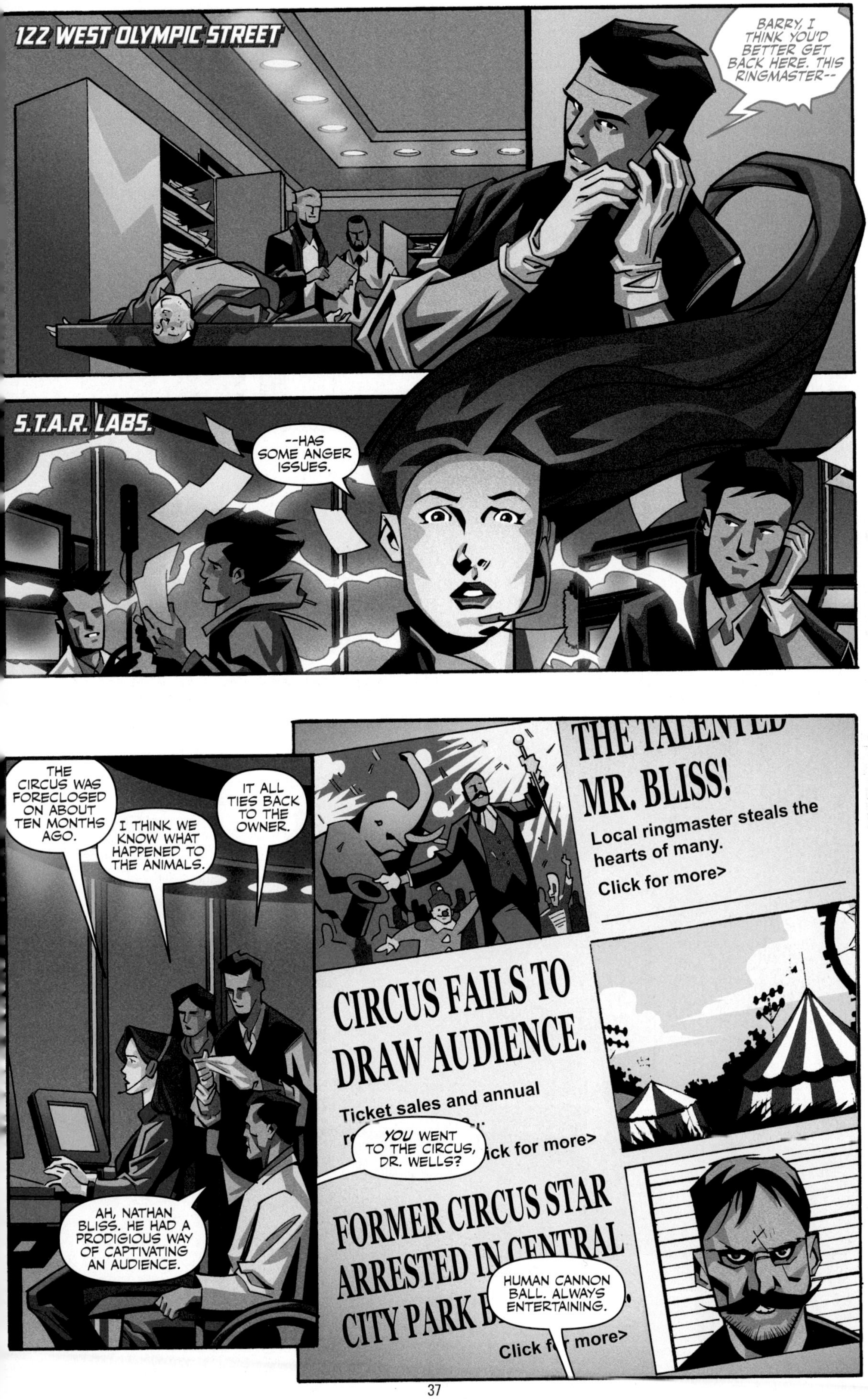
122 WEST OLYMPIC STREET
BARRY, I THINK YOU'D BETTER GET BACK HERE. THIS RINGMASTER--
S.T.A.R. LABS.
--HAS SOME ANGER ISSUES.
THE CIRCUS WAS FORECLOSED ON ABOUT TEN MONTHS AGO.
I THINK WE KNOW WHAT HAPPENED TO THE ANIMALS.
IT ALL TIES BACK TO THE OWNER.
AH, NATHAN BLISS. HE HAD A PRODIGIOUS WAY OF CAPTIVATING AN AUDIENCE.
THE TALENTED MR. BLISS!
Local ringmaster steals the hearts of many.
Click for more>
CIRCUS FAILS TO DRAW AUDIENCE.
Ticket sales and annual
YOU WENT TO THE CIRCUS, DR. WELLS?
FORMER CIRCUS STAR ARRESTED IN CENTRAL CITY PARK
HUMAN CANNON BALL. ALWAYS ENTERTAINING.

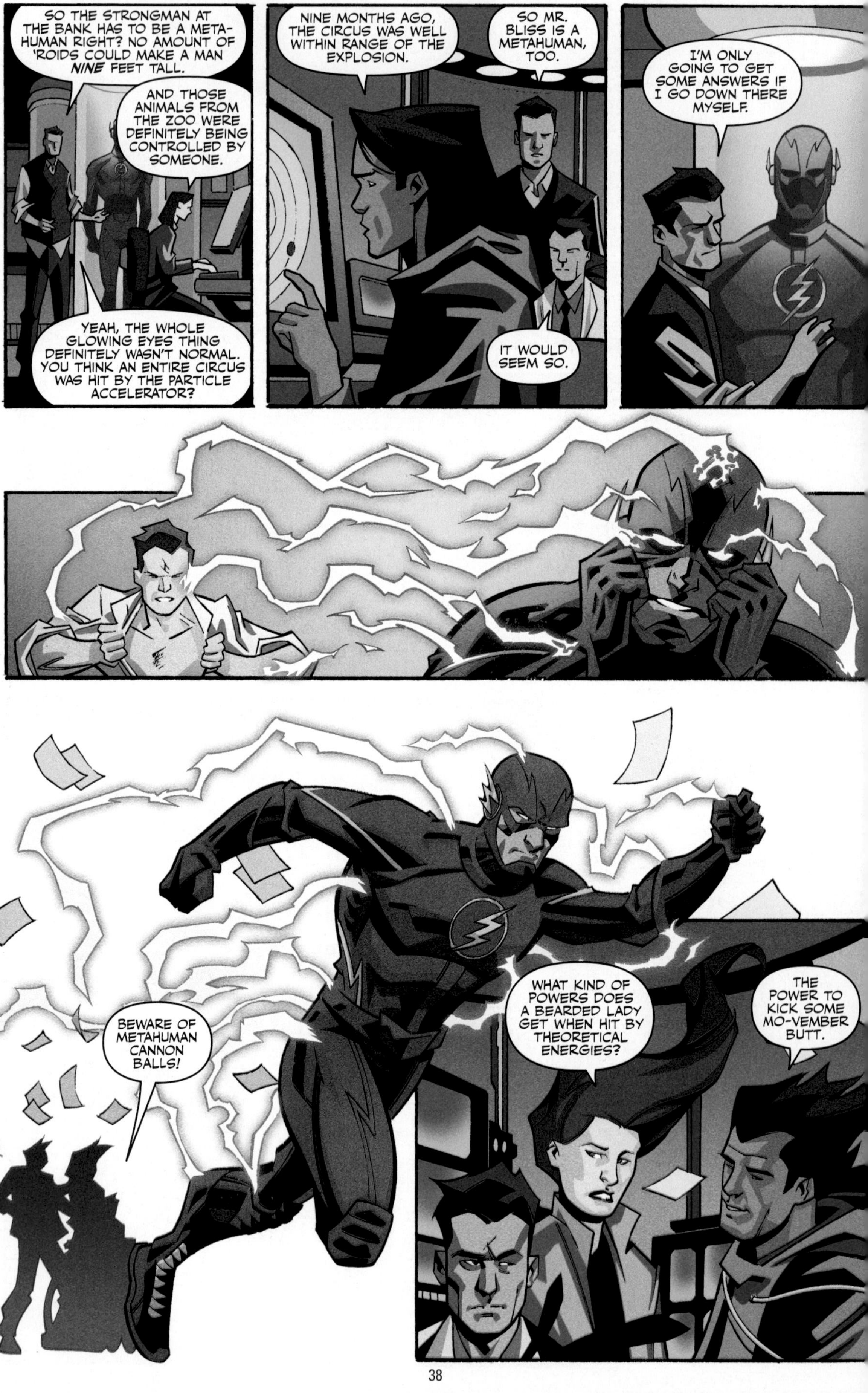
SO THE STRONGMAN AT THE BANK HAS TO BE A METAHUMAN RIGHT? NO AMOUNT OF 'ROIDS COULD MAKE A MAN NINE FEET TALL.
AND THOSE ANIMALS FROM THE ZOO WERE DEFINITELY BEING CONTROLLED BY SOMEONE.
YEAH, THE WHOLE GLOWING EYES THING DEFINITELY WASN'T NORMAL. YOU THINK AN ENTIRE CIRCUS WAS HIT BY THE PARTICLE ACCELERATOR?
NINE MONTHS AGO, THE CIRCUS WAS WELL WITHIN RANGE OF THE EXPLOSION.
SO MR. BLISS IS A METAHUMAN, TOO.
IT WOULD SEEM SO.
I'M ONLY GOING TO GET SOME ANSWERS IF I GO DOWN THERE MYSELF.
BEWARE OF METAHUMAN CANNON BALLS!
WHAT KIND OF POWERS DOES A BEARDED LADY GET WHEN HIT BY THEORETICAL ENERGIES?
THE POWER TO KICK SOME MO-VEMBER BUTT.

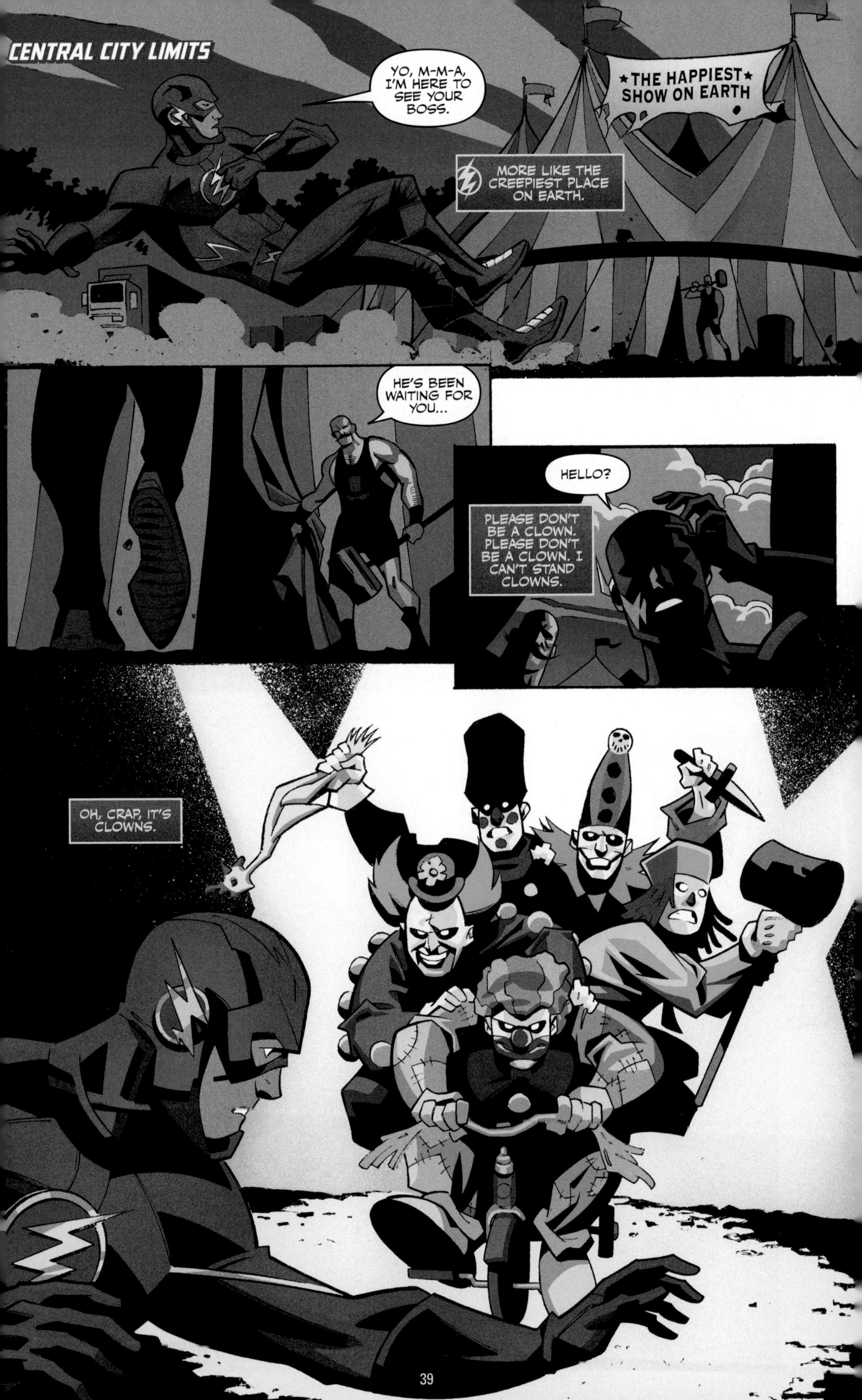
CENTRAL CITY LIMITS
YO, M-M-A, I'M HERE TO SEE YOUR BOSS.
★THE HAPPIEST★ SHOW ON EARTH
MORE LIKE THE CREEPIEST PLACE ON EARTH.
HE'S BEEN WAITING FOR YOU...
HELLO?
PLEASE DON'T BE A CLOWN. PLEASE DON'T BE A CLOWN. I CAN'T STAND CLOWNS.
OH, CRAP, IT'S CLOWNS.

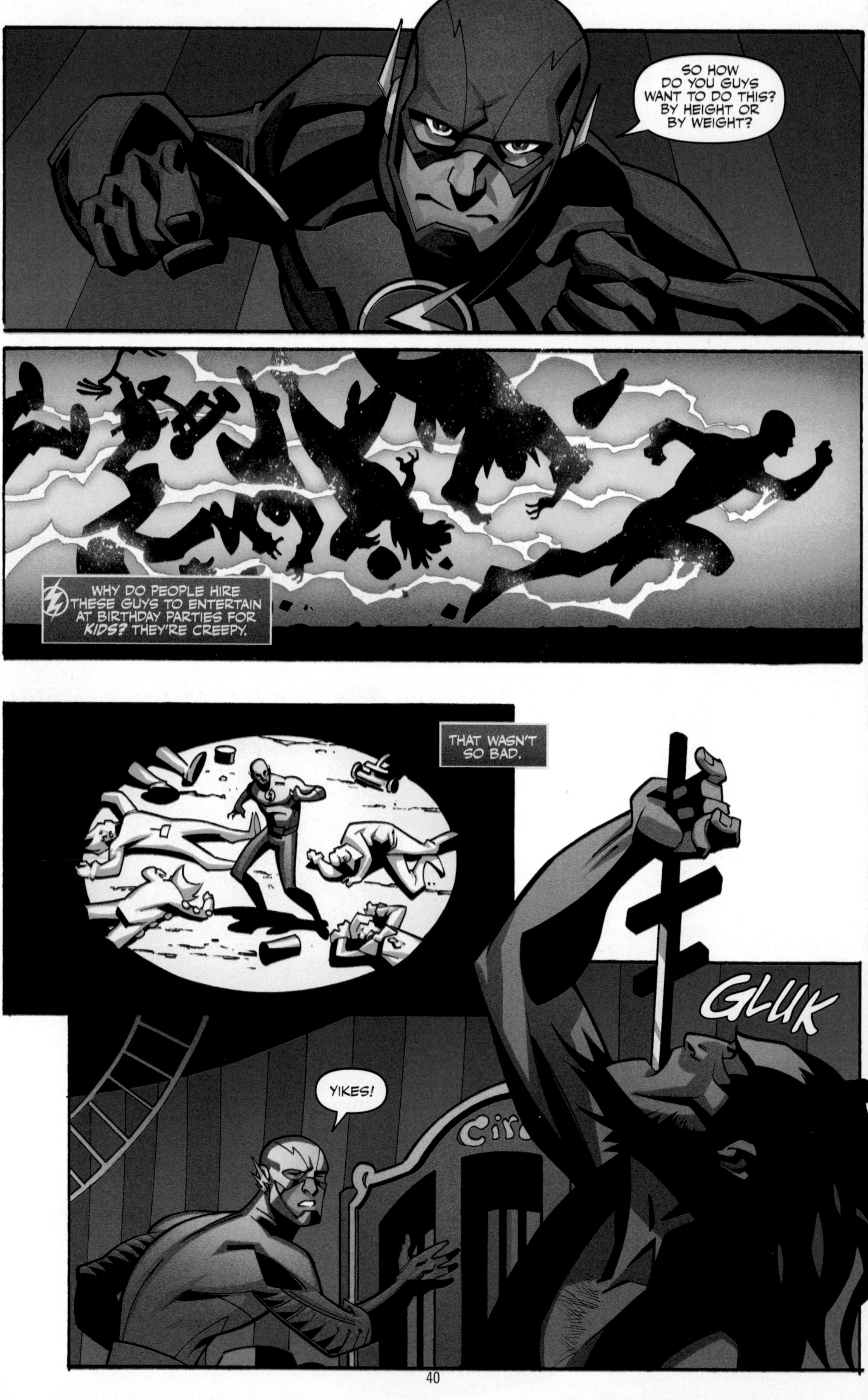
SO HOW DO YOU GUYS WANT TO DO THIS? BY HEIGHT OR BY WEIGHT?
WHY DO PEOPLE HIRE THESE GUYS TO ENTERTAIN AT BIRTHDAY PARTIES FOR KIDS? THEY'RE CREEPY.
THAT WASN'T SO BAD.
GLUK
YIKES!

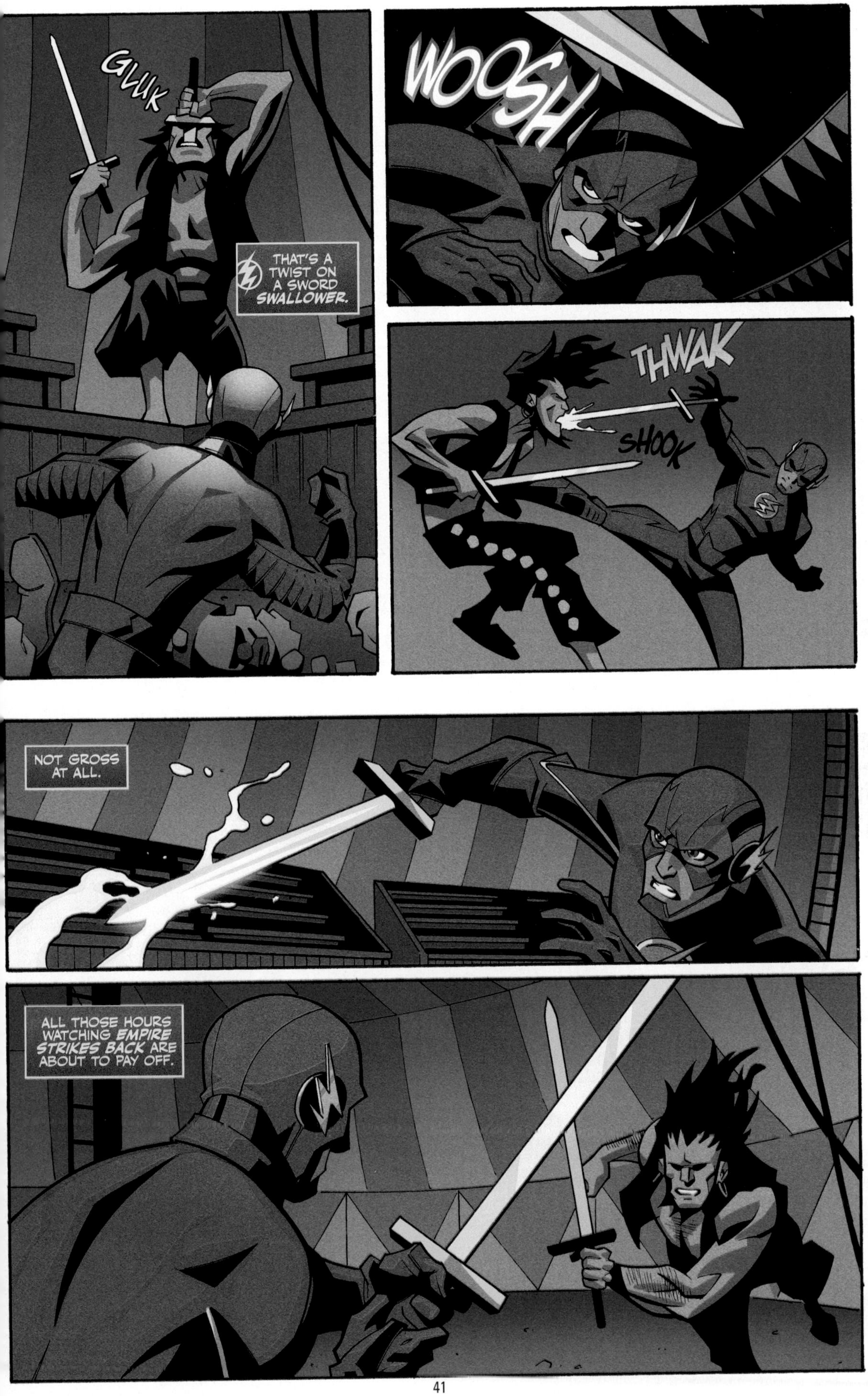
GLUK
THAT'S A TWIST ON A SWORD SWALLOWER.
WOOSH
THWAK
SHOOK
NOT GROSS AT ALL.
ALL THOSE HOURS WATCHING EMPIRE STRIKES BACK ARE ABOUT TO PAY OFF.

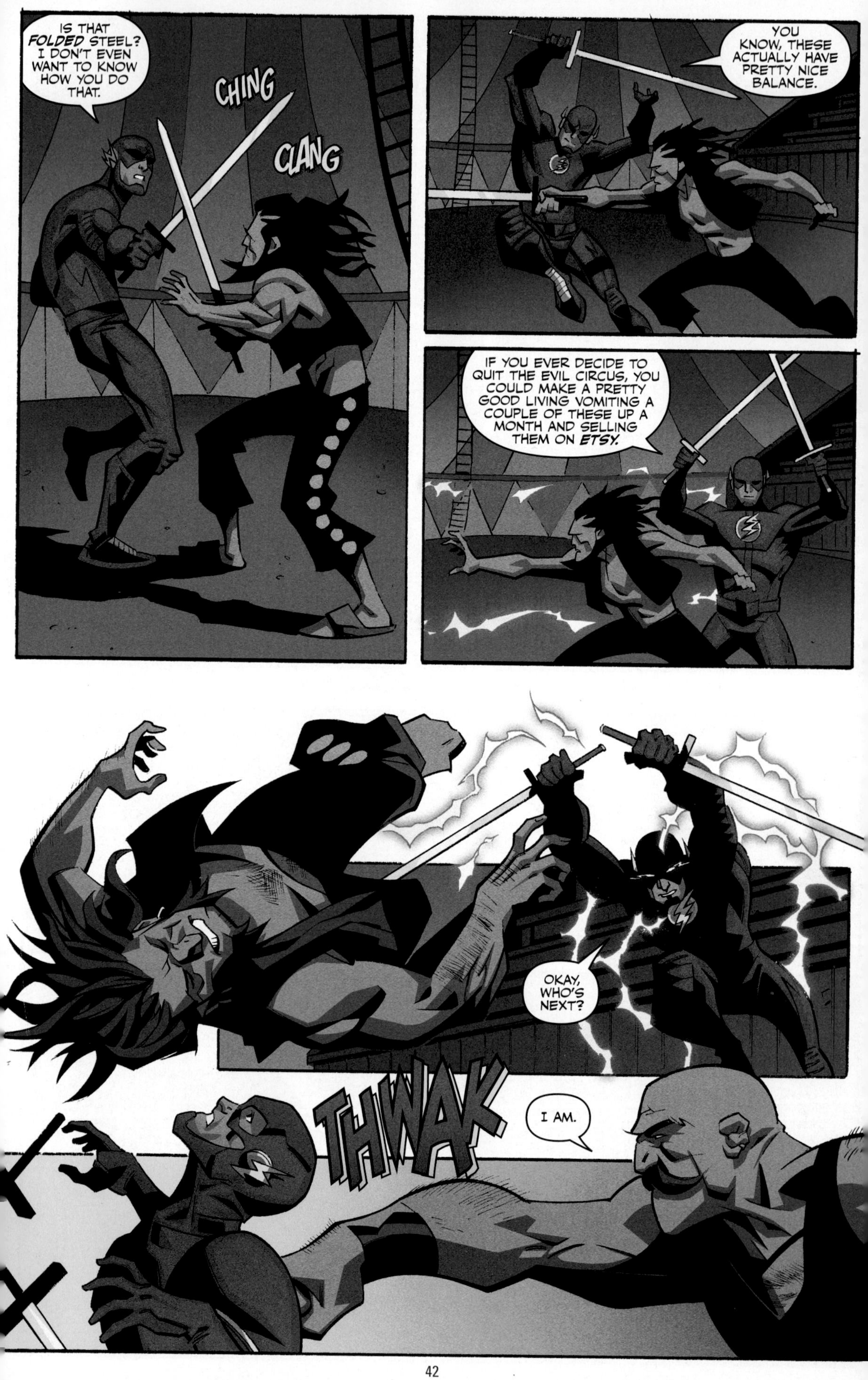
IS THAT FOLDED STEEL? I DON'T EVEN WANT TO KNOW HOW YOU DO THAT.
CHING
CLANG
YOU KNOW, THESE ACTUALLY HAVE PRETTY NICE BALANCE.
IF YOU EVER DECIDE TO QUIT THE EVIL CIRCUS, YOU COULD MAKE A PRETTY GOOD LIVING VOMITING A COUPLE OF THESE UP A MONTH AND SELLING THEM ON ETSY.
OKAY, WHO'S NEXT?
THWAK
I AM.

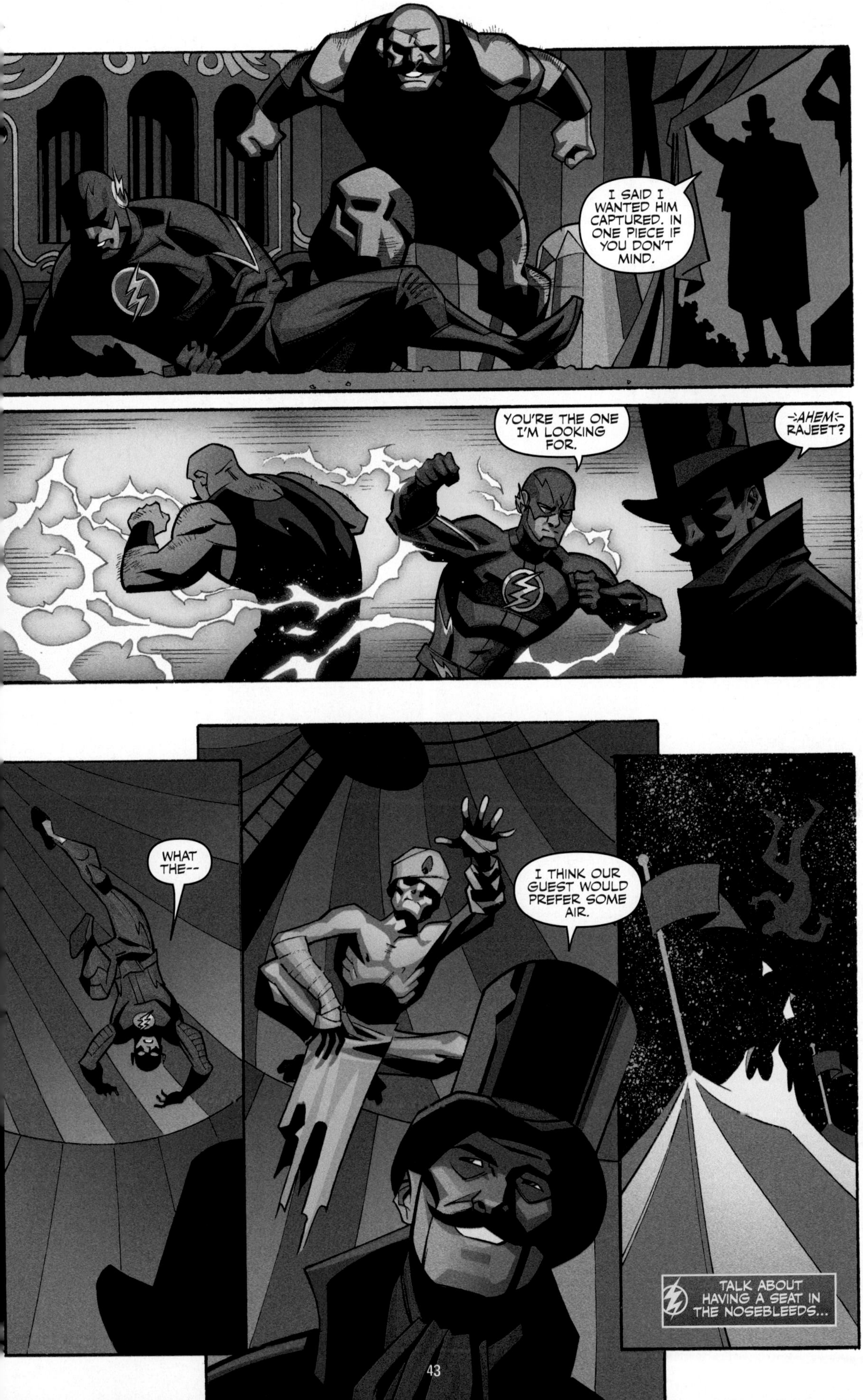

I SAID I WANTED HIM CAPTURED. IN ONE PIECE IF YOU DON'T MIND.
YOU'RE THE ONE I'M LOOKING FOR.
-AHEM- RAJEET?
WHAT THE--
I THINK OUR GUEST WOULD PREFER SOME AIR.
TALK ABOUT HAVING A SEAT IN THE NOSEBLEEDS...

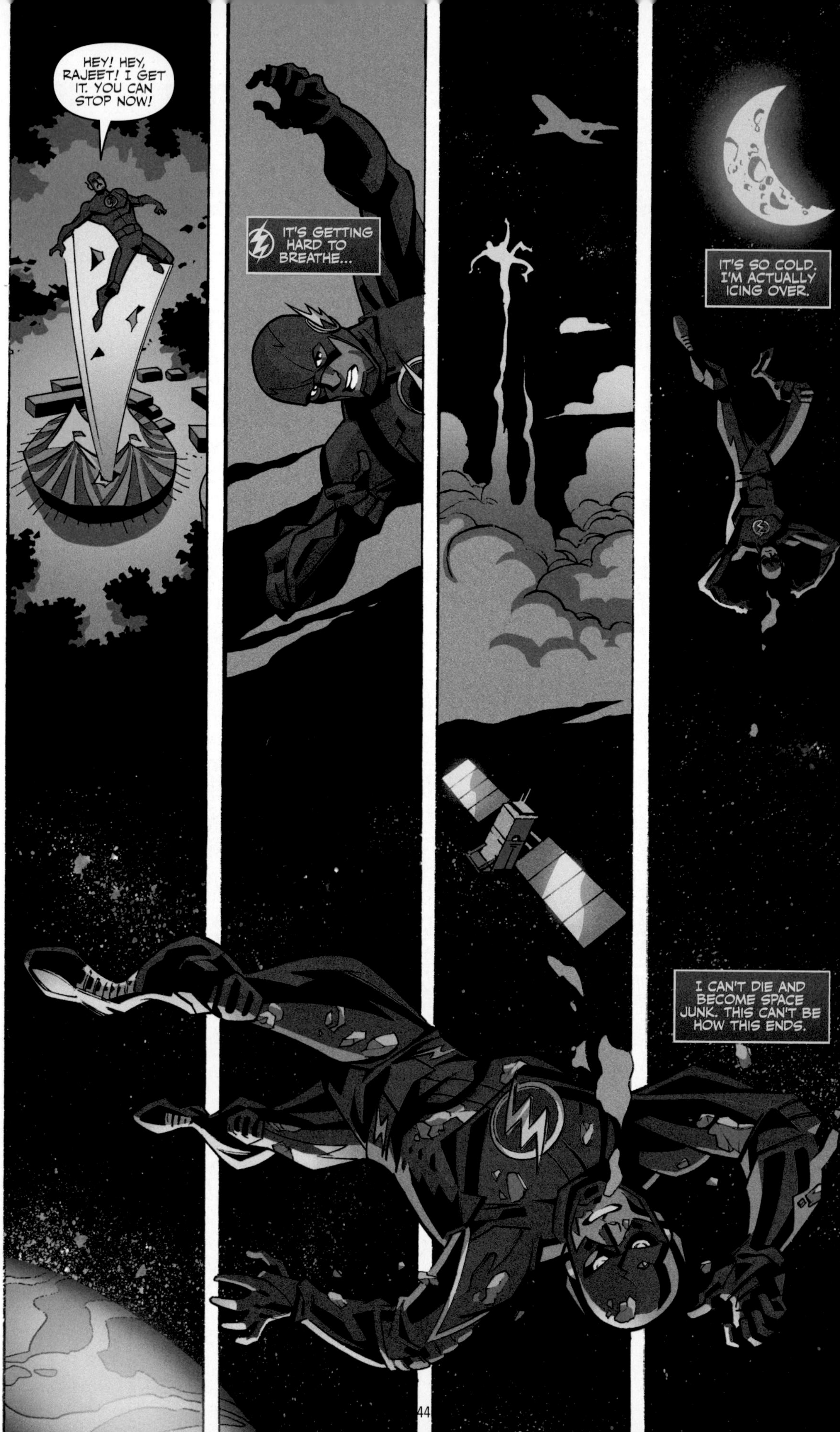
HEY! HEY, RAJEET! I GET IT. YOU CAN STOP NOW!
IT'S GETTING HARD TO BREATHE...
IT'S SO COLD. I'M ACTUALLY ICING OVER.
I CAN'T DIE AND BECOME SPACE JUNK. THIS CAN'T BE HOW THIS ENDS.

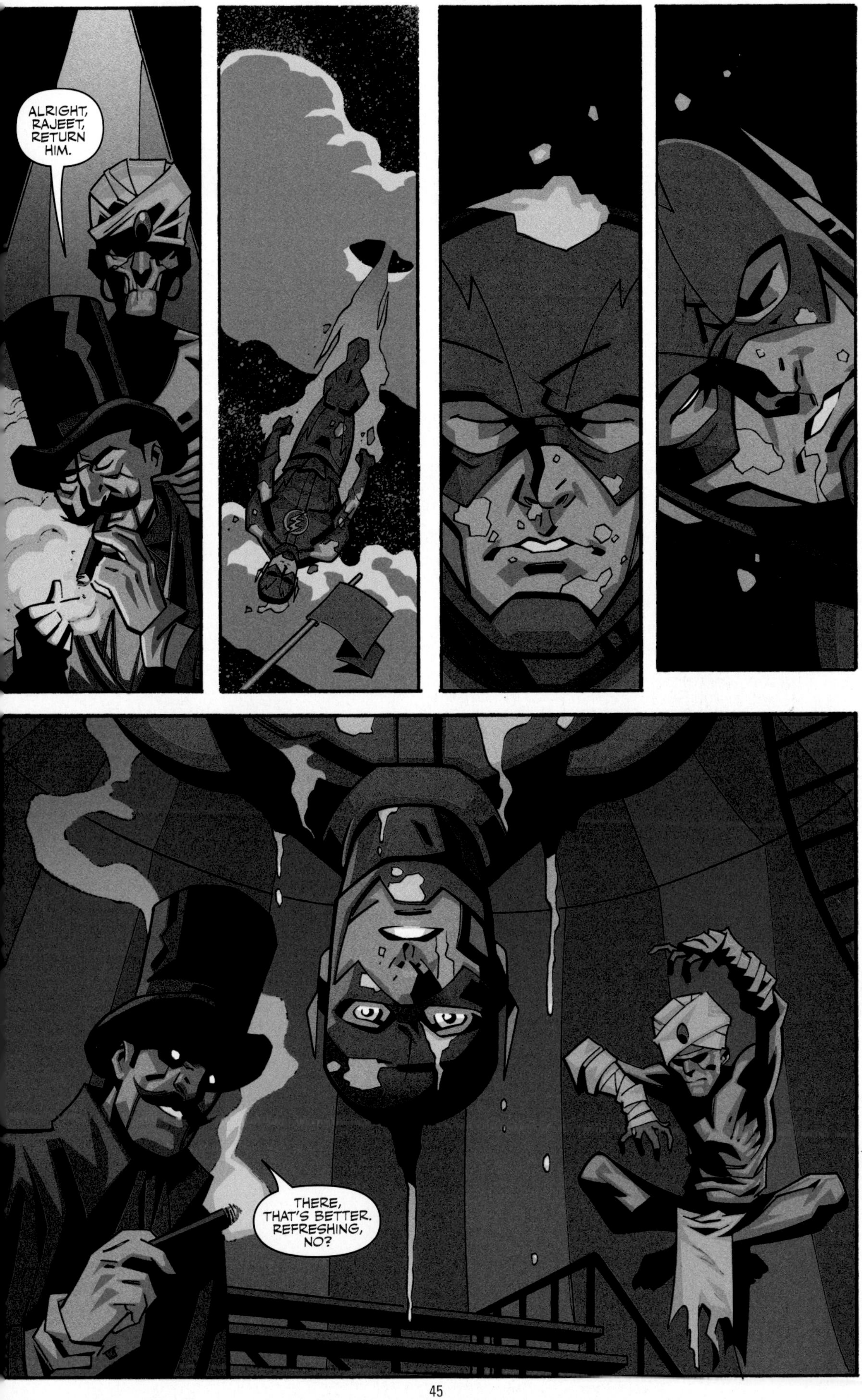
ALRIGHT, RAJEET, RETURN HIM.
THERE, THAT'S BETTER. REFRESHING, NO?

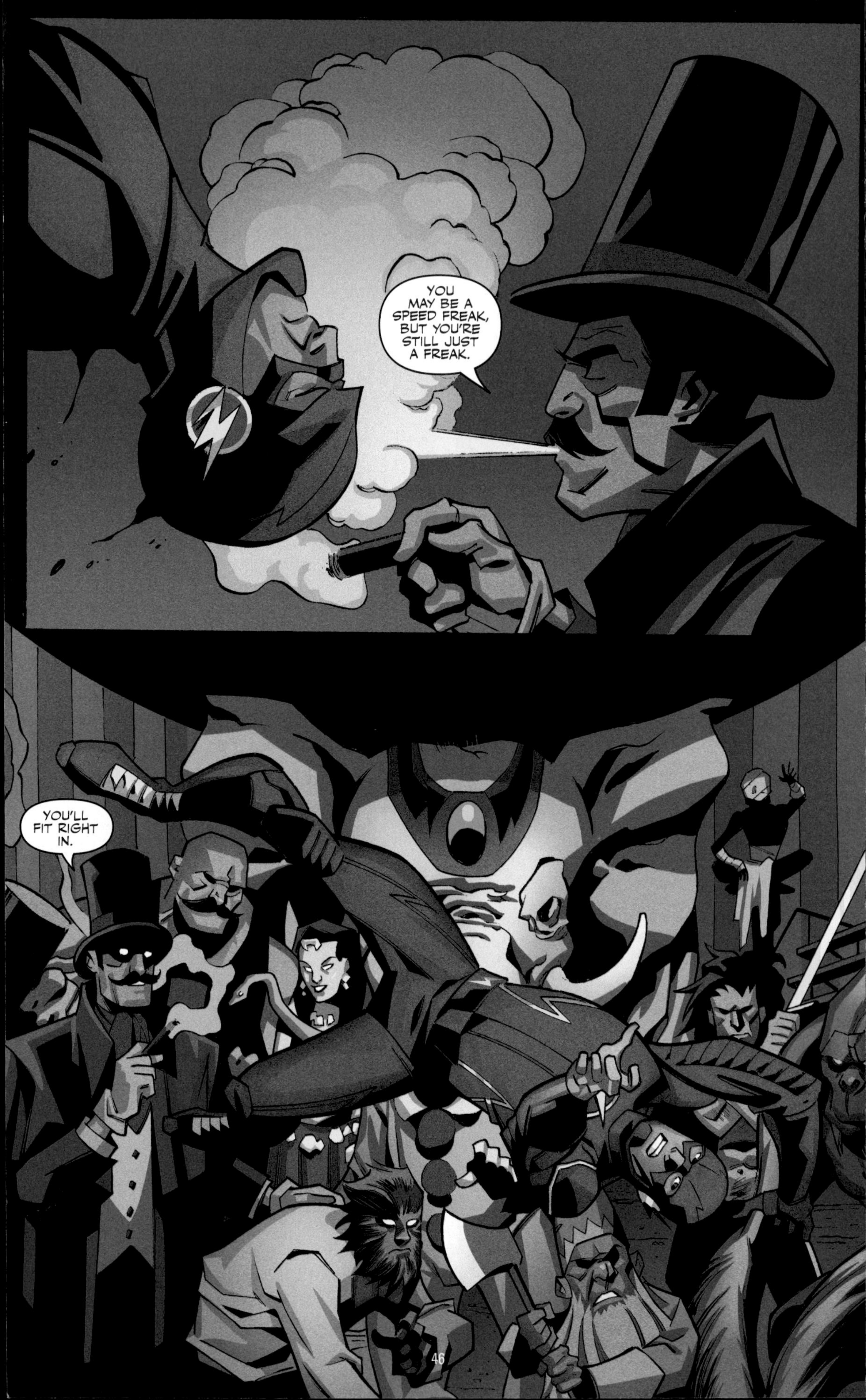
YOU MAY BE A SPEED FREAK, BUT YOU'RE STILL JUST A FREAK.
YOU'LL FIT RIGHT IN.

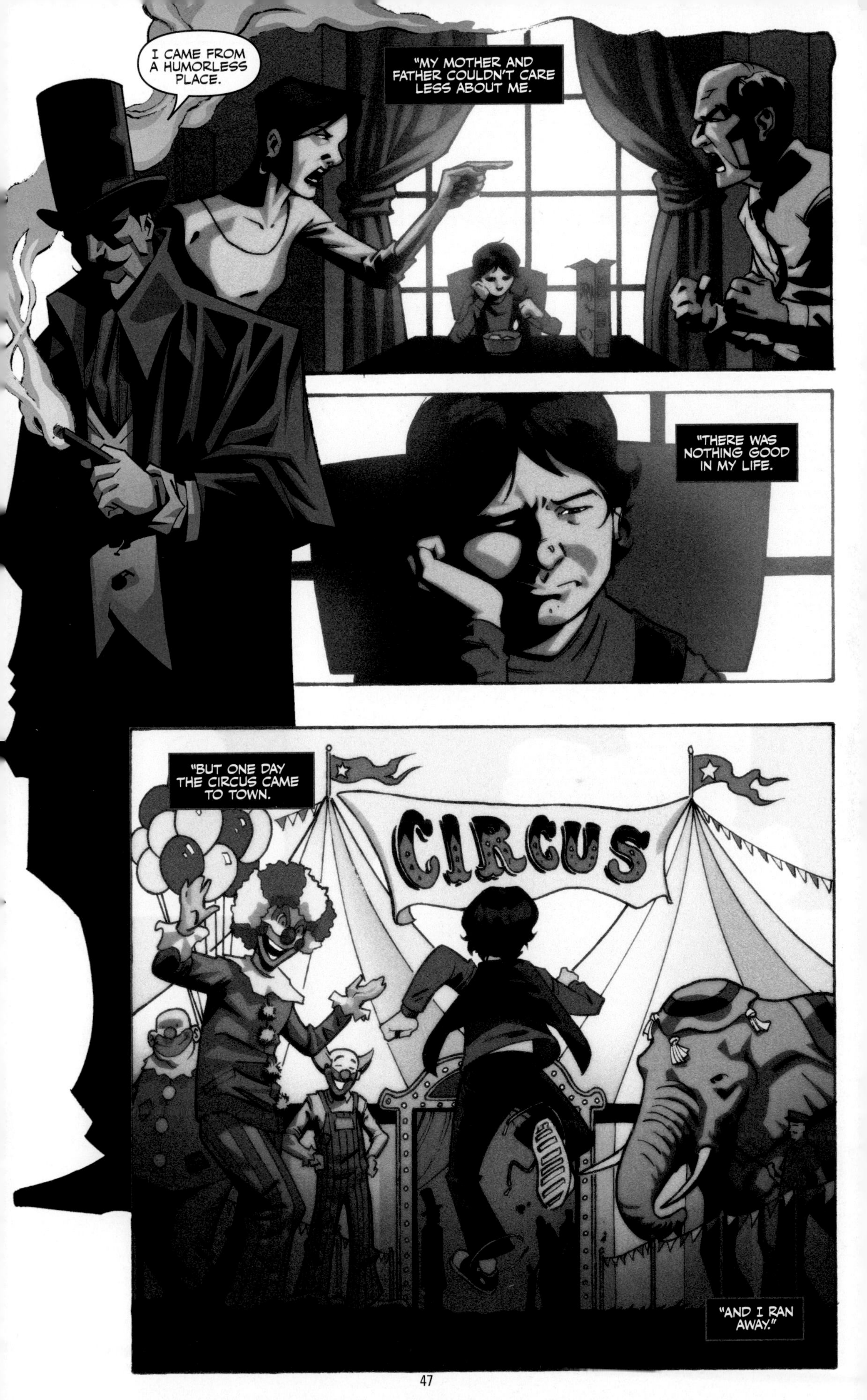
I CAME FROM A HUMORLESS PLACE.
"MY MOTHER AND FATHER COULDN'T CARE LESS ABOUT ME.
"THERE WAS NOTHING GOOD IN MY LIFE.
"BUT ONE DAY THE CIRCUS CAME TO TOWN.
CIRCUS
"AND I RAN AWAY."

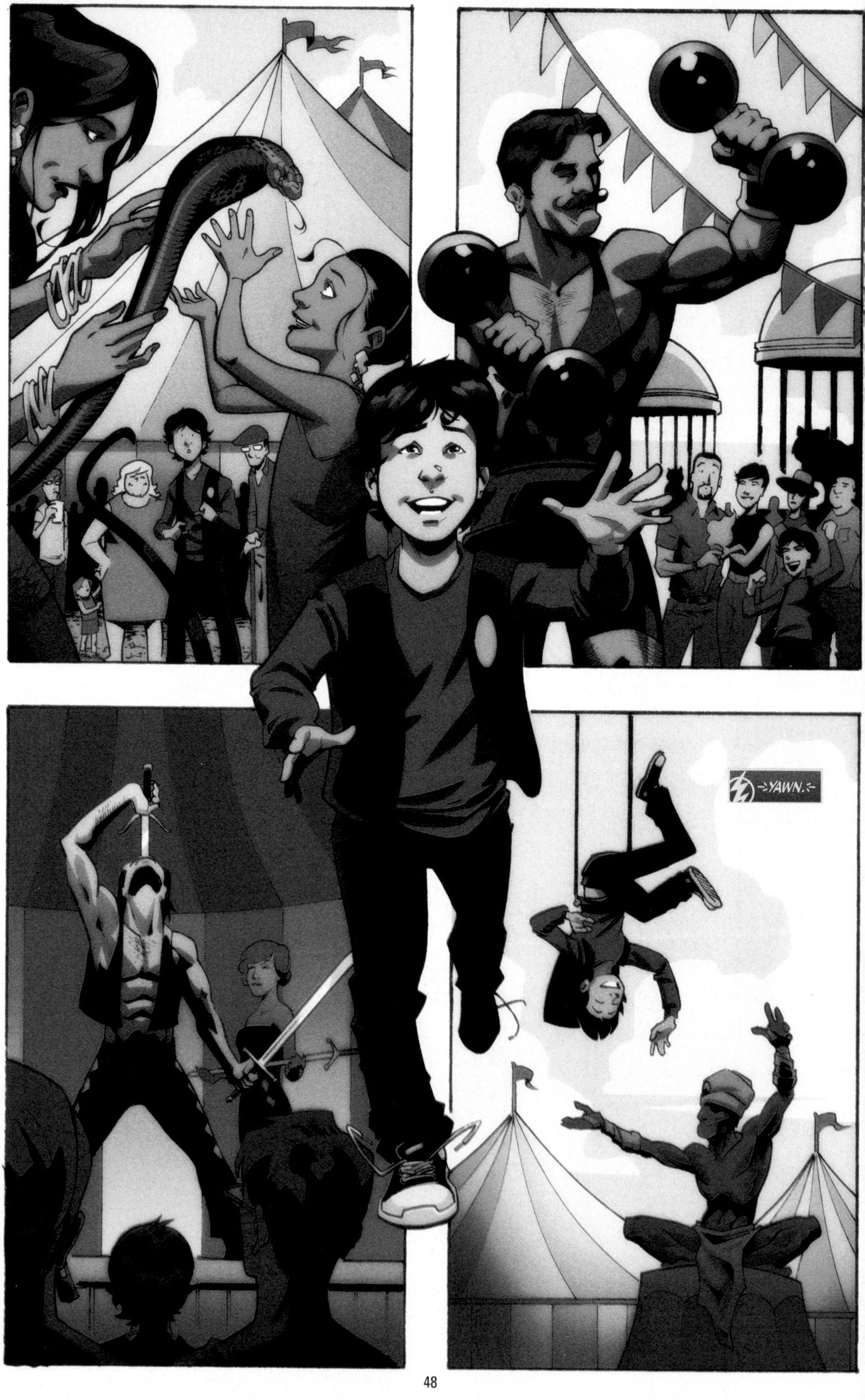
-YAWN.-

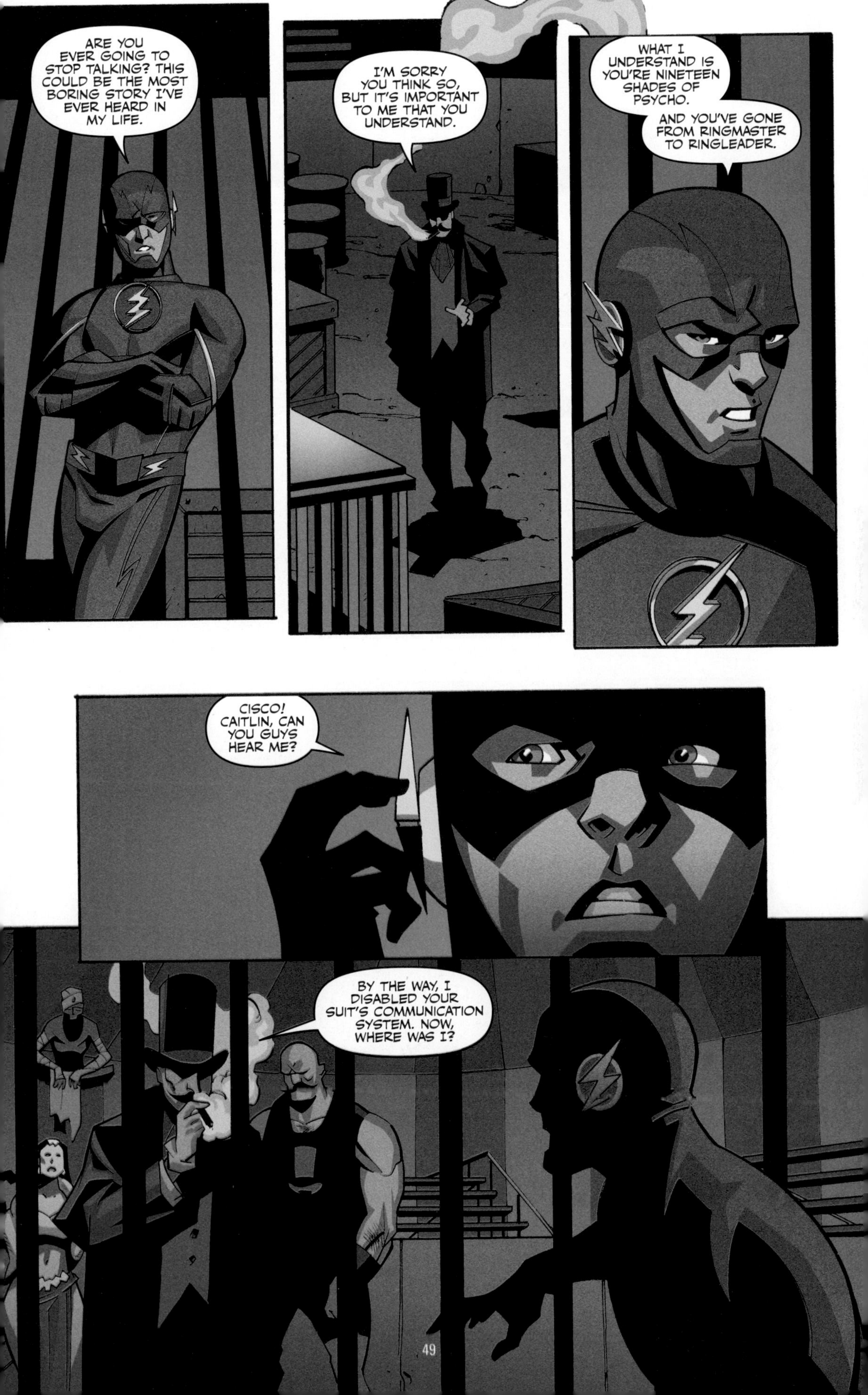
ARE YOU EVER GOING TO STOP TALKING? THIS COULD BE THE MOST BORING STORY I'VE EVER HEARD IN MY LIFE.
I'M SORRY YOU THINK SO, BUT IT'S IMPORTANT TO ME THAT YOU UNDERSTAND.
WHAT I UNDERSTAND IS YOU'RE NINETEEN SHADES OF PSYCHO.
AND YOU'VE GONE FROM RINGMASTER TO RINGLEADER.
CISCO! CAITLIN, CAN YOU GUYS HEAR ME?
BY THE WAY, I DISABLED YOUR SUIT'S COMMUNICATION SYSTEM. NOW, WHERE WAS I?

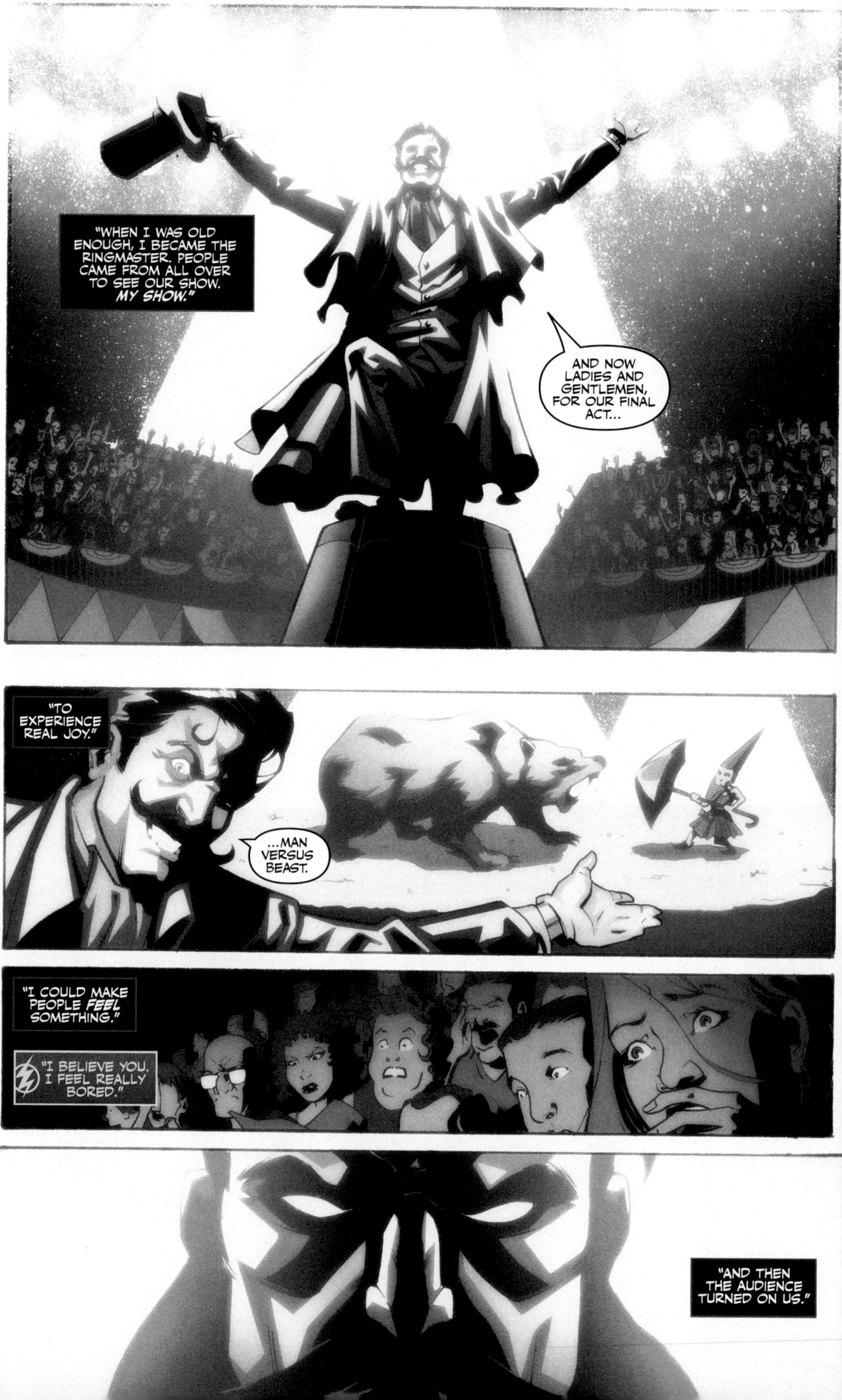
"WHEN I WAS OLD ENOUGH, I BECAME THE RINGMASTER. PEOPLE CAME FROM ALL OVER TO SEE OUR SHOW. MY SHOW."
AND NOW LADIES AND GENTLEMEN, FOR OUR FINAL ACT...
"TO EXPERIENCE REAL JOY."
...MAN VERSUS BEAST.
"I COULD MAKE PEOPLE FEEL SOMETHING."
"I BELIEVE YOU. I FEEL REALLY BORED."
"AND THEN THE AUDIENCE TURNED ON US."

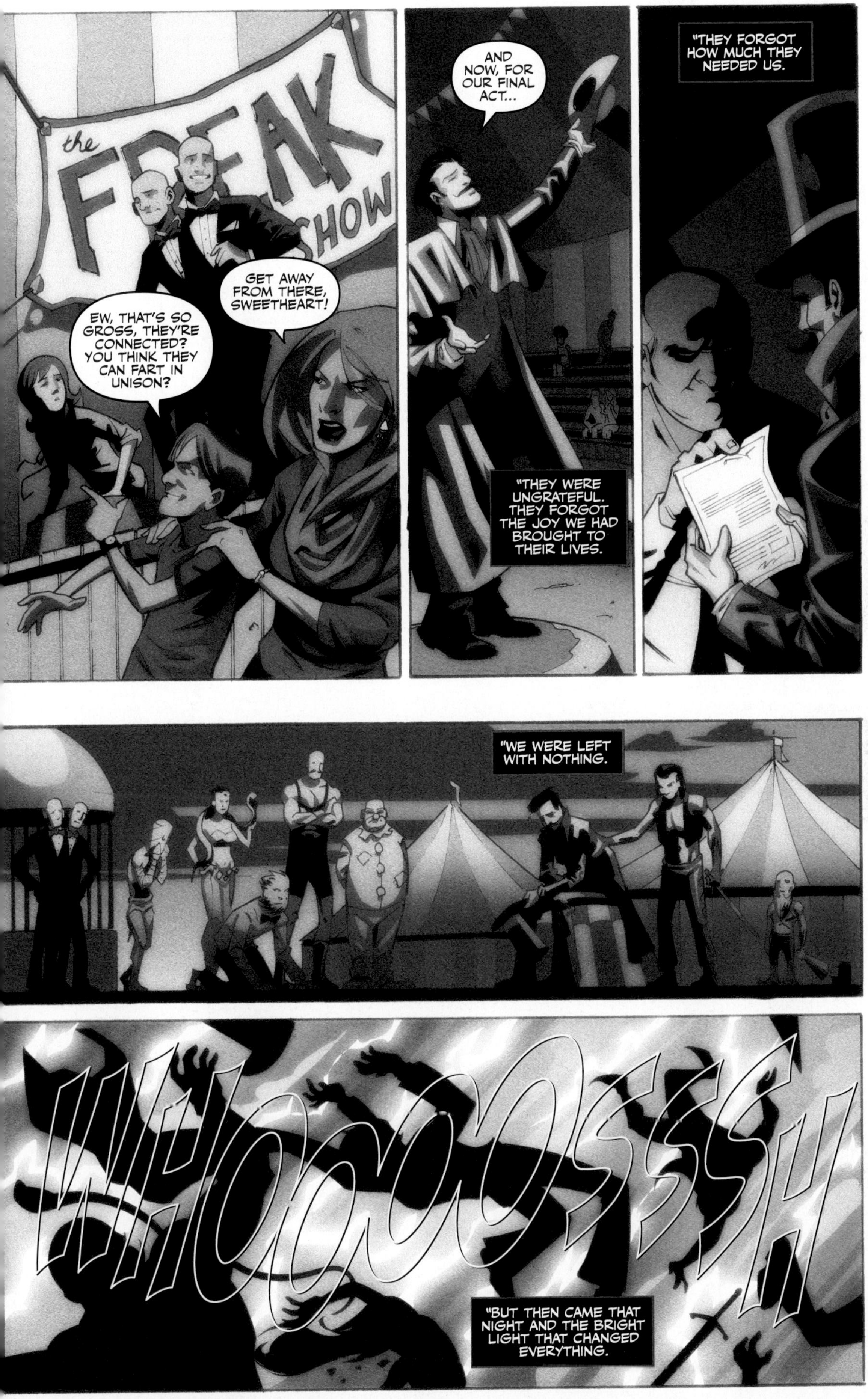
EW, THAT'S SO GROSS, THEY'RE CONNECTED? YOU THINK THEY CAN FART IN UNISON?
GET AWAY FROM THERE, SWEETHEART!
the FREAK SHOW
AND NOW, FOR OUR FINAL ACT...
"THEY WERE UNGRATEFUL. THEY FORGOT THE JOY WE HAD BROUGHT TO THEIR LIVES.
"THEY FORGOT HOW MUCH THEY NEEDED US.
"WE WERE LEFT WITH NOTHING.
WHOOOOOSSSH
"BUT THEN CAME THAT NIGHT AND THE BRIGHT LIGHT THAT CHANGED EVERYTHING.

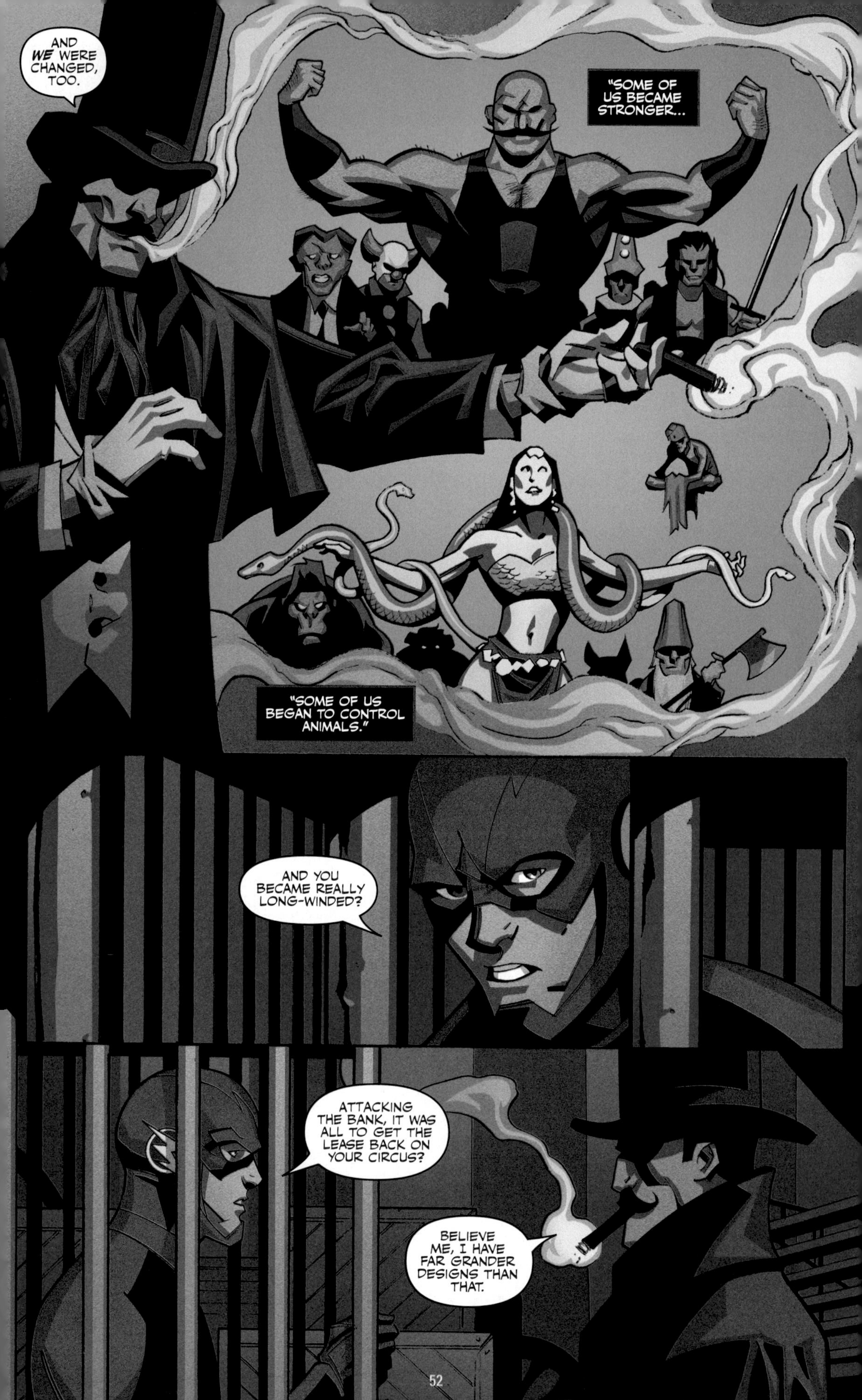
AND WE WERE CHANGED, TOO.
"SOME OF US BECAME STRONGER...
"SOME OF US BEGAN TO CONTROL ANIMALS."
AND YOU BECAME REALLY LONG-WINDED?
ATTACKING THE BANK, IT WAS ALL TO GET THE LEASE BACK ON YOUR CIRCUS?
BELIEVE ME, I HAVE FAR GRANDER DESIGNS THAN THAT.

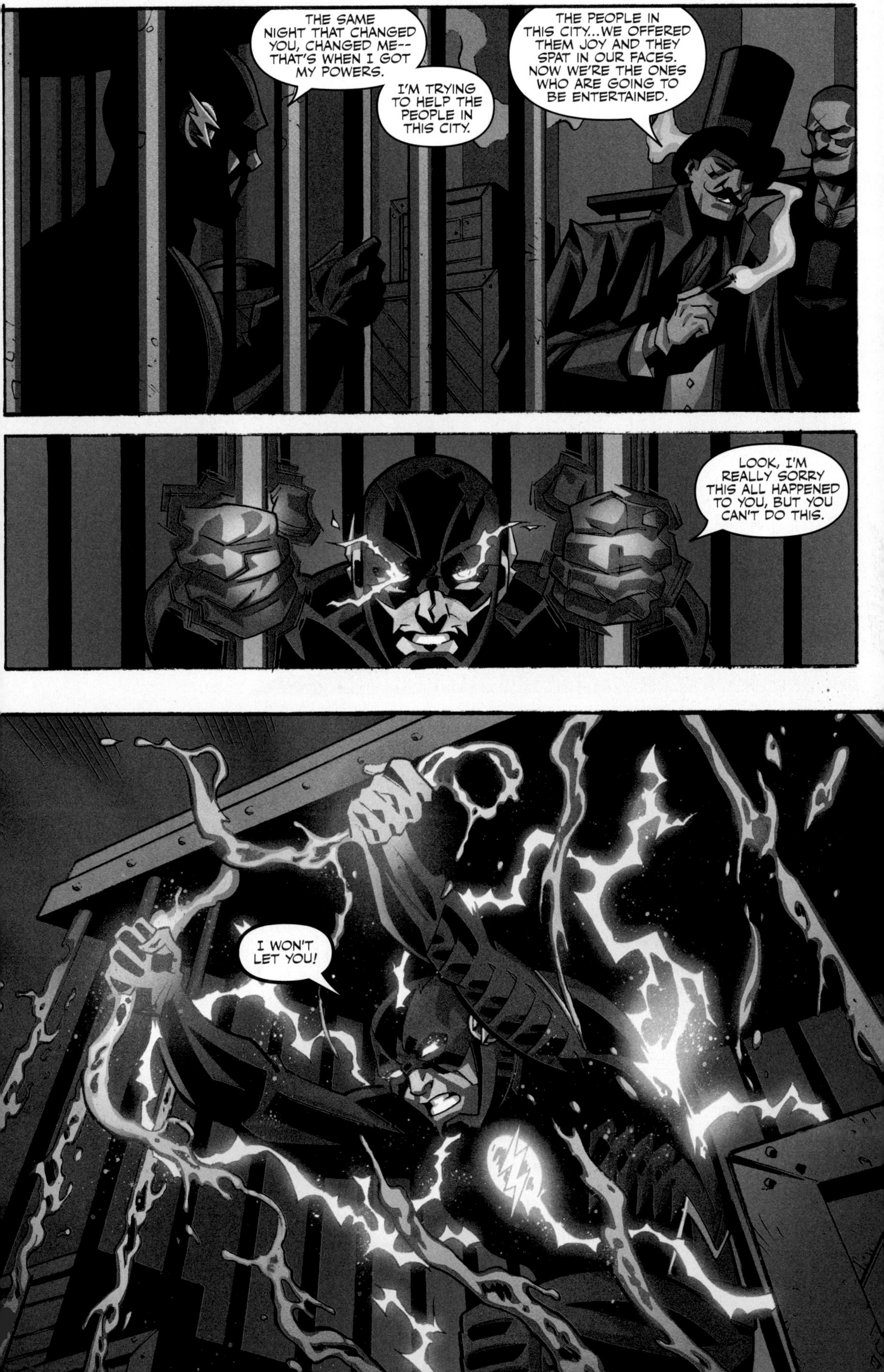

THE SAME NIGHT THAT CHANGED YOU, CHANGED ME-- THAT'S WHEN I GOT MY POWERS.
I'M TRYING TO HELP THE PEOPLE IN THIS CITY.
THE PEOPLE IN THIS CITY...WE OFFERED THEM JOY AND THEY SPAT IN OUR FACES. NOW WE'RE THE ONES WHO ARE GOING TO BE ENTERTAINED.
LOOK, I'M REALLY SORRY THIS ALL HAPPENED TO YOU, BUT YOU CAN'T DO THIS.
I WON'T LET YOU!

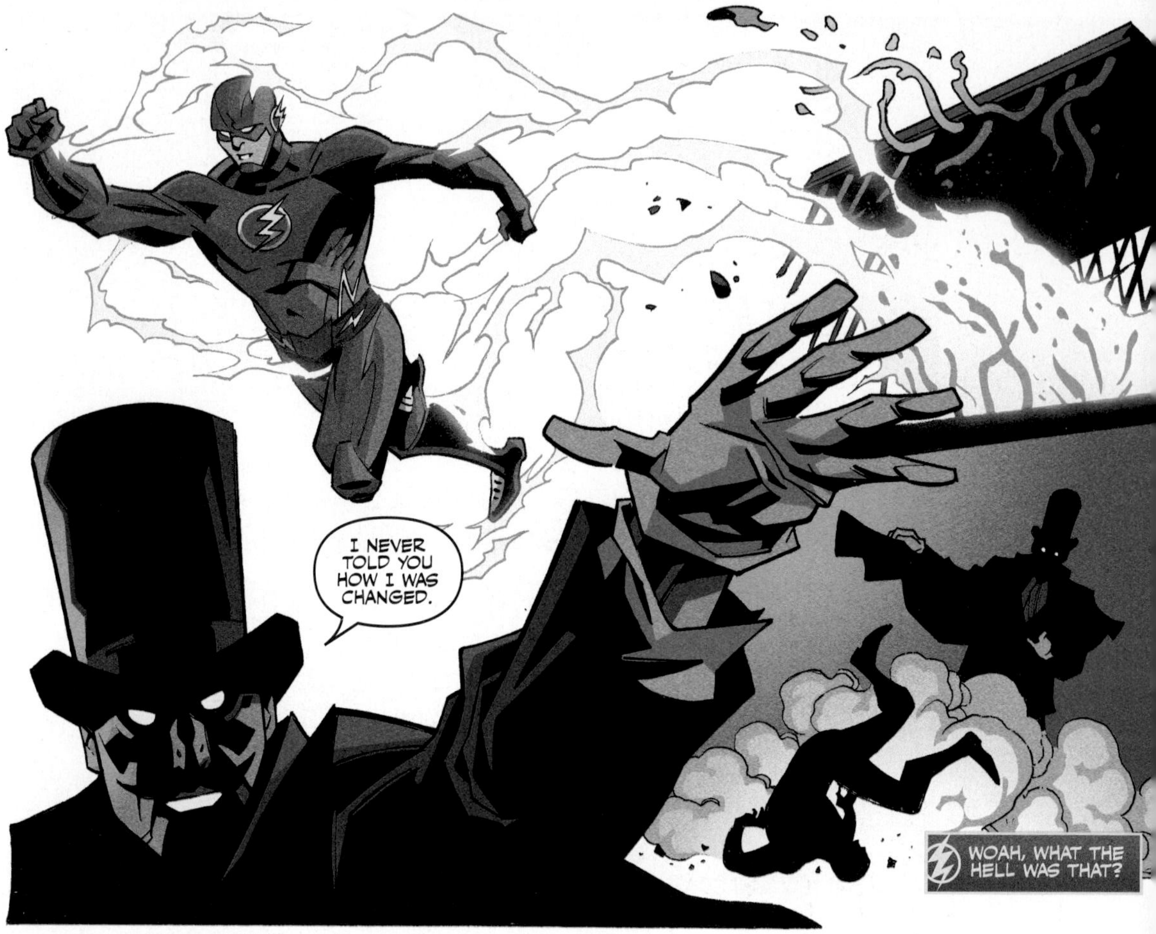
I NEVER TOLD YOU HOW I WAS CHANGED.
WOAH, WHAT THE HELL WAS THAT?

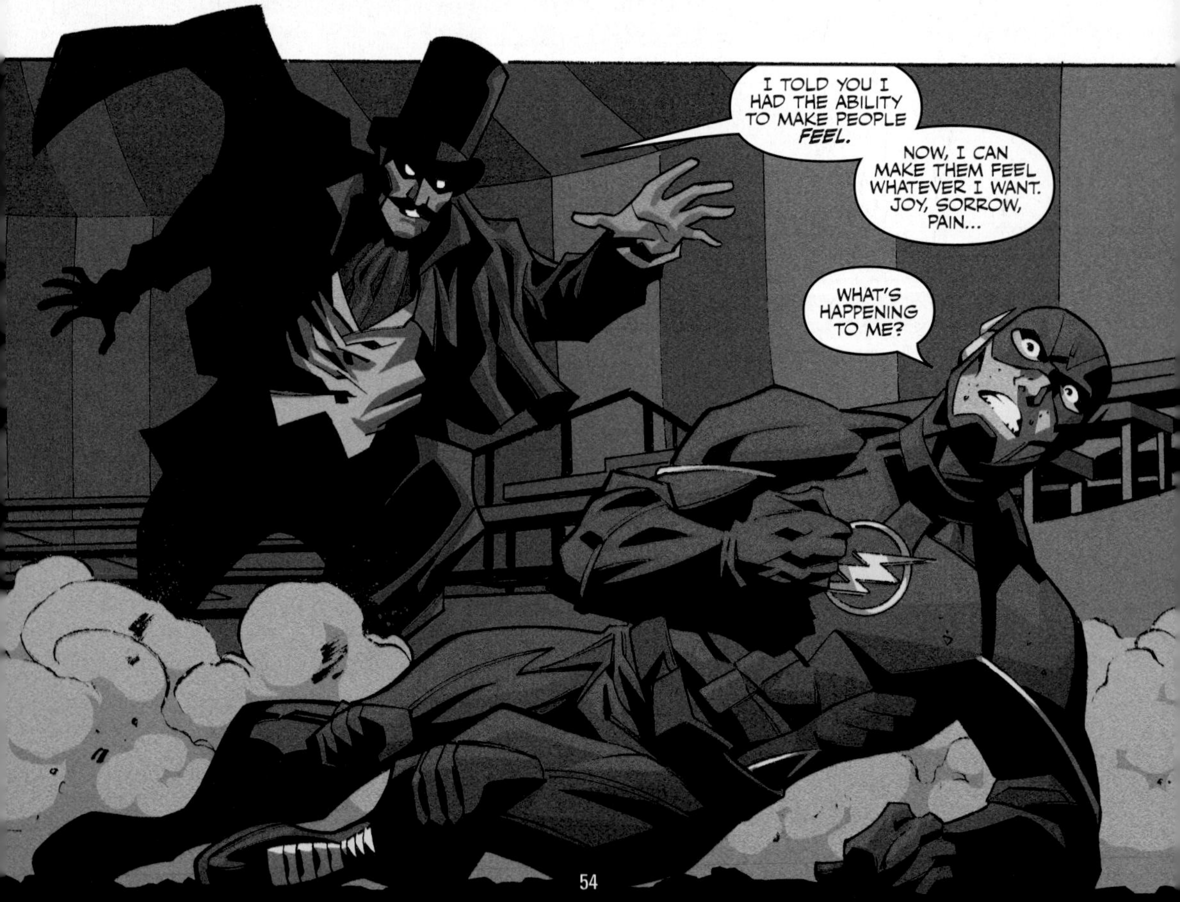
I TOLD YOU I HAD THE ABILITY TO MAKE PEOPLE *FEEL.*
NOW, I CAN MAKE THEM FEEL WHATEVER I WANT. JOY, SORROW, PAIN...
WHAT'S HAPPENING TO ME?

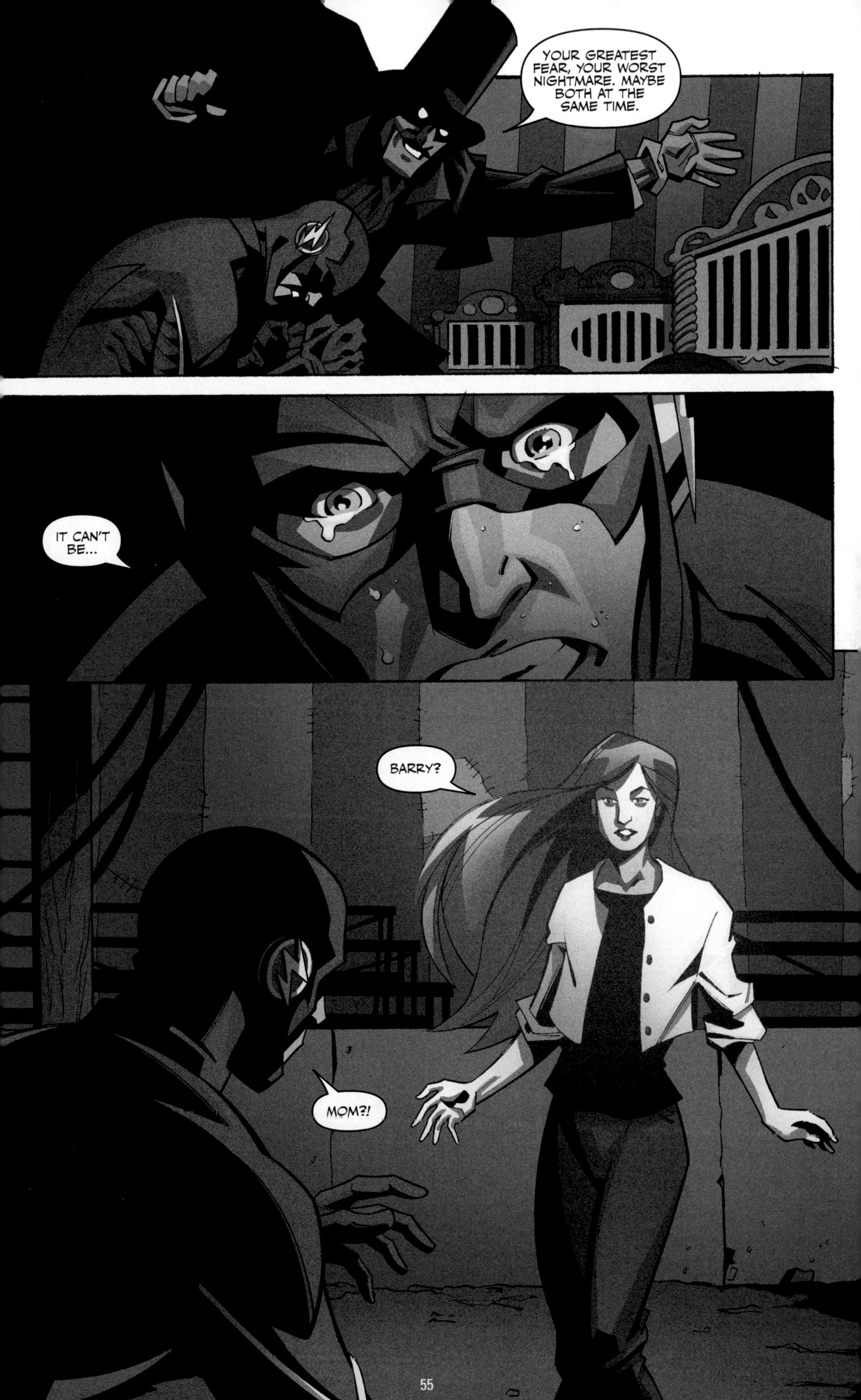
YOUR GREATEST FEAR, YOUR WORST NIGHTMARE. MAYBE BOTH AT THE SAME TIME.
IT CAN'T BE...
BARRY?
MOM?!

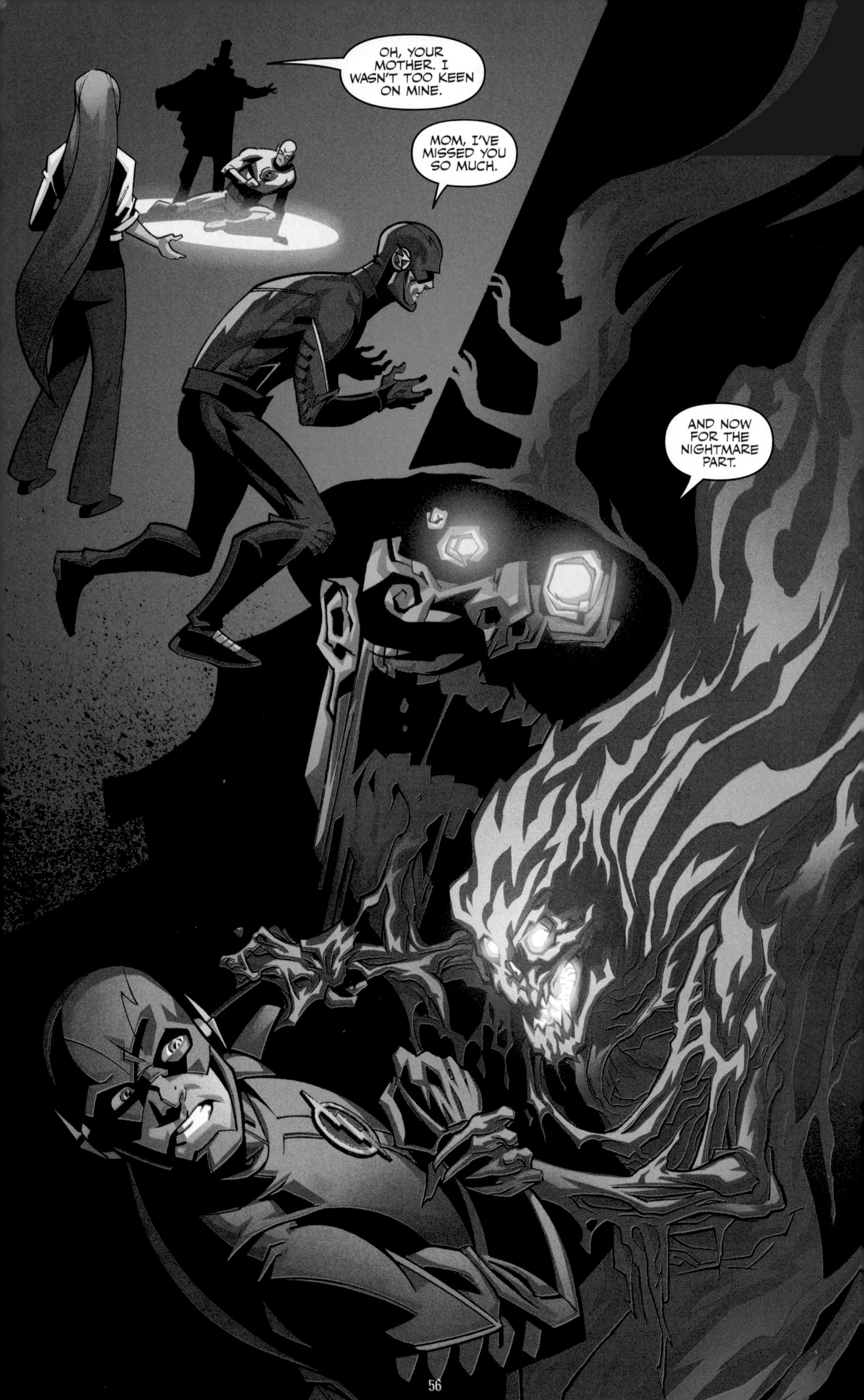
OH, YOUR MOTHER. I WASN'T TOO KEEN ON MINE.
MOM, I'VE MISSED YOU SO MUCH.
AND NOW FOR THE NIGHTMARE PART.

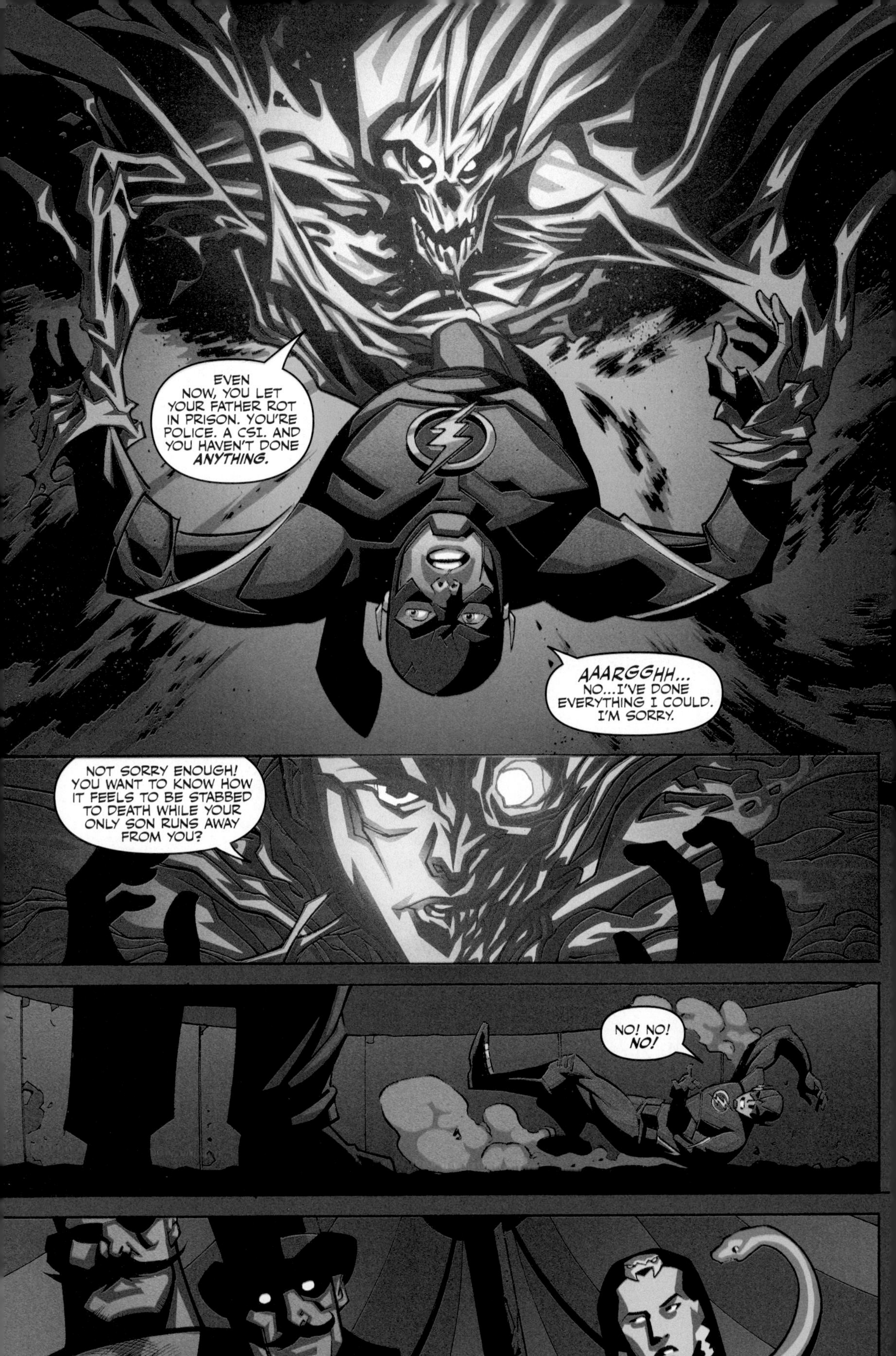
EVEN NOW, YOU LET YOUR FATHER ROT IN PRISON. YOU'RE POLICE. A CSI. AND YOU HAVEN'T DONE *ANYTHING.*
AAARGGHH... NO...I'VE DONE EVERYTHING I COULD. I'M SORRY.
NOT SORRY ENOUGH! YOU WANT TO KNOW HOW IT FEELS TO BE STABBED TO DEATH WHILE YOUR ONLY SON RUNS AWAY FROM YOU?
NO! NO! *NO!*

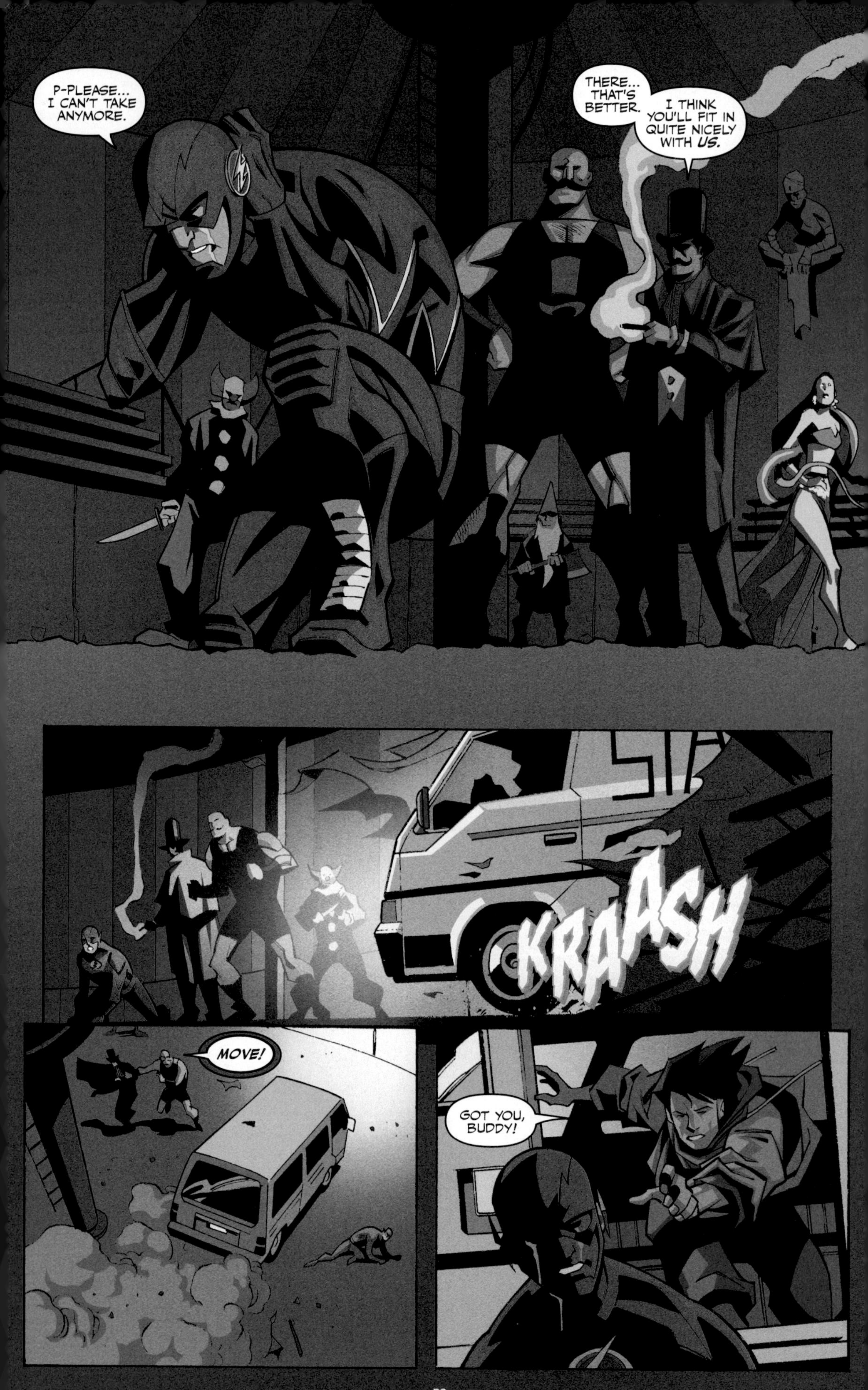

P-PLEASE... I CAN'T TAKE ANYMORE.
THERE... THAT'S BETTER.
I THINK YOU'LL FIT IN QUITE NICELY WITH US.
KRAASH
MOVE!
GOT YOU, BUDDY!

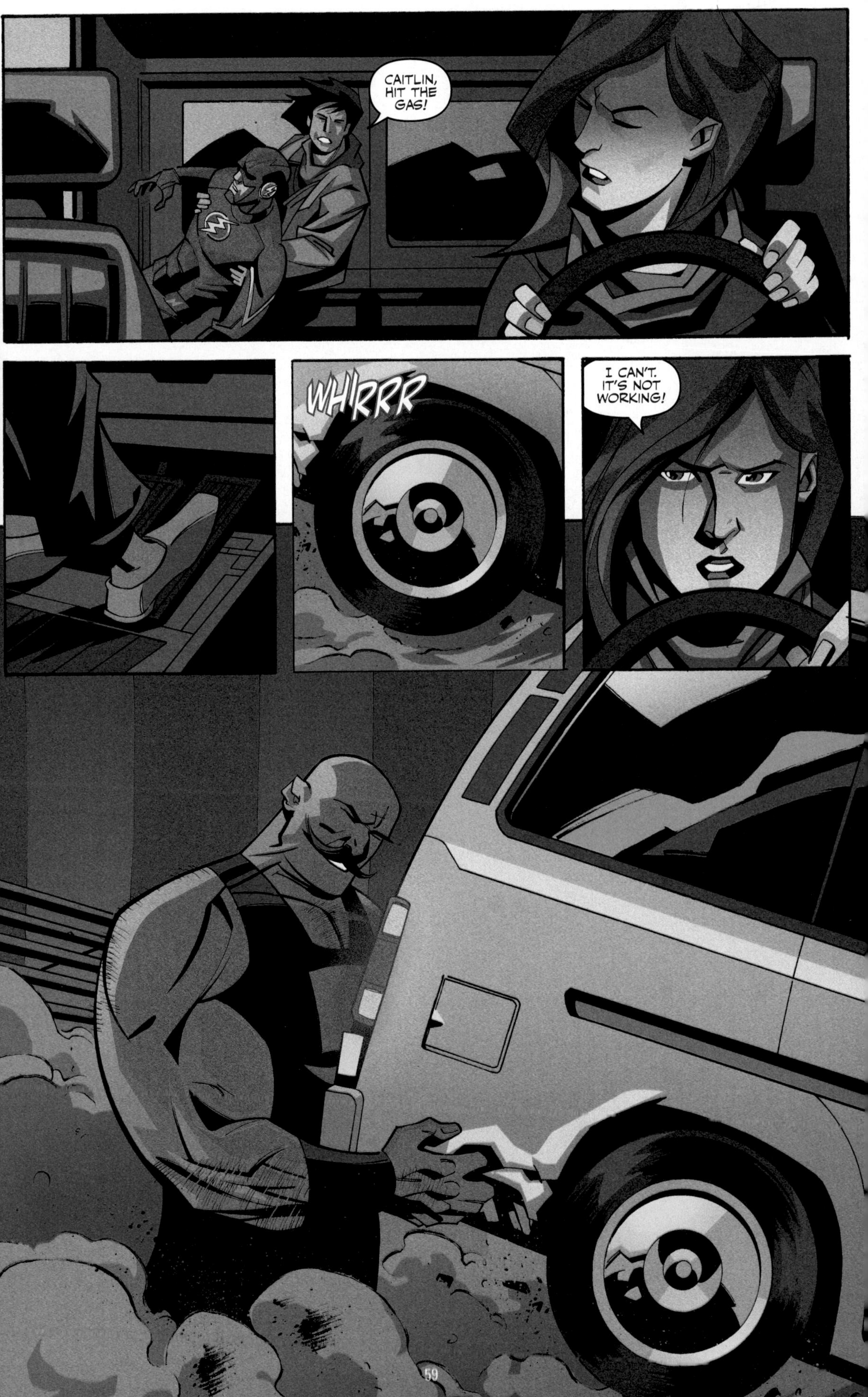
CAITLIN, HIT THE GAS!
WHIRRR
I CAN'T. IT'S NOT WORKING!

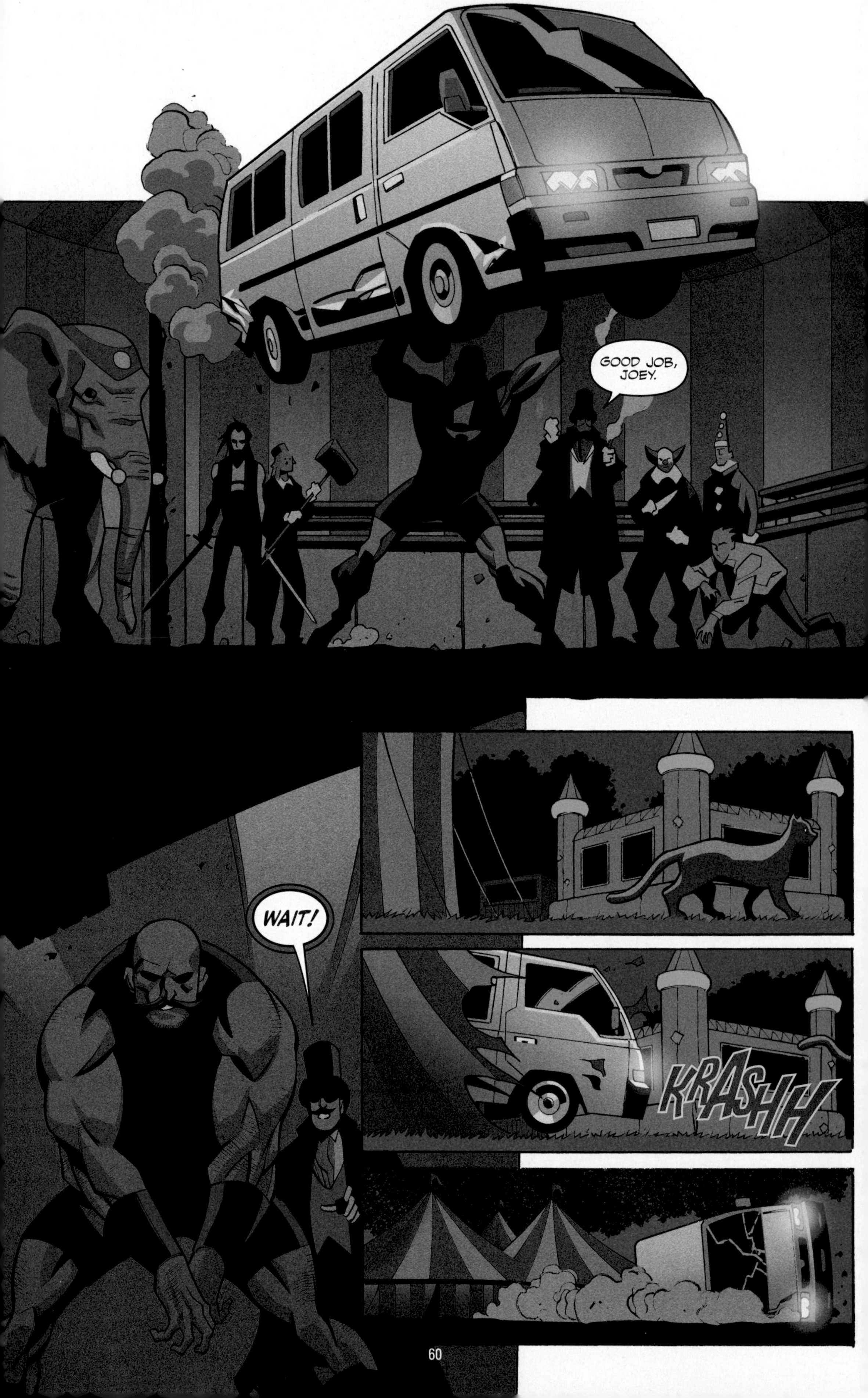
GOOD JOB, JOEY.
WAIT!
KRASHH

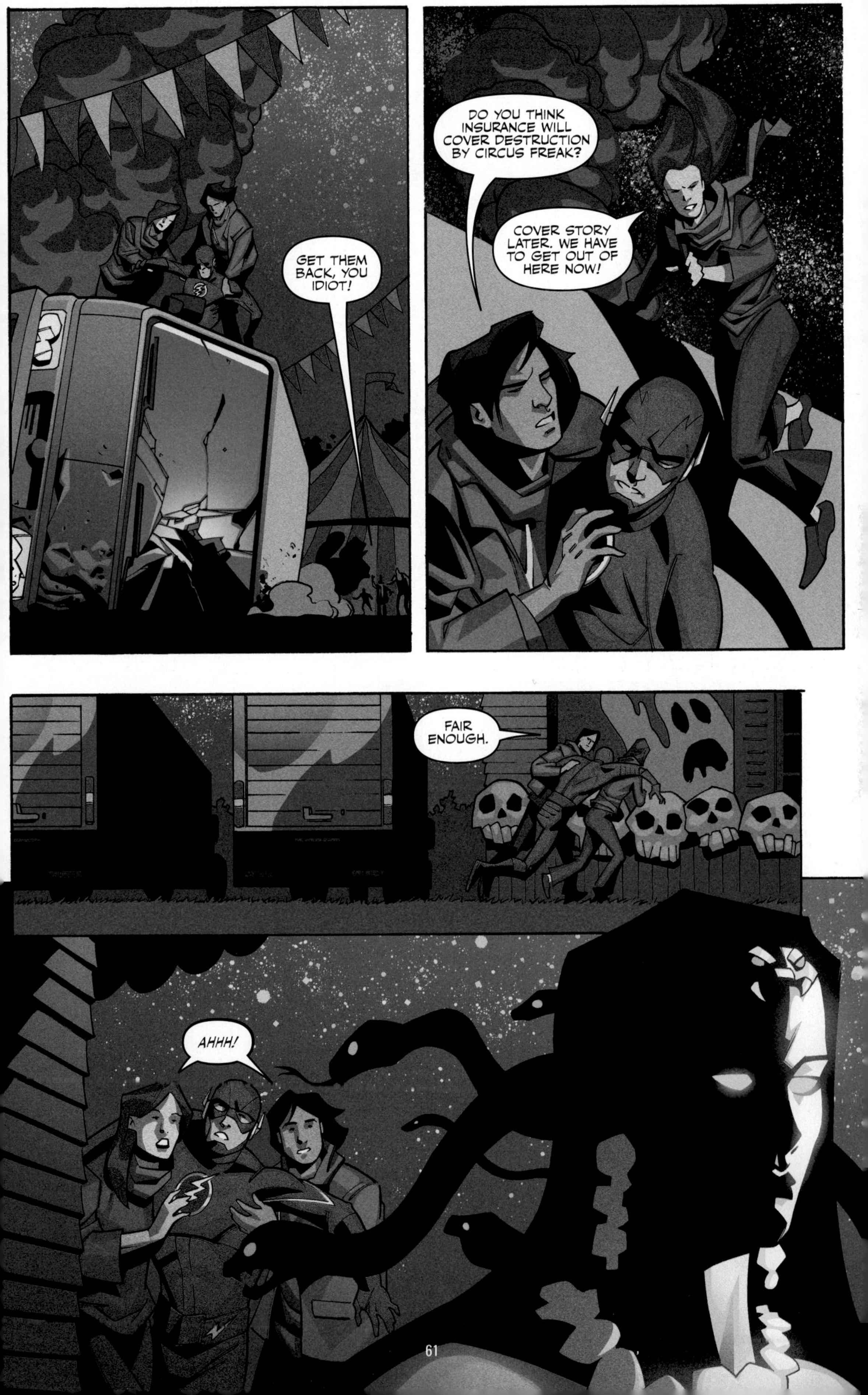
GET THEM BACK, YOU IDIOT!
DO YOU THINK INSURANCE WILL COVER DESTRUCTION BY CIRCUS FREAK?
COVER STORY LATER. WE HAVE TO GET OUT OF HERE NOW!
FAIR ENOUGH.
AHHH!

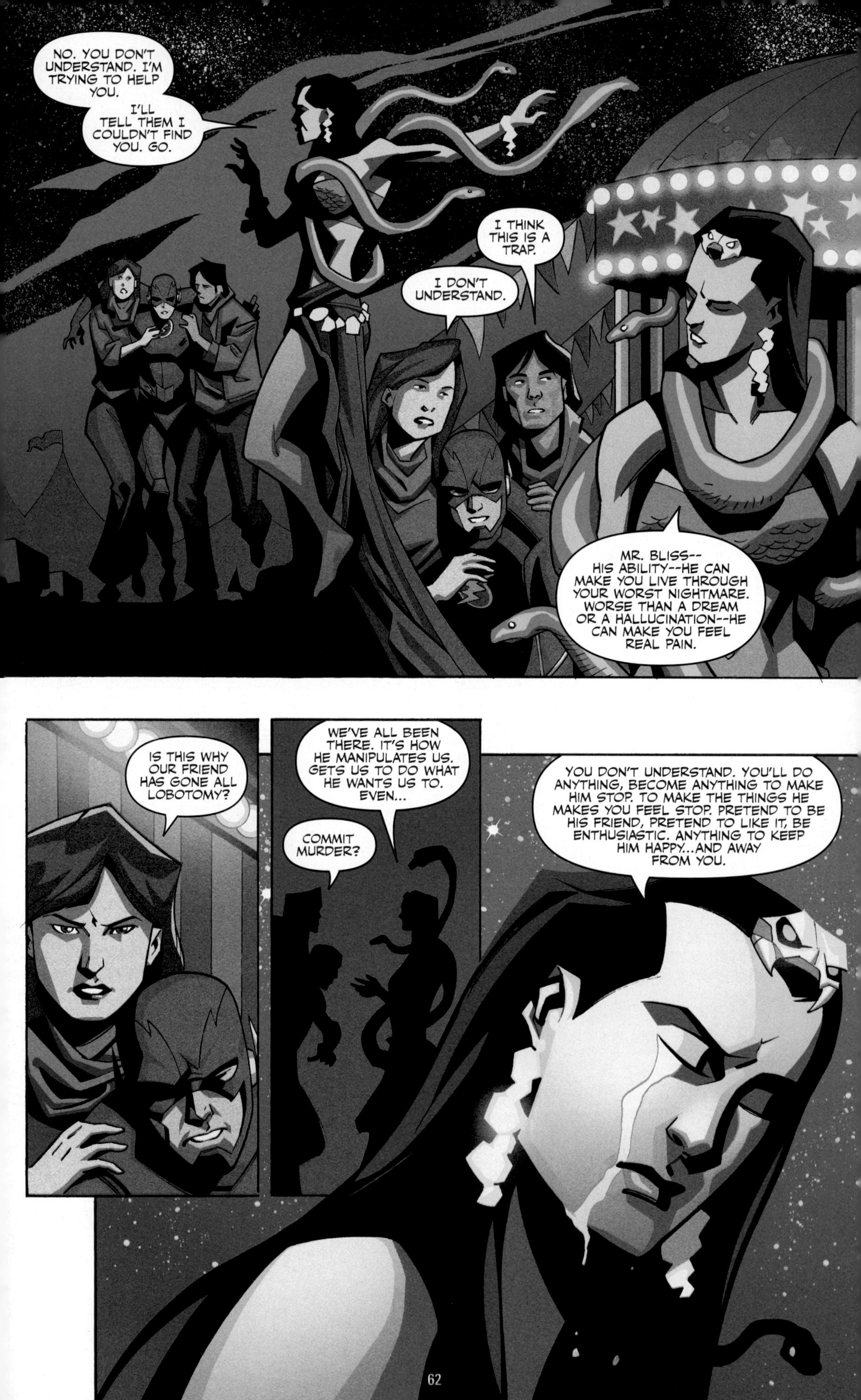
NO. YOU DON'T UNDERSTAND. I'M TRYING TO HELP YOU.
I'LL TELL THEM I COULDN'T FIND YOU. GO.
I THINK THIS IS A TRAP.
I DON'T UNDERSTAND.
MR. BLISS-- HIS ABILITY--HE CAN MAKE YOU LIVE THROUGH YOUR WORST NIGHTMARE. WORSE THAN A DREAM OR A HALLUCINATION--HE CAN MAKE YOU FEEL REAL PAIN.
IS THIS WHY OUR FRIEND HAS GONE ALL LOBOTOMY?
WE'VE ALL BEEN THERE. IT'S HOW HE MANIPULATES US. GETS US TO DO WHAT HE WANTS US TO. EVEN...
COMMIT MURDER?
YOU DON'T UNDERSTAND. YOU'LL DO ANYTHING, BECOME ANYTHING TO MAKE HIM STOP. TO MAKE THE THINGS HE MAKES YOU FEEL STOP. PRETEND TO BE HIS FRIEND, PRETEND TO LIKE IT, BE ENTHUSIASTIC. ANYTHING TO KEEP HIM HAPPY...AND AWAY FROM YOU.

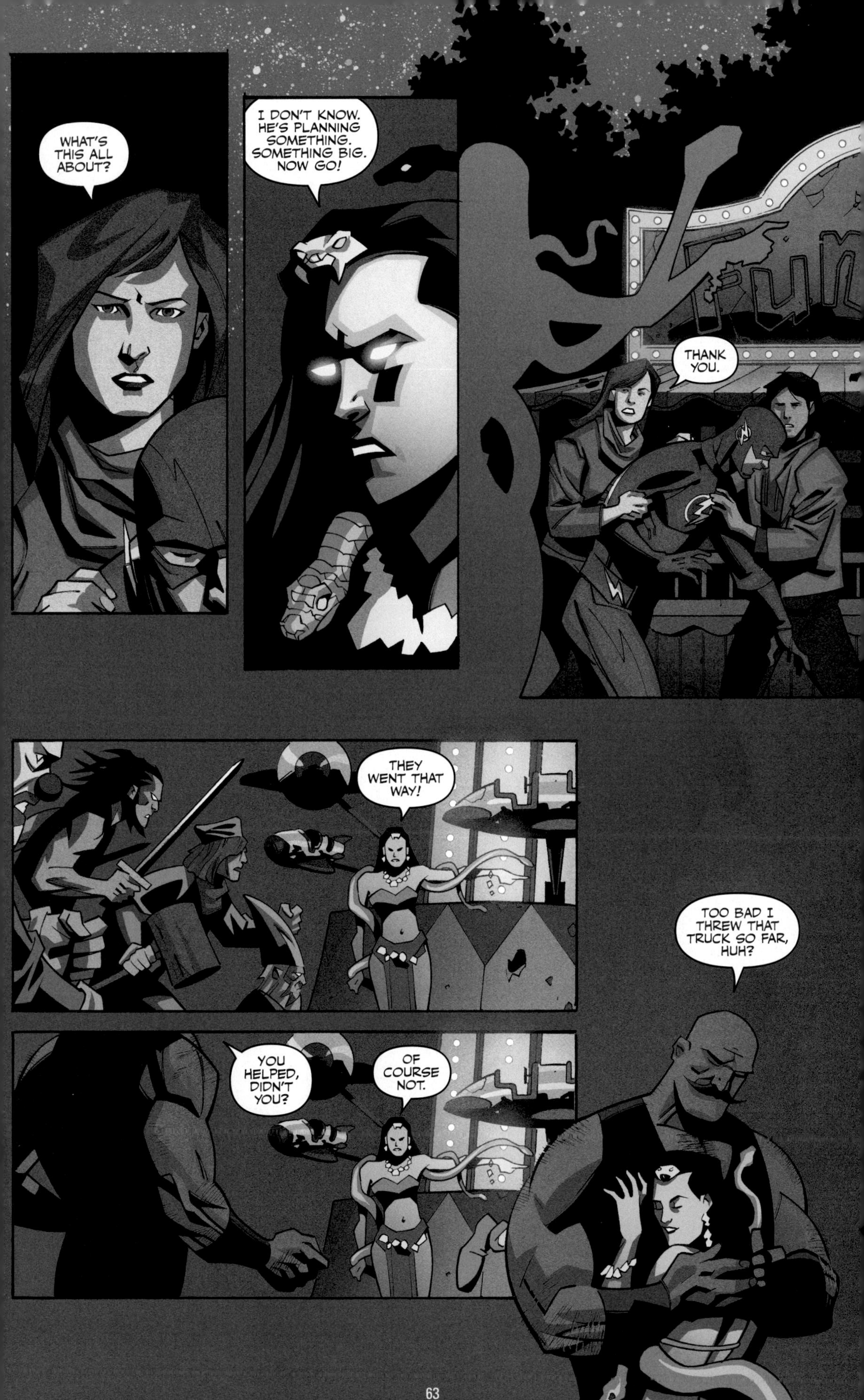
WHAT'S THIS ALL ABOUT?
I DON'T KNOW. HE'S PLANNING SOMETHING. SOMETHING BIG. NOW GO!
THANK YOU.
THEY WENT THAT WAY!
YOU HELPED, DIDN'T YOU?
OF COURSE NOT.
TOO BAD I THREW THAT TRUCK SO FAR, HUH?

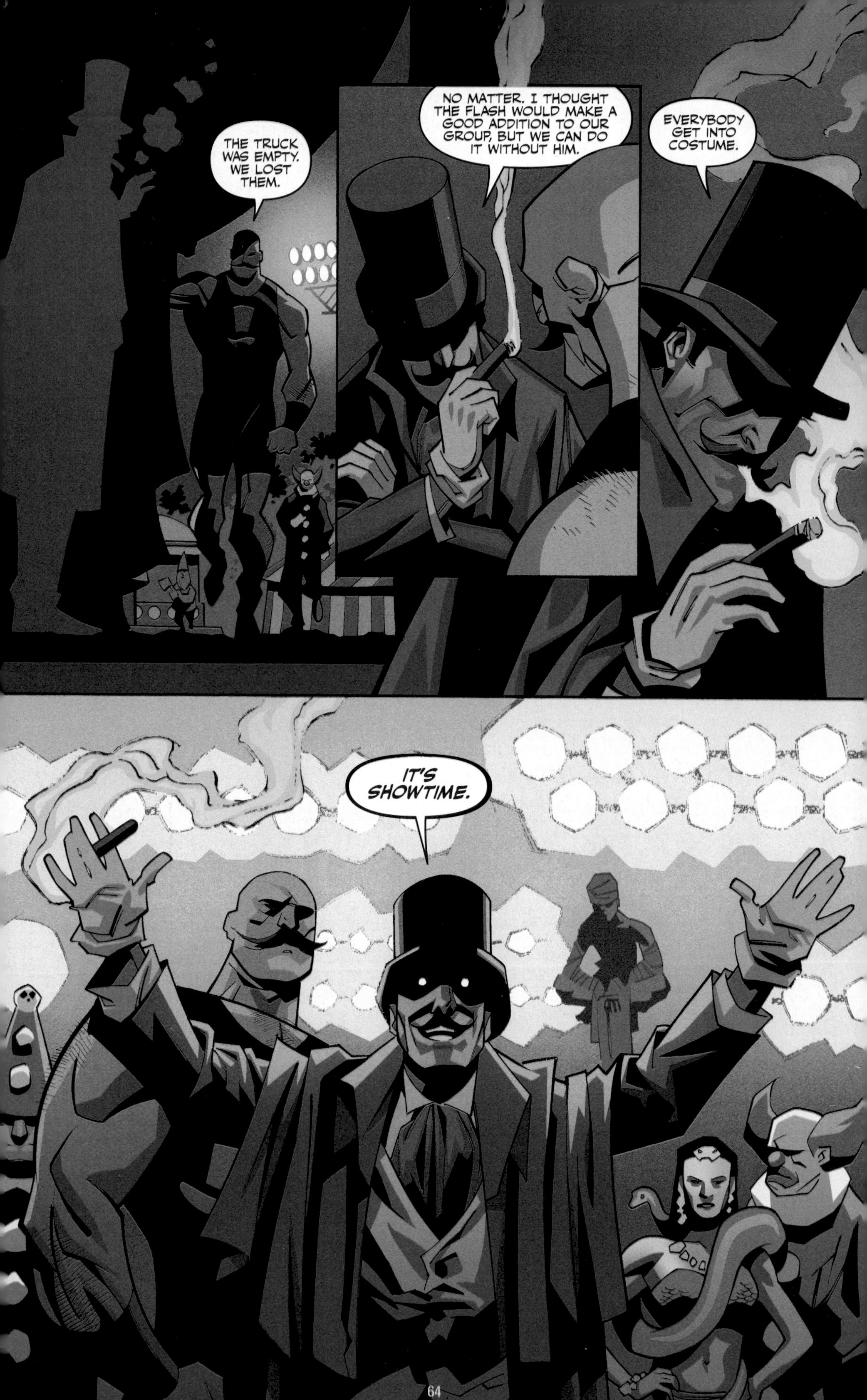
THE TRUCK WAS EMPTY. WE LOST THEM.
NO MATTER. I THOUGHT THE FLASH WOULD MAKE A GOOD ADDITION TO OUR GROUP, BUT WE CAN DO IT WITHOUT HIM.
EVERYBODY GET INTO COSTUME.
IT'S SHOWTIME.

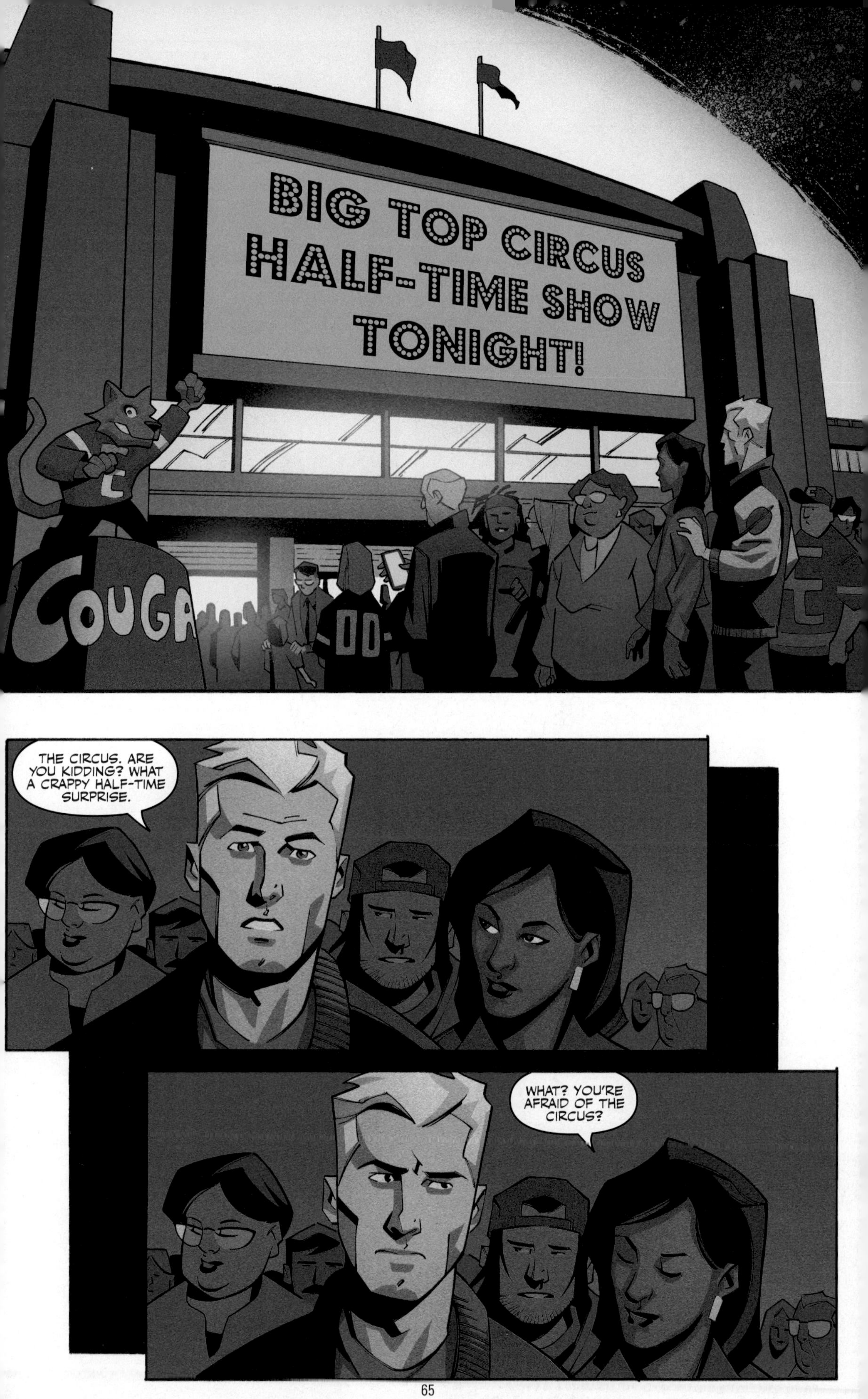
BIG TOP CIRCUS
HALF-TIME SHOW
TONIGHT!
COUGA
00
THE CIRCUS. ARE YOU KIDDING? WHAT A CRAPPY HALF-TIME SURPRISE.
WHAT? YOU'RE AFRAID OF THE CIRCUS?

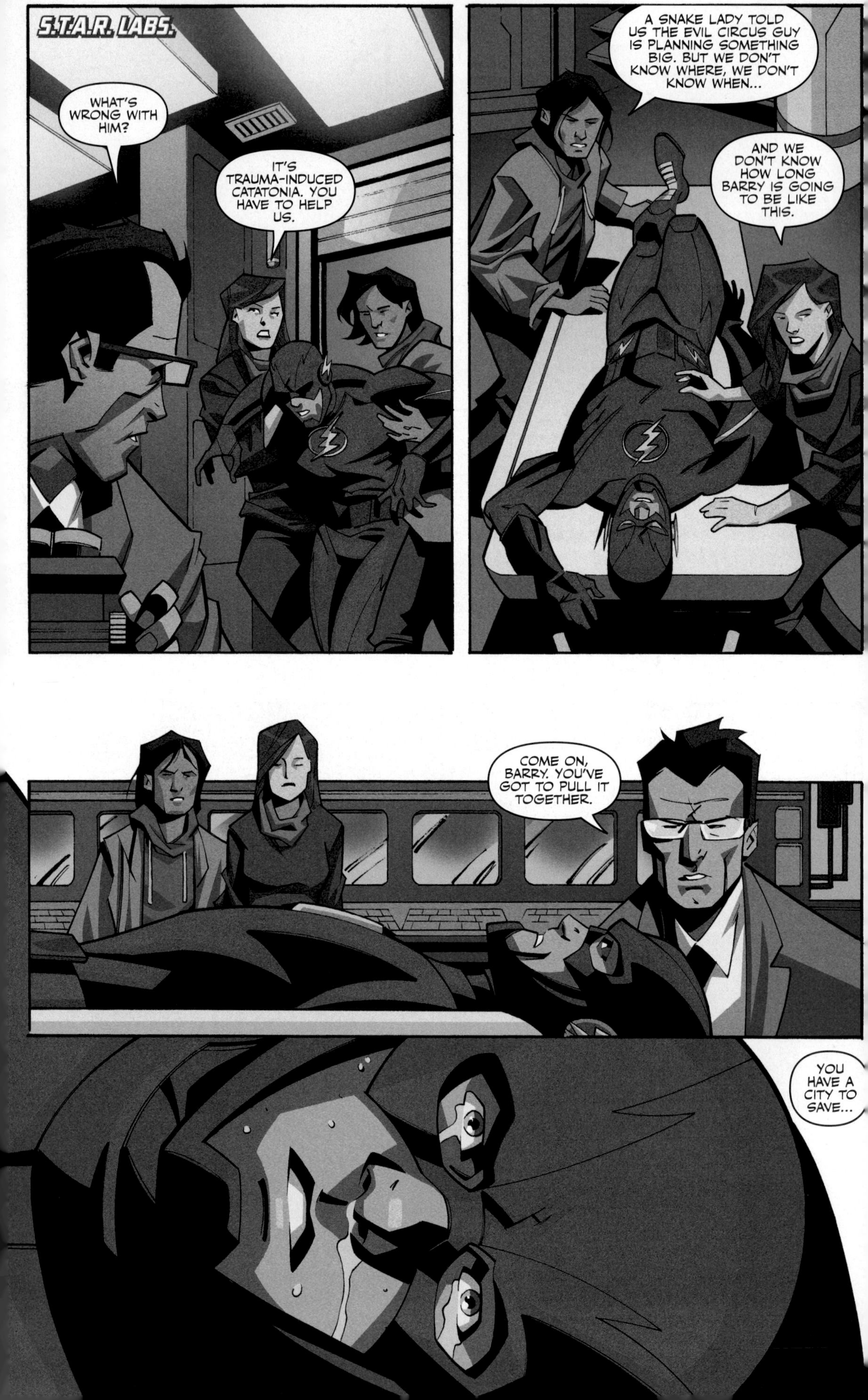
S.T.A.R. LABS.
WHAT'S WRONG WITH HIM?
IT'S TRAUMA-INDUCED CATATONIA. YOU HAVE TO HELP US.
A SNAKE LADY TOLD US THE EVIL CIRCUS GUY IS PLANNING SOMETHING BIG. BUT WE DON'T KNOW WHERE, WE DON'T KNOW WHEN...
AND WE DON'T KNOW HOW LONG BARRY IS GOING TO BE LIKE THIS.
COME ON, BARRY. YOU'VE GOT TO PULL IT TOGETHER.
YOU HAVE A CITY TO SAVE...

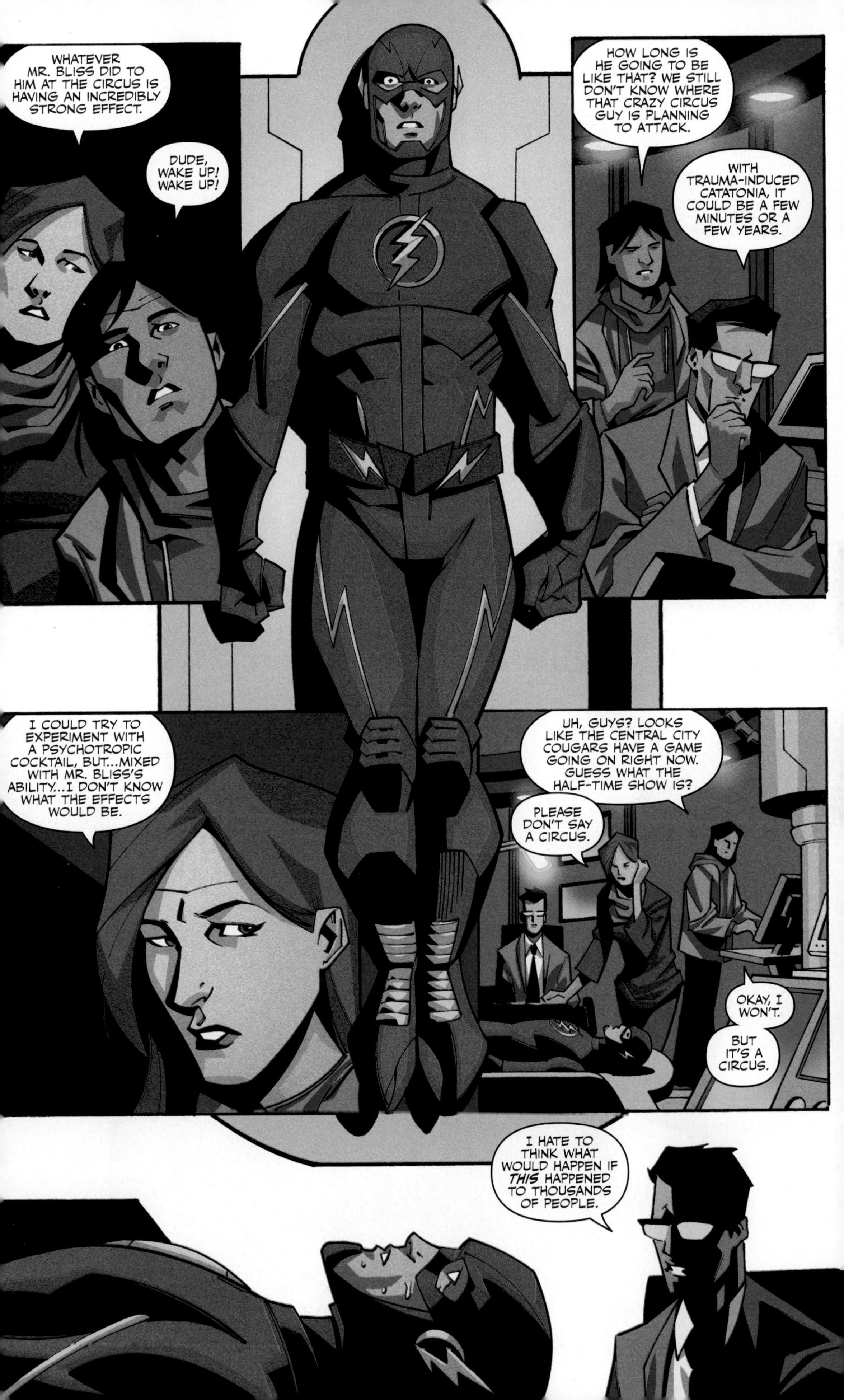
WHATEVER MR. BLISS DID TO HIM AT THE CIRCUS IS HAVING AN INCREDIBLY STRONG EFFECT.
DUDE, WAKE UP! WAKE UP!
HOW LONG IS HE GOING TO BE LIKE THAT? WE STILL DON'T KNOW WHERE THAT CRAZY CIRCUS GUY IS PLANNING TO ATTACK.
WITH TRAUMA-INDUCED CATATONIA, IT COULD BE A FEW MINUTES OR A FEW YEARS.
I COULD TRY TO EXPERIMENT WITH A PSYCHOTROPIC COCKTAIL, BUT...MIXED WITH MR. BLISS'S ABILITY...I DON'T KNOW WHAT THE EFFECTS WOULD BE.
UH, GUYS? LOOKS LIKE THE CENTRAL CITY COUGARS HAVE A GAME GOING ON RIGHT NOW. GUESS WHAT THE HALF-TIME SHOW IS?
PLEASE DON'T SAY A CIRCUS.
OKAY, I WON'T.
BUT IT'S A CIRCUS.
I HATE TO THINK WHAT WOULD HAPPEN IF *THIS* HAPPENED TO THOUSANDS OF PEOPLE.

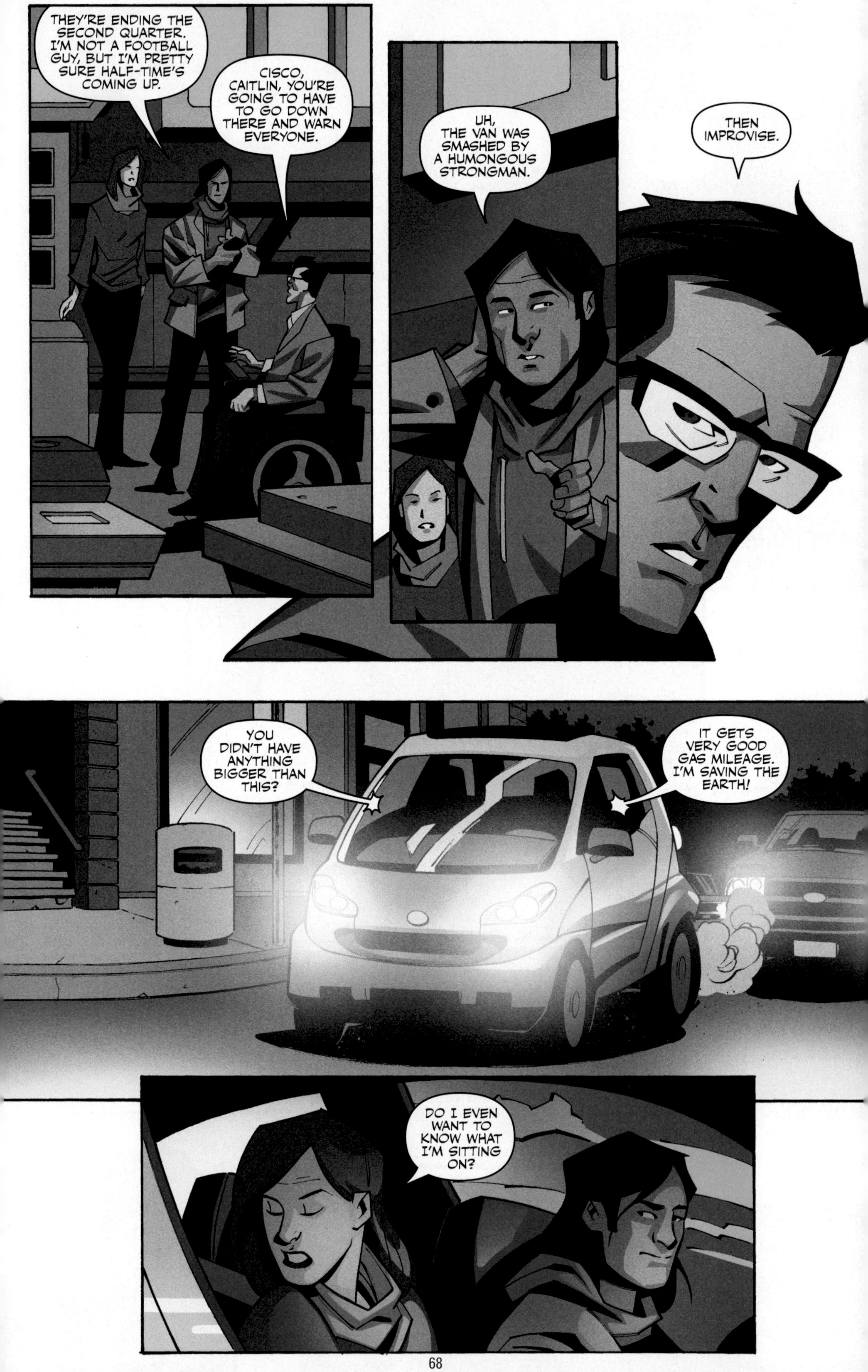
THEY'RE ENDING THE SECOND QUARTER. I'M NOT A FOOTBALL GUY, BUT I'M PRETTY SURE HALF-TIME'S COMING UP.
CISCO, CAITLIN, YOU'RE GOING TO HAVE TO GO DOWN THERE AND WARN EVERYONE.
UH, THE VAN WAS SMASHED BY A HUMONGOUS STRONGMAN.
THEN IMPROVISE.
YOU DIDN'T HAVE ANYTHING BIGGER THAN THIS?
IT GETS VERY GOOD GAS MILEAGE. I'M SAVING THE EARTH!
DO I EVEN WANT TO KNOW WHAT I'M SITTING ON?

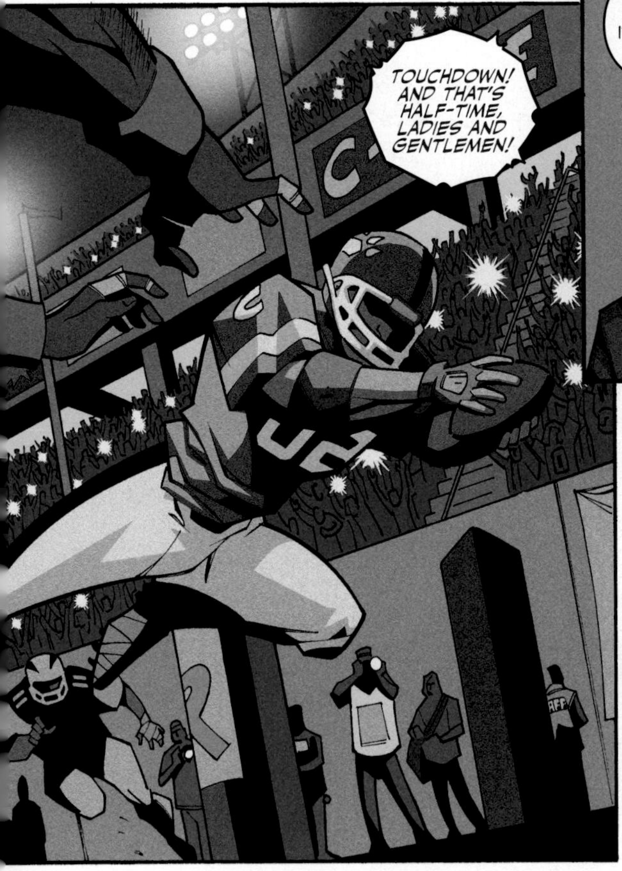
TOUCHDOWN! AND THAT'S HALF-TIME, LADIES AND GENTLEMEN!

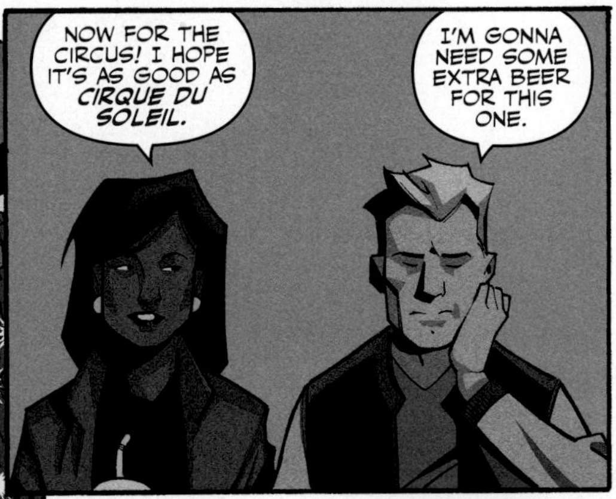
NOW FOR THE CIRCUS! I HOPE IT'S AS GOOD AS *CIRQUE DU SOLEIL.*
I'M GONNA NEED SOME EXTRA BEER FOR THIS ONE.

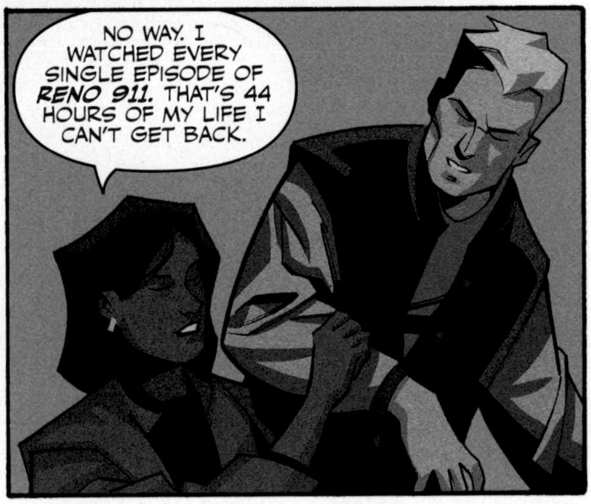
NO WAY. I WATCHED EVERY SINGLE EPISODE OF *RENO 911.* THAT'S 44 HOURS OF MY LIFE I CAN'T GET BACK.

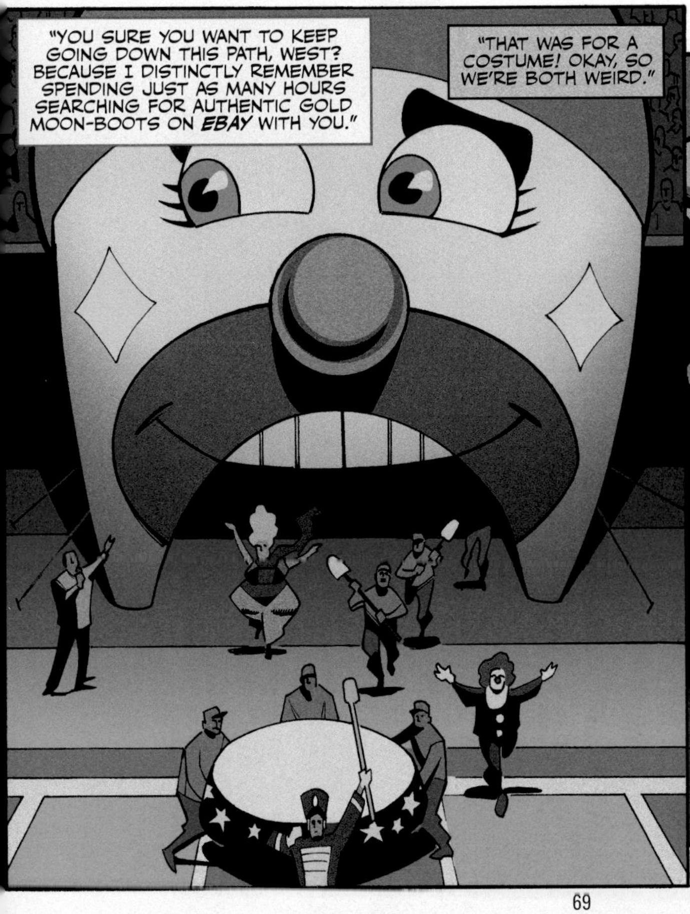
"YOU SURE YOU WANT TO KEEP GOING DOWN THIS PATH, WEST? BECAUSE I DISTINCTLY REMEMBER SPENDING JUST AS MANY HOURS SEARCHING FOR AUTHENTIC GOLD MOON-BOOTS ON *EBAY* WITH YOU."
"THAT WAS FOR A COSTUME! OKAY, SO WE'RE BOTH WEIRD."

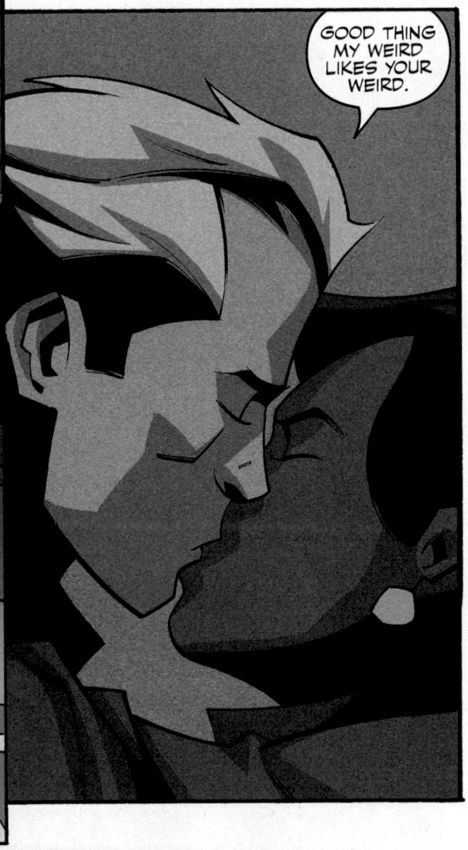
GOOD THING MY WEIRD LIKES YOUR WEIRD.

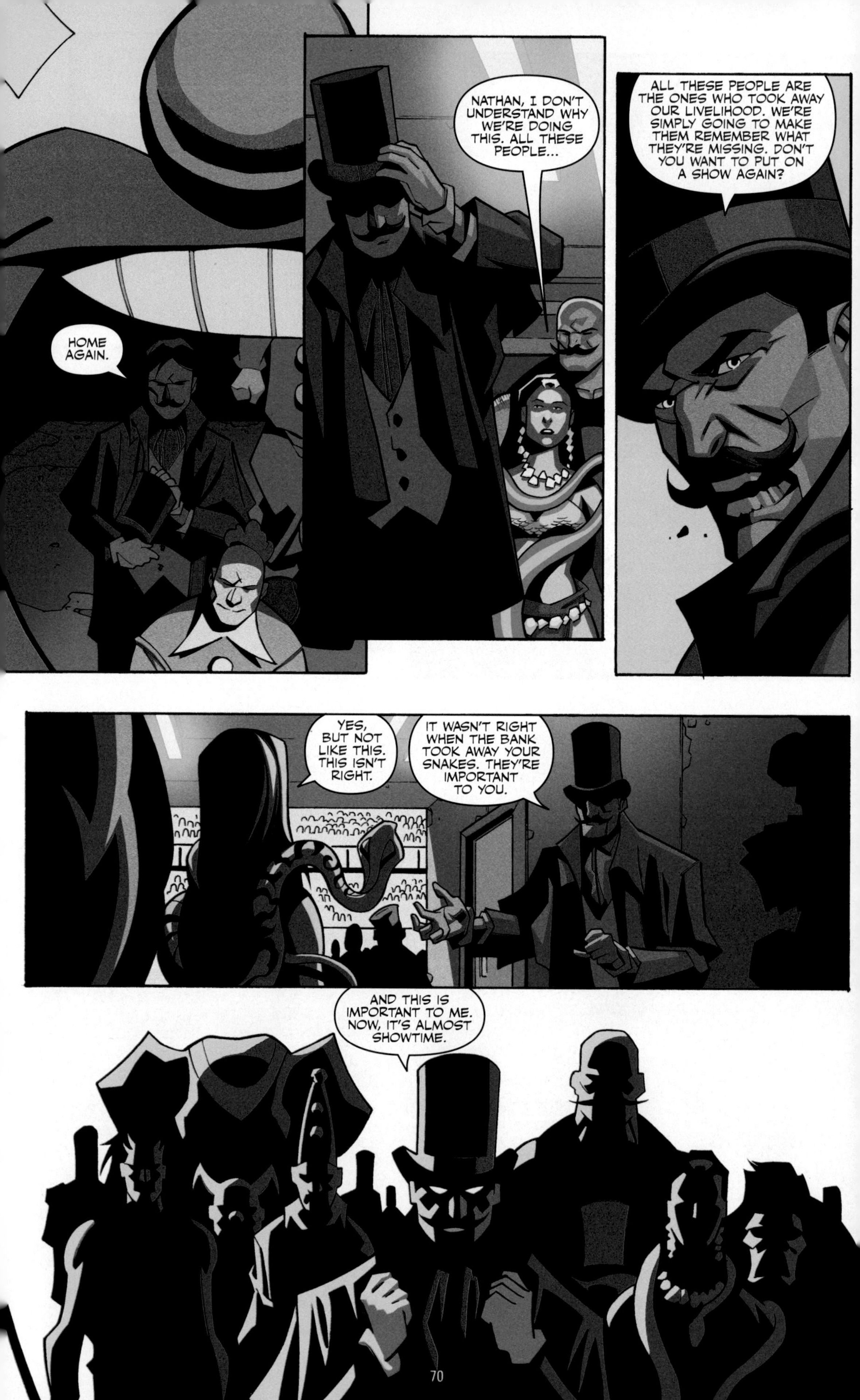
HOME AGAIN.
NATHAN, I DON'T UNDERSTAND WHY WE'RE DOING THIS. ALL THESE PEOPLE...
ALL THESE PEOPLE ARE THE ONES WHO TOOK AWAY OUR LIVELIHOOD. WE'RE SIMPLY GOING TO MAKE THEM REMEMBER WHAT THEY'RE MISSING. DON'T YOU WANT TO PUT ON A SHOW AGAIN?
YES, BUT NOT LIKE THIS. THIS ISN'T RIGHT.
IT WASN'T RIGHT WHEN THE BANK TOOK AWAY YOUR SNAKES. THEY'RE IMPORTANT TO YOU.
AND THIS IS IMPORTANT TO ME. NOW, IT'S ALMOST SHOWTIME.

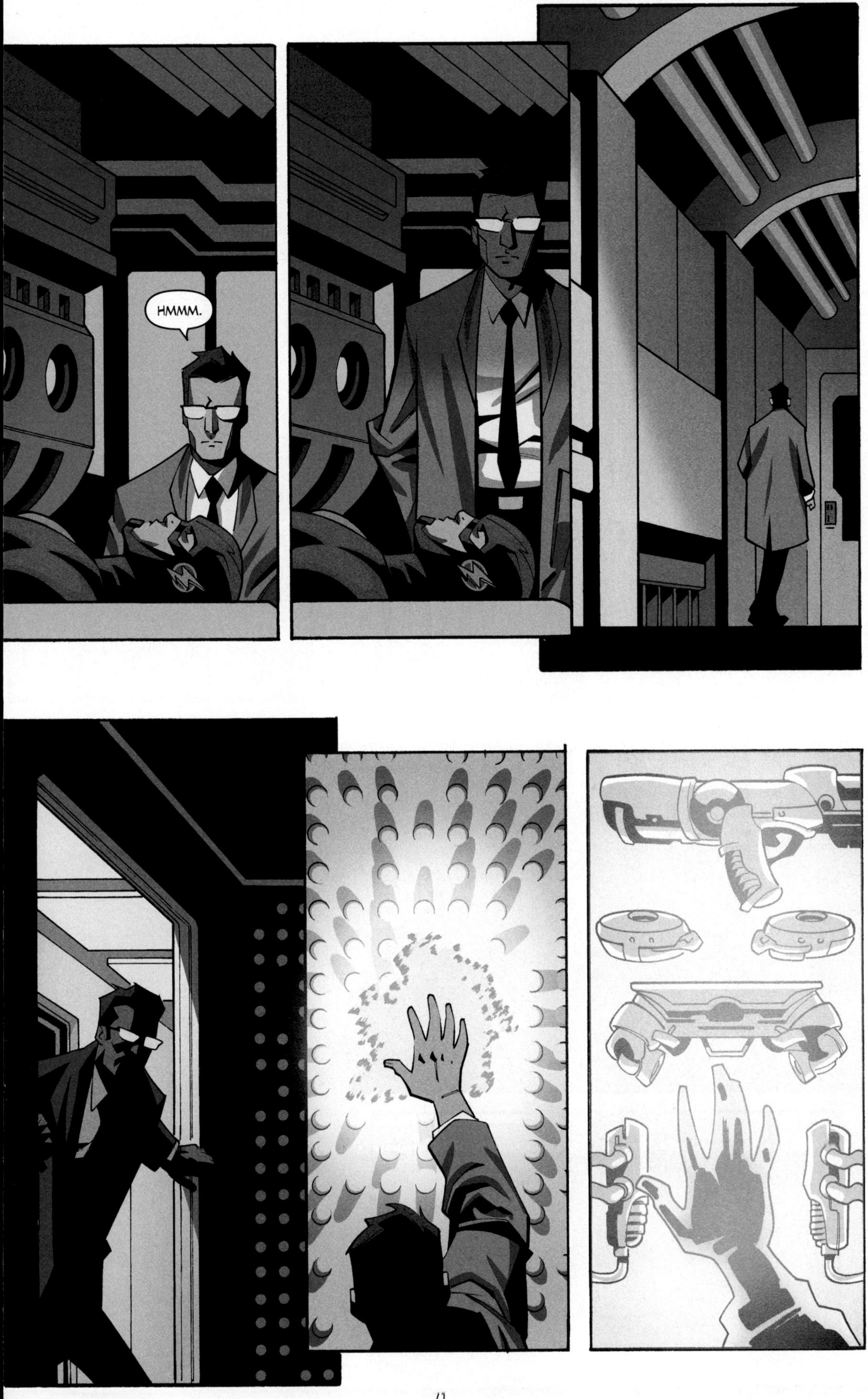
HMMM.

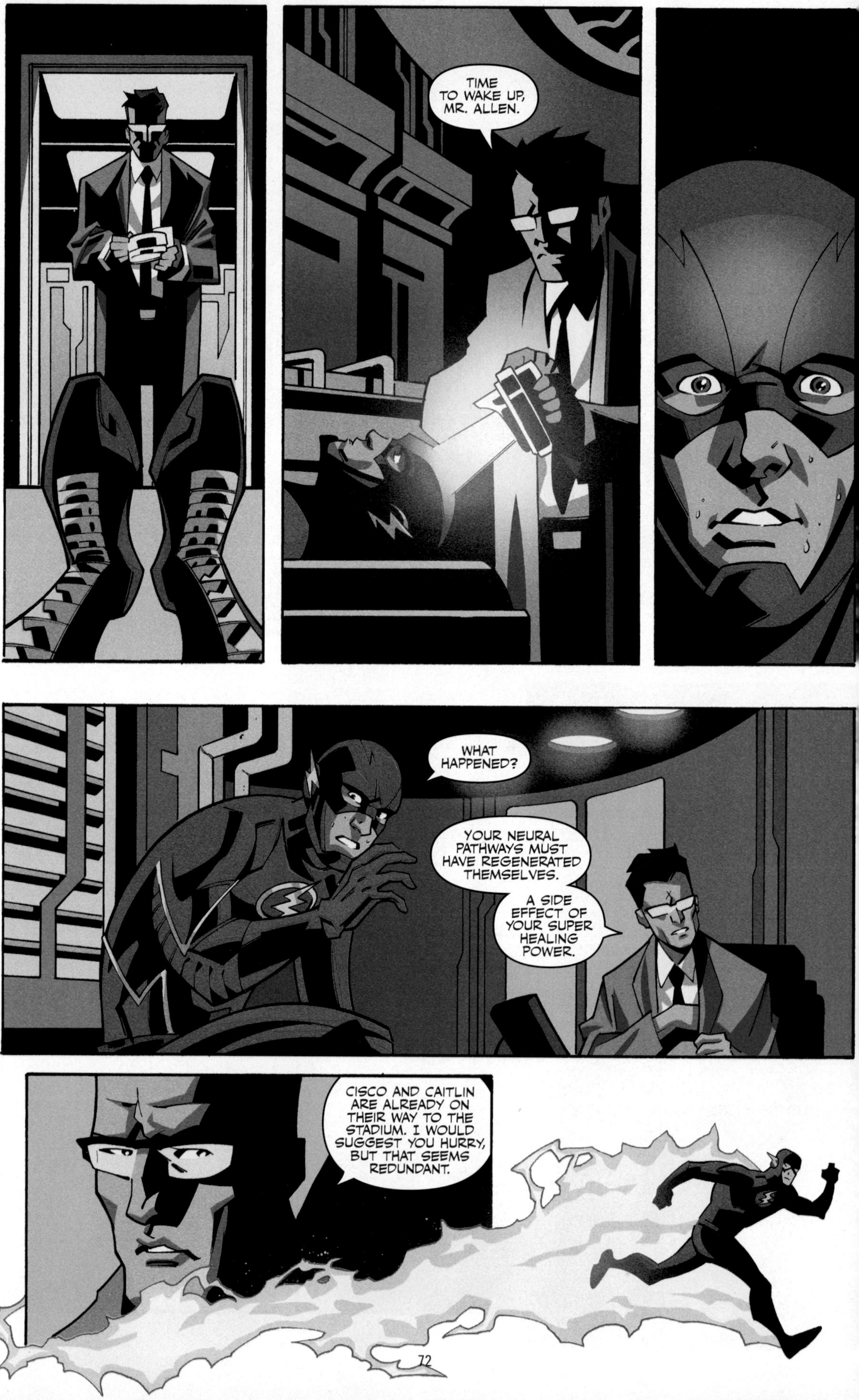
TIME TO WAKE UP, MR. ALLEN.
WHAT HAPPENED?
YOUR NEURAL PATHWAYS MUST HAVE REGENERATED THEMSELVES.
A SIDE EFFECT OF YOUR SUPER HEALING POWER.
CISCO AND CAITLIN ARE ALREADY ON THEIR WAY TO THE STADIUM. I WOULD SUGGEST YOU HURRY, BUT THAT SEEMS REDUNDANT.

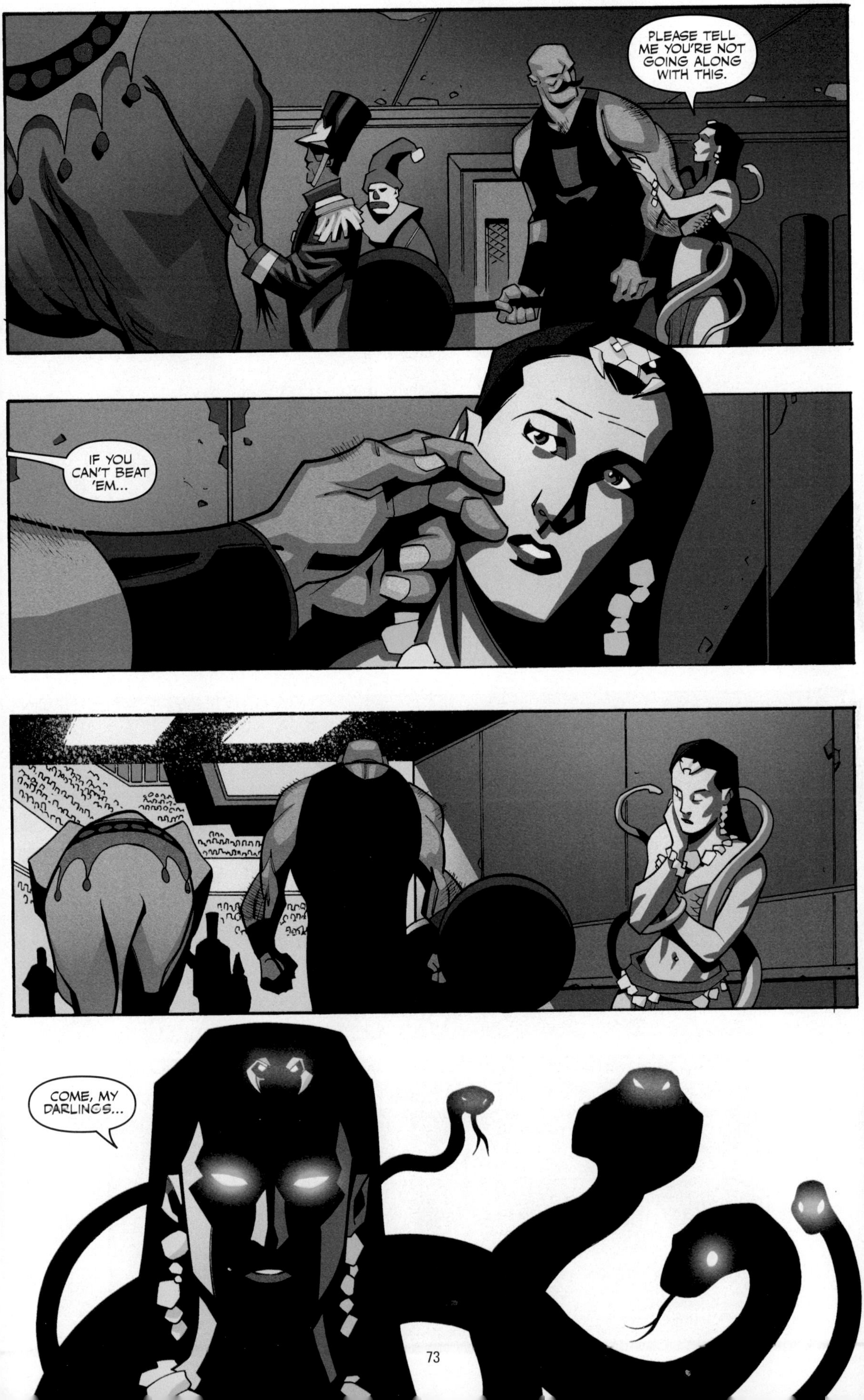
PLEASE TELL ME YOU'RE NOT GOING ALONG WITH THIS.
IF YOU CAN'T BEAT 'EM...
COME, MY DARLINGS...

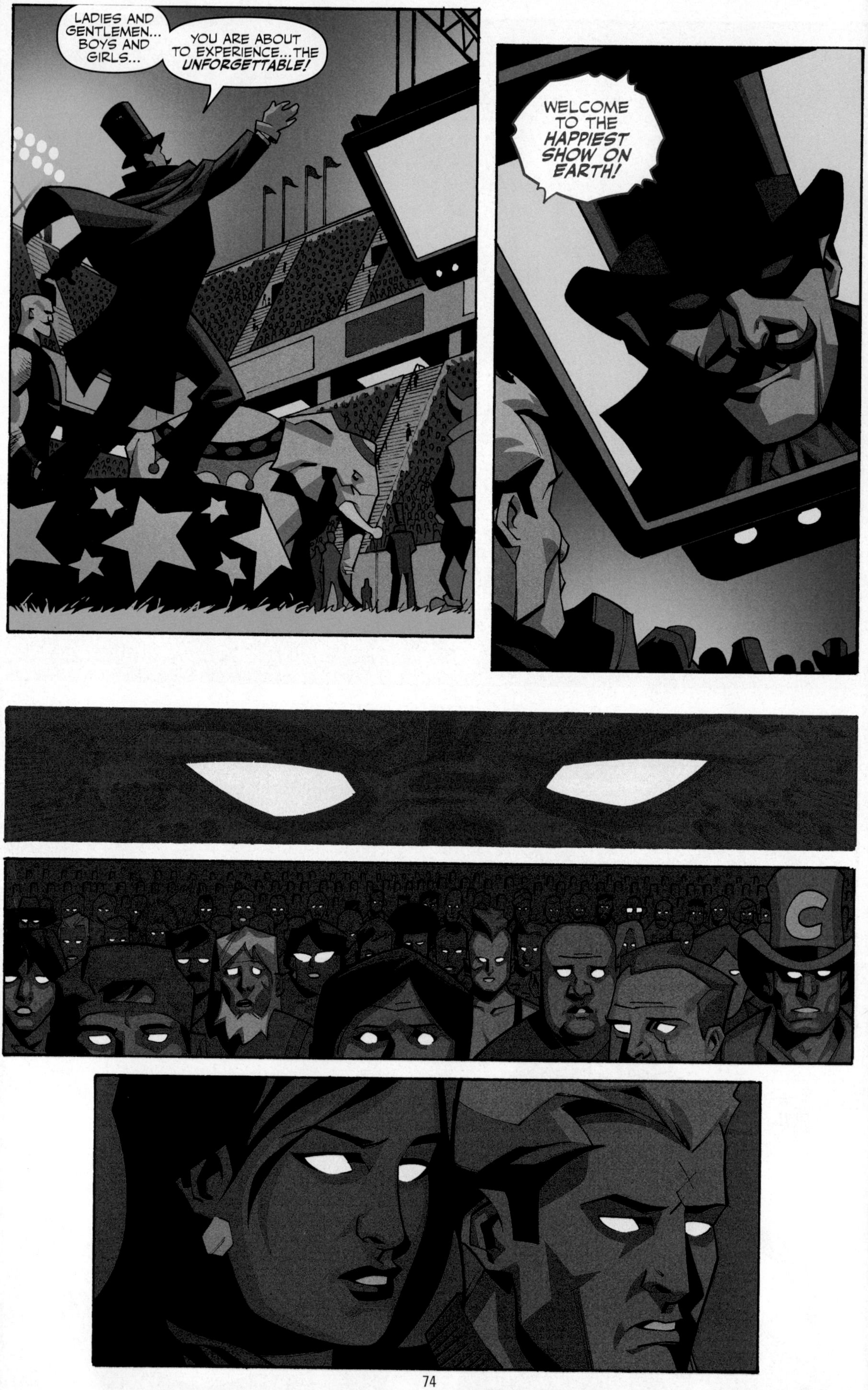
LADIES AND GENTLEMEN... BOYS AND GIRLS...
YOU ARE ABOUT TO EXPERIENCE...THE *UNFORGETTABLE!*
WELCOME TO THE *HAPPIEST SHOW ON EARTH!*

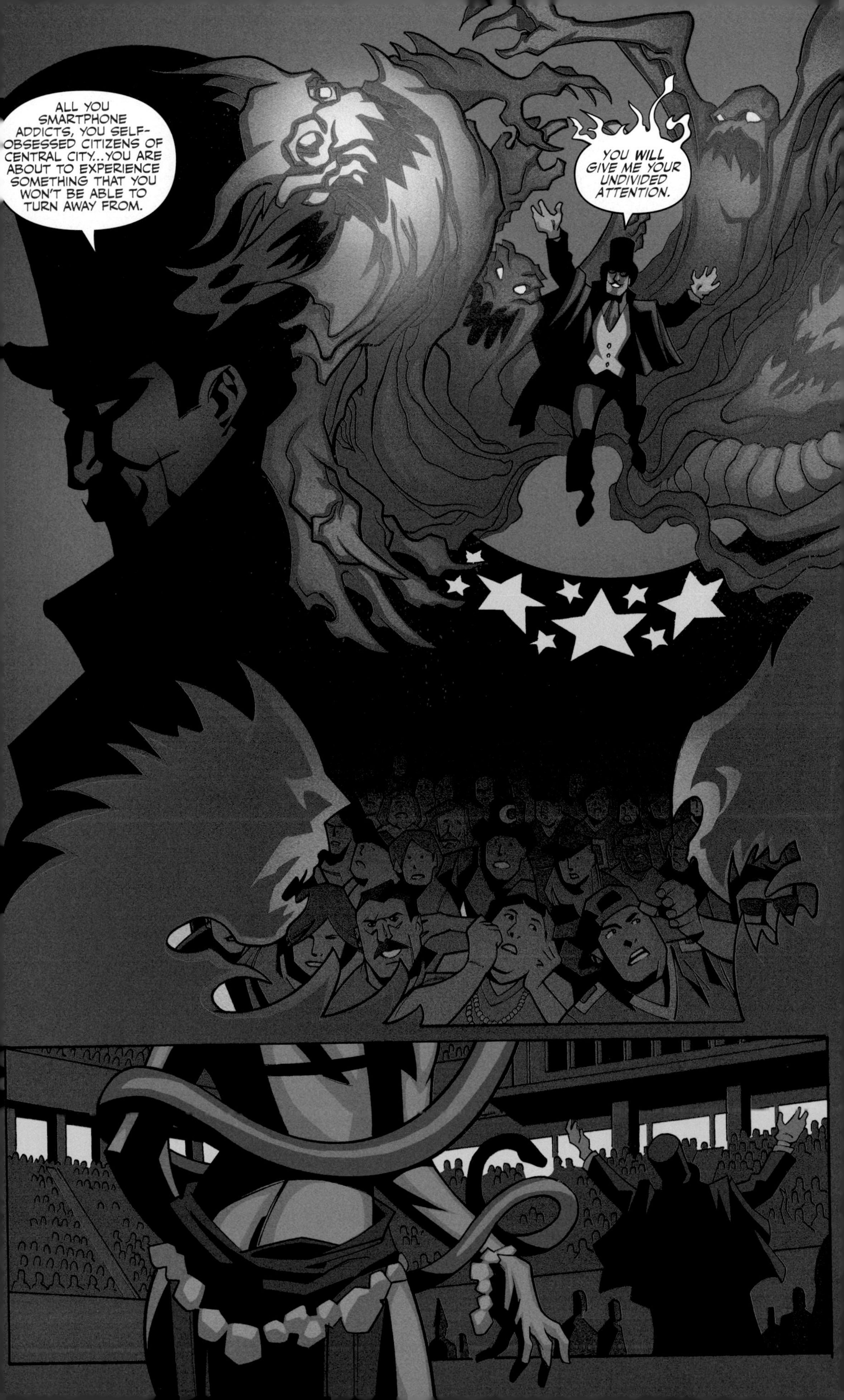
ALL YOU SMARTPHONE ADDICTS, YOU SELF-OBSESSED CITIZENS OF CENTRAL CITY...YOU ARE ABOUT TO EXPERIENCE SOMETHING THAT YOU WON'T BE ABLE TO TURN AWAY FROM.
YOU WILL GIVE ME YOUR UNDIVIDED ATTENTION.

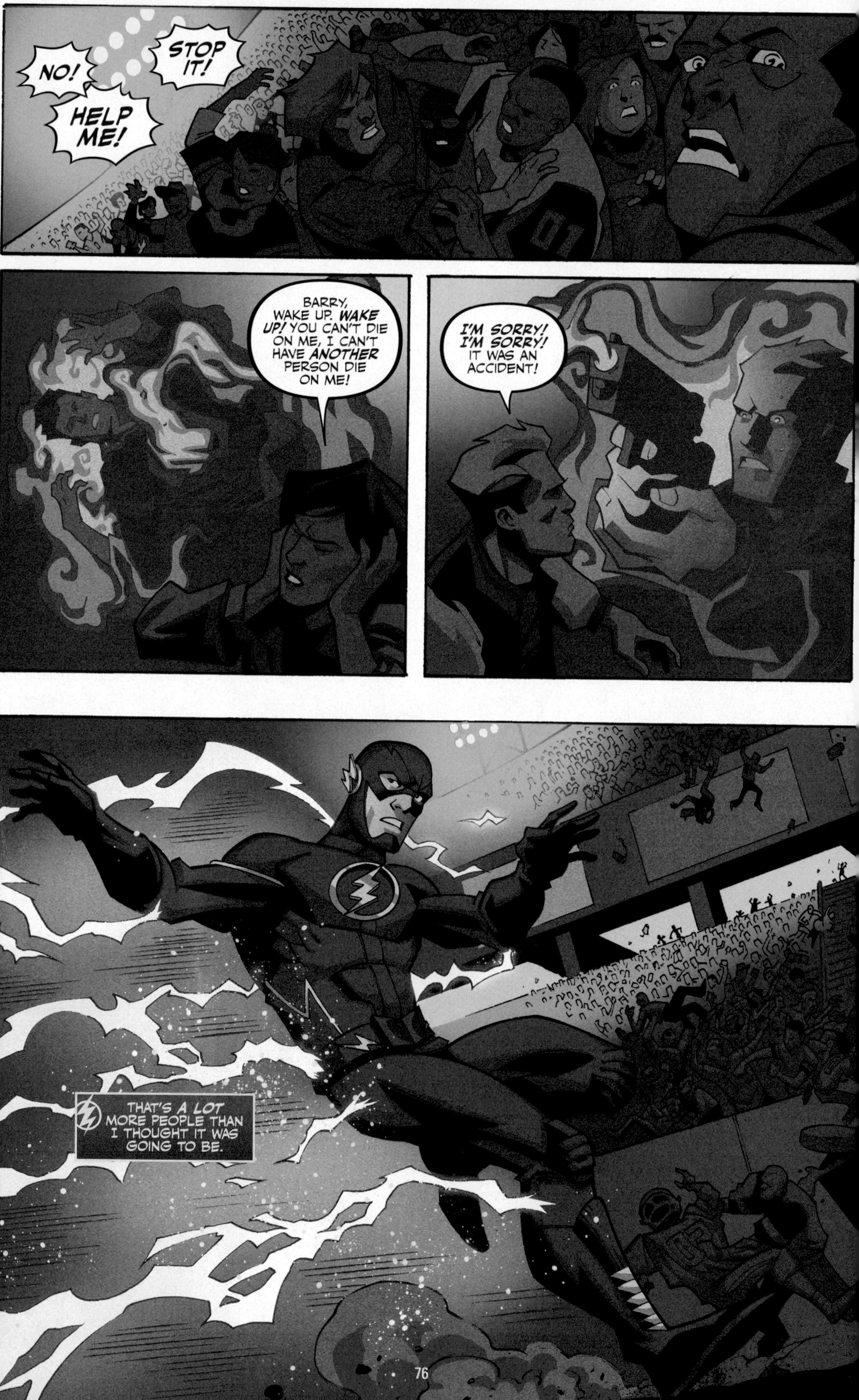
NO!
STOP IT!
HELP ME!
BARRY, WAKE UP. WAKE UP! YOU CAN'T DIE ON ME, I CAN'T HAVE ANOTHER PERSON DIE ON ME!
I'M SORRY! I'M SORRY! IT WAS AN ACCIDENT!
THAT'S A LOT MORE PEOPLE THAN I THOUGHT IT WAS GOING TO BE.

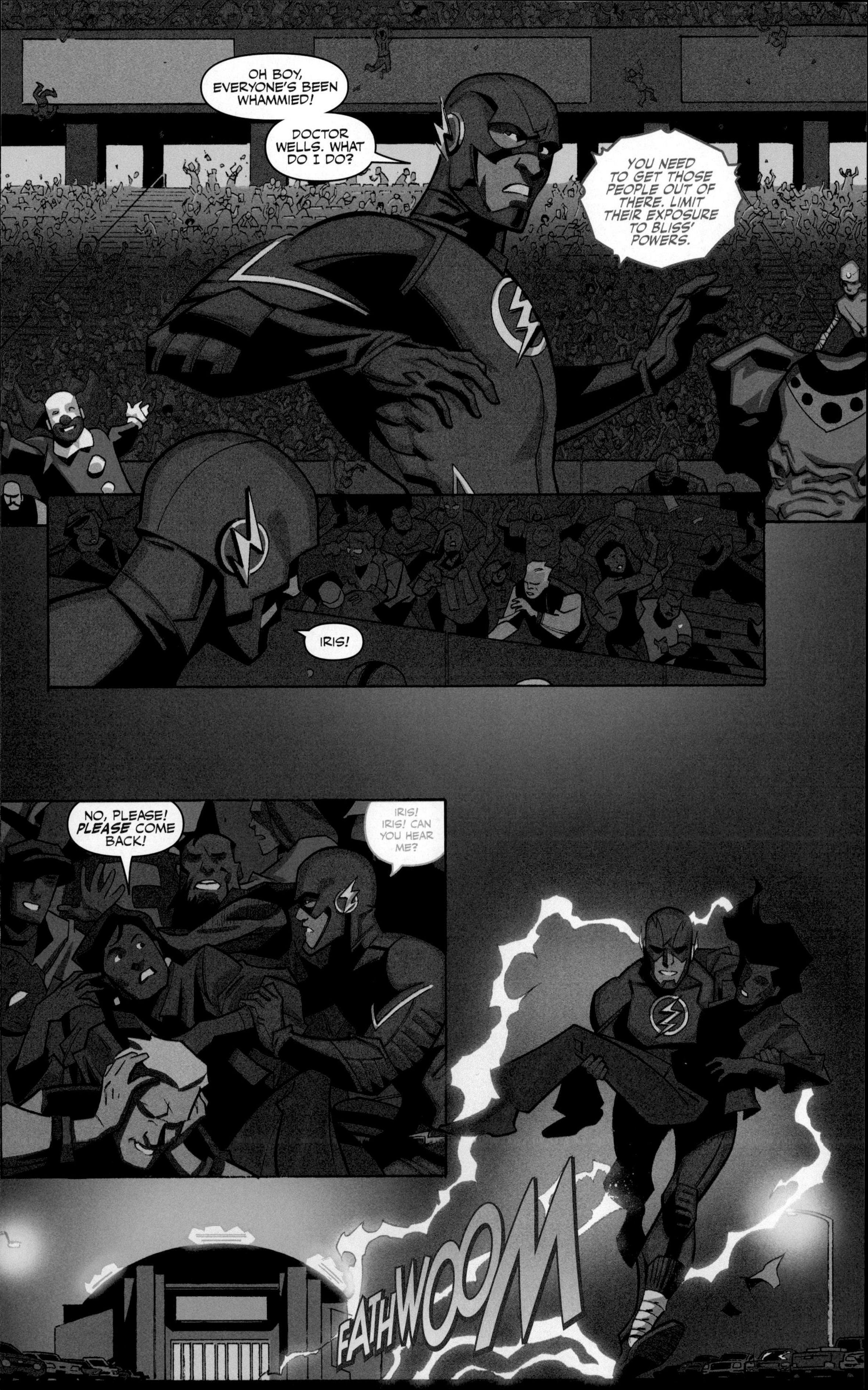
OH BOY, EVERYONE'S BEEN WHAMMIED!
DOCTOR WELLS. WHAT DO I DO?
YOU NEED TO GET THOSE PEOPLE OUT OF THERE. LIMIT THEIR EXPOSURE TO BLISS' POWERS.
IRIS!
NO, PLEASE! ***PLEASE*** COME BACK!
IRIS! IRIS! CAN YOU HEAR ME?
FATHWOOM

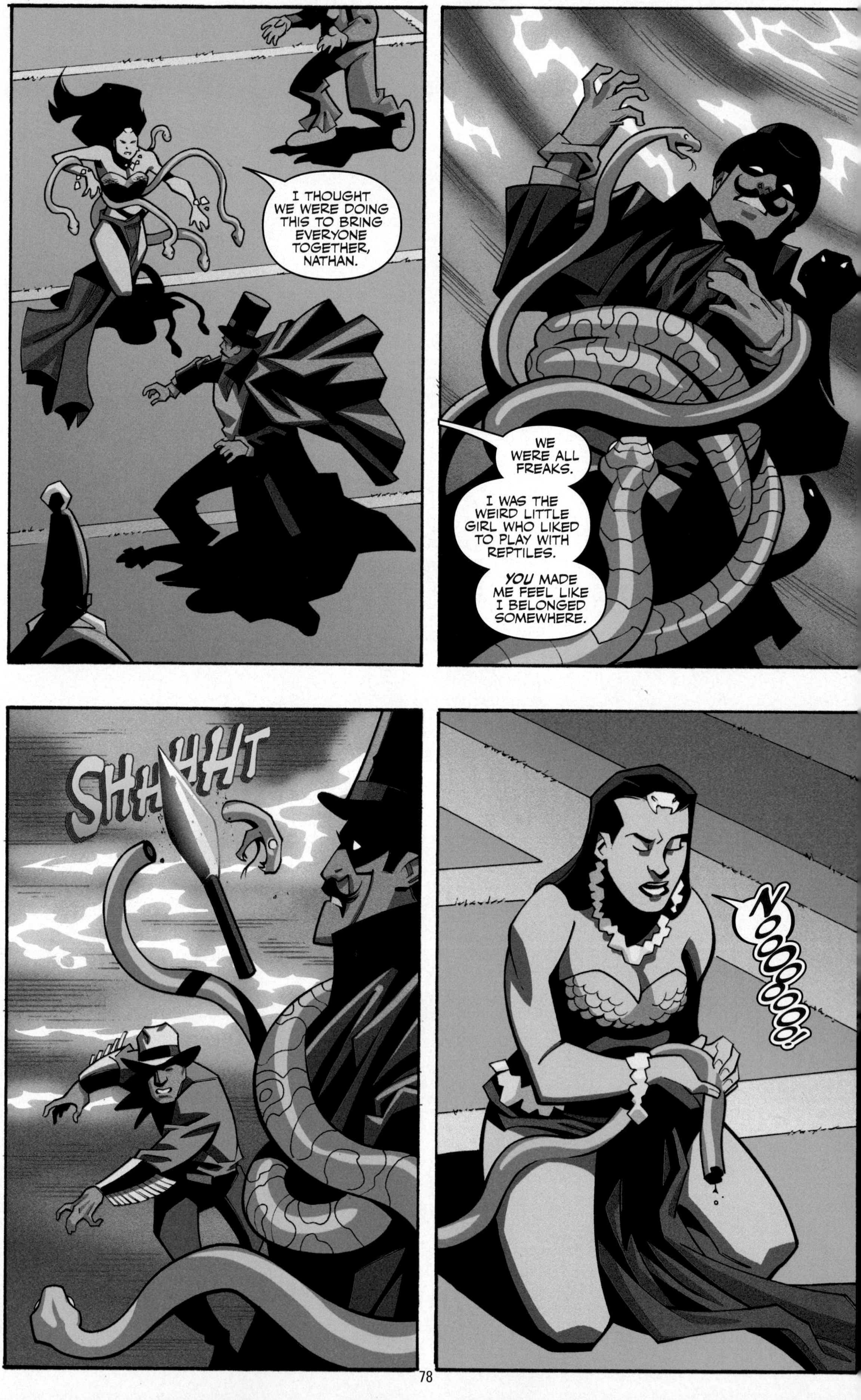
I THOUGHT WE WERE DOING THIS TO BRING EVERYONE TOGETHER, NATHAN.
WE WERE ALL FREAKS.
I WAS THE WEIRD LITTLE GIRL WHO LIKED TO PLAY WITH REPTILES.
YOU MADE ME FEEL LIKE I BELONGED SOMEWHERE.
SHHHHT
NOOOOOO!

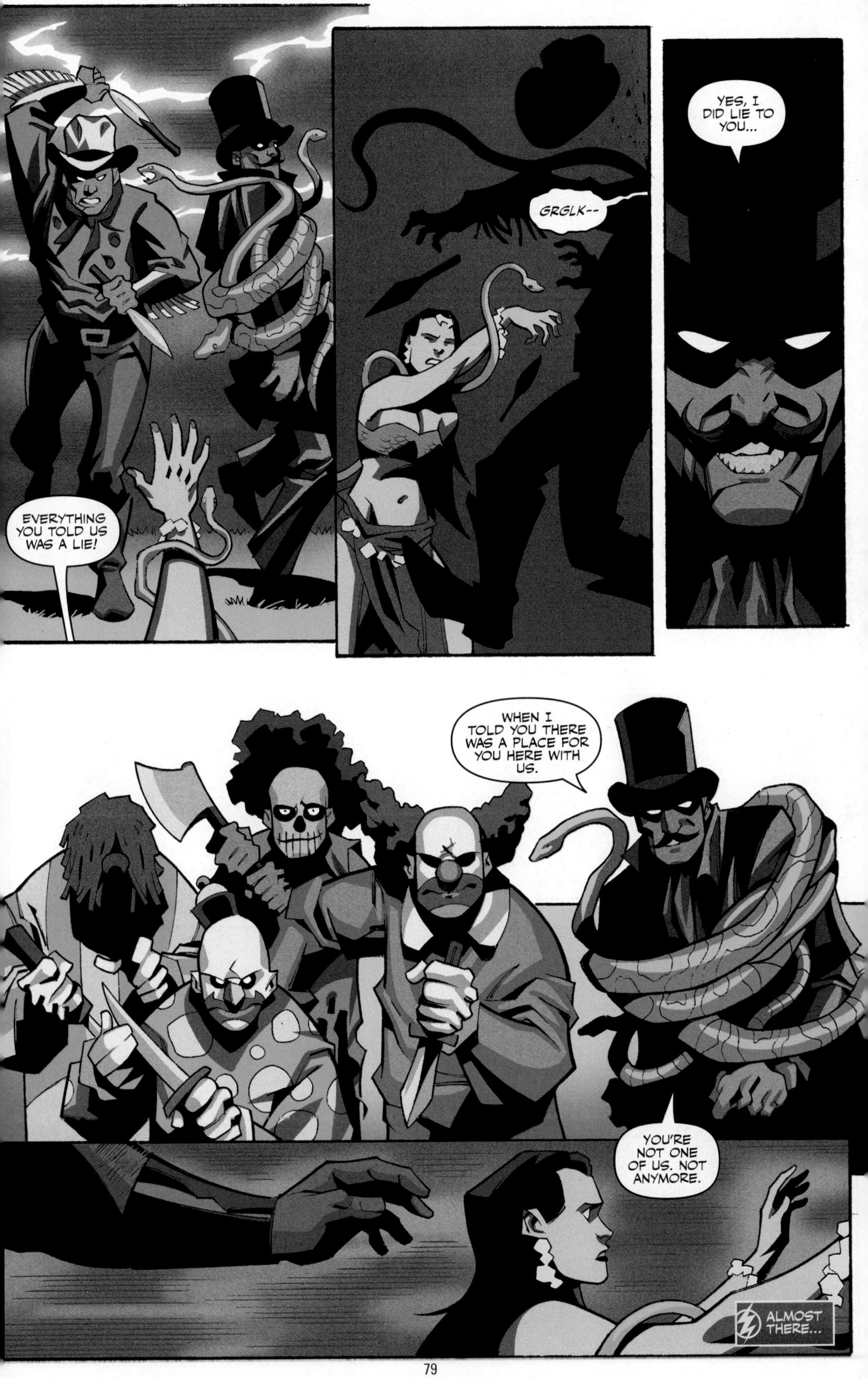

EVERYTHING YOU TOLD US WAS A LIE!
GRGLK--
YES, I DID LIE TO YOU...
WHEN I TOLD YOU THERE WAS A PLACE FOR YOU HERE WITH US.
YOU'RE NOT ONE OF US. NOT ANYMORE.
ALMOST THERE...

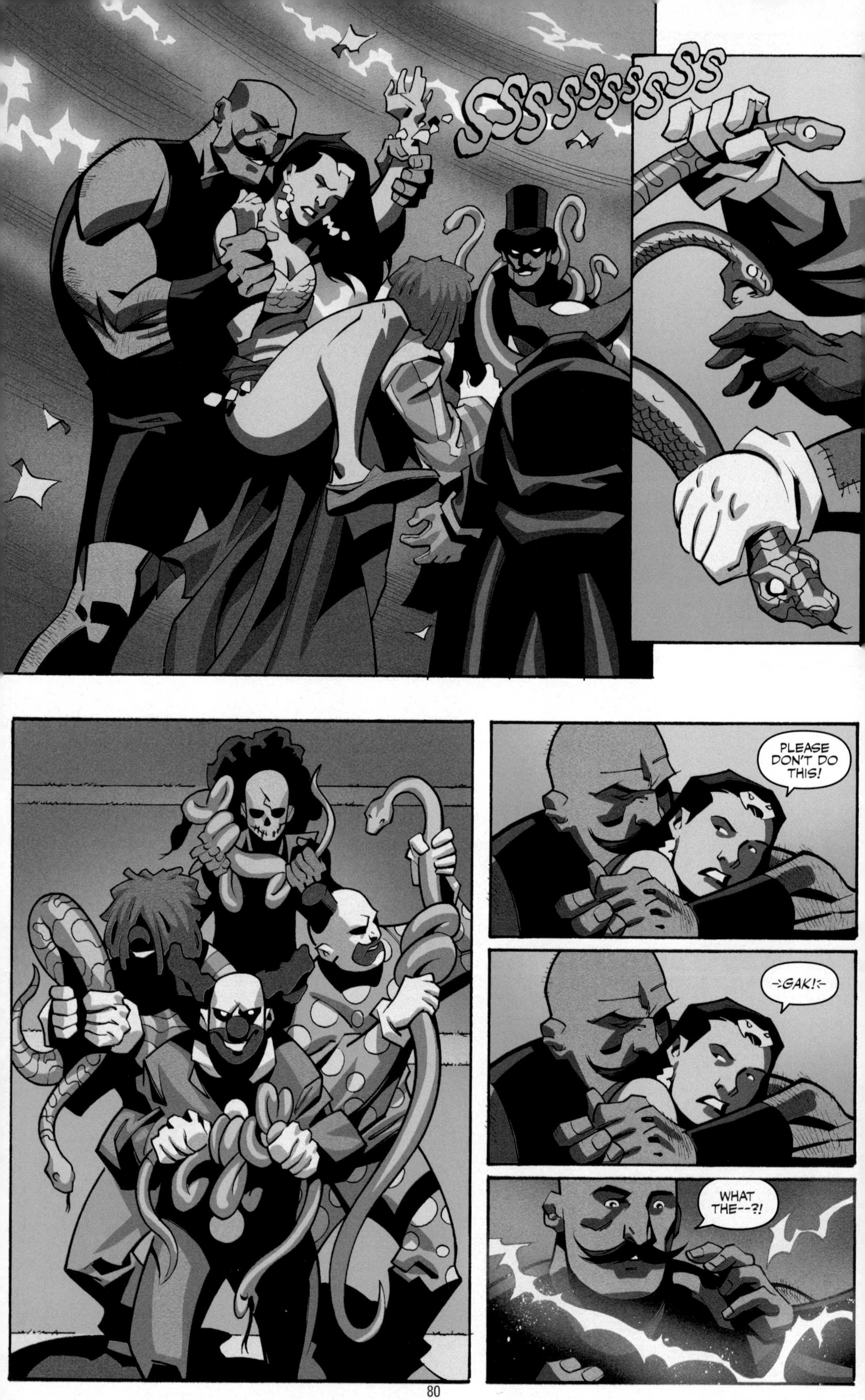
SSSSSSSSSS
PLEASE DON'T DO THIS!
-GAK!-
WHAT THE--?!

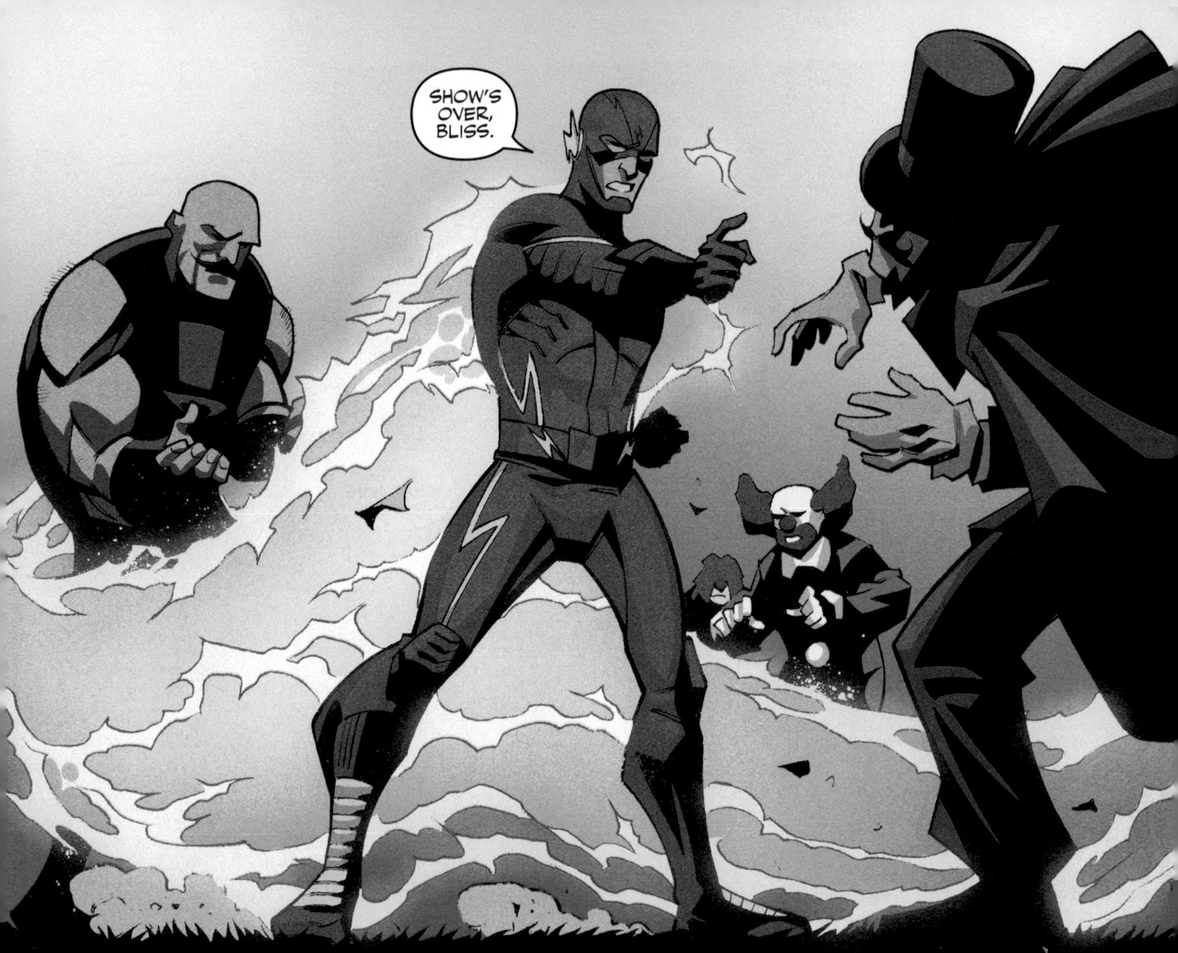
SHOW'S OVER, BLISS.

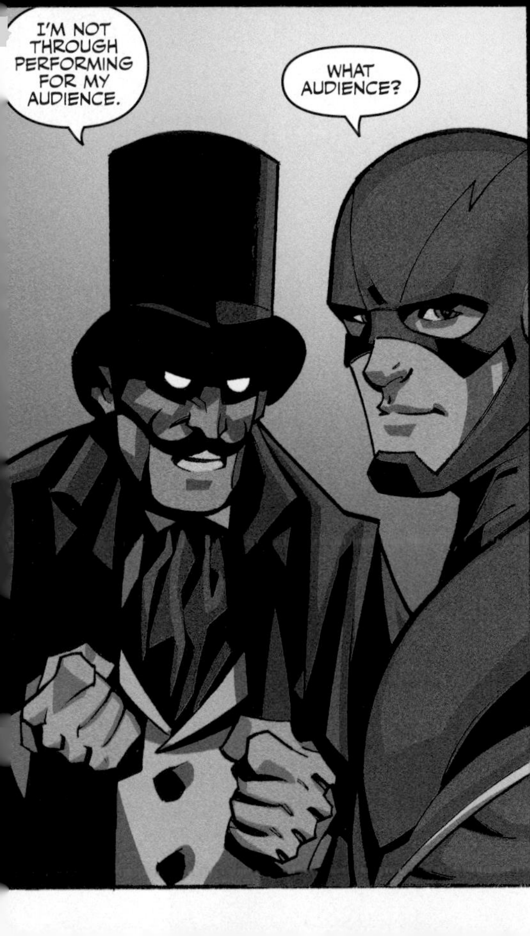
I'M NOT THROUGH PERFORMING FOR MY AUDIENCE.
WHAT AUDIENCE?

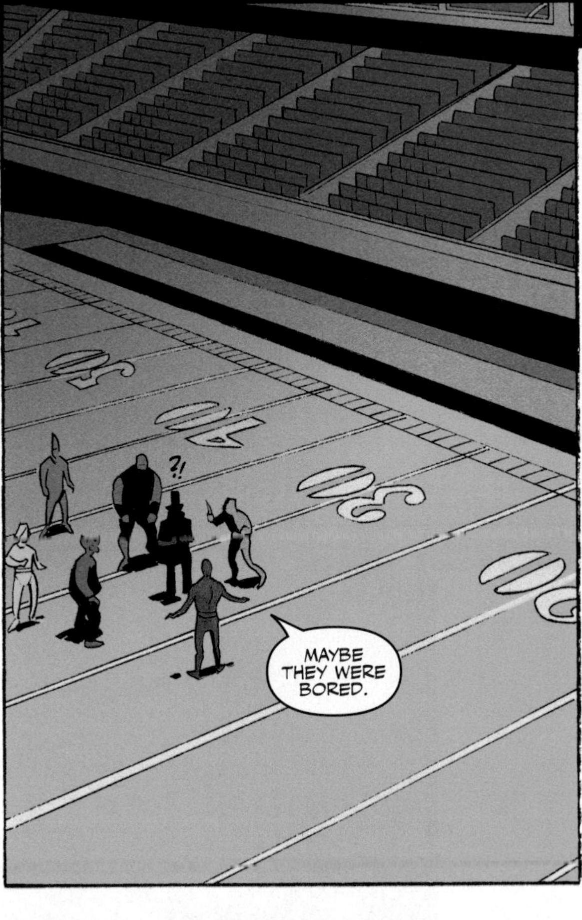
?!
MAYBE THEY WERE BORED.

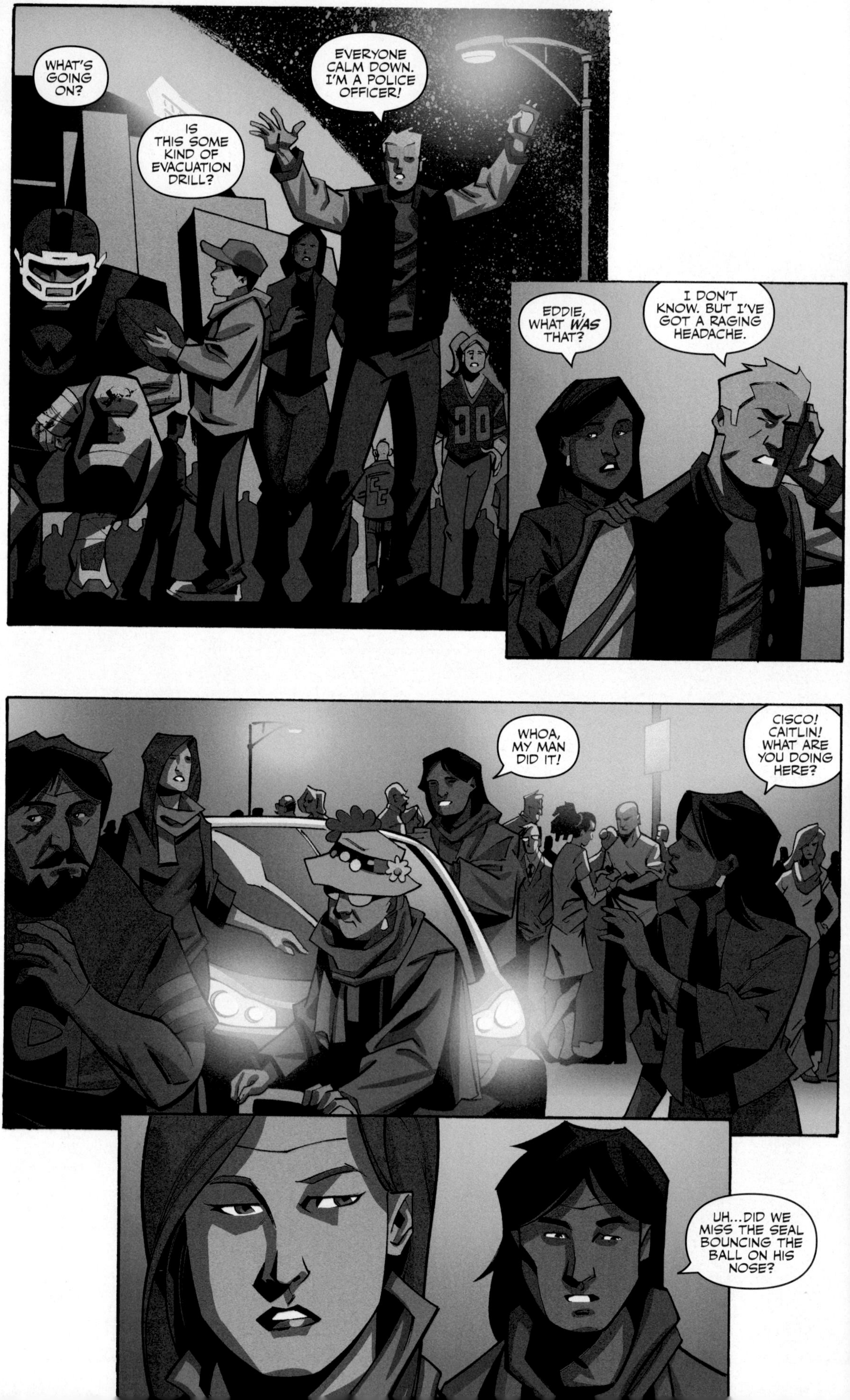
WHAT'S GOING ON?
IS THIS SOME KIND OF EVACUATION DRILL?
EVERYONE CALM DOWN. I'M A POLICE OFFICER!
EDDIE, WHAT *WAS* THAT?
I DON'T KNOW. BUT I'VE GOT A RAGING HEADACHE.
WHOA, MY MAN DID IT!
CISCO! CAITLIN! WHAT ARE YOU DOING HERE?
UH...DID WE MISS THE SEAL BOUNCING THE BALL ON HIS NOSE?

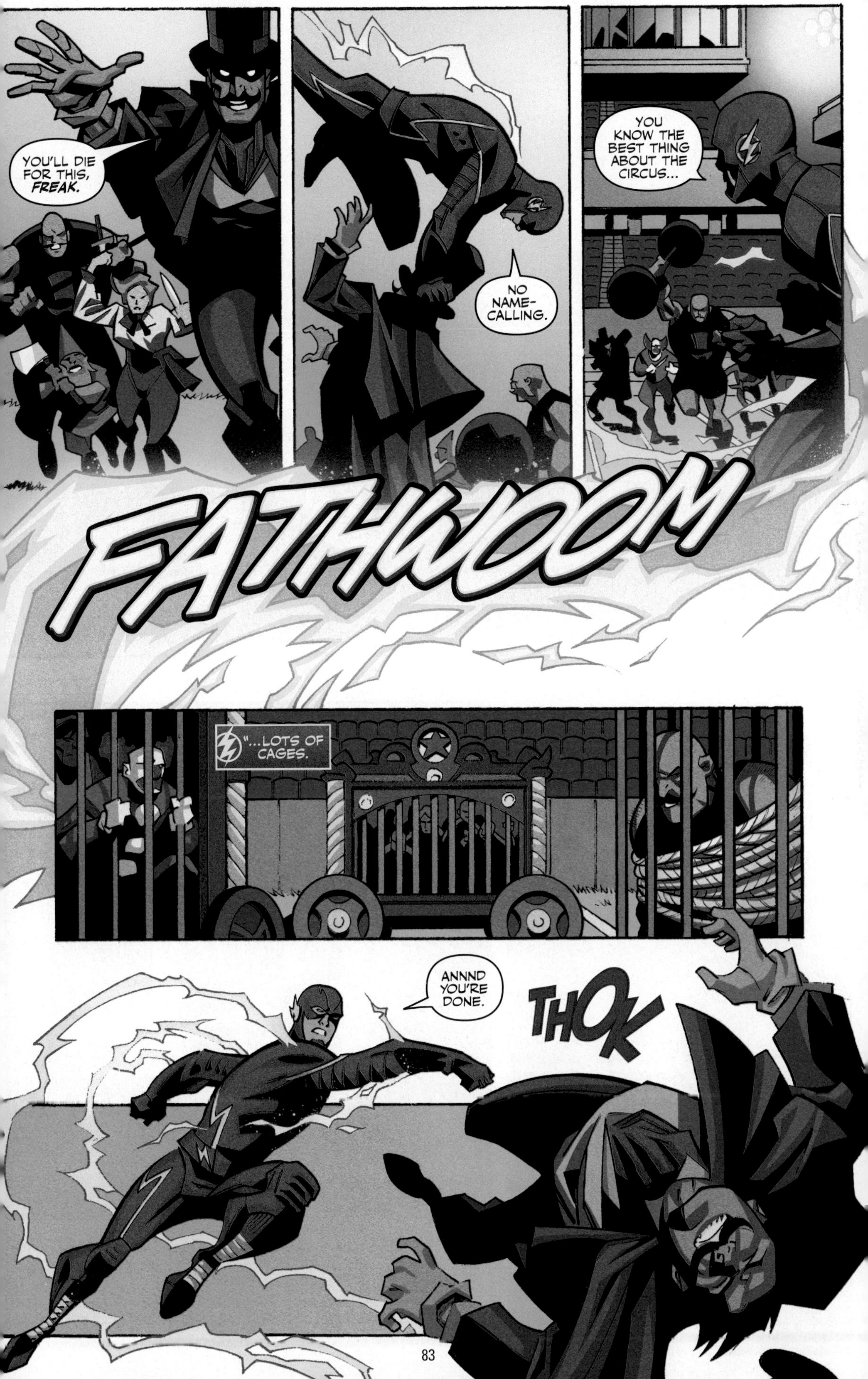

YOU'LL DIE FOR THIS, *FREAK.*
NO NAME-CALLING.
YOU KNOW THE BEST THING ABOUT THE CIRCUS...
FATHWOOM
"...LOTS OF CAGES.
ANNND YOU'RE DONE.
THOK

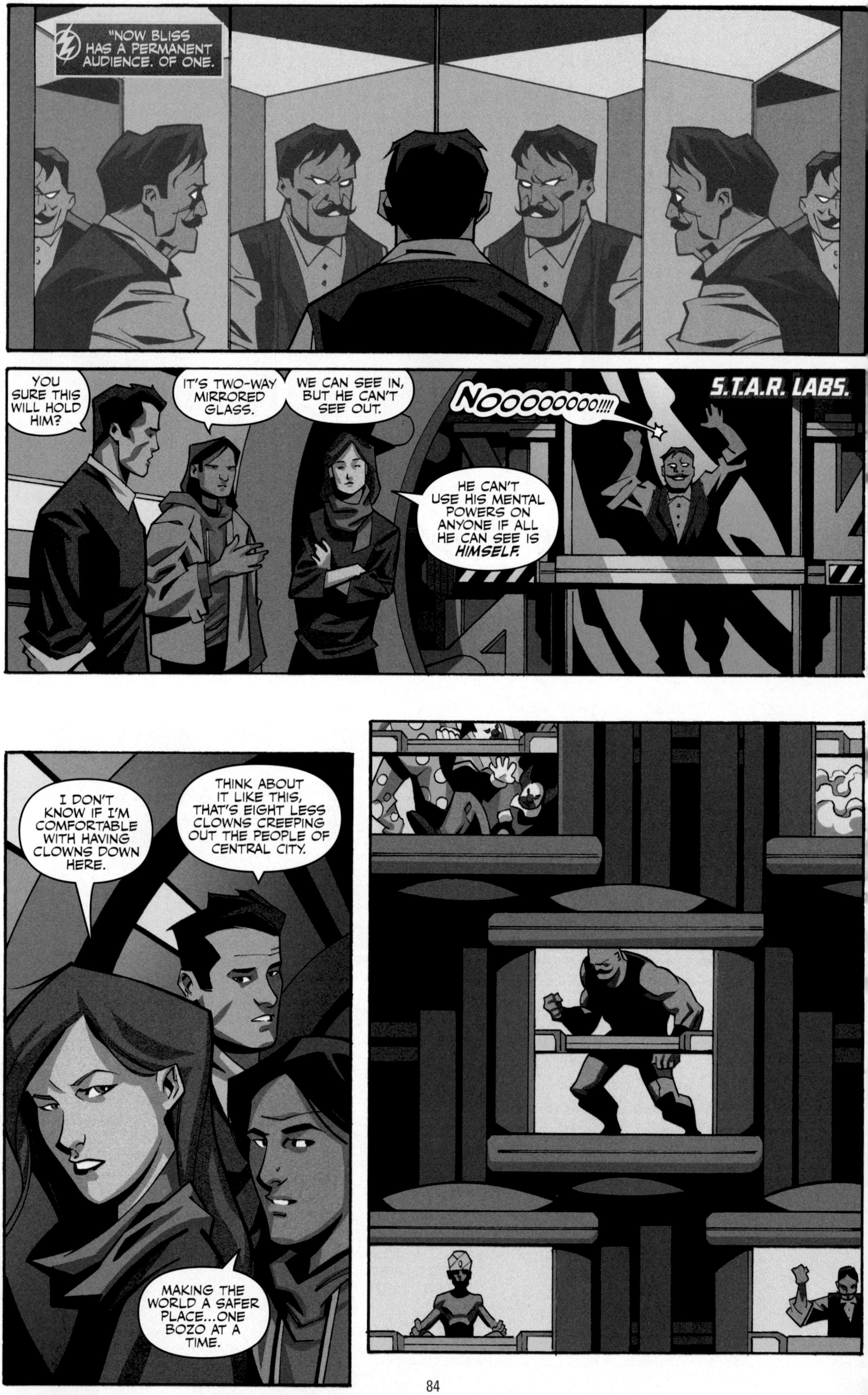
"NOW BLISS HAS A PERMANENT AUDIENCE. OF ONE.
YOU SURE THIS WILL HOLD HIM?
IT'S TWO-WAY MIRRORED GLASS.
WE CAN SEE IN, BUT HE CAN'T SEE OUT.
S.T.A.R. LABS.
NOOOOOOOO!!!!
HE CAN'T USE HIS MENTAL POWERS ON ANYONE IF ALL HE CAN SEE IS HIMSELF.
I DON'T KNOW IF I'M COMFORTABLE WITH HAVING CLOWNS DOWN HERE.
THINK ABOUT IT LIKE THIS, THAT'S EIGHT LESS CLOWNS CREEPING OUT THE PEOPLE OF CENTRAL CITY.
MAKING THE WORLD A SAFER PLACE...ONE BOZO AT A TIME.

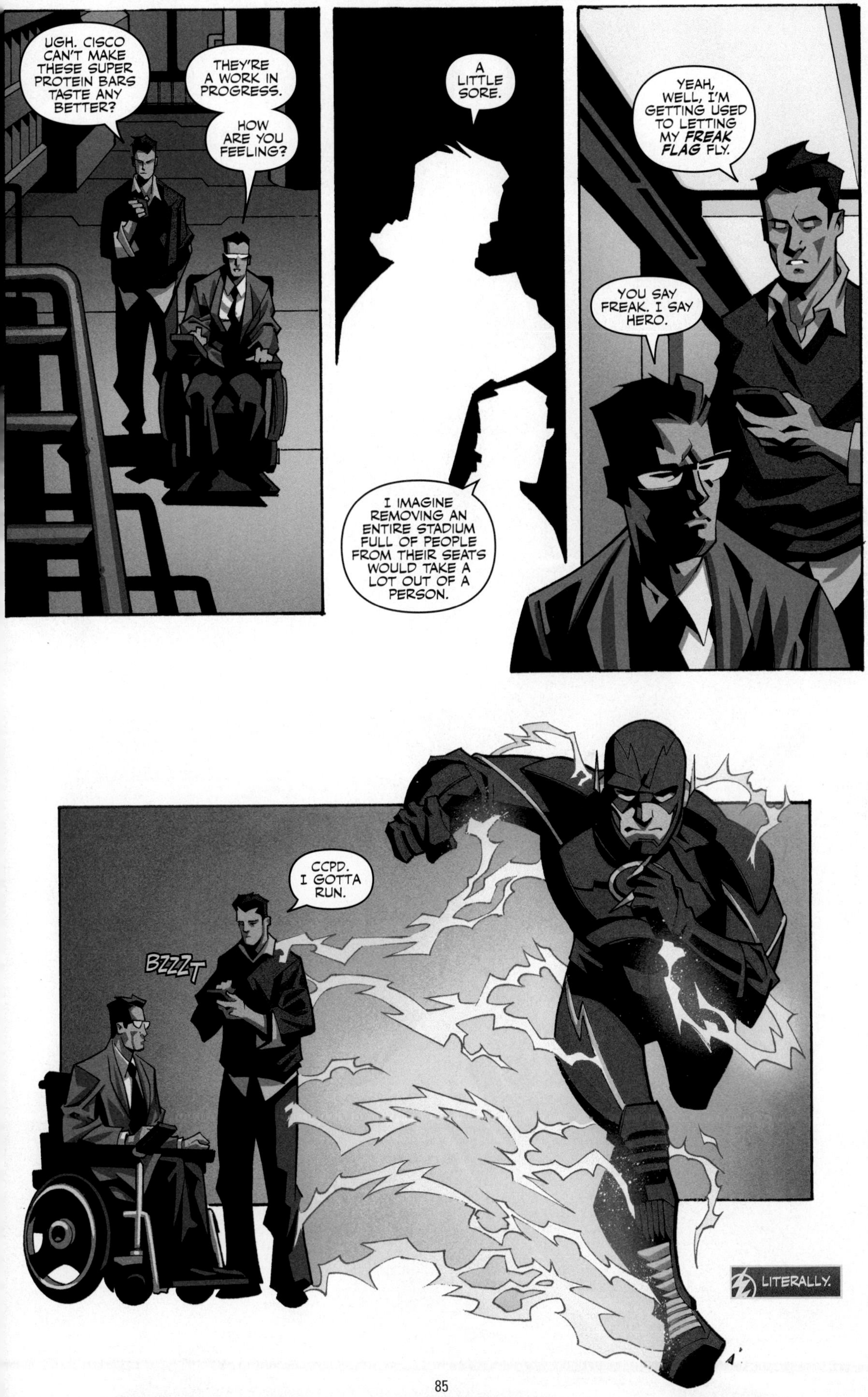
UGH. CISCO CAN'T MAKE THESE SUPER PROTEIN BARS TASTE ANY BETTER?
THEY'RE A WORK IN PROGRESS.
HOW ARE YOU FEELING?
A LITTLE SORE.
I IMAGINE REMOVING AN ENTIRE STADIUM FULL OF PEOPLE FROM THEIR SEATS WOULD TAKE A LOT OUT OF A PERSON.
YEAH, WELL, I'M GETTING USED TO LETTING MY FREAK FLAG FLY.
YOU SAY FREAK. I SAY HERO.
BZZZT
CCPD. I GOTTA RUN.
LITERALLY.

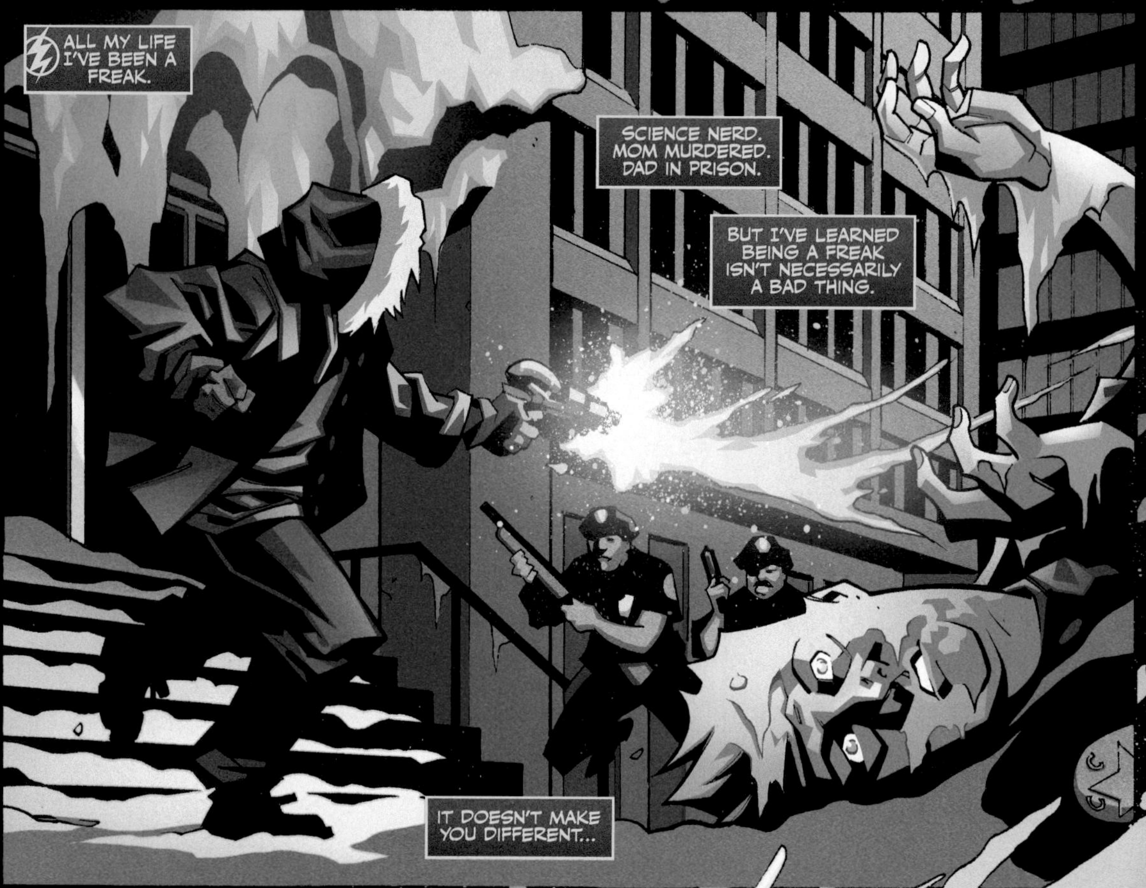
ALL MY LIFE I'VE BEEN A FREAK.
SCIENCE NERD. MOM MURDERED. DAD IN PRISON.
BUT I'VE LEARNED BEING A FREAK ISN'T NECESSARILY A BAD THING.
IT DOESN'T MAKE YOU DIFFERENT...

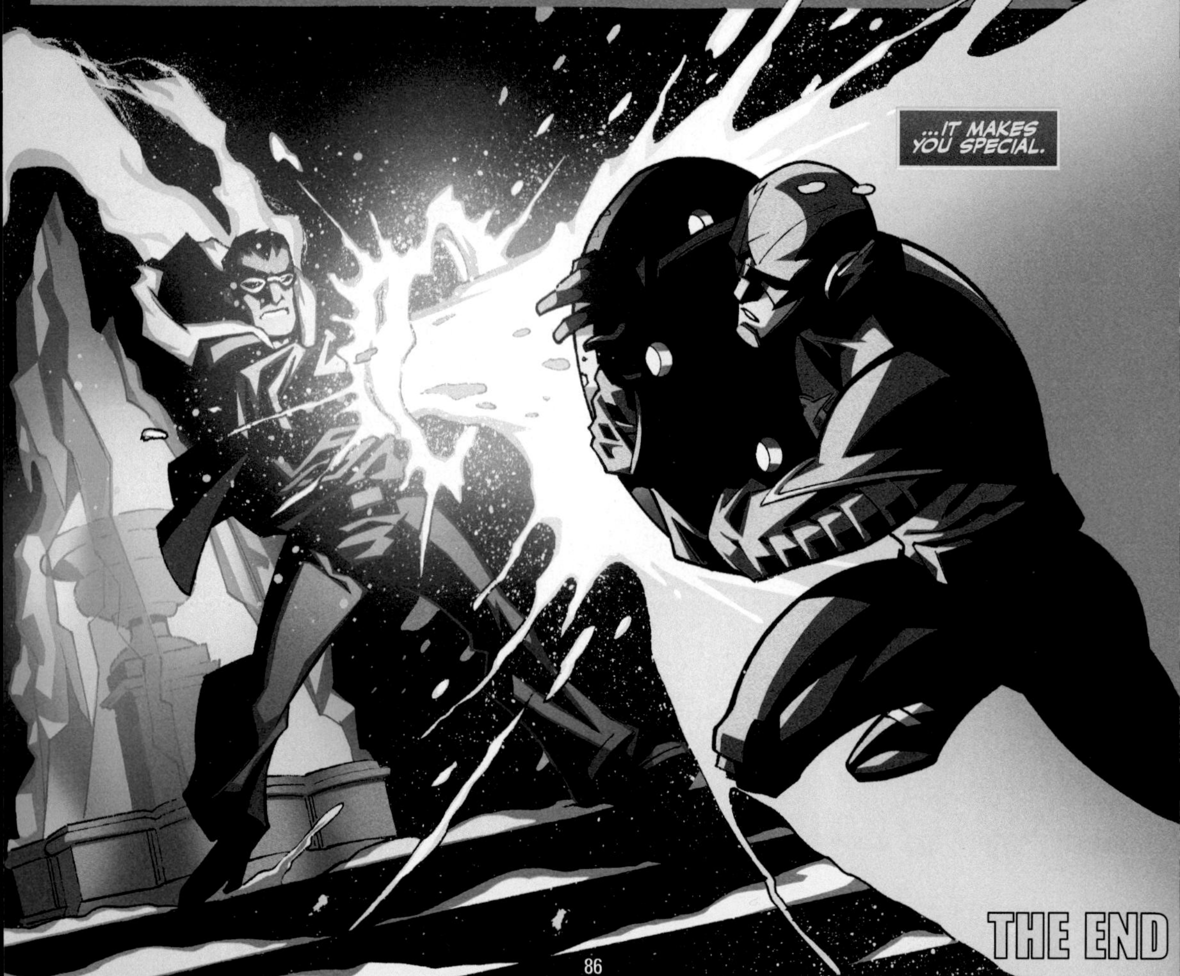
...IT MAKES YOU SPECIAL.
THE END

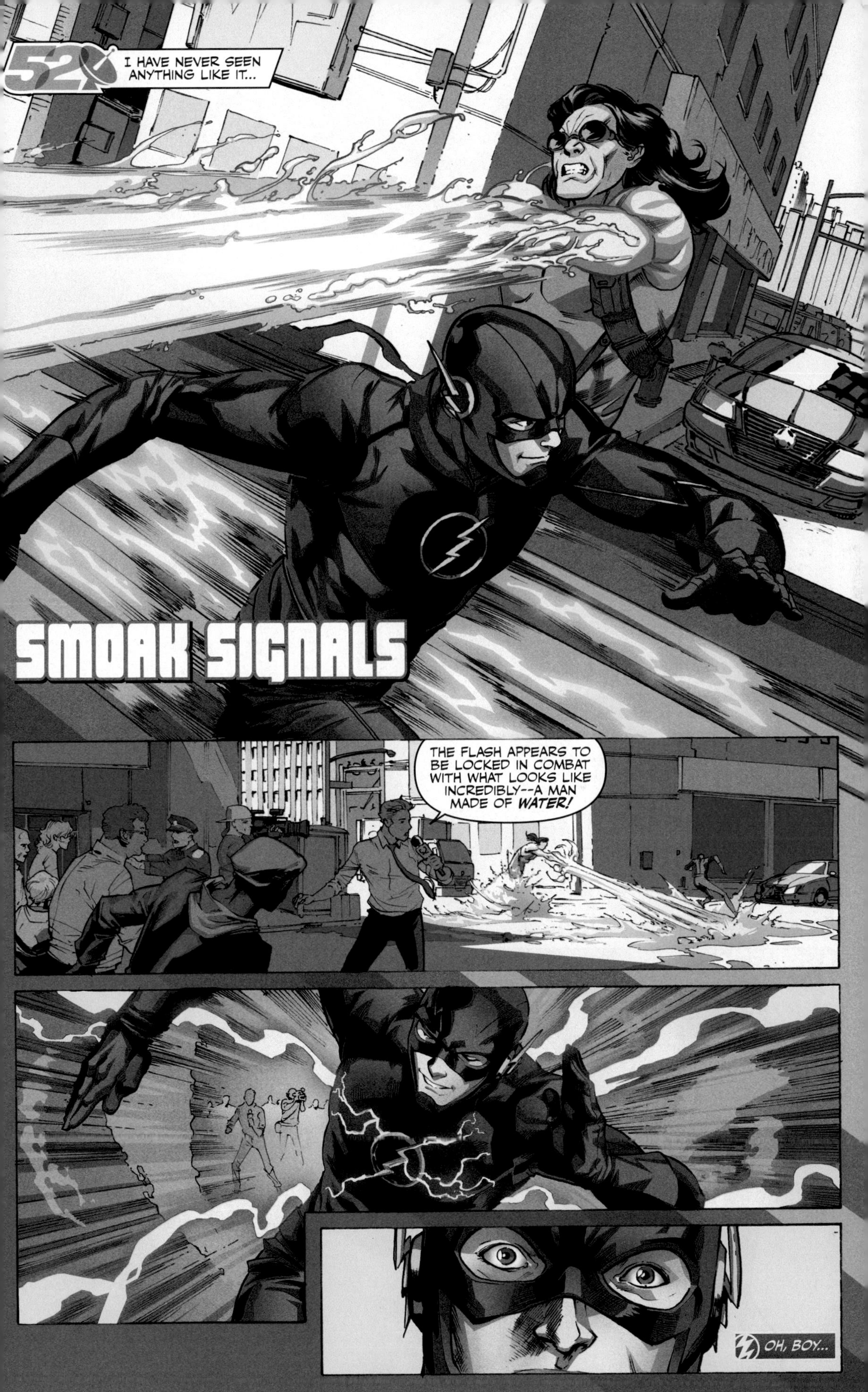
I HAVE NEVER SEEN ANYTHING LIKE IT...
SMOAK SIGNALS
THE FLASH APPEARS TO BE LOCKED IN COMBAT WITH WHAT LOOKS LIKE INCREDIBLY--A MAN MADE OF *WATER!*
OH, BOY...

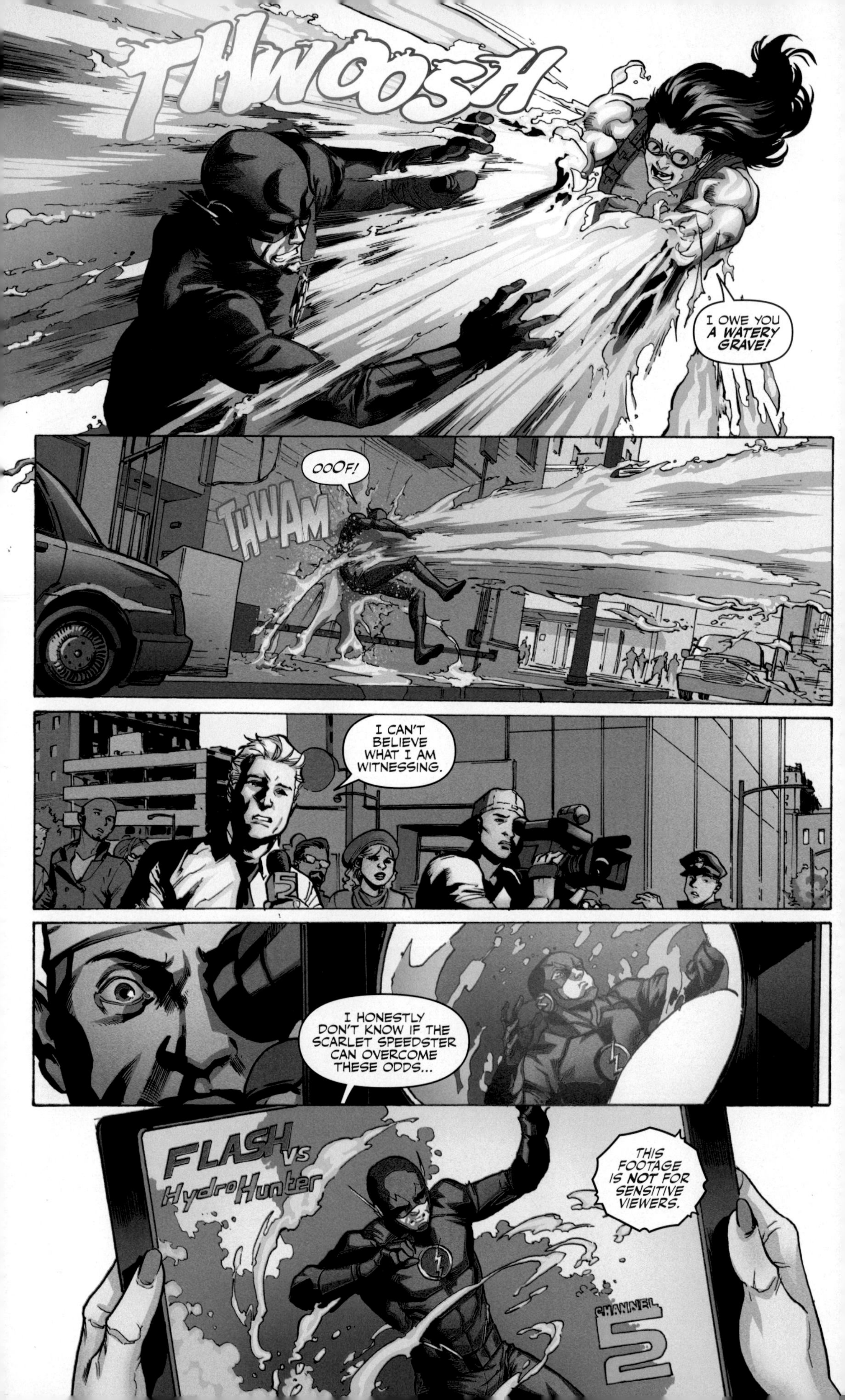
THWOOSH
I OWE YOU A WATERY GRAVE!
OOOF!
THWAM
I CAN'T BELIEVE WHAT I AM WITNESSING.
I HONESTLY DON'T KNOW IF THE SCARLET SPEEDSTER CAN OVERCOME THESE ODDS...
FLASH VS HydroHunter
THIS FOOTAGE IS NOT FOR SENSITIVE VIEWERS.
CHANNEL 5

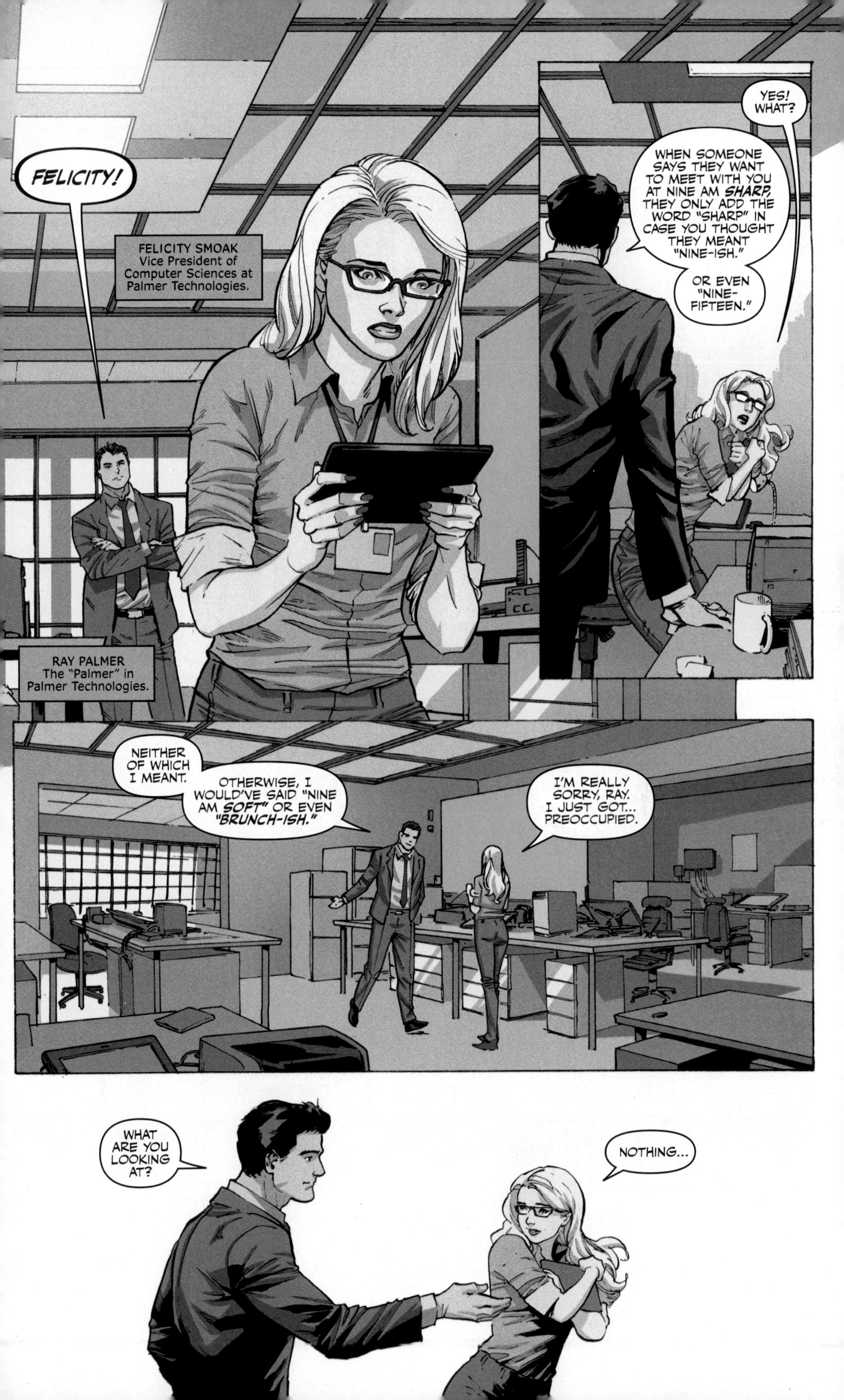
FELICITY!
FELICITY SMOAK Vice President of Computer Sciences at Palmer Technologies.
RAY PALMER The "Palmer" in Palmer Technologies.
YES! WHAT?
WHEN SOMEONE SAYS THEY WANT TO MEET WITH YOU AT NINE AM SHARP, THEY ONLY ADD THE WORD "SHARP" IN CASE YOU THOUGHT THEY MEANT "NINE-ISH."
OR EVEN "NINE-FIFTEEN."
NEITHER OF WHICH I MEANT.
OTHERWISE, I WOULD'VE SAID "NINE AM SOFT" OR EVEN "BRUNCH-ISH."
I'M REALLY SORRY, RAY. I JUST GOT... PREOCCUPIED.
WHAT ARE YOU LOOKING AT?
NOTHING...

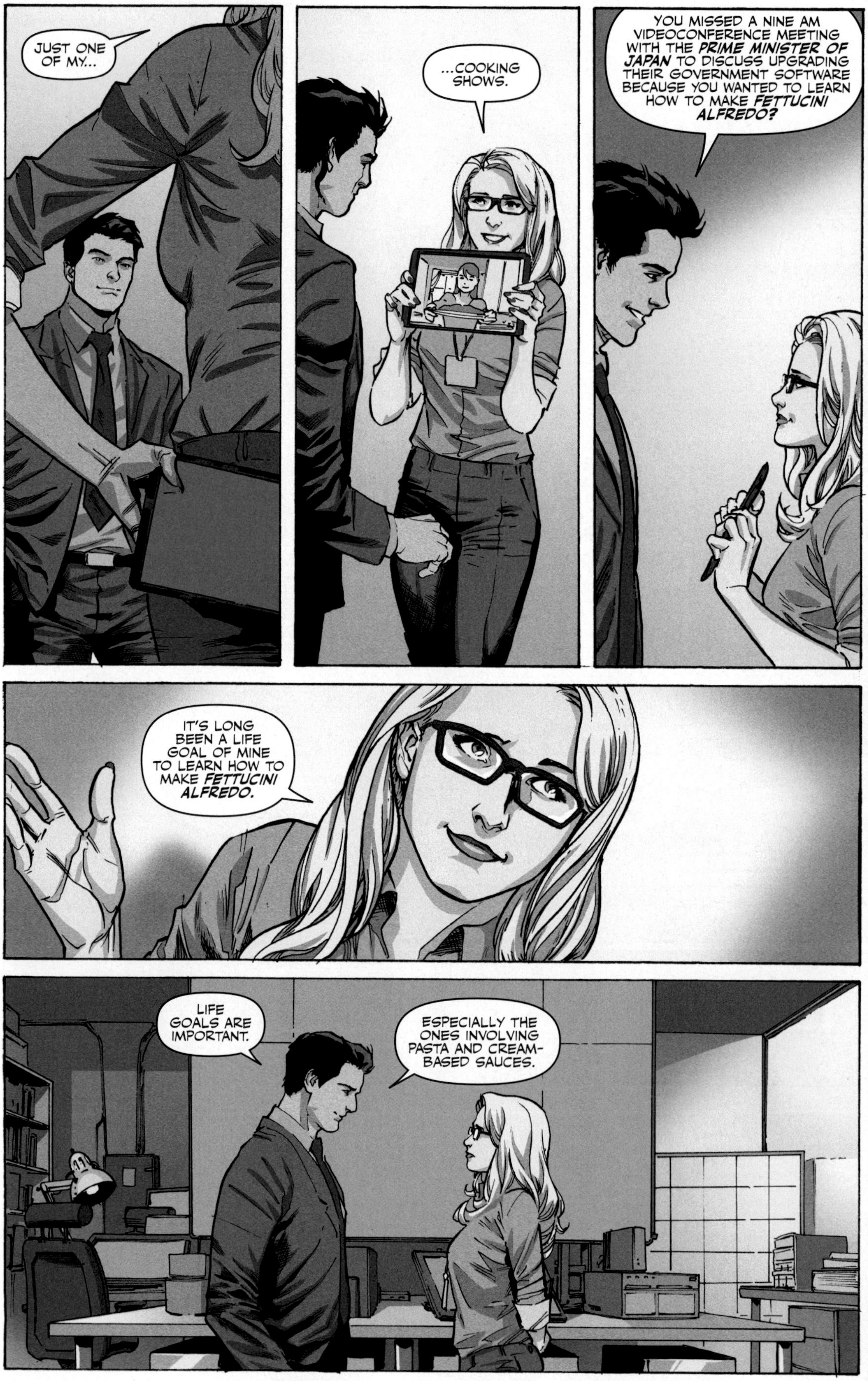
JUST ONE OF MY...
...COOKING SHOWS.
YOU MISSED A NINE AM VIDEOCONFERENCE MEETING WITH THE PRIME MINISTER OF JAPAN TO DISCUSS UPGRADING THEIR GOVERNMENT SOFTWARE BECAUSE YOU WANTED TO LEARN HOW TO MAKE FETTUCINI ALFREDO?
IT'S LONG BEEN A LIFE GOAL OF MINE TO LEARN HOW TO MAKE FETTUCINI ALFREDO.
LIFE GOALS ARE IMPORTANT.
ESPECIALLY THE ONES INVOLVING PASTA AND CREAM-BASED SAUCES.

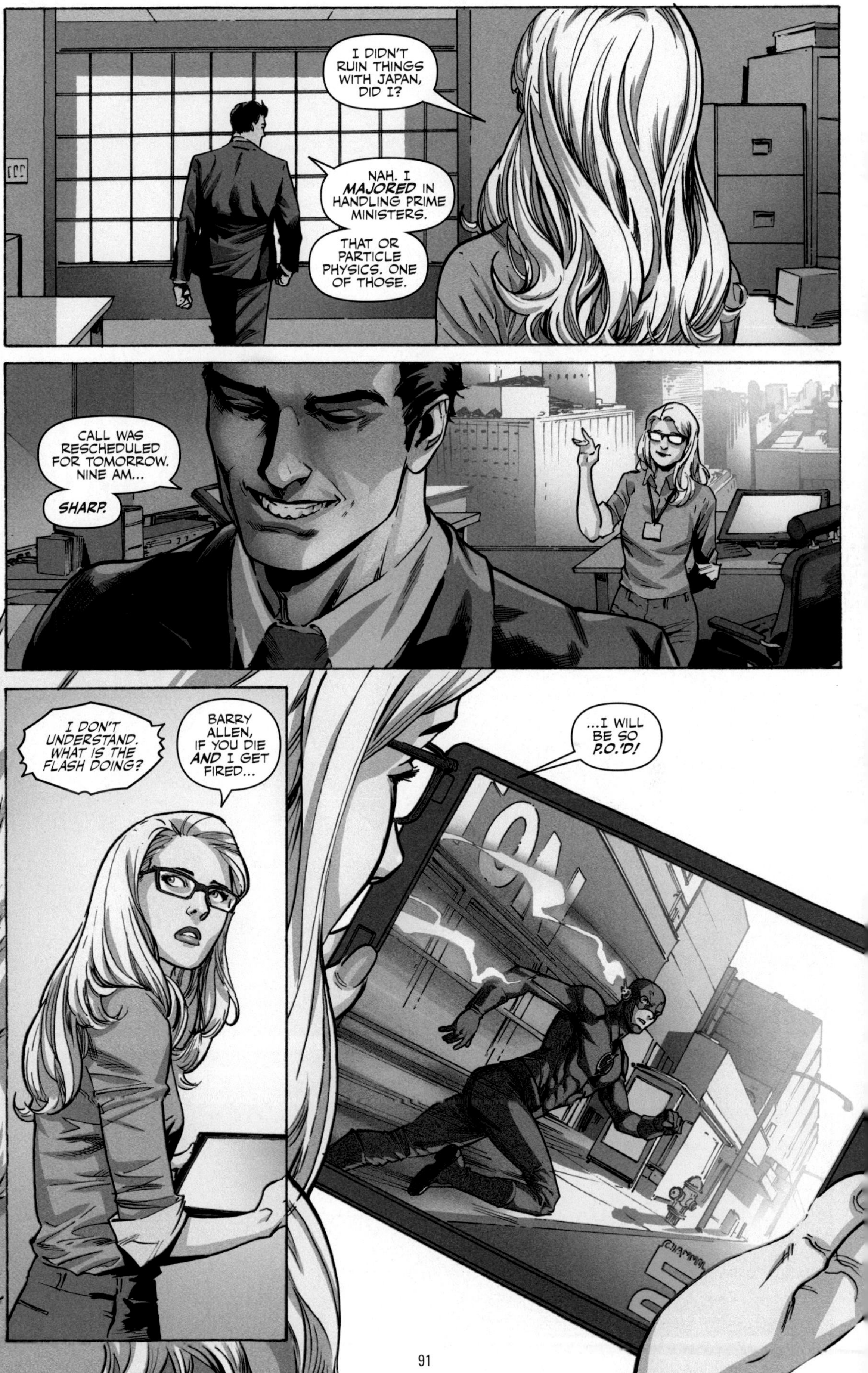
I DIDN'T RUIN THINGS WITH JAPAN, DID I?
NAH. I MAJORED IN HANDLING PRIME MINISTERS.
THAT OR PARTICLE PHYSICS. ONE OF THOSE.
CALL WAS RESCHEDULED FOR TOMORROW. NINE AM...
SHARP.
I DON'T UNDERSTAND. WHAT IS THE FLASH DOING?
BARRY ALLEN, IF YOU DIE AND I GET FIRED...
...I WILL BE SO P.O.'D!

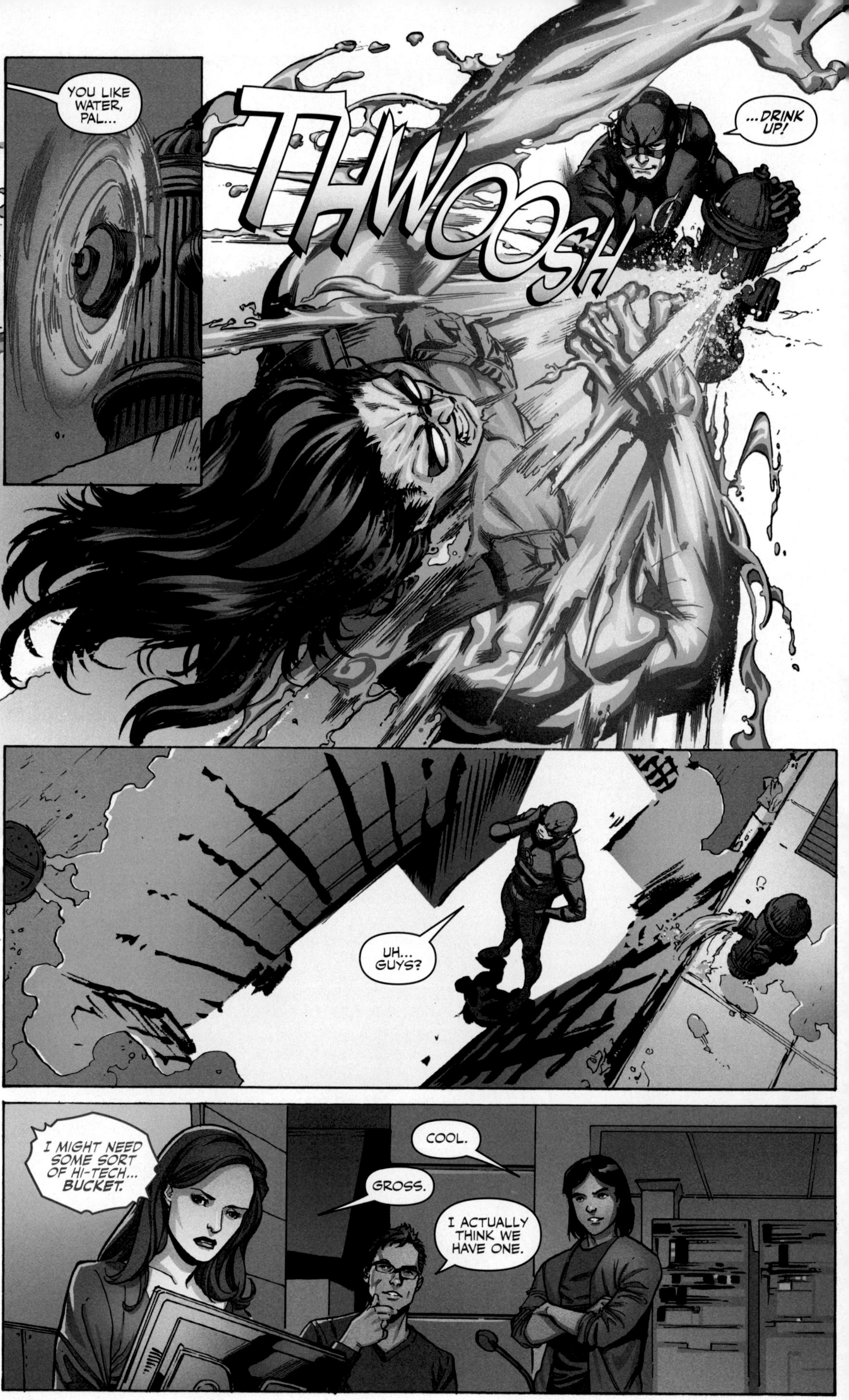
YOU LIKE WATER, PAL...
THWOOSH
...DRINK UP!
UH... GUYS?
I MIGHT NEED SOME SORT OF HI-TECH... BUCKET.
COOL.
GROSS.
I ACTUALLY THINK WE HAVE ONE.

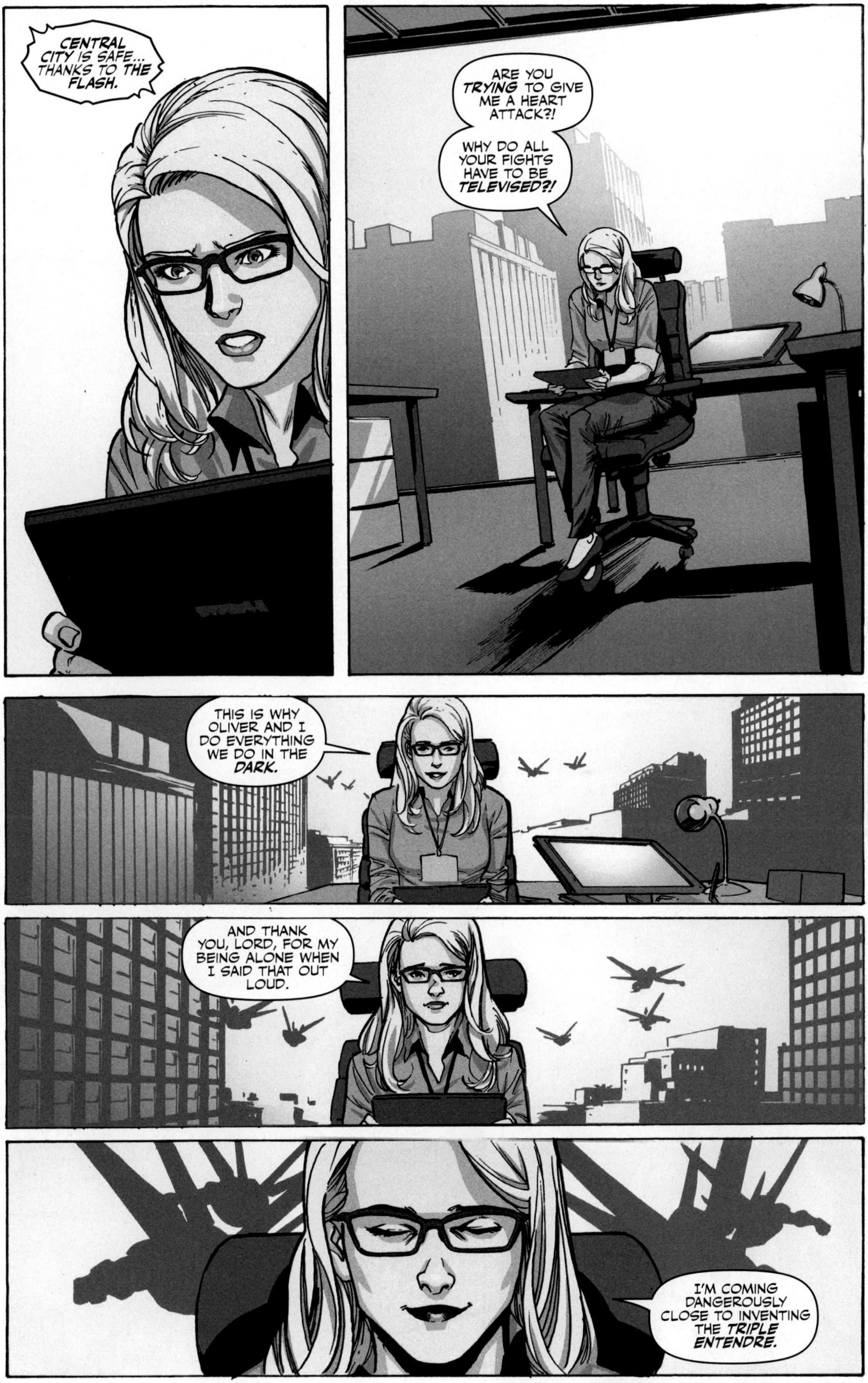
CENTRAL CITY IS SAFE... THANKS TO THE FLASH.
ARE YOU TRYING TO GIVE ME A HEART ATTACK?!
WHY DO ALL YOUR FIGHTS HAVE TO BE TELEVISED?!
THIS IS WHY OLIVER AND I DO EVERYTHING WE DO IN THE DARK.
AND THANK YOU, LORD, FOR MY BEING ALONE WHEN I SAID THAT OUT LOUD.
I'M COMING DANGEROUSLY CLOSE TO INVENTING THE TRIPLE ENTENDRE.

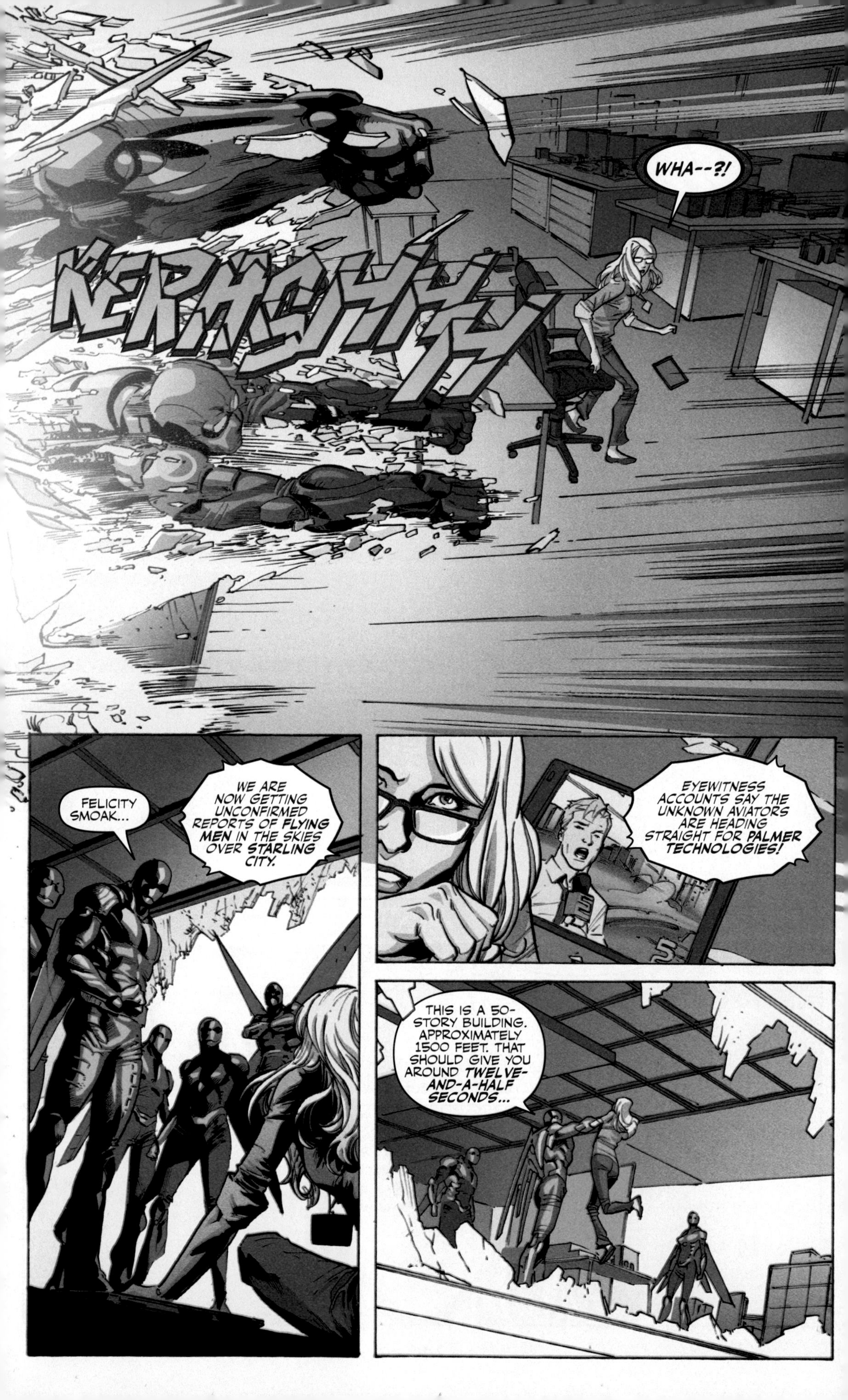
WHA--?!
FELICITY SMOAK...
WE ARE NOW GETTING UNCONFIRMED REPORTS OF FLYING MEN IN THE SKIES OVER STARLING CITY.
EYEWITNESS ACCOUNTS SAY THE UNKNOWN AVIATORS ARE HEADING STRAIGHT FOR PALMER TECHNOLOGIES!
THIS IS A 50-STORY BUILDING. APPROXIMATELY 1500 FEET. THAT SHOULD GIVE YOU AROUND TWELVE-AND-A-HALF SECONDS...

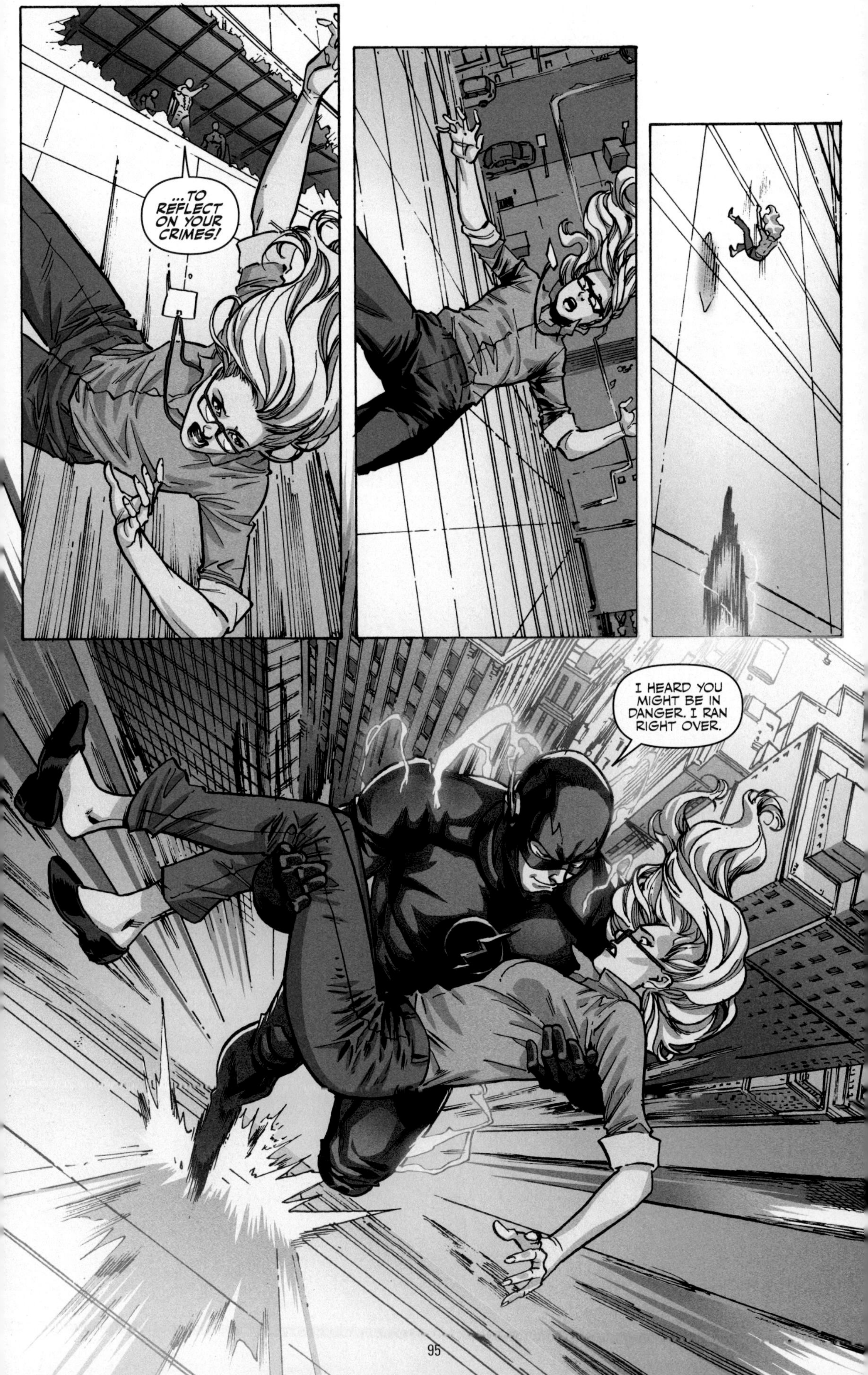
...TO REFLECT ON YOUR CRIMES!
I HEARD YOU MIGHT BE IN DANGER. I RAN RIGHT OVER.

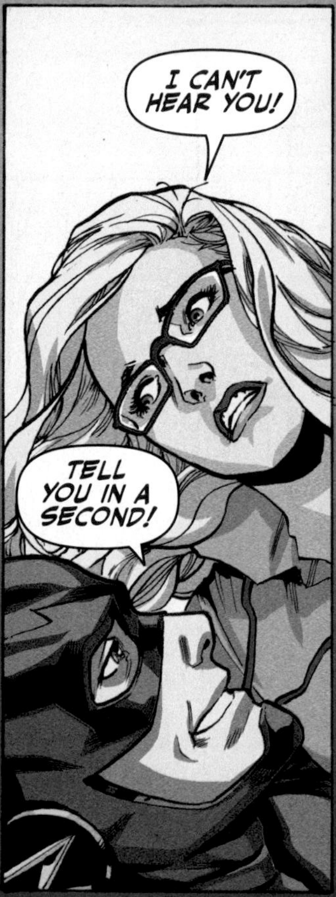
I CAN'T HEAR YOU!
TELL YOU IN A SECOND!

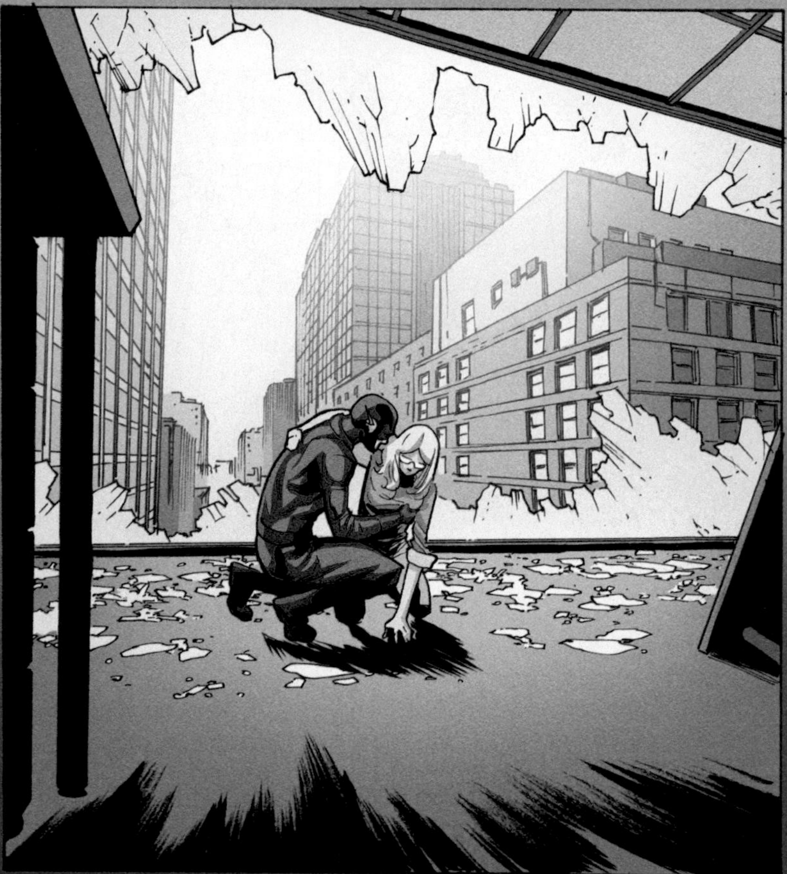

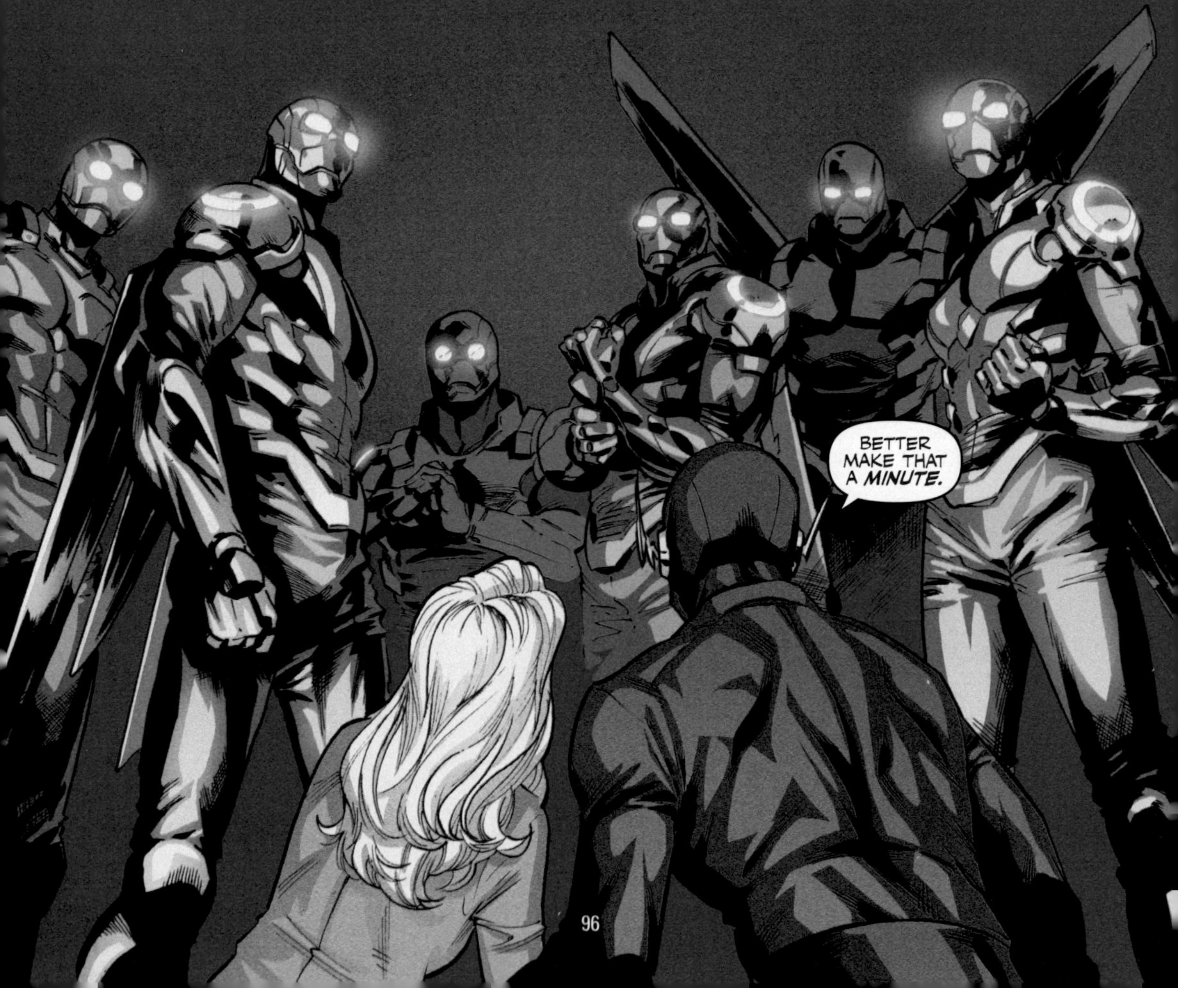
BETTER MAKE THAT A *MINUTE*.

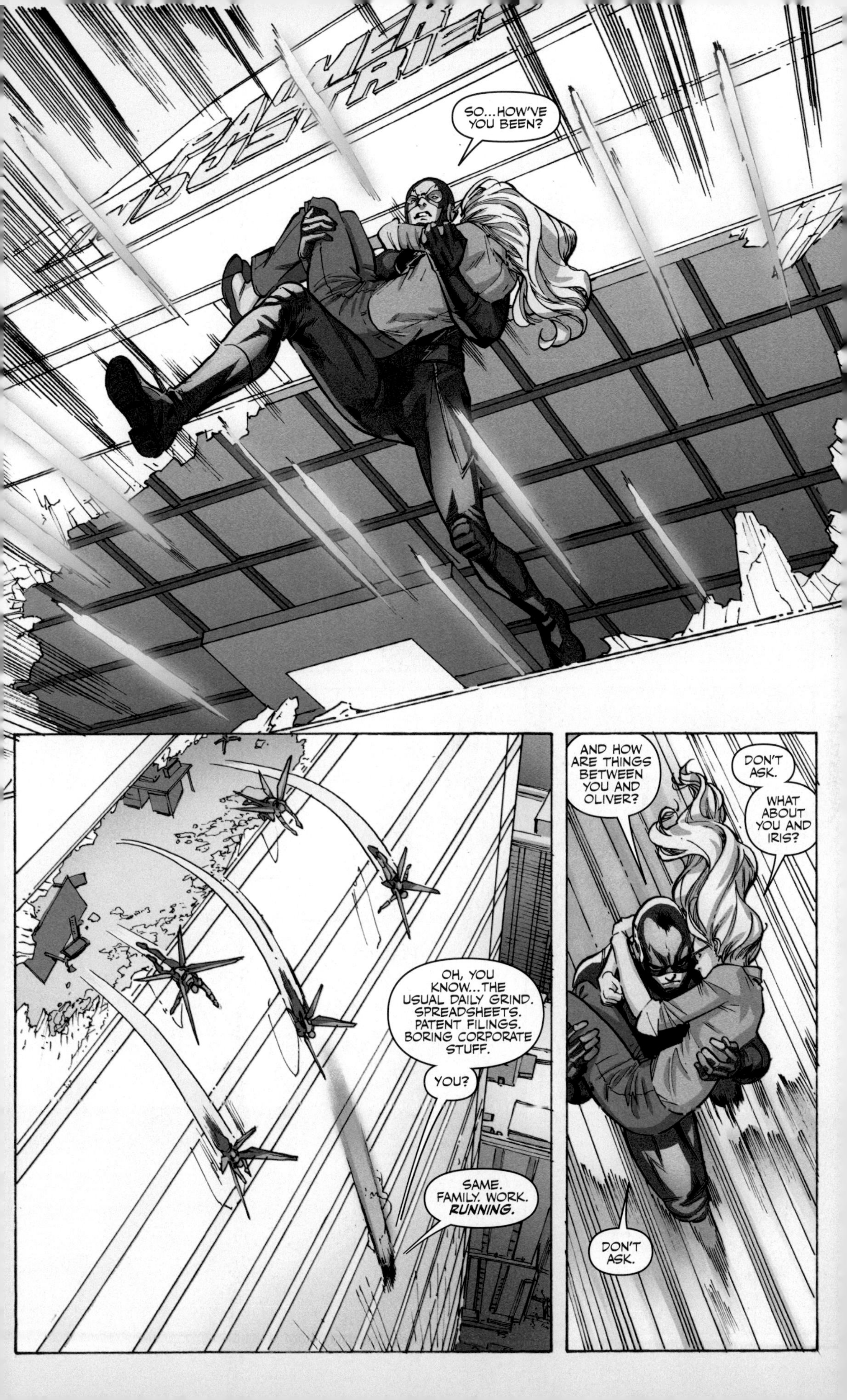
SO...HOW'VE YOU BEEN?
OH, YOU KNOW...THE USUAL DAILY GRIND. SPREADSHEETS. PATENT FILINGS. BORING CORPORATE STUFF.
YOU?
SAME. FAMILY. WORK. *RUNNING.*
AND HOW ARE THINGS BETWEEN YOU AND OLIVER?
DON'T ASK.
WHAT ABOUT YOU AND IRIS?
DON'T ASK.

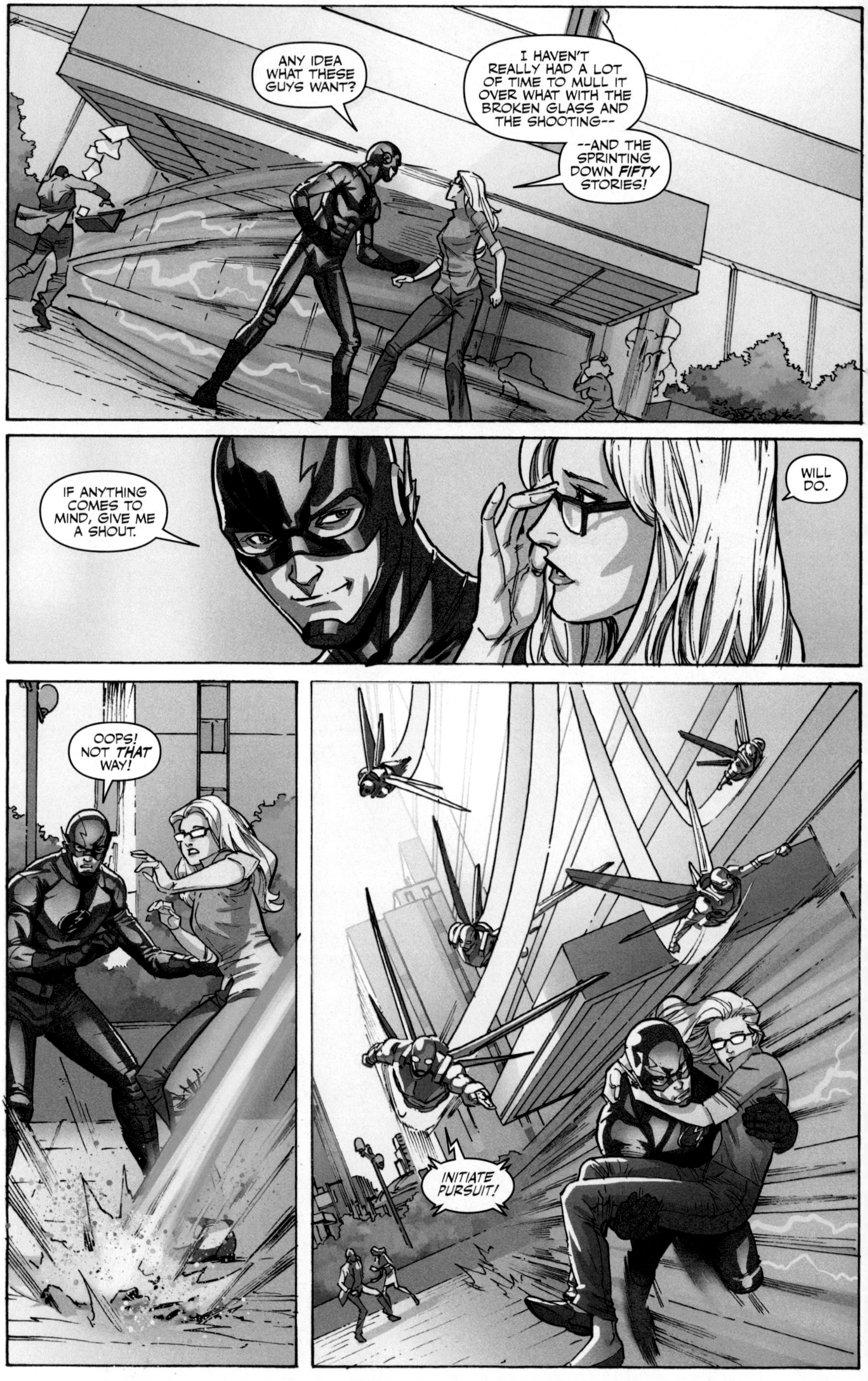
ANY IDEA WHAT THESE GUYS WANT?
I HAVEN'T REALLY HAD A LOT OF TIME TO MULL IT OVER WHAT WITH THE BROKEN GLASS AND THE SHOOTING--
--AND THE SPRINTING DOWN FIFTY STORIES!
IF ANYTHING COMES TO MIND, GIVE ME A SHOUT.
WILL DO.
OOPS! NOT THAT WAY!
INITIATE PURSUIT!

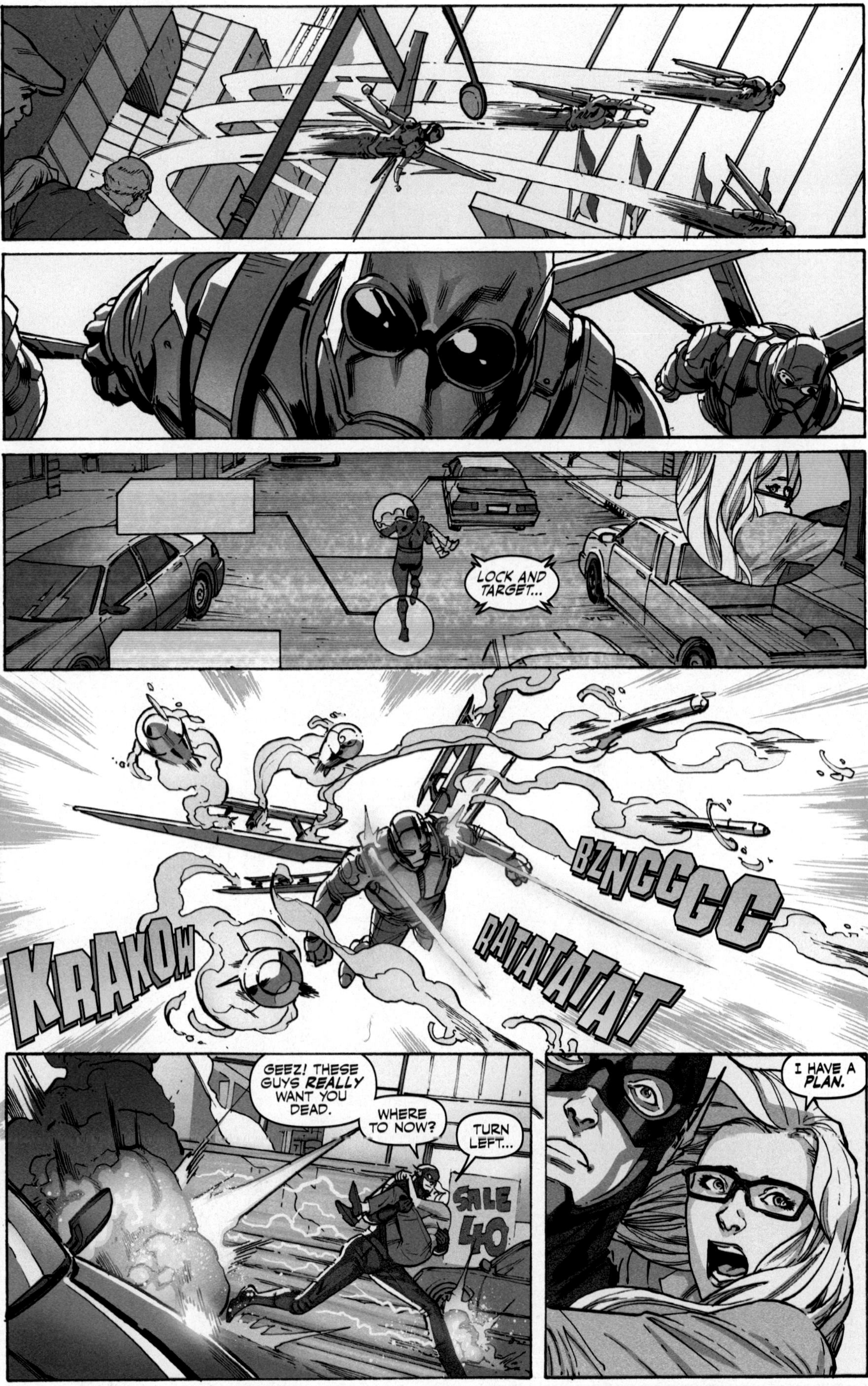
LOCK AND TARGET...
BZNGGGGG
KRAKOW
RATATATATAT
GEEZ! THESE GUYS REALLY WANT YOU DEAD.
WHERE TO NOW?
TURN LEFT...
SALE 40
I HAVE A PLAN.

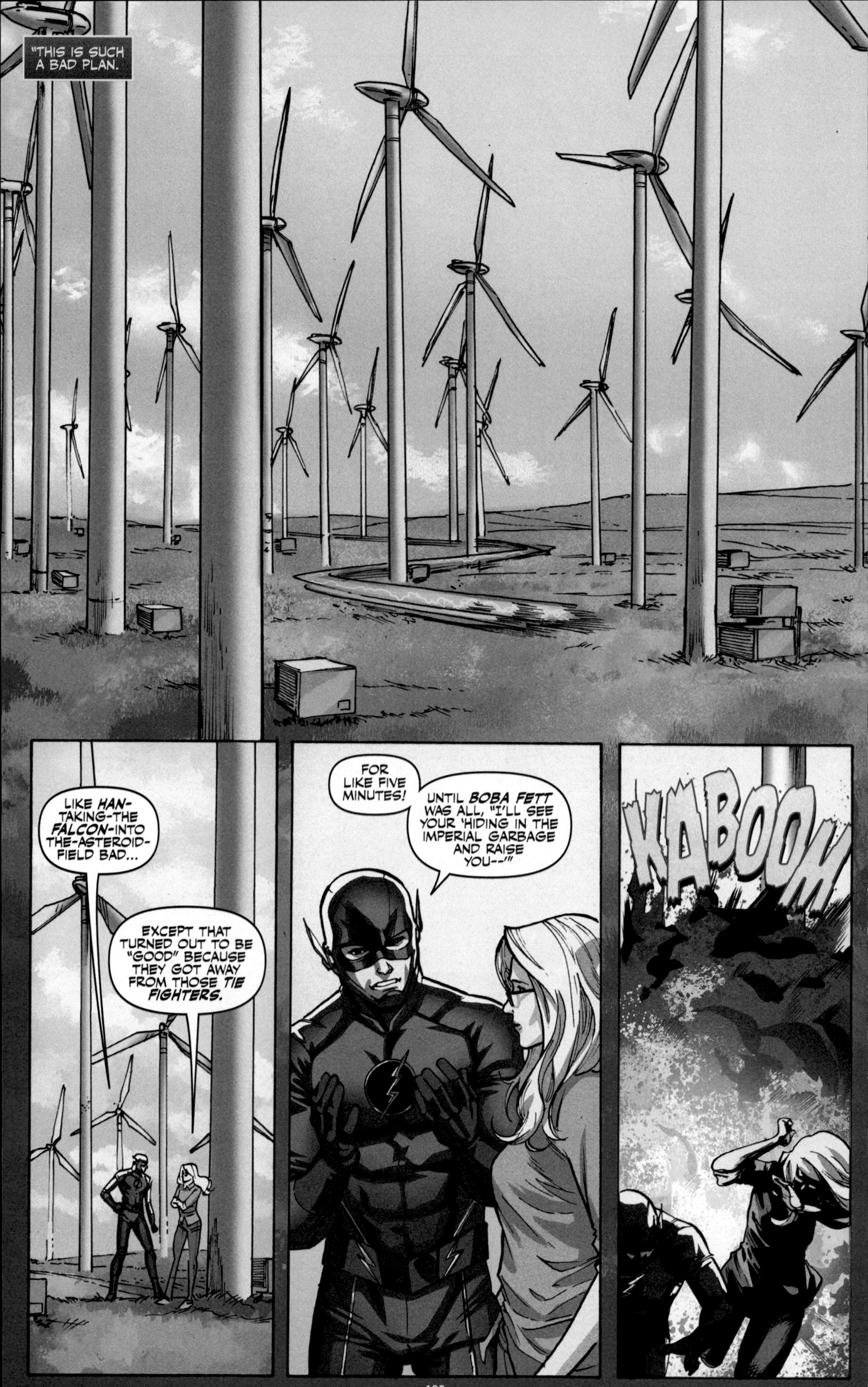
"THIS IS SUCH A BAD PLAN.
LIKE HAN-TAKING-THE FALCON-INTO THE-ASTEROID-FIELD BAD...
EXCEPT THAT TURNED OUT TO BE "GOOD" BECAUSE THEY GOT AWAY FROM THOSE TIE FIGHTERS.
FOR LIKE FIVE MINUTES!
UNTIL BOBA FETT WAS ALL, "I'LL SEE YOUR 'HIDING IN THE IMPERIAL GARBAGE AND RAISE YOU--'"
KABOOM

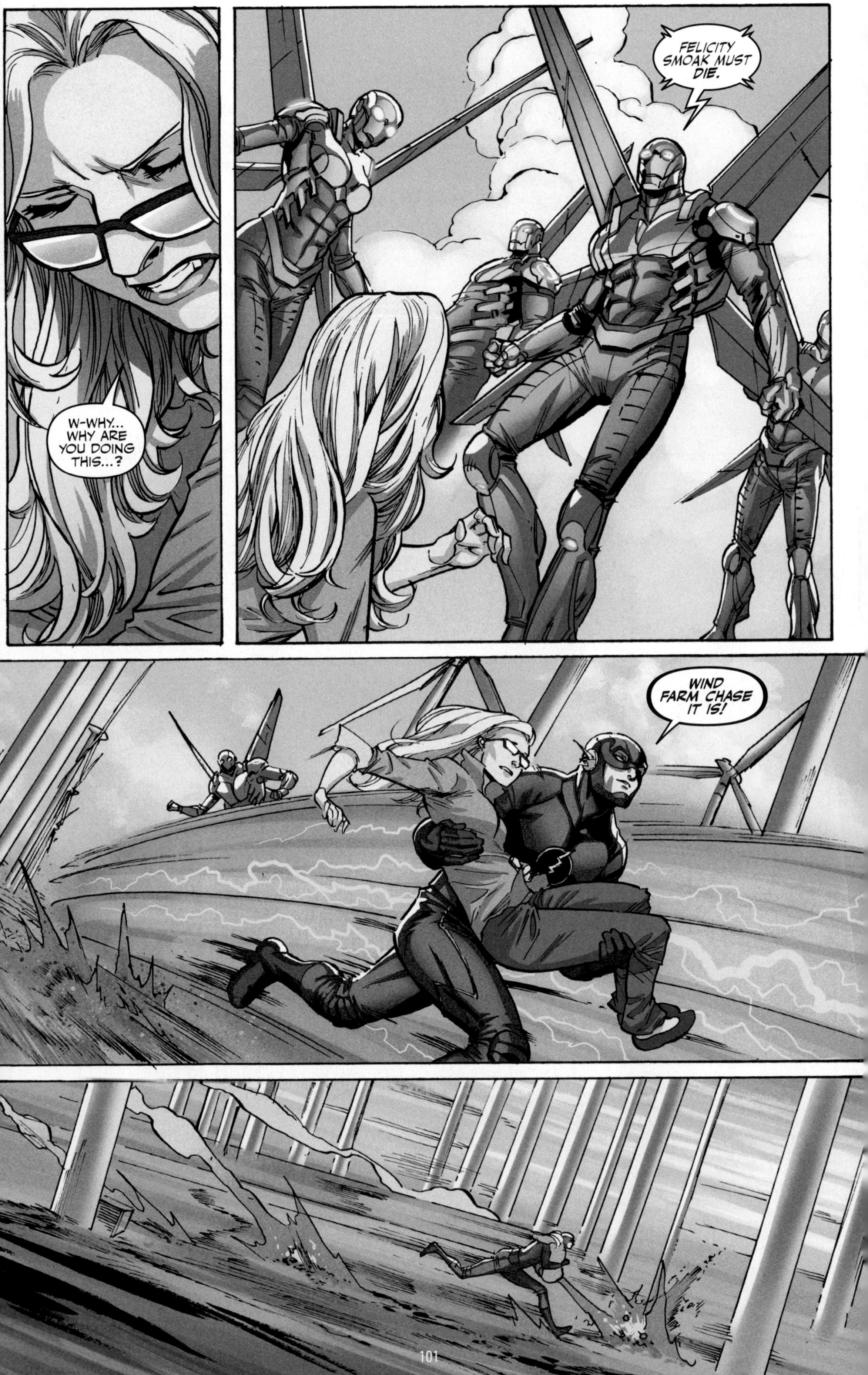
W-WHY... WHY ARE YOU DOING THIS...?
FELICITY SMOAK MUST DIE.
WIND FARM CHASE IT IS!

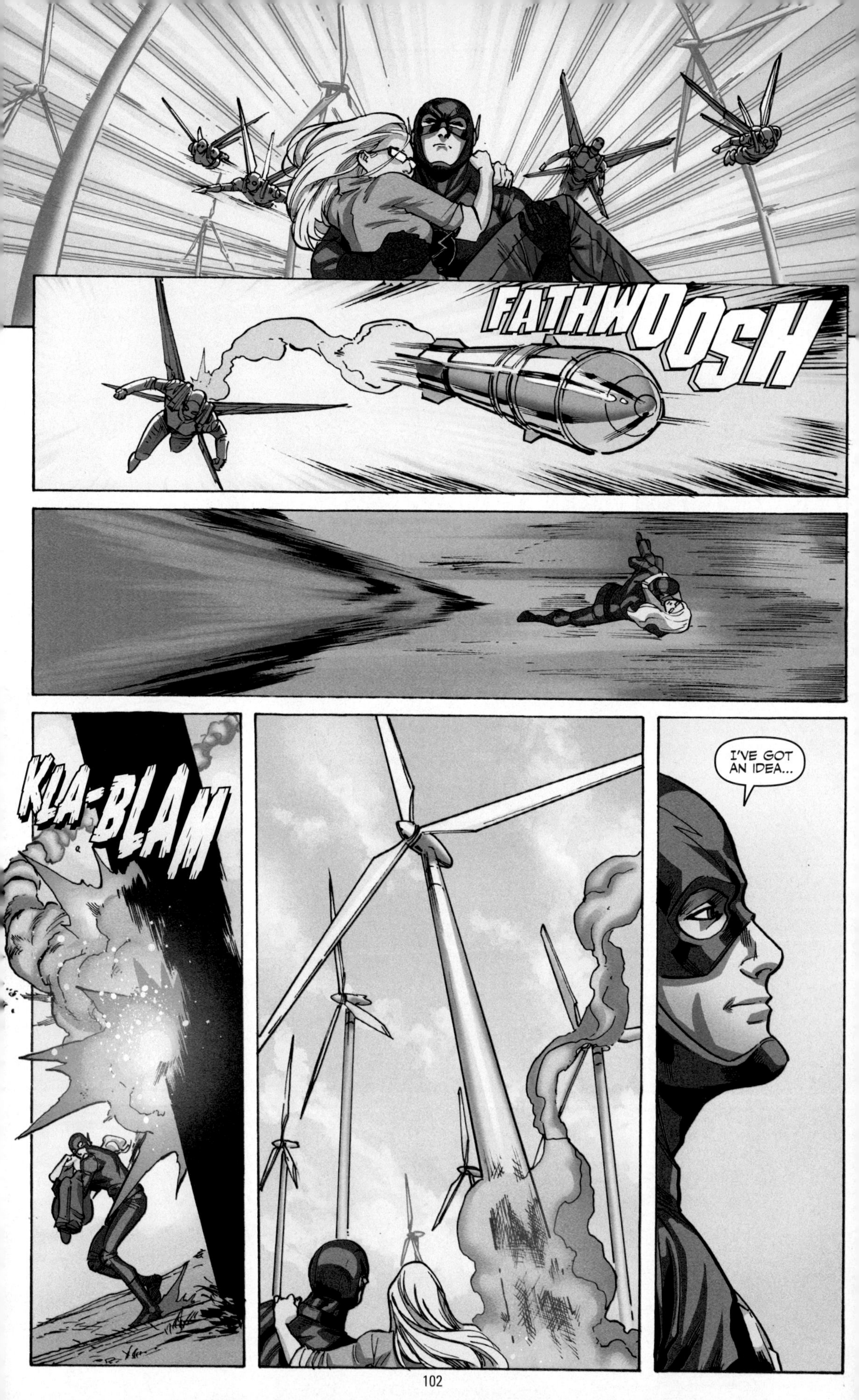
FATHWOOSH
KLA-BLAM
I'VE GOT AN IDEA...

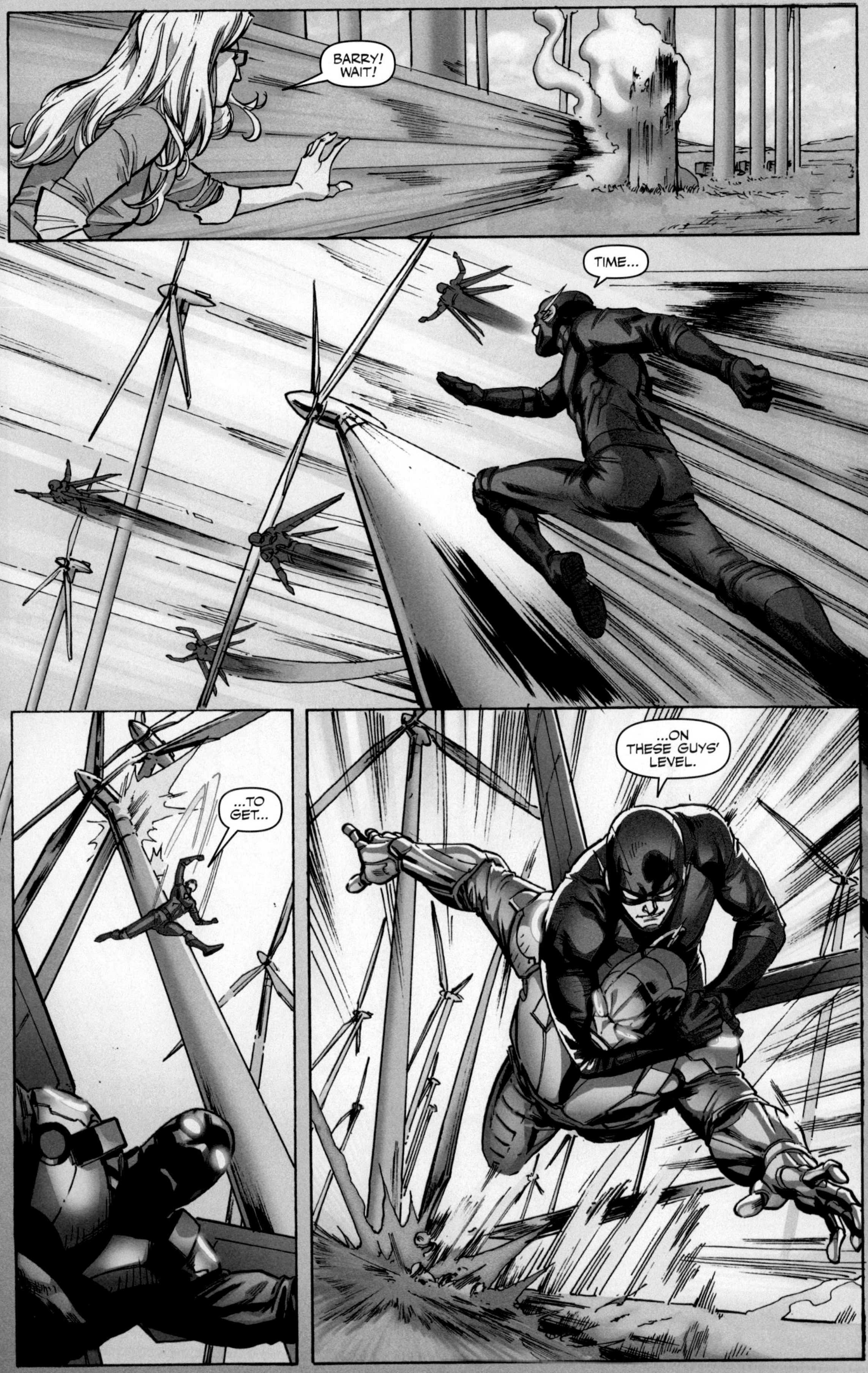
BARRY! WAIT!
TIME...
...TO GET...
...ON THESE GUYS' LEVEL.

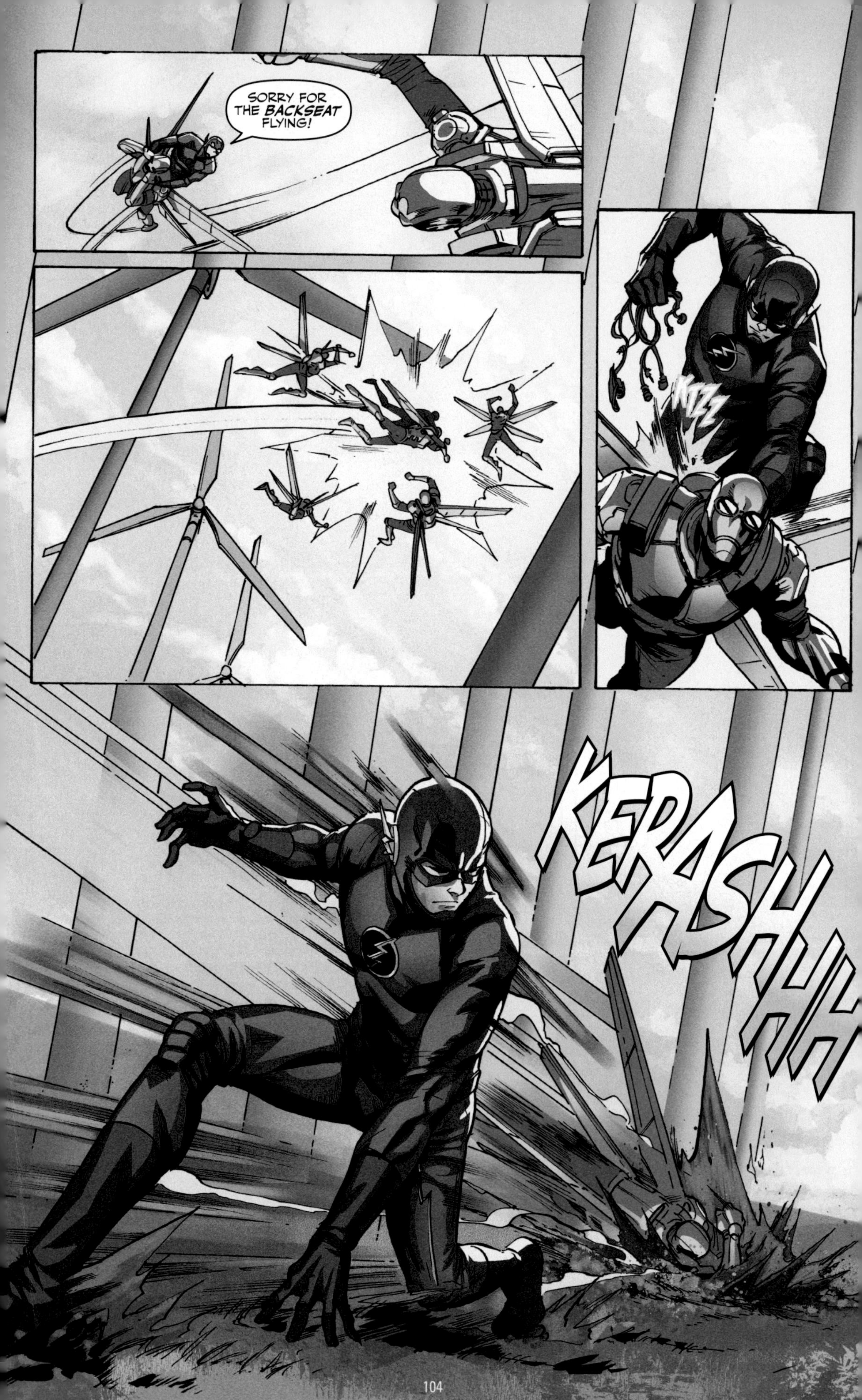
SORRY FOR THE BACKSEAT FLYING!
KTZZ
KERASHHH

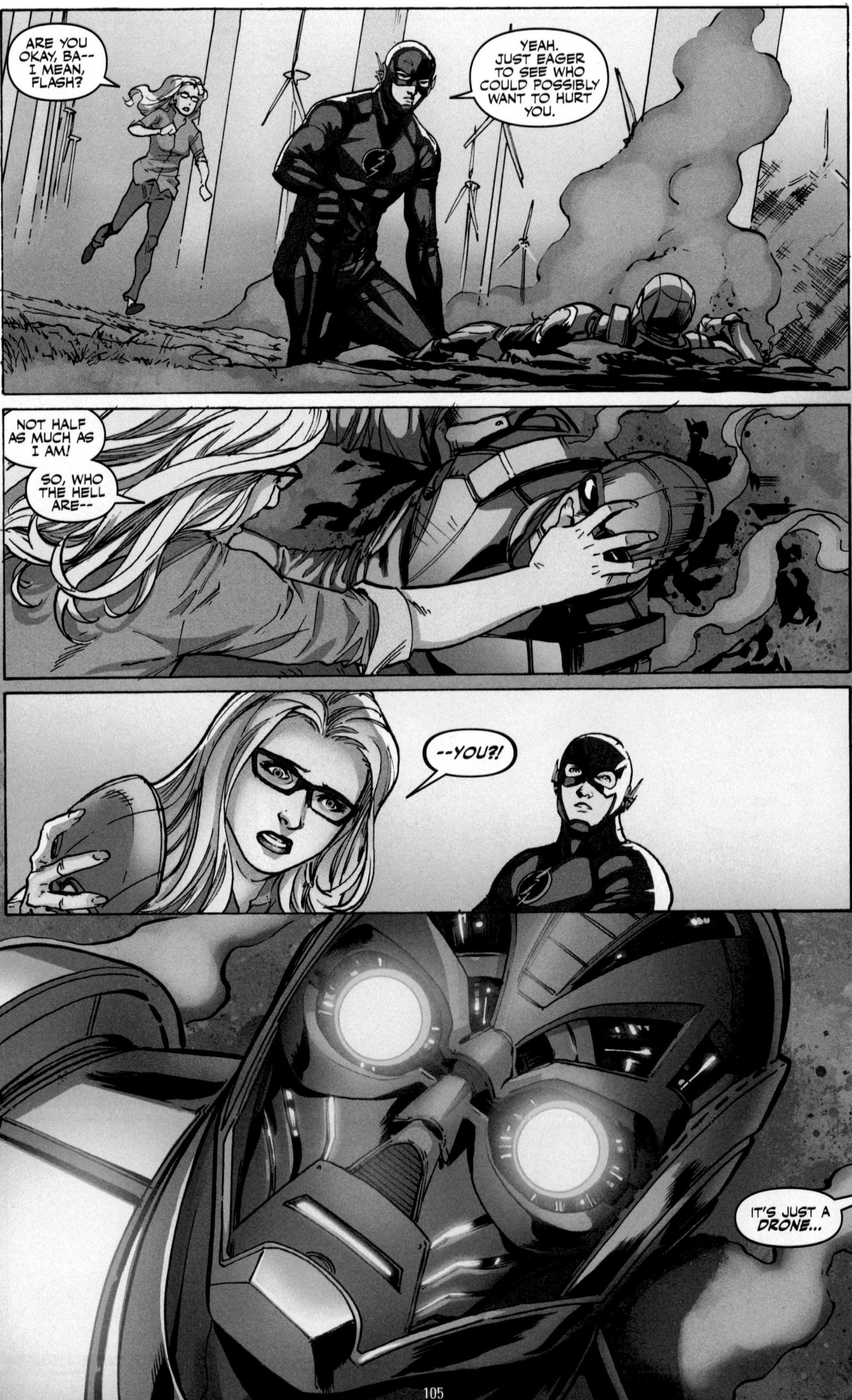
ARE YOU OKAY, BA-- I MEAN, FLASH?
YEAH. JUST EAGER TO SEE WHO COULD POSSIBLY WANT TO HURT YOU.
NOT HALF AS MUCH AS I AM!
SO, WHO THE HELL ARE--
--YOU?!
IT'S JUST A DRONE...

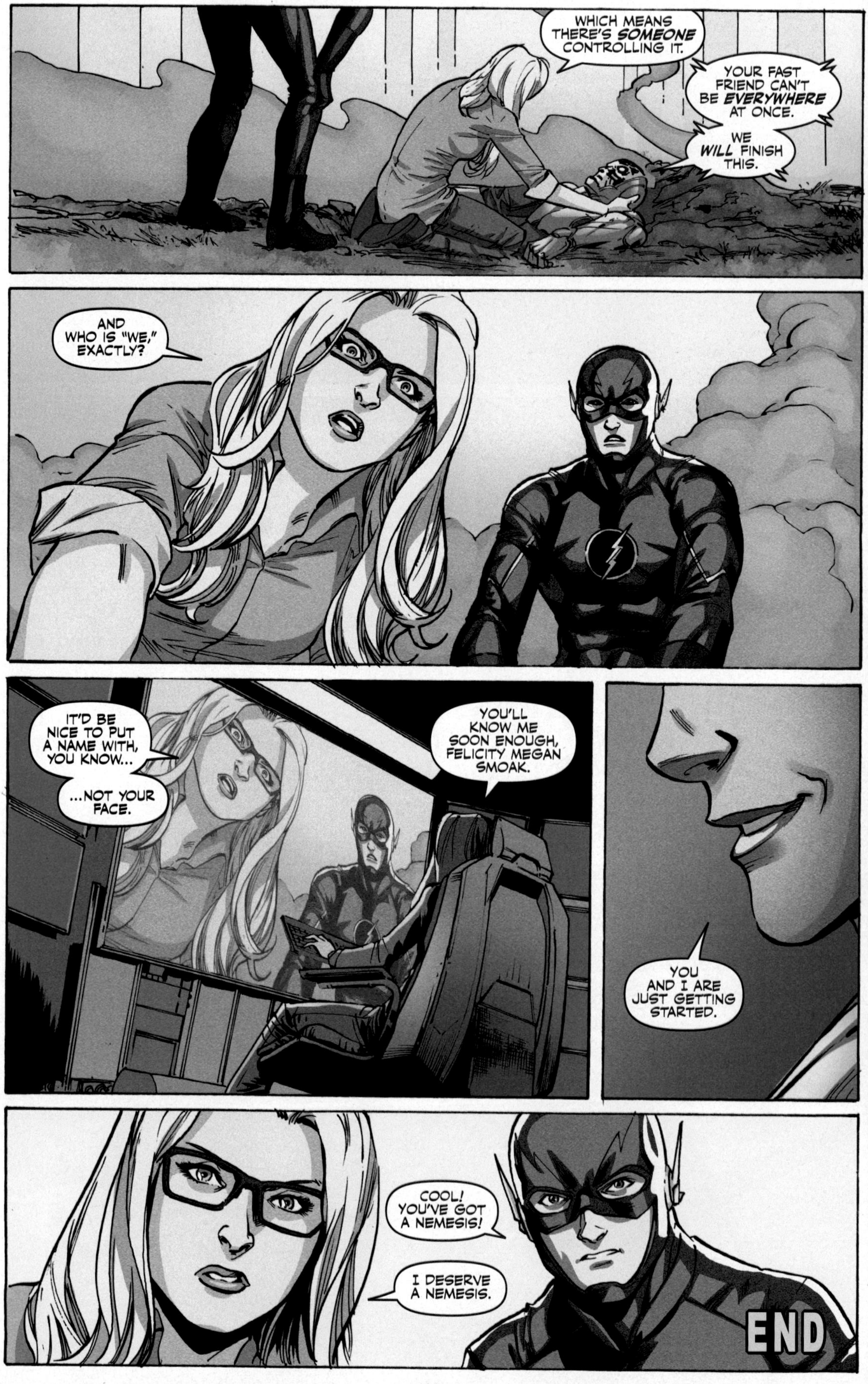
WHICH MEANS THERE'S SOMEONE CONTROLLING IT.
YOUR FAST FRIEND CAN'T BE EVERYWHERE AT ONCE.
WE WILL FINISH THIS.
AND WHO IS "WE," EXACTLY?
IT'D BE NICE TO PUT A NAME WITH, YOU KNOW...
...NOT YOUR FACE.
YOU'LL KNOW ME SOON ENOUGH, FELICITY MEGAN SMOAK.
YOU AND I ARE JUST GETTING STARTED.
COOL! YOU'VE GOT A NEMESIS!
I DESERVE A NEMESIS.
END

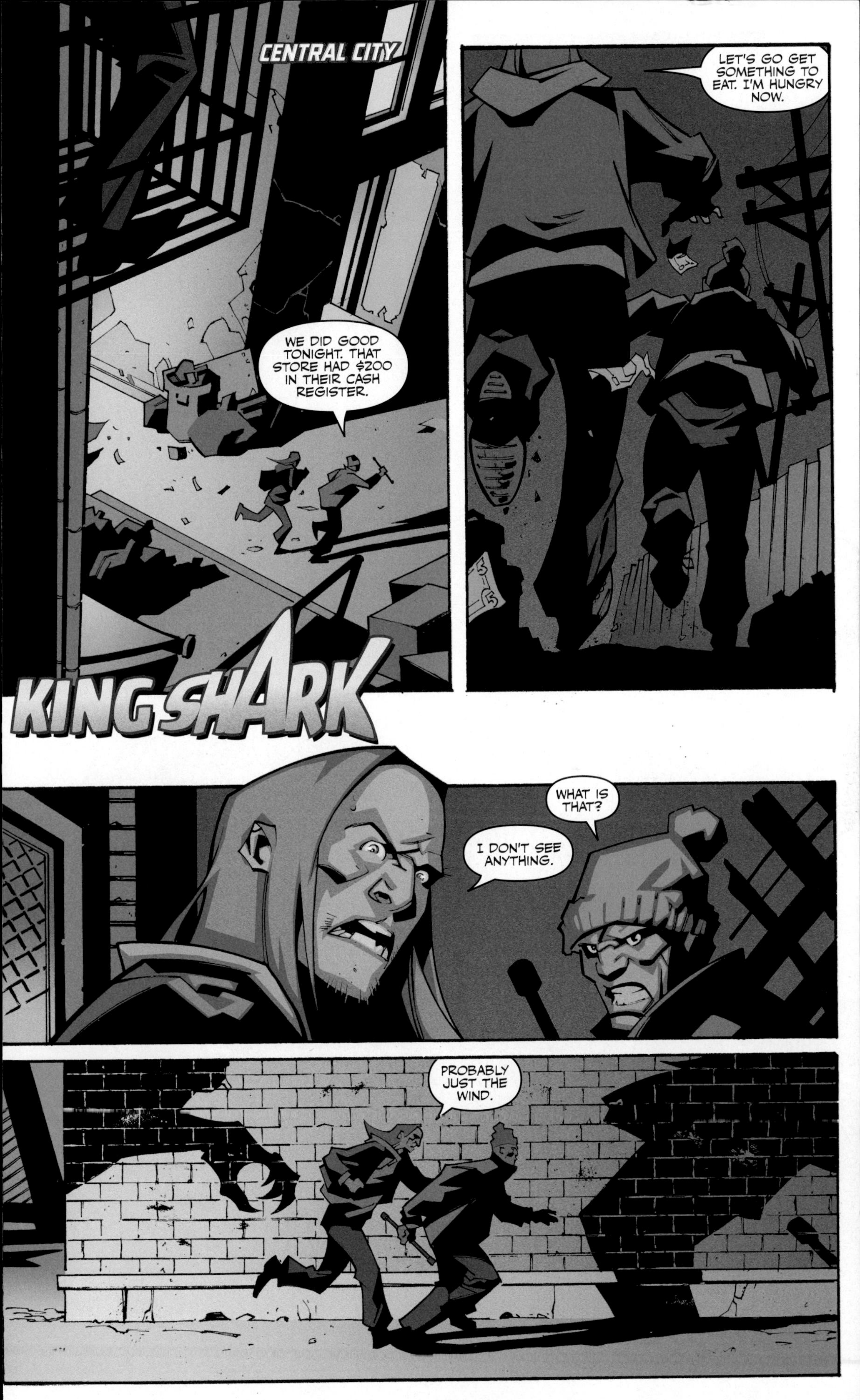
CENTRAL CITY
WE DID GOOD TONIGHT. THAT STORE HAD $200 IN THEIR CASH REGISTER.
LET'S GO GET SOMETHING TO EAT. I'M HUNGRY NOW.
KING SHARK
WHAT IS THAT?
I DON'T SEE ANYTHING.
PROBABLY JUST THE WIND.

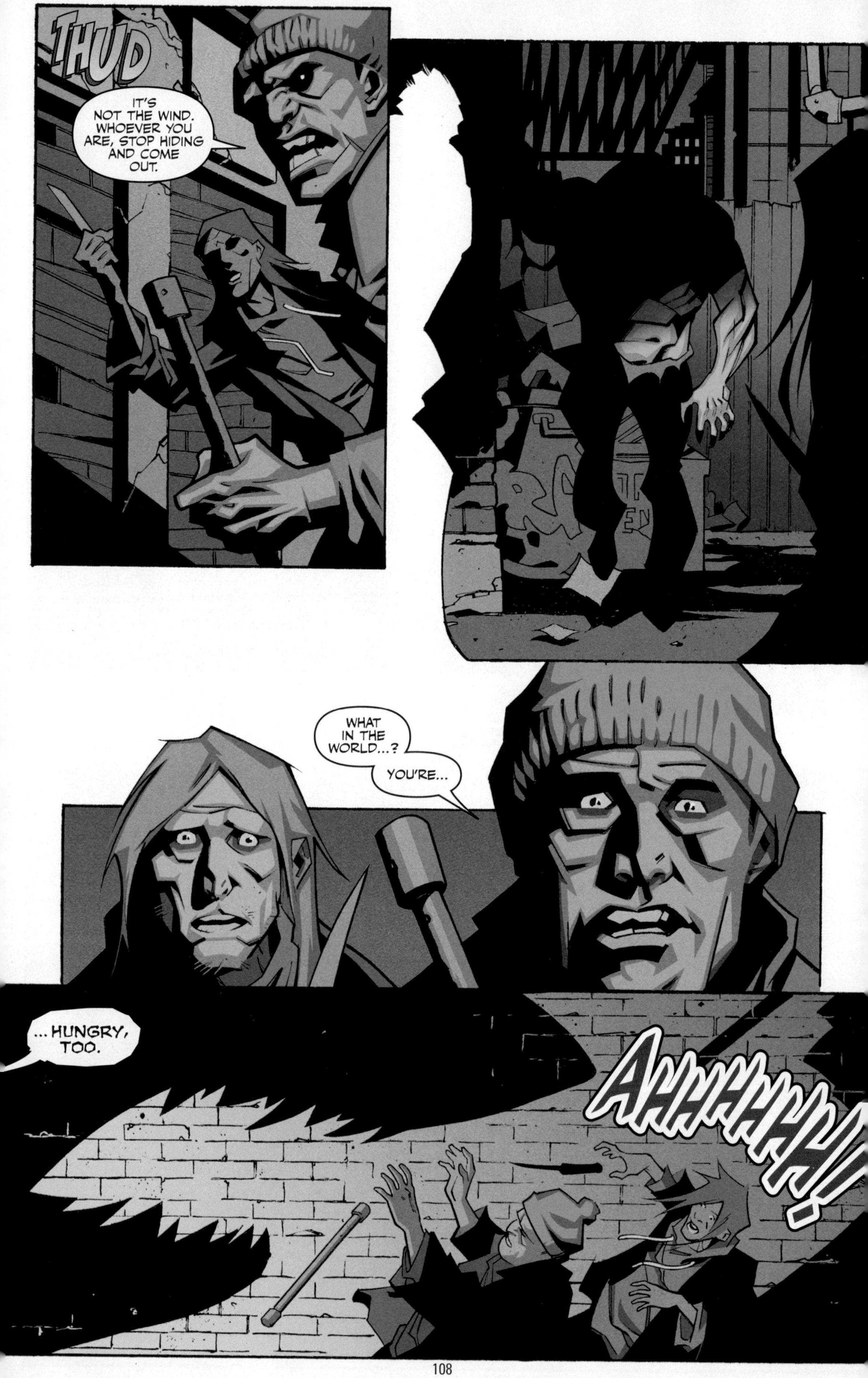
THUD
IT'S NOT THE WIND. WHOEVER YOU ARE, STOP HIDING AND COME OUT.
WHAT IN THE WORLD...?
YOU'RE...
...HUNGRY, TOO.
AHHHHHH!!

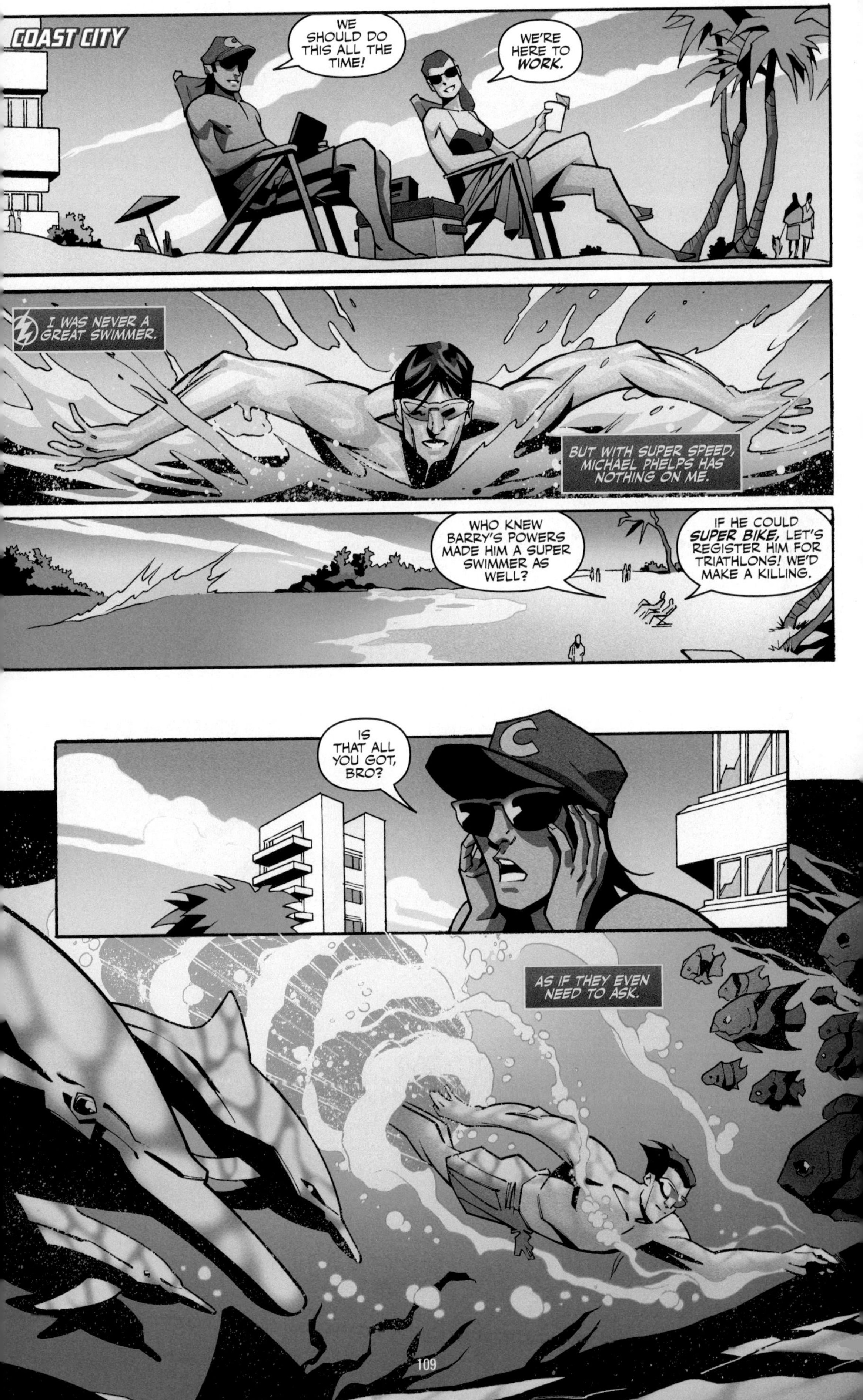
COAST CITY
WE SHOULD DO THIS ALL THE TIME!
WE'RE HERE TO WORK.
I WAS NEVER A GREAT SWIMMER.
BUT WITH SUPER SPEED, MICHAEL PHELPS HAS NOTHING ON ME.
WHO KNEW BARRY'S POWERS MADE HIM A SUPER SWIMMER AS WELL?
IF HE COULD SUPER BIKE, LET'S REGISTER HIM FOR TRIATHLONS! WE'D MAKE A KILLING.
IS THAT ALL YOU GOT, BRO?
AS IF THEY EVEN NEED TO ASK.

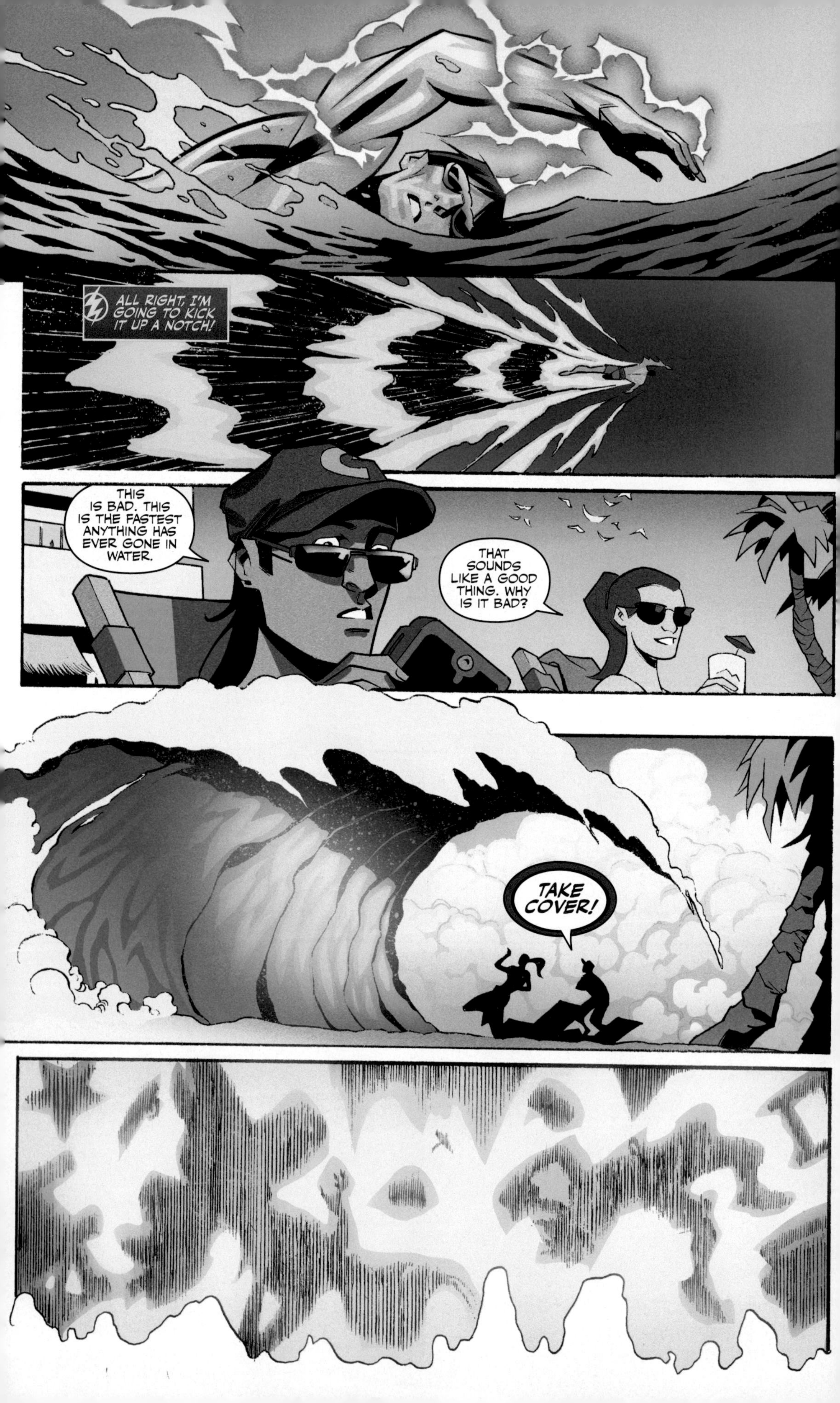
ALL RIGHT, I'M GOING TO KICK IT UP A NOTCH!
THIS IS BAD. THIS IS THE FASTEST ANYTHING HAS EVER GONE IN WATER.
THAT SOUNDS LIKE A GOOD THING. WHY IS IT BAD?
TAKE COVER!

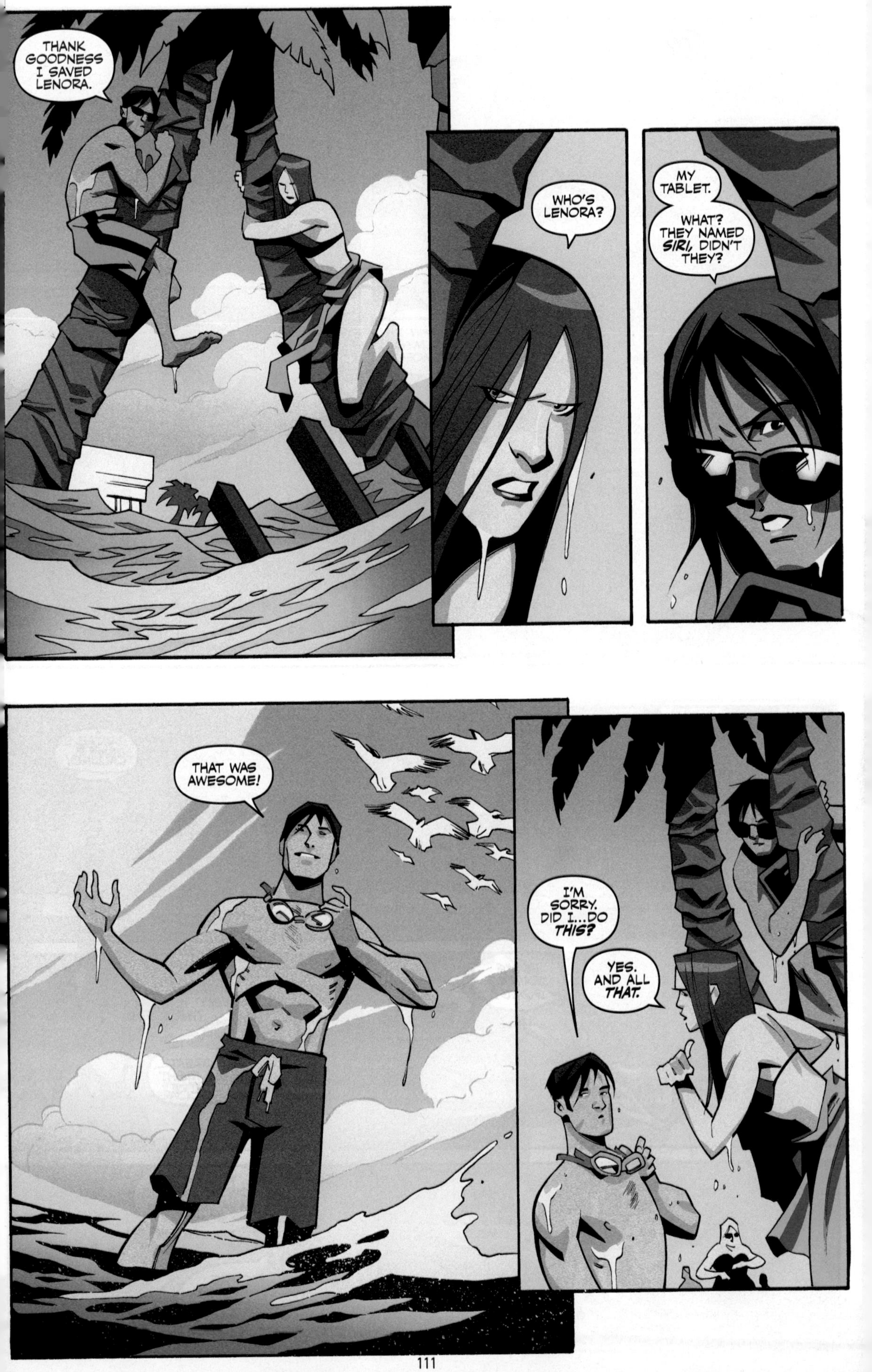
THANK GOODNESS I SAVED LENORA.
WHO'S LENORA?
MY TABLET.
WHAT? THEY NAMED *SIRI,* DIDN'T THEY?
THAT WAS AWESOME!
I'M SORRY. DID I...DO *THIS?*
YES. AND ALL *THAT.*

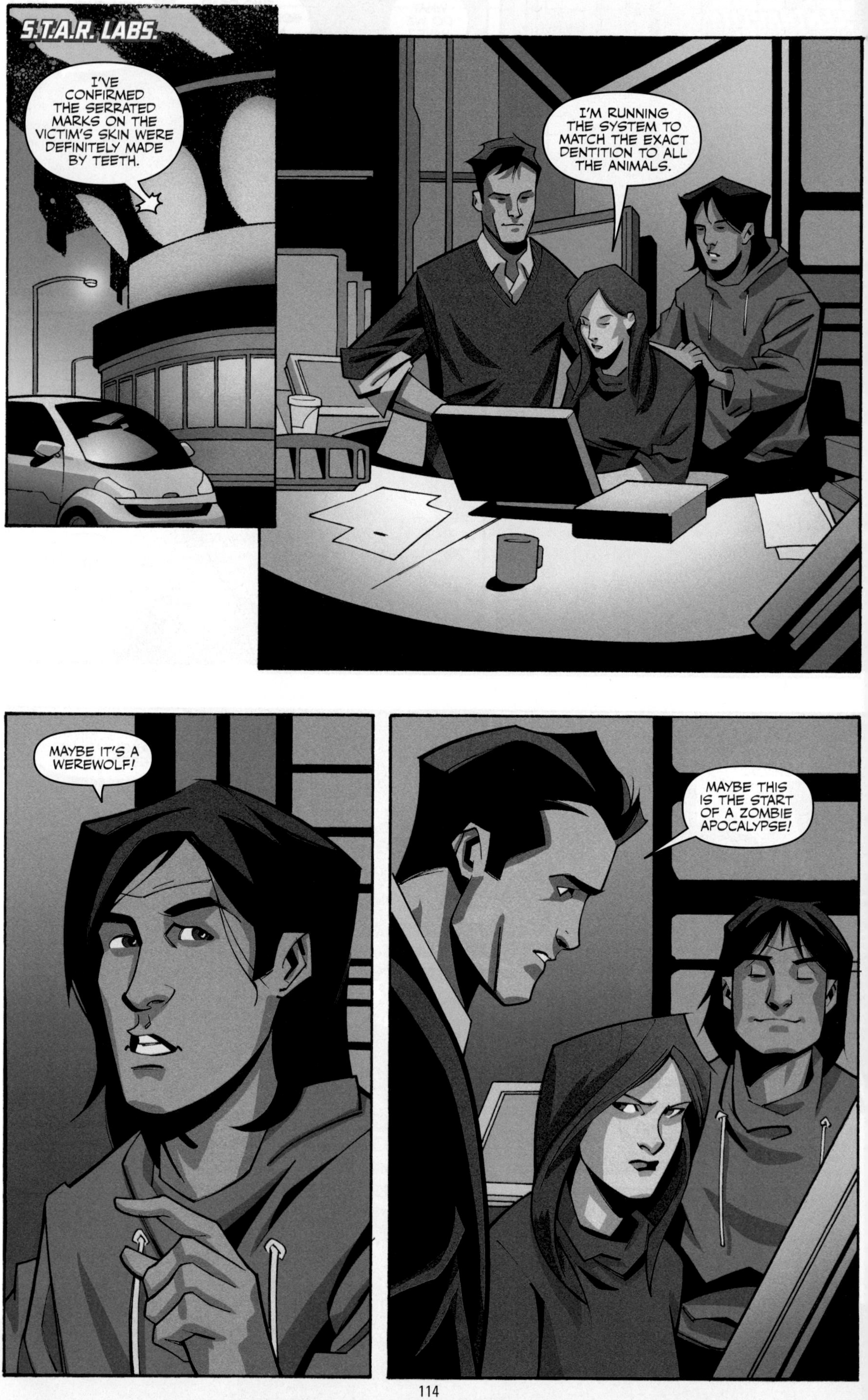
S.T.A.R. LABS.
I'VE CONFIRMED THE SERRATED MARKS ON THE VICTIM'S SKIN WERE DEFINITELY MADE BY TEETH.
I'M RUNNING THE SYSTEM TO MATCH THE EXACT DENTITION TO ALL THE ANIMALS.
MAYBE IT'S A WEREWOLF!
MAYBE THIS IS THE START OF A ZOMBIE APOCALYPSE!

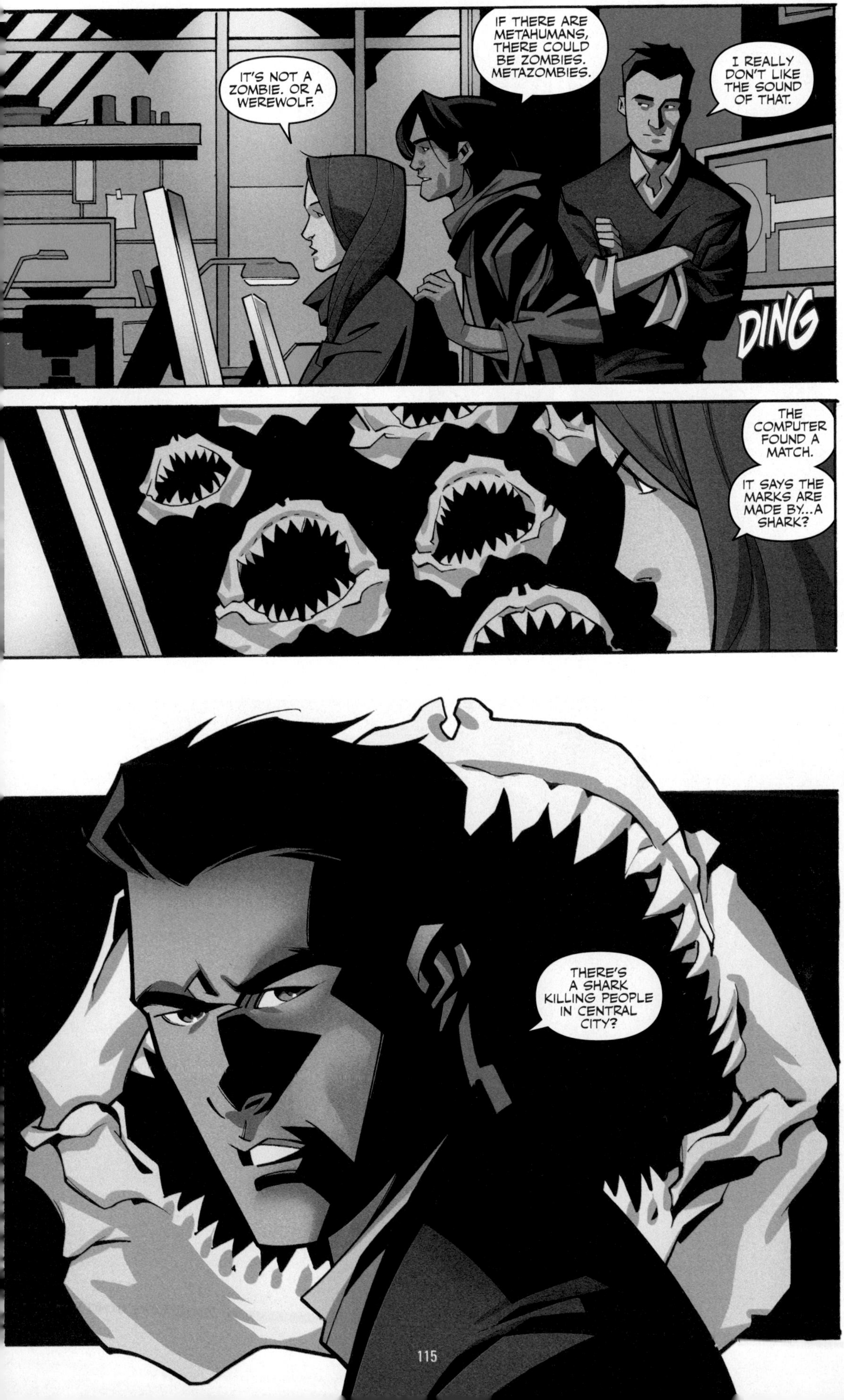

IT'S NOT A ZOMBIE. OR A WEREWOLF.
IF THERE ARE METAHUMANS, THERE COULD BE ZOMBIES. METAZOMBIES.
I REALLY DON'T LIKE THE SOUND OF THAT.
DING
THE COMPUTER FOUND A MATCH.
IT SAYS THE MARKS ARE MADE BY...A SHARK?
THERE'S A SHARK KILLING PEOPLE IN CENTRAL CITY?

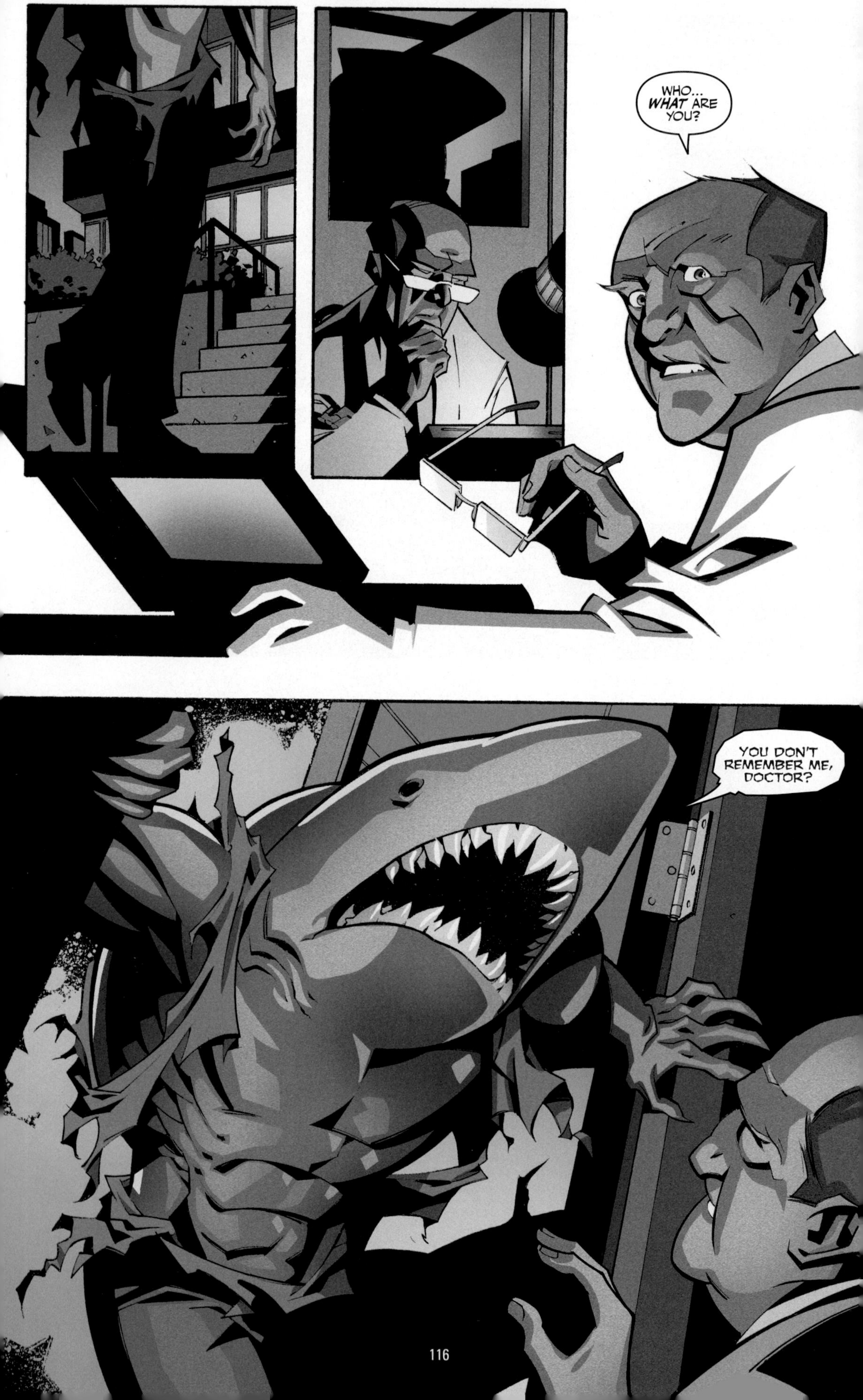
WHO... *WHAT* ARE YOU?
YOU DON'T REMEMBER ME, DOCTOR?

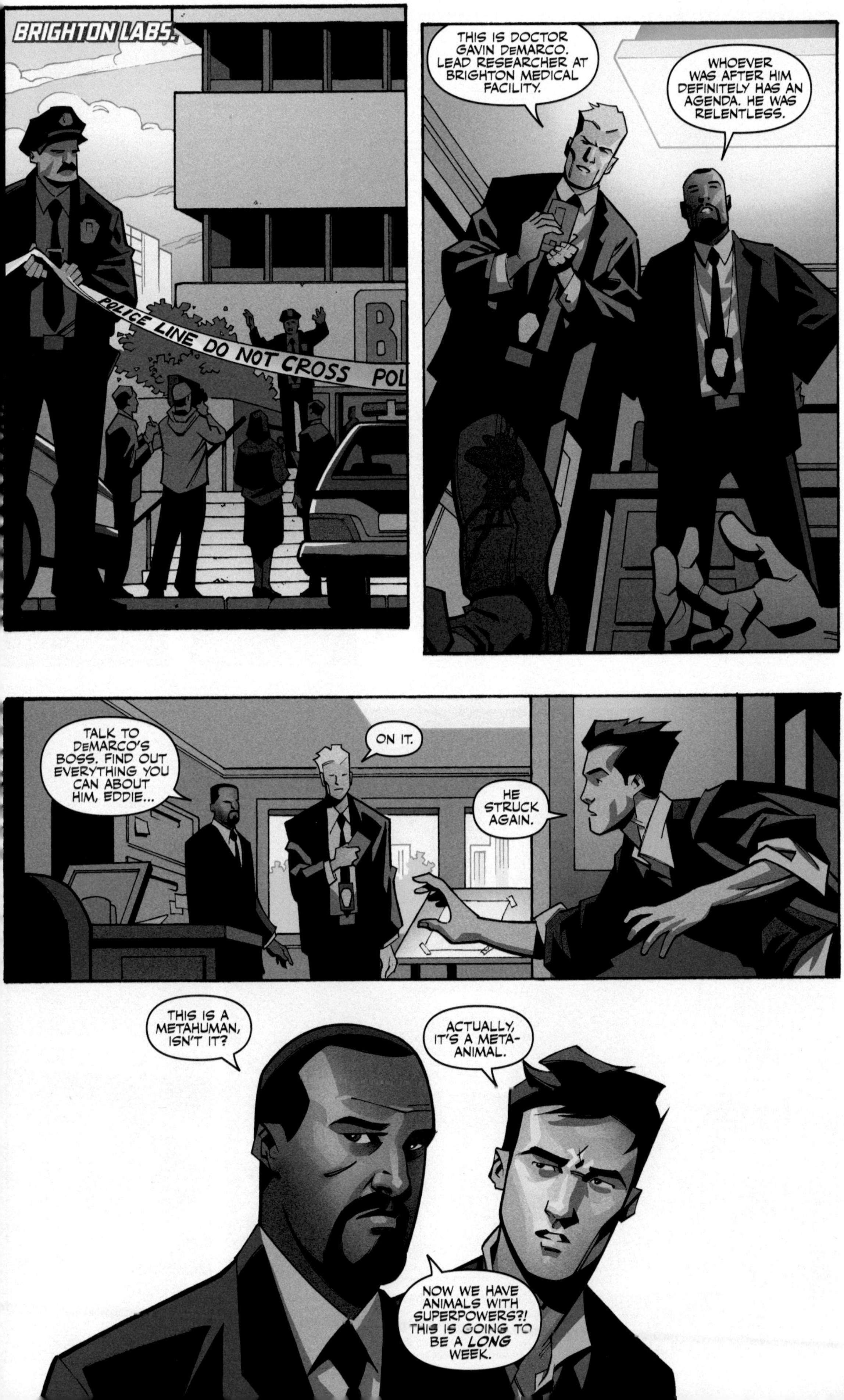
BRIGHTON LABS.
POLICE LINE DO NOT CROSS POL
THIS IS DOCTOR GAVIN DeMARCO. LEAD RESEARCHER AT BRIGHTON MEDICAL FACILITY.
WHOEVER WAS AFTER HIM DEFINITELY HAS AN AGENDA. HE WAS RELENTLESS.
TALK TO DeMARCO'S BOSS. FIND OUT EVERYTHING YOU CAN ABOUT HIM, EDDIE...
ON IT.
HE STRUCK AGAIN.
THIS IS A METAHUMAN, ISN'T IT?
ACTUALLY, IT'S A META-ANIMAL.
NOW WE HAVE ANIMALS WITH SUPERPOWERS?! THIS IS GOING TO BE A LONG WEEK.

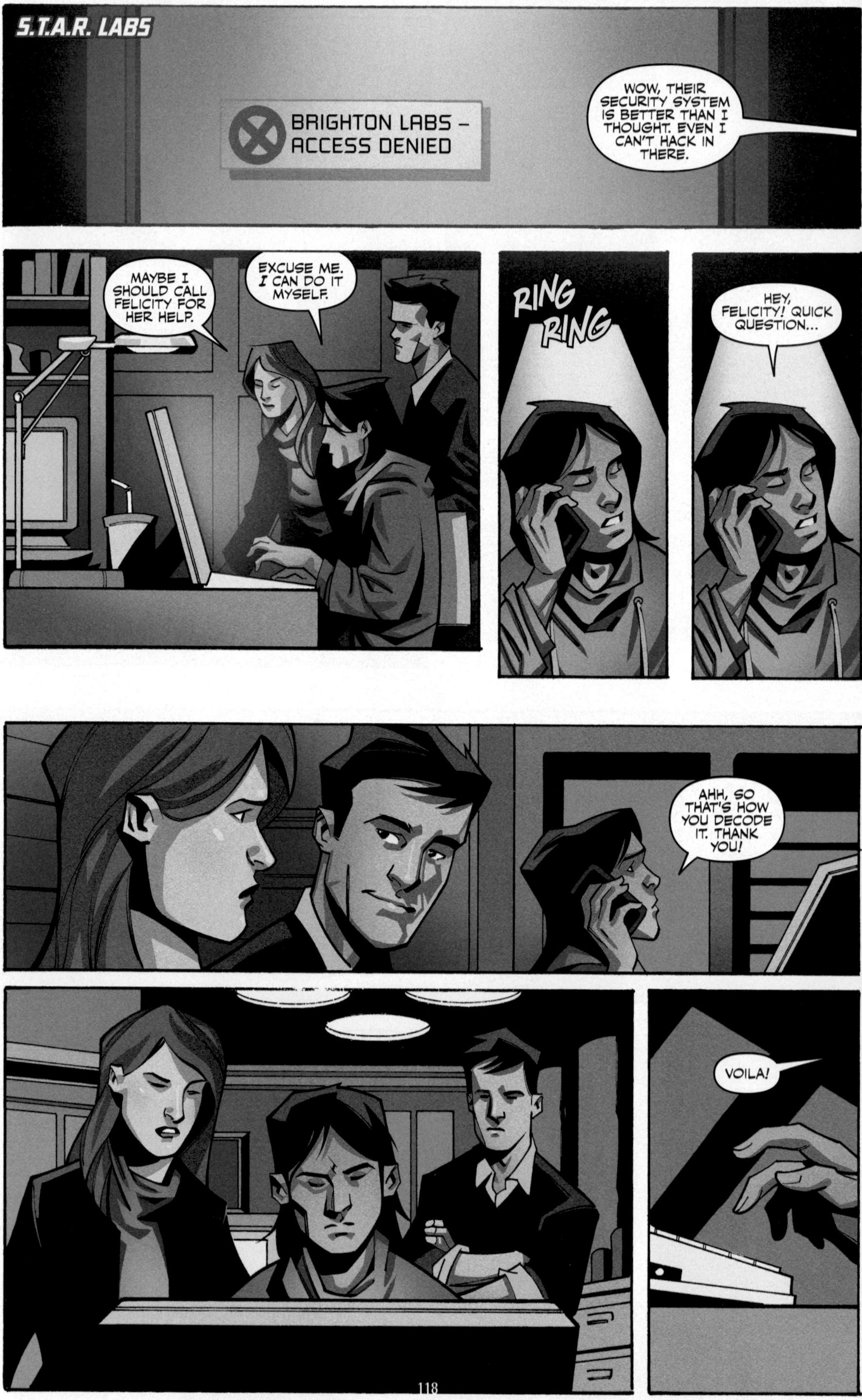
S.T.A.R. LABS
BRIGHTON LABS – ACCESS DENIED
WOW, THEIR SECURITY SYSTEM IS BETTER THAN I THOUGHT. EVEN I CAN'T HACK IN THERE.
MAYBE I SHOULD CALL FELICITY FOR HER HELP.
EXCUSE ME. I CAN DO IT MYSELF.
RING RING
HEY, FELICITY! QUICK QUESTION...
AHH, SO THAT'S HOW YOU DECODE IT. THANK YOU!
VOILA!

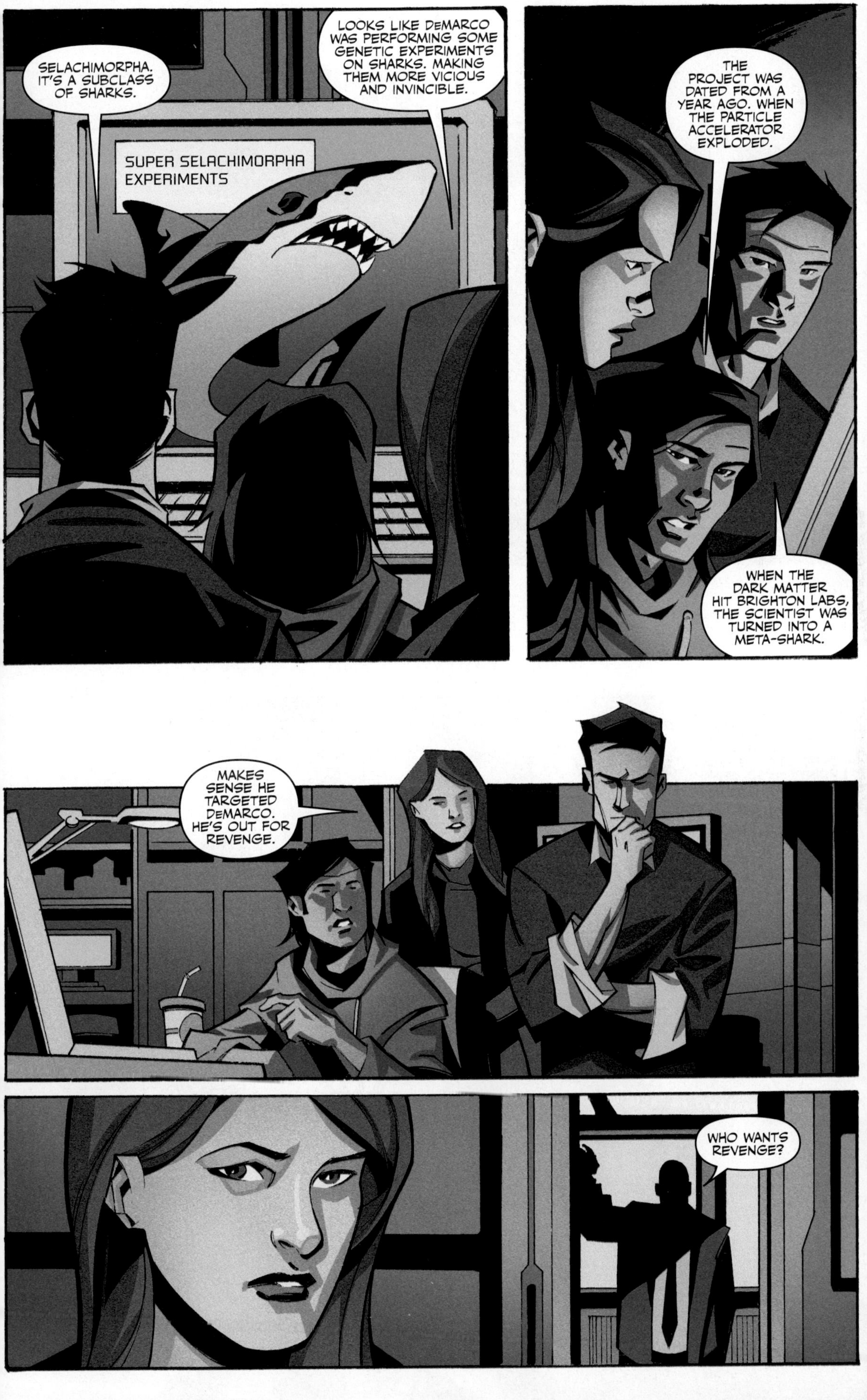
SELACHIMORPHA. IT'S A SUBCLASS OF SHARKS.
LOOKS LIKE DeMARCO WAS PERFORMING SOME GENETIC EXPERIMENTS ON SHARKS. MAKING THEM MORE VICIOUS AND INVINCIBLE.
SUPER SELACHIMORPHA EXPERIMENTS
THE PROJECT WAS DATED FROM A YEAR AGO. WHEN THE PARTICLE ACCELERATOR EXPLODED.
WHEN THE DARK MATTER HIT BRIGHTON LABS, THE SCIENTIST WAS TURNED INTO A META-SHARK.
MAKES SENSE HE TARGETED DeMARCO. HE'S OUT FOR REVENGE.
WHO WANTS REVENGE?

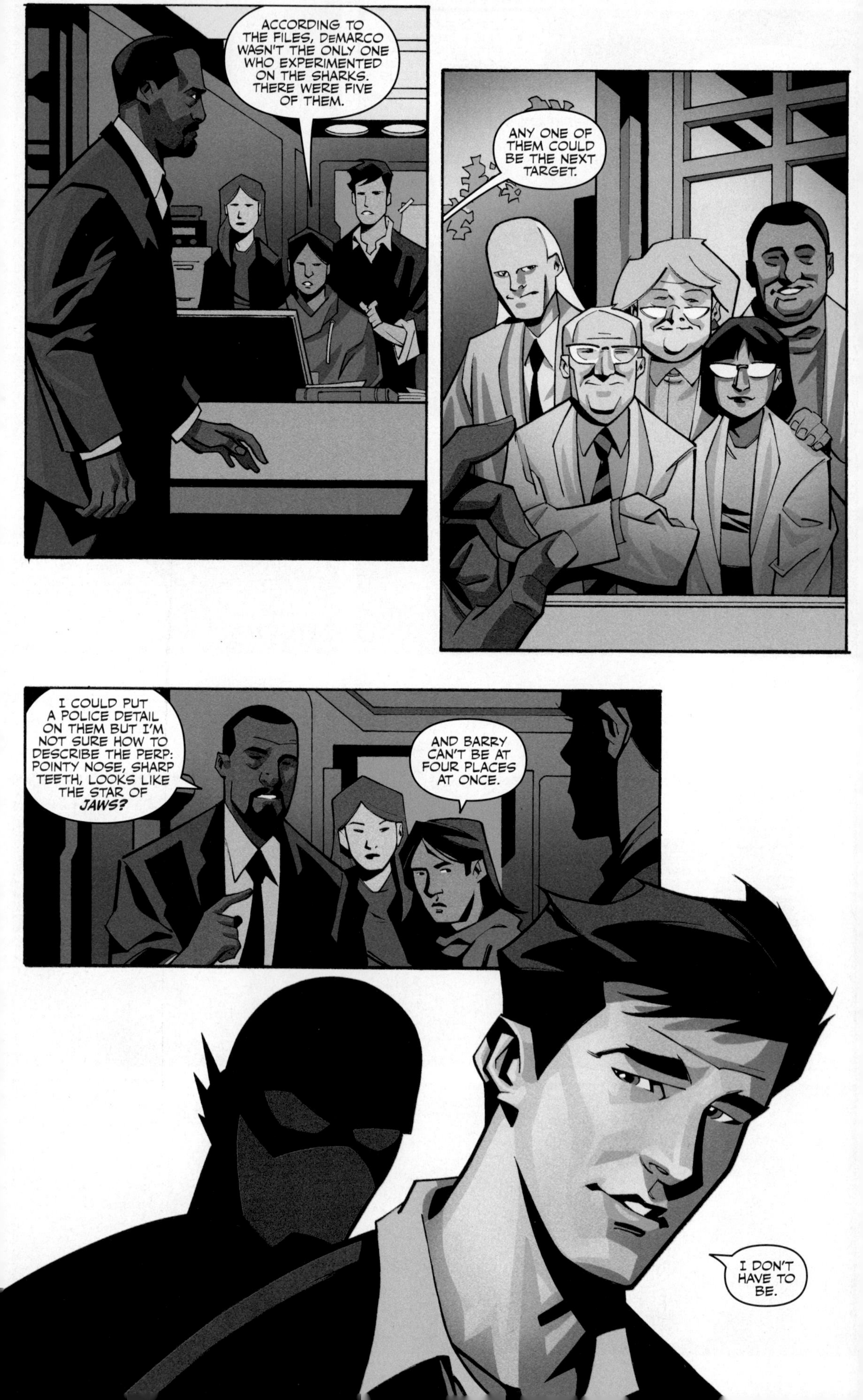
ACCORDING TO THE FILES, DeMARCO WASN'T THE ONLY ONE WHO EXPERIMENTED ON THE SHARKS. THERE WERE FIVE OF THEM.
ANY ONE OF THEM COULD BE THE NEXT TARGET.
I COULD PUT A POLICE DETAIL ON THEM BUT I'M NOT SURE HOW TO DESCRIBE THE PERP: POINTY NOSE, SHARP TEETH, LOOKS LIKE THE STAR OF JAWS?
AND BARRY CAN'T BE AT FOUR PLACES AT ONCE.
I DON'T HAVE TO BE.

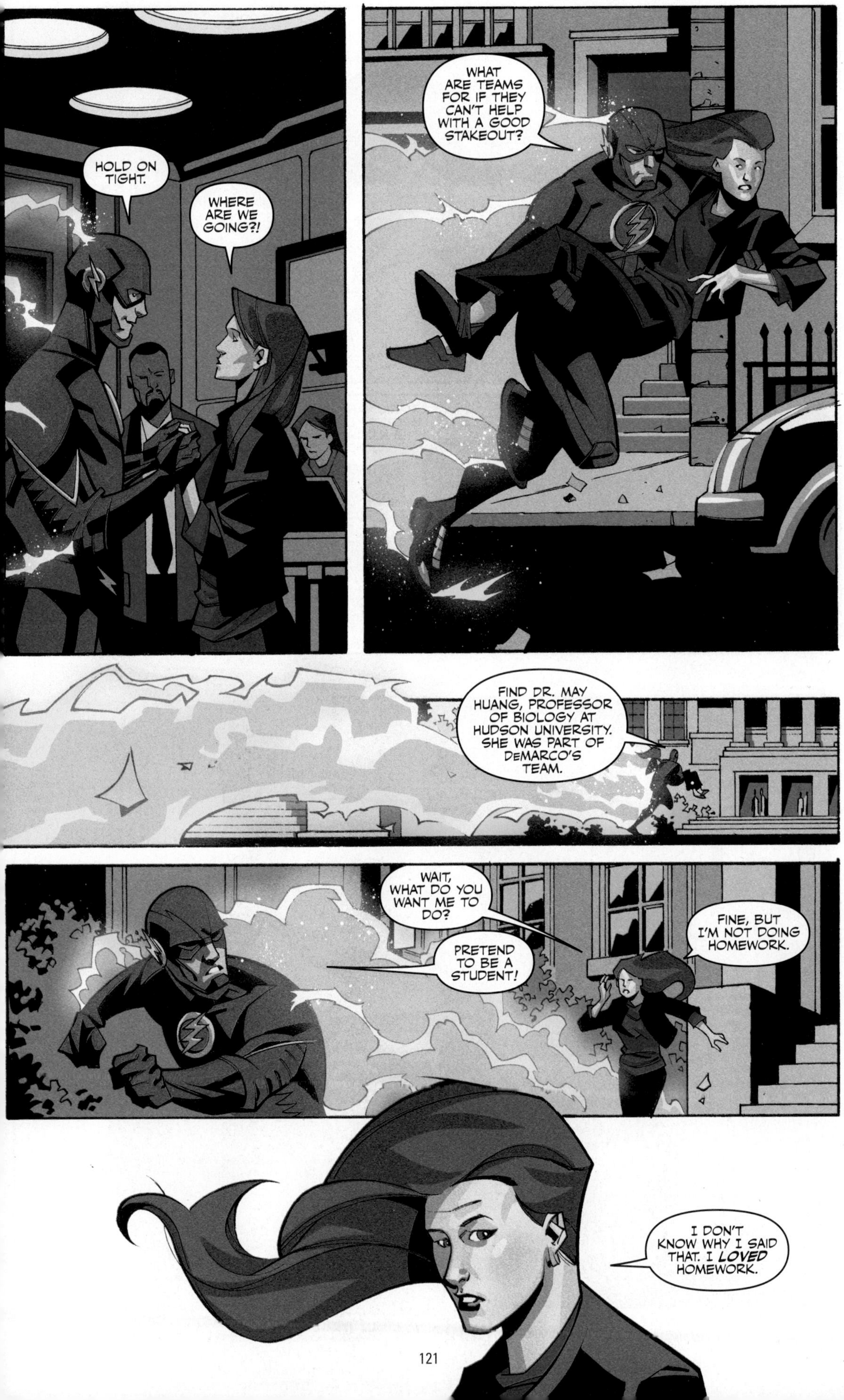
HOLD ON TIGHT.
WHERE ARE WE GOING?!
WHAT ARE TEAMS FOR IF THEY CAN'T HELP WITH A GOOD STAKEOUT?
FIND DR. MAY HUANG, PROFESSOR OF BIOLOGY AT HUDSON UNIVERSITY. SHE WAS PART OF DeMARCO'S TEAM.
WAIT, WHAT DO YOU WANT ME TO DO?
PRETEND TO BE A STUDENT!
FINE, BUT I'M NOT DOING HOMEWORK.
I DON'T KNOW WHY I SAID THAT. I *LOVED* HOMEWORK.

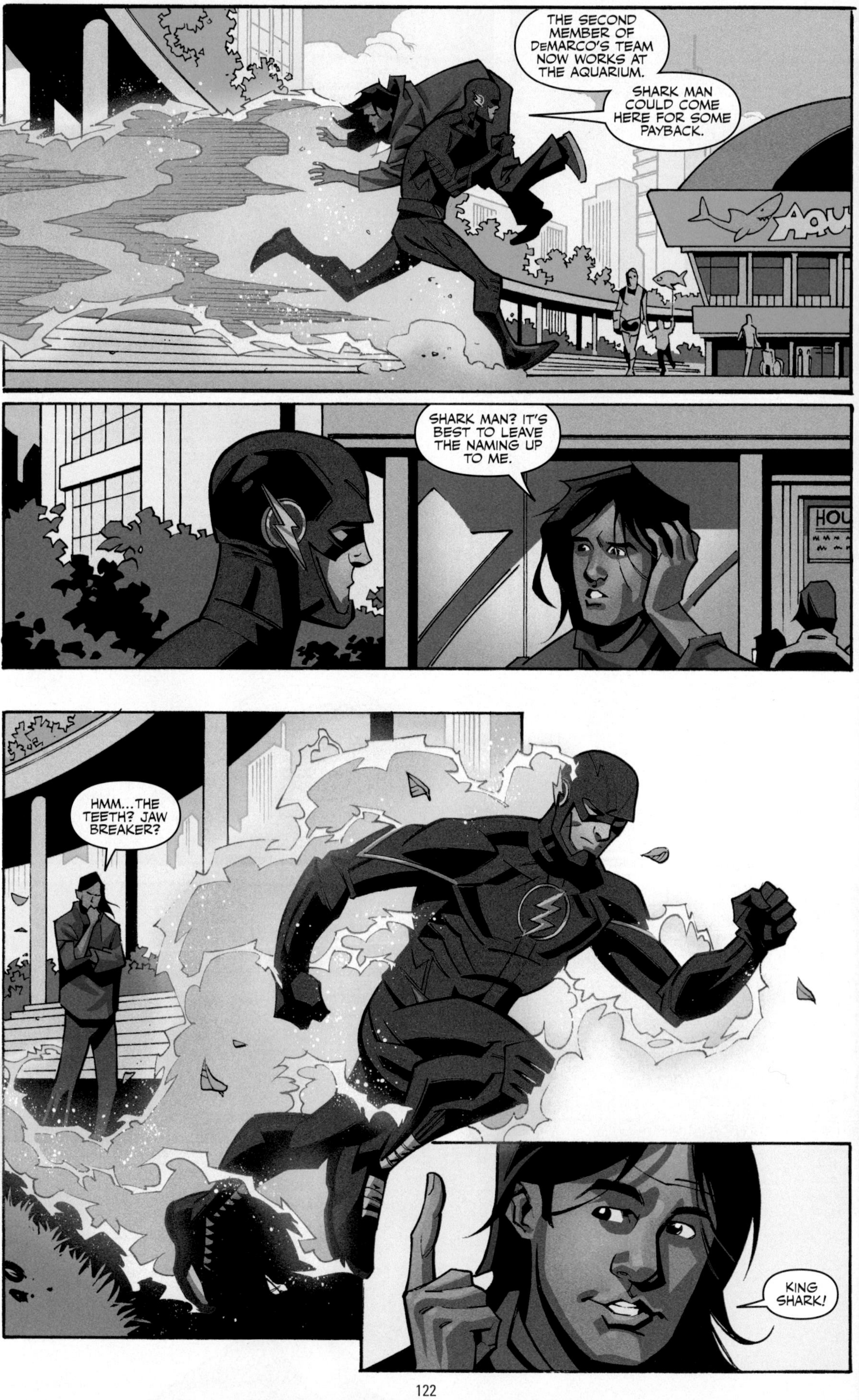
THE SECOND MEMBER OF DeMARCO'S TEAM NOW WORKS AT THE AQUARIUM.
SHARK MAN COULD COME HERE FOR SOME PAYBACK.
AQU
SHARK MAN? IT'S BEST TO LEAVE THE NAMING UP TO ME.
HOU
HMM...THE TEETH? JAW BREAKER?
KING SHARK!

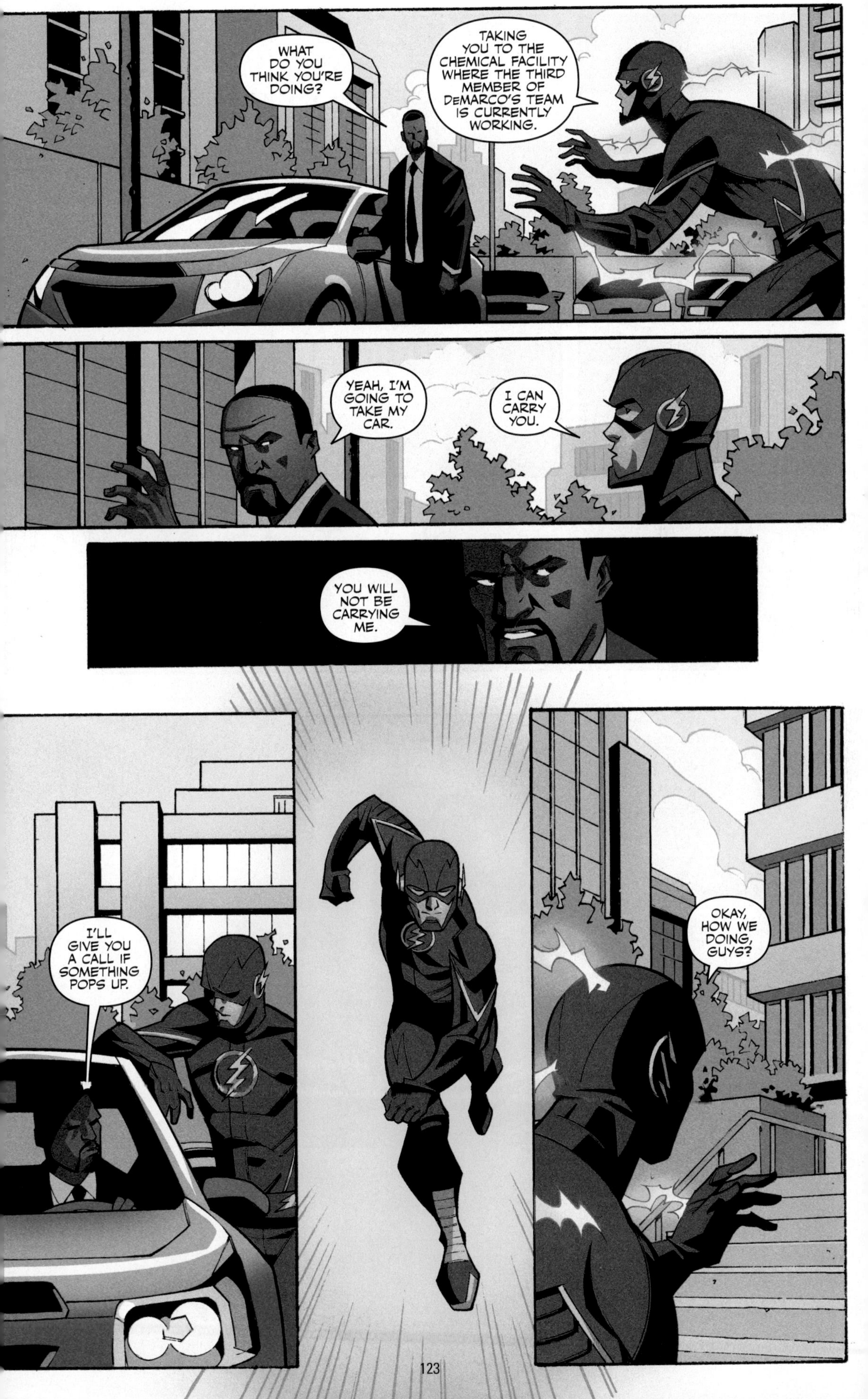
WHAT DO YOU THINK YOU'RE DOING?
TAKING YOU TO THE CHEMICAL FACILITY WHERE THE THIRD MEMBER OF DeMARCO'S TEAM IS CURRENTLY WORKING.
YEAH, I'M GOING TO TAKE MY CAR.
I CAN CARRY YOU.
YOU WILL NOT BE CARRYING ME.
I'LL GIVE YOU A CALL IF SOMETHING POPS UP.
OKAY, HOW WE DOING, GUYS?

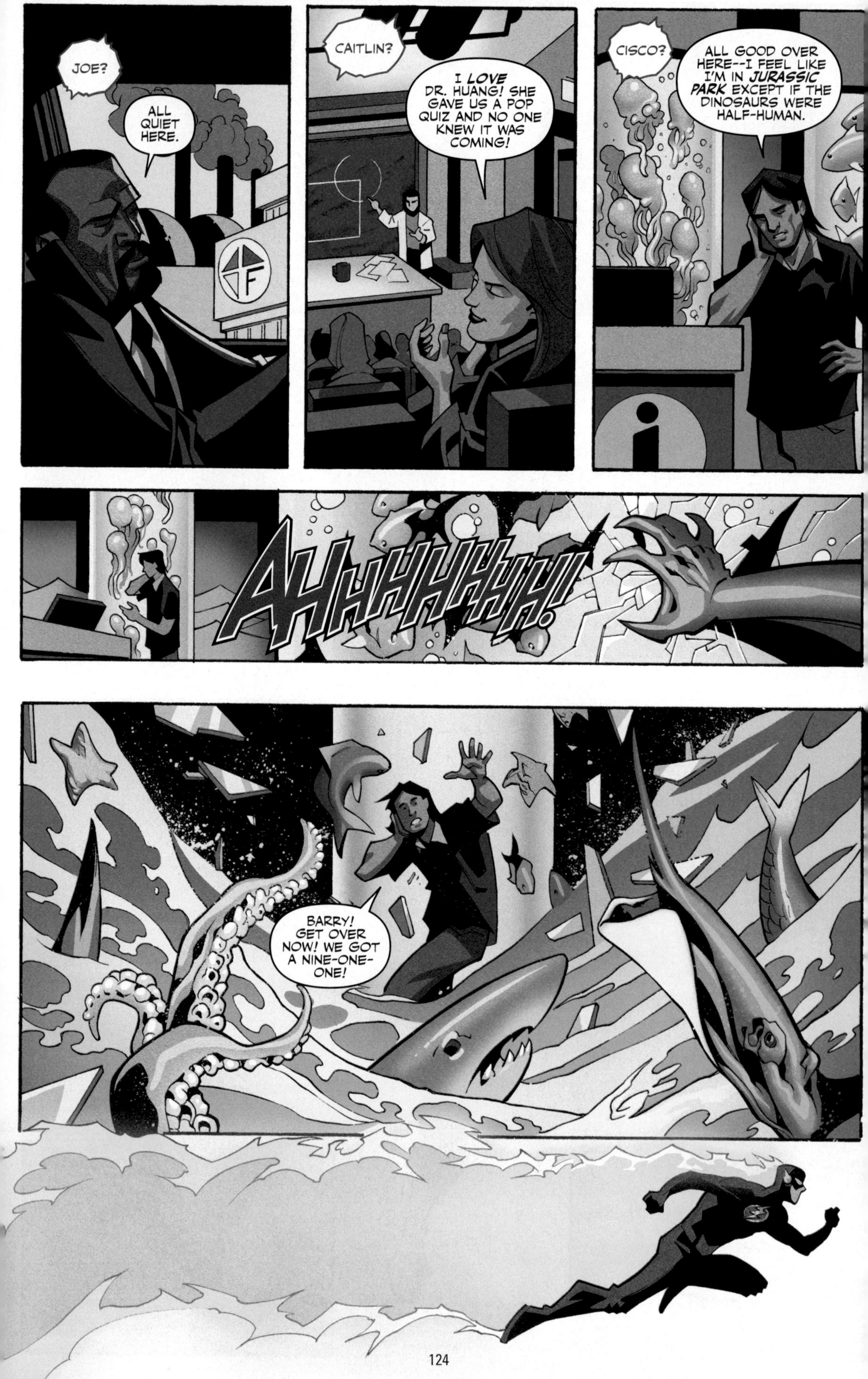
JOE?
ALL QUIET HERE.
CAITLIN?
I LOVE DR. HUANG! SHE GAVE US A POP QUIZ AND NO ONE KNEW IT WAS COMING!
CISCO?
ALL GOOD OVER HERE--I FEEL LIKE I'M IN JURASSIC PARK EXCEPT IF THE DINOSAURS WERE HALF-HUMAN.
AHHHHHHH!
BARRY! GET OVER NOW! WE GOT A NINE-ONE-ONE!

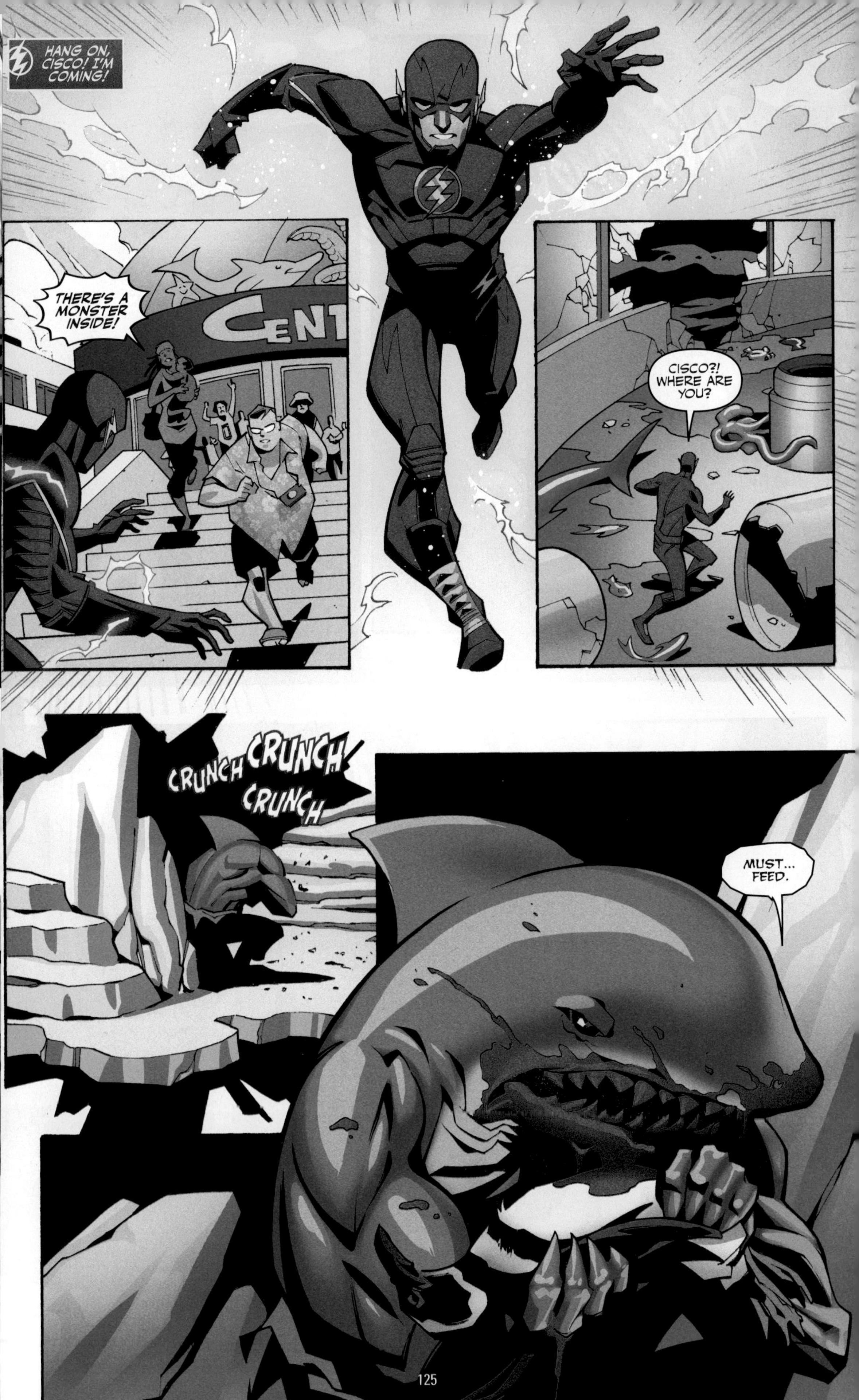
HANG ON, CISCO! I'M COMING!
THERE'S A MONSTER INSIDE!
CENT
CISCO?! WHERE ARE YOU?
CRUNCH CRUNCH! CRUNCH
MUST... FEED.

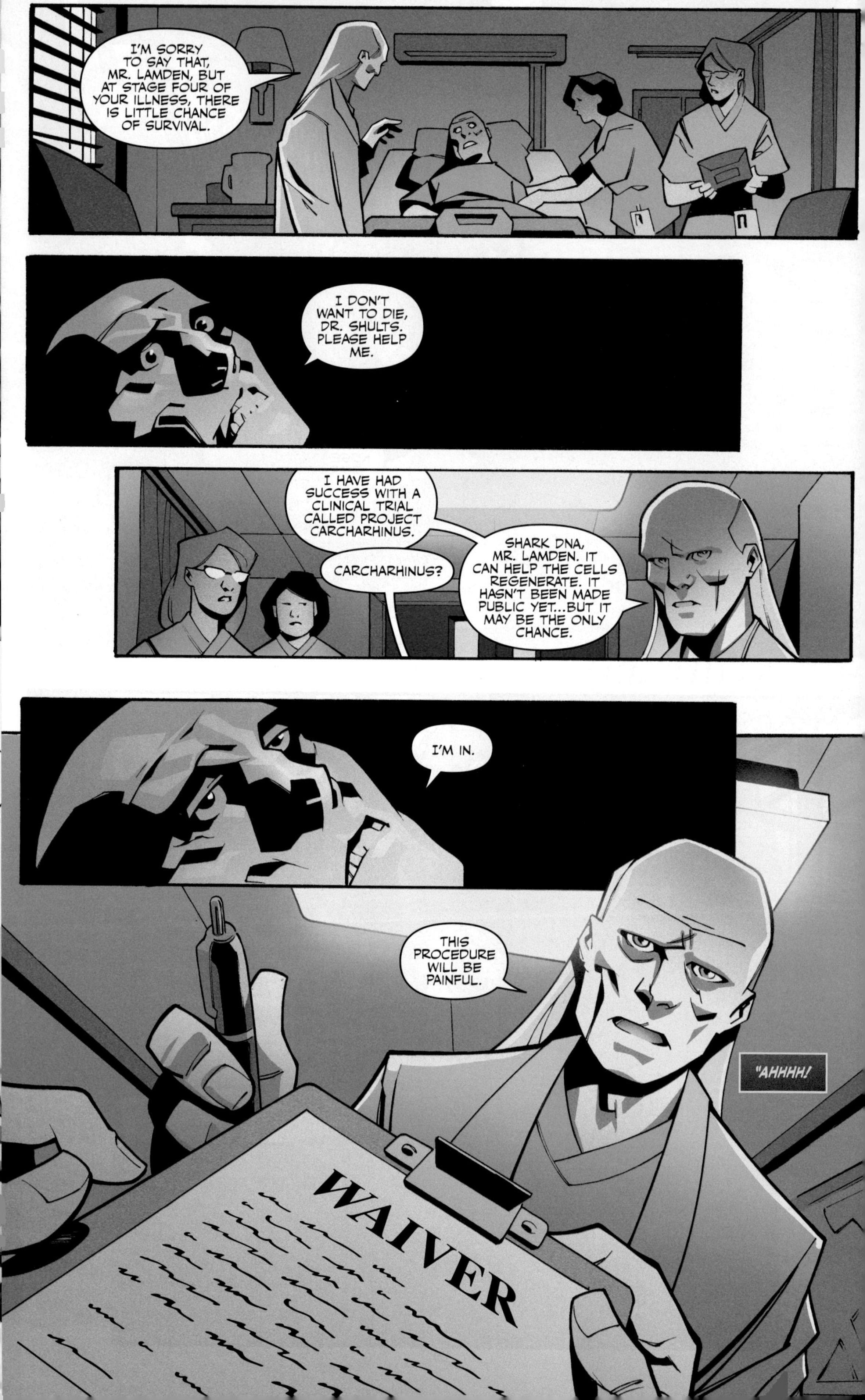
I'M SORRY TO SAY THAT, MR. LAMDEN, BUT AT STAGE FOUR OF YOUR ILLNESS, THERE IS LITTLE CHANCE OF SURVIVAL.
I DON'T WANT TO DIE, DR. SHULTS. PLEASE HELP ME.
I HAVE HAD SUCCESS WITH A CLINICAL TRIAL CALLED PROJECT CARCHARHINUS.
CARCHARHINUS?
SHARK DNA, MR. LAMDEN. IT CAN HELP THE CELLS REGENERATE. IT HASN'T BEEN MADE PUBLIC YET...BUT IT MAY BE THE ONLY CHANCE.
I'M IN.
THIS PROCEDURE WILL BE PAINFUL.
"AHHHH!
WAIVER

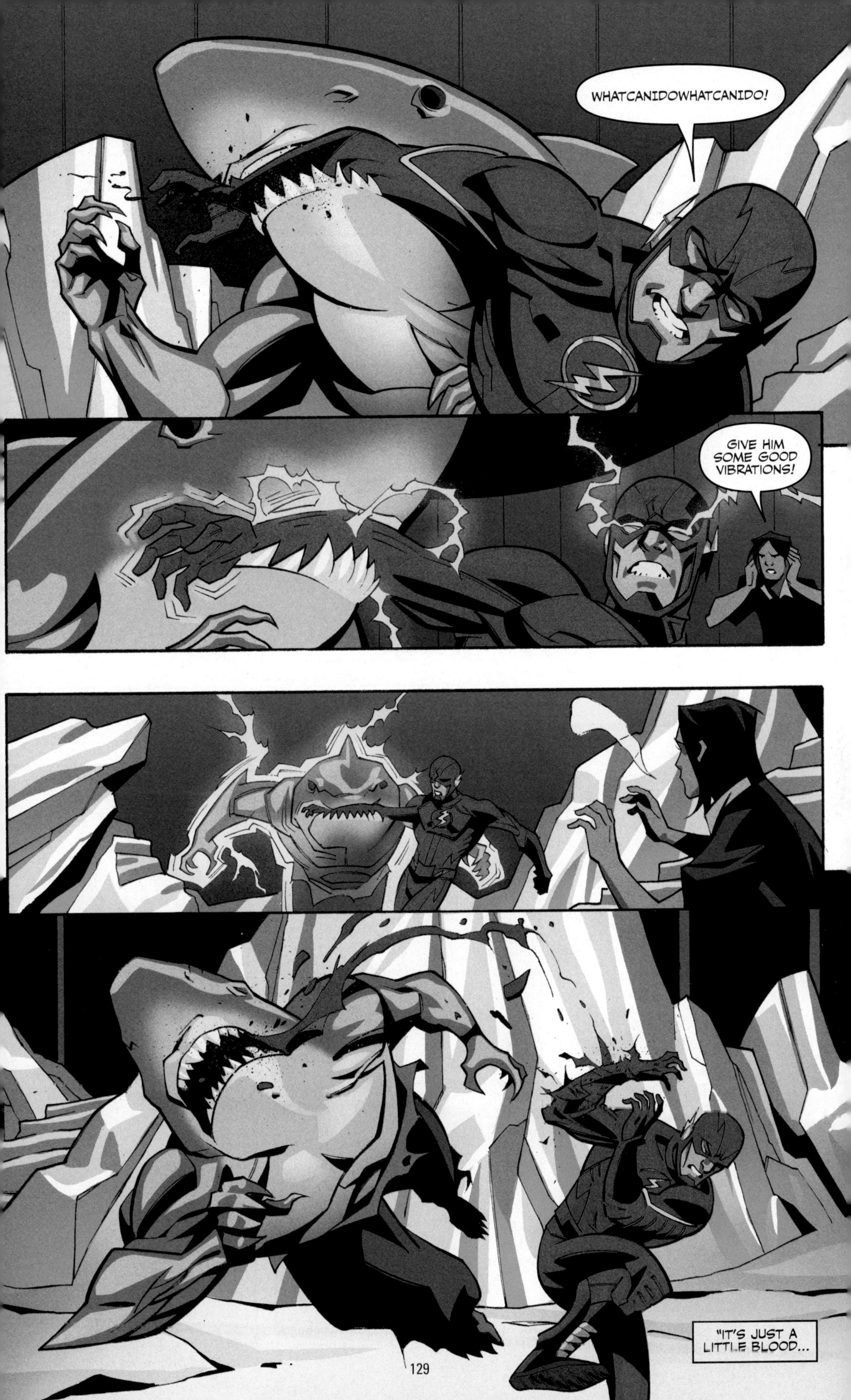
WHATCANIDOWHATCANIDO!
GIVE HIM SOME GOOD VIBRATIONS!
"IT'S JUST A LITTLE BLOOD...

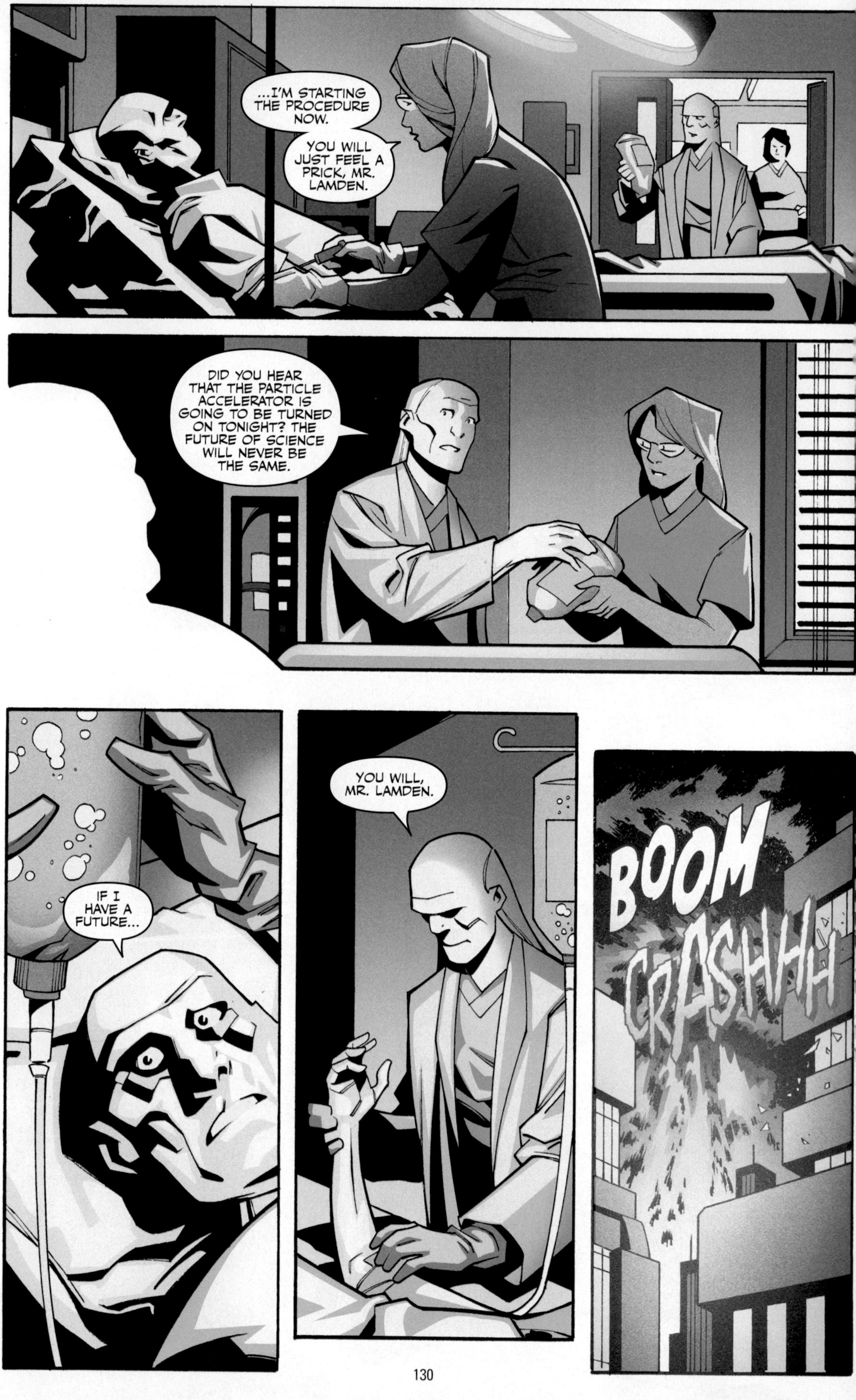
...I'M STARTING THE PROCEDURE NOW.
YOU WILL JUST FEEL A PRICK, MR. LAMDEN.
DID YOU HEAR THAT THE PARTICLE ACCELERATOR IS GOING TO BE TURNED ON TONIGHT? THE FUTURE OF SCIENCE WILL NEVER BE THE SAME.
IF I HAVE A FUTURE...
YOU WILL, MR. LAMDEN.
BOOM
CRASHHH

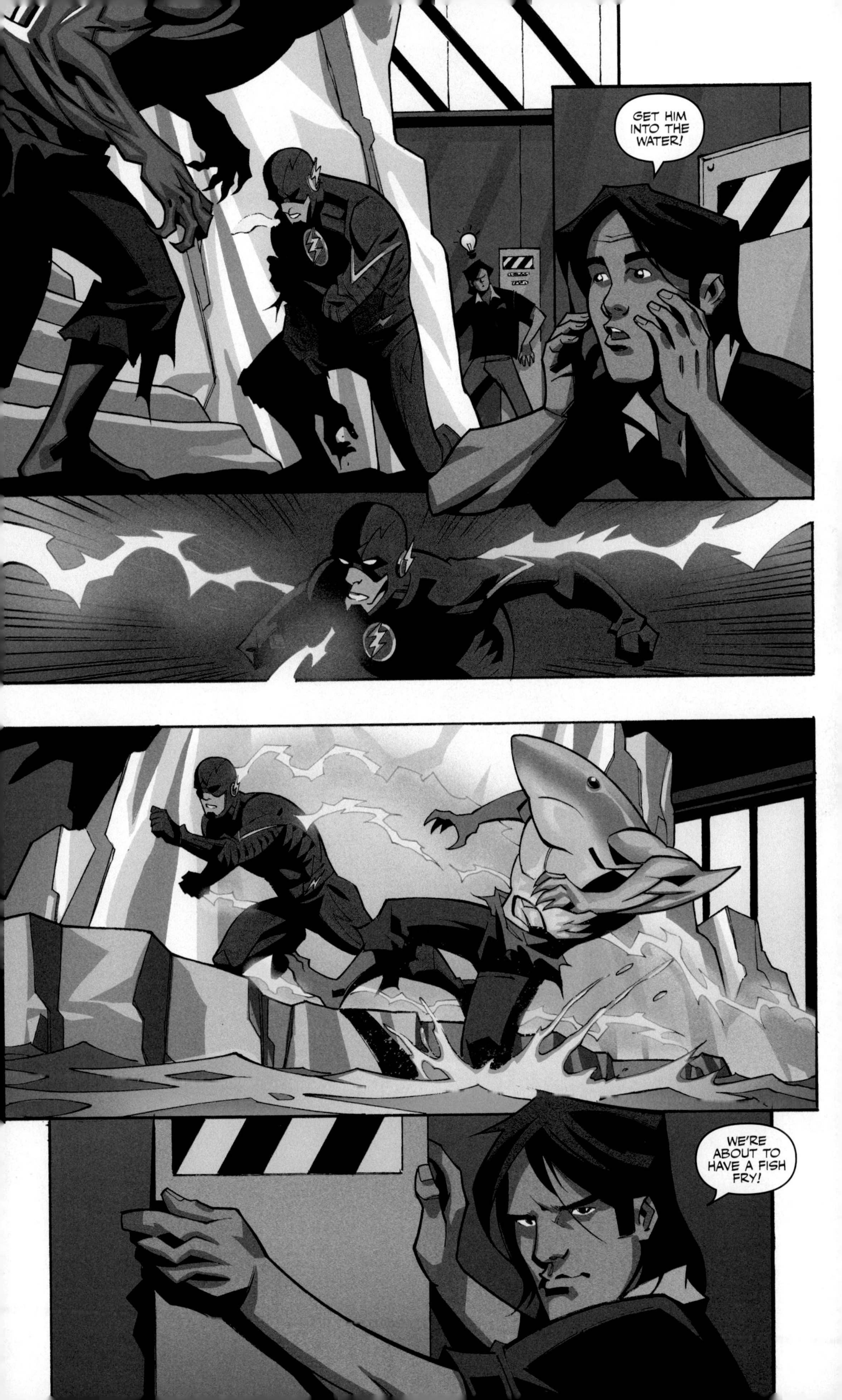
GET HIM INTO THE WATER!
WE'RE ABOUT TO HAVE A FISH FRY!

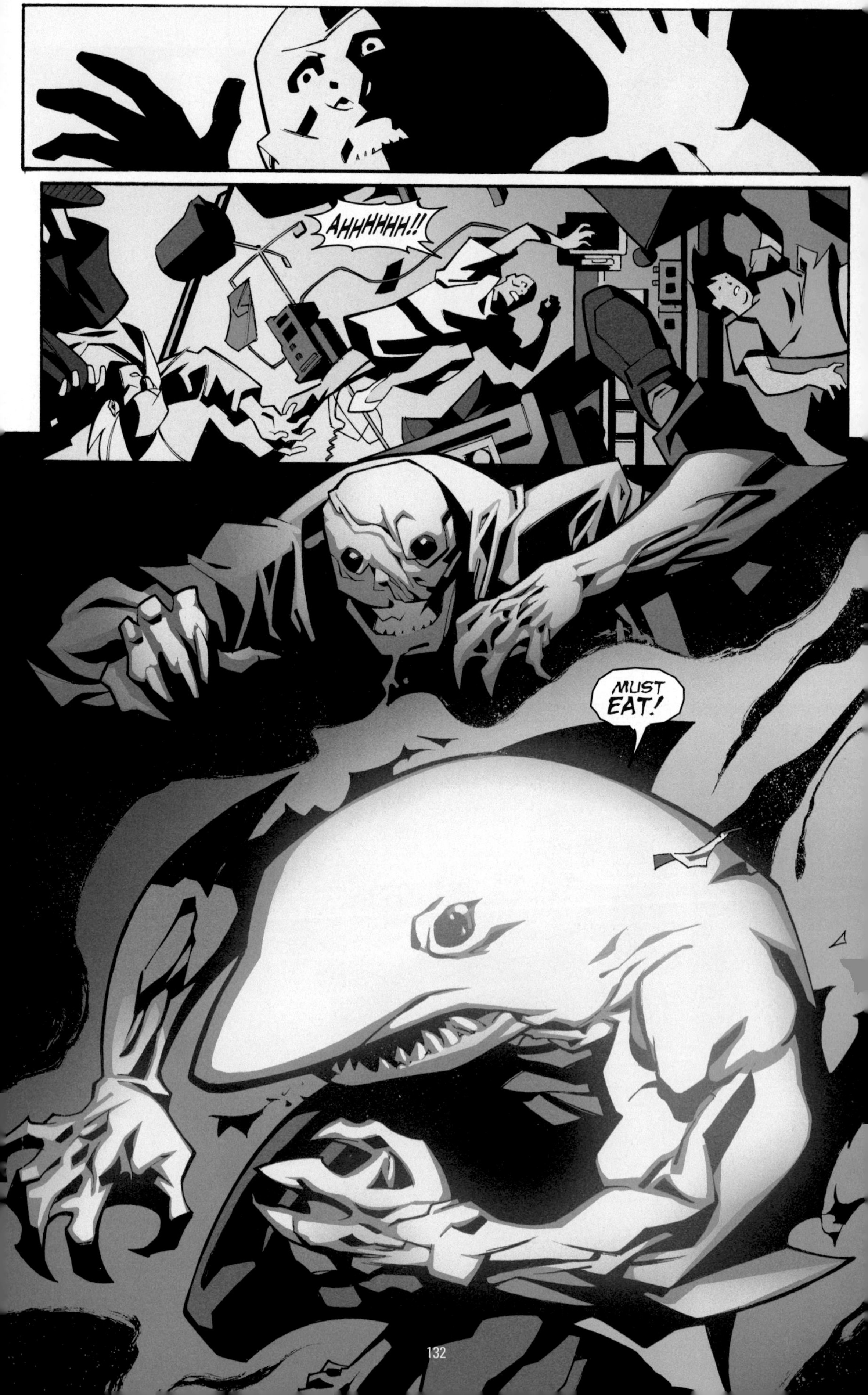
AHHHHHH!!
MUST EAT!

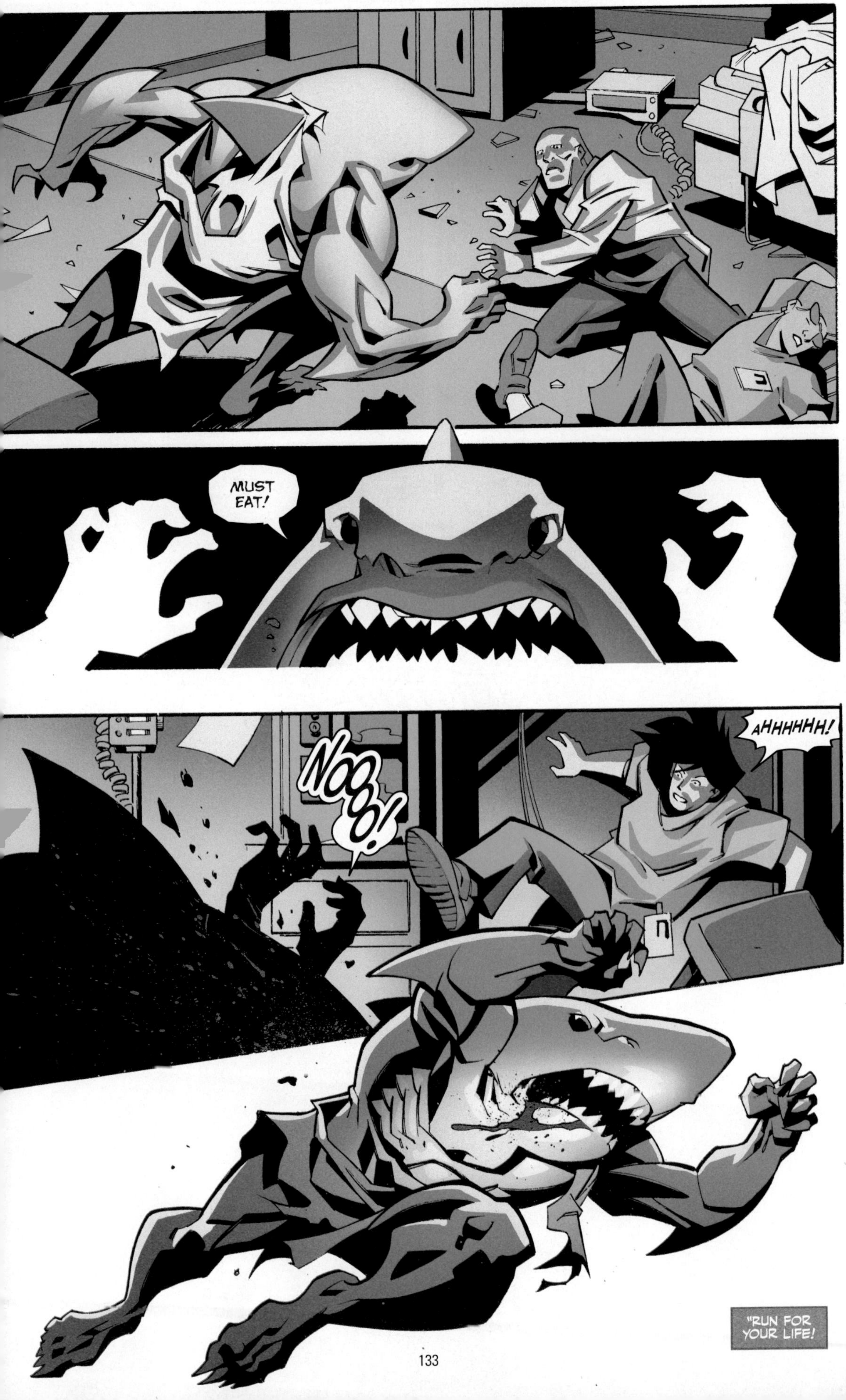
MUST EAT!
NOOOO!
AHHHHHH!
"RUN FOR YOUR LIFE!

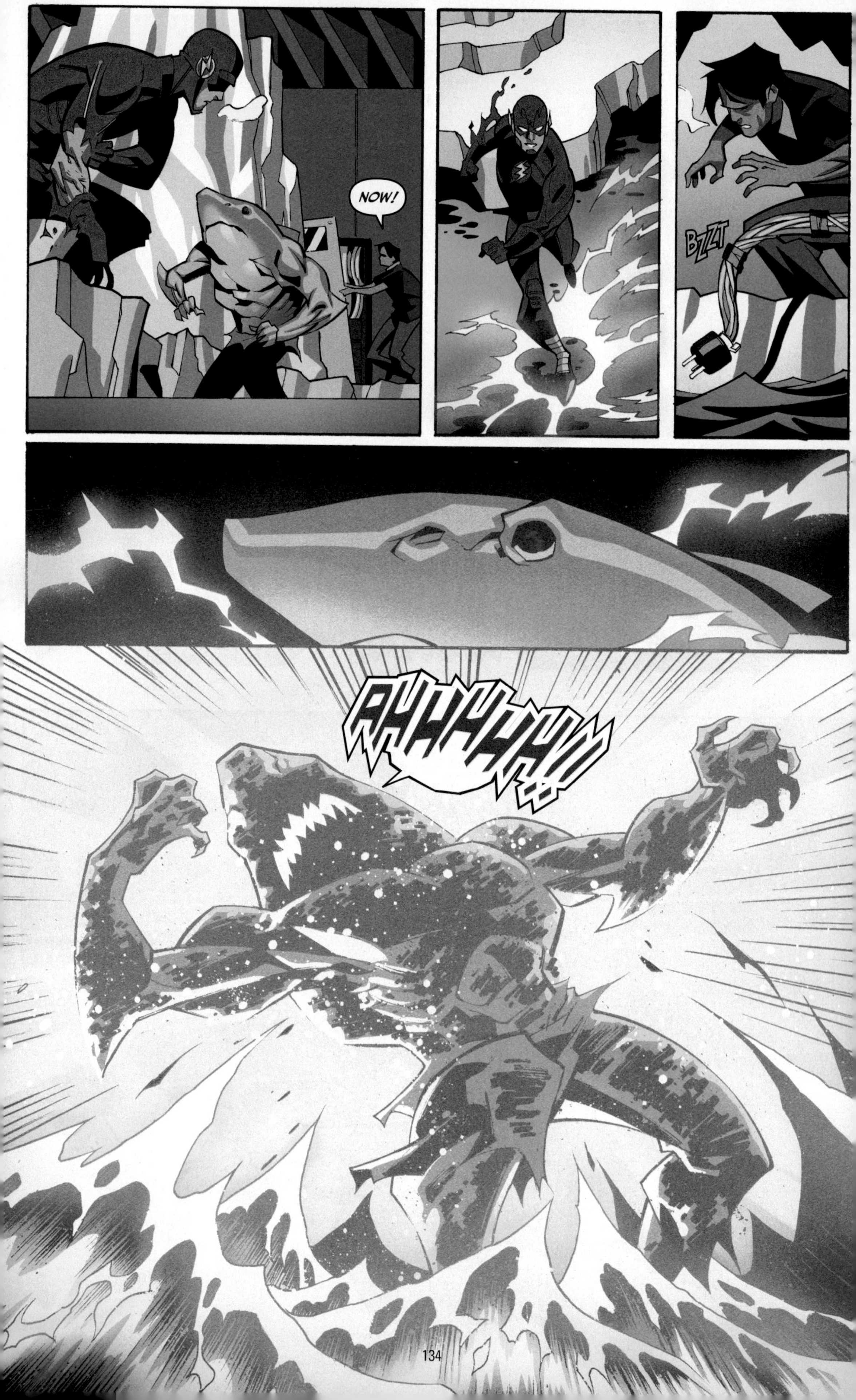
NOW!
BZZZT
AHHHHHHH!!

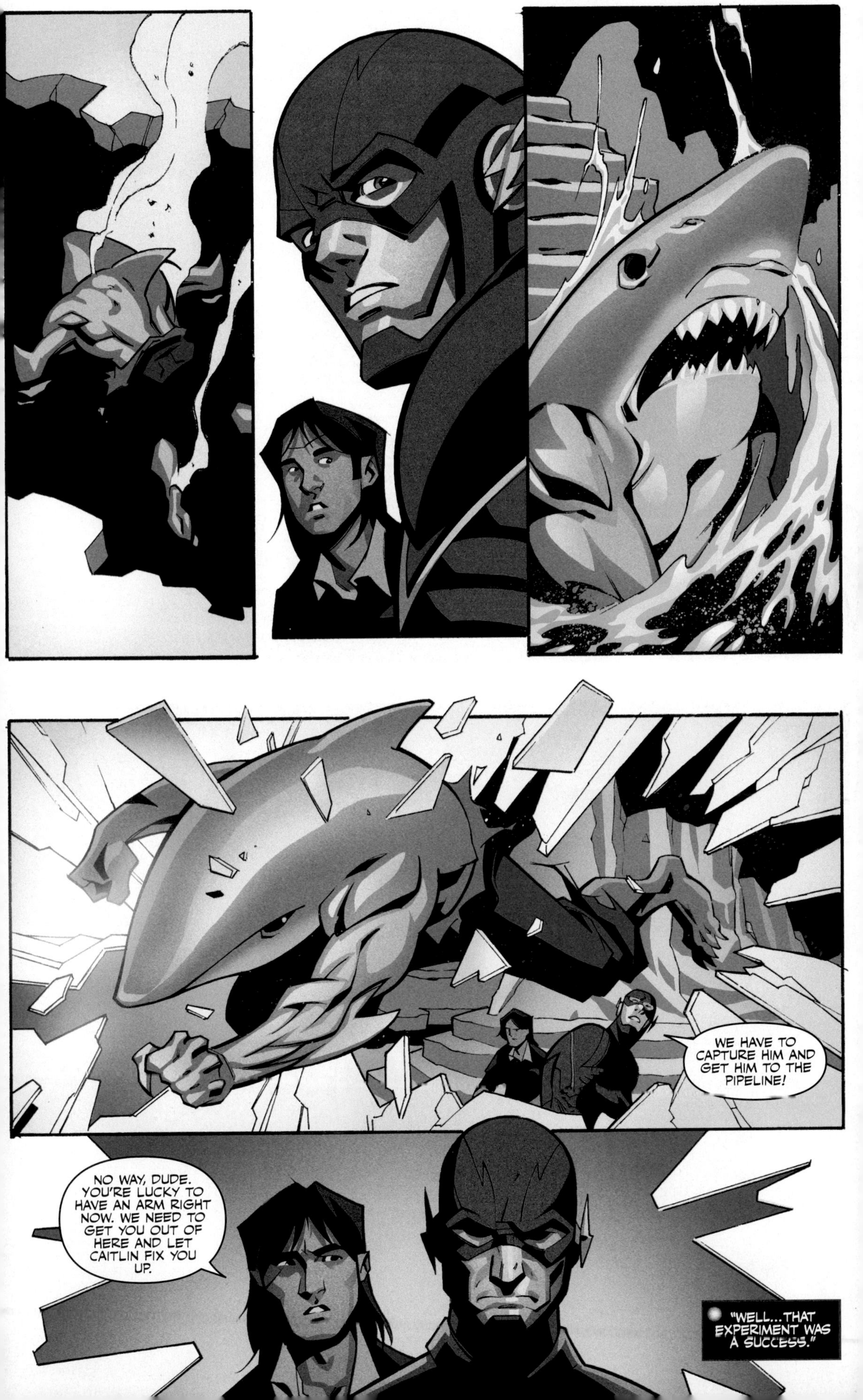
WE HAVE TO CAPTURE HIM AND GET HIM TO THE PIPELINE!
NO WAY, DUDE. YOU'RE LUCKY TO HAVE AN ARM RIGHT NOW. WE NEED TO GET YOU OUT OF HERE AND LET CAITLIN FIX YOU UP.
"WELL...THAT EXPERIMENT WAS A SUCCESS."

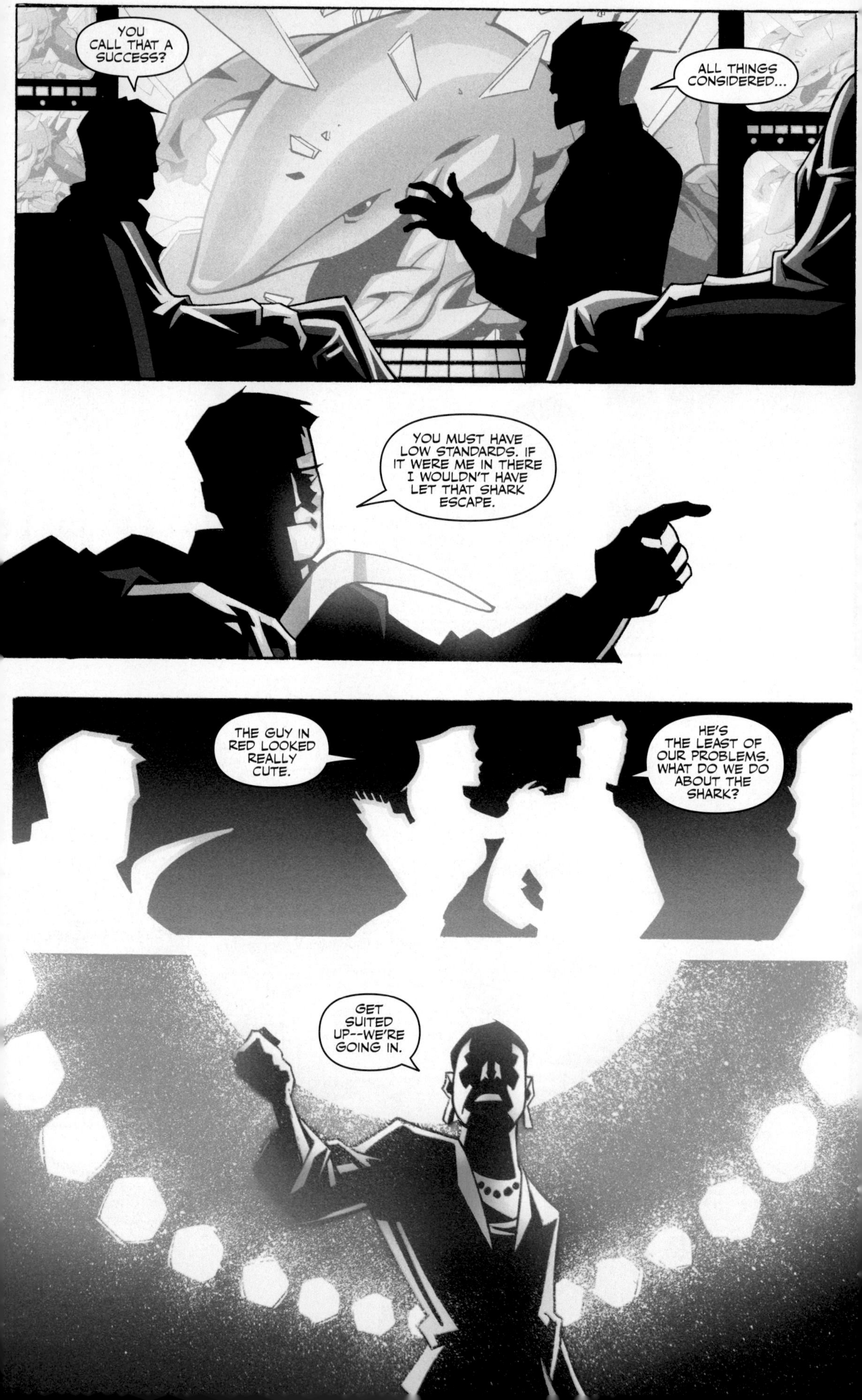
YOU CALL THAT A SUCCESS?
ALL THINGS CONSIDERED...
YOU MUST HAVE LOW STANDARDS. IF IT WERE ME IN THERE I WOULDN'T HAVE LET THAT SHARK ESCAPE.
THE GUY IN RED LOOKED REALLY CUTE.
HE'S THE LEAST OF OUR PROBLEMS. WHAT DO WE DO ABOUT THE SHARK?
GET SUITED UP--WE'RE GOING IN.

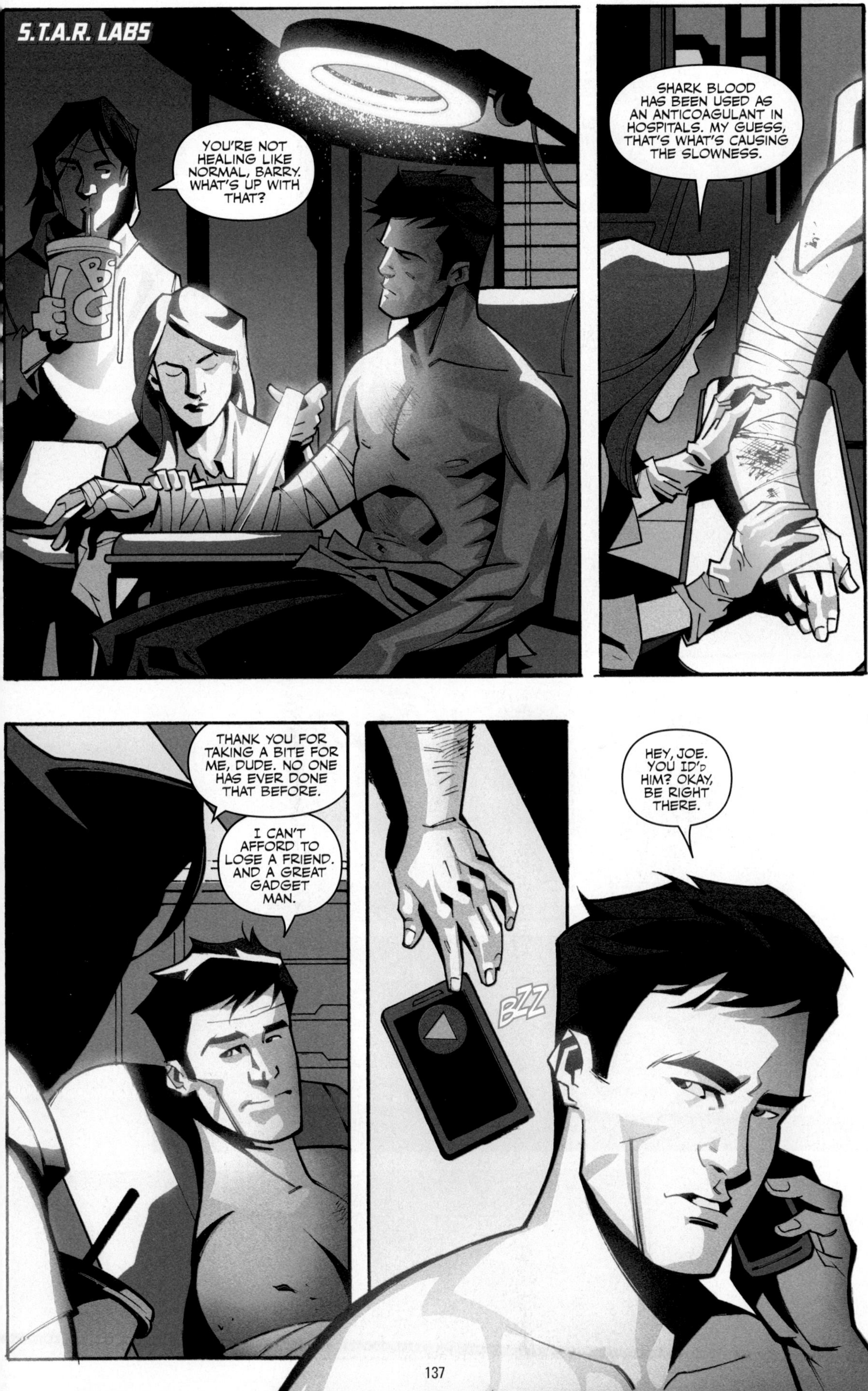
S.T.A.R. LABS
YOU'RE NOT HEALING LIKE NORMAL, BARRY. WHAT'S UP WITH THAT?
SHARK BLOOD HAS BEEN USED AS AN ANTICOAGULANT IN HOSPITALS. MY GUESS, THAT'S WHAT'S CAUSING THE SLOWNESS.
THANK YOU FOR TAKING A BITE FOR ME, DUDE. NO ONE HAS EVER DONE THAT BEFORE.
I CAN'T AFFORD TO LOSE A FRIEND. AND A GREAT GADGET MAN.
BZZ
HEY, JOE. YOU ID'D HIM? OKAY, BE RIGHT THERE.

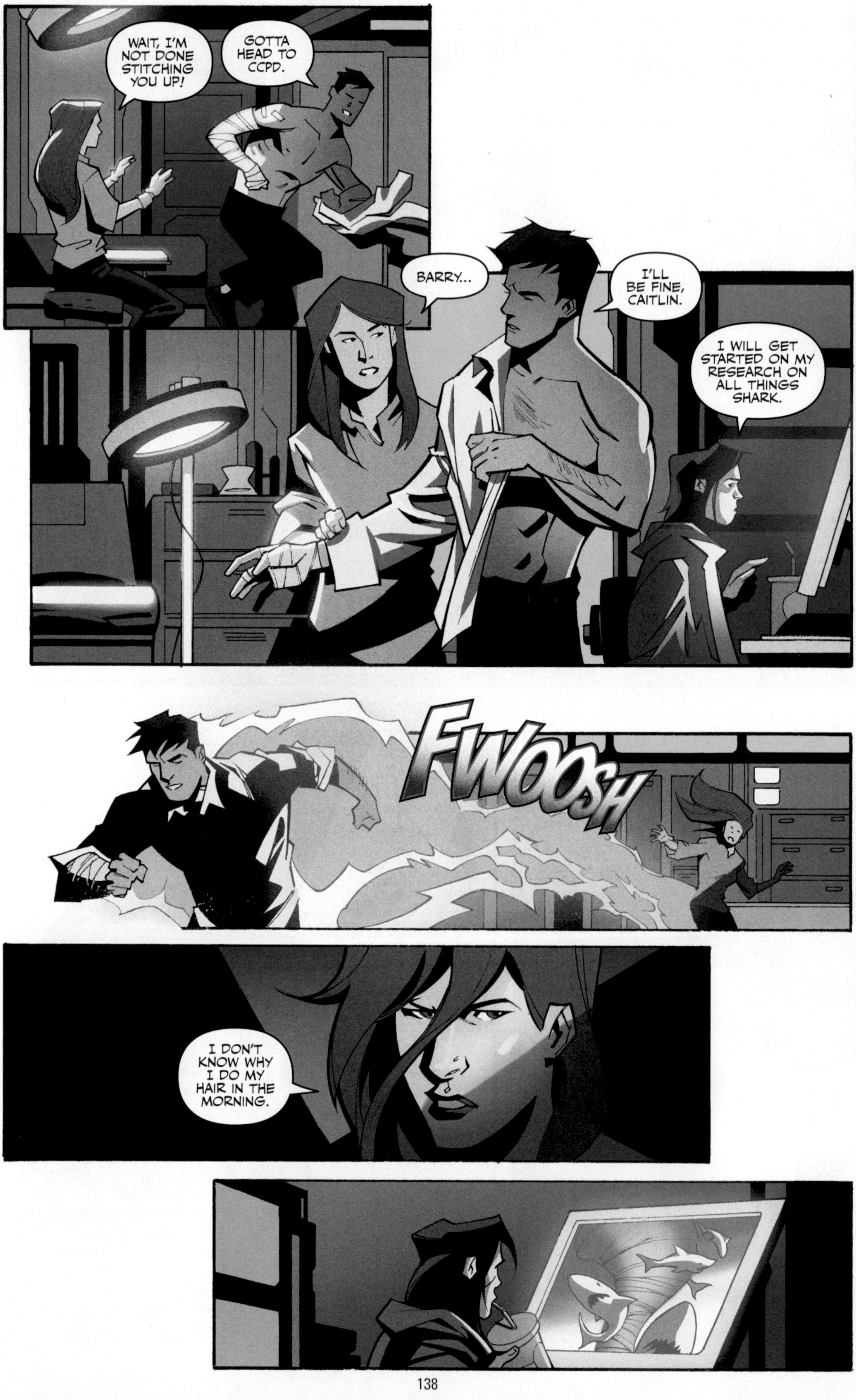
WAIT, I'M NOT DONE STITCHING YOU UP!
GOTTA HEAD TO CCPD.
BARRY...
I'LL BE FINE, CAITLIN.
I WILL GET STARTED ON MY RESEARCH ON ALL THINGS SHARK.
FWOOSH
I DON'T KNOW WHY I DO MY HAIR IN THE MORNING.

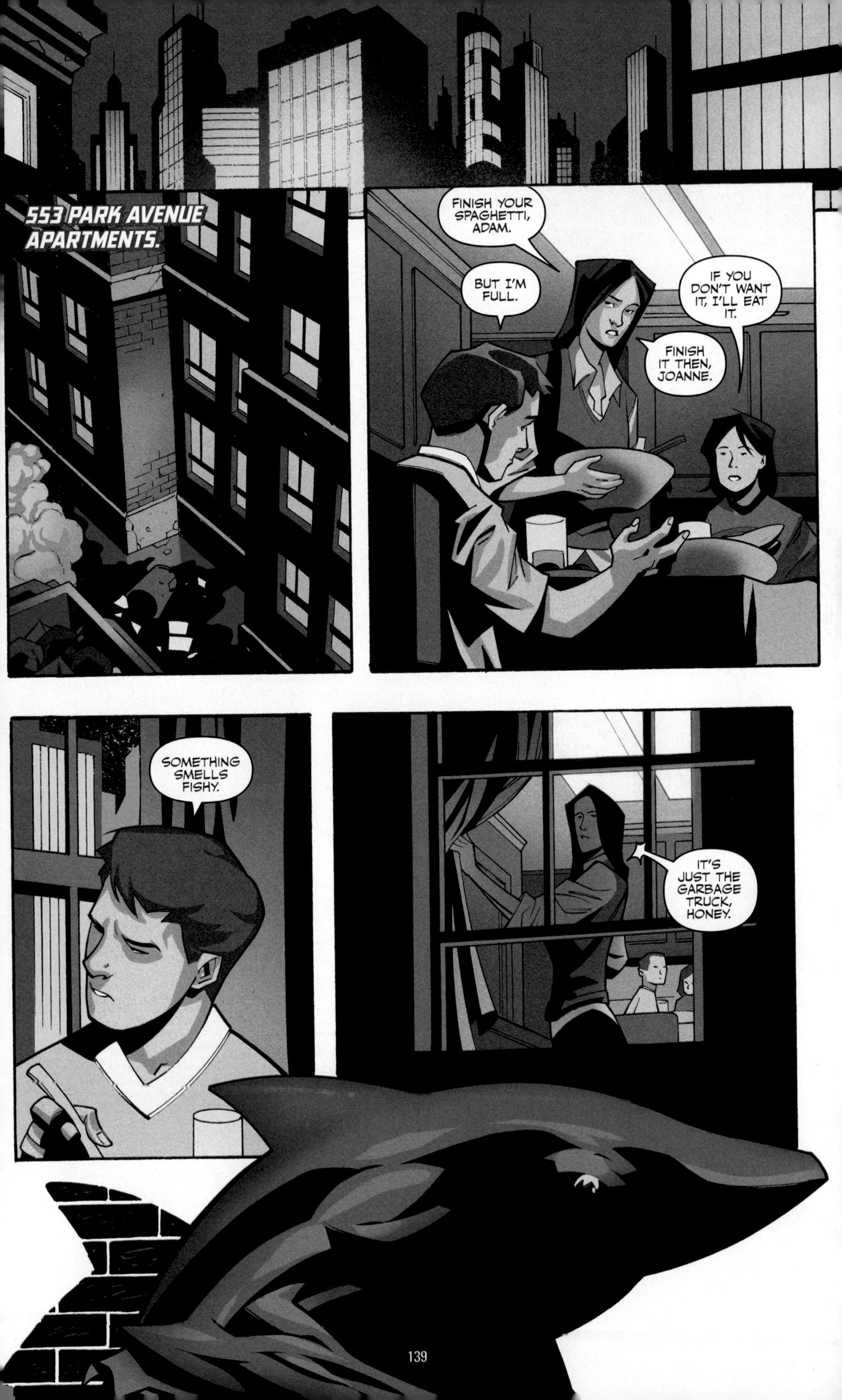
553 PARK AVENUE APARTMENTS.
FINISH YOUR SPAGHETTI, ADAM.
BUT I'M FULL.
IF YOU DON'T WANT IT, I'LL EAT IT.
FINISH IT THEN, JOANNE.
SOMETHING SMELLS FISHY.
IT'S JUST THE GARBAGE TRUCK, HONEY.

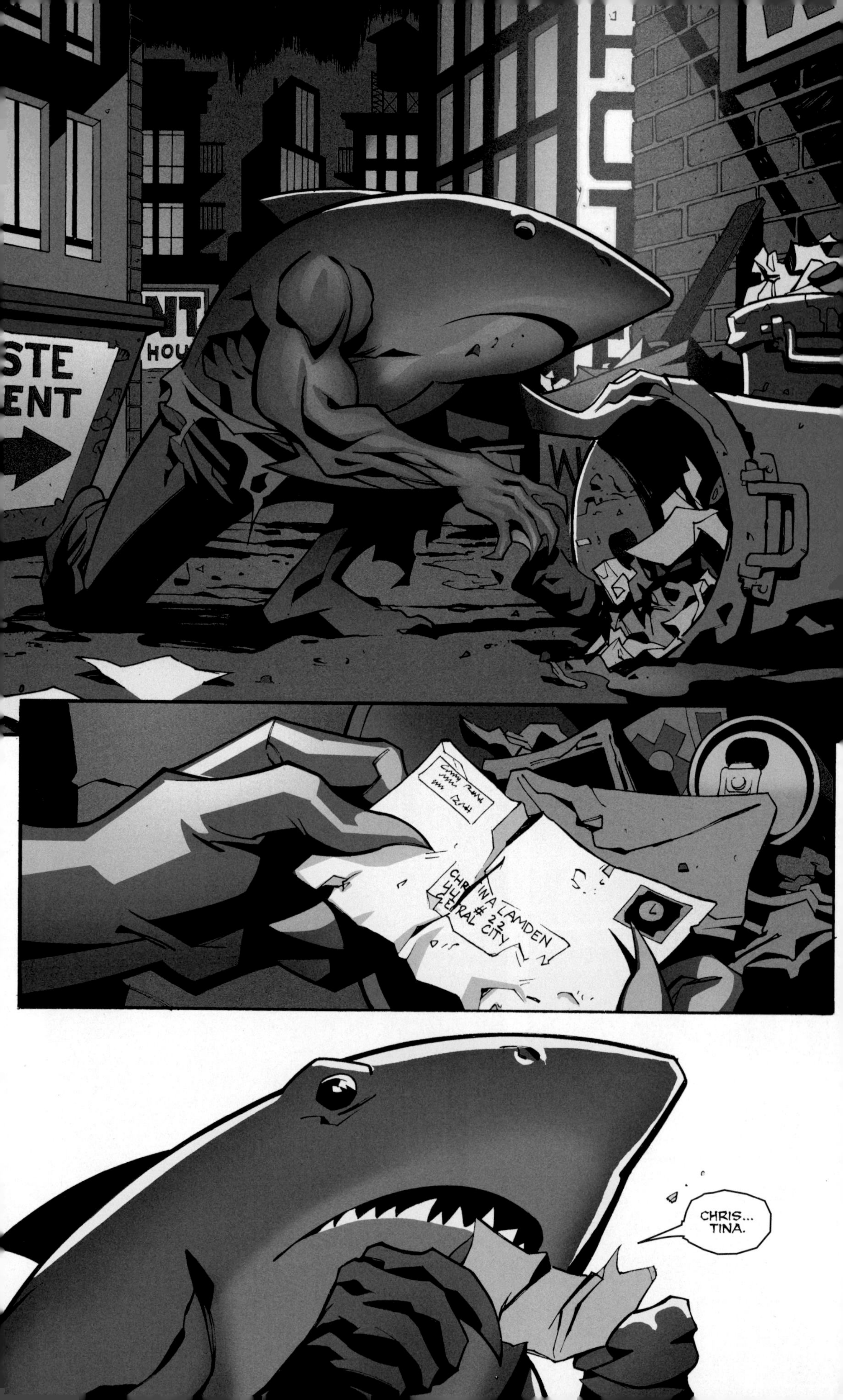
CHRIS... TINA.

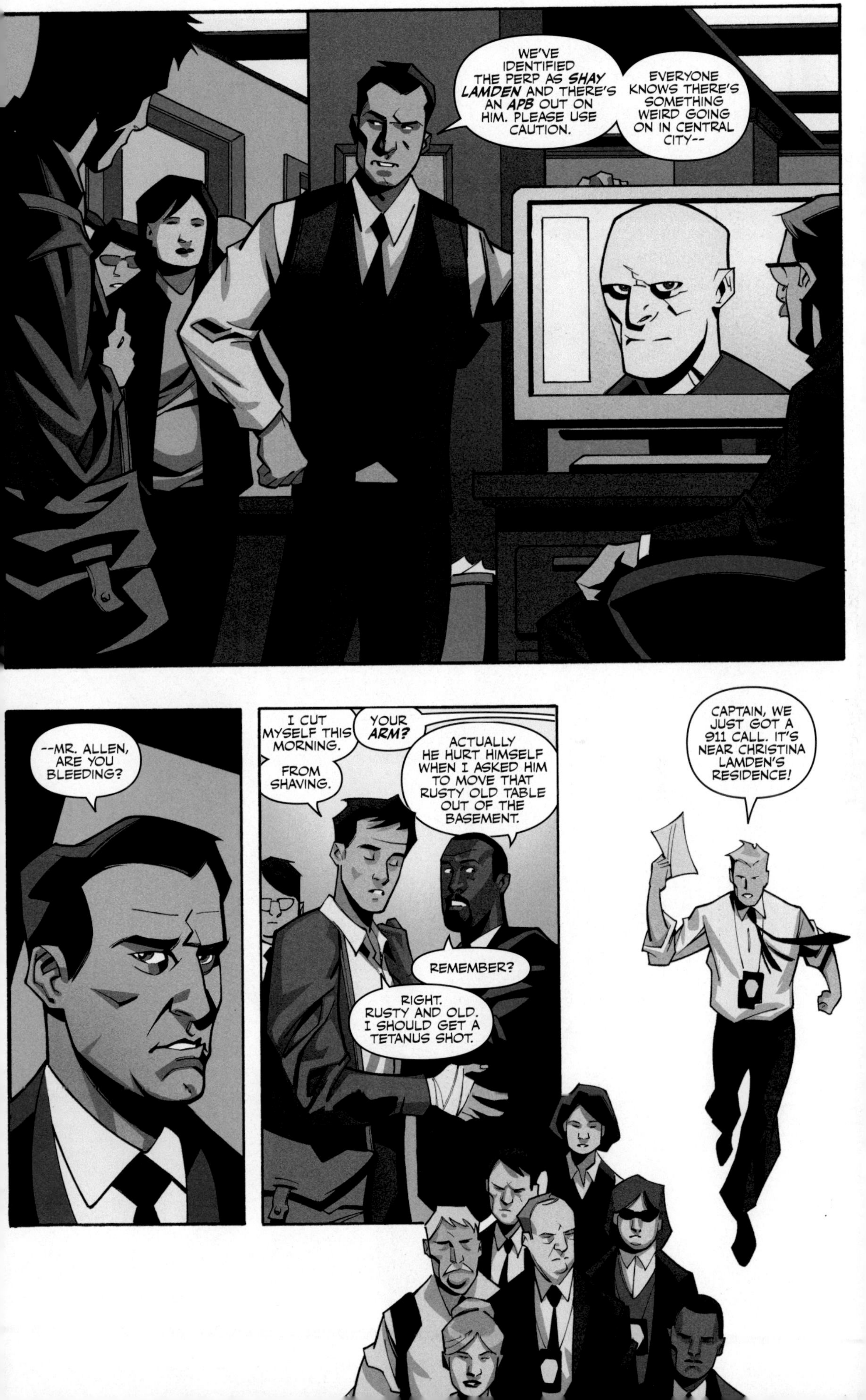
WE'VE IDENTIFIED THE PERP AS SHAY LAMDEN AND THERE'S AN APB OUT ON HIM. PLEASE USE CAUTION.
EVERYONE KNOWS THERE'S SOMETHING WEIRD GOING ON IN CENTRAL CITY--
--MR. ALLEN, ARE YOU BLEEDING?
YOUR ARM?
I CUT MYSELF THIS MORNING.
FROM SHAVING.
ACTUALLY HE HURT HIMSELF WHEN I ASKED HIM TO MOVE THAT RUSTY OLD TABLE OUT OF THE BASEMENT.
REMEMBER?
RIGHT. RUSTY AND OLD. I SHOULD GET A TETANUS SHOT.
CAPTAIN, WE JUST GOT A 911 CALL. IT'S NEAR CHRISTINA LAMDEN'S RESIDENCE!

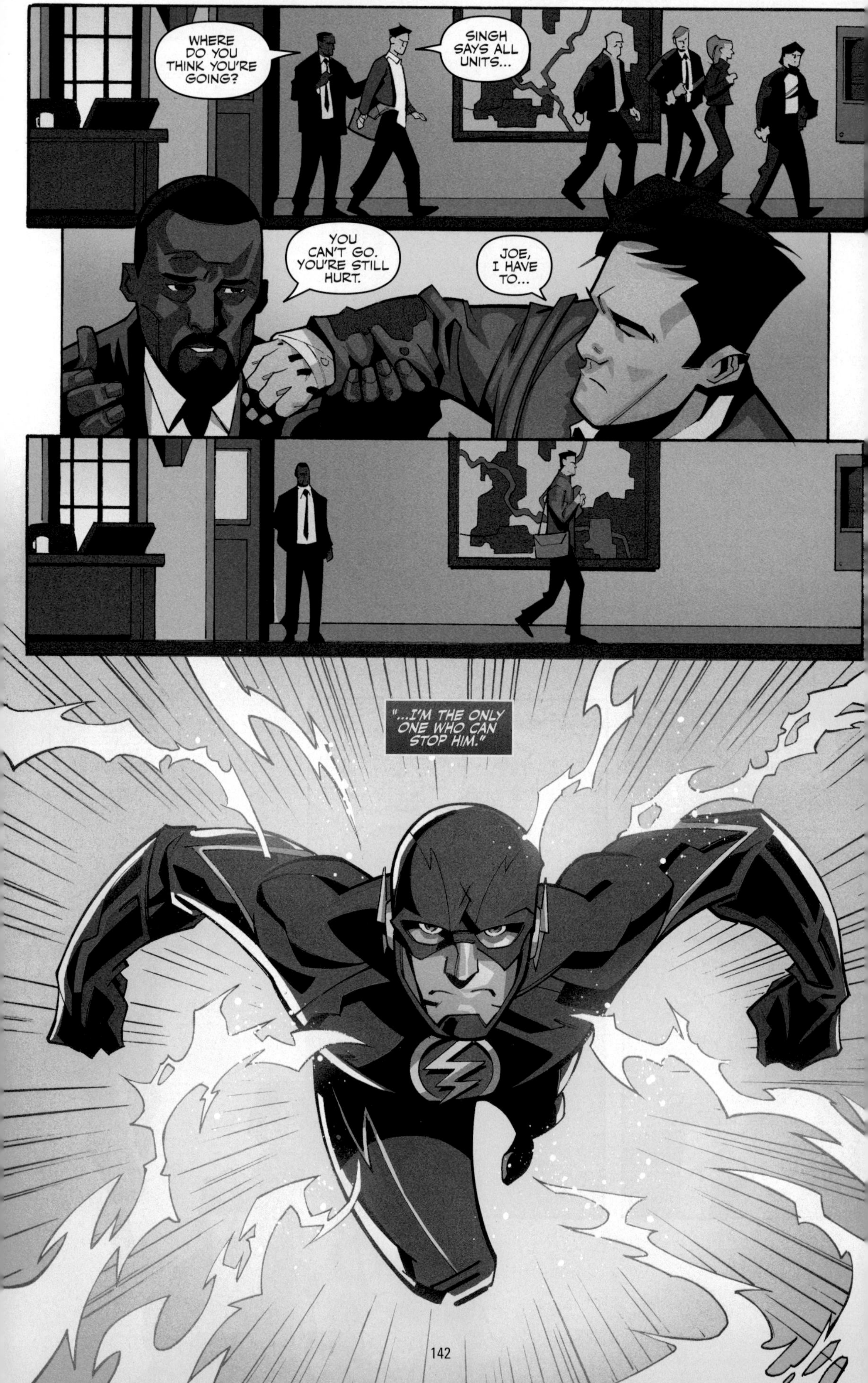
WHERE DO YOU THINK YOU'RE GOING?
SINGH SAYS ALL UNITS...
YOU CAN'T GO. YOU'RE STILL HURT.
JOE, I HAVE TO...
"...I'M THE ONLY ONE WHO CAN STOP HIM."

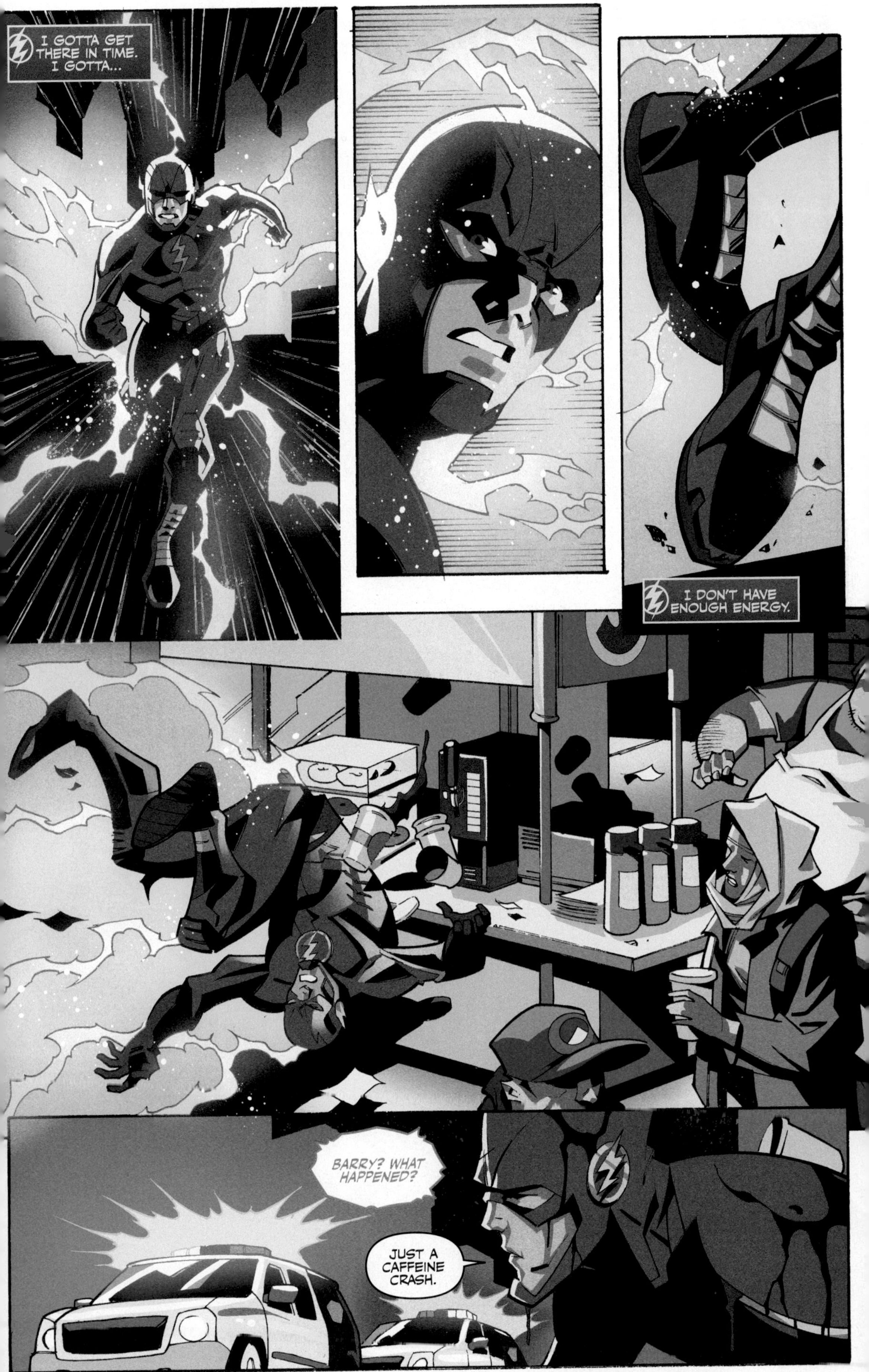
I GOTTA GET THERE IN TIME. I GOTTA...
I DON'T HAVE ENOUGH ENERGY.
BARRY? WHAT HAPPENED?
JUST A CAFFEINE CRASH.

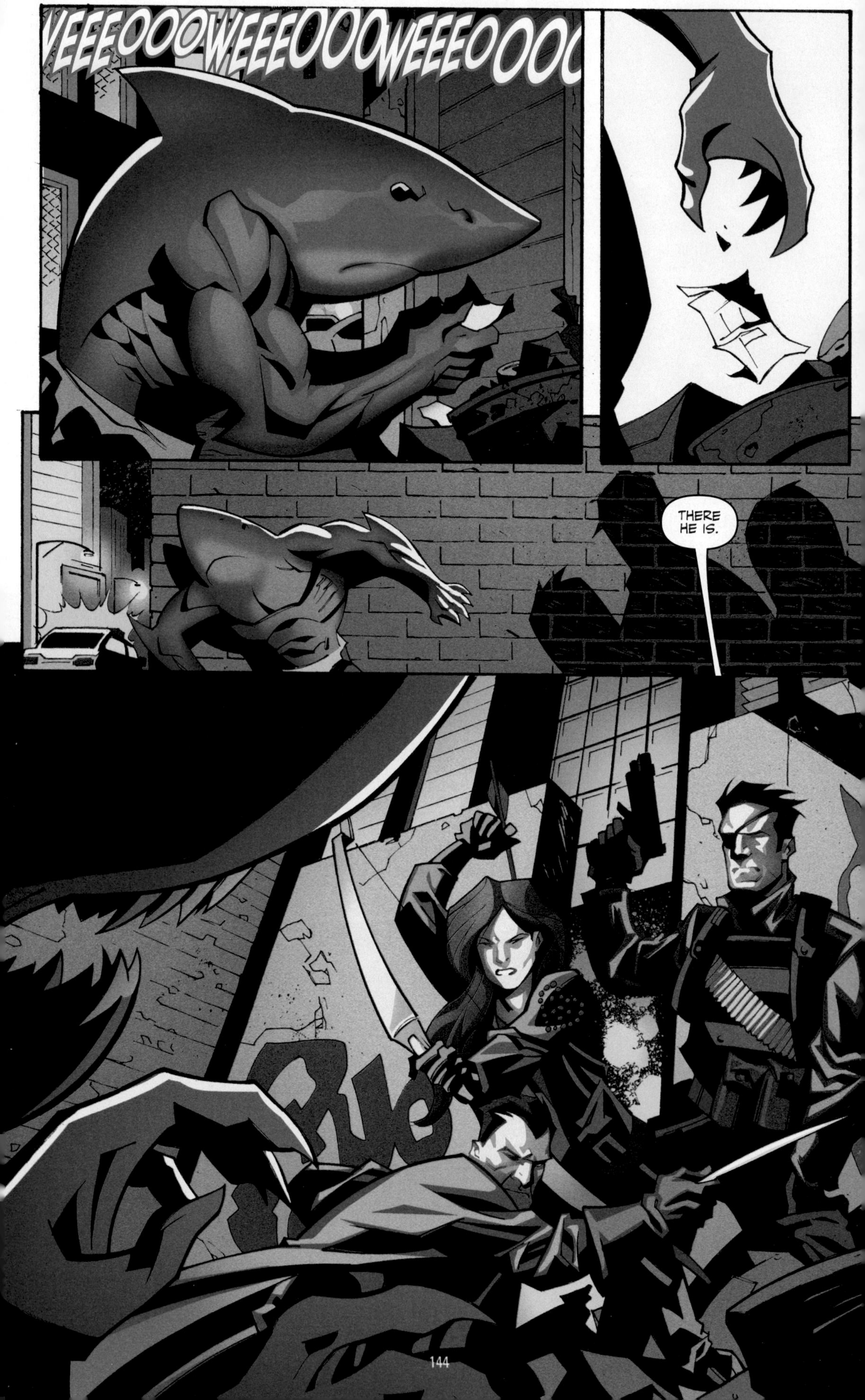
WEEEOOOWEEEOOOWEEEOOO
THERE HE IS.

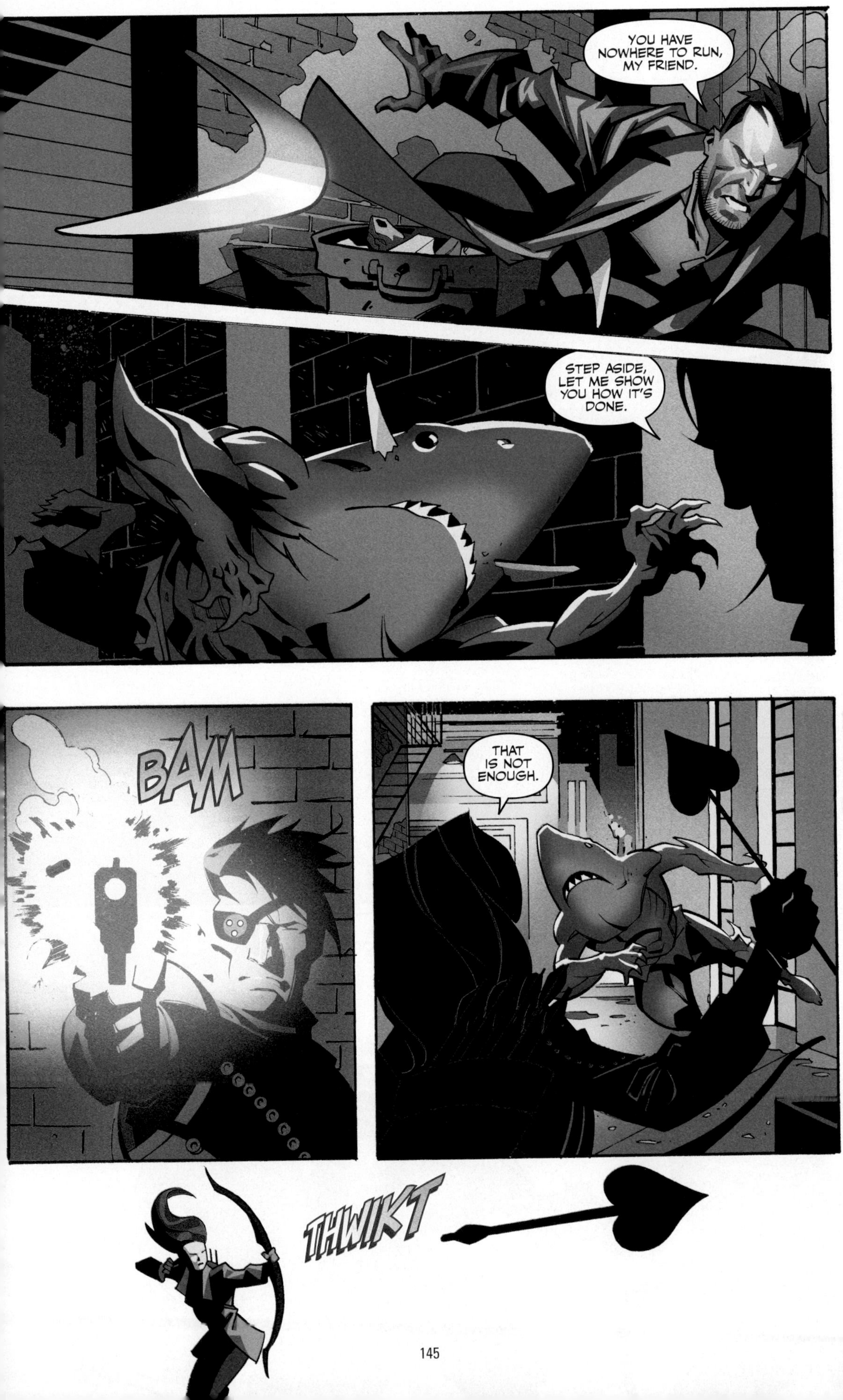
YOU HAVE NOWHERE TO RUN, MY FRIEND.
STEP ASIDE, LET ME SHOW YOU HOW IT'S DONE.
BAM
THAT IS NOT ENOUGH.
THWIKT

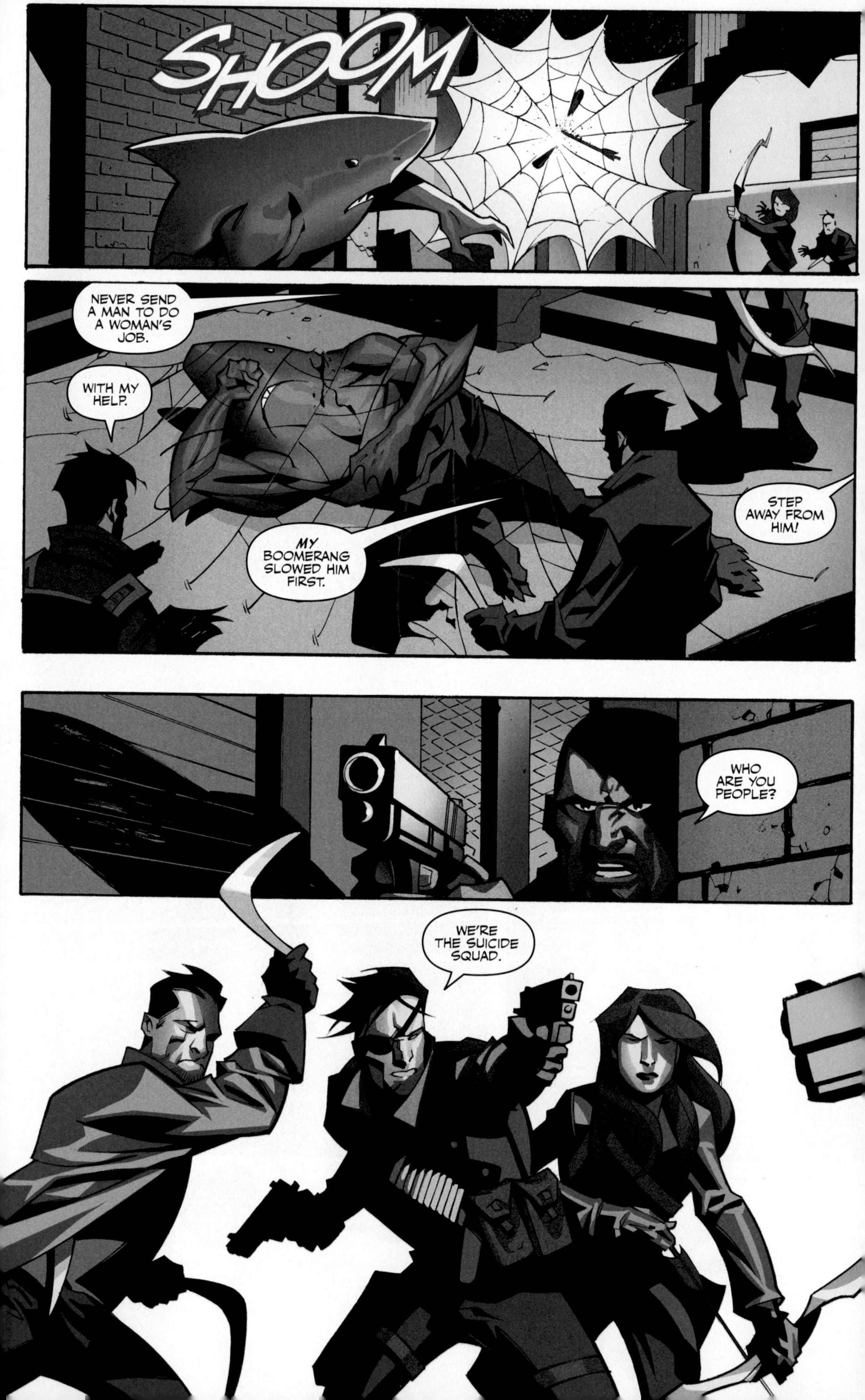
SHOOM
NEVER SEND A MAN TO DO A WOMAN'S JOB.
WITH MY HELP.
MY BOOMERANG SLOWED HIM FIRST.
STEP AWAY FROM HIM!
WHO ARE YOU PEOPLE?
WE'RE THE SUICIDE SQUAD.

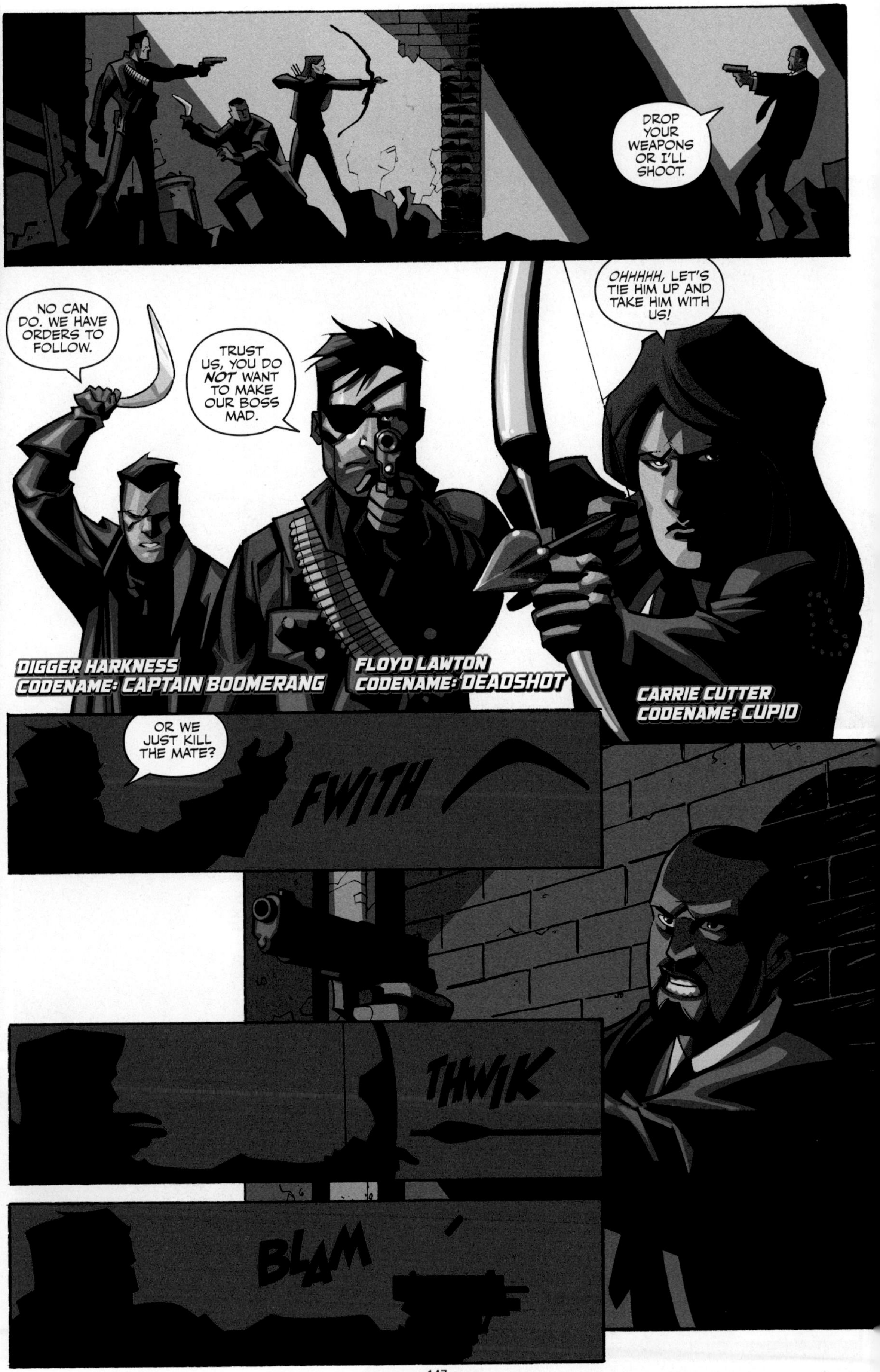

DROP YOUR WEAPONS OR I'LL SHOOT.
NO CAN DO. WE HAVE ORDERS TO FOLLOW.
TRUST US, YOU DO NOT WANT TO MAKE OUR BOSS MAD.
OHHHHH, LET'S TIE HIM UP AND TAKE HIM WITH US!
DIGGER HARKNESS
CODENAME: CAPTAIN BOOMERANG
FLOYD LAWTON
CODENAME: DEADSHOT
CARRIE CUTTER
CODENAME: CUPID
OR WE JUST KILL THE MATE?
FWITH
THWIK
BLAM

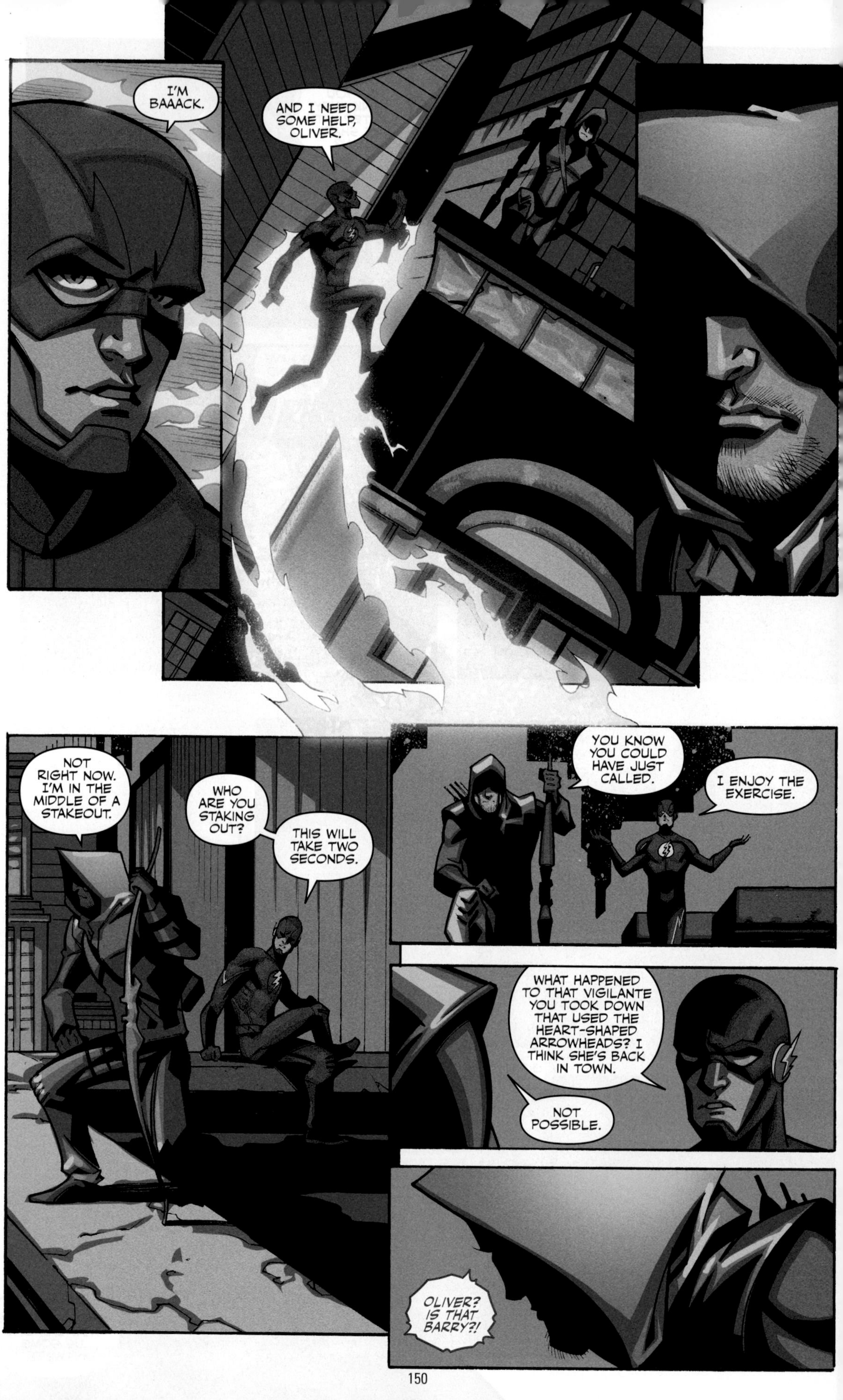
I'M BAAACK.
AND I NEED SOME HELP, OLIVER.
NOT RIGHT NOW. I'M IN THE MIDDLE OF A STAKEOUT.
WHO ARE YOU STAKING OUT?
THIS WILL TAKE TWO SECONDS.
YOU KNOW YOU COULD HAVE JUST CALLED.
I ENJOY THE EXERCISE.
WHAT HAPPENED TO THAT VIGILANTE YOU TOOK DOWN THAT USED THE HEART-SHAPED ARROWHEADS? I THINK SHE'S BACK IN TOWN.
NOT POSSIBLE.
OLIVER? IS THAT BARRY?!

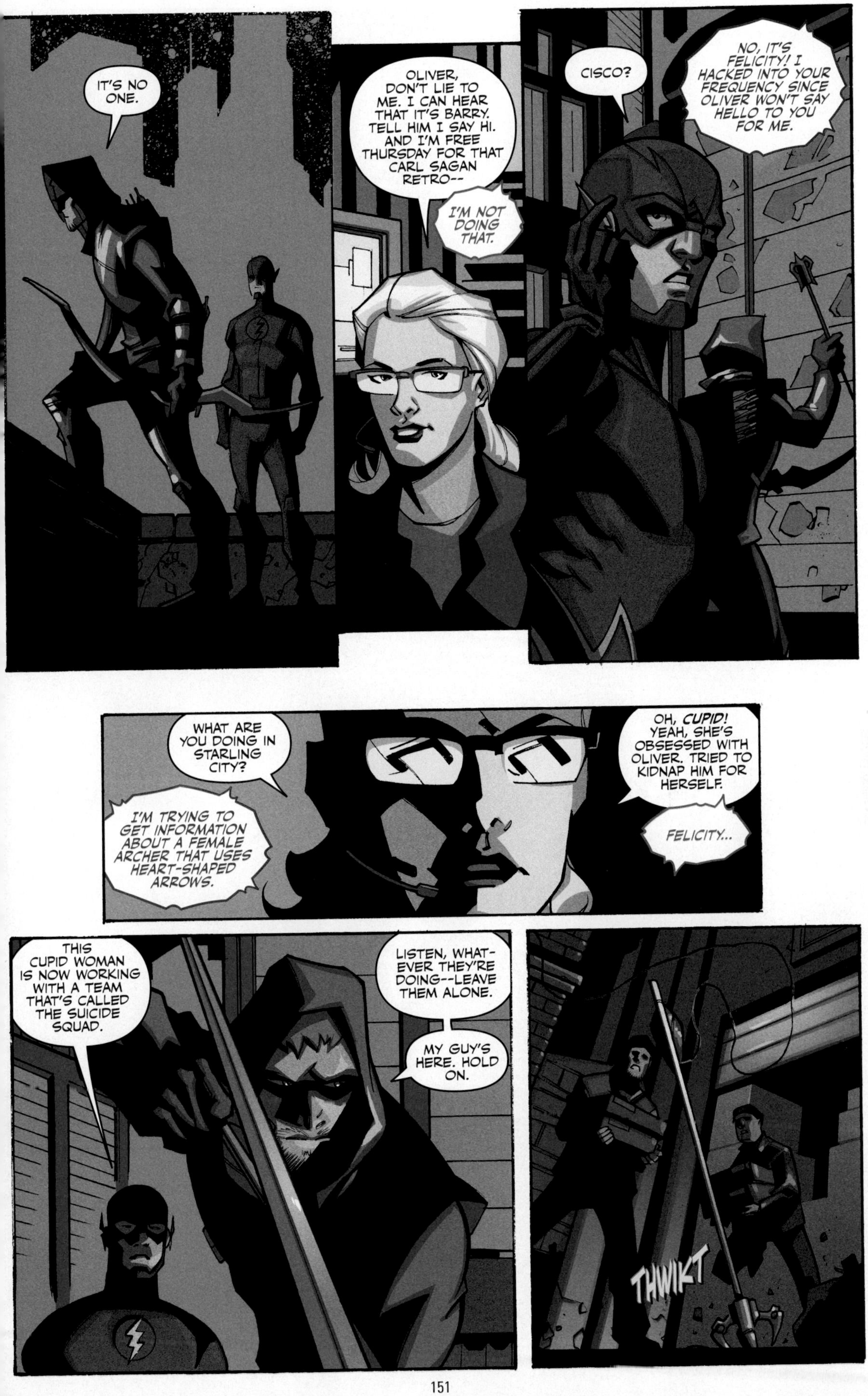
IT'S NO ONE.
OLIVER, DON'T LIE TO ME. I CAN HEAR THAT IT'S BARRY. TELL HIM I SAY HI. AND I'M FREE THURSDAY FOR THAT CARL SAGAN RETRO--
I'M NOT DOING THAT.
CISCO?
NO, IT'S FELICITY! I HACKED INTO YOUR FREQUENCY SINCE OLIVER WON'T SAY HELLO TO YOU FOR ME.
WHAT ARE YOU DOING IN STARLING CITY?
I'M TRYING TO GET INFORMATION ABOUT A FEMALE ARCHER THAT USES HEART-SHAPED ARROWS.
OH, CUPID! YEAH, SHE'S OBSESSED WITH OLIVER. TRIED TO KIDNAP HIM FOR HERSELF.
FELICITY...
THIS CUPID WOMAN IS NOW WORKING WITH A TEAM THAT'S CALLED THE SUICIDE SQUAD.
LISTEN, WHATEVER THEY'RE DOING--LEAVE THEM ALONE.
MY GUY'S HERE. HOLD ON.
THWIKT

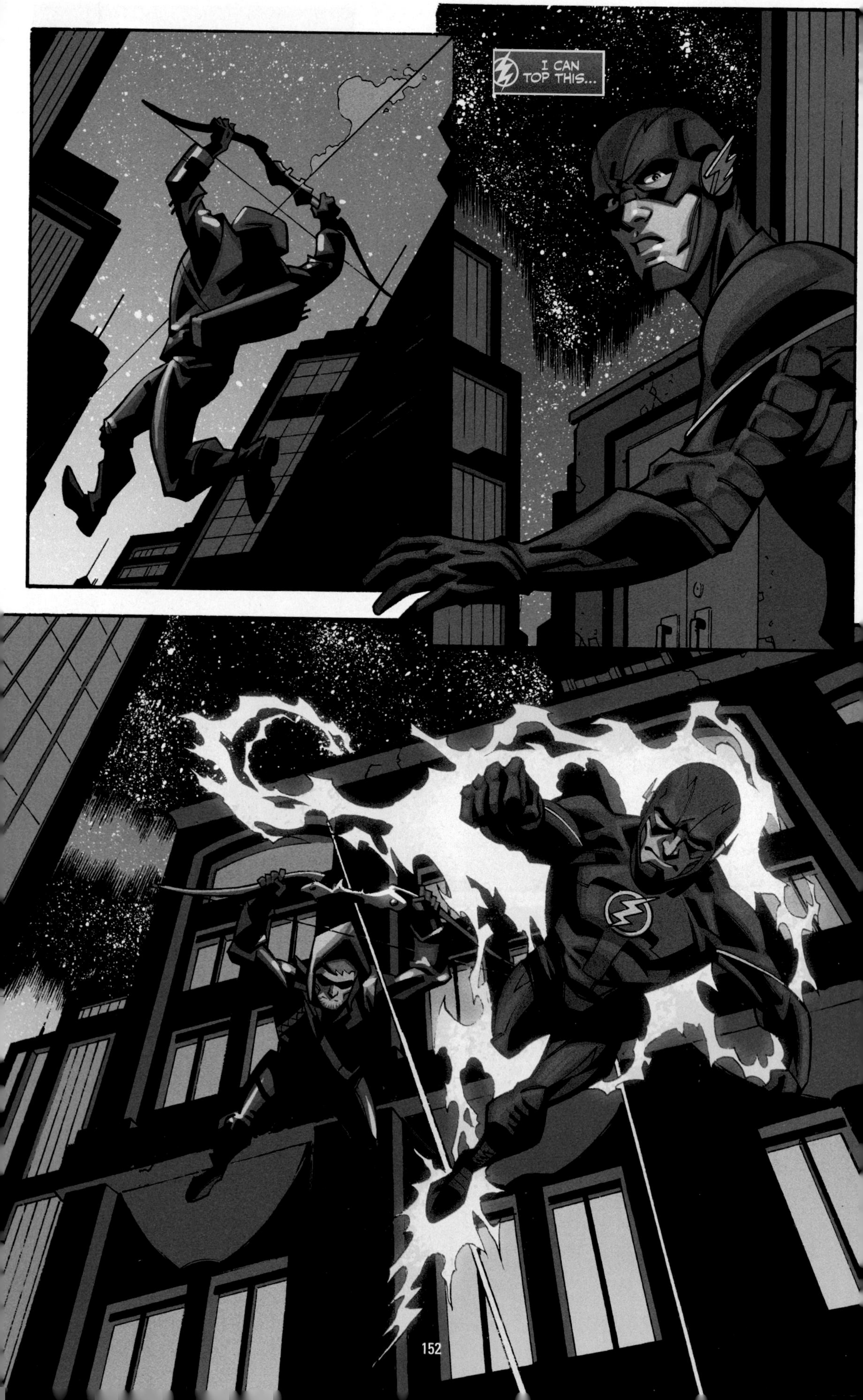
I CAN TOP THIS...

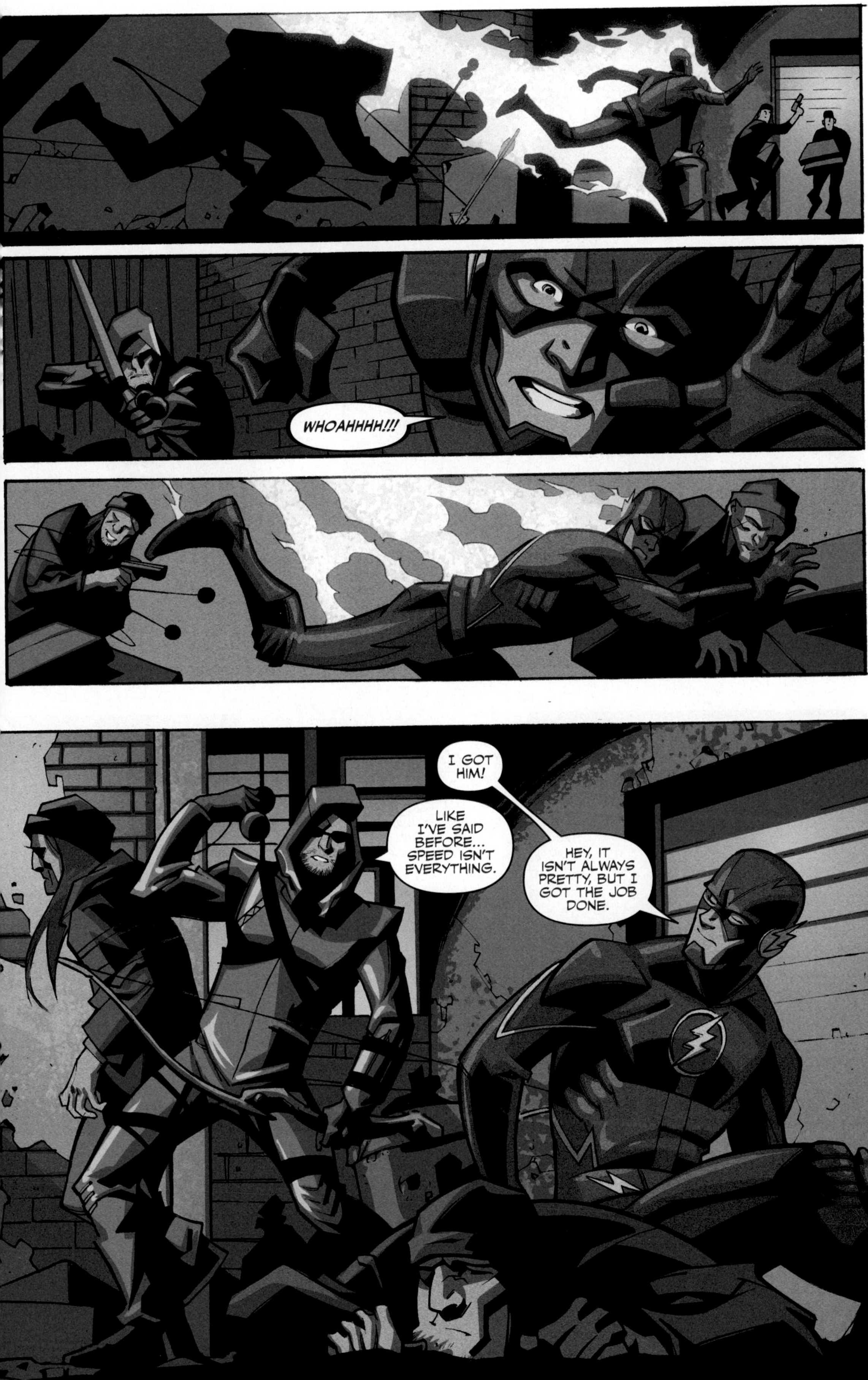
WHOAHHHH!!!
I GOT HIM!
LIKE I'VE SAID BEFORE... SPEED ISN'T EVERYTHING.
HEY, IT ISN'T ALWAYS PRETTY, BUT I GOT THE JOB DONE.

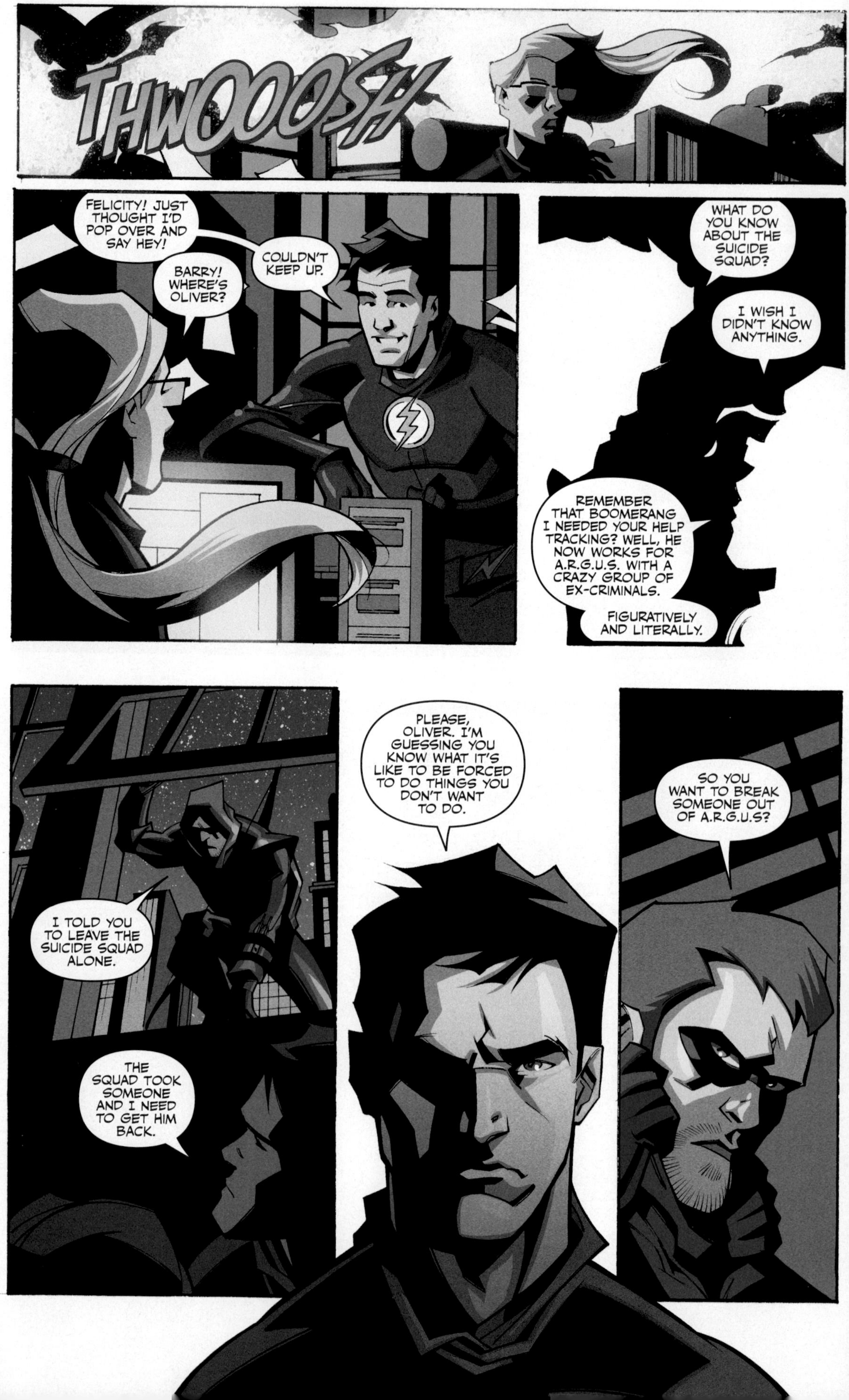
THWOOOSH
FELICITY! JUST THOUGHT I'D POP OVER AND SAY HEY!
BARRY! WHERE'S OLIVER?
COULDN'T KEEP UP.
WHAT DO YOU KNOW ABOUT THE SUICIDE SQUAD?
I WISH I DIDN'T KNOW ANYTHING.
REMEMBER THAT BOOMERANG I NEEDED YOUR HELP TRACKING? WELL, HE NOW WORKS FOR A.R.G.U.S. WITH A CRAZY GROUP OF EX-CRIMINALS.
FIGURATIVELY AND LITERALLY.
I TOLD YOU TO LEAVE THE SUICIDE SQUAD ALONE.
THE SQUAD TOOK SOMEONE AND I NEED TO GET HIM BACK.
PLEASE, OLIVER. I'M GUESSING YOU KNOW WHAT IT'S LIKE TO BE FORCED TO DO THINGS YOU DON'T WANT TO DO.
SO YOU WANT TO BREAK SOMEONE OUT OF A.R.G.U.S?

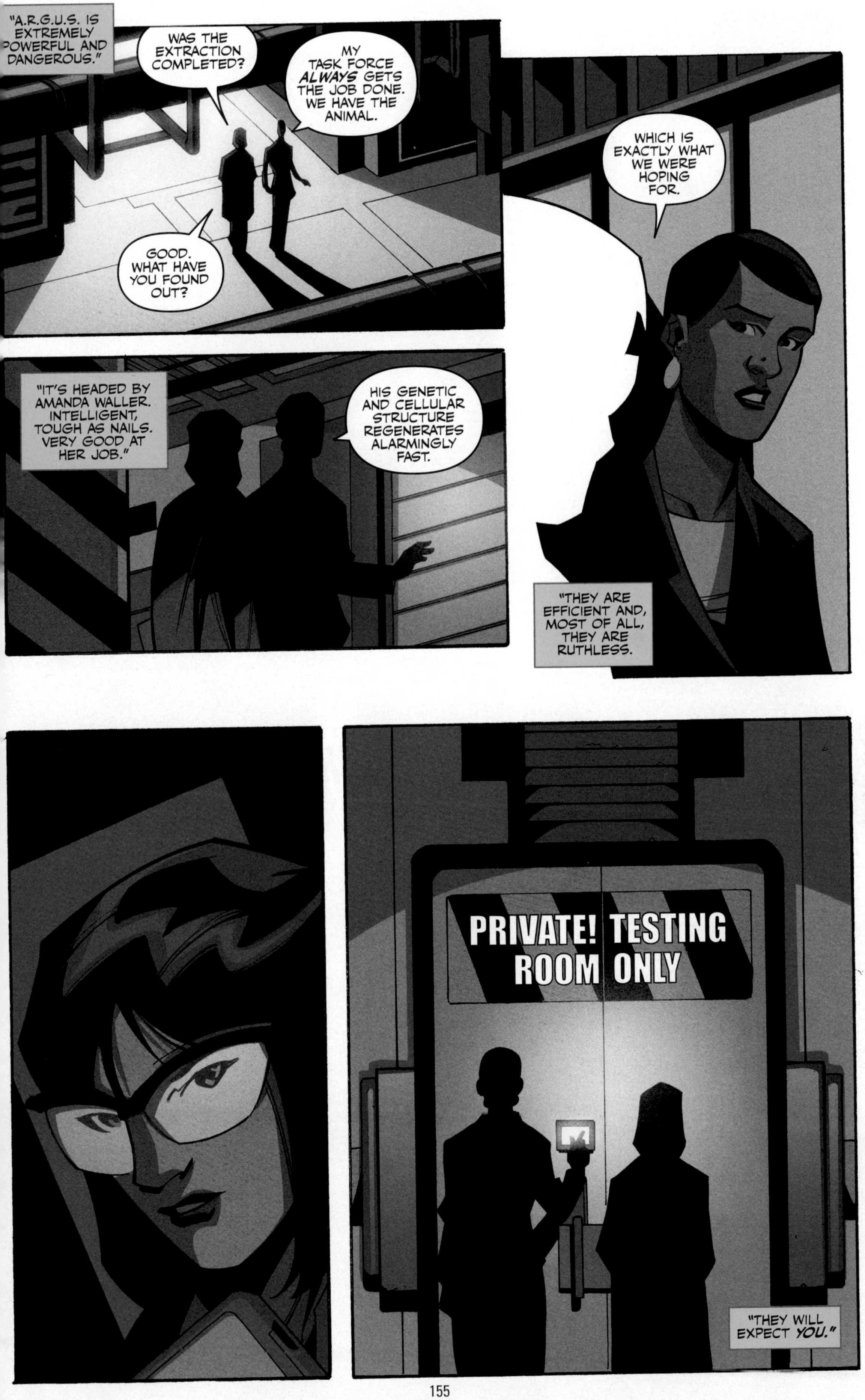
"A.R.G.U.S. IS EXTREMELY POWERFUL AND DANGEROUS."
WAS THE EXTRACTION COMPLETED?
MY TASK FORCE *ALWAYS* GETS THE JOB DONE. WE HAVE THE ANIMAL.
GOOD. WHAT HAVE YOU FOUND OUT?
WHICH IS EXACTLY WHAT WE WERE HOPING FOR.
"IT'S HEADED BY AMANDA WALLER. INTELLIGENT, TOUGH AS NAILS. VERY GOOD AT HER JOB."
HIS GENETIC AND CELLULAR STRUCTURE REGENERATES ALARMINGLY FAST.
"THEY ARE EFFICIENT AND, MOST OF ALL, THEY ARE RUTHLESS.
PRIVATE! TESTING ROOM ONLY
"THEY WILL EXPECT *YOU*."

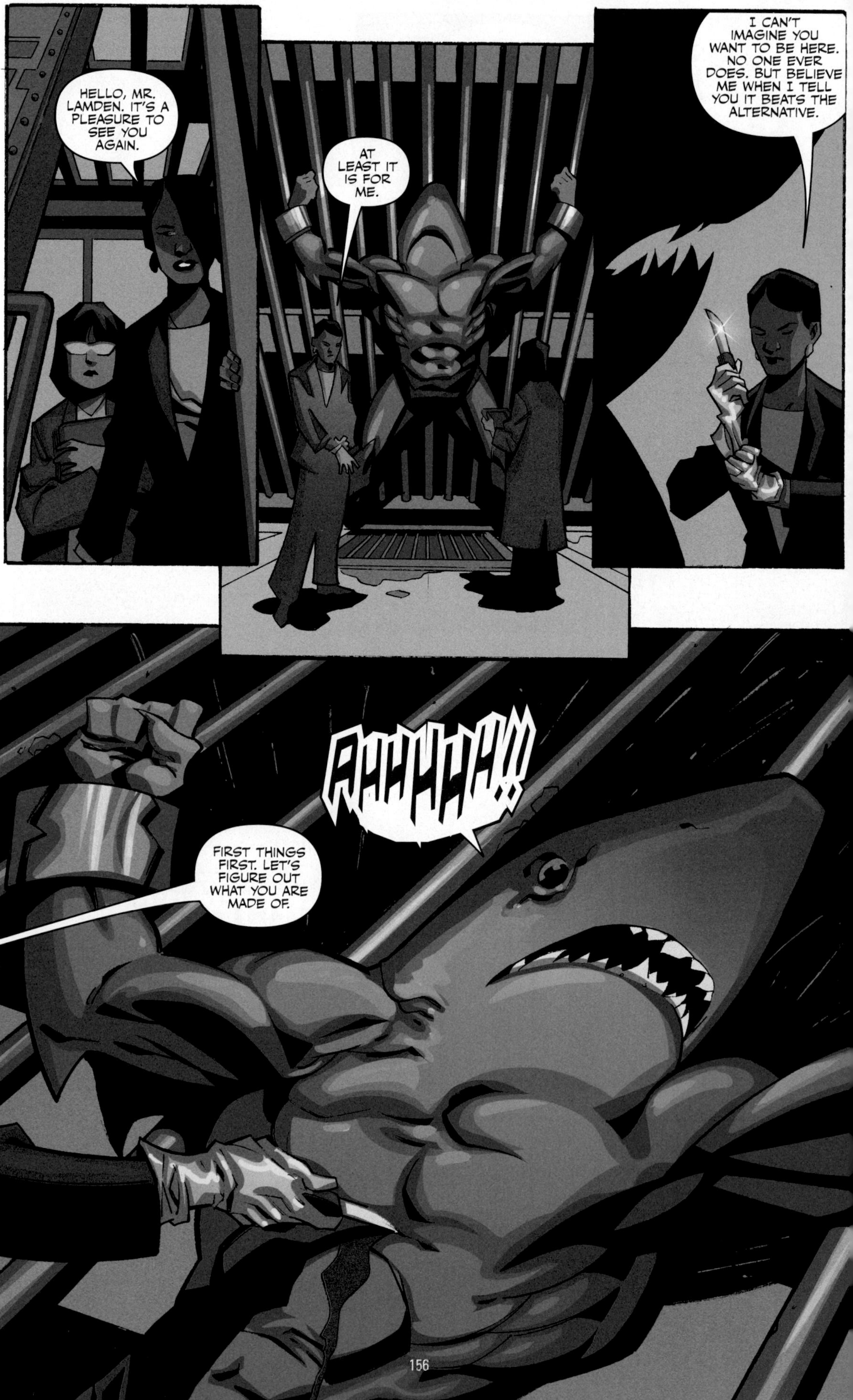
HELLO, MR. LAMDEN. IT'S A PLEASURE TO SEE YOU AGAIN.
AT LEAST IT IS FOR ME.
I CAN'T IMAGINE YOU WANT TO BE HERE. NO ONE EVER DOES. BUT BELIEVE ME WHEN I TELL YOU IT BEATS THE ALTERNATIVE.
FIRST THINGS FIRST. LET'S FIGURE OUT WHAT YOU ARE MADE OF.

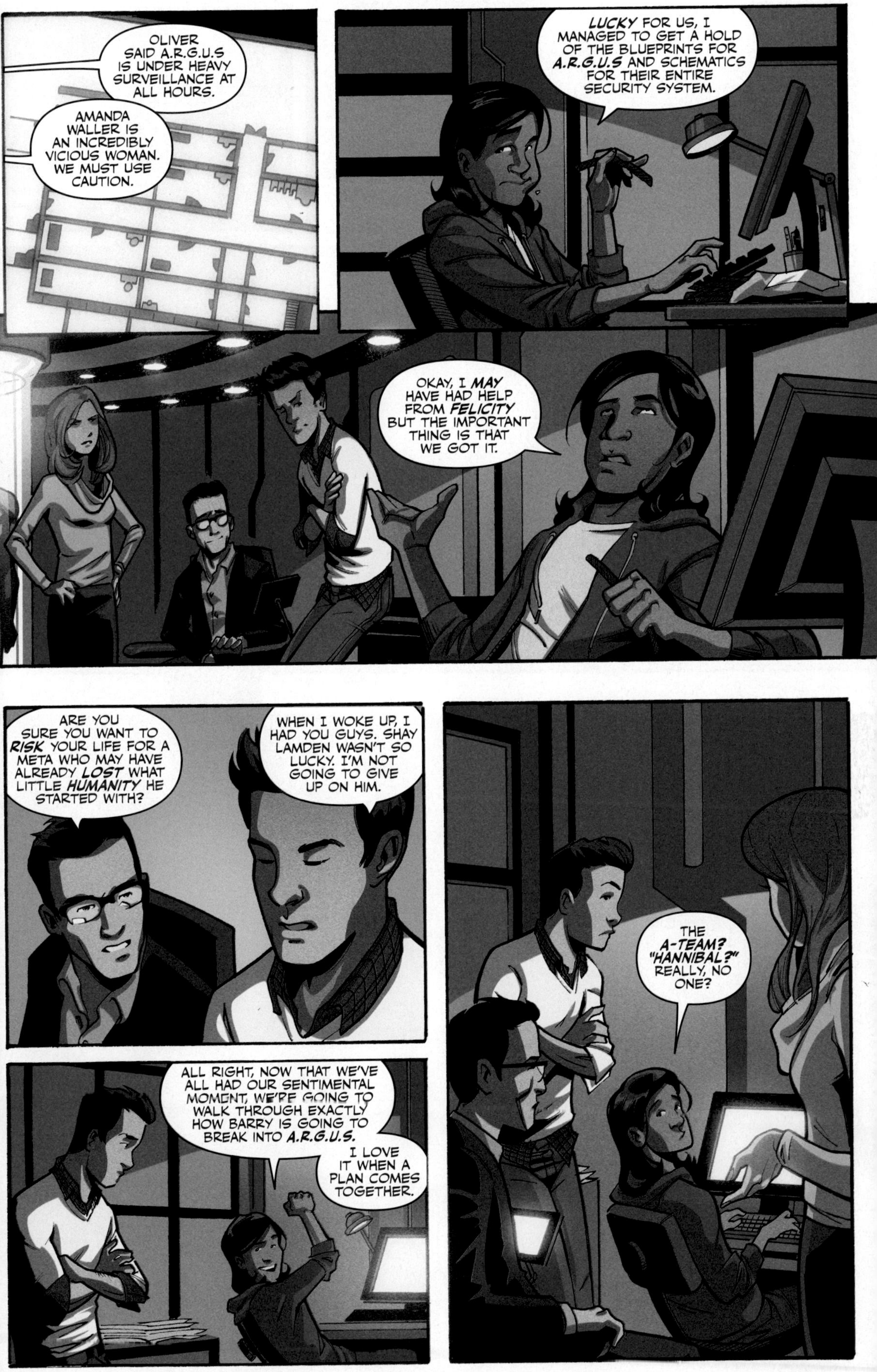
OLIVER SAID A.R.G.U.S IS UNDER HEAVY SURVEILLANCE AT ALL HOURS.
AMANDA WALLER IS AN INCREDIBLY VICIOUS WOMAN. WE MUST USE CAUTION.
LUCKY FOR US, I MANAGED TO GET A HOLD OF THE BLUEPRINTS FOR A.R.G.U.S AND SCHEMATICS FOR THEIR ENTIRE SECURITY SYSTEM.
OKAY, I MAY HAVE HAD HELP FROM FELICITY BUT THE IMPORTANT THING IS THAT WE GOT IT.
ARE YOU SURE YOU WANT TO RISK YOUR LIFE FOR A META WHO MAY HAVE ALREADY LOST WHAT LITTLE HUMANITY HE STARTED WITH?
WHEN I WOKE UP, I HAD YOU GUYS. SHAY LAMDEN WASN'T SO LUCKY. I'M NOT GOING TO GIVE UP ON HIM.
ALL RIGHT, NOW THAT WE'VE ALL HAD OUR SENTIMENTAL MOMENT, WE'RE GOING TO WALK THROUGH EXACTLY HOW BARRY IS GOING TO BREAK INTO A.R.G.U.S.
I LOVE IT WHEN A PLAN COMES TOGETHER.
THE A-TEAM? "HANNIBAL?" REALLY, NO ONE?

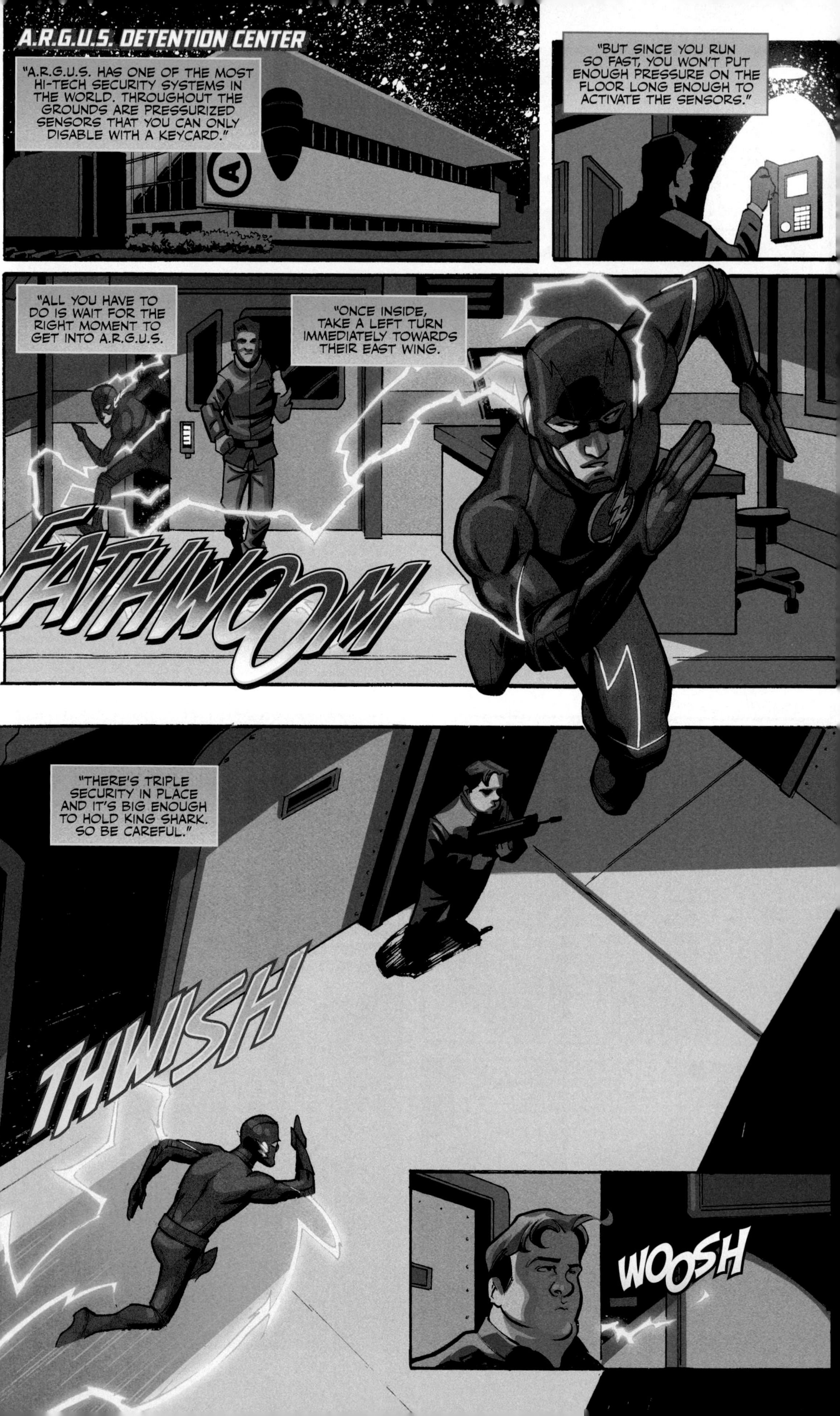
A.R.G.U.S. DETENTION CENTER
"A.R.G.U.S. HAS ONE OF THE MOST HI-TECH SECURITY SYSTEMS IN THE WORLD. THROUGHOUT THE GROUNDS ARE PRESSURIZED SENSORS THAT YOU CAN ONLY DISABLE WITH A KEYCARD."
"BUT SINCE YOU RUN SO FAST, YOU WON'T PUT ENOUGH PRESSURE ON THE FLOOR LONG ENOUGH TO ACTIVATE THE SENSORS."
"ALL YOU HAVE TO DO IS WAIT FOR THE RIGHT MOMENT TO GET INTO A.R.G.U.S.
"ONCE INSIDE, TAKE A LEFT TURN IMMEDIATELY TOWARDS THEIR EAST WING.
FATHWOOM
"THERE'S TRIPLE SECURITY IN PLACE AND IT'S BIG ENOUGH TO HOLD KING SHARK. SO BE CAREFUL."
THWISH
WOOSH

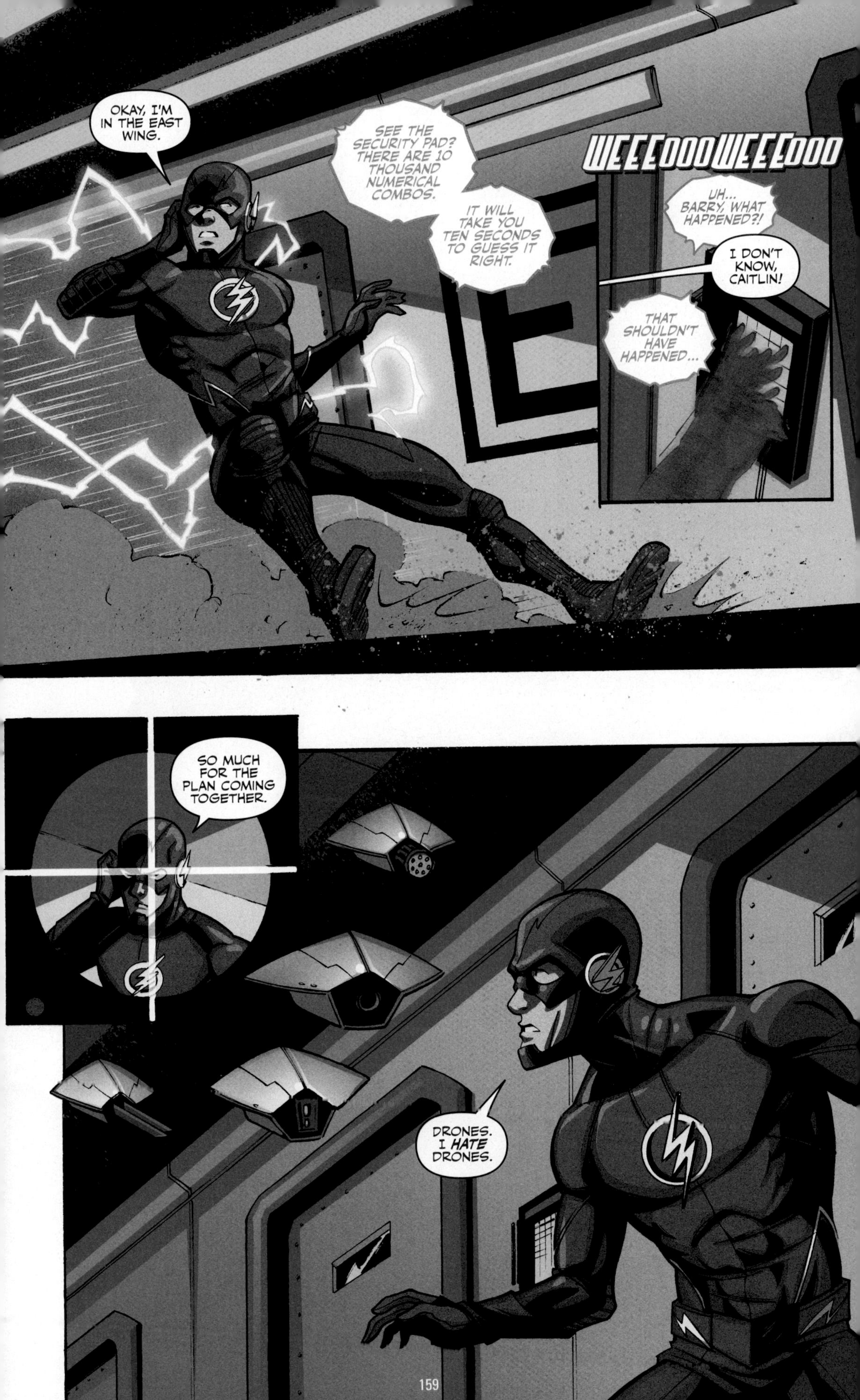
OKAY, I'M IN THE EAST WING.
SEE THE SECURITY PAD? THERE ARE 10 THOUSAND NUMERICAL COMBOS.
IT WILL TAKE YOU TEN SECONDS TO GUESS IT RIGHT.
WEEEOOOWEEEOOO
UH... BARRY, WHAT HAPPENED?!
I DON'T KNOW, CAITLIN!
THAT SHOULDN'T HAVE HAPPENED...
SO MUCH FOR THE PLAN COMING TOGETHER.
DRONES. I HATE DRONES.

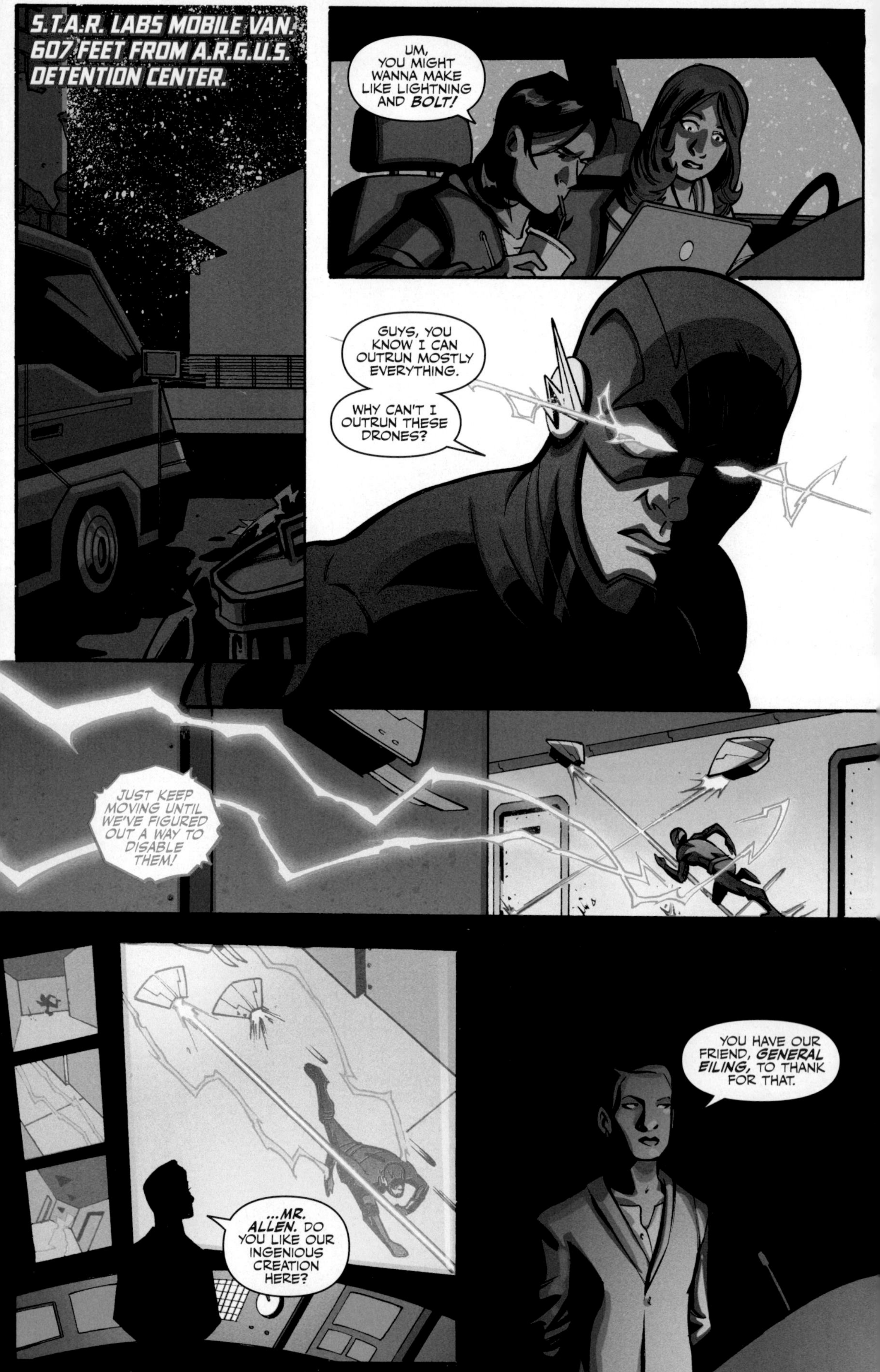
S.T.A.R. LABS MOBILE VAN. 607 FEET FROM A.R.G.U.S. DETENTION CENTER.
UM, YOU MIGHT WANNA MAKE LIKE LIGHTNING AND *BOLT!*
GUYS, YOU KNOW I CAN OUTRUN MOSTLY EVERYTHING.
WHY CAN'T I OUTRUN THESE DRONES?
JUST KEEP MOVING UNTIL WE'VE FIGURED OUT A WAY TO DISABLE THEM!
...*MR. ALLEN.* DO YOU LIKE OUR INGENIOUS CREATION HERE?
YOU HAVE OUR FRIEND, *GENERAL EILING,* TO THANK FOR THAT.

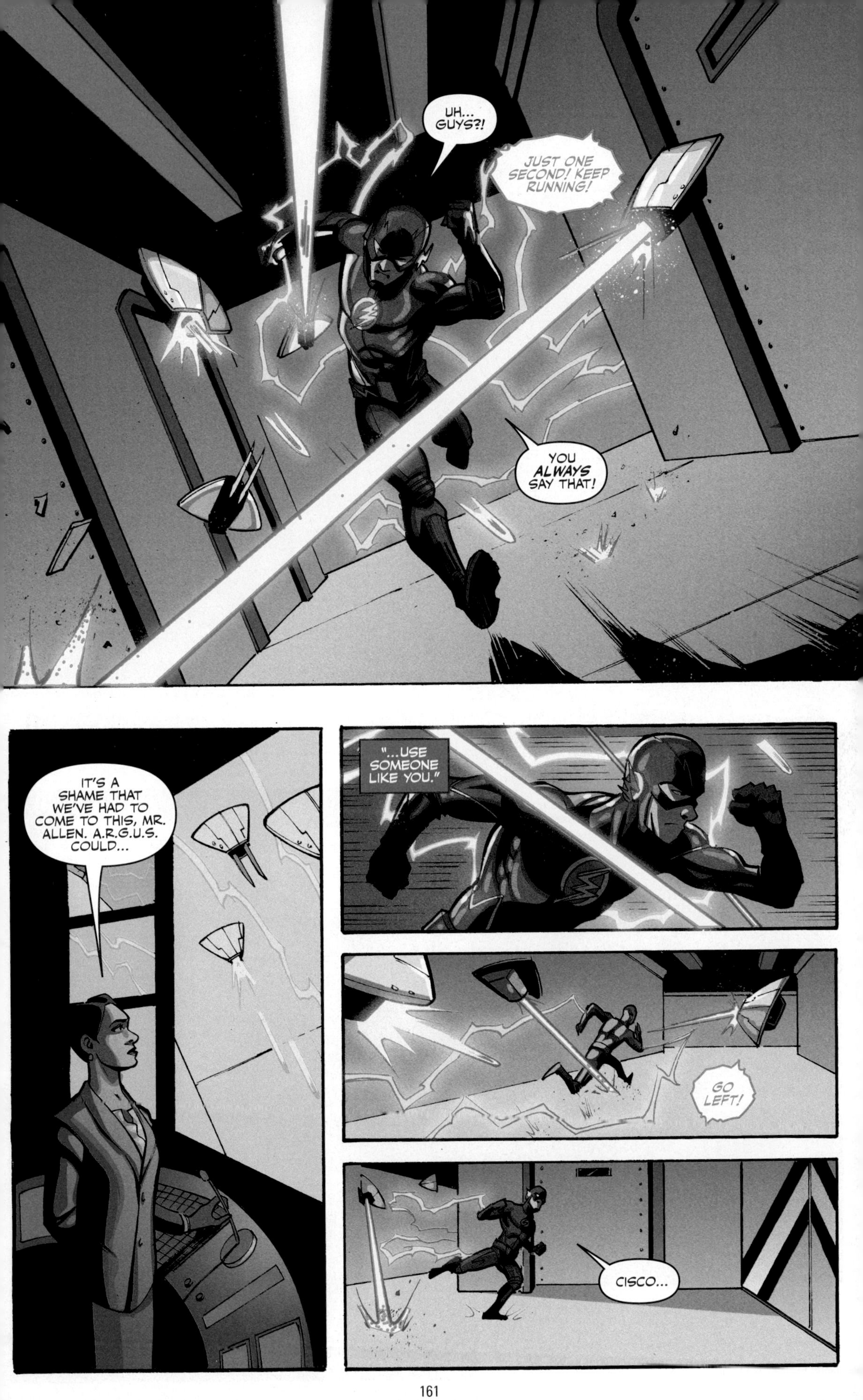
UH... GUYS?!
JUST ONE SECOND! KEEP RUNNING!
YOU ALWAYS SAY THAT!
IT'S A SHAME THAT WE'VE HAD TO COME TO THIS, MR. ALLEN. A.R.G.U.S. COULD...
"...USE SOMEONE LIKE YOU."
GO LEFT!
CISCO...

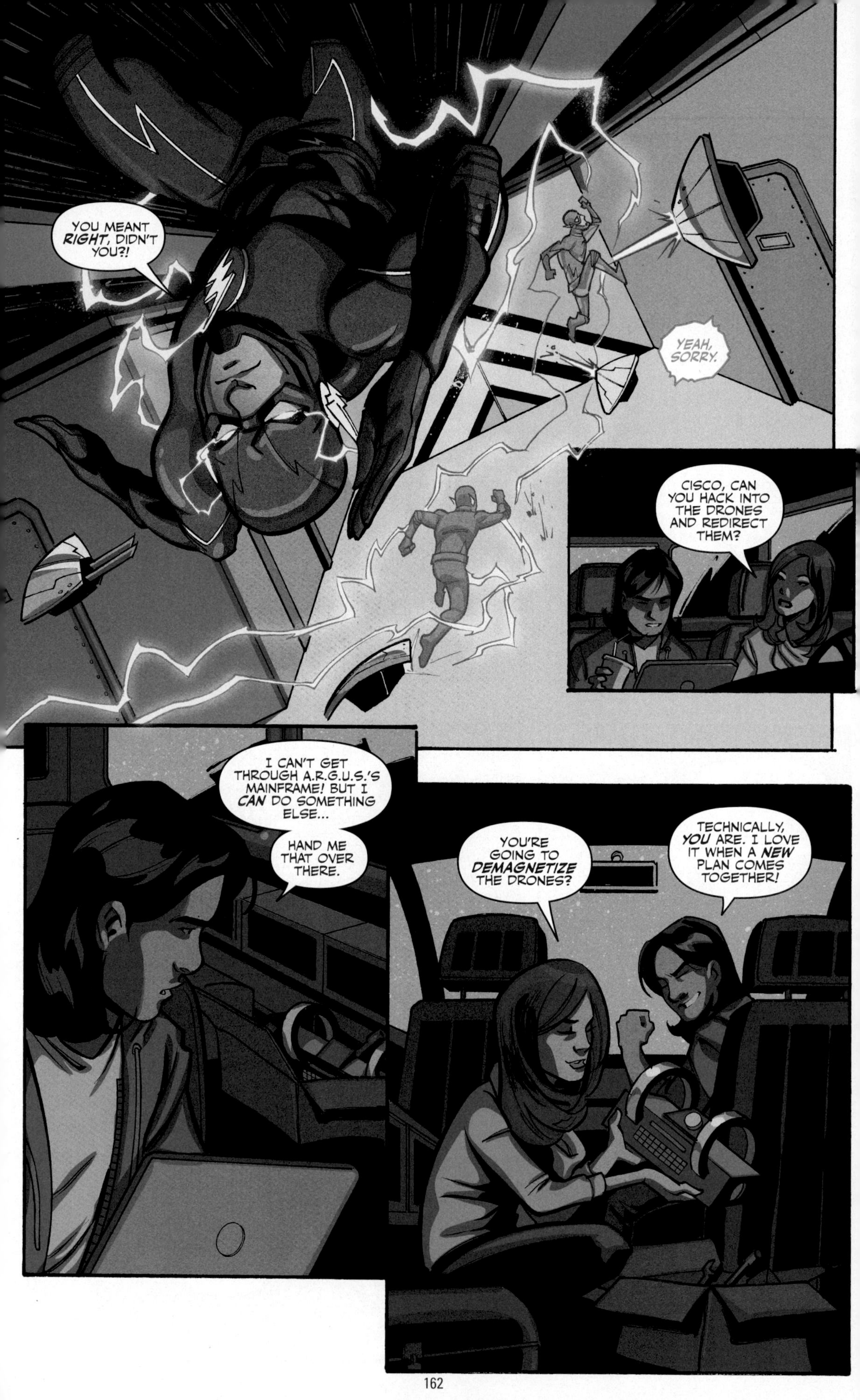
YOU MEANT RIGHT, DIDN'T YOU?!
YEAH, SORRY.
CISCO, CAN YOU HACK INTO THE DRONES AND REDIRECT THEM?
I CAN'T GET THROUGH A.R.G.U.S.'S MAINFRAME! BUT I CAN DO SOMETHING ELSE...
HAND ME THAT OVER THERE.
YOU'RE GOING TO DEMAGNETIZE THE DRONES?
TECHNICALLY, YOU ARE. I LOVE IT WHEN A NEW PLAN COMES TOGETHER!

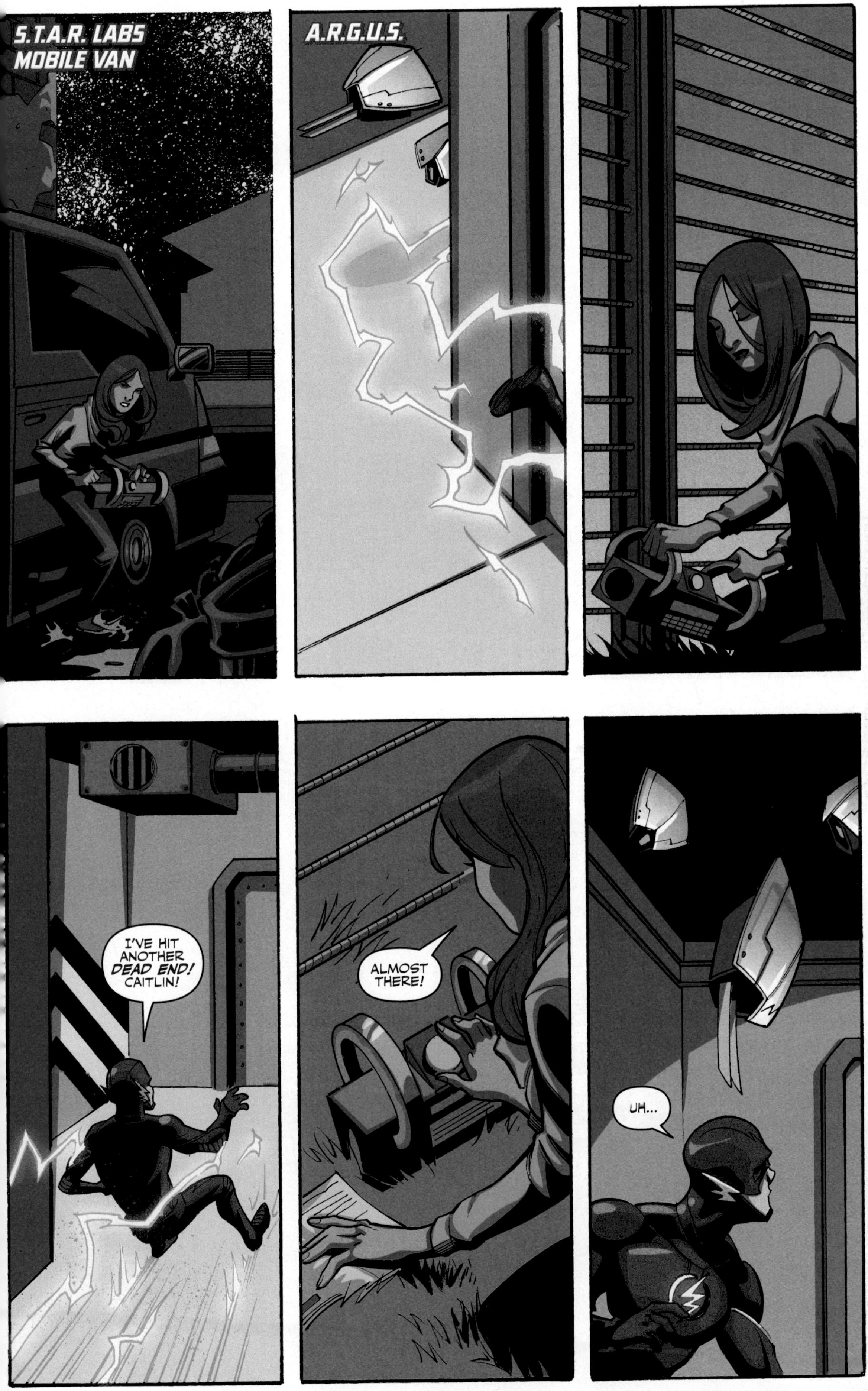
S.T.A.R. LABS MOBILE VAN
A.R.G.U.S.
I'VE HIT ANOTHER DEAD END! CAITLIN!
ALMOST THERE!
UH...

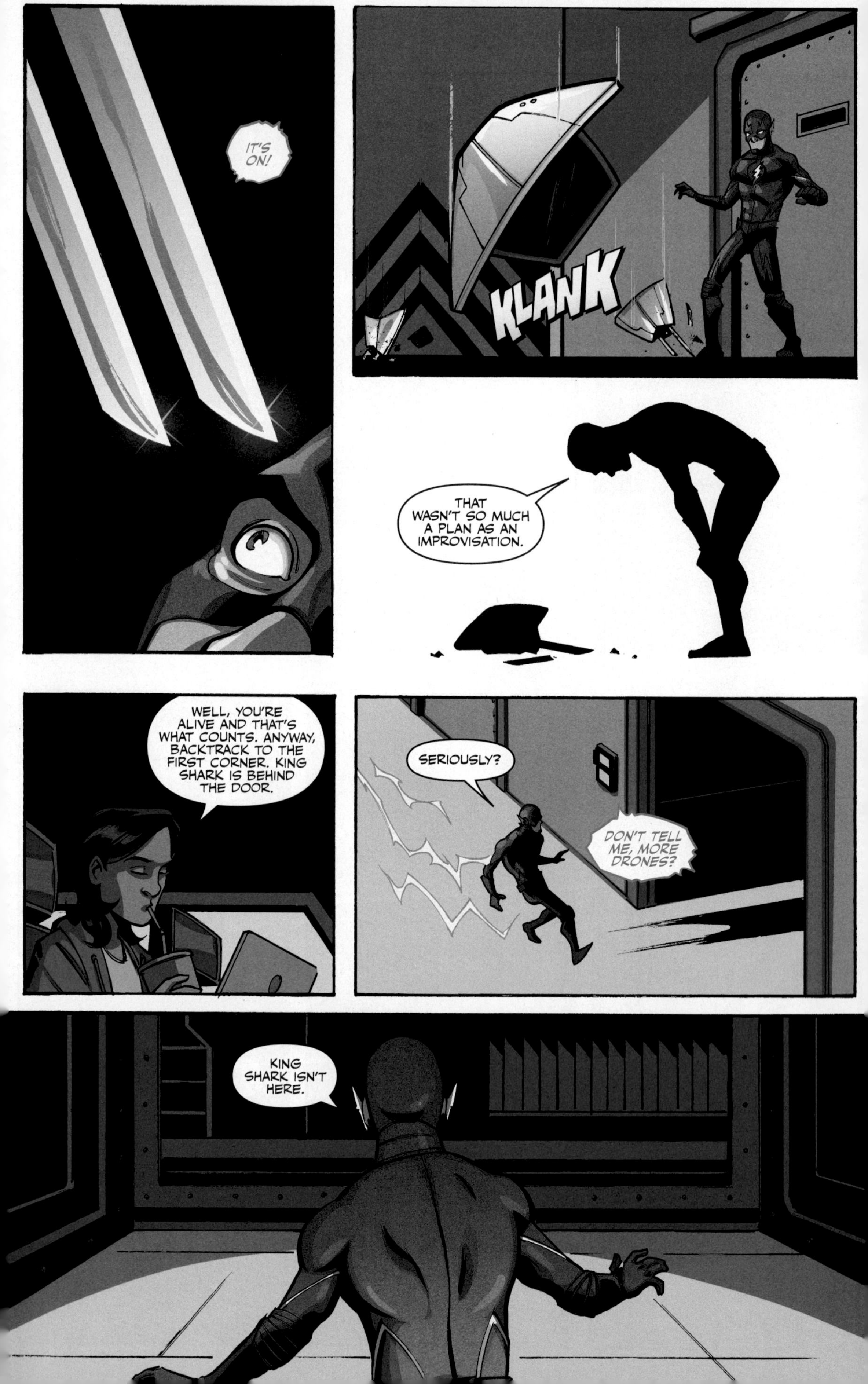
IT'S ON!
KLANK
THAT WASN'T SO MUCH A PLAN AS AN IMPROVISATION.
WELL, YOU'RE ALIVE AND THAT'S WHAT COUNTS. ANYWAY, BACKTRACK TO THE FIRST CORNER. KING SHARK IS BEHIND THE DOOR.
SERIOUSLY?
DON'T TELL ME, MORE DRONES?
KING SHARK ISN'T HERE.

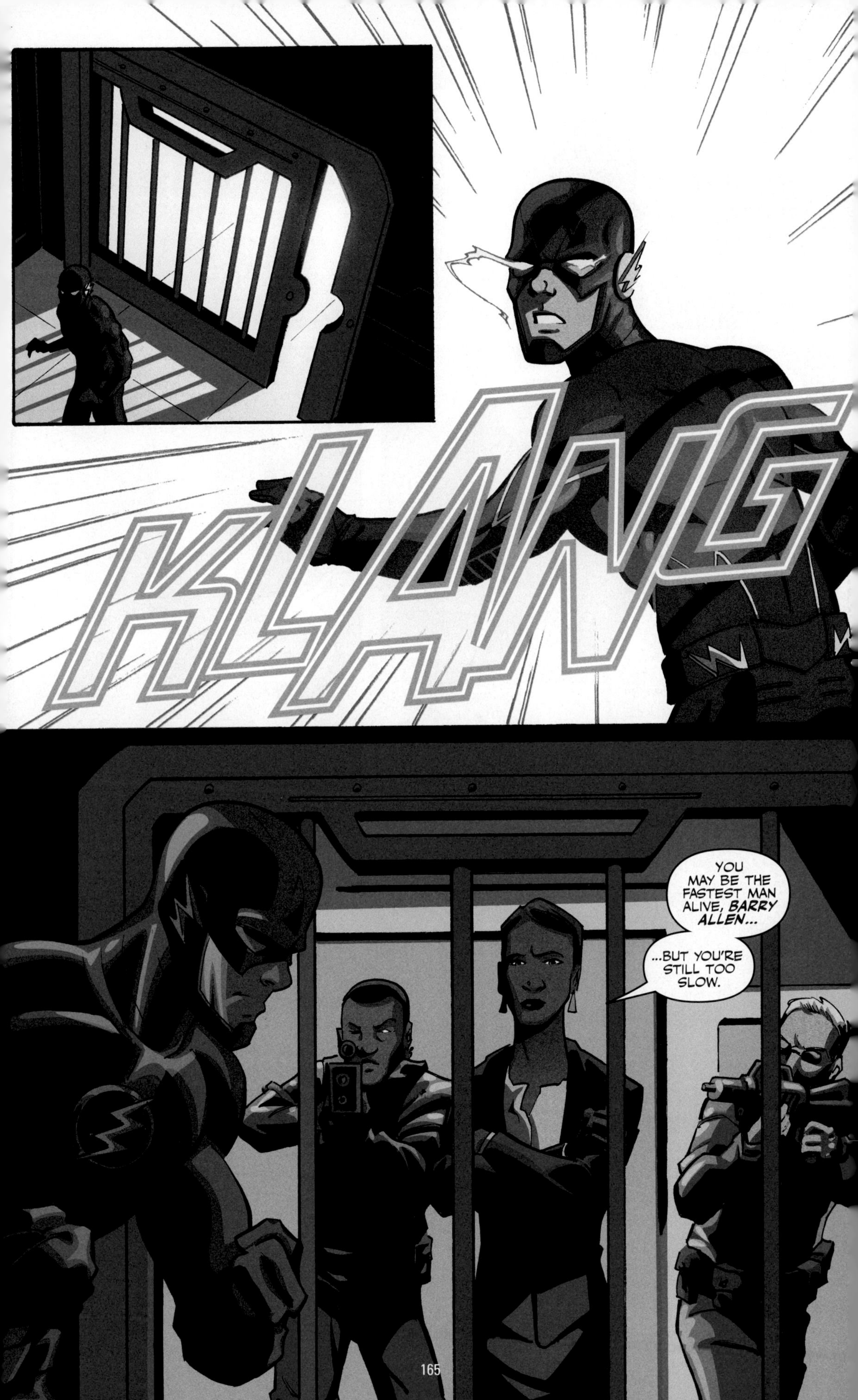
KLANG
YOU MAY BE THE FASTEST MAN ALIVE, BARRY ALLEN...
...BUT YOU'RE STILL TOO SLOW.

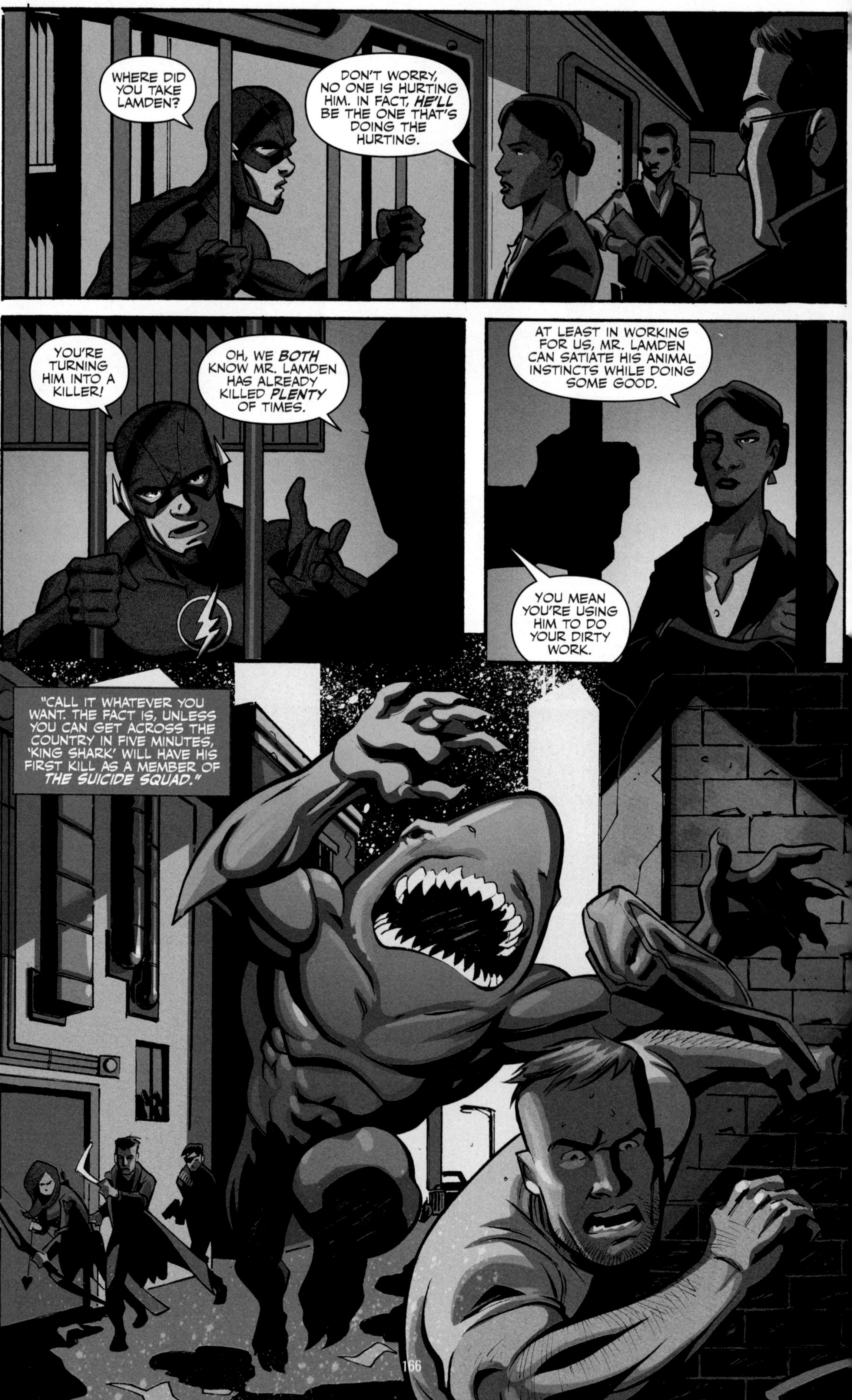

WHERE DID YOU TAKE LAMDEN?
DON'T WORRY, NO ONE IS HURTING HIM. IN FACT, HE'LL BE THE ONE THAT'S DOING THE HURTING.
YOU'RE TURNING HIM INTO A KILLER!
OH, WE BOTH KNOW MR. LAMDEN HAS ALREADY KILLED PLENTY OF TIMES.
AT LEAST IN WORKING FOR US, MR. LAMDEN CAN SATIATE HIS ANIMAL INSTINCTS WHILE DOING SOME GOOD.
YOU MEAN YOU'RE USING HIM TO DO YOUR DIRTY WORK.
"CALL IT WHATEVER YOU WANT. THE FACT IS, UNLESS YOU CAN GET ACROSS THE COUNTRY IN FIVE MINUTES, 'KING SHARK' WILL HAVE HIS FIRST KILL AS A MEMBER OF THE SUICIDE SQUAD."

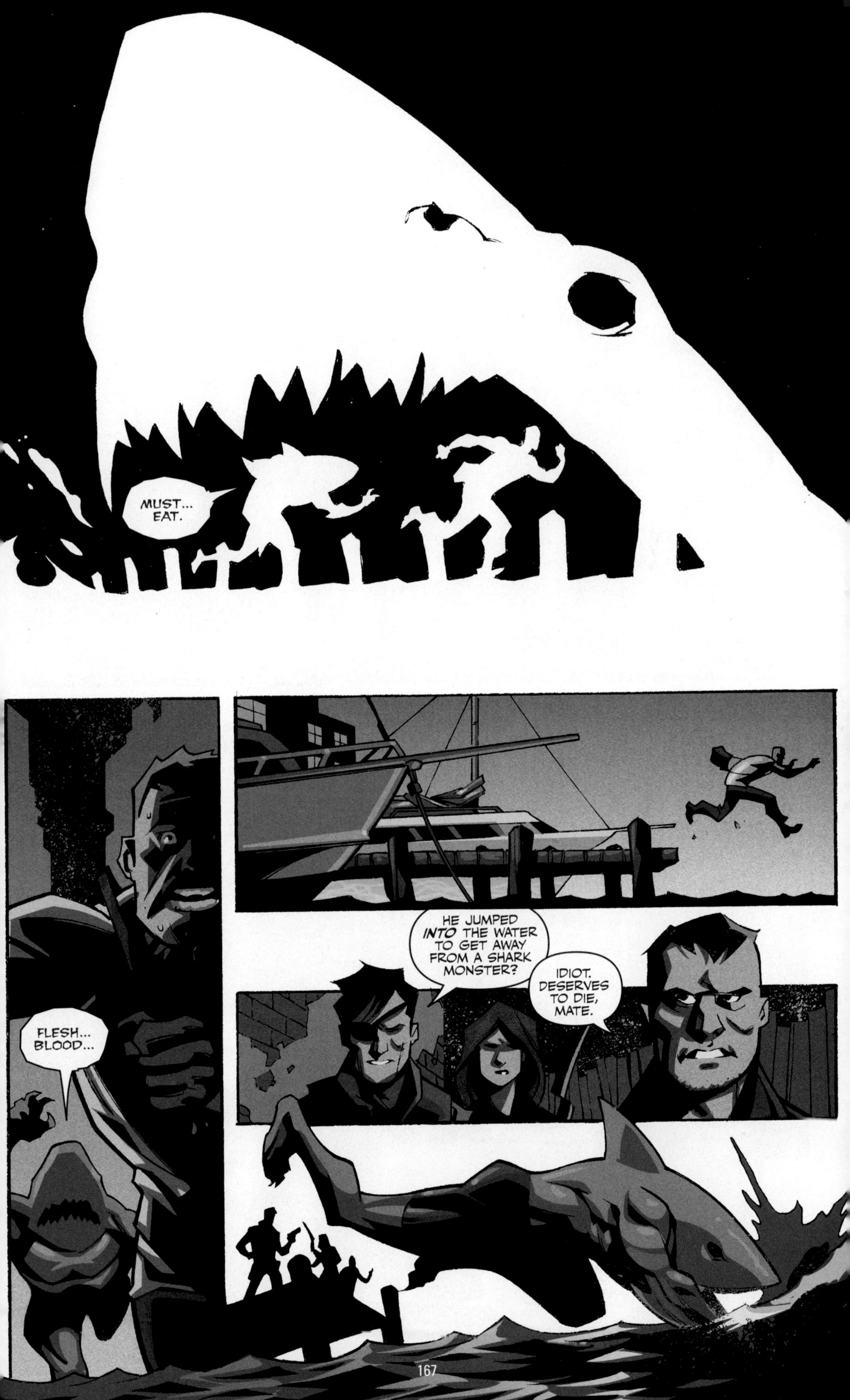
MUST... EAT.
FLESH... BLOOD...
HE JUMPED INTO THE WATER TO GET AWAY FROM A SHARK MONSTER?
IDIOT. DESERVES TO DIE, MATE.

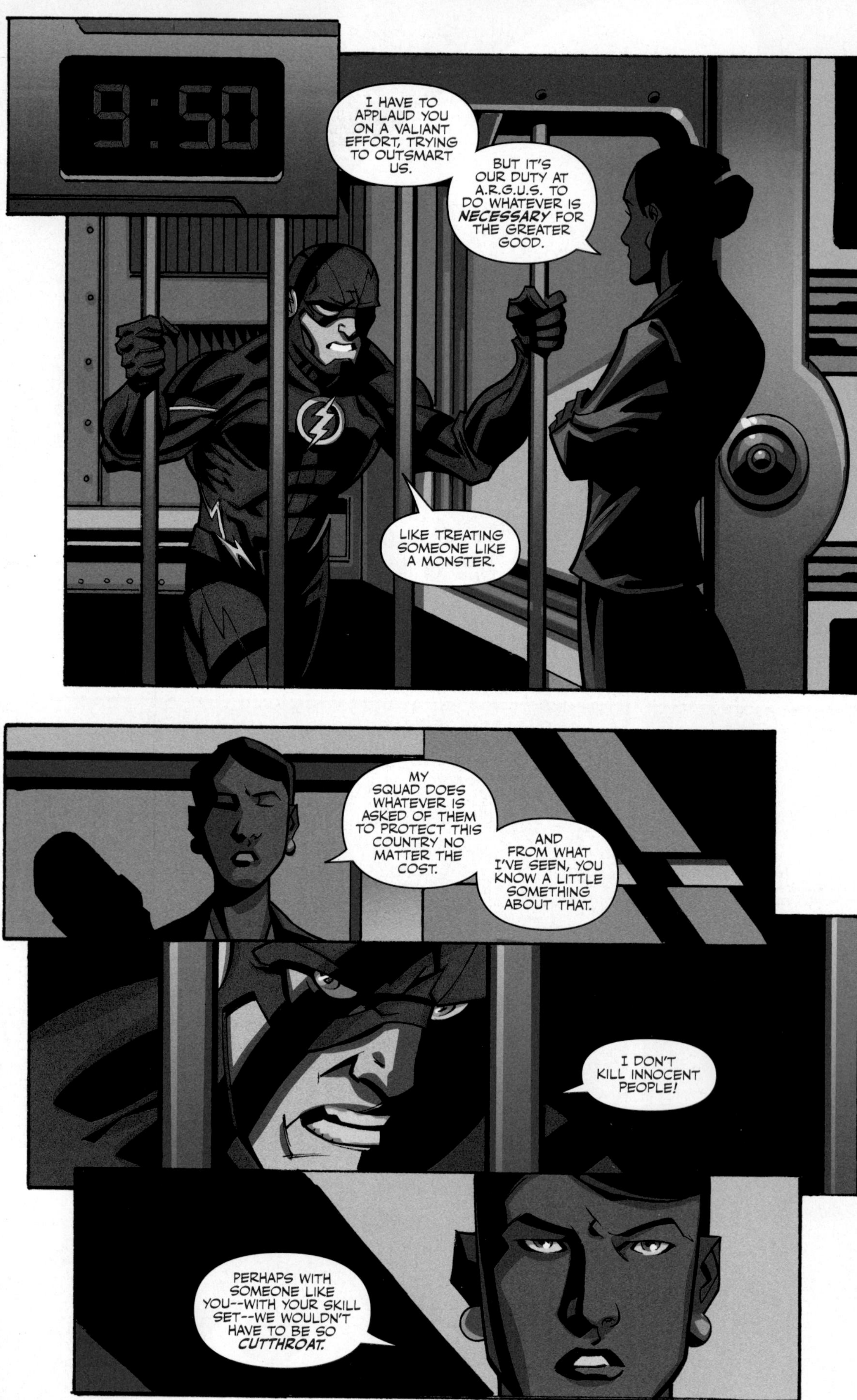
9:50
I HAVE TO APPLAUD YOU ON A VALIANT EFFORT, TRYING TO OUTSMART US.
BUT IT'S OUR DUTY AT A.R.G.U.S. TO DO WHATEVER IS NECESSARY FOR THE GREATER GOOD.
LIKE TREATING SOMEONE LIKE A MONSTER.
MY SQUAD DOES WHATEVER IS ASKED OF THEM TO PROTECT THIS COUNTRY NO MATTER THE COST.
AND FROM WHAT I'VE SEEN, YOU KNOW A LITTLE SOMETHING ABOUT THAT.
I DON'T KILL INNOCENT PEOPLE!
PERHAPS WITH SOMEONE LIKE YOU--WITH YOUR SKILL SET--WE WOULDN'T HAVE TO BE SO CUTTHROAT.

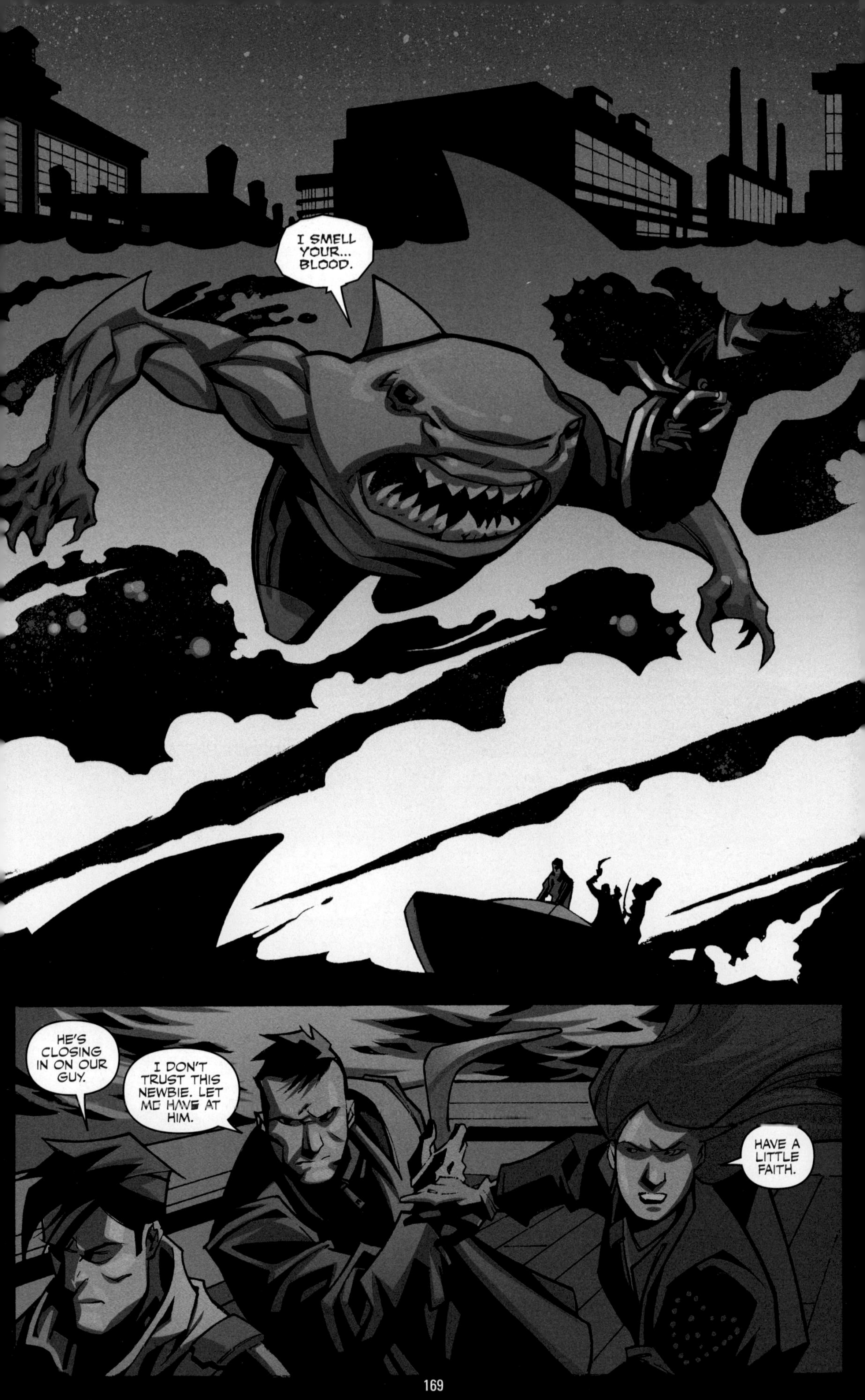

I SMELL YOUR... BLOOD.
HE'S CLOSING IN ON OUR GUY.
I DON'T TRUST THIS NEWBIE. LET ME HAVE AT HIM.
HAVE A LITTLE FAITH.

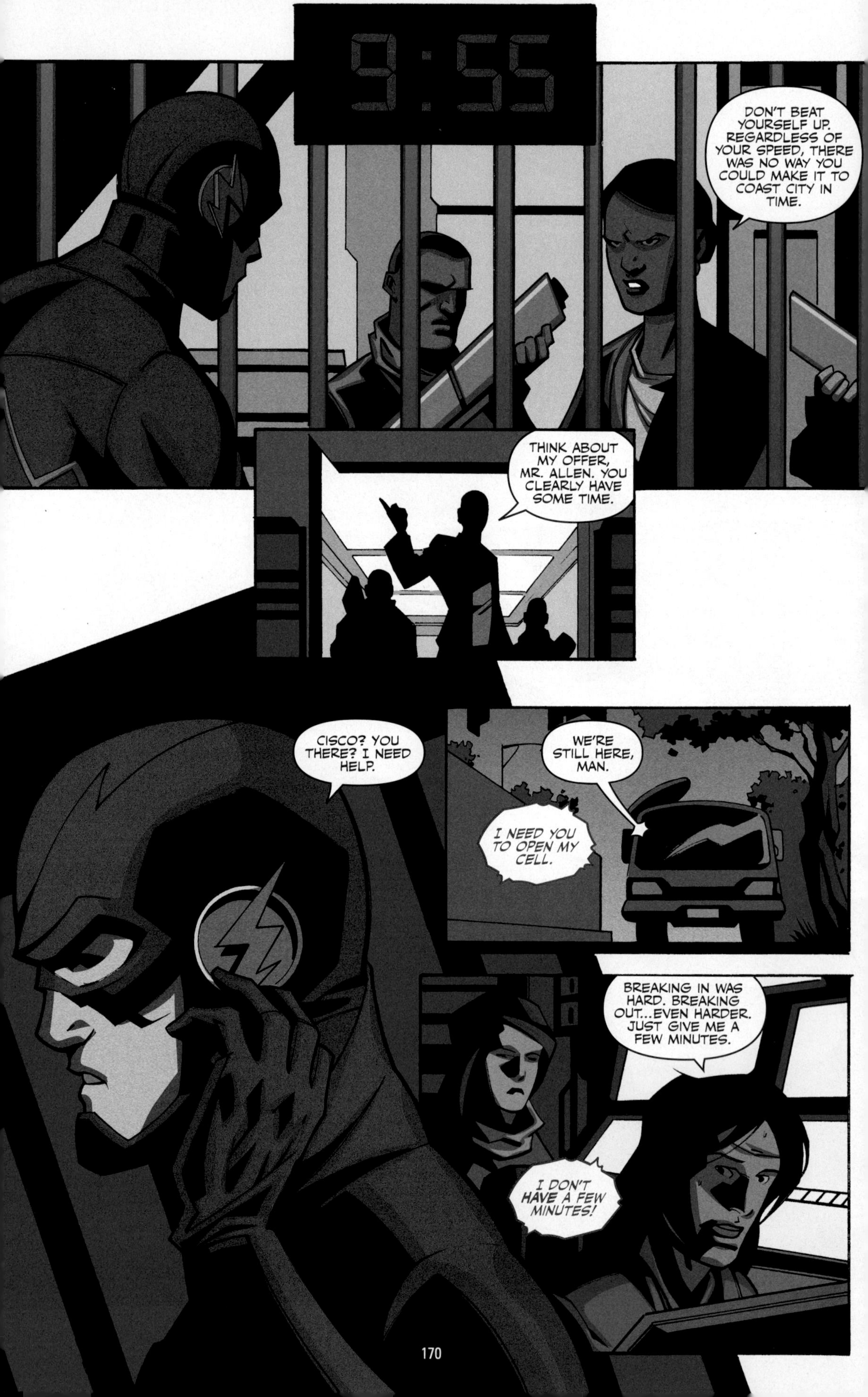
9:55
DON'T BEAT YOURSELF UP. REGARDLESS OF YOUR SPEED, THERE WAS NO WAY YOU COULD MAKE IT TO COAST CITY IN TIME.
THINK ABOUT MY OFFER, MR. ALLEN. YOU CLEARLY HAVE SOME TIME.
CISCO? YOU THERE? I NEED HELP.
WE'RE STILL HERE, MAN.
I NEED YOU TO OPEN MY CELL.
BREAKING IN WAS HARD. BREAKING OUT...EVEN HARDER. JUST GIVE ME A FEW MINUTES.
I DON'T HAVE A FEW MINUTES!

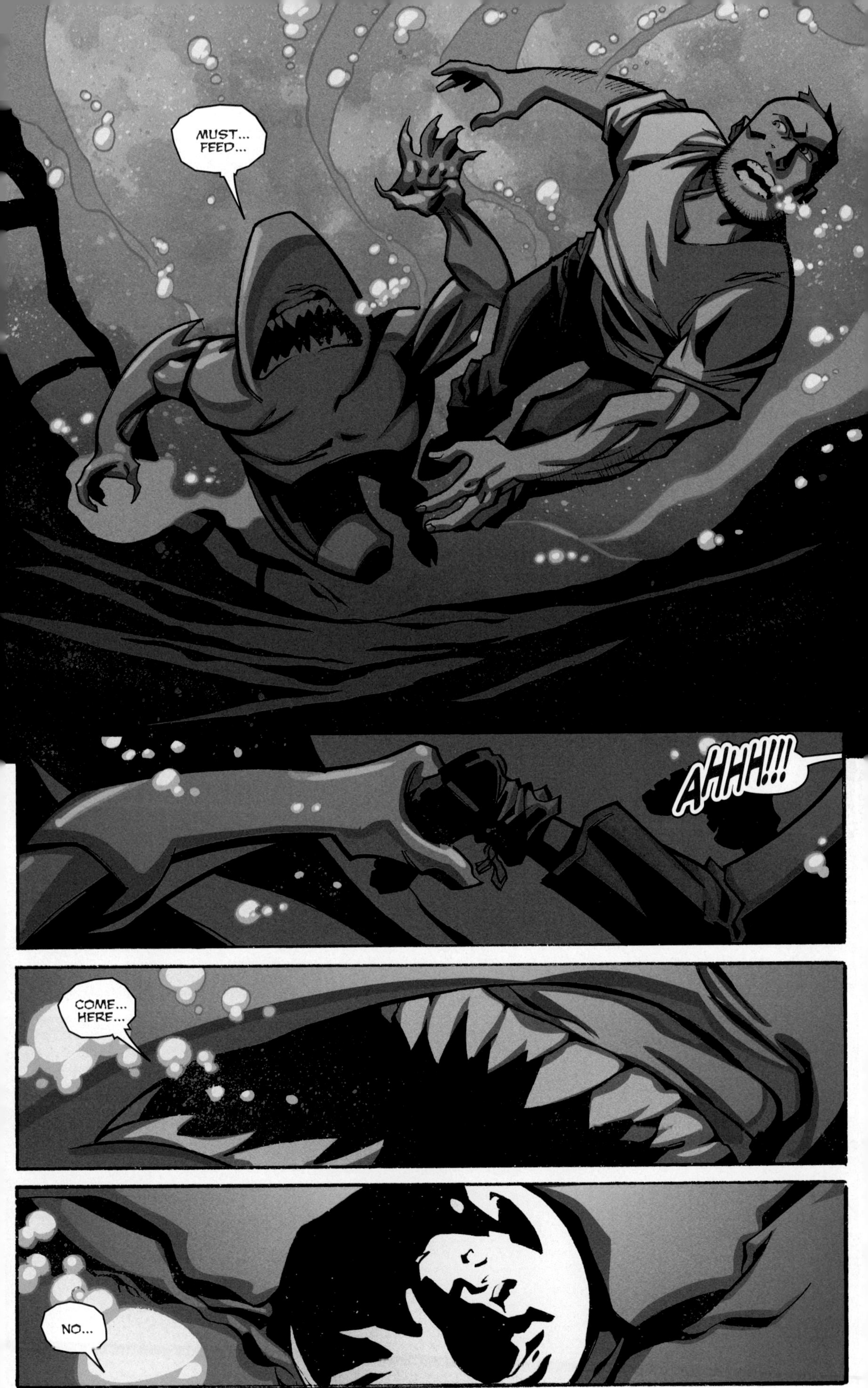
MUST... FEED...
AHHH!!!
COME... HERE...
NO...

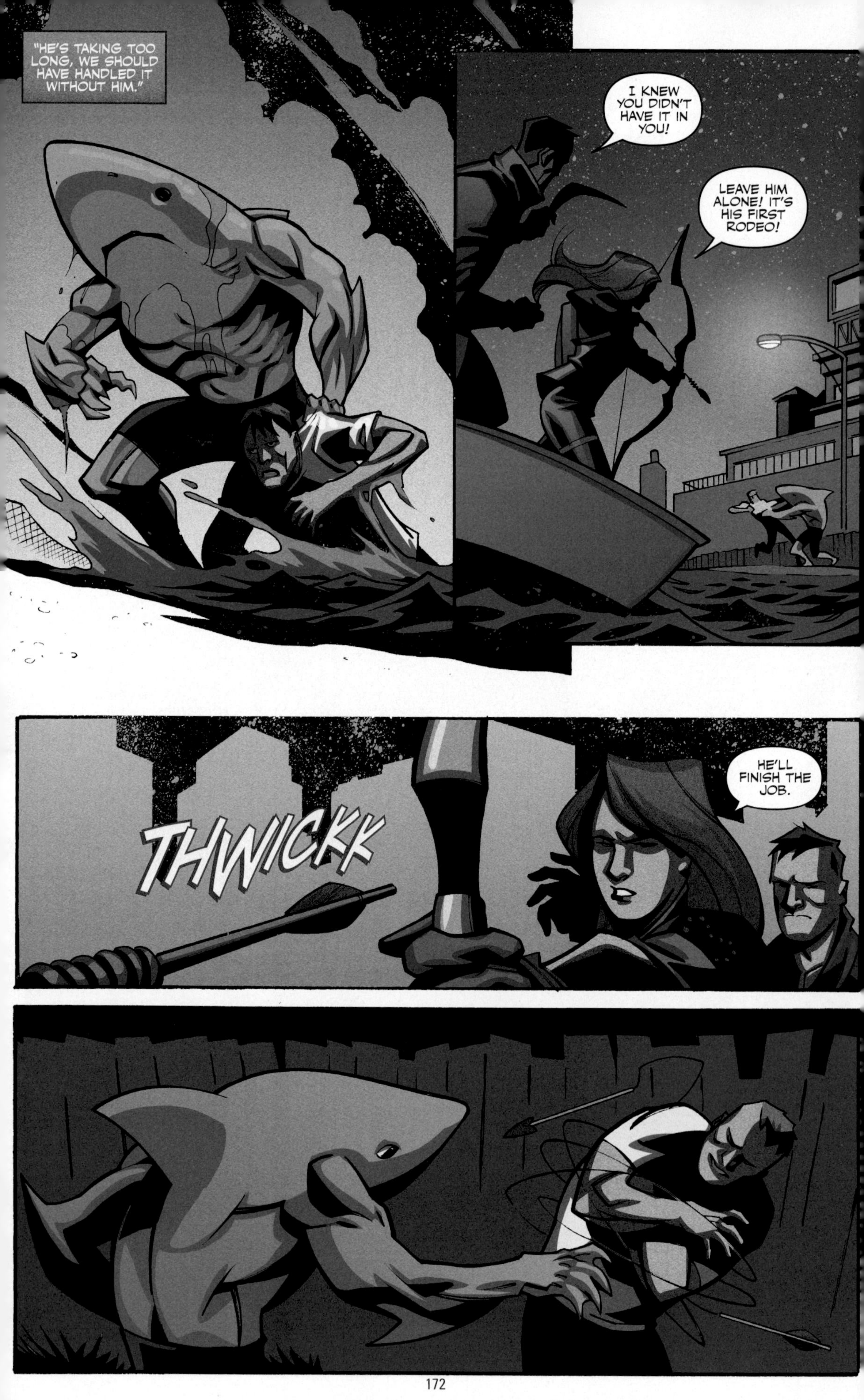
"HE'S TAKING TOO LONG, WE SHOULD HAVE HANDLED IT WITHOUT HIM."
I KNEW YOU DIDN'T HAVE IT IN YOU!
LEAVE HIM ALONE! IT'S HIS FIRST RODEO!
THWICKK
HE'LL FINISH THE JOB.

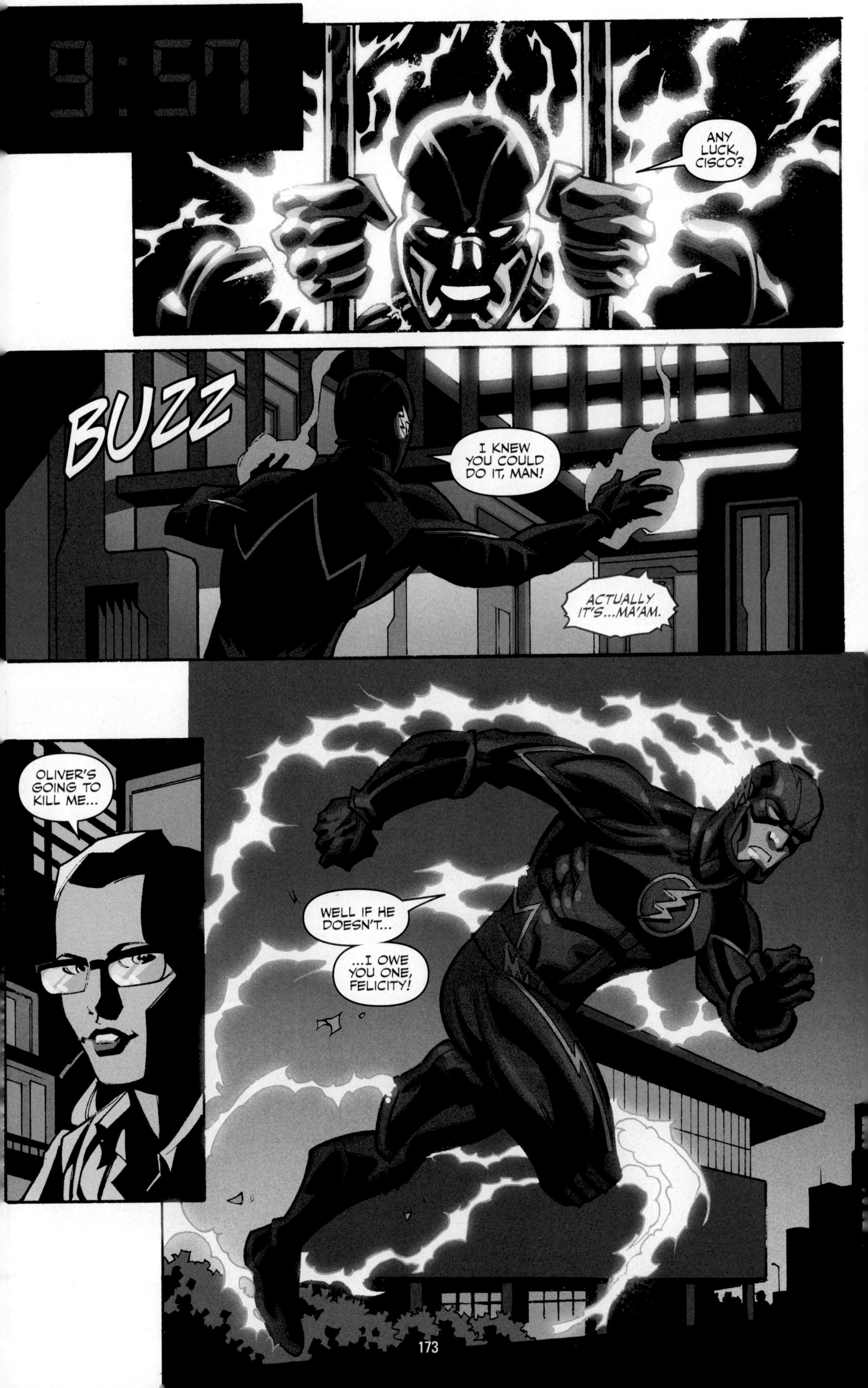
9:57
ANY LUCK, CISCO?
BUZZ
I KNEW YOU COULD DO IT, MAN!
ACTUALLY IT'S...MA'AM.
OLIVER'S GOING TO KILL ME...
WELL IF HE DOESN'T...
...I OWE YOU ONE, FELICITY!

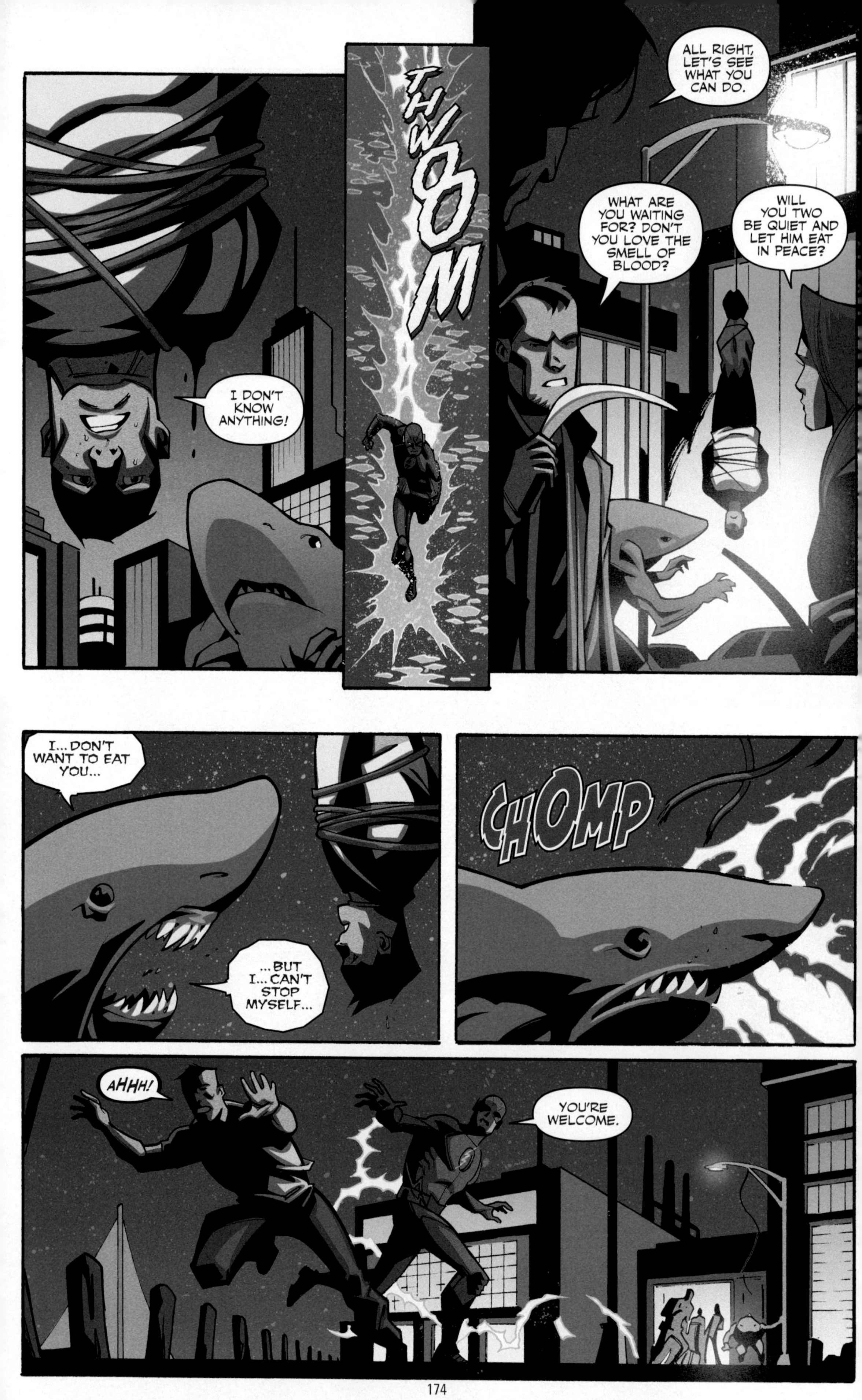

I DON'T KNOW ANYTHING!
THWOOM
ALL RIGHT, LET'S SEE WHAT YOU CAN DO.
WHAT ARE YOU WAITING FOR? DON'T YOU LOVE THE SMELL OF BLOOD?
WILL YOU TWO BE QUIET AND LET HIM EAT IN PEACE?
I... DON'T WANT TO EAT YOU...
...BUT I... CAN'T STOP MYSELF...
CHOMP
AHHH!
YOU'RE WELCOME.

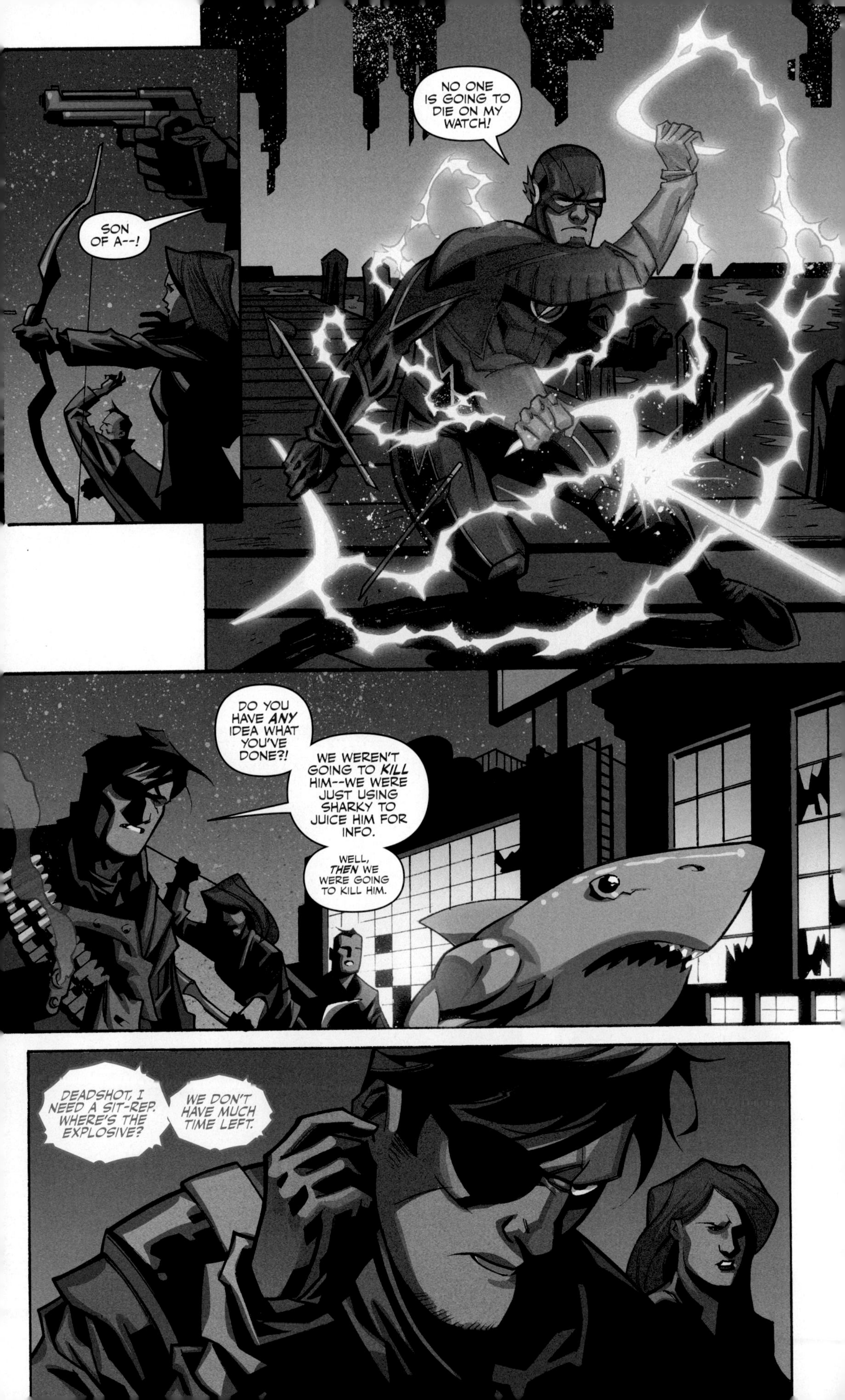

SON OF A--!
NO ONE IS GOING TO DIE ON MY WATCH!
DO YOU HAVE ANY IDEA WHAT YOU'VE DONE?!
WE WEREN'T GOING TO KILL HIM--WE WERE JUST USING SHARKY TO JUICE HIM FOR INFO.
WELL, THEN WE WERE GOING TO KILL HIM.
DEADSHOT, I NEED A SIT-REP. WHERE'S THE EXPLOSIVE?
WE DON'T HAVE MUCH TIME LEFT.

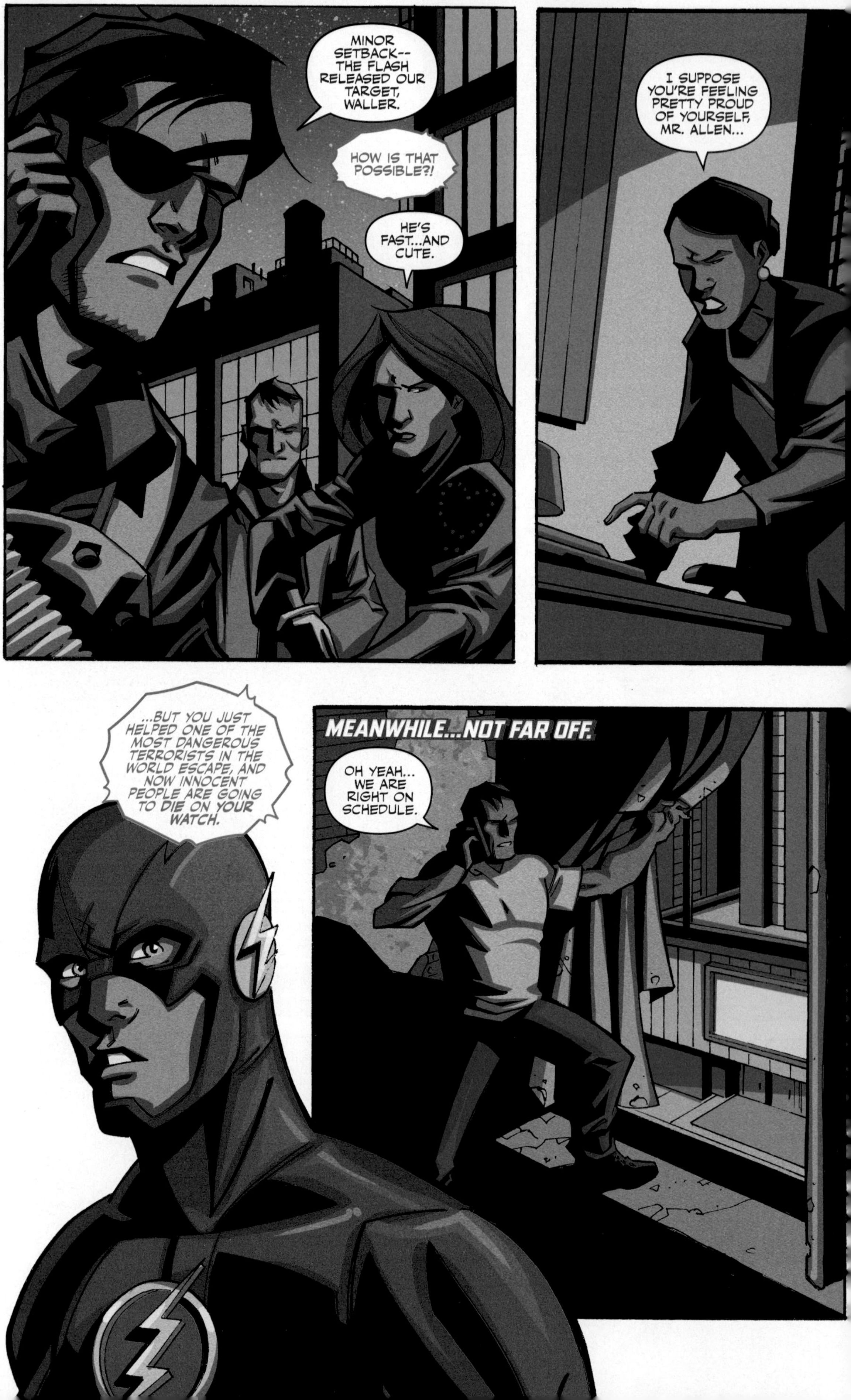
MINOR SETBACK-- THE FLASH RELEASED OUR TARGET, WALLER.
HOW IS THAT POSSIBLE?!
HE'S FAST...AND CUTE.
I SUPPOSE YOU'RE FEELING PRETTY PROUD OF YOURSELF, MR. ALLEN...
...BUT YOU JUST HELPED ONE OF THE MOST DANGEROUS TERRORISTS IN THE WORLD ESCAPE, AND NOW INNOCENT PEOPLE ARE GOING TO DIE ON YOUR WATCH.
MEANWHILE...NOT FAR OFF.
OH YEAH... WE ARE RIGHT ON SCHEDULE.

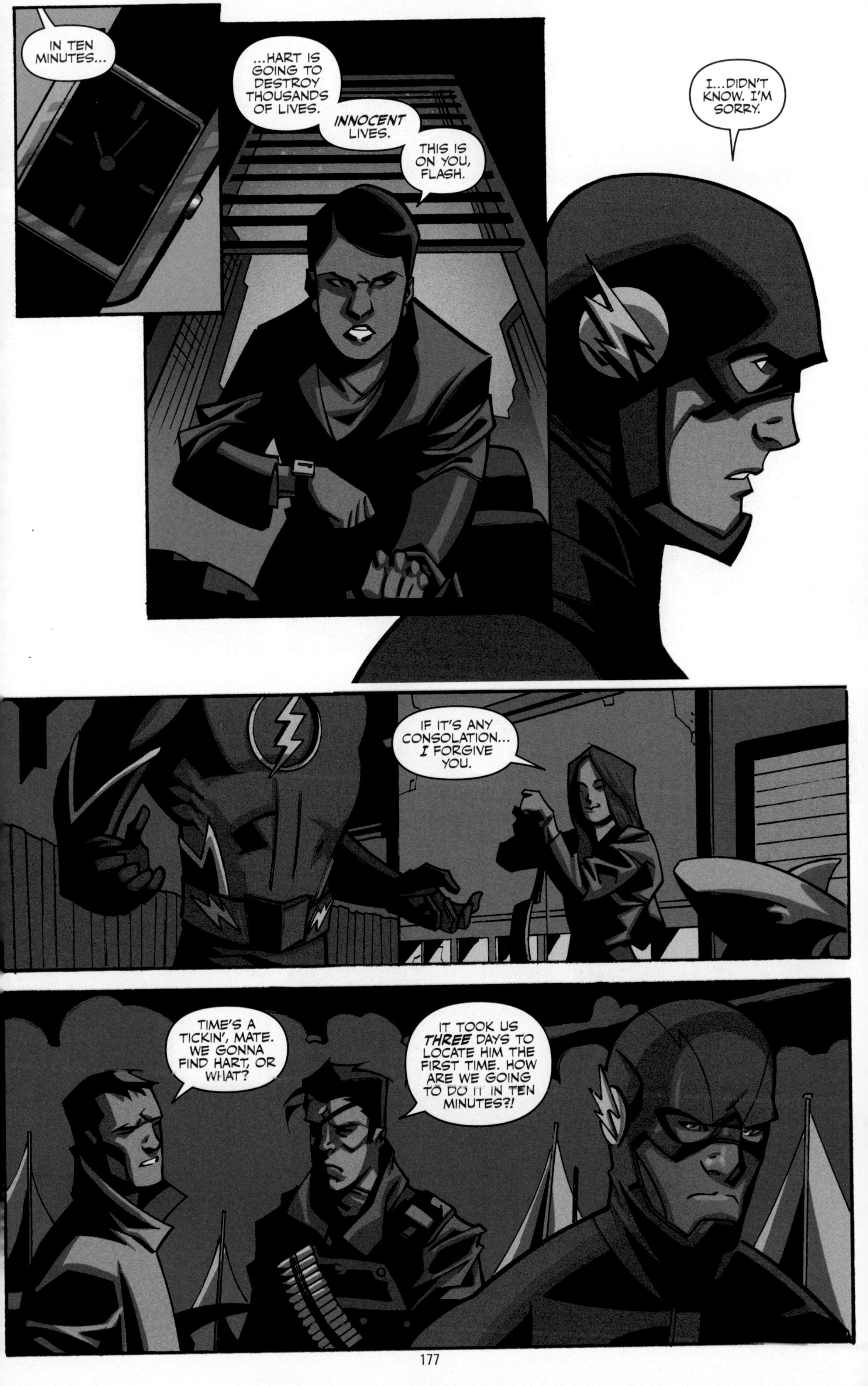
IN TEN MINUTES...
...HART IS GOING TO DESTROY THOUSANDS OF LIVES.
INNOCENT LIVES.
THIS IS ON YOU, FLASH.
I...DIDN'T KNOW. I'M SORRY.
IF IT'S ANY CONSOLATION... *I* FORGIVE YOU.
TIME'S A TICKIN', MATE. WE GONNA FIND HART, OR WHAT?
IT TOOK US *THREE* DAYS TO LOCATE HIM THE FIRST TIME. HOW ARE WE GOING TO DO IT IN TEN MINUTES?!

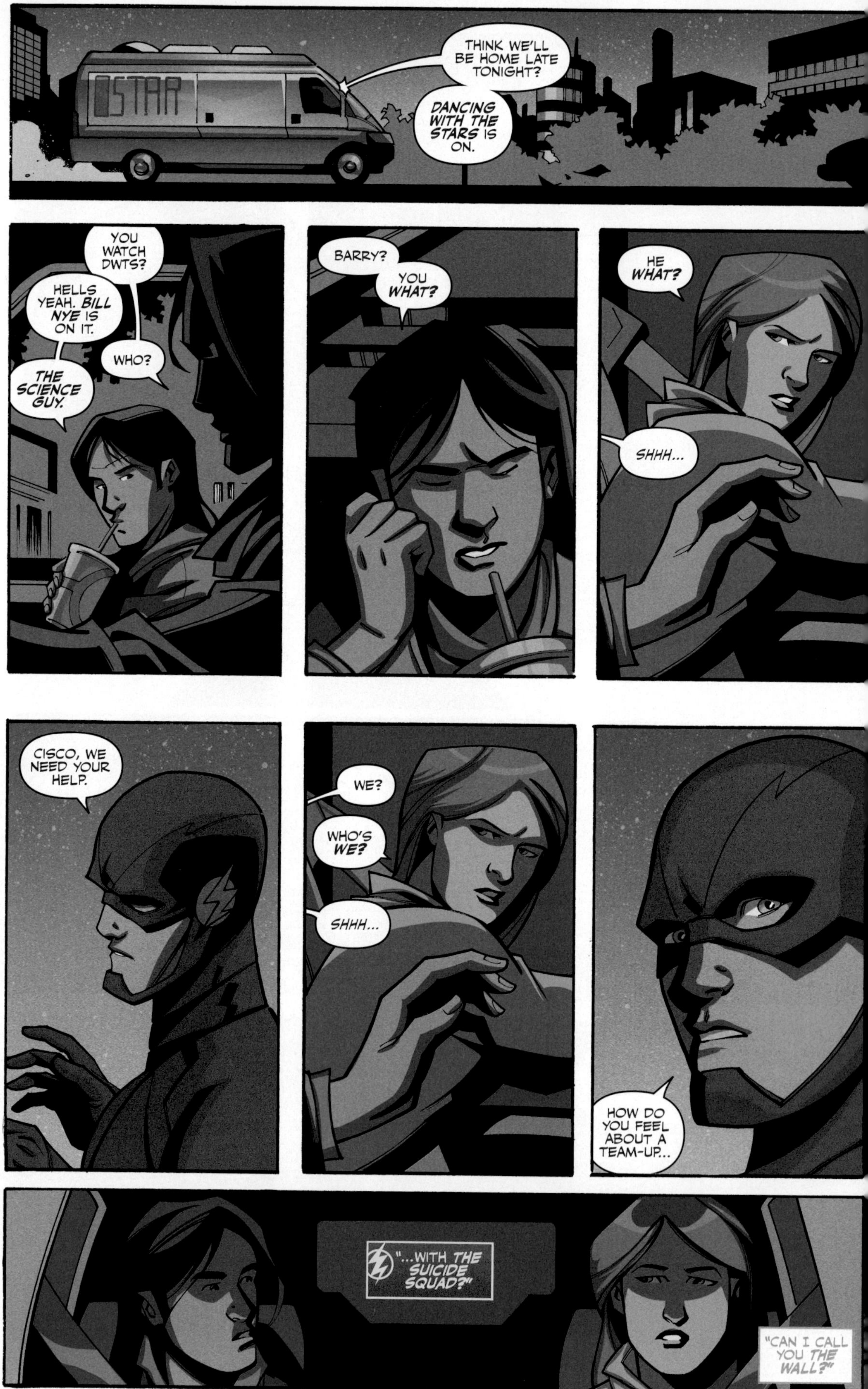

STAR
THINK WE'LL BE HOME LATE TONIGHT?
DANCING WITH THE STARS IS ON.
YOU WATCH DWTS?
HELLS YEAH. *BILL NYE* IS ON IT.
WHO?
THE SCIENCE GUY.
BARRY?
YOU *WHAT?*
HE *WHAT?*
SHHH...
CISCO, WE NEED YOUR HELP.
WE?
WHO'S *WE?*
SHHH...
HOW DO YOU FEEL ABOUT A TEAM-UP...
"...WITH *THE SUICIDE SQUAD?*"
"CAN I CALL YOU *THE WALL?*"

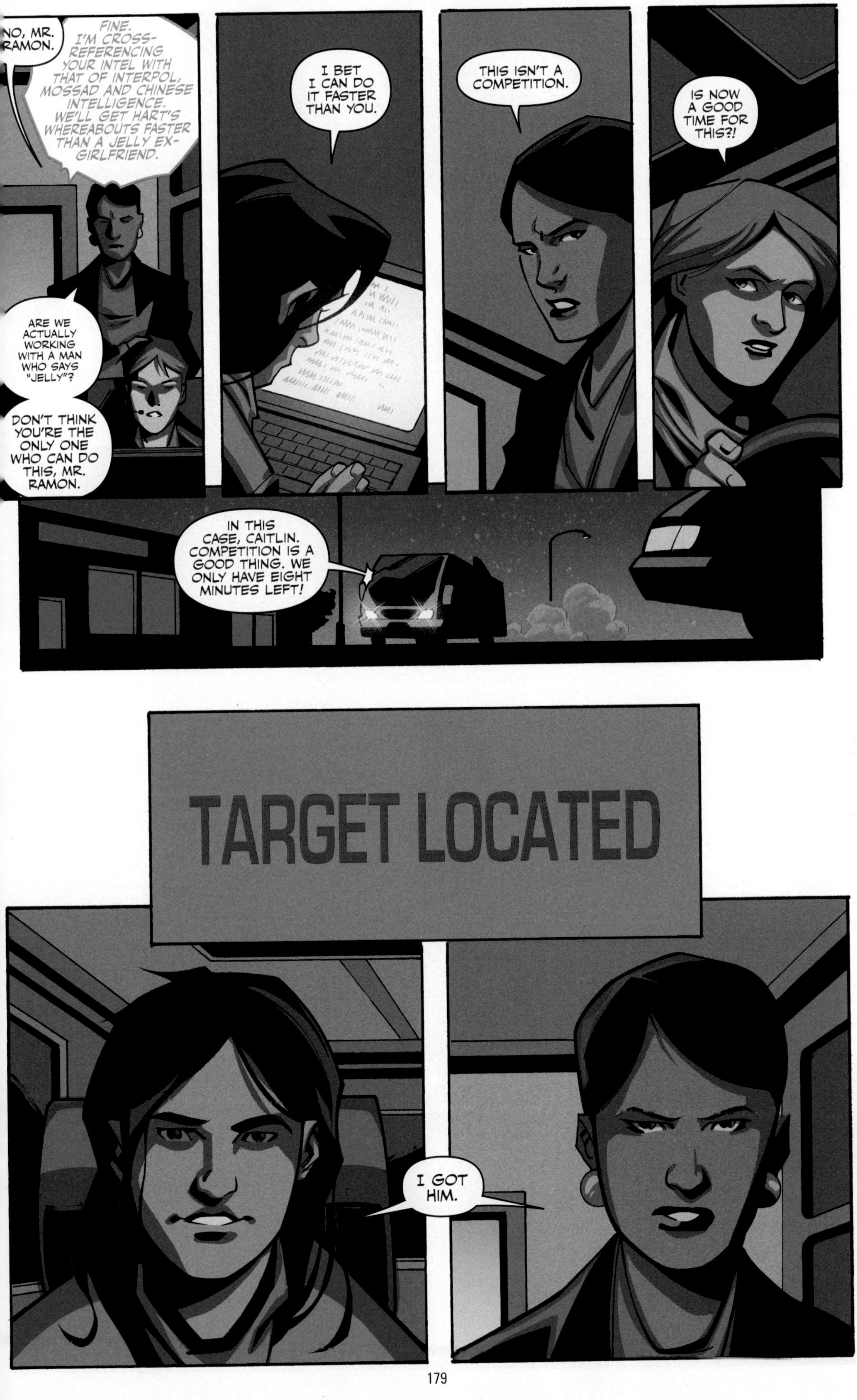
NO, MR. RAMON.
FINE. I'M CROSS-REFERENCING YOUR INTEL WITH THAT OF INTERPOL, MOSSAD AND CHINESE INTELLIGENCE. WE'LL GET HART'S WHEREABOUTS FASTER THAN A JELLY EX-GIRLFRIEND.
ARE WE ACTUALLY WORKING WITH A MAN WHO SAYS "JELLY"?
DON'T THINK YOU'RE THE ONLY ONE WHO CAN DO THIS, MR. RAMON.
I BET I CAN DO IT FASTER THAN YOU.
THIS ISN'T A COMPETITION.
IS NOW A GOOD TIME FOR THIS?!
IN THIS CASE, CAITLIN. COMPETITION IS A GOOD THING. WE ONLY HAVE EIGHT MINUTES LEFT!
TARGET LOCATED
I GOT HIM.

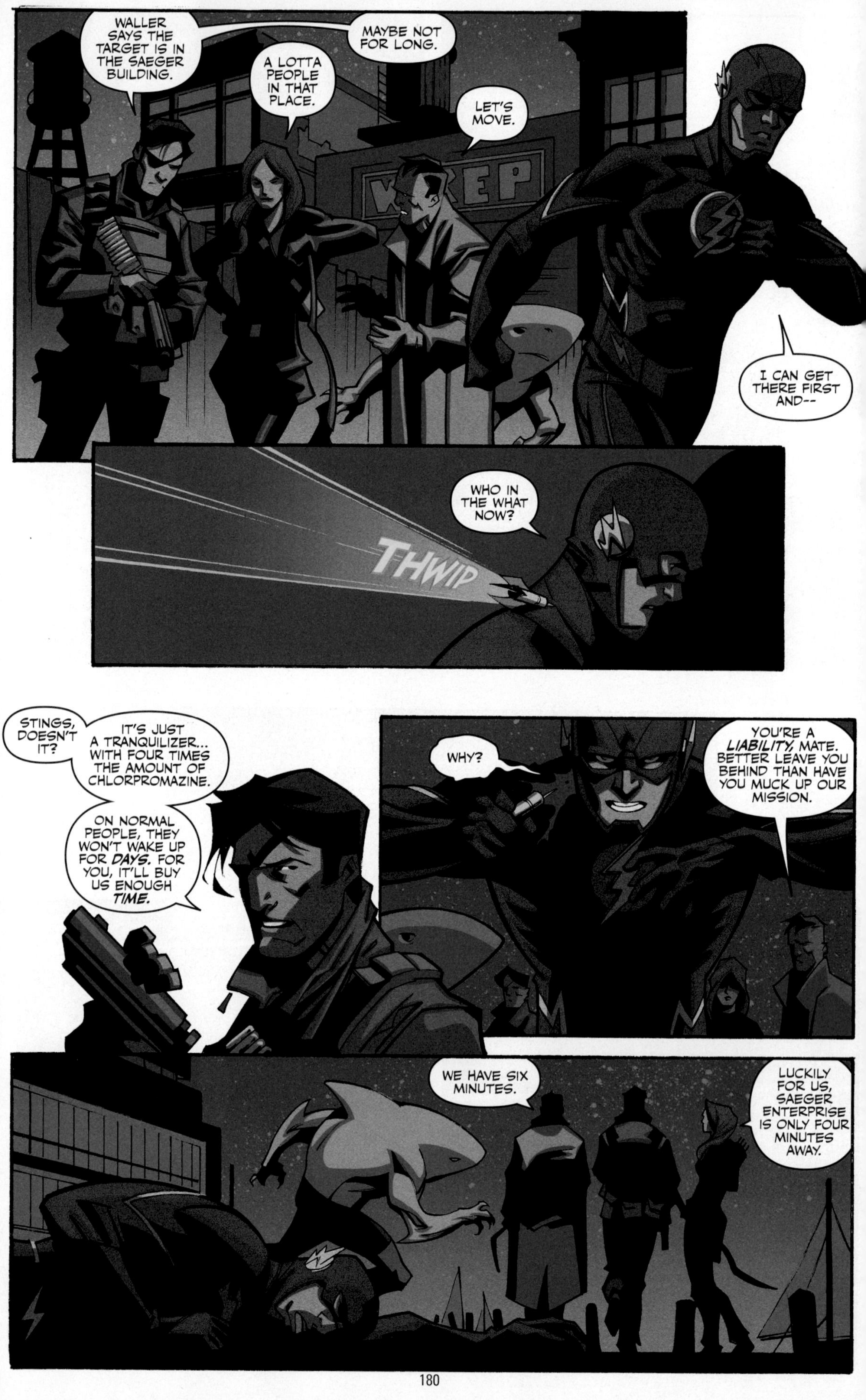
WALLER SAYS THE TARGET IS IN THE SAEGER BUILDING.
A LOTTA PEOPLE IN THAT PLACE.
MAYBE NOT FOR LONG.
LET'S MOVE.
I CAN GET THERE FIRST AND--
THWIP
WHO IN THE WHAT NOW?
STINGS, DOESN'T IT?
IT'S JUST A TRANQUILIZER... WITH FOUR TIMES THE AMOUNT OF CHLORPROMAZINE.
ON NORMAL PEOPLE, THEY WON'T WAKE UP FOR *DAYS.* FOR YOU, IT'LL BUY US ENOUGH *TIME.*
WHY?
YOU'RE A *LIABILITY,* MATE. BETTER LEAVE YOU BEHIND THAN HAVE YOU MUCK UP OUR MISSION.
WE HAVE SIX MINUTES.
LUCKILY FOR US, SAEGER ENTERPRISE IS ONLY FOUR MINUTES AWAY.

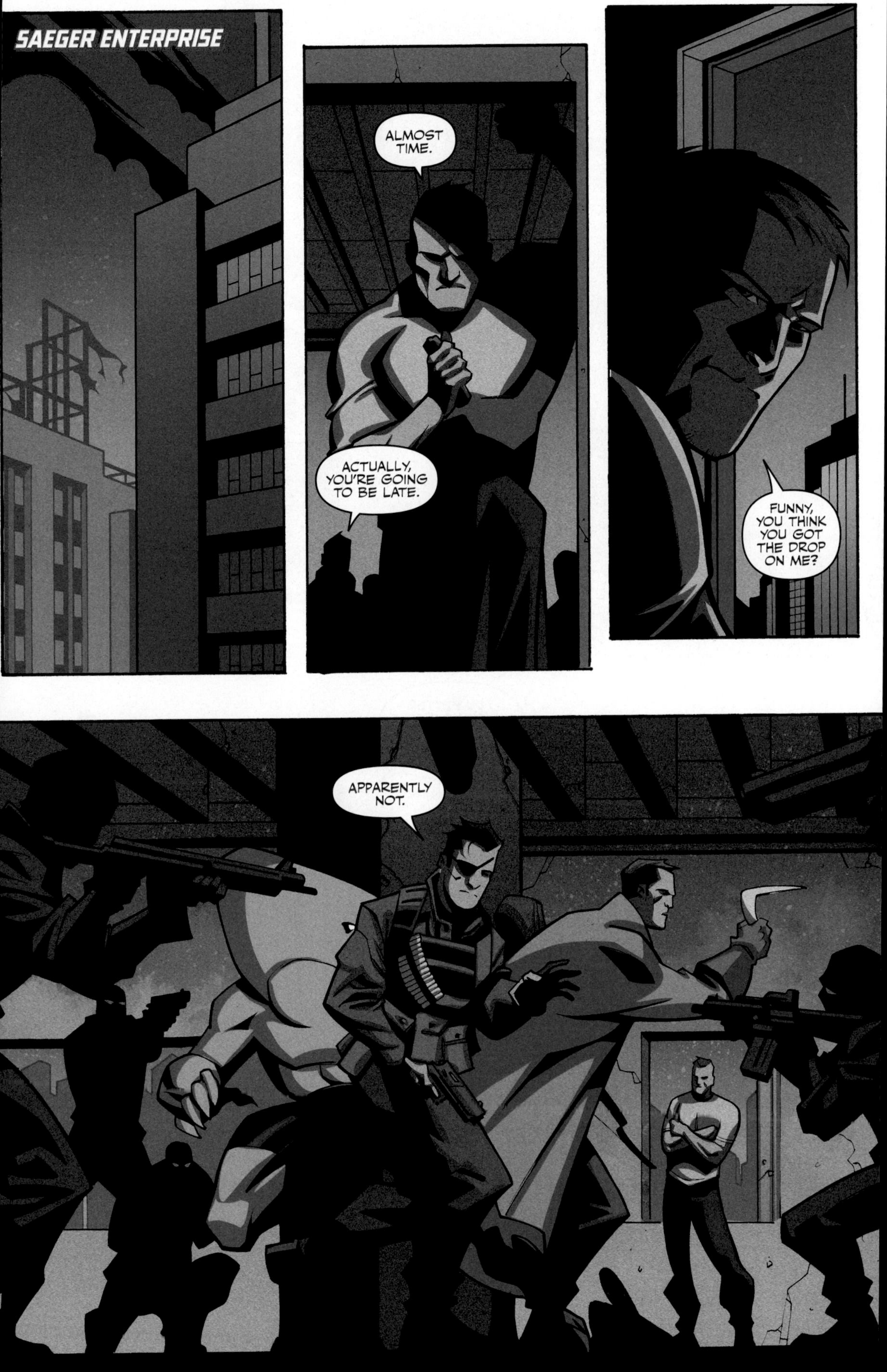
SAEGER ENTERPRISE
ALMOST TIME.
ACTUALLY, YOU'RE GOING TO BE LATE.
FUNNY, YOU THINK YOU GOT THE DROP ON ME?
APPARENTLY NOT.

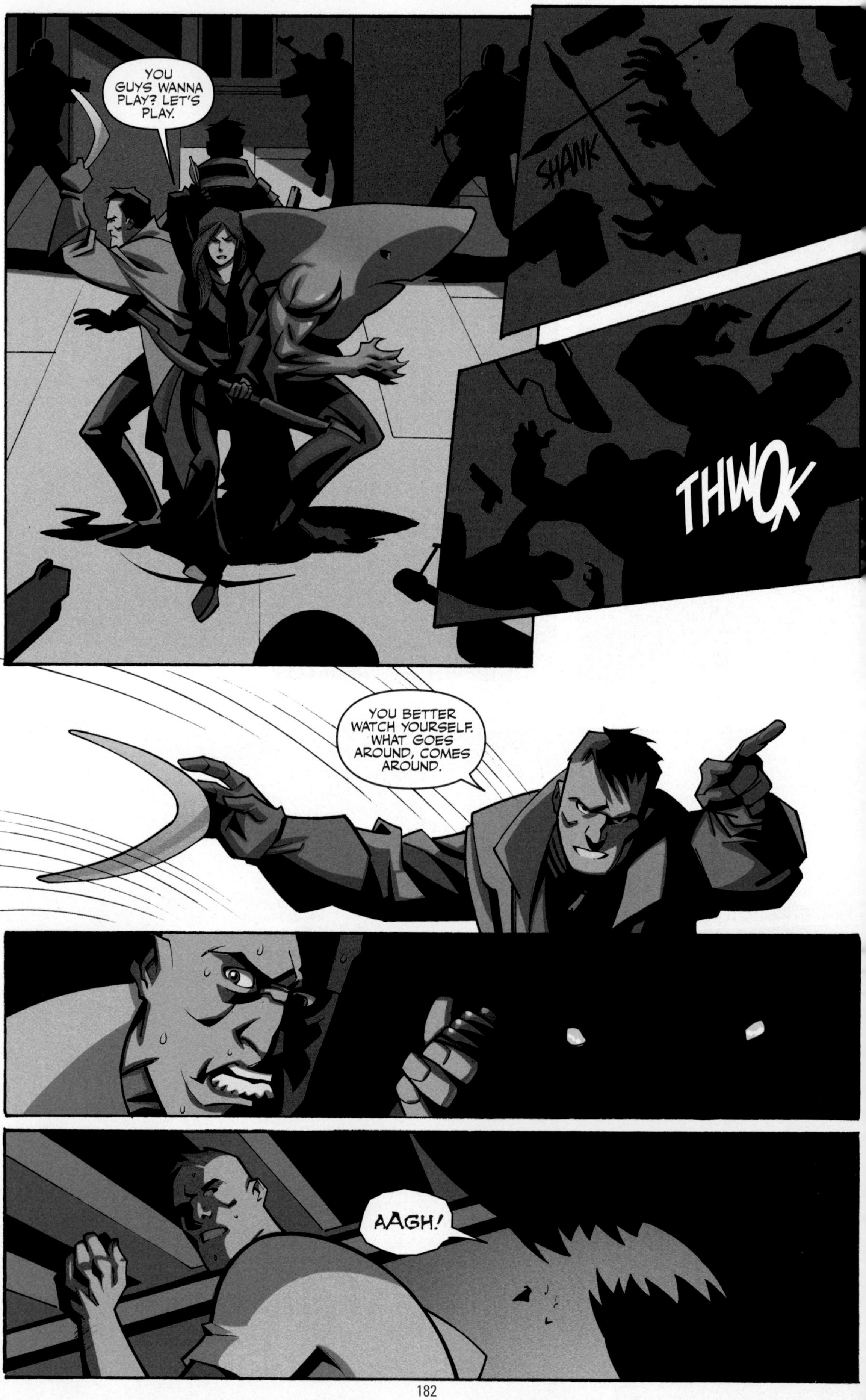
YOU GUYS WANNA PLAY? LET'S PLAY.
SHANK
THWOK
YOU BETTER WATCH YOURSELF. WHAT GOES AROUND, COMES AROUND.
AAGH!

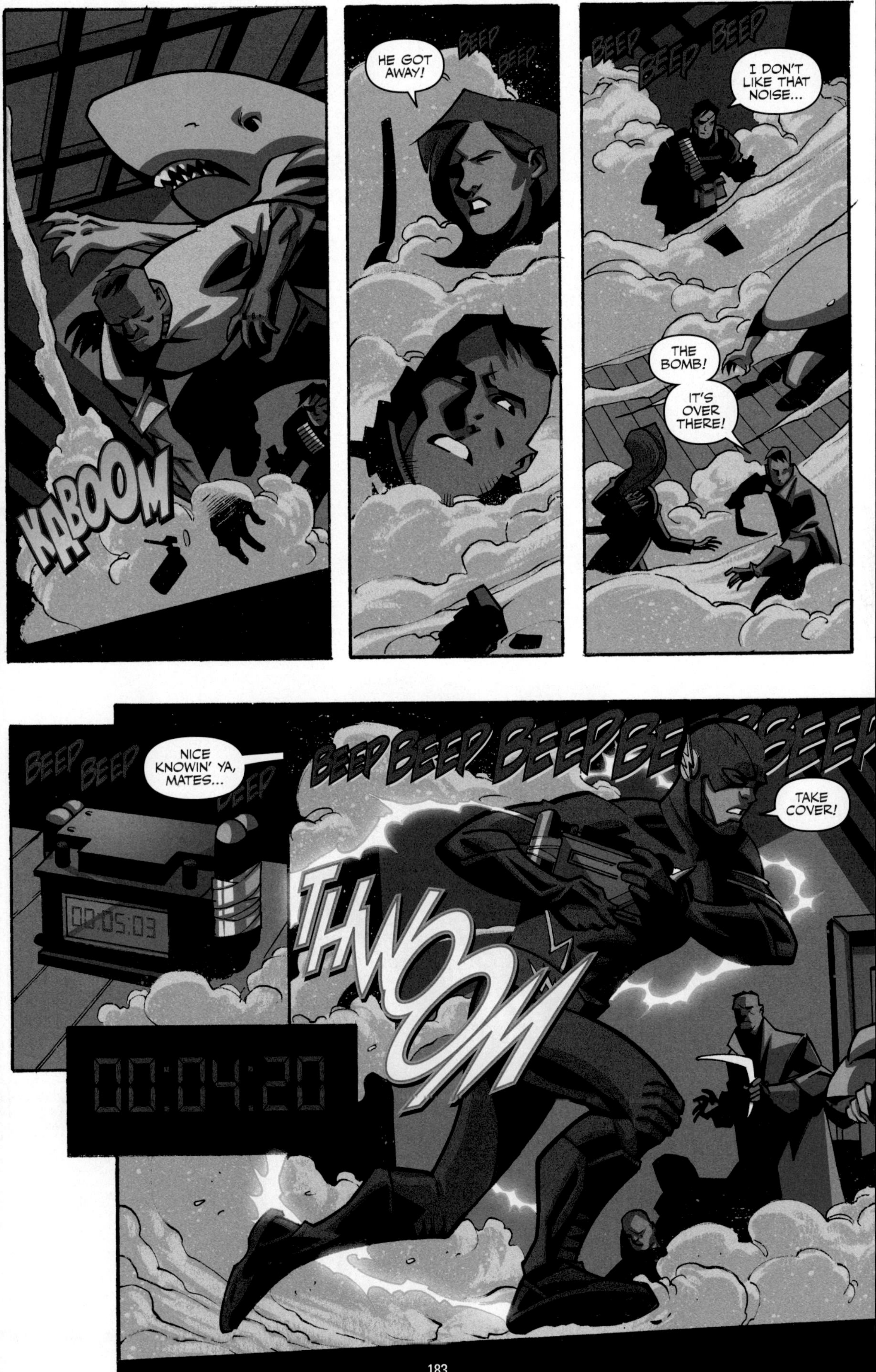
KABOOM
BEEP BEEP
HE GOT AWAY!
BEEP BEEP BEEP
I DON'T LIKE THAT NOISE...
THE BOMB!
IT'S OVER THERE!
BEEP BEEP
NICE KNOWIN' YA, MATES...
00:05:03
BEEP BEEP BEEP
TAKE COVER!
THWOOM
00:04:20

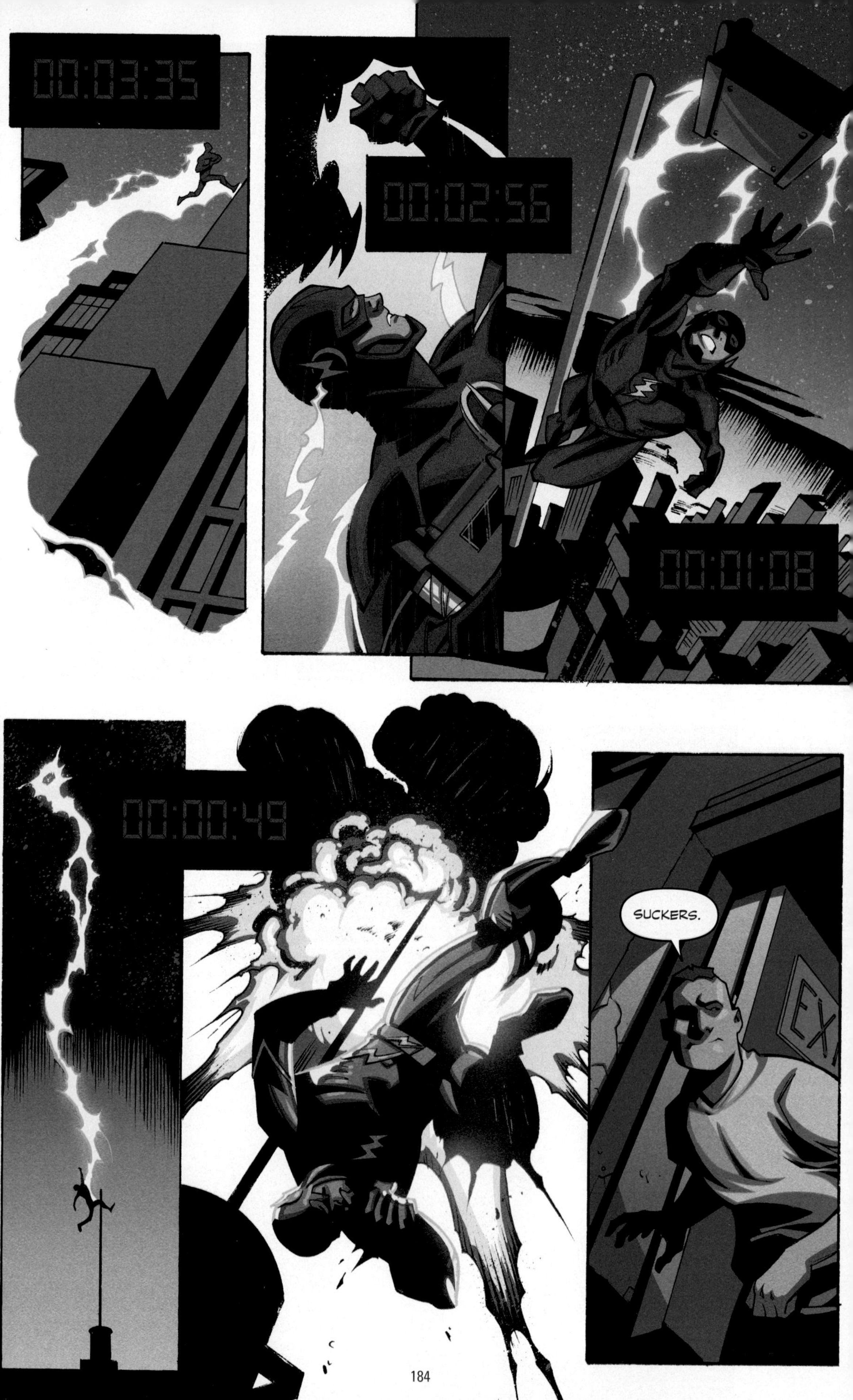
00:03:35
00:02:56
00:01:08
00:00:49
SUCKERS.
EX

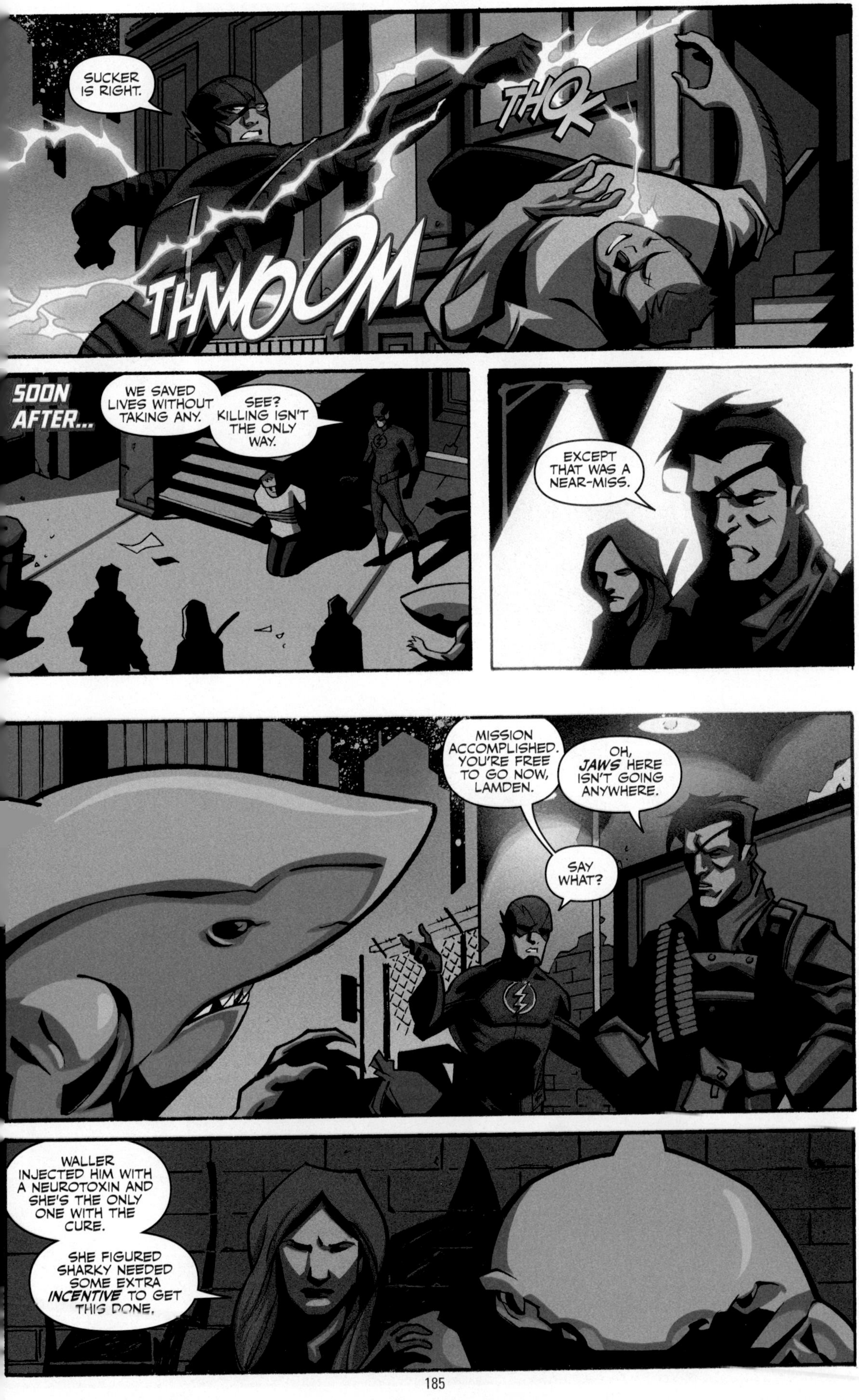
SUCKER IS RIGHT.
THOK
THWOOM
SOON AFTER...
WE SAVED LIVES WITHOUT TAKING ANY.
SEE? KILLING ISN'T THE ONLY WAY.
EXCEPT THAT WAS A NEAR-MISS.
MISSION ACCOMPLISHED. YOU'RE FREE TO GO NOW, LAMDEN.
OH, JAWS HERE ISN'T GOING ANYWHERE.
SAY WHAT?
WALLER INJECTED HIM WITH A NEUROTOXIN AND SHE'S THE ONLY ONE WITH THE CURE.
SHE FIGURED SHARKY NEEDED SOME EXTRA INCENTIVE TO GET THIS DONE.

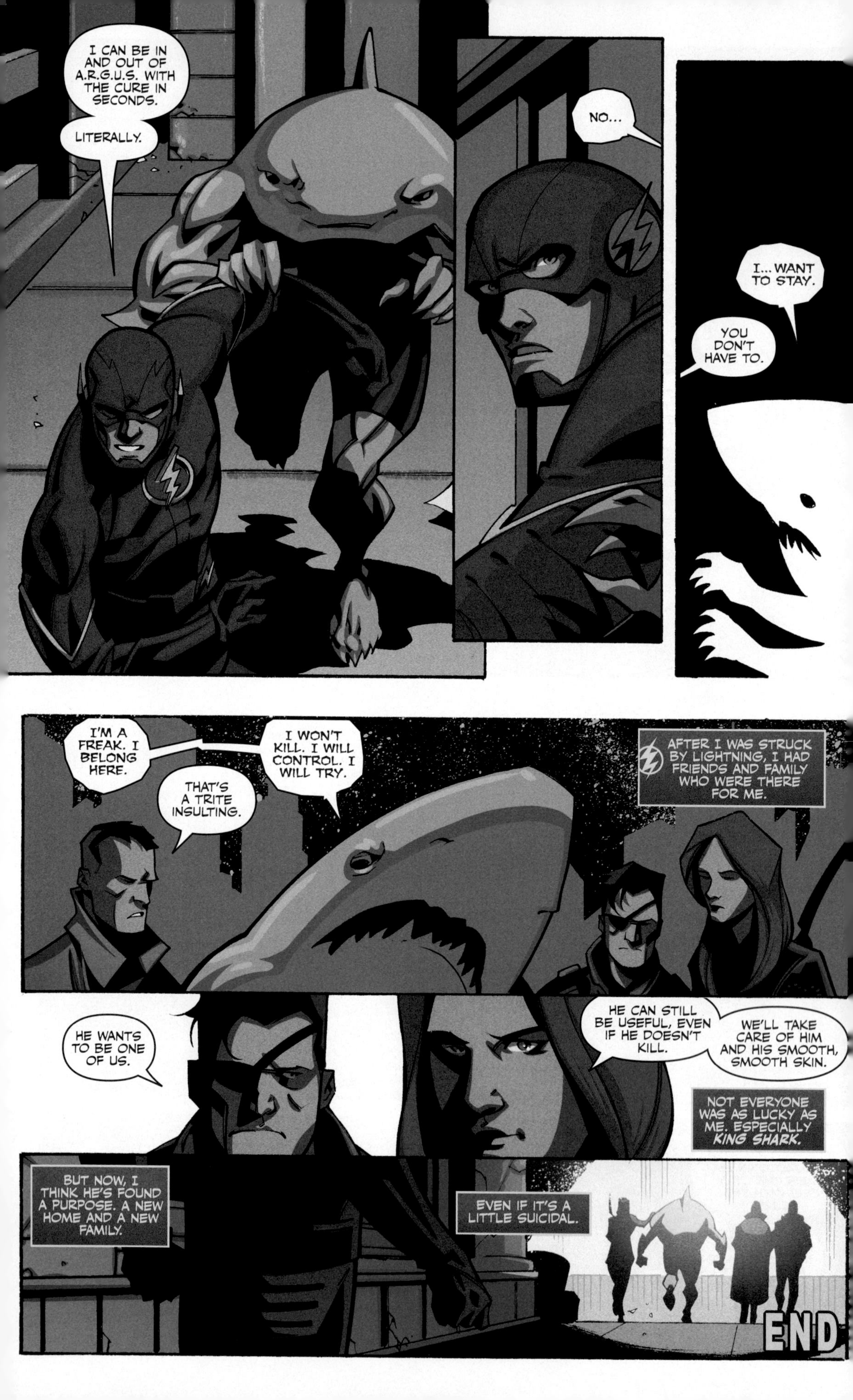
I CAN BE IN AND OUT OF A.R.G.U.S. WITH THE CURE IN SECONDS.
LITERALLY.
NO...
I... WANT TO STAY.
YOU DON'T HAVE TO.
I'M A FREAK. I BELONG HERE.
I WON'T KILL. I WILL CONTROL. I WILL TRY.
THAT'S A TRITE INSULTING.
AFTER I WAS STRUCK BY LIGHTNING, I HAD FRIENDS AND FAMILY WHO WERE THERE FOR ME.
HE WANTS TO BE ONE OF US.
HE CAN STILL BE USEFUL, EVEN IF HE DOESN'T KILL.
WE'LL TAKE CARE OF HIM AND HIS SMOOTH, SMOOTH SKIN.
NOT EVERYONE WAS AS LUCKY AS ME. ESPECIALLY *KING SHARK*.
BUT NOW, I THINK HE'S FOUND A PURPOSE. A NEW HOME AND A NEW FAMILY.
EVEN IF IT'S A LITTLE SUICIDAL.
END

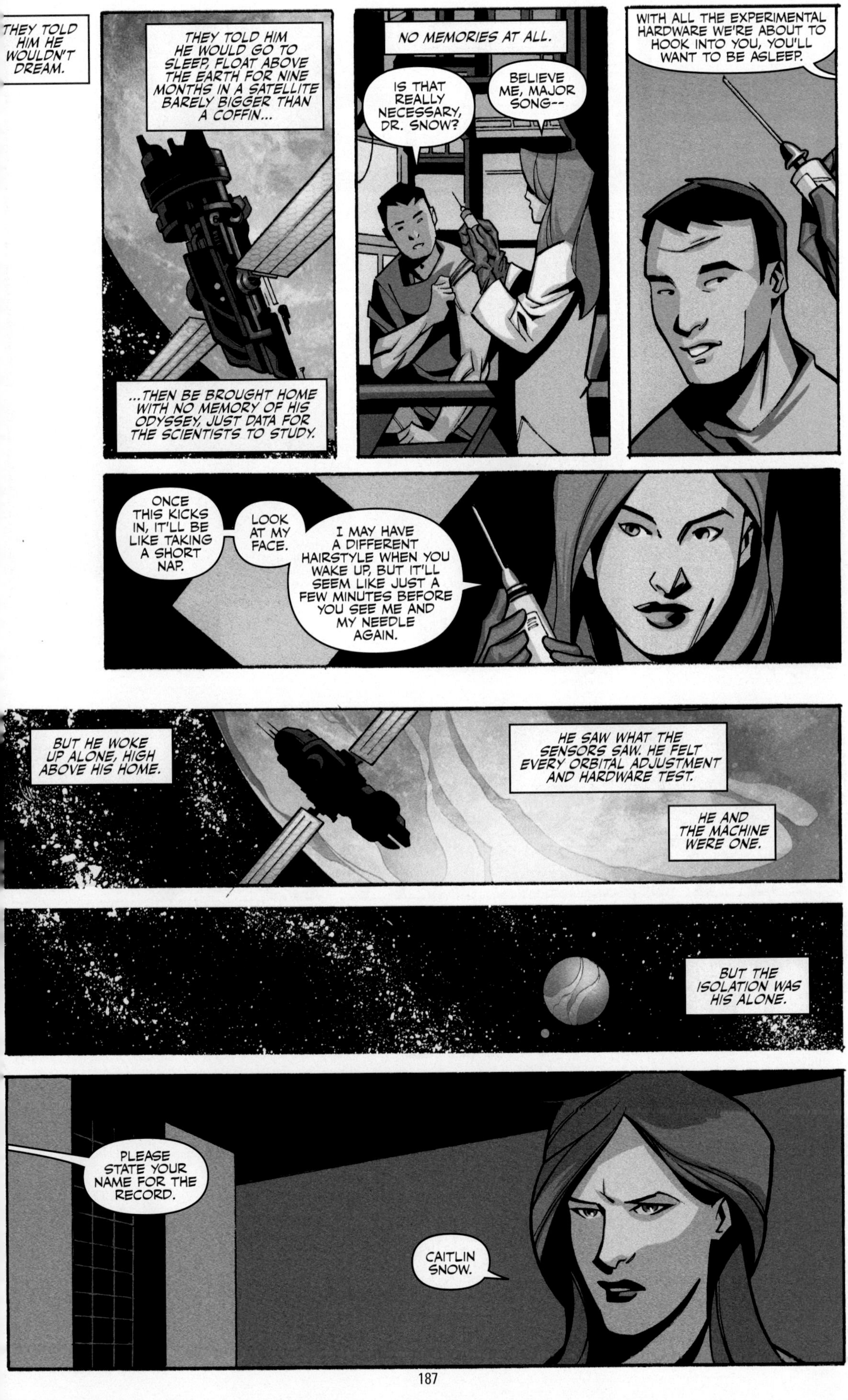
THEY TOLD HIM HE WOULDN'T DREAM.
THEY TOLD HIM HE WOULD GO TO SLEEP, FLOAT ABOVE THE EARTH FOR NINE MONTHS IN A SATELLITE BARELY BIGGER THAN A COFFIN...
...THEN BE BROUGHT HOME WITH NO MEMORY OF HIS ODYSSEY, JUST DATA FOR THE SCIENTISTS TO STUDY.
NO MEMORIES AT ALL.
IS THAT REALLY NECESSARY, DR. SNOW?
BELIEVE ME, MAJOR SONG--
WITH ALL THE EXPERIMENTAL HARDWARE WE'RE ABOUT TO HOOK INTO YOU, YOU'LL WANT TO BE ASLEEP.
ONCE THIS KICKS IN, IT'LL BE LIKE TAKING A SHORT NAP.
LOOK AT MY FACE.
I MAY HAVE A DIFFERENT HAIRSTYLE WHEN YOU WAKE UP, BUT IT'LL SEEM LIKE JUST A FEW MINUTES BEFORE YOU SEE ME AND MY NEEDLE AGAIN.
BUT HE WOKE UP ALONE, HIGH ABOVE HIS HOME.
HE SAW WHAT THE SENSORS SAW. HE FELT EVERY ORBITAL ADJUSTMENT AND HARDWARE TEST.
HE AND THE MACHINE WERE ONE.
BUT THE ISOLATION WAS HIS ALONE.
PLEASE STATE YOUR NAME FOR THE RECORD.
CAITLIN SNOW.

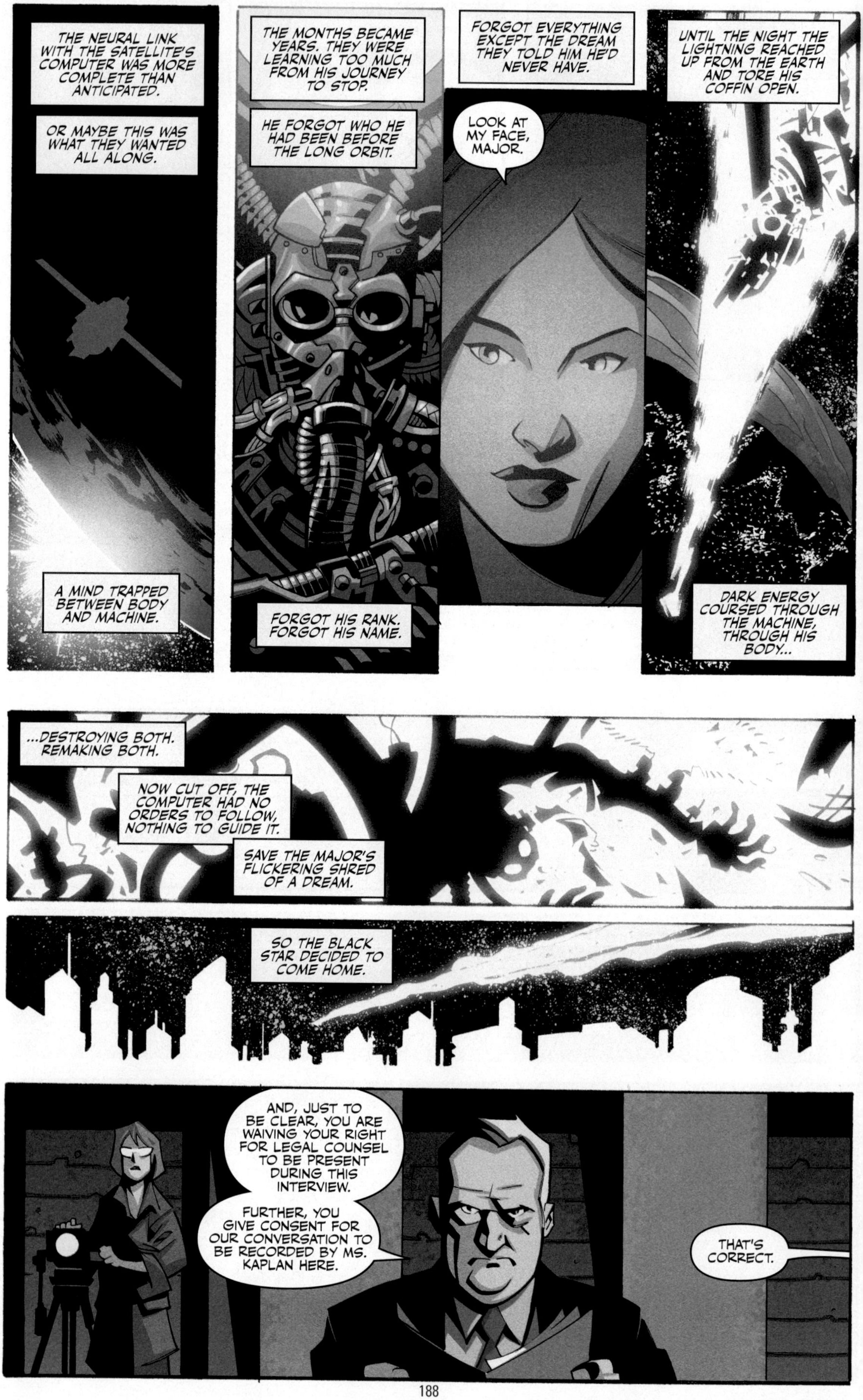
THE NEURAL LINK WITH THE SATELLITE'S COMPUTER WAS MORE COMPLETE THAN ANTICIPATED.
OR MAYBE THIS WAS WHAT THEY WANTED ALL ALONG.
A MIND TRAPPED BETWEEN BODY AND MACHINE.
THE MONTHS BECAME YEARS. THEY WERE LEARNING TOO MUCH FROM HIS JOURNEY TO STOP.
HE FORGOT WHO HE HAD BEEN BEFORE THE LONG ORBIT.
FORGOT HIS RANK. FORGOT HIS NAME.
FORGOT EVERYTHING EXCEPT THE DREAM THEY TOLD HIM HE'D NEVER HAVE.
LOOK AT MY FACE, MAJOR.
UNTIL THE NIGHT THE LIGHTNING REACHED UP FROM THE EARTH AND TORE HIS COFFIN OPEN.
DARK ENERGY COURSED THROUGH THE MACHINE, THROUGH HIS BODY...
...DESTROYING BOTH. REMAKING BOTH.
NOW CUT OFF, THE COMPUTER HAD NO ORDERS TO FOLLOW, NOTHING TO GUIDE IT.
SAVE THE MAJOR'S FLICKERING SHRED OF A DREAM.
SO THE BLACK STAR DECIDED TO COME HOME.
AND, JUST TO BE CLEAR, YOU ARE WAIVING YOUR RIGHT FOR LEGAL COUNSEL TO BE PRESENT DURING THIS INTERVIEW.
FURTHER, YOU GIVE CONSENT FOR OUR CONVERSATION TO BE RECORDED BY MS. KAPLAN HERE.
THAT'S CORRECT.

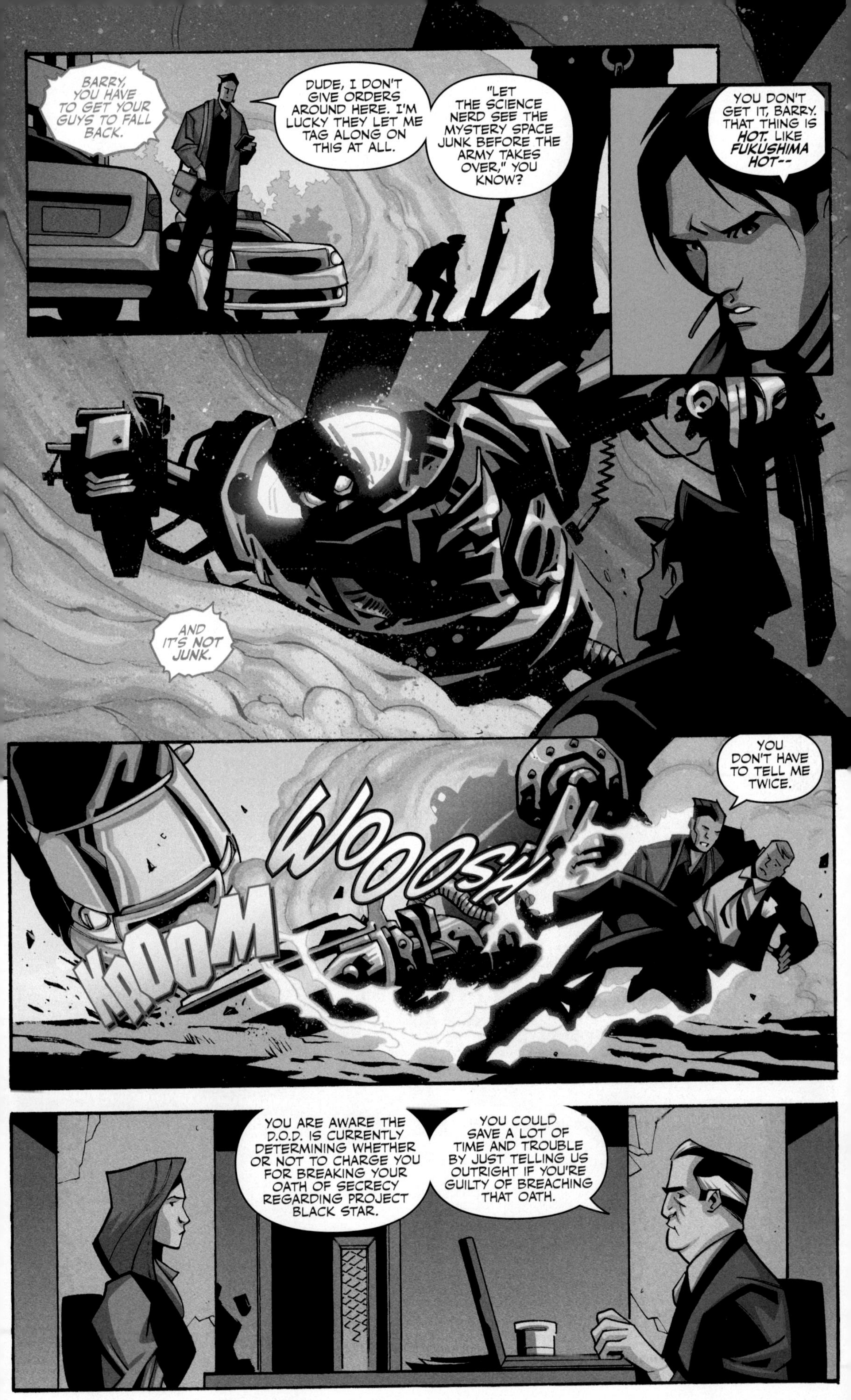
BARRY, YOU HAVE TO GET YOUR GUYS TO FALL BACK.
DUDE, I DON'T GIVE ORDERS AROUND HERE. I'M LUCKY THEY LET ME TAG ALONG ON THIS AT ALL.
"LET THE SCIENCE NERD SEE THE MYSTERY SPACE JUNK BEFORE THE ARMY TAKES OVER," YOU KNOW?
YOU DON'T GET IT, BARRY. THAT THING IS HOT. LIKE FUKUSHIMA HOT--
AND IT'S NOT JUNK.
WOOOSH
KROOOM
YOU DON'T HAVE TO TELL ME TWICE.
YOU ARE AWARE THE D.O.D. IS CURRENTLY DETERMINING WHETHER OR NOT TO CHARGE YOU FOR BREAKING YOUR OATH OF SECRECY REGARDING PROJECT BLACK STAR.
YOU COULD SAVE A LOT OF TIME AND TROUBLE BY JUST TELLING US OUTRIGHT IF YOU'RE GUILTY OF BREACHING THAT OATH.

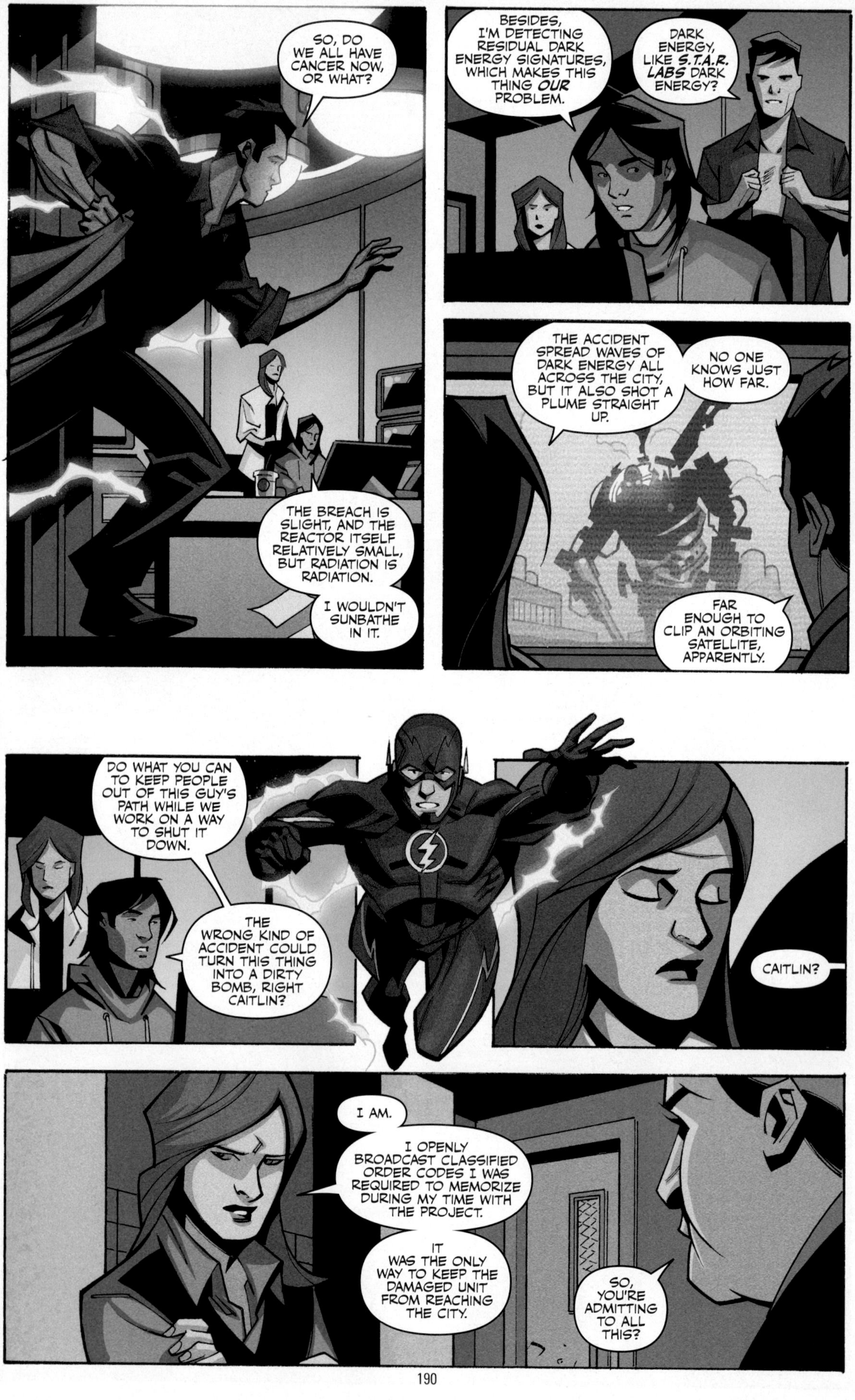

SO, DO WE ALL HAVE CANCER NOW, OR WHAT?
THE BREACH IS SLIGHT, AND THE REACTOR ITSELF RELATIVELY SMALL, BUT RADIATION IS RADIATION.
I WOULDN'T SUNBATHE IN IT.
BESIDES, I'M DETECTING RESIDUAL DARK ENERGY SIGNATURES, WHICH MAKES THIS THING OUR PROBLEM.
DARK ENERGY, LIKE S.T.A.R. LABS DARK ENERGY?
THE ACCIDENT SPREAD WAVES OF DARK ENERGY ALL ACROSS THE CITY, BUT IT ALSO SHOT A PLUME STRAIGHT UP.
NO ONE KNOWS JUST HOW FAR.
FAR ENOUGH TO CLIP AN ORBITING SATELLITE, APPARENTLY.
DO WHAT YOU CAN TO KEEP PEOPLE OUT OF THIS GUY'S PATH WHILE WE WORK ON A WAY TO SHUT IT DOWN.
THE WRONG KIND OF ACCIDENT COULD TURN THIS THING INTO A DIRTY BOMB, RIGHT CAITLIN?
CAITLIN?
I AM.
I OPENLY BROADCAST CLASSIFIED ORDER CODES I WAS REQUIRED TO MEMORIZE DURING MY TIME WITH THE PROJECT.
IT WAS THE ONLY WAY TO KEEP THE DAMAGED UNIT FROM REACHING THE CITY.
SO, YOU'RE ADMITTING TO ALL THIS?

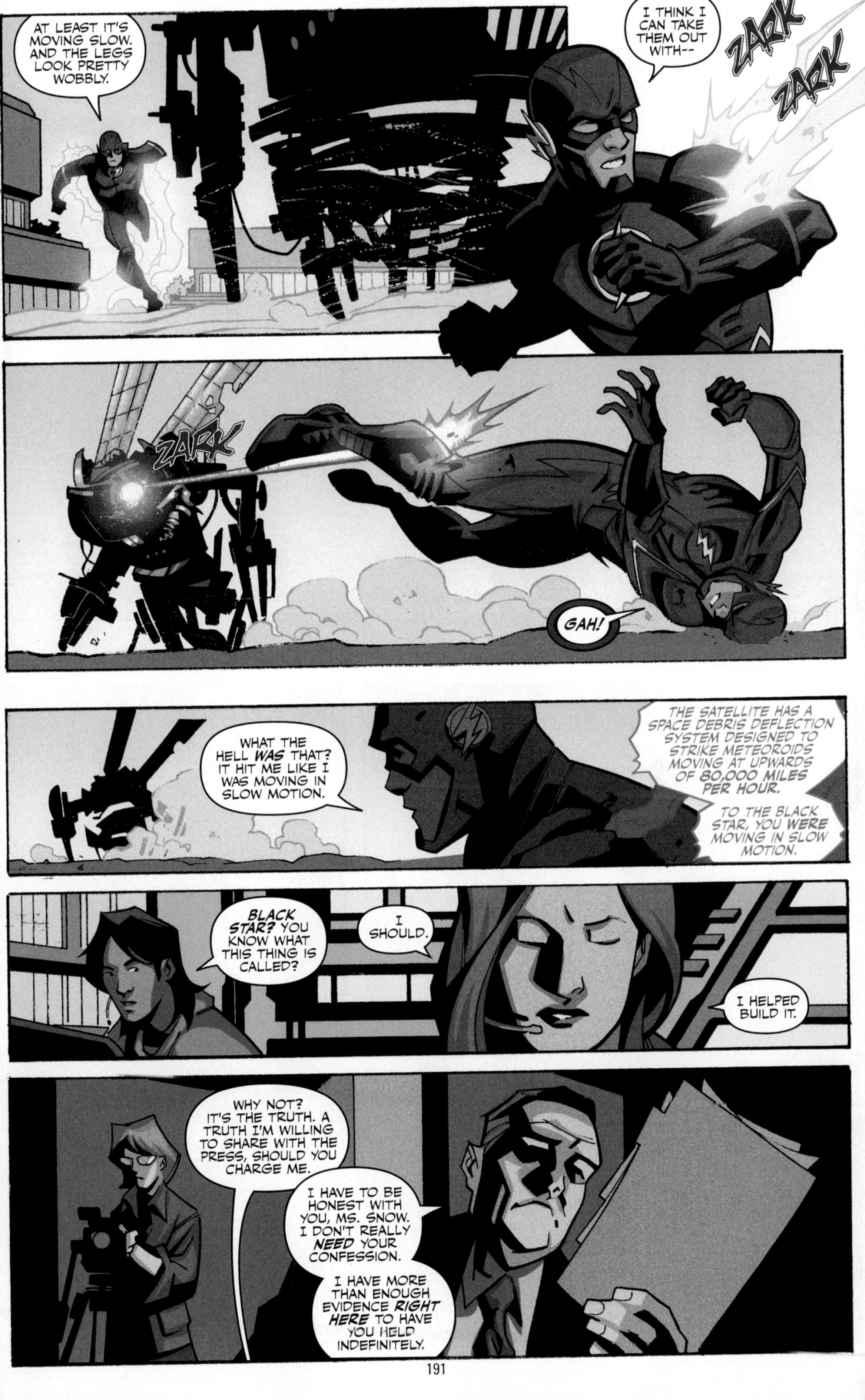

AT LEAST IT'S MOVING SLOW. AND THE LEGS LOOK PRETTY WOBBLY.
I THINK I CAN TAKE THEM OUT WITH--
ZARK
ZARK
ZARK
GAH!
WHAT THE HELL WAS THAT? IT HIT ME LIKE I WAS MOVING IN SLOW MOTION.
THE SATELLITE HAS A SPACE DEBRIS DEFLECTION SYSTEM DESIGNED TO STRIKE METEOROIDS MOVING AT UPWARDS OF 80,000 MILES PER HOUR.
TO THE BLACK STAR, YOU WERE MOVING IN SLOW MOTION.
BLACK STAR? YOU KNOW WHAT THIS THING IS CALLED?
I SHOULD.
I HELPED BUILD IT.
WHY NOT? IT'S THE TRUTH. A TRUTH I'M WILLING TO SHARE WITH THE PRESS, SHOULD YOU CHARGE ME.
I HAVE TO BE HONEST WITH YOU, MS. SNOW. I DON'T REALLY NEED YOUR CONFESSION.
I HAVE MORE THAN ENOUGH EVIDENCE RIGHT HERE TO HAVE YOU HELD INDEFINITELY.

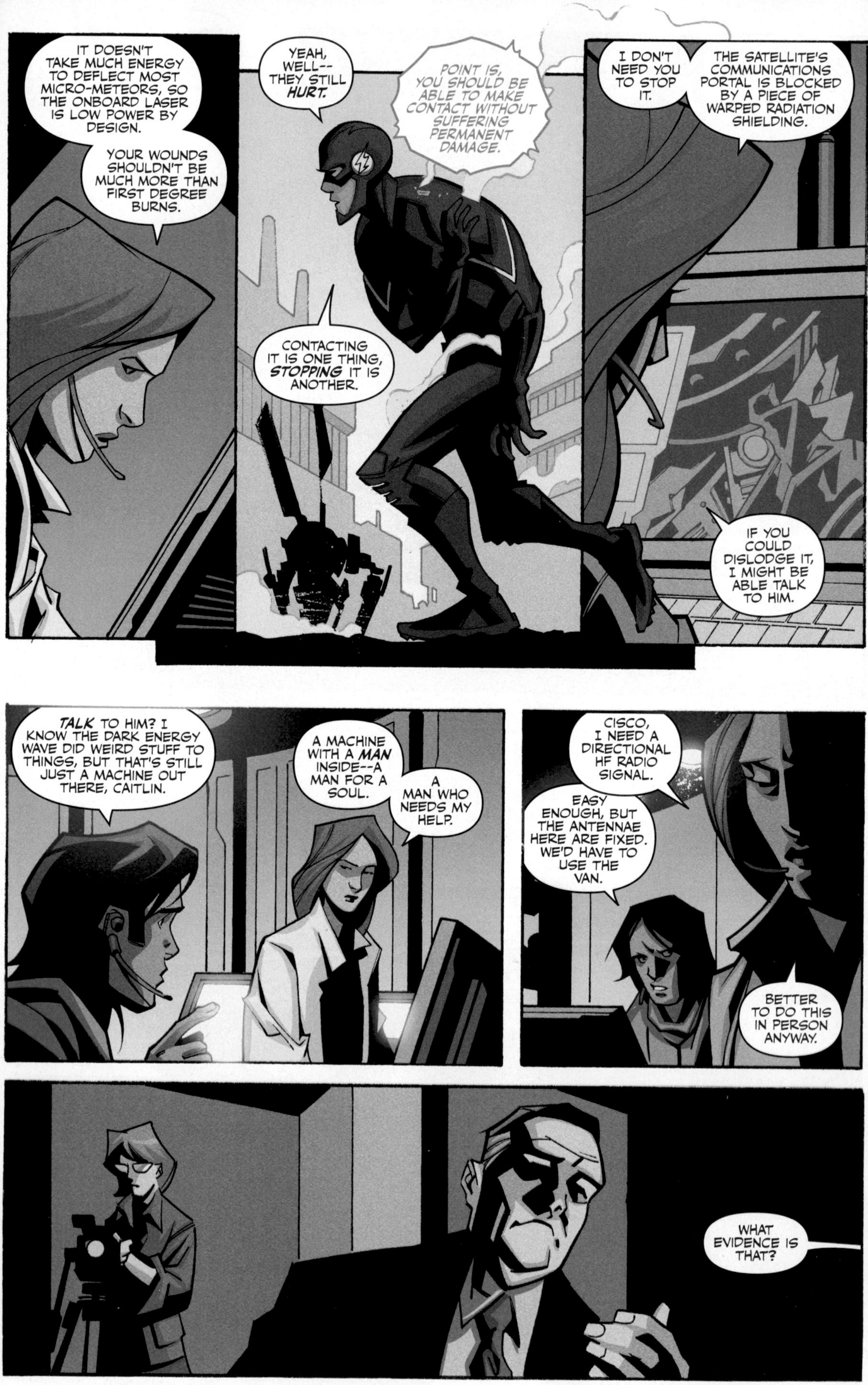

IT DOESN'T TAKE MUCH ENERGY TO DEFLECT MOST MICRO-METEORS, SO THE ONBOARD LASER IS LOW POWER BY DESIGN.
YOUR WOUNDS SHOULDN'T BE MUCH MORE THAN FIRST DEGREE BURNS.
YEAH, WELL-- THEY STILL HURT.
POINT IS, YOU SHOULD BE ABLE TO MAKE CONTACT WITHOUT SUFFERING PERMANENT DAMAGE.
CONTACTING IT IS ONE THING, STOPPING IT IS ANOTHER.
I DON'T NEED YOU TO STOP IT.
THE SATELLITE'S COMMUNICATIONS PORTAL IS BLOCKED BY A PIECE OF WARPED RADIATION SHIELDING.
IF YOU COULD DISLODGE IT, I MIGHT BE ABLE TALK TO HIM.
TALK TO HIM? I KNOW THE DARK ENERGY WAVE DID WEIRD STUFF TO THINGS, BUT THAT'S STILL JUST A MACHINE OUT THERE, CAITLIN.
A MACHINE WITH A MAN INSIDE--A MAN FOR A SOUL.
A MAN WHO NEEDS MY HELP.
CISCO, I NEED A DIRECTIONAL HF RADIO SIGNAL.
EASY ENOUGH, BUT THE ANTENNAE HERE ARE FIXED. WE'D HAVE TO USE THE VAN.
BETTER TO DO THIS IN PERSON ANYWAY.
WHAT EVIDENCE IS THAT?

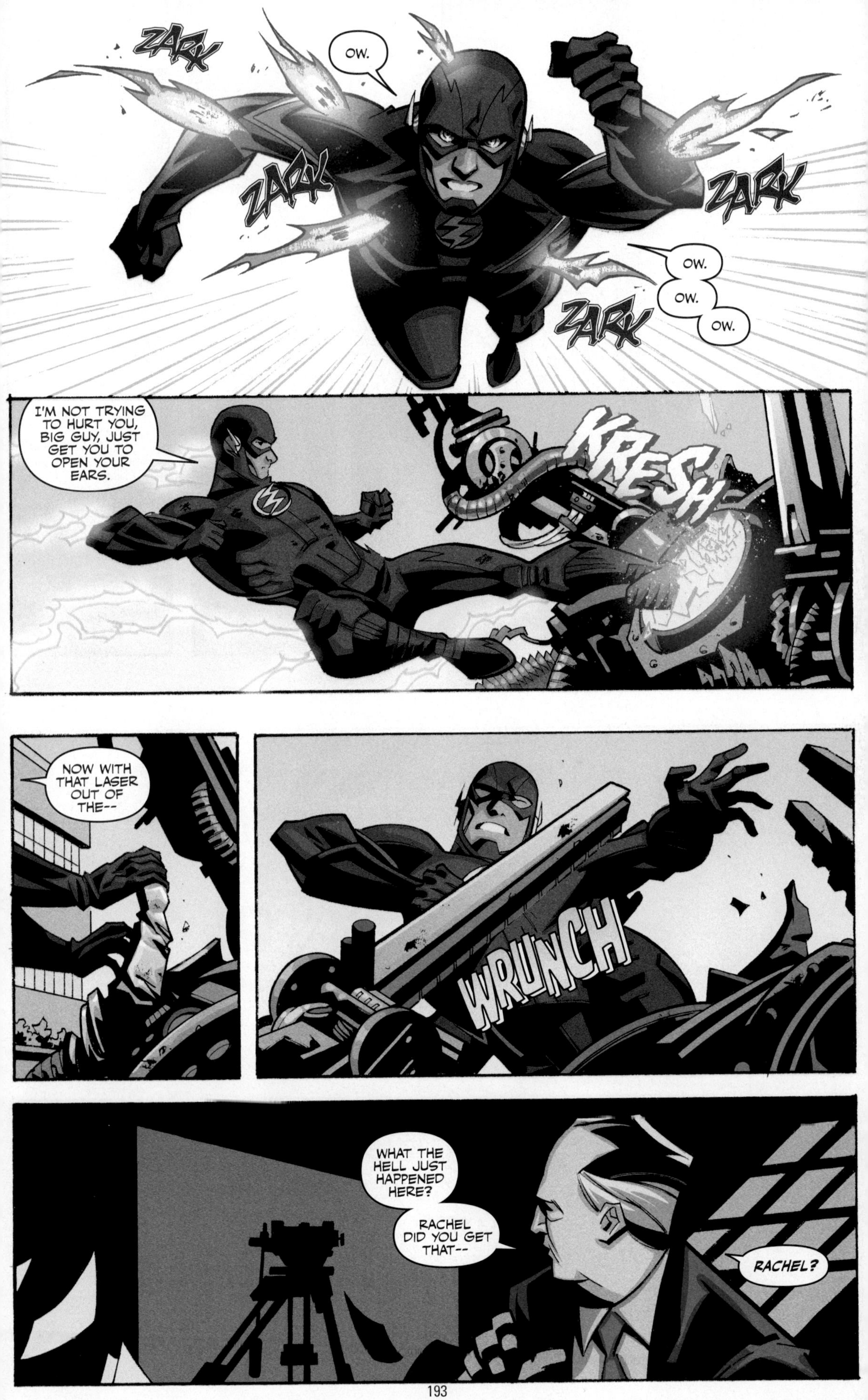
ZARK
OW.
ZARK
ZARK
OW.
OW.
ZARK
OW.
I'M NOT TRYING TO HURT YOU, BIG GUY, JUST GET YOU TO OPEN YOUR EARS.
KRESH
NOW WITH THAT LASER OUT OF THE--
WRUNCH
WHAT THE HELL JUST HAPPENED HERE?
RACHEL DID YOU GET THAT--
RACHEL?

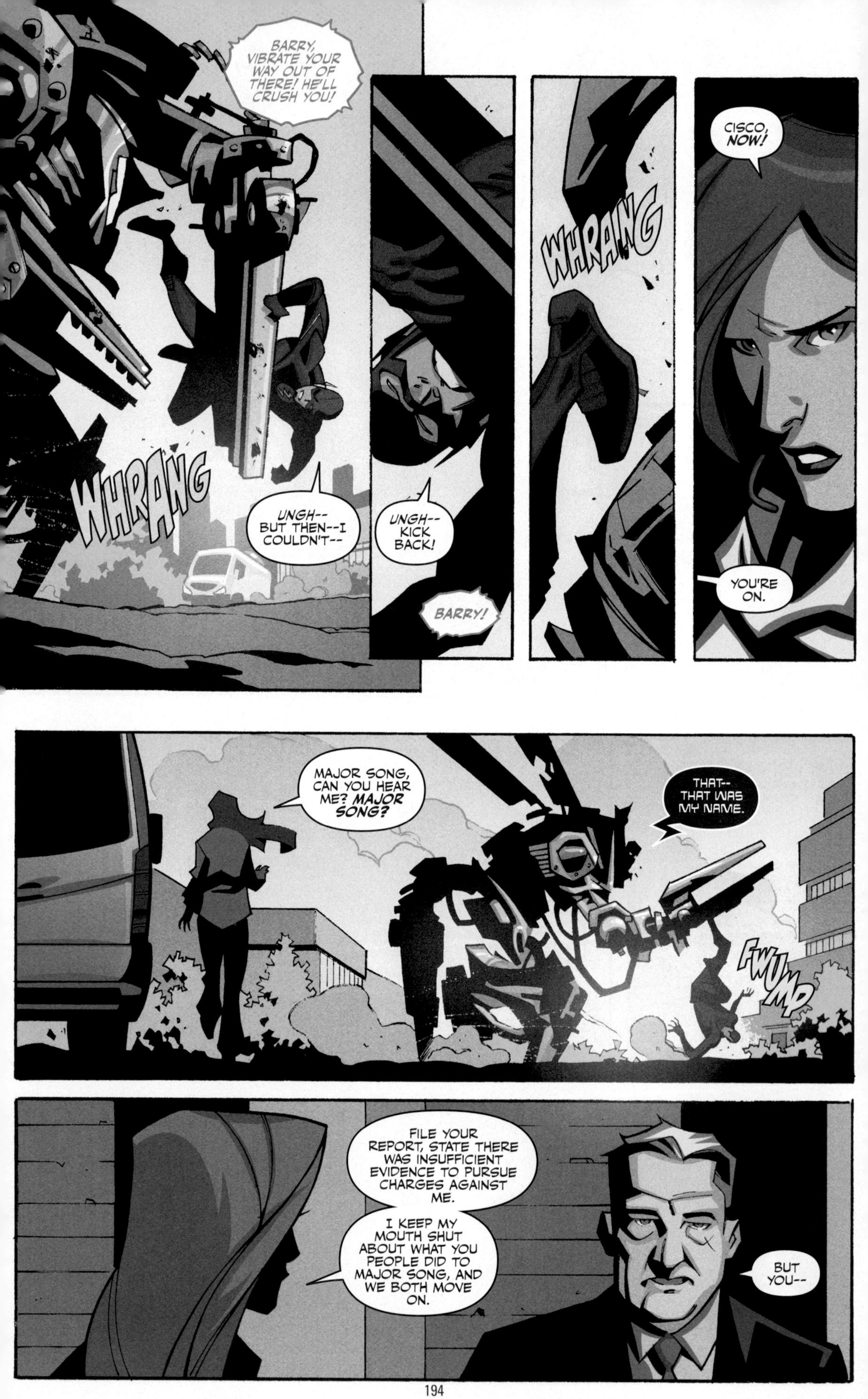
BARRY, VIBRATE YOUR WAY OUT OF THERE! HE'LL CRUSH YOU!
WHRANG
UNGH-- BUT THEN--I COULDN'T--
UNGH-- KICK BACK!
BARRY!
WHRANG
CISCO, NOW!
YOU'RE ON.
MAJOR SONG, CAN YOU HEAR ME? MAJOR SONG?
THAT-- THAT WAS MY NAME.
FWUMP
FILE YOUR REPORT, STATE THERE WAS INSUFFICIENT EVIDENCE TO PURSUE CHARGES AGAINST ME.
I KEEP MY MOUTH SHUT ABOUT WHAT YOU PEOPLE DID TO MAJOR SONG, AND WE BOTH MOVE ON.
BUT YOU--

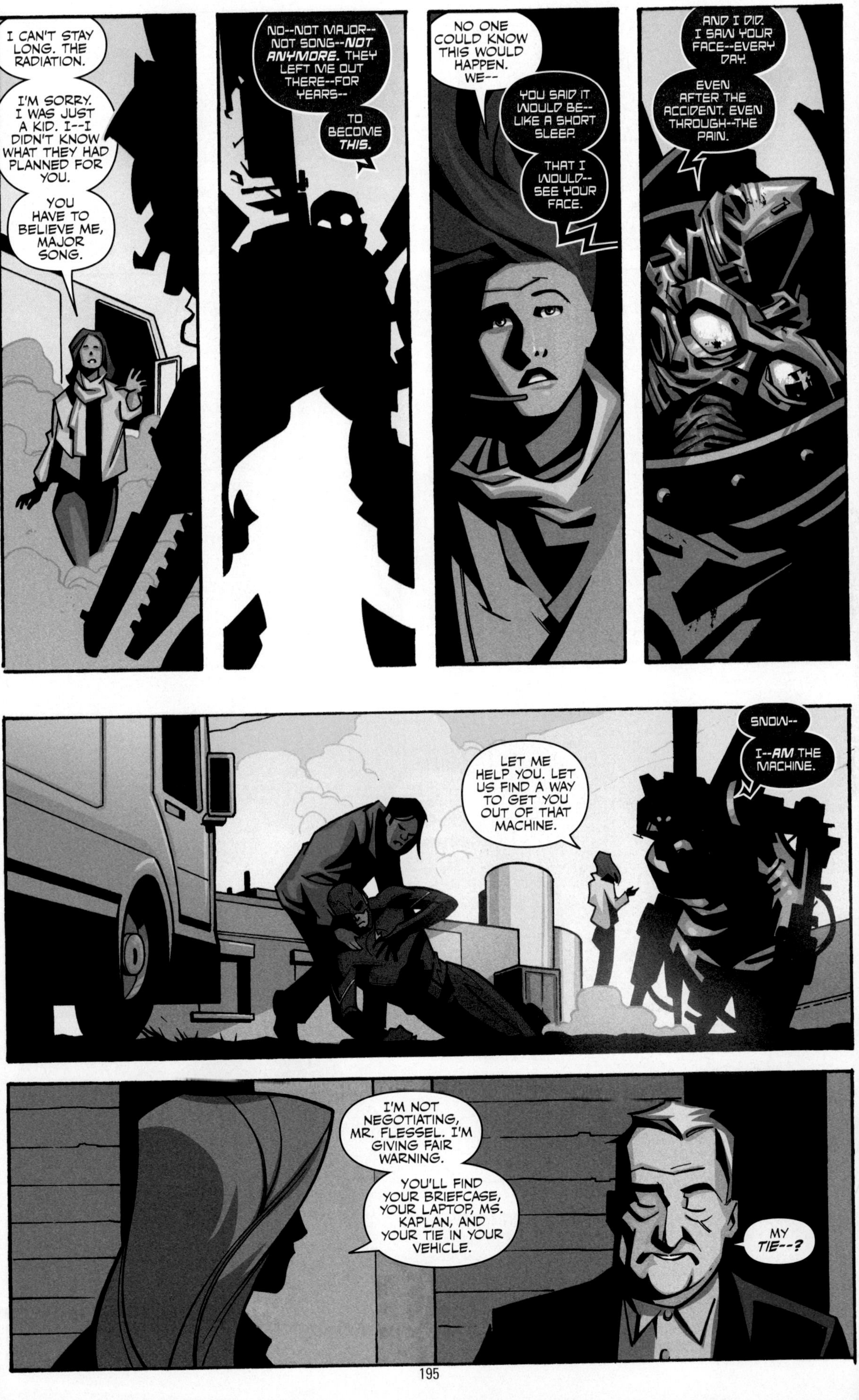
I CAN'T STAY LONG. THE RADIATION.
I'M SORRY. I WAS JUST A KID. I--I DIDN'T KNOW WHAT THEY HAD PLANNED FOR YOU.
YOU HAVE TO BELIEVE ME, MAJOR SONG.
NO--NOT MAJOR--NOT SONG--NOT ANYMORE. THEY LEFT ME OUT THERE--FOR YEARS--
TO BECOME THIS.
NO ONE COULD KNOW THIS WOULD HAPPEN. WE--
YOU SAID IT WOULD BE--LIKE A SHORT SLEEP.
THAT I WOULD--SEE YOUR FACE.
AND I DID. I SAW YOUR FACE--EVERY DAY.
EVEN AFTER THE ACCIDENT. EVEN THROUGH--THE PAIN.
LET ME HELP YOU. LET US FIND A WAY TO GET YOU OUT OF THAT MACHINE.
SNOW--
I--AM THE MACHINE.
I'M NOT NEGOTIATING, MR. FLESSEL. I'M GIVING FAIR WARNING.
YOU'LL FIND YOUR BRIEFCASE, YOUR LAPTOP, MS. KAPLAN, AND YOUR TIE IN YOUR VEHICLE.
MY TIE--?

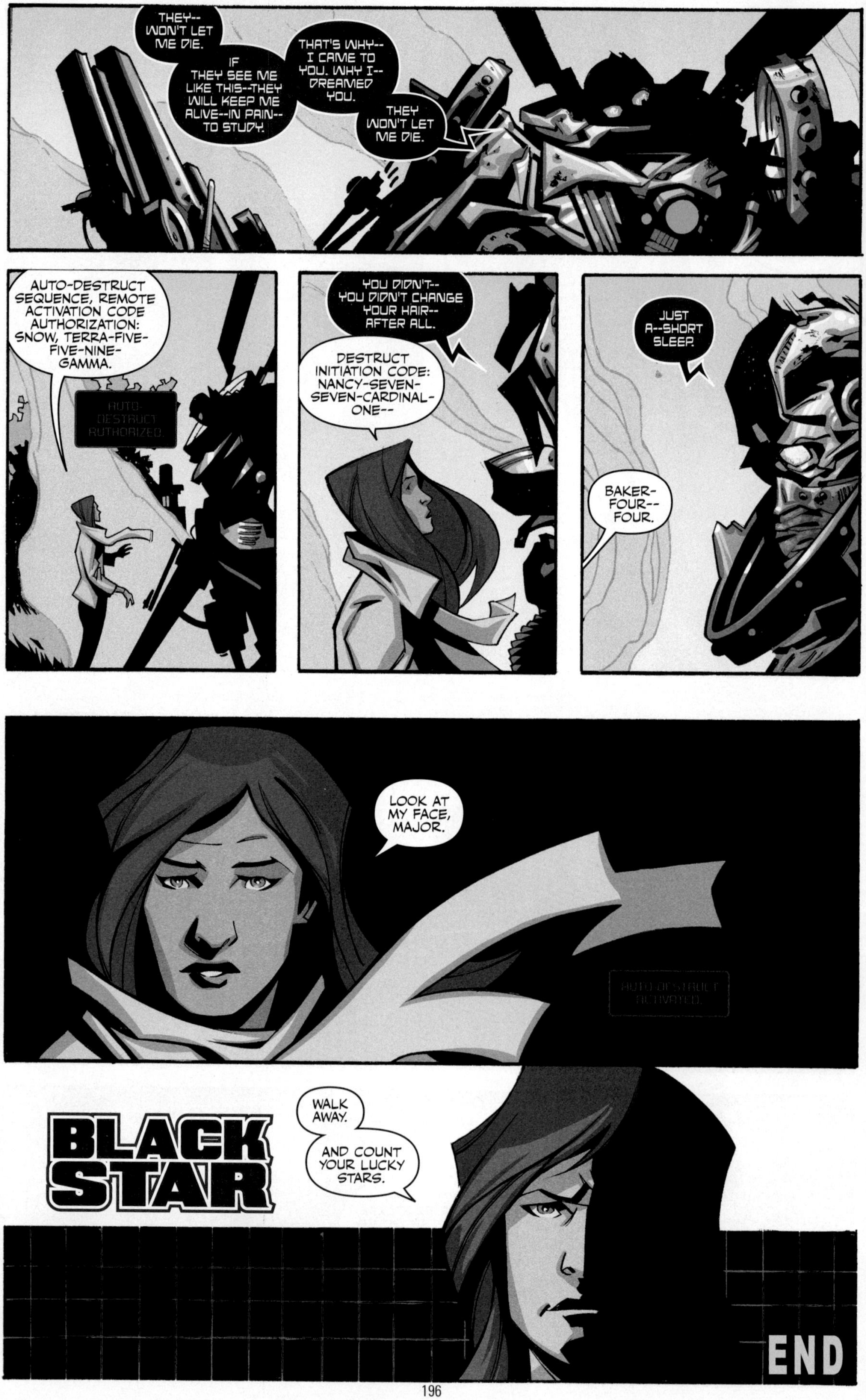
THEY-- WON'T LET ME DIE.
IF THEY SEE ME LIKE THIS--THEY WILL KEEP ME ALIVE--IN PAIN-- TO STUDY.
THAT'S WHY-- I CAME TO YOU. WHY I-- DREAMED YOU.
THEY WON'T LET ME DIE.
AUTO-DESTRUCT SEQUENCE, REMOTE ACTIVATION CODE AUTHORIZATION: SNOW, TERRA-FIVE-FIVE-NINE-GAMMA.
AUTO-DESTRUCT AUTHORIZED.
YOU DIDN'T-- YOU DIDN'T CHANGE YOUR HAIR-- AFTER ALL.
DESTRUCT INITIATION CODE: NANCY-SEVEN-SEVEN-CARDINAL-ONE--
JUST A--SHORT SLEEP.
BAKER-FOUR--FOUR.
LOOK AT MY FACE, MAJOR.
AUTO-DESTRUCT ACTIVATED.
BLACK STAR
WALK AWAY.
AND COUNT YOUR LUCKY STARS.
END

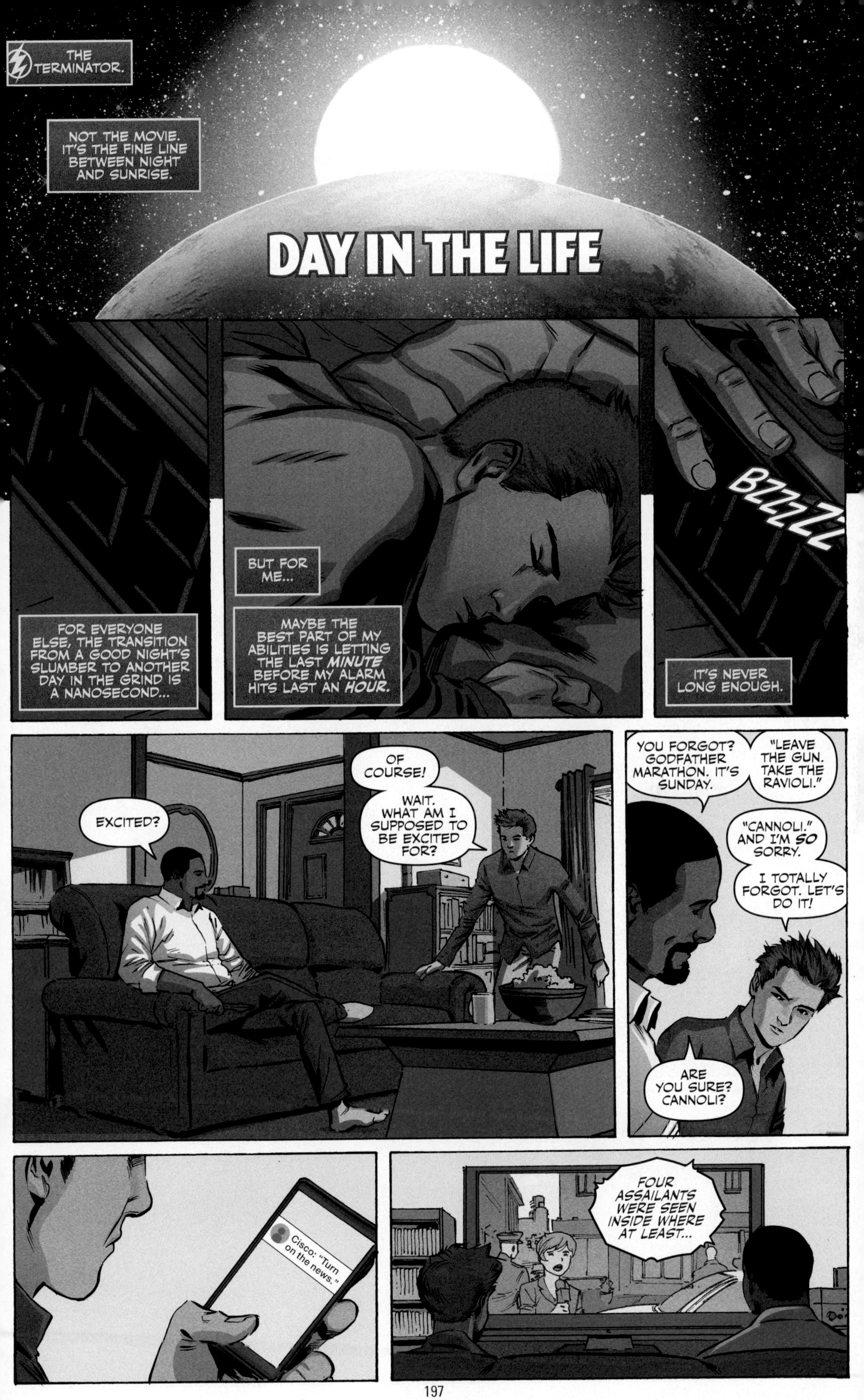
THE TERMINATOR.
NOT THE MOVIE. IT'S THE FINE LINE BETWEEN NIGHT AND SUNRISE.
DAY IN THE LIFE
FOR EVERYONE ELSE, THE TRANSITION FROM A GOOD NIGHT'S SLUMBER TO ANOTHER DAY IN THE GRIND IS A NANOSECOND...
BUT FOR ME...
MAYBE THE BEST PART OF MY ABILITIES IS LETTING THE LAST MINUTE BEFORE MY ALARM HITS LAST AN HOUR.
BZZZZZ
IT'S NEVER LONG ENOUGH.
EXCITED?
OF COURSE!
WAIT. WHAT AM I SUPPOSED TO BE EXCITED FOR?
YOU FORGOT? GODFATHER MARATHON. IT'S SUNDAY.
"LEAVE THE GUN. TAKE THE RAVIOLI."
"CANNOLI." AND I'M SO SORRY.
I TOTALLY FORGOT. LET'S DO IT!
ARE YOU SURE? CANNOLI?
Cisco: "Turn on the news."
FOUR ASSAILANTS WERE SEEN INSIDE WHERE AT LEAST...

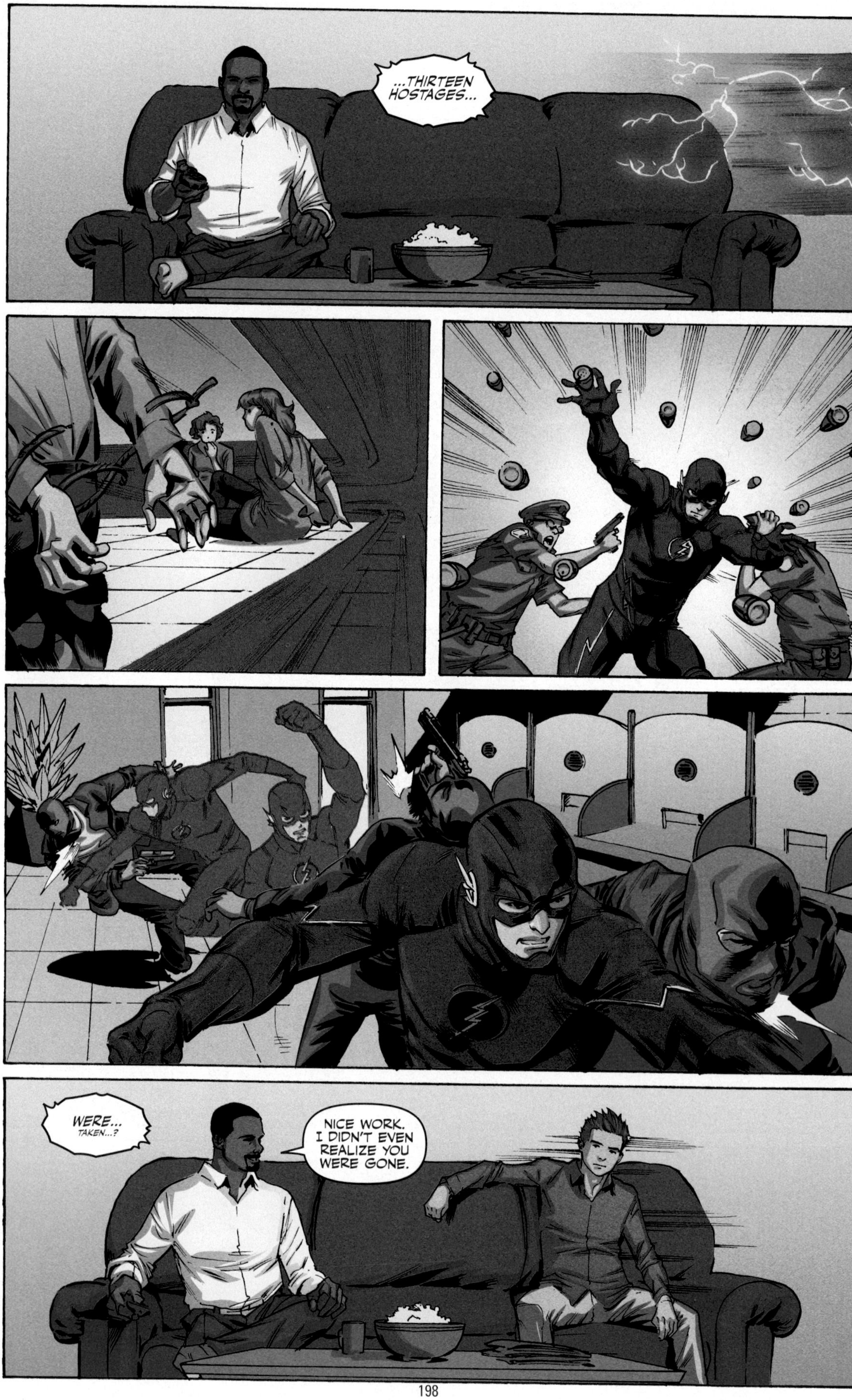
...THIRTEEN HOSTAGES...
WERE... TAKEN...?
NICE WORK. I DIDN'T EVEN REALIZE YOU WERE GONE.

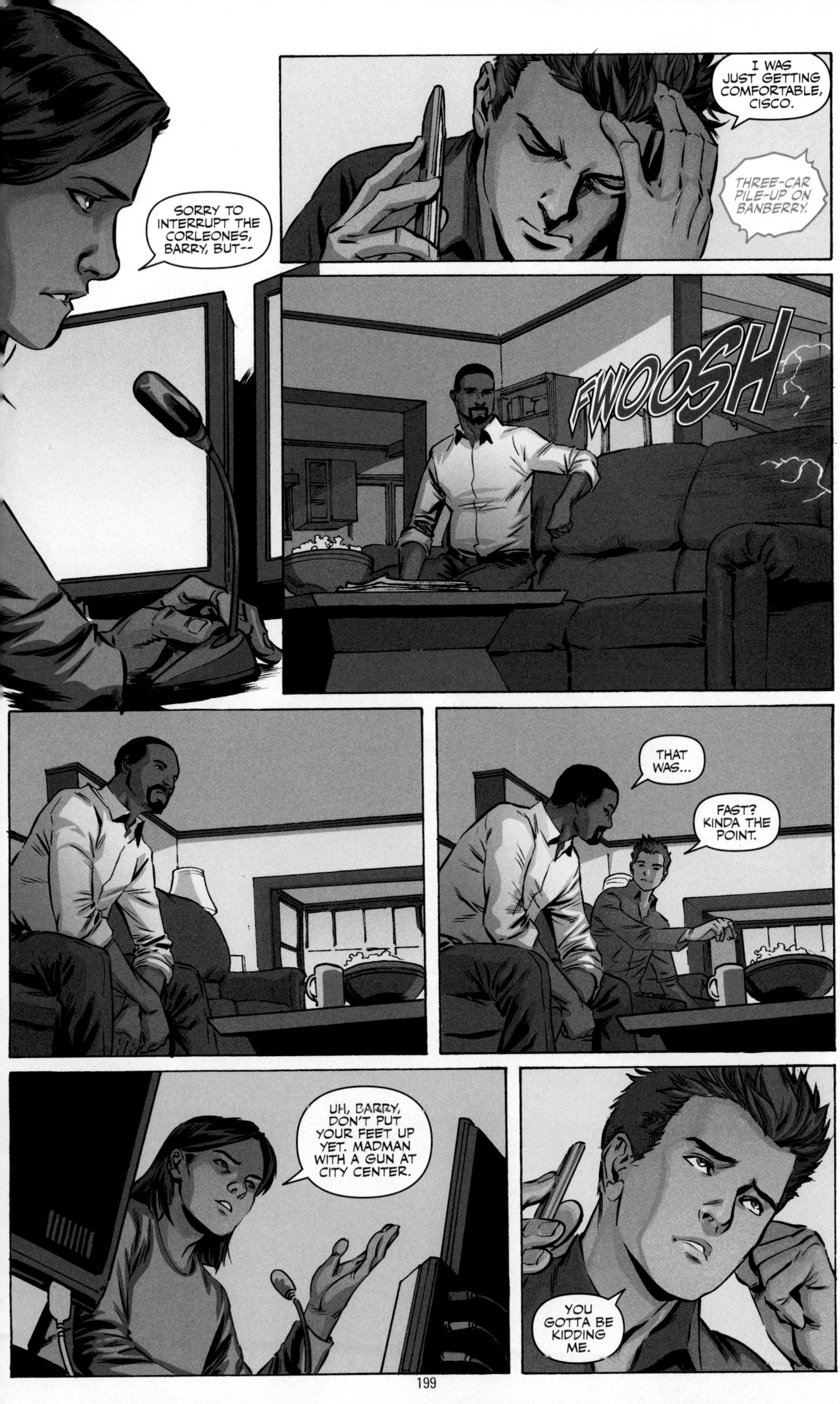
I WAS JUST GETTING COMFORTABLE, CISCO.
SORRY TO INTERRUPT THE CORLEONES, BARRY, BUT--
THREE-CAR PILE-UP ON BANBERRY.
FWOOSH
THAT WAS...
FAST? KINDA THE POINT.
UH, BARRY, DON'T PUT YOUR FEET UP YET. MADMAN WITH A GUN AT CITY CENTER.
YOU GOTTA BE KIDDING ME.

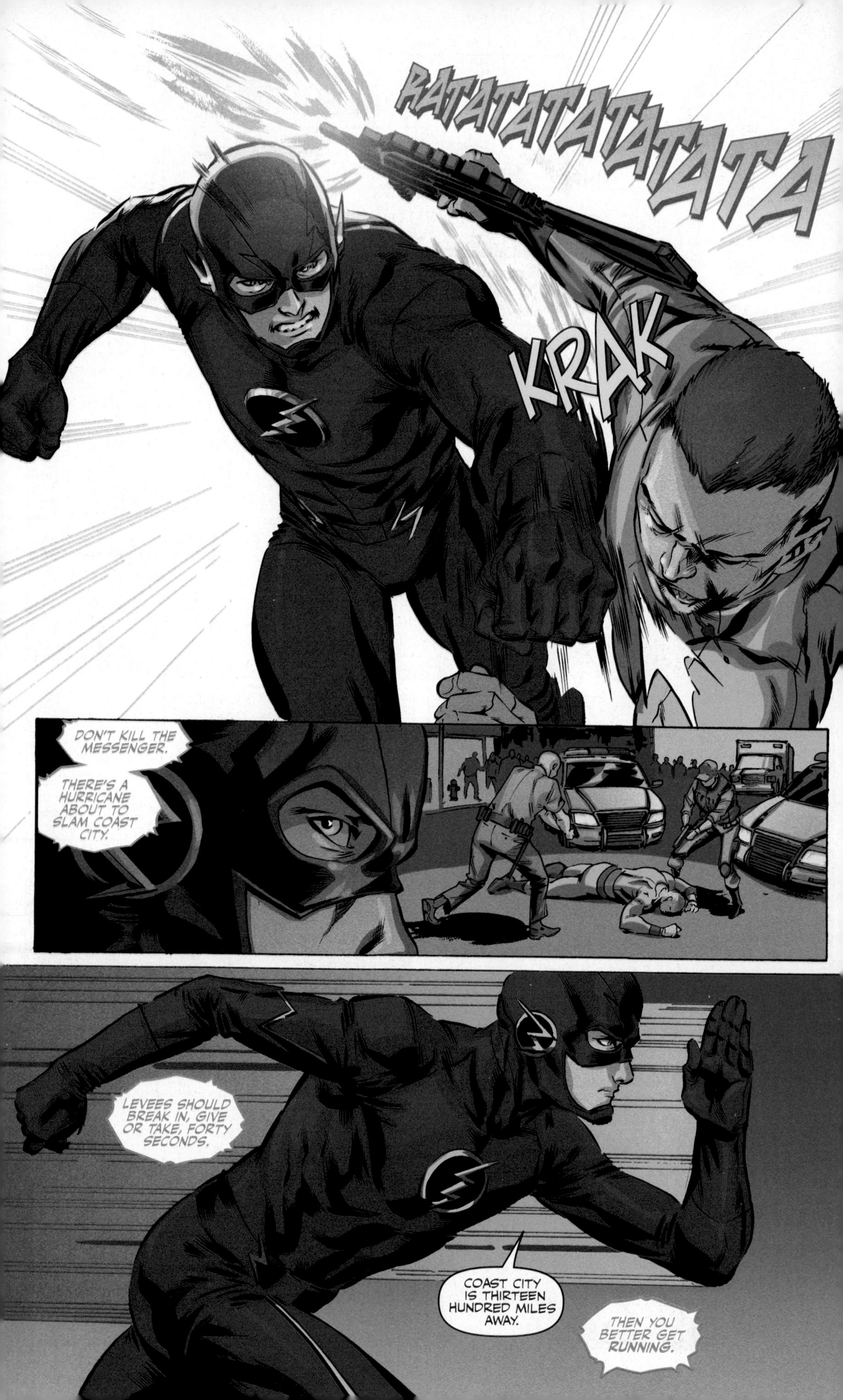
RATATATATATATATA
KRAK
DON'T KILL THE MESSENGER.
THERE'S A HURRICANE ABOUT TO SLAM COAST CITY.
LEVEES SHOULD BREAK IN, GIVE OR TAKE, FORTY SECONDS.
COAST CITY IS THIRTEEN HUNDRED MILES AWAY.
THEN YOU BETTER GET RUNNING.

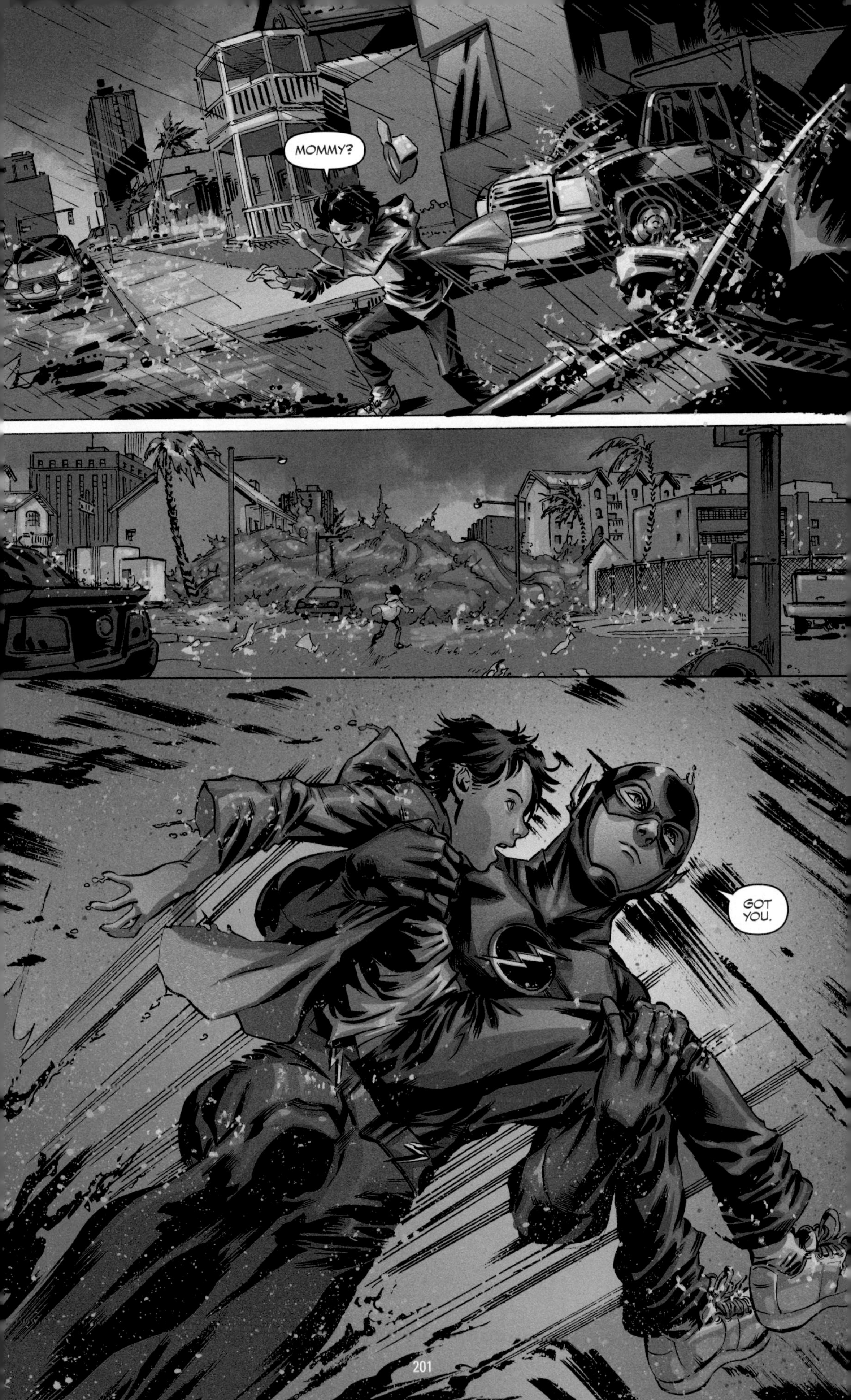
MOMMY?
GOT YOU.

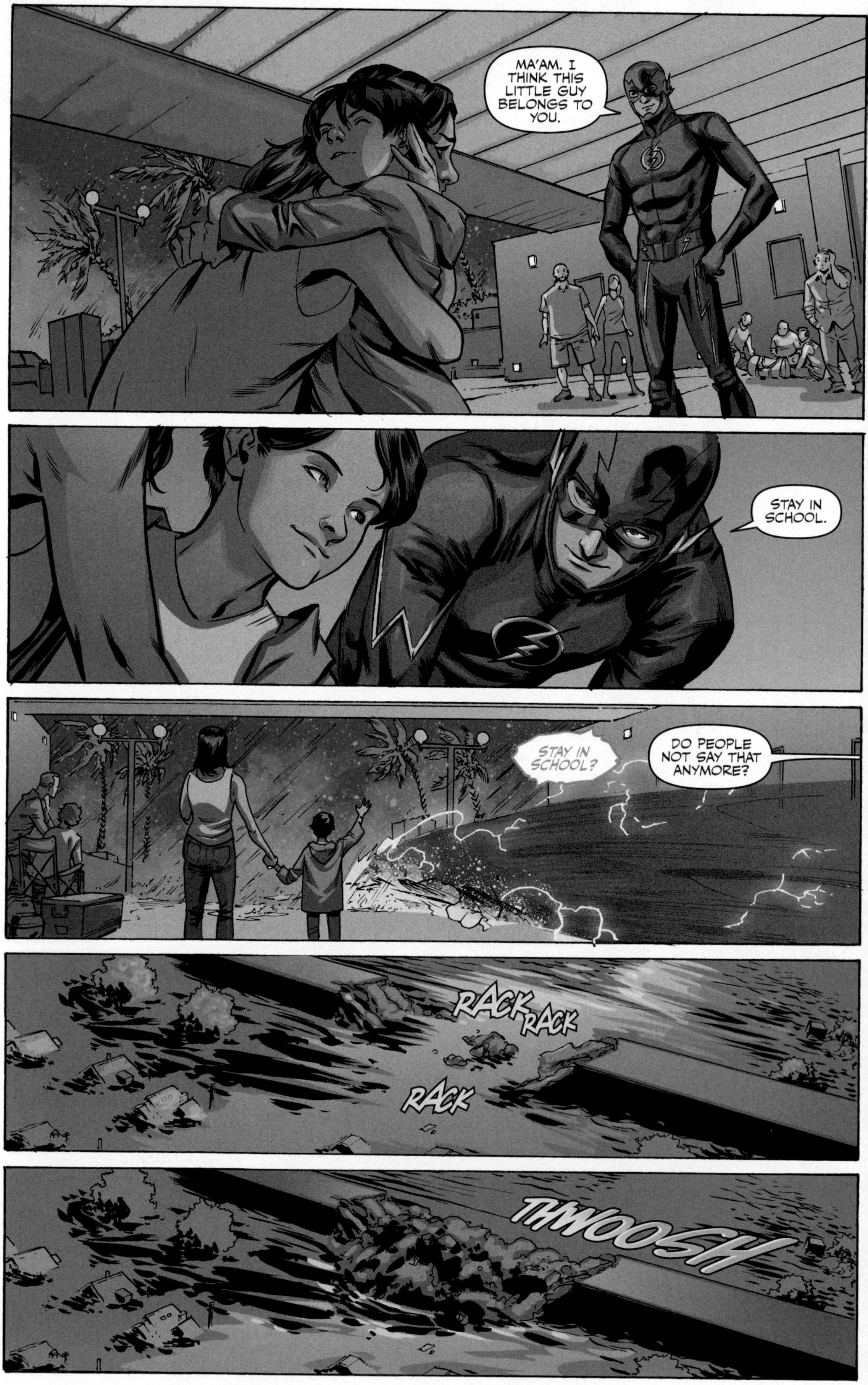
MA'AM. I THINK THIS LITTLE GUY BELONGS TO YOU.
STAY IN SCHOOL.
STAY IN SCHOOL?
DO PEOPLE NOT SAY THAT ANYMORE?
RACK RACK
RACK
THWOOSH

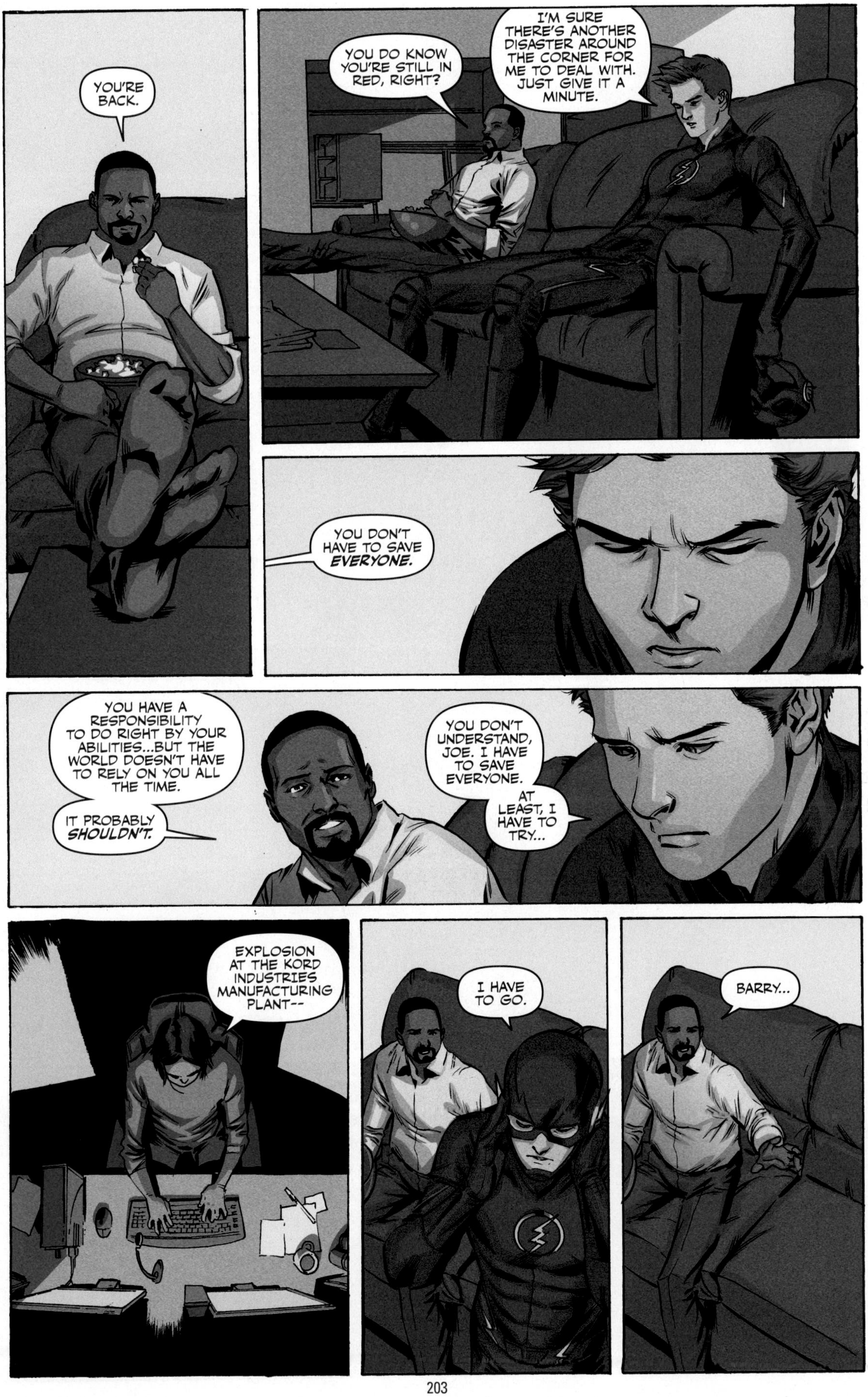
YOU'RE BACK.
YOU DO KNOW YOU'RE STILL IN RED, RIGHT?
I'M SURE THERE'S ANOTHER DISASTER AROUND THE CORNER FOR ME TO DEAL WITH. JUST GIVE IT A MINUTE.
YOU DON'T HAVE TO SAVE EVERYONE.
YOU HAVE A RESPONSIBILITY TO DO RIGHT BY YOUR ABILITIES...BUT THE WORLD DOESN'T HAVE TO RELY ON YOU ALL THE TIME.
IT PROBABLY SHOULDN'T.
YOU DON'T UNDERSTAND, JOE. I HAVE TO SAVE EVERYONE.
AT LEAST, I HAVE TO TRY...
EXPLOSION AT THE KORD INDUSTRIES MANUFACTURING PLANT--
I HAVE TO GO.
BARRY...

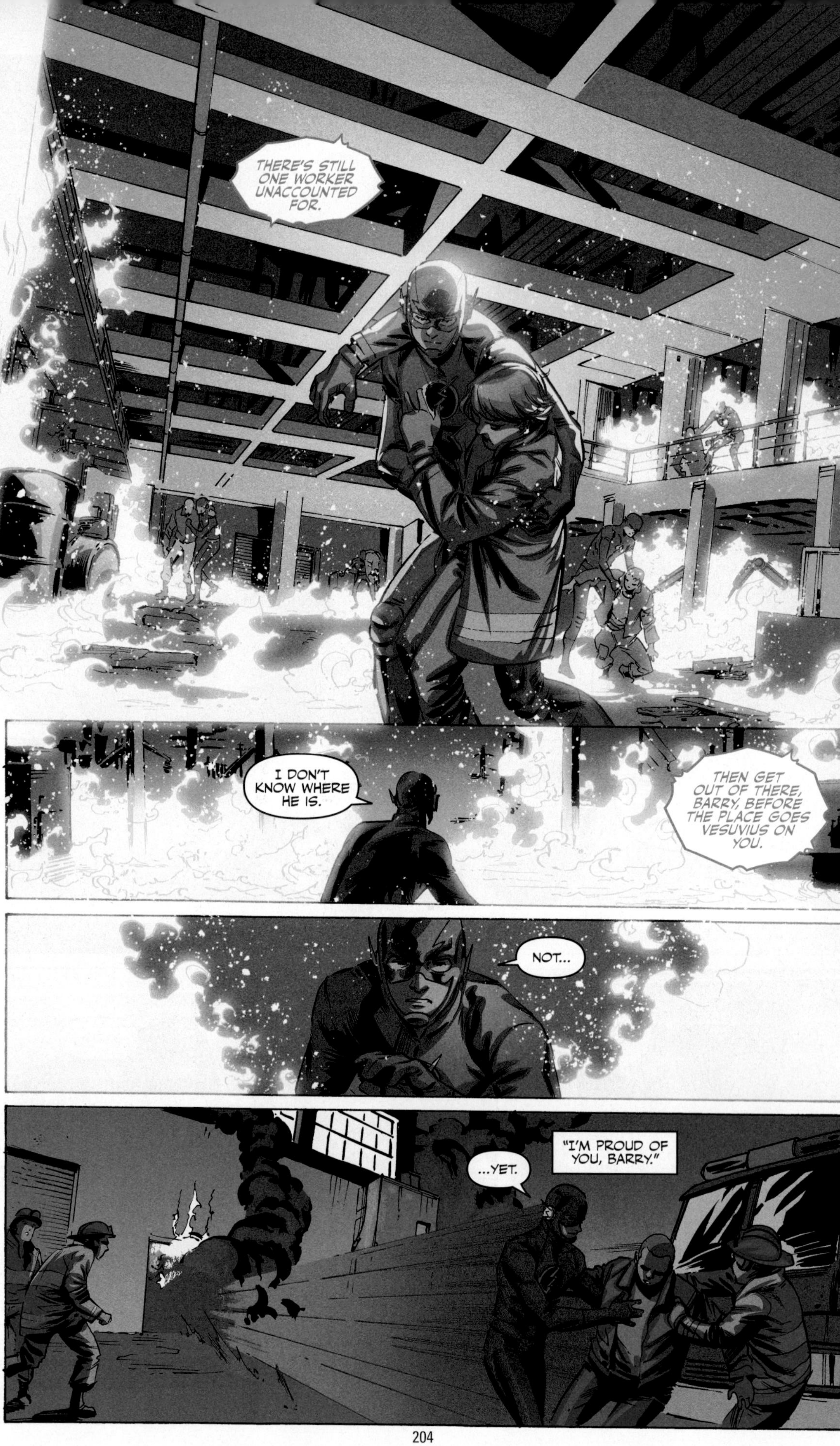
THERE'S STILL ONE WORKER UNACCOUNTED FOR.
I DON'T KNOW WHERE HE IS.
THEN GET OUT OF THERE, BARRY, BEFORE THE PLACE GOES VESUVIUS ON YOU.
NOT...
...YET.
"I'M PROUD OF YOU, BARRY."

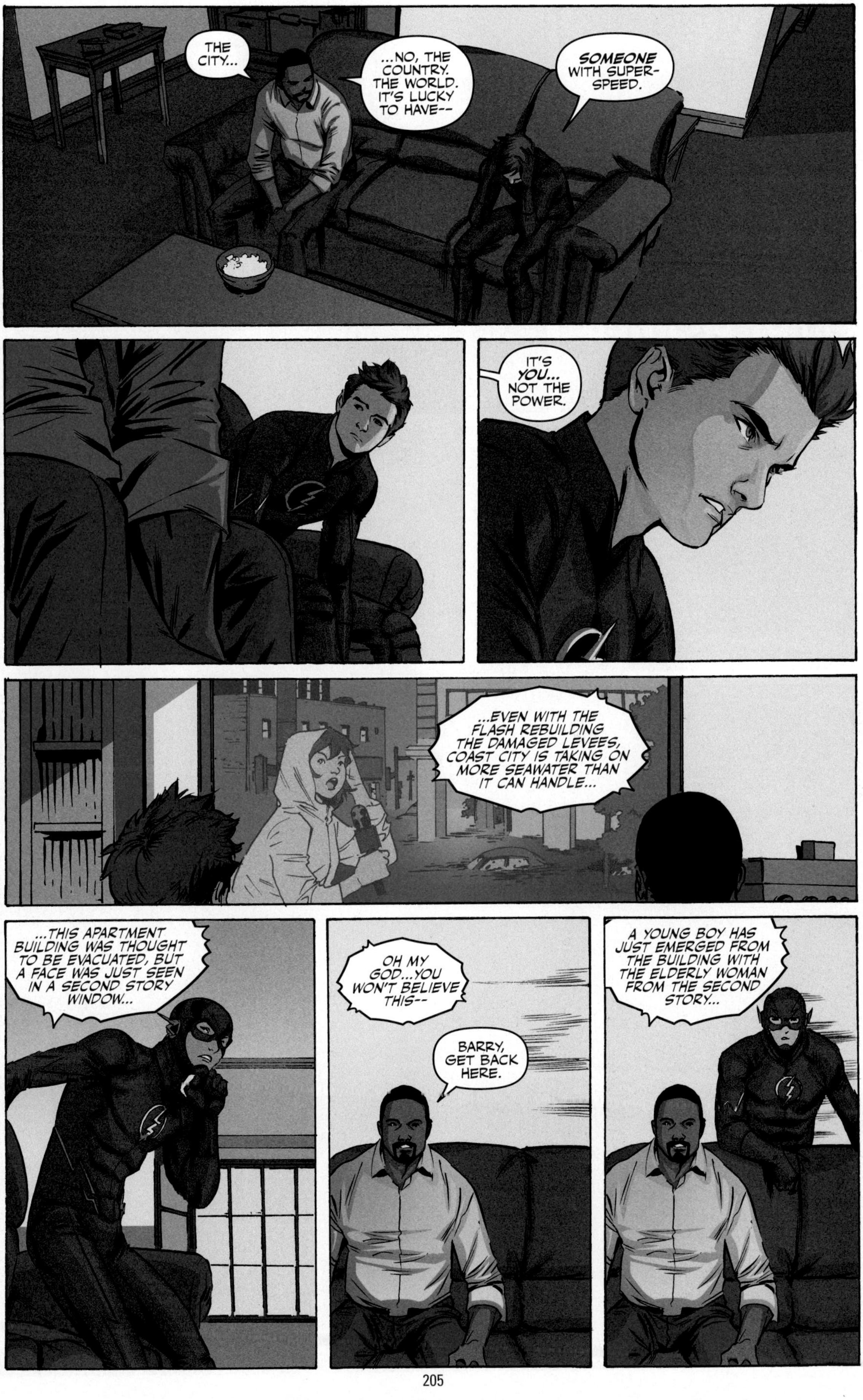
THE CITY...
...NO, THE COUNTRY. THE WORLD. IT'S LUCKY TO HAVE--
SOMEONE WITH SUPER-SPEED.
IT'S YOU... NOT THE POWER.
...EVEN WITH THE FLASH REBUILDING THE DAMAGED LEVEES, COAST CITY IS TAKING ON MORE SEAWATER THAN IT CAN HANDLE...
...THIS APARTMENT BUILDING WAS THOUGHT TO BE EVACUATED, BUT A FACE WAS JUST SEEN IN A SECOND STORY WINDOW...
OH MY GOD...YOU WON'T BELIEVE THIS--
BARRY, GET BACK HERE.
A YOUNG BOY HAS JUST EMERGED FROM THE BUILDING WITH THE ELDERLY WOMAN FROM THE SECOND STORY...

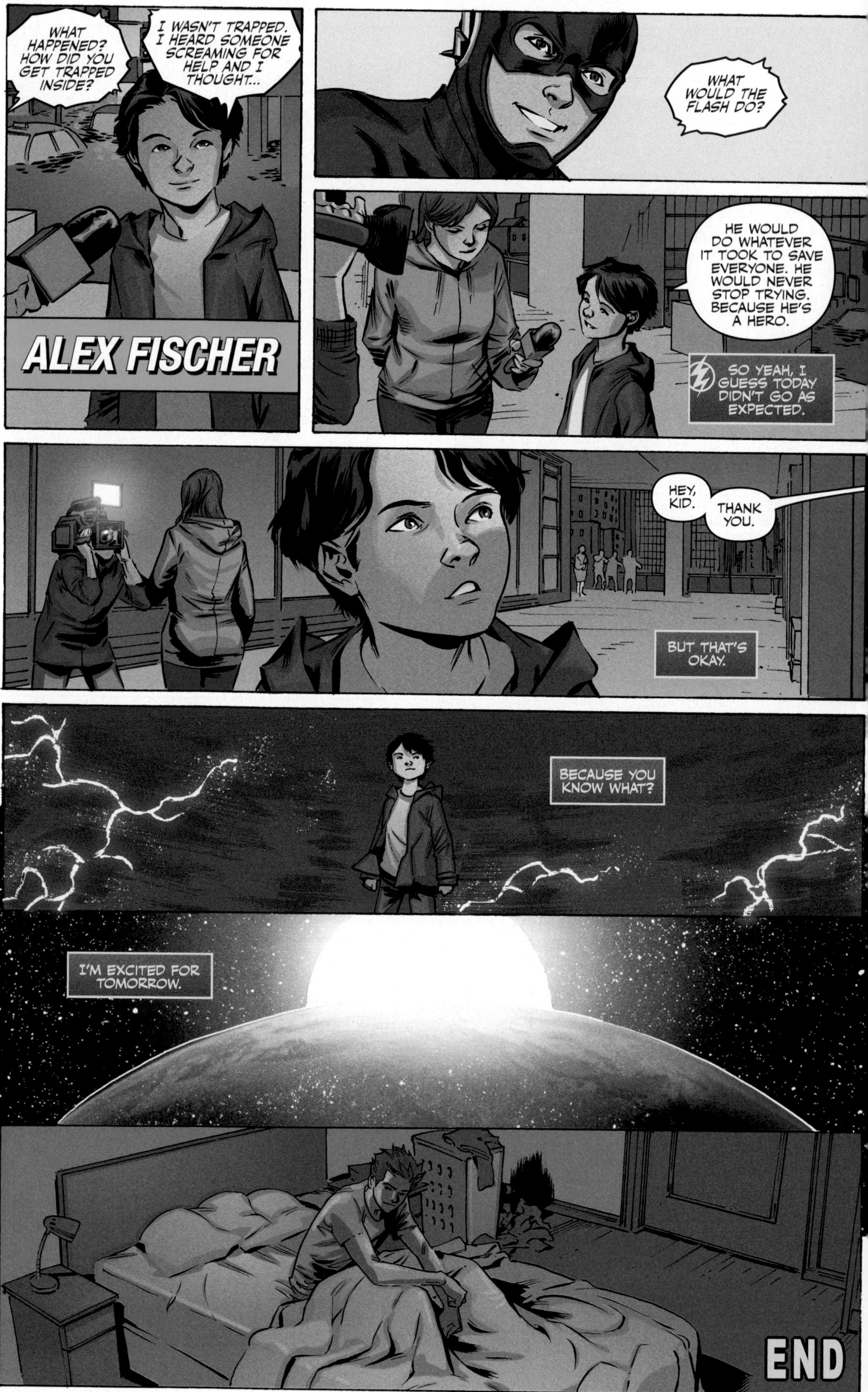
WHAT HAPPENED? HOW DID YOU GET TRAPPED INSIDE?
I WASN'T TRAPPED. I HEARD SOMEONE SCREAMING FOR HELP AND I THOUGHT...
ALEX FISCHER
WHAT WOULD THE FLASH DO?
HE WOULD DO WHATEVER IT TOOK TO SAVE EVERYONE. HE WOULD NEVER STOP TRYING. BECAUSE HE'S A HERO.
SO YEAH, I GUESS TODAY DIDN'T GO AS EXPECTED.
HEY, KID.
THANK YOU.
BUT THAT'S OKAY.
BECAUSE YOU KNOW WHAT?
I'M EXCITED FOR TOMORROW.
END

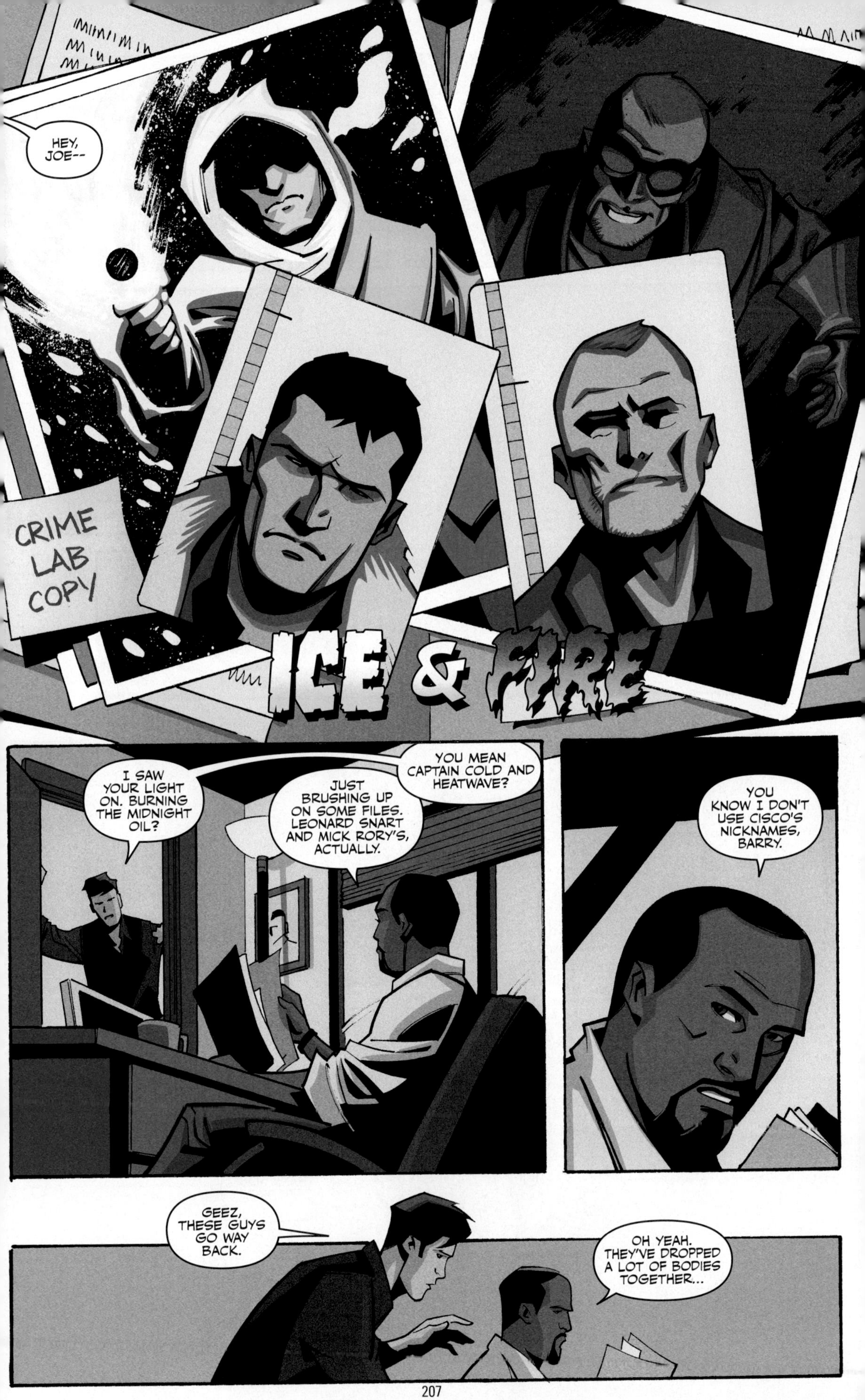

HEY, JOE--
CRIME LAB COPY
ICE & FIRE
I SAW YOUR LIGHT ON. BURNING THE MIDNIGHT OIL?
JUST BRUSHING UP ON SOME FILES. LEONARD SNART AND MICK RORY'S, ACTUALLY.
YOU MEAN CAPTAIN COLD AND HEATWAVE?
YOU KNOW I DON'T USE CISCO'S NICKNAMES, BARRY.
GEEZ, THESE GUYS GO WAY BACK.
OH YEAH. THEY'VE DROPPED A LOT OF BODIES TOGETHER...

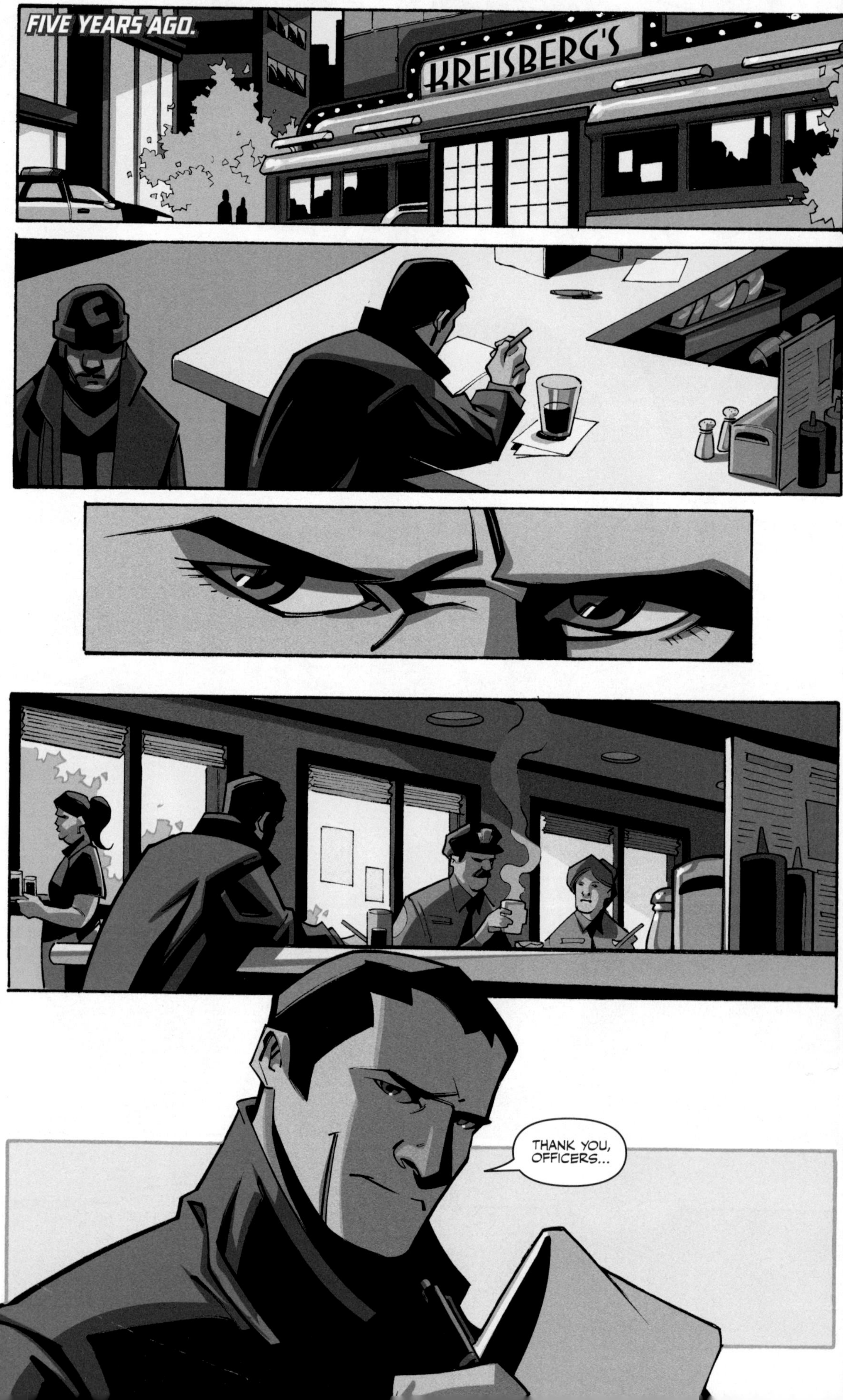
FIVE YEARS AGO.
KREISBERG'S
THANK YOU, OFFICERS...

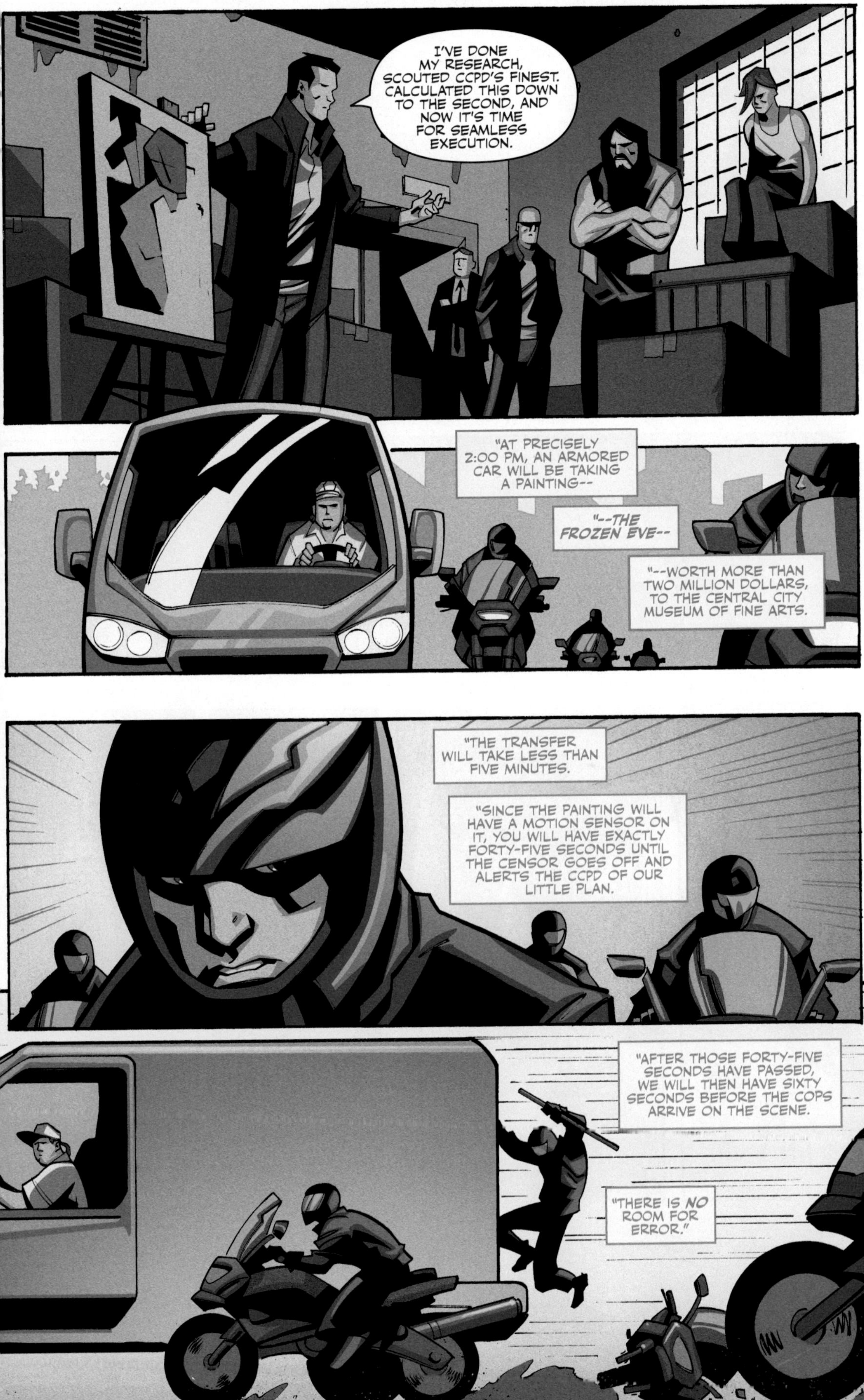
I'VE DONE MY RESEARCH, SCOUTED CCPD'S FINEST. CALCULATED THIS DOWN TO THE SECOND, AND NOW IT'S TIME FOR SEAMLESS EXECUTION.
"AT PRECISELY 2:00 PM, AN ARMORED CAR WILL BE TAKING A PAINTING--
"--THE FROZEN EVE--
"--WORTH MORE THAN TWO MILLION DOLLARS, TO THE CENTRAL CITY MUSEUM OF FINE ARTS.
"THE TRANSFER WILL TAKE LESS THAN FIVE MINUTES.
"SINCE THE PAINTING WILL HAVE A MOTION SENSOR ON IT, YOU WILL HAVE EXACTLY FORTY-FIVE SECONDS UNTIL THE CENSOR GOES OFF AND ALERTS THE CCPD OF OUR LITTLE PLAN.
"AFTER THOSE FORTY-FIVE SECONDS HAVE PASSED, WE WILL THEN HAVE SIXTY SECONDS BEFORE THE COPS ARRIVE ON THE SCENE.
"THERE IS NO ROOM FOR ERROR."

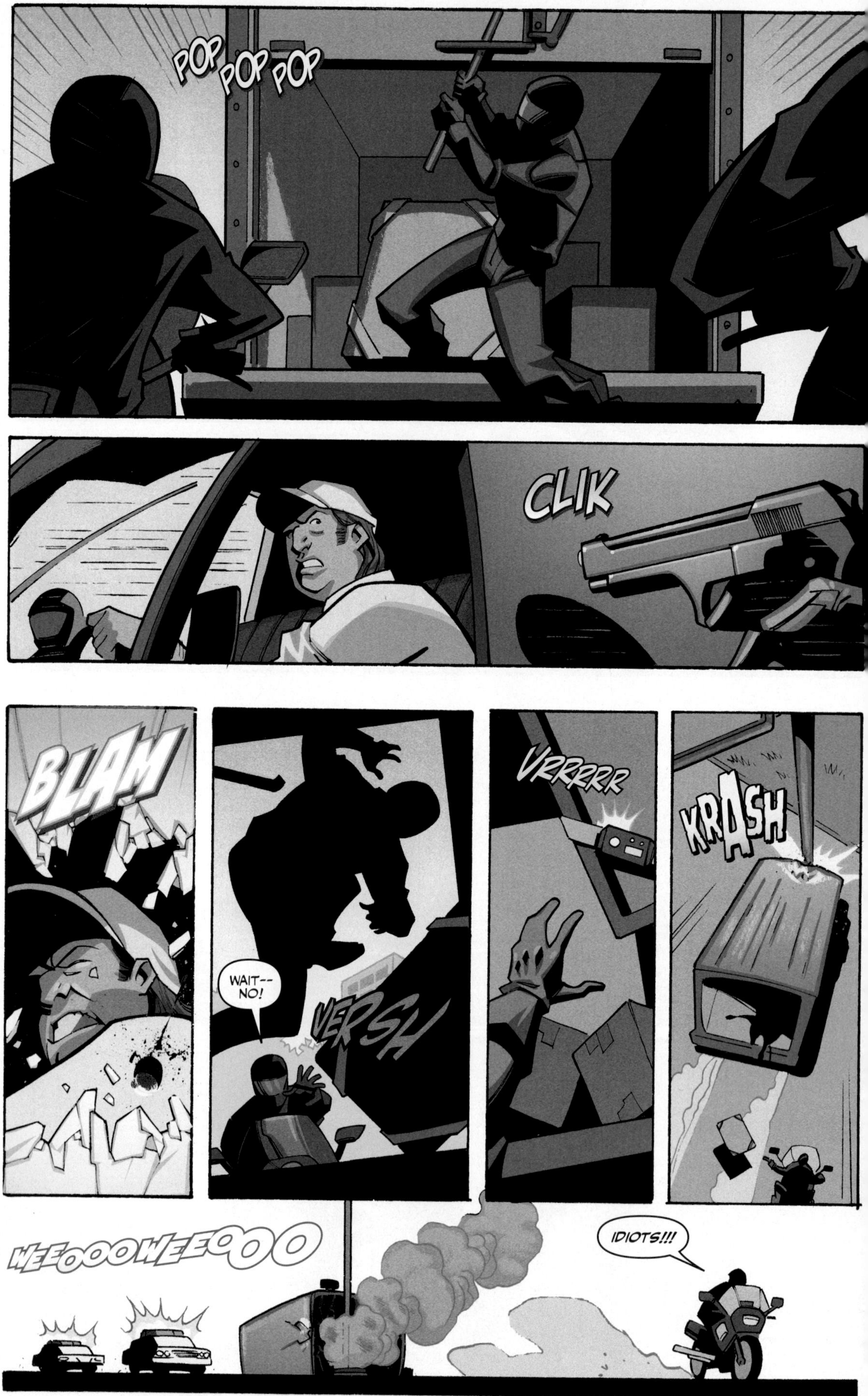
POP
POP
POP
CLIK
BLAM
WAIT-- NO!
VERSH
VRRRRR
KRASH
WEEOOOWEEOOO
IDIOTS!!!

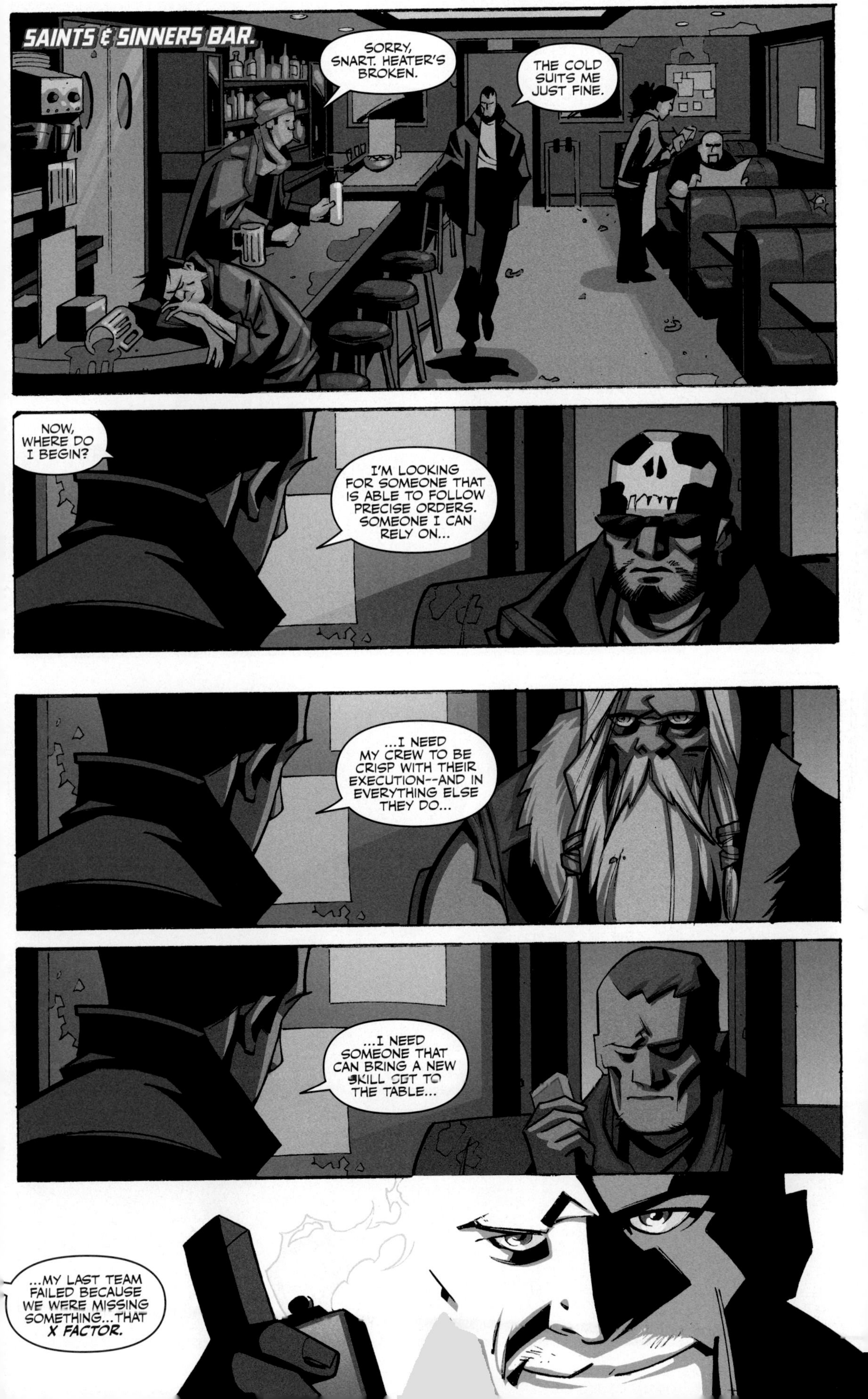
SAINTS & SINNERS BAR.
SORRY, SNART. HEATER'S BROKEN.
THE COLD SUITS ME JUST FINE.
NOW, WHERE DO I BEGIN?
I'M LOOKING FOR SOMEONE THAT IS ABLE TO FOLLOW PRECISE ORDERS. SOMEONE I CAN RELY ON...
...I NEED MY CREW TO BE CRISP WITH THEIR EXECUTION--AND IN EVERYTHING ELSE THEY DO...
...I NEED SOMEONE THAT CAN BRING A NEW SKILL SET TO THE TABLE...
...MY LAST TEAM FAILED BECAUSE WE WERE MISSING SOMETHING...THAT *X FACTOR.*

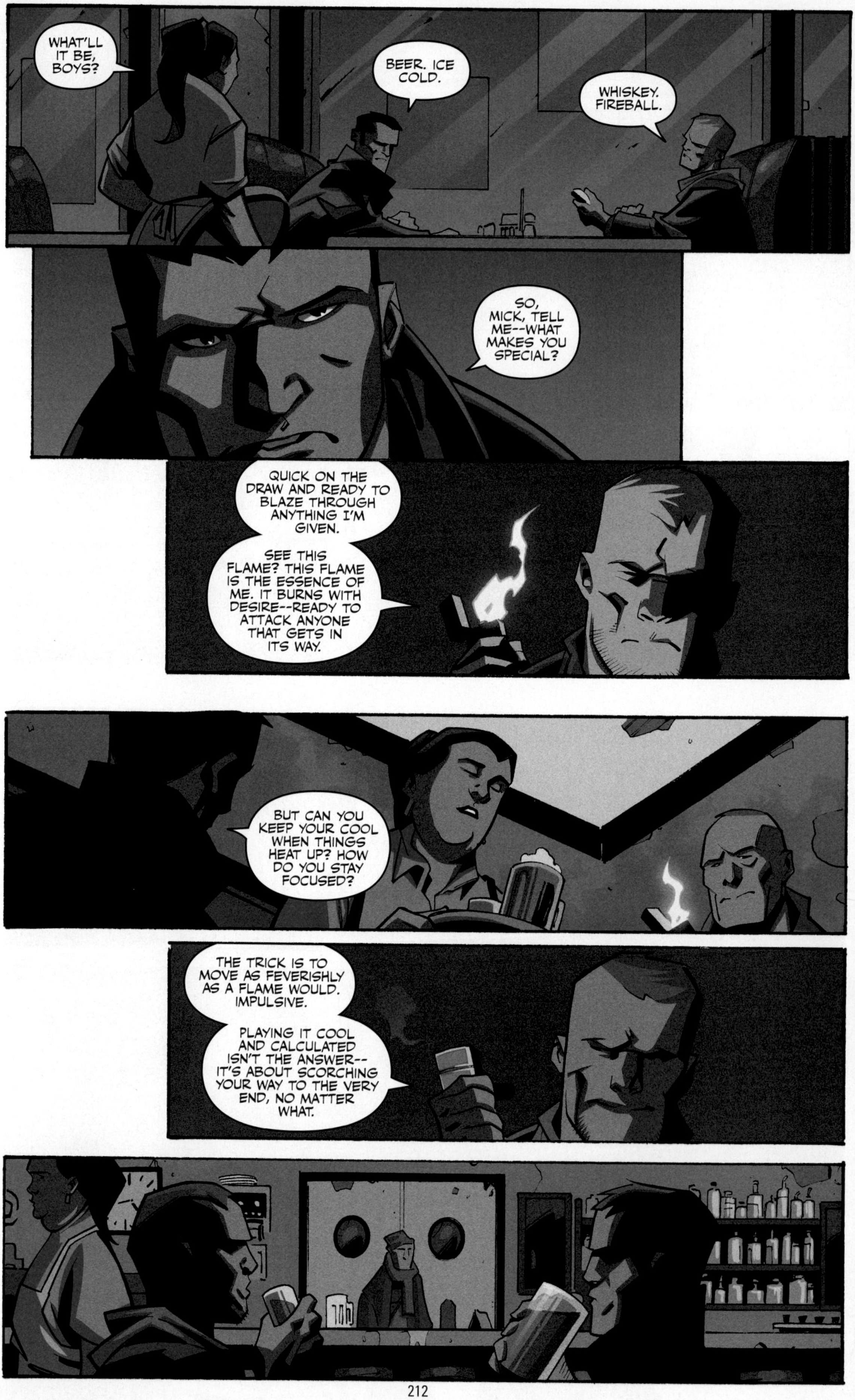
WHAT'LL IT BE, BOYS?
BEER. ICE COLD.
WHISKEY. FIREBALL.
SO, MICK, TELL ME--WHAT MAKES YOU SPECIAL?
QUICK ON THE DRAW AND READY TO BLAZE THROUGH ANYTHING I'M GIVEN.
SEE THIS FLAME? THIS FLAME IS THE ESSENCE OF ME. IT BURNS WITH DESIRE--READY TO ATTACK ANYONE THAT GETS IN ITS WAY.
BUT CAN YOU KEEP YOUR COOL WHEN THINGS HEAT UP? HOW DO YOU STAY FOCUSED?
THE TRICK IS TO MOVE AS FEVERISHLY AS A FLAME WOULD. IMPULSIVE.
PLAYING IT COOL AND CALCULATED ISN'T THE ANSWER--IT'S ABOUT SCORCHING YOUR WAY TO THE VERY END, NO MATTER WHAT.

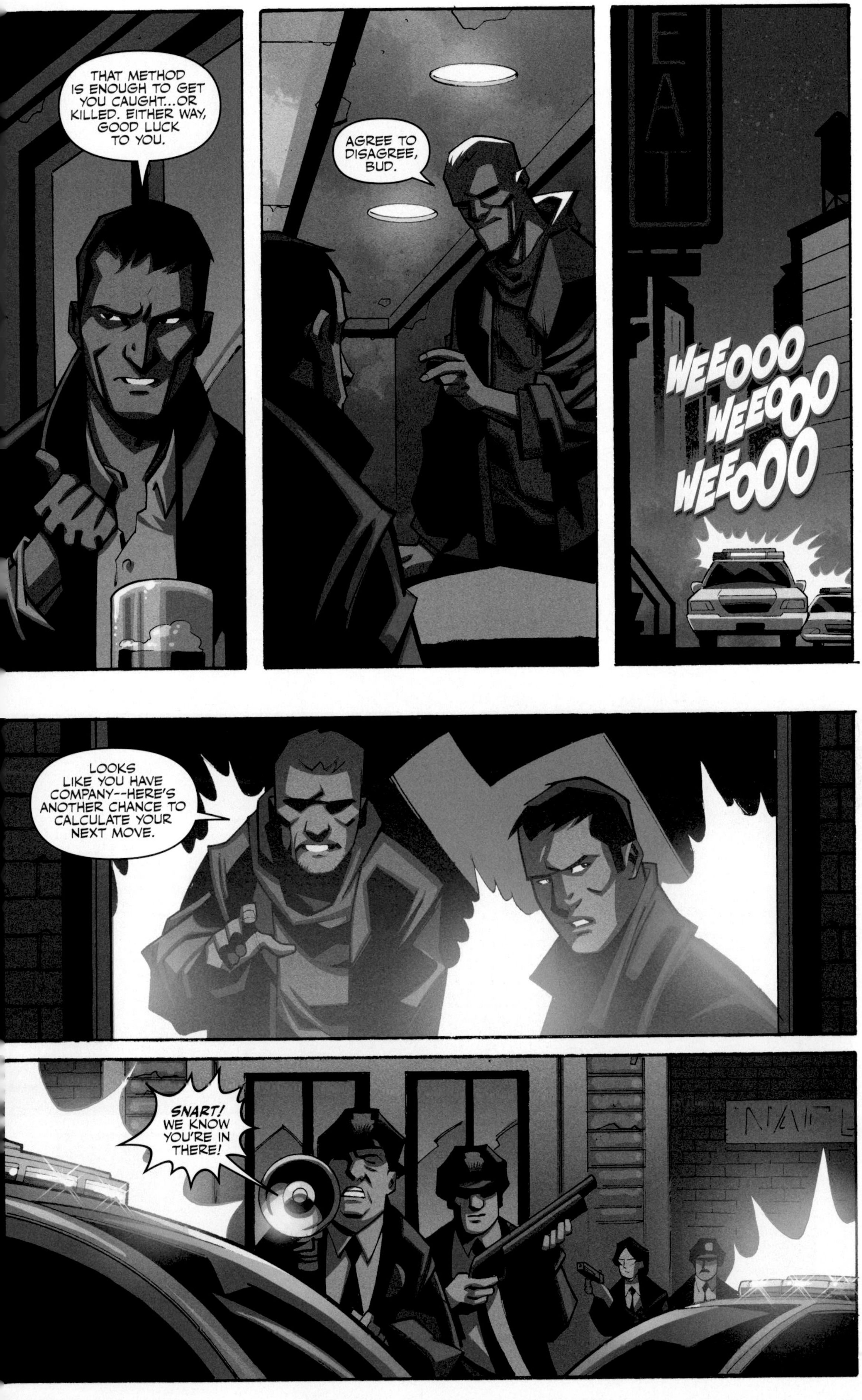
THAT METHOD IS ENOUGH TO GET YOU CAUGHT...OR KILLED. EITHER WAY, GOOD LUCK TO YOU.
AGREE TO DISAGREE, BUD.
EAT
WEEOOO WEEOOO WEEOOO
LOOKS LIKE YOU HAVE COMPANY--HERE'S ANOTHER CHANCE TO CALCULATE YOUR NEXT MOVE.
SNART! WE KNOW YOU'RE IN THERE!

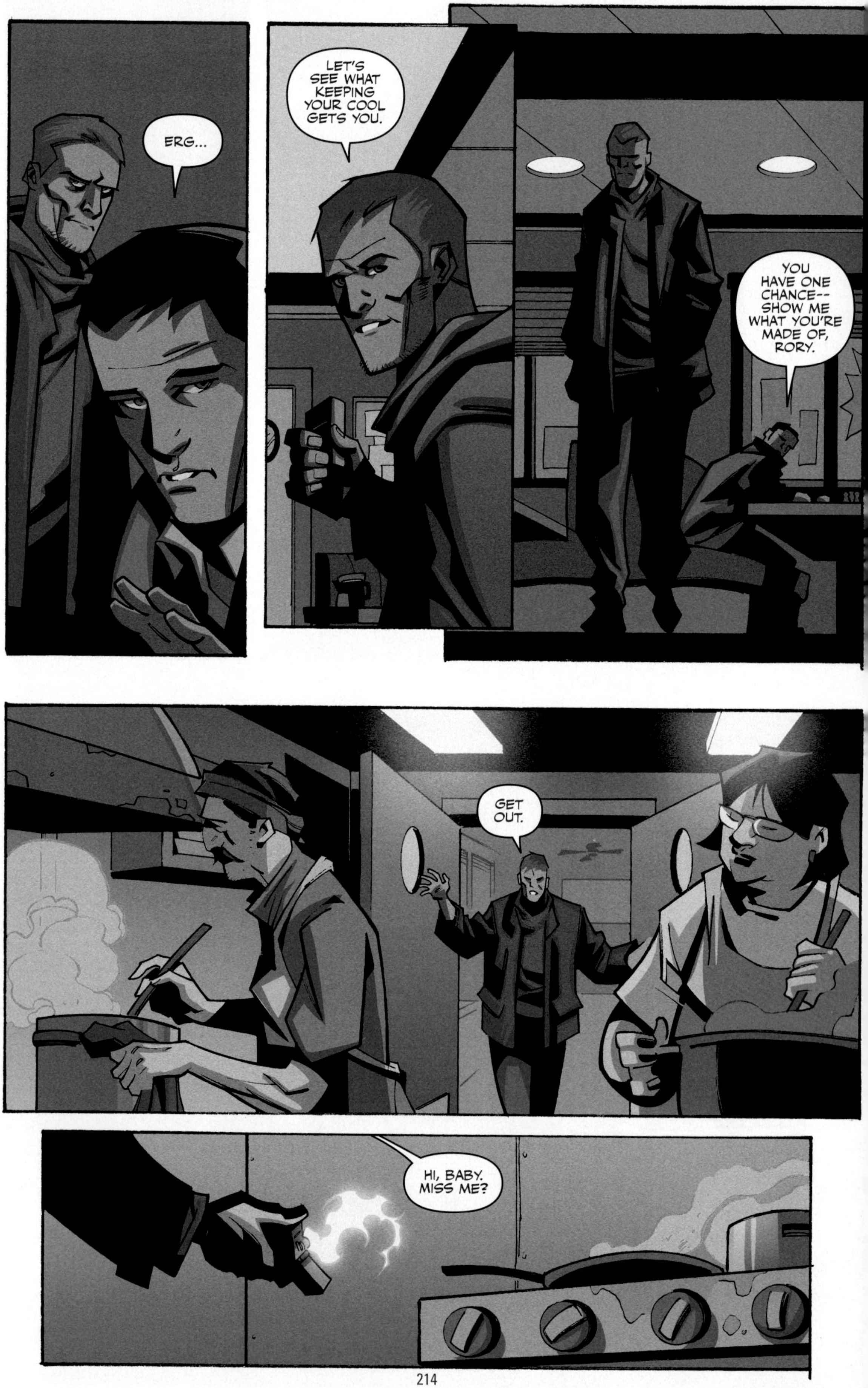

ERG...
LET'S SEE WHAT KEEPING YOUR COOL GETS YOU.
YOU HAVE ONE CHANCE-- SHOW ME WHAT YOU'RE MADE OF, RORY.
GET OUT.
HI, BABY. MISS ME?

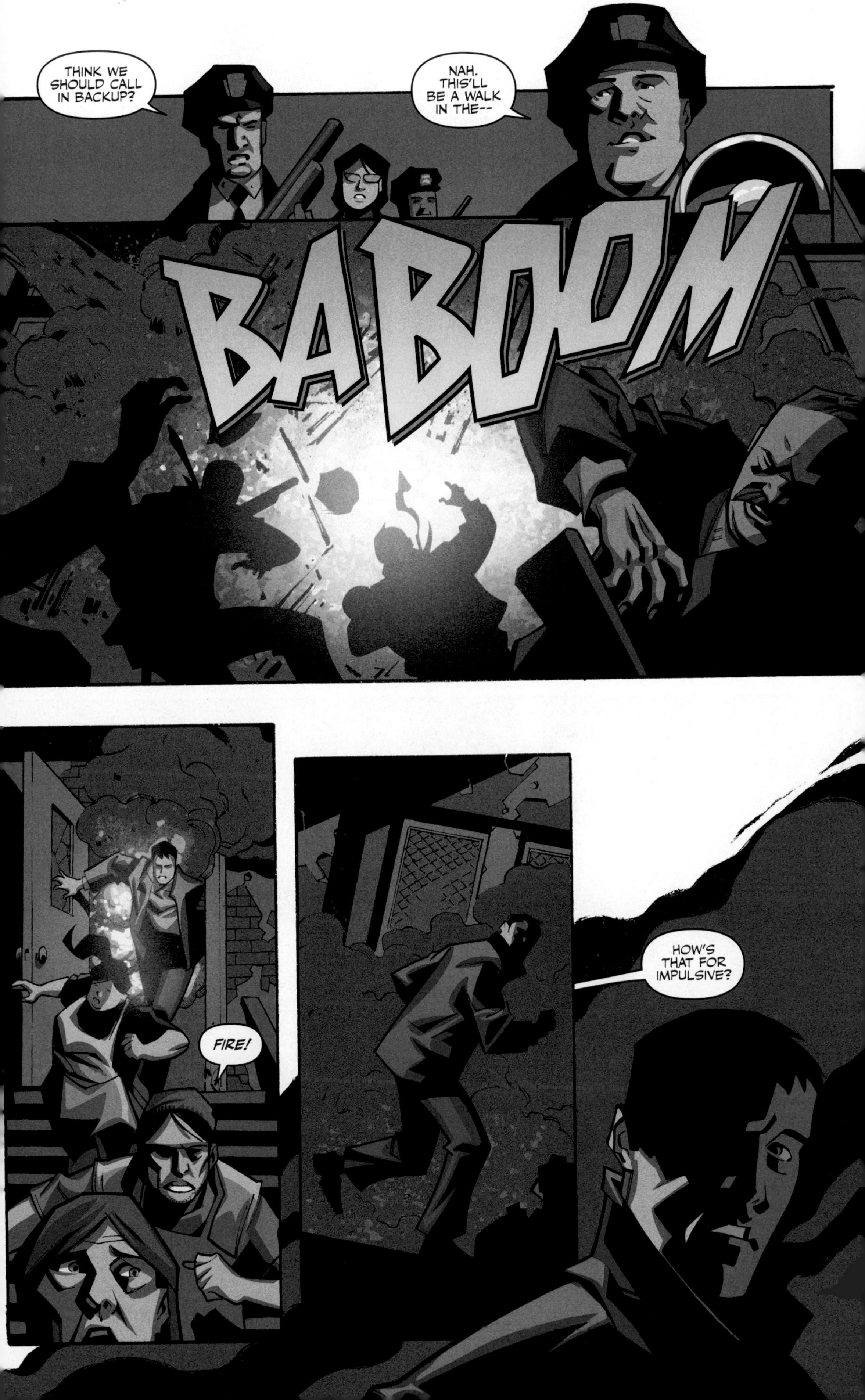
THINK WE SHOULD CALL IN BACKUP?
NAH. THIS'LL BE A WALK IN THE--
BABOOM
FIRE!
HOW'S THAT FOR IMPULSIVE?

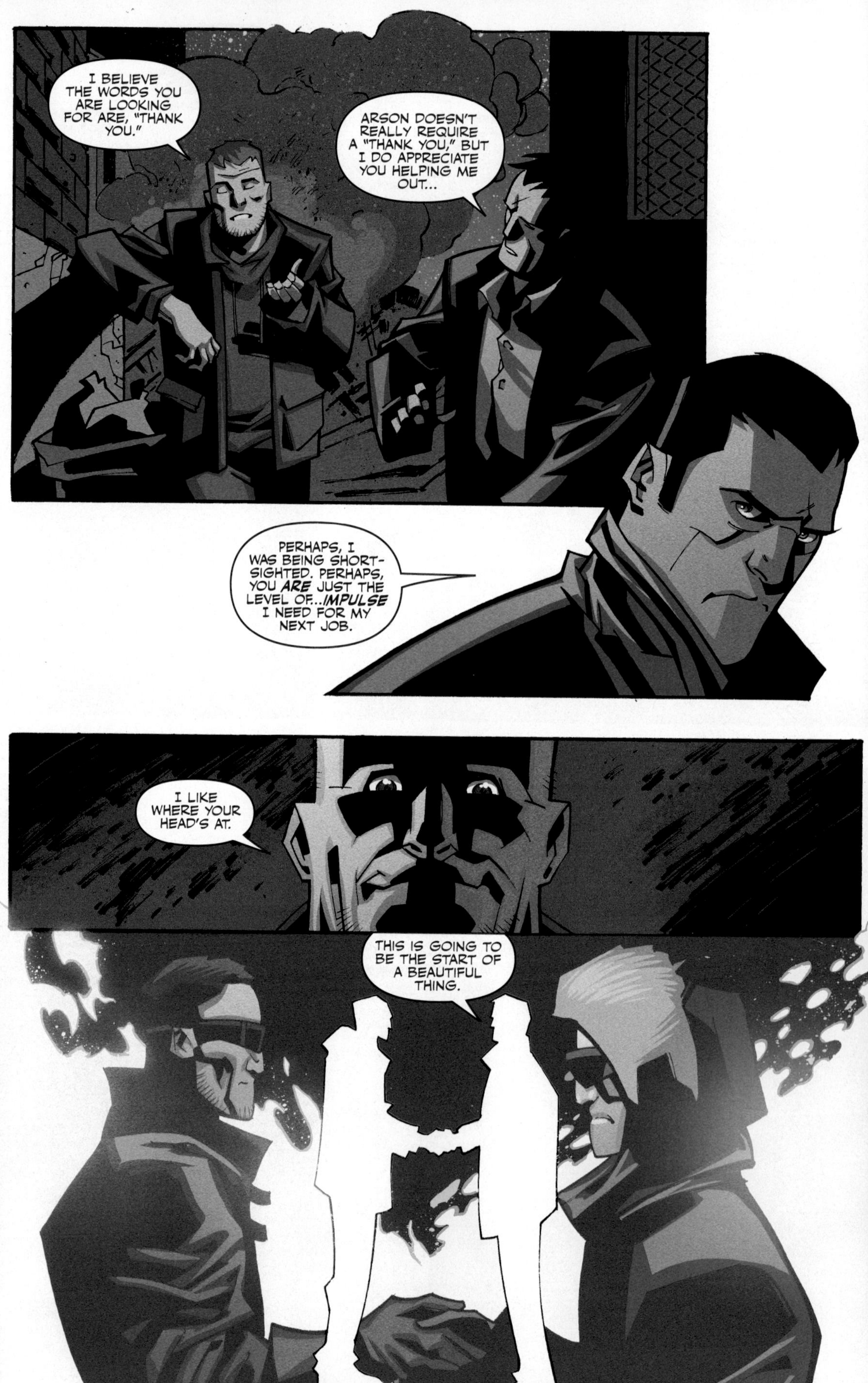
I BELIEVE THE WORDS YOU ARE LOOKING FOR ARE, "THANK YOU."
ARSON DOESN'T REALLY REQUIRE A "THANK YOU," BUT I DO APPRECIATE YOU HELPING ME OUT...
PERHAPS, I WAS BEING SHORT-SIGHTED. PERHAPS, YOU **ARE** JUST THE LEVEL OF...**IMPULSE** I NEED FOR MY NEXT JOB.
I LIKE WHERE YOUR HEAD'S AT.
THIS IS GOING TO BE THE START OF A BEAUTIFUL THING.

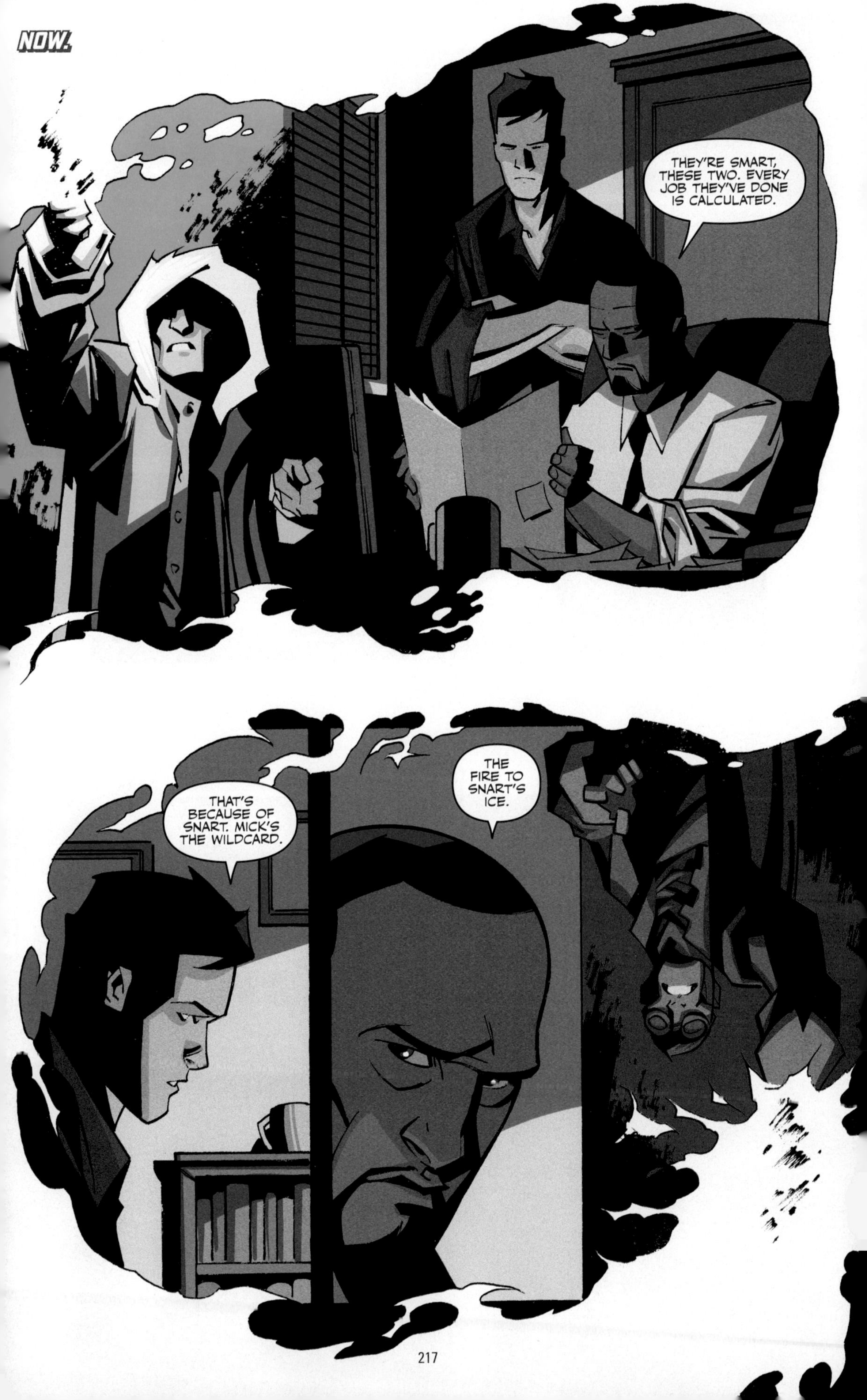
NOW.
THEY'RE SMART, THESE TWO. EVERY JOB THEY'VE DONE IS CALCULATED.
THAT'S BECAUSE OF SNART. MICK'S THE WILDCARD.
THE FIRE TO SNART'S ICE.

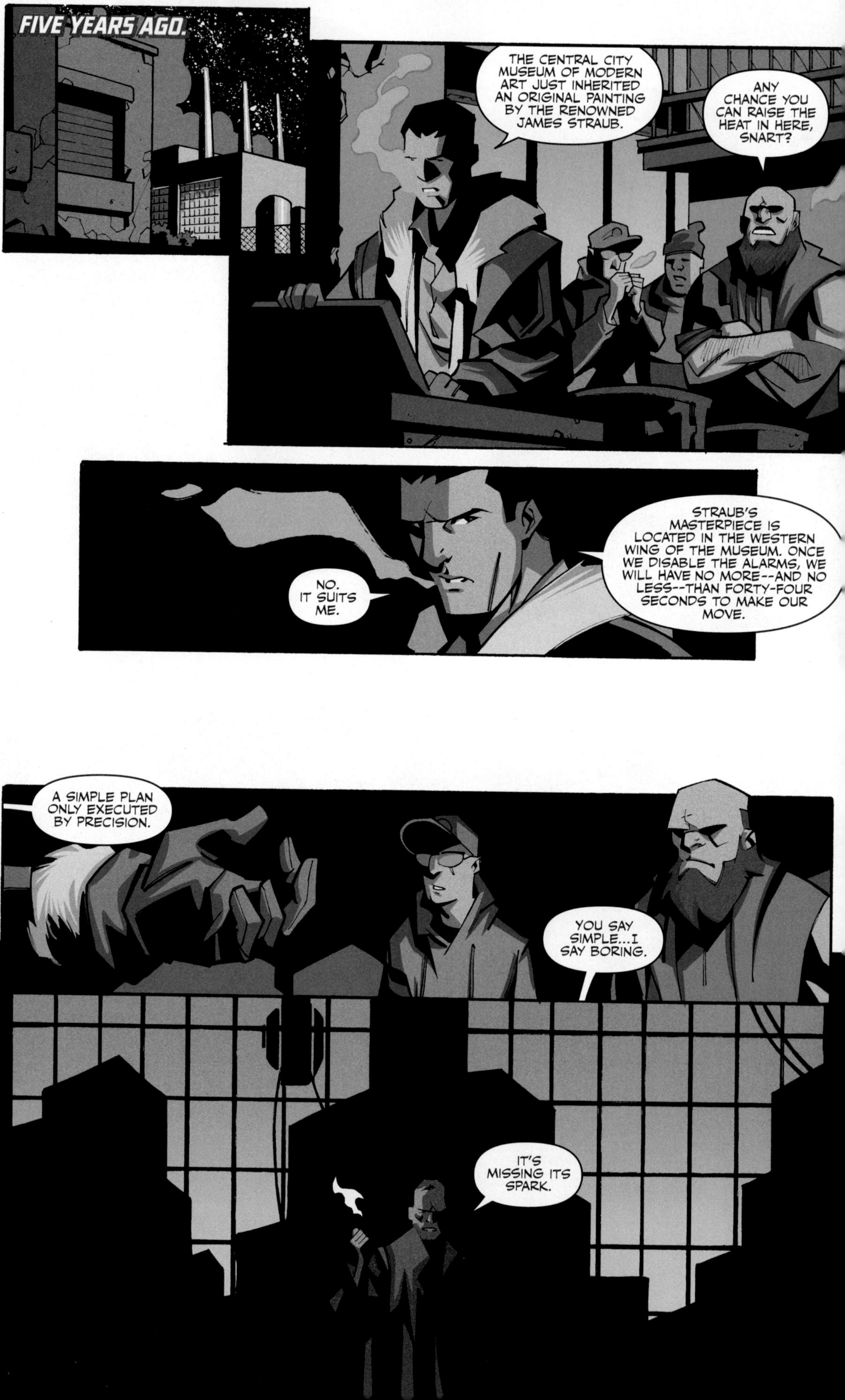
FIVE YEARS AGO.
THE CENTRAL CITY MUSEUM OF MODERN ART JUST INHERITED AN ORIGINAL PAINTING BY THE RENOWNED JAMES STRAUB.
ANY CHANCE YOU CAN RAISE THE HEAT IN HERE, SNART?
NO. IT SUITS ME.
STRAUB'S MASTERPIECE IS LOCATED IN THE WESTERN WING OF THE MUSEUM. ONCE WE DISABLE THE ALARMS, WE WILL HAVE NO MORE--AND NO LESS--THAN FORTY-FOUR SECONDS TO MAKE OUR MOVE.
A SIMPLE PLAN ONLY EXECUTED BY PRECISION.
YOU SAY SIMPLE...I SAY BORING.
IT'S MISSING ITS SPARK.

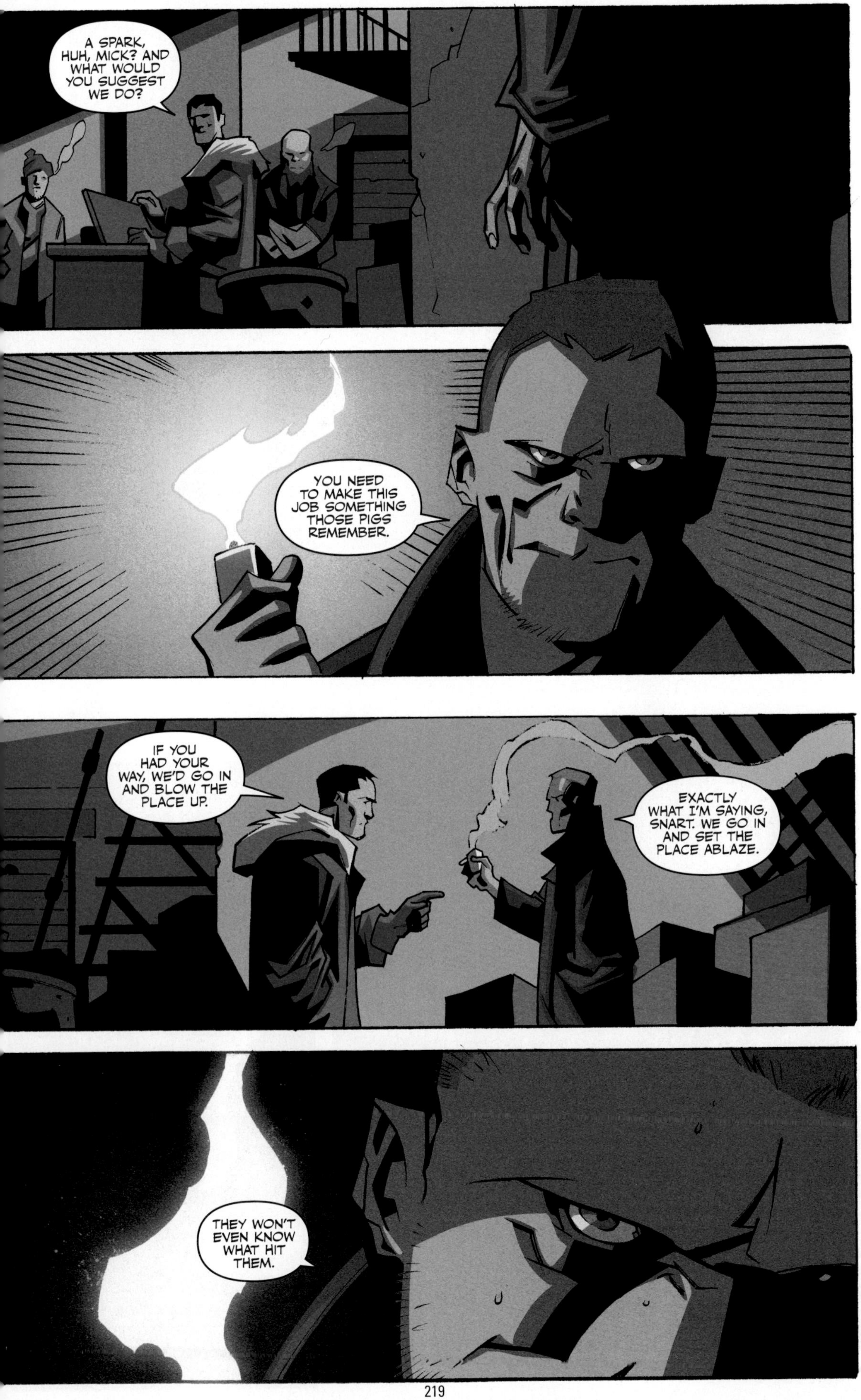
A SPARK, HUH, MICK? AND WHAT WOULD YOU SUGGEST WE DO?
YOU NEED TO MAKE THIS JOB SOMETHING THOSE PIGS REMEMBER.
IF YOU HAD YOUR WAY, WE'D GO IN AND BLOW THE PLACE UP.
EXACTLY WHAT I'M SAYING, SNART. WE GO IN AND SET THE PLACE ABLAZE.
THEY WON'T EVEN KNOW WHAT HIT THEM.

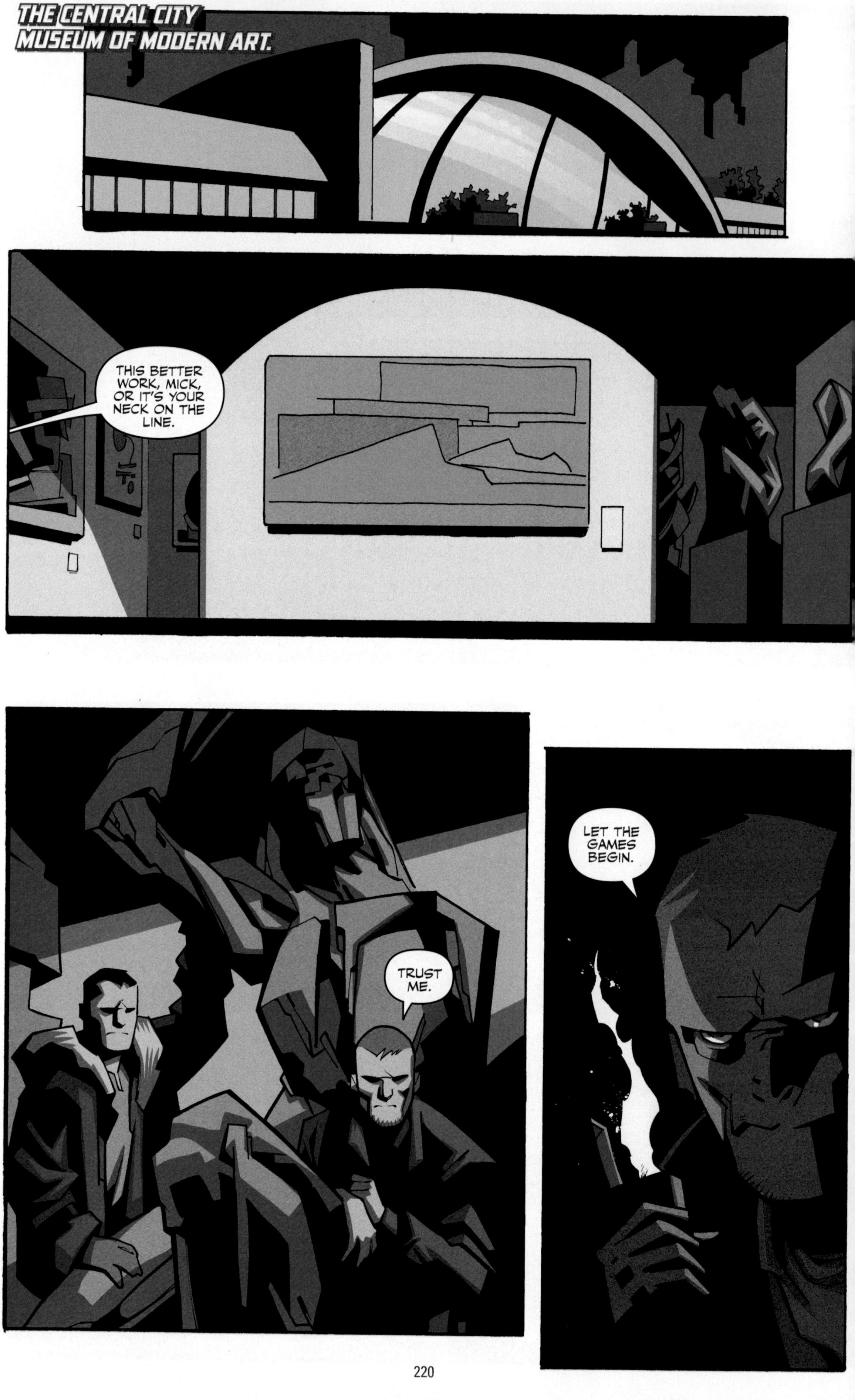
THE CENTRAL CITY MUSEUM OF MODERN ART.
THIS BETTER WORK, MICK, OR IT'S YOUR NECK ON THE LINE.
TRUST ME.
LET THE GAMES BEGIN.

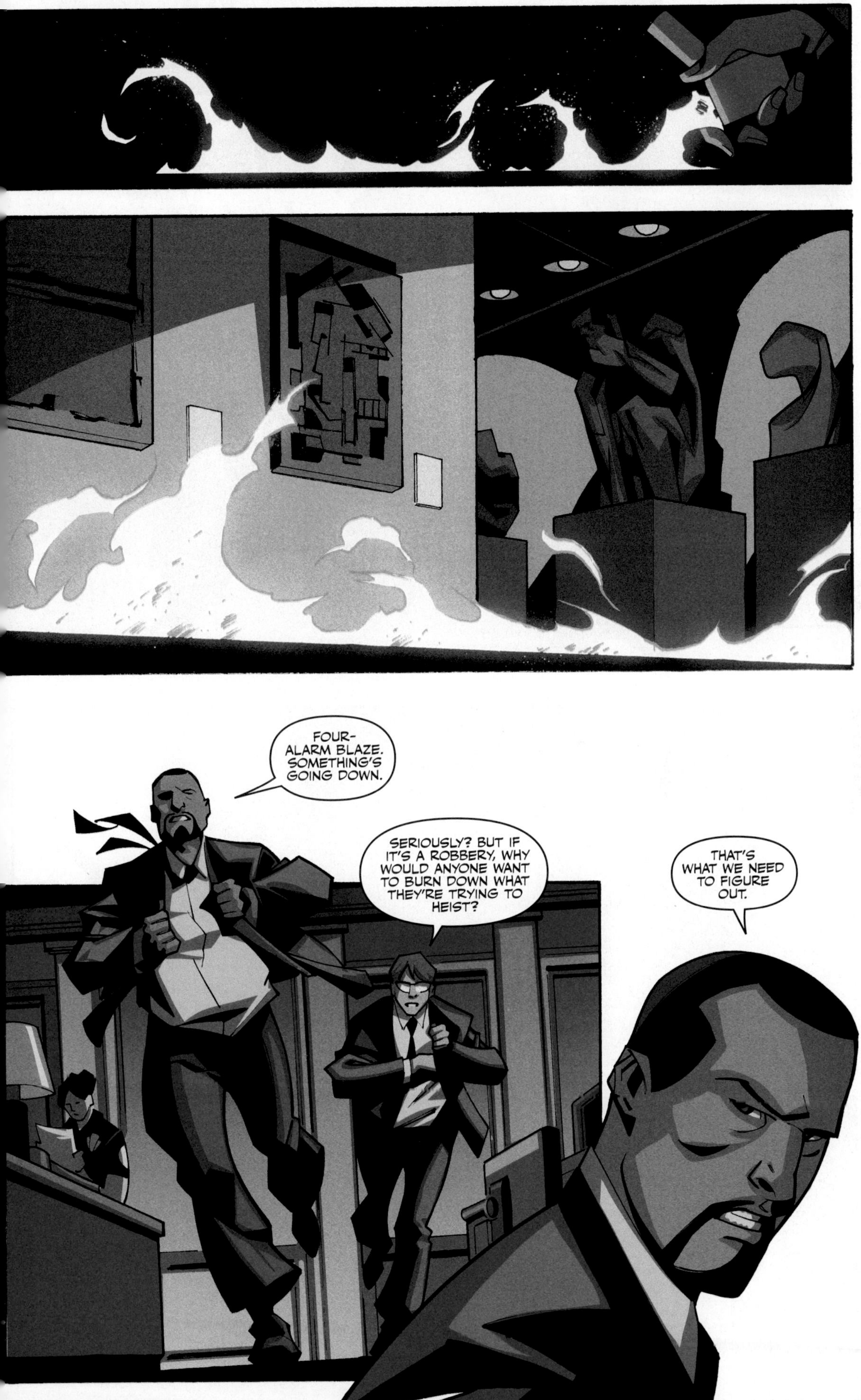
FOUR-ALARM BLAZE. SOMETHING'S GOING DOWN.
SERIOUSLY? BUT IF IT'S A ROBBERY, WHY WOULD ANYONE WANT TO BURN DOWN WHAT THEY'RE TRYING TO HEIST?
THAT'S WHAT WE NEED TO FIGURE OUT.

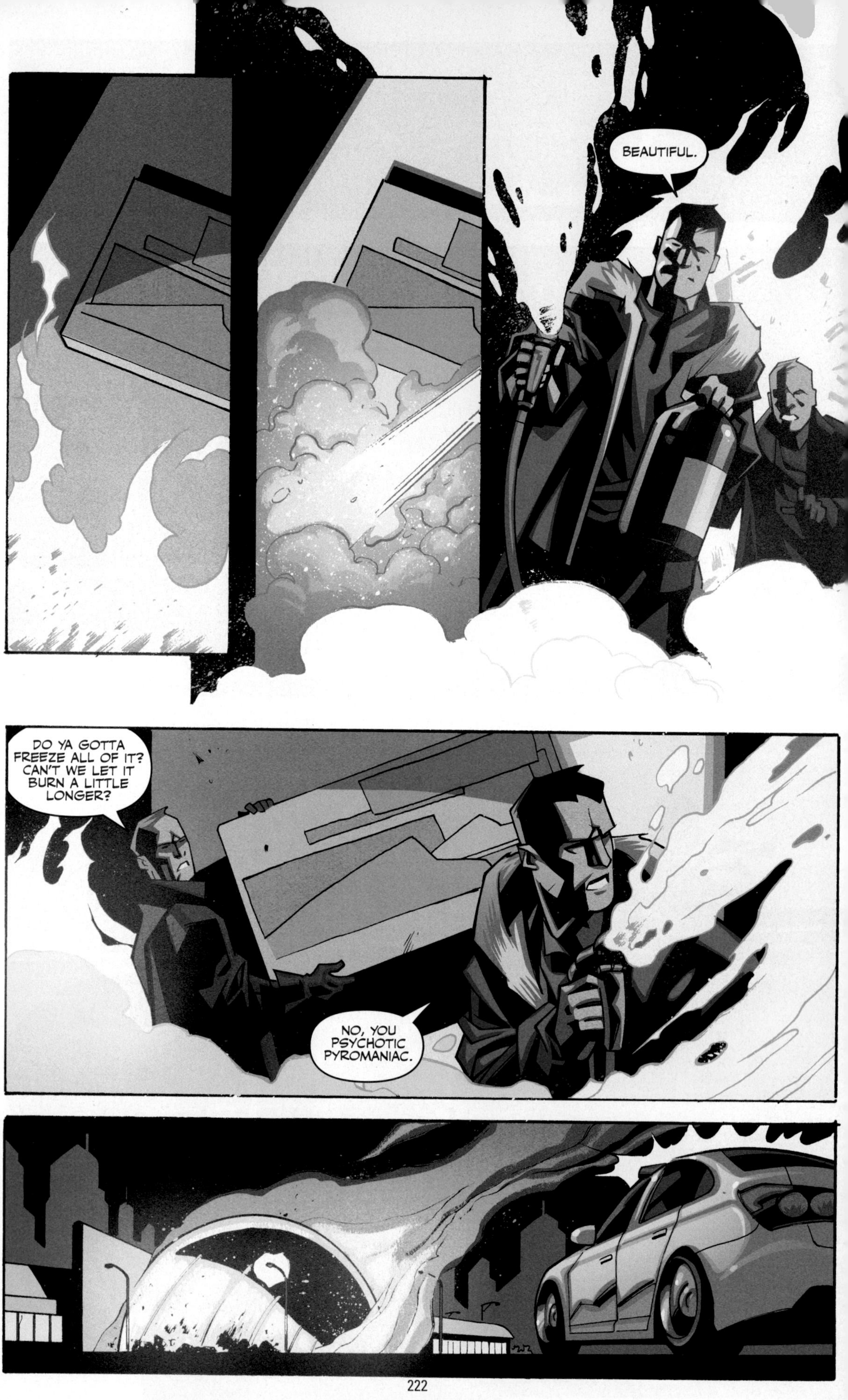
BEAUTIFUL.
DO YA GOTTA FREEZE ALL OF IT? CAN'T WE LET IT BURN A LITTLE LONGER?
NO, YOU PSYCHOTIC PYROMANIAC.

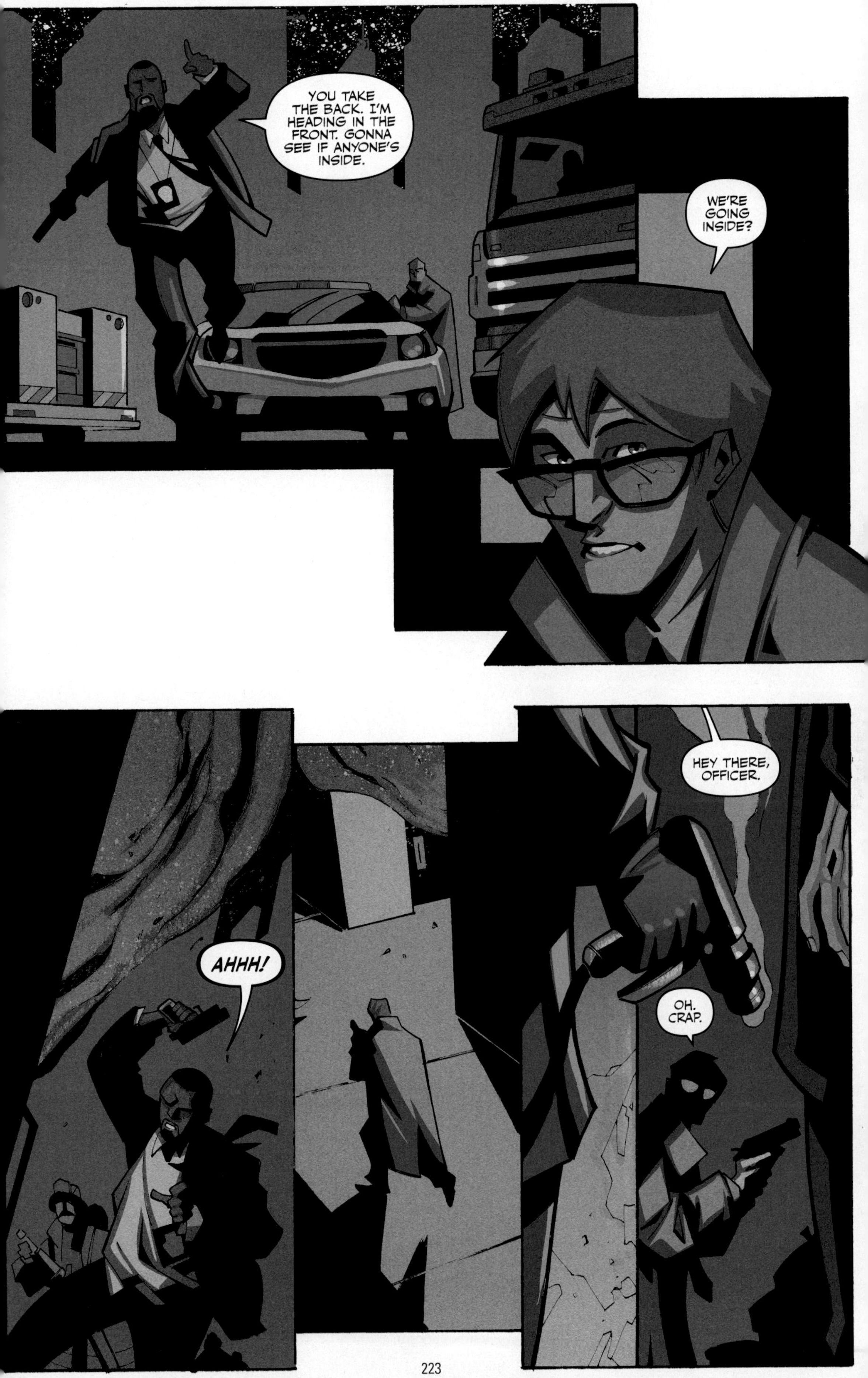
YOU TAKE THE BACK. I'M HEADING IN THE FRONT. GONNA SEE IF ANYONE'S INSIDE.
WE'RE GOING INSIDE?
AHHH!
HEY THERE, OFFICER.
OH. CRAP.

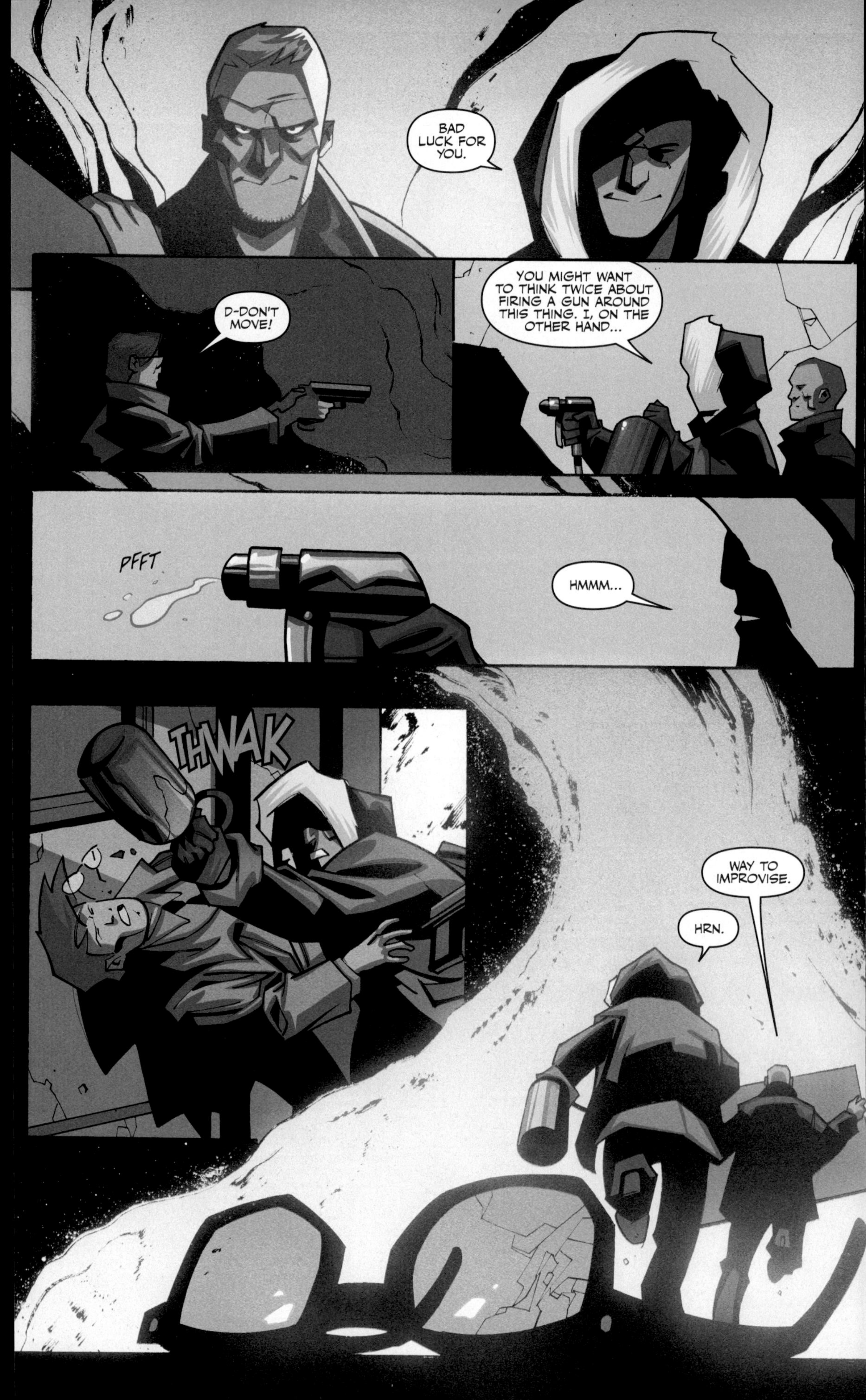

BAD LUCK FOR YOU.
D-DON'T MOVE!
YOU MIGHT WANT TO THINK TWICE ABOUT FIRING A GUN AROUND THIS THING. I, ON THE OTHER HAND...
PFFT
HMMM...
THWAK
WAY TO IMPROVISE.
HRN.

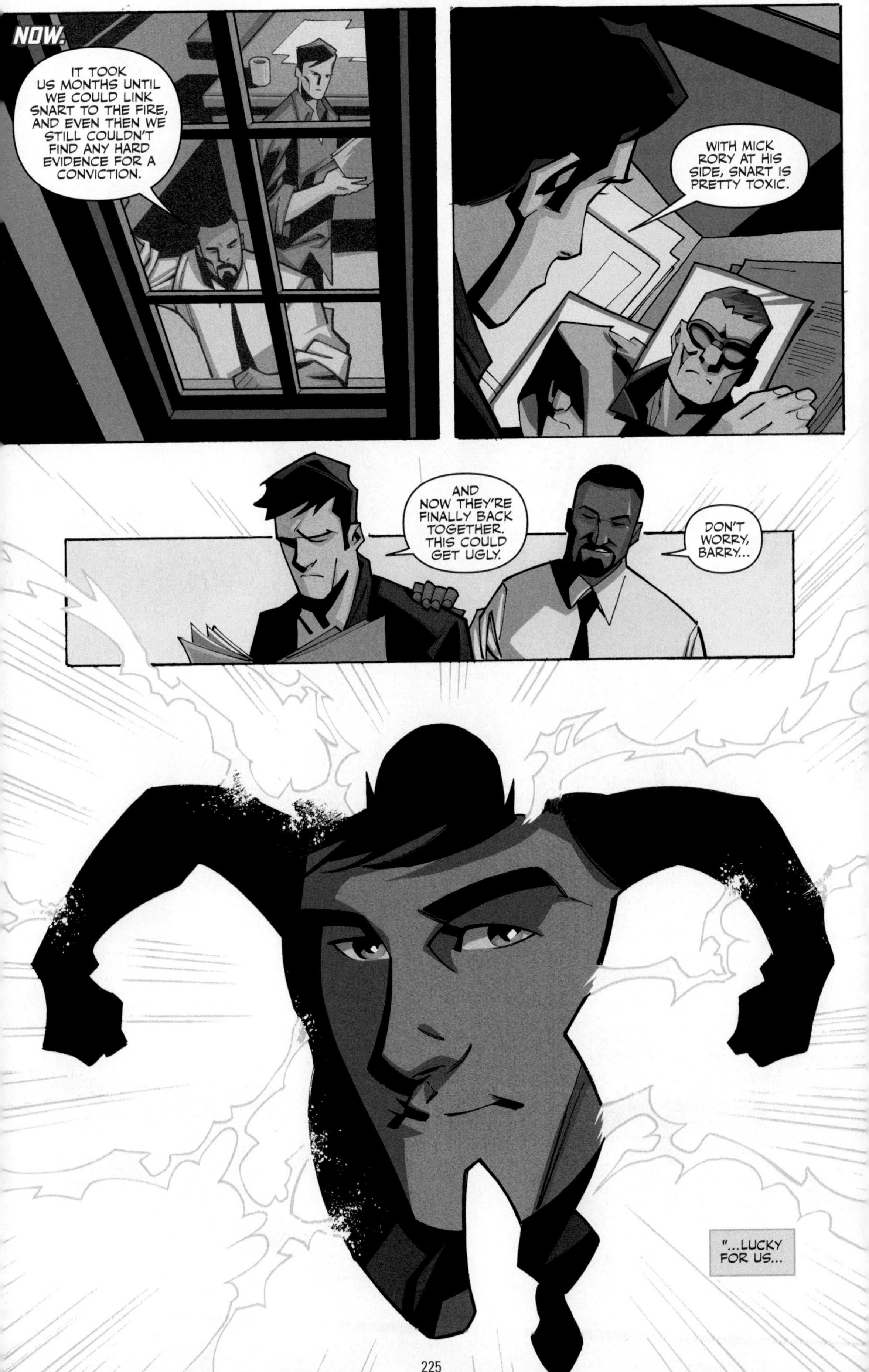
NOW.
IT TOOK US MONTHS UNTIL WE COULD LINK SNART TO THE FIRE, AND EVEN THEN WE STILL COULDN'T FIND ANY HARD EVIDENCE FOR A CONVICTION.
WITH MICK RORY AT HIS SIDE, SNART IS PRETTY TOXIC.
AND NOW THEY'RE FINALLY BACK TOGETHER. THIS COULD GET UGLY.
DON'T WORRY, BARRY...
"...LUCKY FOR US...

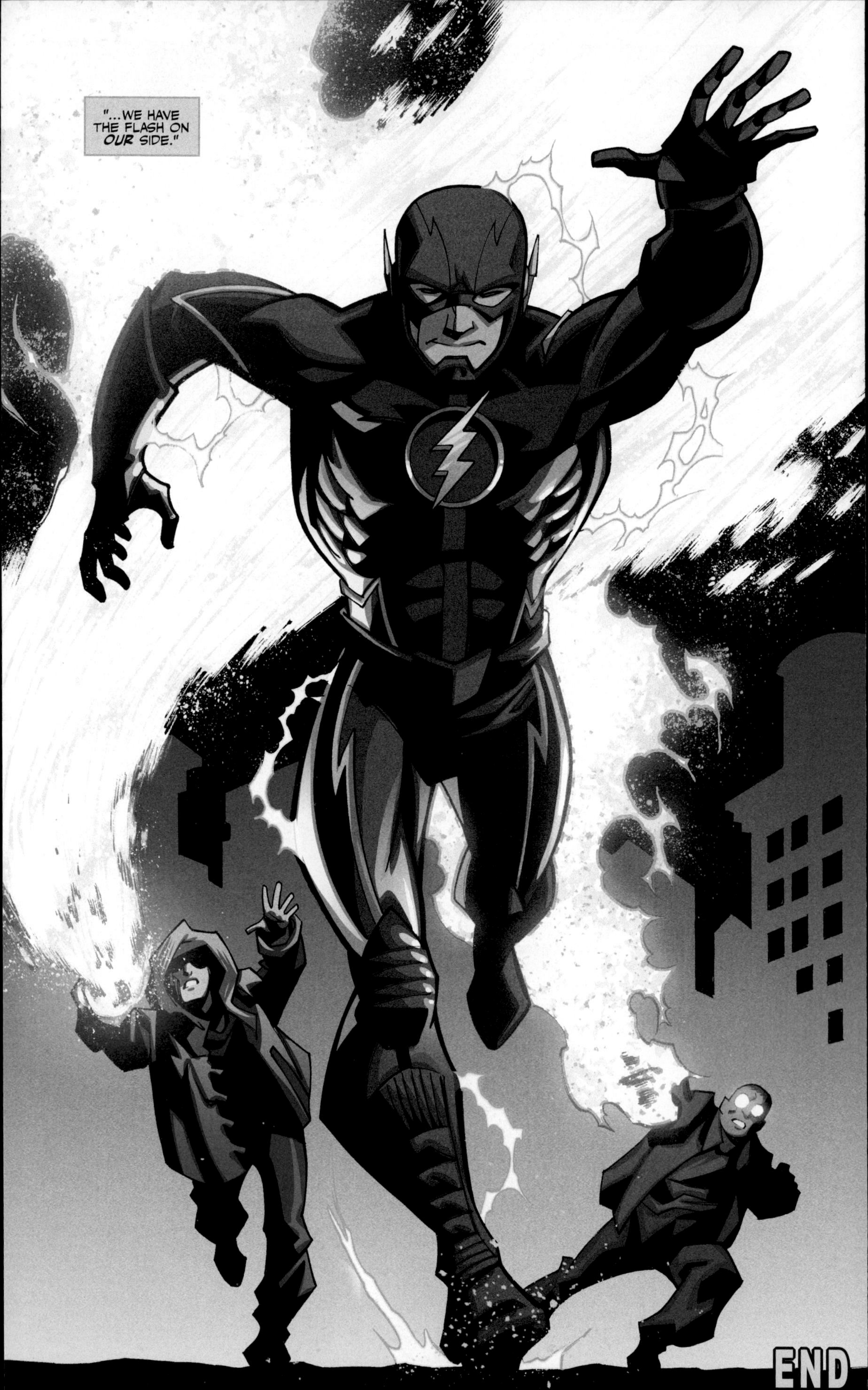
"...WE HAVE THE FLASH ON OUR SIDE."
END

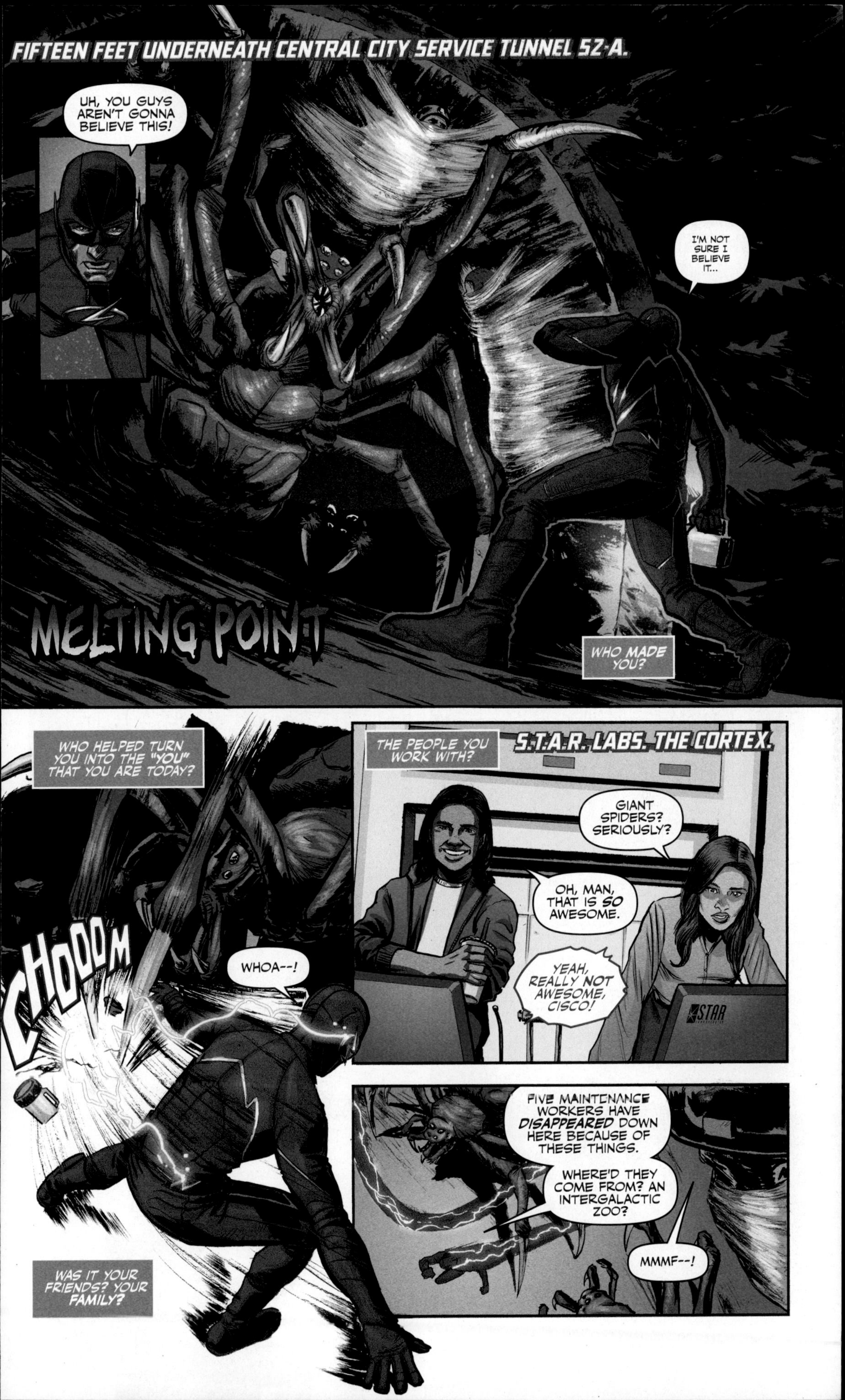

FIFTEEN FEET UNDERNEATH CENTRAL CITY SERVICE TUNNEL 52-A.
UH, YOU GUYS AREN'T GONNA BELIEVE THIS!
I'M NOT SURE I BELIEVE IT...
MELTING POINT
WHO MADE YOU?
WHO HELPED TURN YOU INTO THE "YOU" THAT YOU ARE TODAY?
THE PEOPLE YOU WORK WITH?
S.T.A.R. LABS. THE CORTEX.
GIANT SPIDERS? SERIOUSLY?
OH, MAN, THAT IS SO AWESOME.
YEAH, REALLY NOT AWESOME, CISCO!
CHOOOM
WHOA--!
FIVE MAINTENANCE WORKERS HAVE DISAPPEARED DOWN HERE BECAUSE OF THESE THINGS.
WHERE'D THEY COME FROM? AN INTERGALACTIC ZOO?
MMMF--!
WAS IT YOUR FRIENDS? YOUR FAMILY?

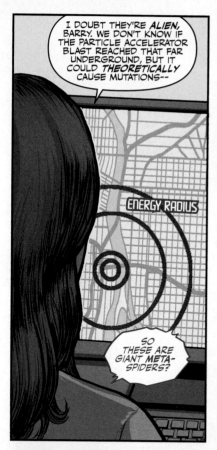

I DOUBT THEY'RE *ALIEN*, BARRY. WE DON'T KNOW IF THE PARTICLE ACCELERATOR BLAST REACHED THAT FAR UNDERGROUND, BUT IT COULD *THEORETICALLY* CAUSE MUTATIONS--

ENERGY RADIUS

SO THESE ARE GIANT *META-SPIDERS*?

GIANT. META. SPIDERS. LIVING UNDER CENTRAL CITY.

I...I'M GONNA NEED TO SIT DOWN.

CENTRAL'S MOST COMMON ARACHNID IS *THE AGRIOPE AURANTIA*, A SPIDER KNOWN FOR RAPIDLY PRODUCING HUGE WEBS. THEY'RE TYPICALLY NON-AGGRESSIVE--

THESE GUYS ARE PRETTY AGGRESSIVE! WHAT DO I DO HERE?

UM, TRY NOT TO GET WEBBED UP AND GET THOSE WORKERS OUT OF THERE?

EASIER SAID THAN DONE.

OR WAS THERE ONE PERSON WHO HELPED YOU THE MOST...

...SOMEONE WHO REACHED DOWN FROM THEIR PLACE *HIGH ABOVE* YOU...AND PULLED YOU UP TO *THEIR* LEVEL?

FWAAASH

OH.

YOU OKAY, CAITLIN?

VRRR RRR VRRR VRRR

I...I JUST GOT A MESSAGE...

I HAVE TO GO TO A *FUNERAL*.

WHO *MADE* YOU? AND MORE IMPORTANTLY...

228

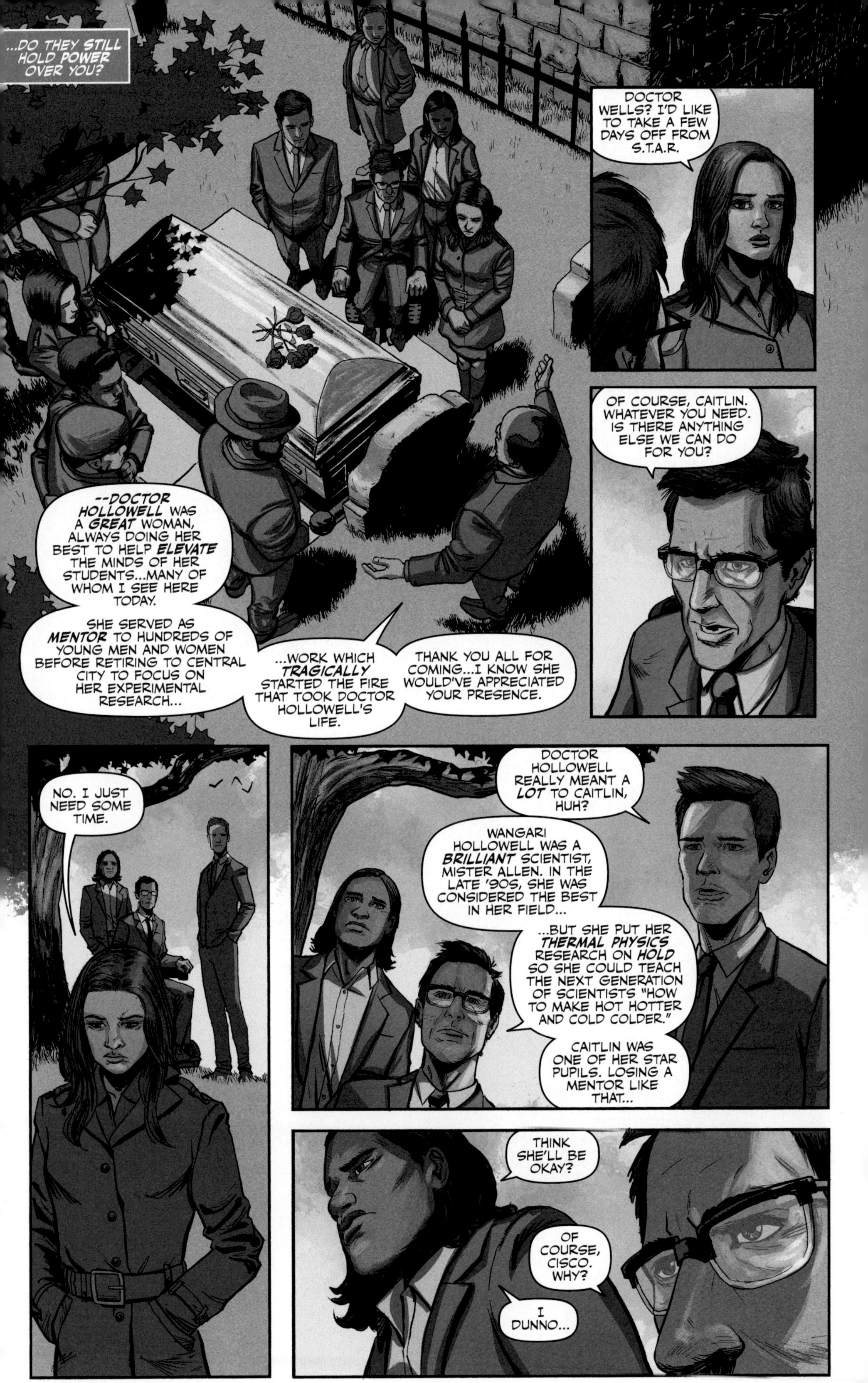

...DO THEY STILL HOLD POWER OVER YOU?
--DOCTOR HOLLOWELL WAS A GREAT WOMAN, ALWAYS DOING HER BEST TO HELP ELEVATE THE MINDS OF HER STUDENTS...MANY OF WHOM I SEE HERE TODAY.
SHE SERVED AS MENTOR TO HUNDREDS OF YOUNG MEN AND WOMEN BEFORE RETIRING TO CENTRAL CITY TO FOCUS ON HER EXPERIMENTAL RESEARCH...
...WORK WHICH TRAGICALLY STARTED THE FIRE THAT TOOK DOCTOR HOLLOWELL'S LIFE.
THANK YOU ALL FOR COMING...I KNOW SHE WOULD'VE APPRECIATED YOUR PRESENCE.
DOCTOR WELLS? I'D LIKE TO TAKE A FEW DAYS OFF FROM S.T.A.R.
OF COURSE, CAITLIN. WHATEVER YOU NEED. IS THERE ANYTHING ELSE WE CAN DO FOR YOU?
NO. I JUST NEED SOME TIME.
DOCTOR HOLLOWELL REALLY MEANT A LOT TO CAITLIN, HUH?
WANGARI HOLLOWELL WAS A BRILLIANT SCIENTIST, MISTER ALLEN. IN THE LATE '90S, SHE WAS CONSIDERED THE BEST IN HER FIELD...
...BUT SHE PUT HER THERMAL PHYSICS RESEARCH ON HOLD SO SHE COULD TEACH THE NEXT GENERATION OF SCIENTISTS "HOW TO MAKE HOT HOTTER AND COLD COLDER."
CAITLIN WAS ONE OF HER STAR PUPILS. LOSING A MENTOR LIKE THAT...
THINK SHE'LL BE OKAY?
OF COURSE, CISCO. WHY?
I DUNNO...

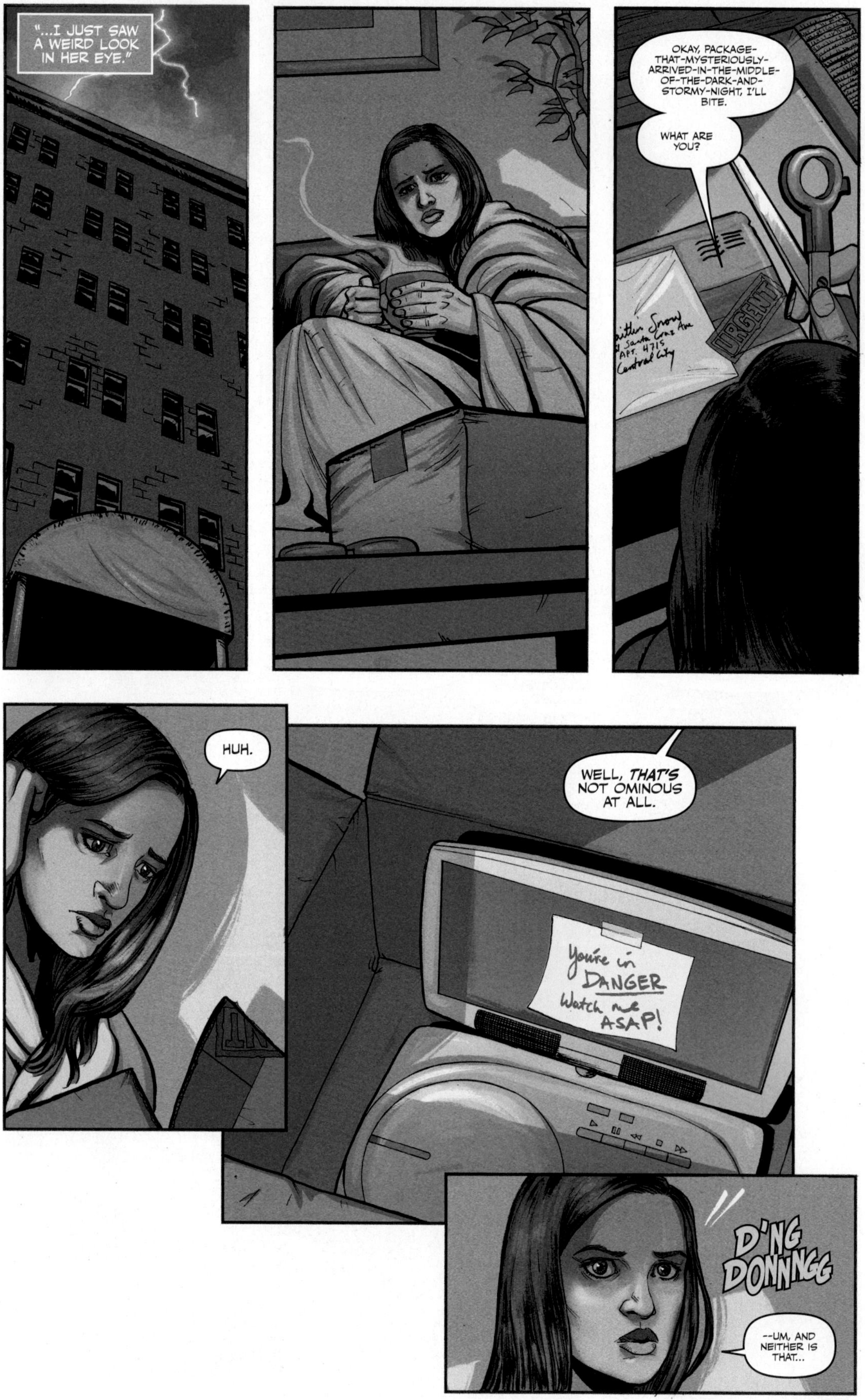
"...I JUST SAW A WEIRD LOOK IN HER EYE."
OKAY, PACKAGE-THAT-MYSTERIOUSLY-ARRIVED-IN-THE-MIDDLE-OF-THE-DARK-AND-STORMY-NIGHT, I'LL BITE.
WHAT ARE YOU?
Apt. 4715
Central City
URGENT
HUH.
WELL, THAT'S NOT OMINOUS AT ALL.
You're in DANGER Watch me ASAP!
D'NG DONNNGG
--UM, AND NEITHER IS THAT...

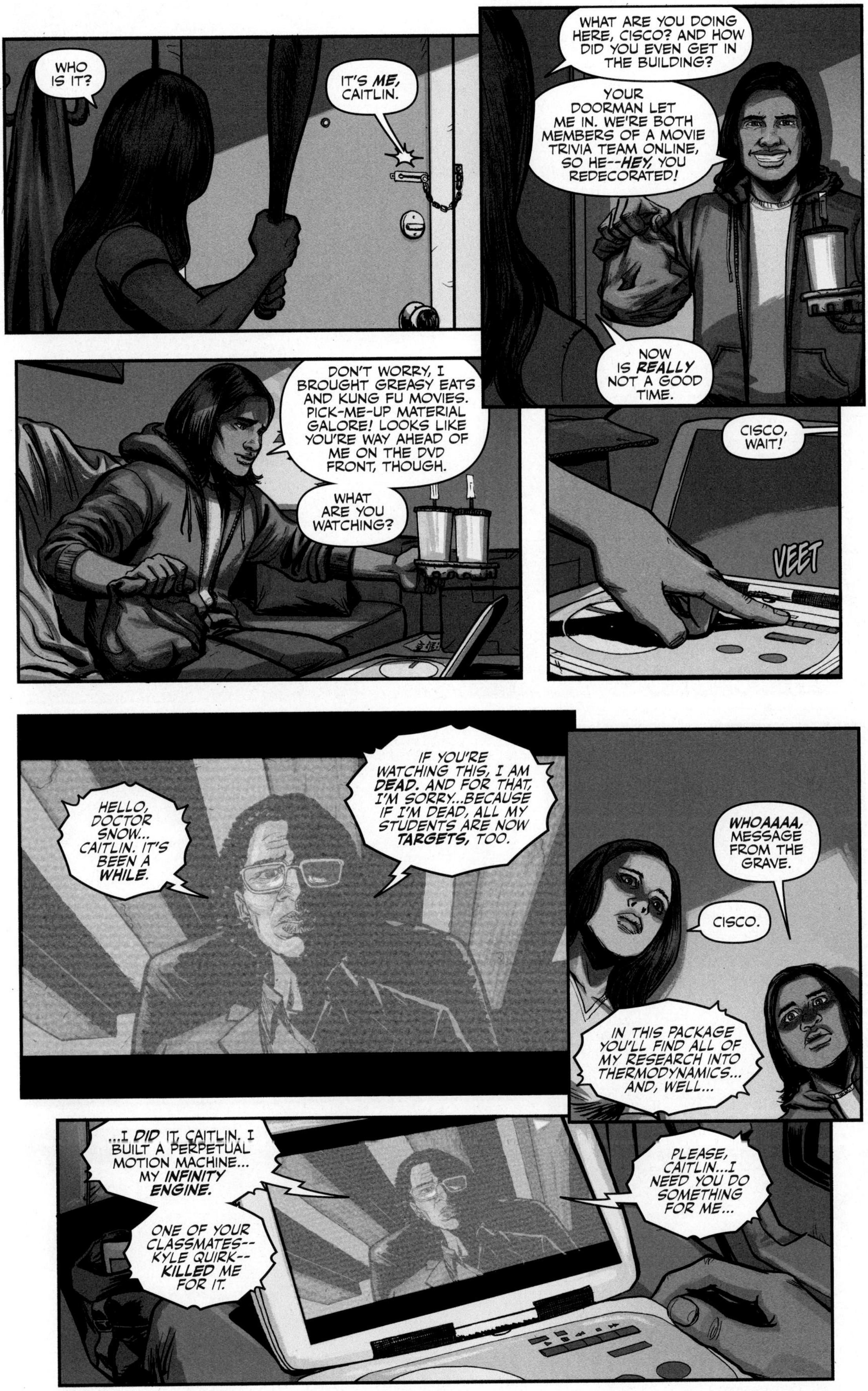
WHO IS IT?
IT'S ME, CAITLIN.
WHAT ARE YOU DOING HERE, CISCO? AND HOW DID YOU EVEN GET IN THE BUILDING?
YOUR DOORMAN LET ME IN. WE'RE BOTH MEMBERS OF A MOVIE TRIVIA TEAM ONLINE, SO HE--HEY, YOU REDECORATED!
NOW IS REALLY NOT A GOOD TIME.
DON'T WORRY, I BROUGHT GREASY EATS AND KUNG FU MOVIES. PICK-ME-UP MATERIAL GALORE! LOOKS LIKE YOU'RE WAY AHEAD OF ME ON THE DVD FRONT, THOUGH.
WHAT ARE YOU WATCHING?
CISCO, WAIT!
VEET
HELLO, DOCTOR SNOW... CAITLIN. IT'S BEEN A WHILE.
IF YOU'RE WATCHING THIS, I AM DEAD. AND FOR THAT, I'M SORRY...BECAUSE IF I'M DEAD, ALL MY STUDENTS ARE NOW TARGETS, TOO.
WHOAAAA, MESSAGE FROM THE GRAVE.
CISCO.
IN THIS PACKAGE YOU'LL FIND ALL OF MY RESEARCH INTO THERMODYNAMICS... AND, WELL...
...I DID IT, CAITLIN. I BUILT A PERPETUAL MOTION MACHINE... MY INFINITY ENGINE.
ONE OF YOUR CLASSMATES--KYLE QUIRK--KILLED ME FOR IT.
PLEASE, CAITLIN...I NEED YOU DO SOMETHING FOR ME...

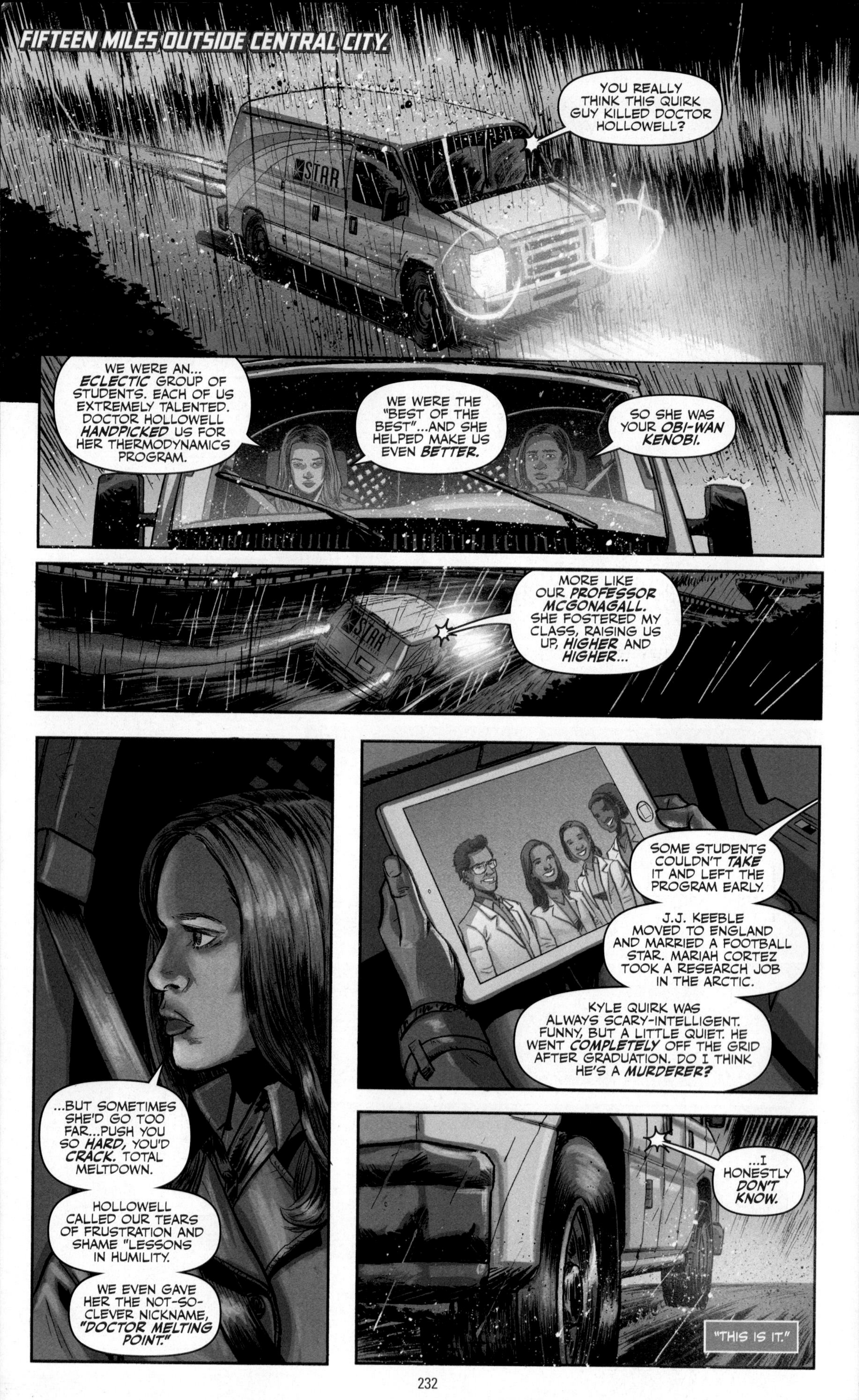
FIFTEEN MILES OUTSIDE CENTRAL CITY.
YOU REALLY THINK THIS QUIRK GUY KILLED DOCTOR HOLLOWELL?
WE WERE AN... ECLECTIC GROUP OF STUDENTS. EACH OF US EXTREMELY TALENTED. DOCTOR HOLLOWELL HANDPICKED US FOR HER THERMODYNAMICS PROGRAM.
WE WERE THE "BEST OF THE BEST"...AND SHE HELPED MAKE US EVEN BETTER.
SO SHE WAS YOUR OBI-WAN KENOBI.
MORE LIKE OUR PROFESSOR MCGONAGALL. SHE FOSTERED MY CLASS, RAISING US UP, HIGHER AND HIGHER...
...BUT SOMETIMES SHE'D GO TOO FAR...PUSH YOU SO HARD, YOU'D CRACK. TOTAL MELTDOWN.
HOLLOWELL CALLED OUR TEARS OF FRUSTRATION AND SHAME "LESSONS IN HUMILITY.
WE EVEN GAVE HER THE NOT-SO-CLEVER NICKNAME, "DOCTOR MELTING POINT."
SOME STUDENTS COULDN'T TAKE IT AND LEFT THE PROGRAM EARLY.
J.J. KEEBLE MOVED TO ENGLAND AND MARRIED A FOOTBALL STAR. MARIAH CORTEZ TOOK A RESEARCH JOB IN THE ARCTIC.
KYLE QUIRK WAS ALWAYS SCARY-INTELLIGENT. FUNNY, BUT A LITTLE QUIET. HE WENT COMPLETELY OFF THE GRID AFTER GRADUATION. DO I THINK HE'S A MURDERER?
...I HONESTLY DON'T KNOW.
"THIS IS IT."

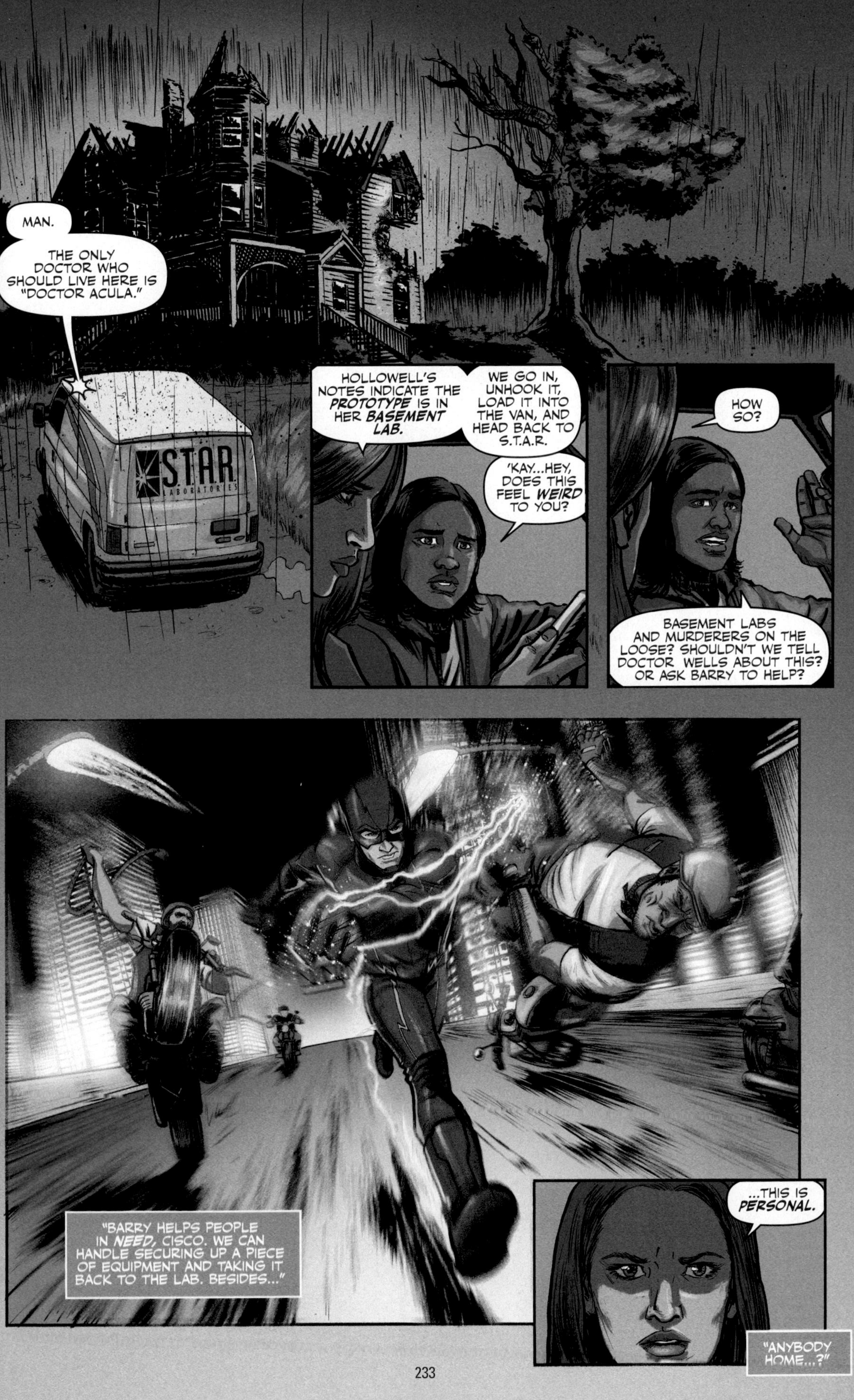

MAN.
THE ONLY DOCTOR WHO SHOULD LIVE HERE IS "DOCTOR ACULA."
S.T.A.R. LABORATORIES
HOLLOWELL'S NOTES INDICATE THE *PROTOTYPE* IS IN HER *BASEMENT LAB.*
WE GO IN, UNHOOK IT, LOAD IT INTO THE VAN, AND HEAD BACK TO S.T.A.R.
'KAY...HEY, DOES THIS FEEL *WEIRD* TO YOU?
HOW SO?
BASEMENT LABS AND MURDERERS ON THE LOOSE? SHOULDN'T WE TELL DOCTOR WELLS ABOUT THIS? OR ASK BARRY TO HELP?
"BARRY HELPS PEOPLE IN *NEED,* CISCO. WE CAN HANDLE SECURING UP A PIECE OF EQUIPMENT AND TAKING IT BACK TO THE LAB. BESIDES..."
...THIS IS *PERSONAL.*
"ANYBODY HOME...?"

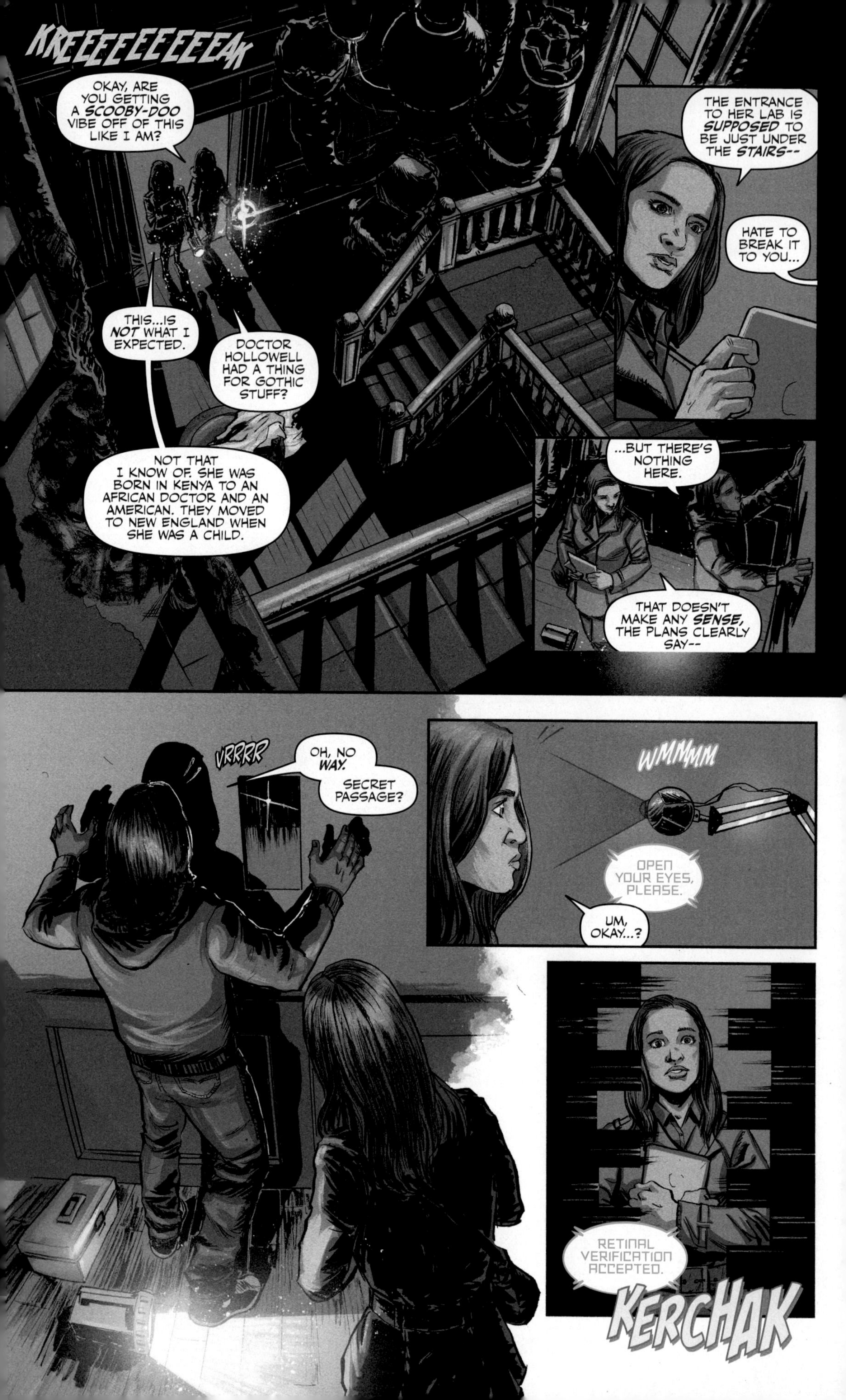
KREEEEEEEEEEAK
OKAY, ARE YOU GETTING A SCOOBY-DOO VIBE OFF OF THIS LIKE I AM?
THIS...IS NOT WHAT I EXPECTED.
DOCTOR HOLLOWELL HAD A THING FOR GOTHIC STUFF?
NOT THAT I KNOW OF. SHE WAS BORN IN KENYA TO AN AFRICAN DOCTOR AND AN AMERICAN. THEY MOVED TO NEW ENGLAND WHEN SHE WAS A CHILD.
THE ENTRANCE TO HER LAB IS SUPPOSED TO BE JUST UNDER THE STAIRS--
HATE TO BREAK IT TO YOU...
...BUT THERE'S NOTHING HERE.
THAT DOESN'T MAKE ANY SENSE, THE PLANS CLEARLY SAY--
VRRRR
OH, NO WAY.
SECRET PASSAGE?
WMMMM
OPEN YOUR EYES, PLEASE.
UM, OKAY...?
RETINAL VERIFICATION ACCEPTED.
KERCHAK

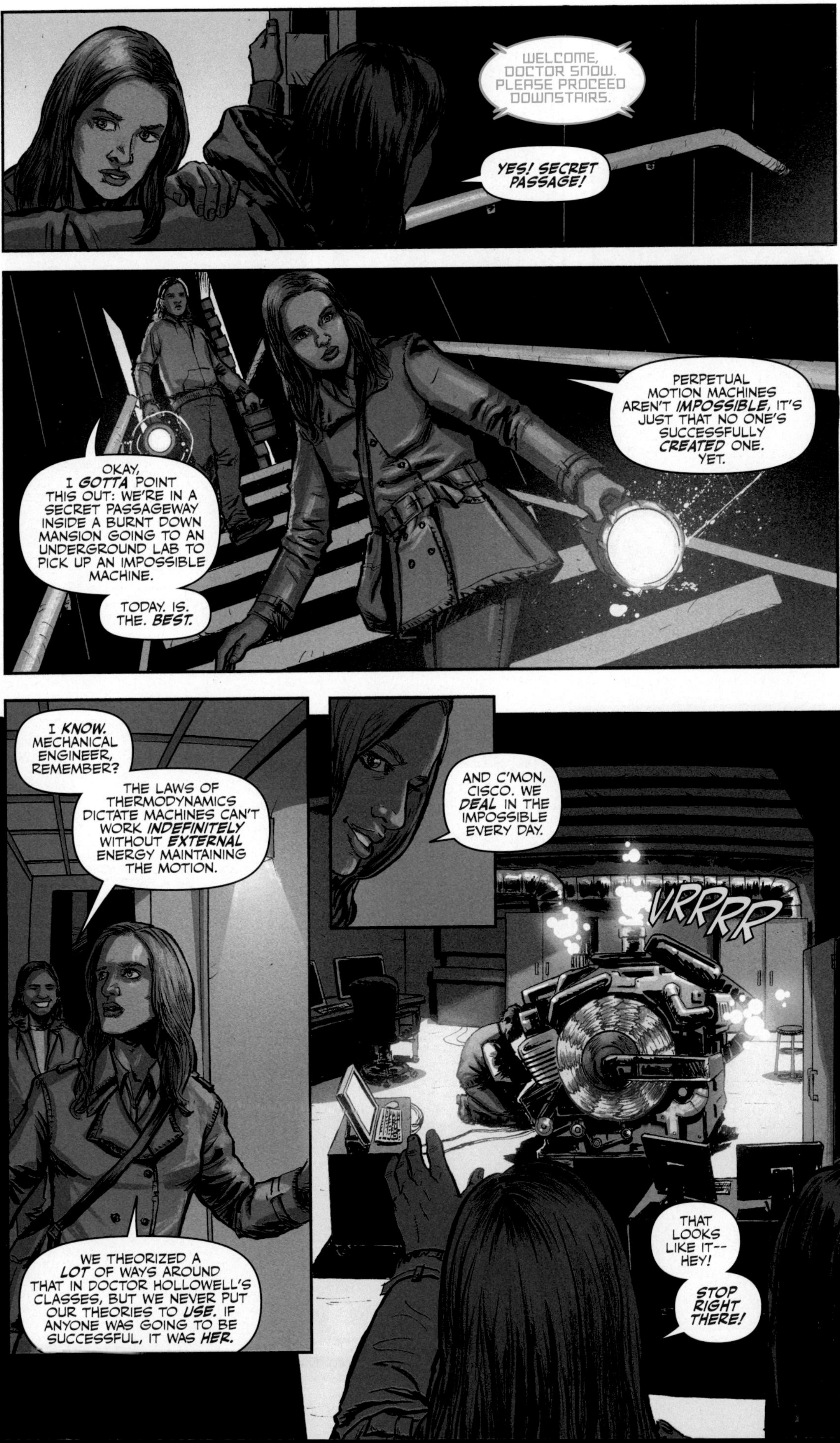
WELCOME, DOCTOR SNOW. PLEASE PROCEED DOWNSTAIRS.
YES! SECRET PASSAGE!
PERPETUAL MOTION MACHINES AREN'T IMPOSSIBLE, IT'S JUST THAT NO ONE'S SUCCESSFULLY CREATED ONE. YET.
OKAY, I GOTTA POINT THIS OUT: WE'RE IN A SECRET PASSAGEWAY INSIDE A BURNT DOWN MANSION GOING TO AN UNDERGROUND LAB TO PICK UP AN IMPOSSIBLE MACHINE.
TODAY. IS. THE. BEST.
I KNOW. MECHANICAL ENGINEER, REMEMBER?
THE LAWS OF THERMODYNAMICS DICTATE MACHINES CAN'T WORK INDEFINITELY WITHOUT EXTERNAL ENERGY MAINTAINING THE MOTION.
WE THEORIZED A LOT OF WAYS AROUND THAT IN DOCTOR HOLLOWELL'S CLASSES, BUT WE NEVER PUT OUR THEORIES TO USE. IF ANYONE WAS GOING TO BE SUCCESSFUL, IT WAS HER.
AND C'MON, CISCO. WE DEAL IN THE IMPOSSIBLE EVERY DAY.
VRRRR
THAT LOOKS LIKE IT-- HEY!
STOP RIGHT THERE!

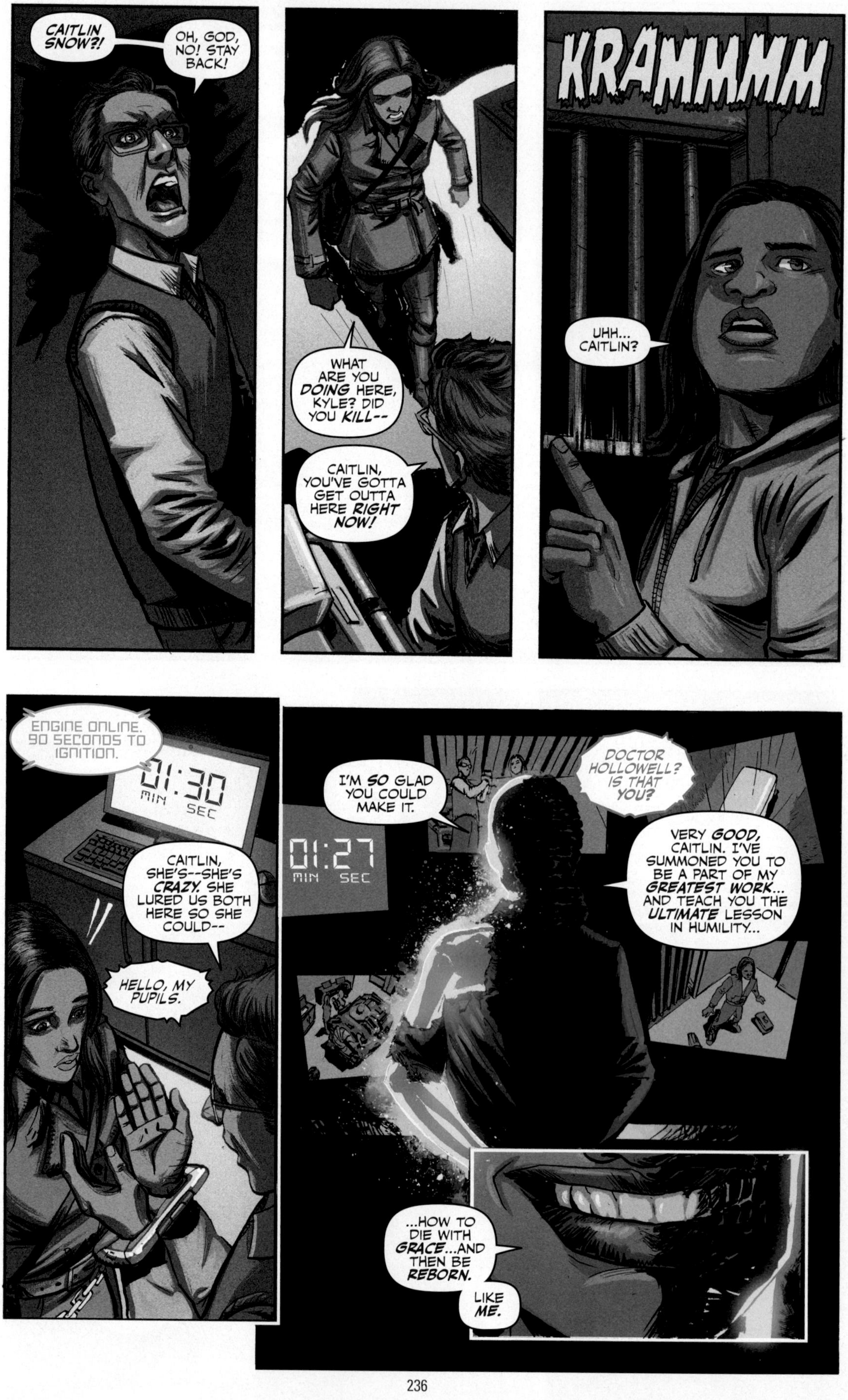
CAITLIN SNOW?!
OH, GOD, NO! STAY BACK!
WHAT ARE YOU DOING HERE, KYLE? DID YOU KILL--
CAITLIN, YOU'VE GOTTA GET OUTTA HERE RIGHT NOW!
KRAMMMM
UHH... CAITLIN?
ENGINE ONLINE. 90 SECONDS TO IGNITION.
01:30 MIN SEC
CAITLIN, SHE'S--SHE'S CRAZY. SHE LURED US BOTH HERE SO SHE COULD--
HELLO, MY PUPILS.
01:27 MIN SEC
I'M SO GLAD YOU COULD MAKE IT.
DOCTOR HOLLOWELL? IS THAT YOU?
VERY GOOD, CAITLIN. I'VE SUMMONED YOU TO BE A PART OF MY GREATEST WORK... AND TEACH YOU THE ULTIMATE LESSON IN HUMILITY...
...HOW TO DIE WITH GRACE...AND THEN BE REBORN.
LIKE ME.

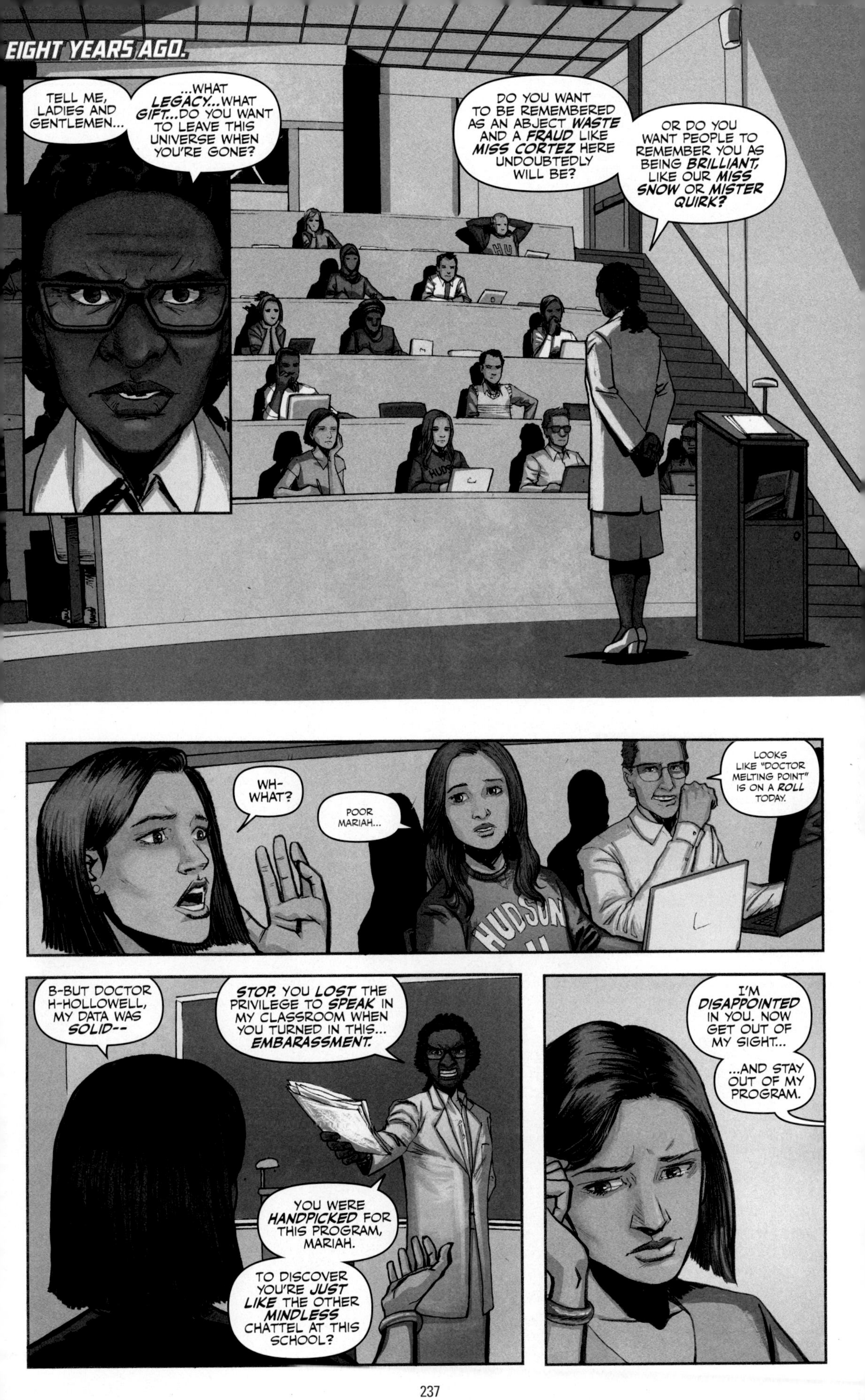
EIGHT YEARS AGO.
TELL ME, LADIES AND GENTLEMEN...
...WHAT LEGACY...WHAT GIFT...DO YOU WANT TO LEAVE THIS UNIVERSE WHEN YOU'RE GONE?
DO YOU WANT TO BE REMEMBERED AS AN ABJECT WASTE AND A FRAUD LIKE MISS CORTEZ HERE UNDOUBTEDLY WILL BE?
OR DO YOU WANT PEOPLE TO REMEMBER YOU AS BEING BRILLIANT, LIKE OUR MISS SNOW OR MISTER QUIRK?
WH-WHAT?
POOR MARIAH...
LOOKS LIKE "DOCTOR MELTING POINT" IS ON A ROLL TODAY.
HUDSON U
B-BUT DOCTOR H-HOLLOWELL, MY DATA WAS SOLID--
STOP. YOU LOST THE PRIVILEGE TO SPEAK IN MY CLASSROOM WHEN YOU TURNED IN THIS... EMBARASSMENT.
YOU WERE HANDPICKED FOR THIS PROGRAM, MARIAH.
TO DISCOVER YOU'RE JUST LIKE THE OTHER MINDLESS CHATTEL AT THIS SCHOOL?
I'M DISAPPOINTED IN YOU. NOW GET OUT OF MY SIGHT...
...AND STAY OUT OF MY PROGRAM.

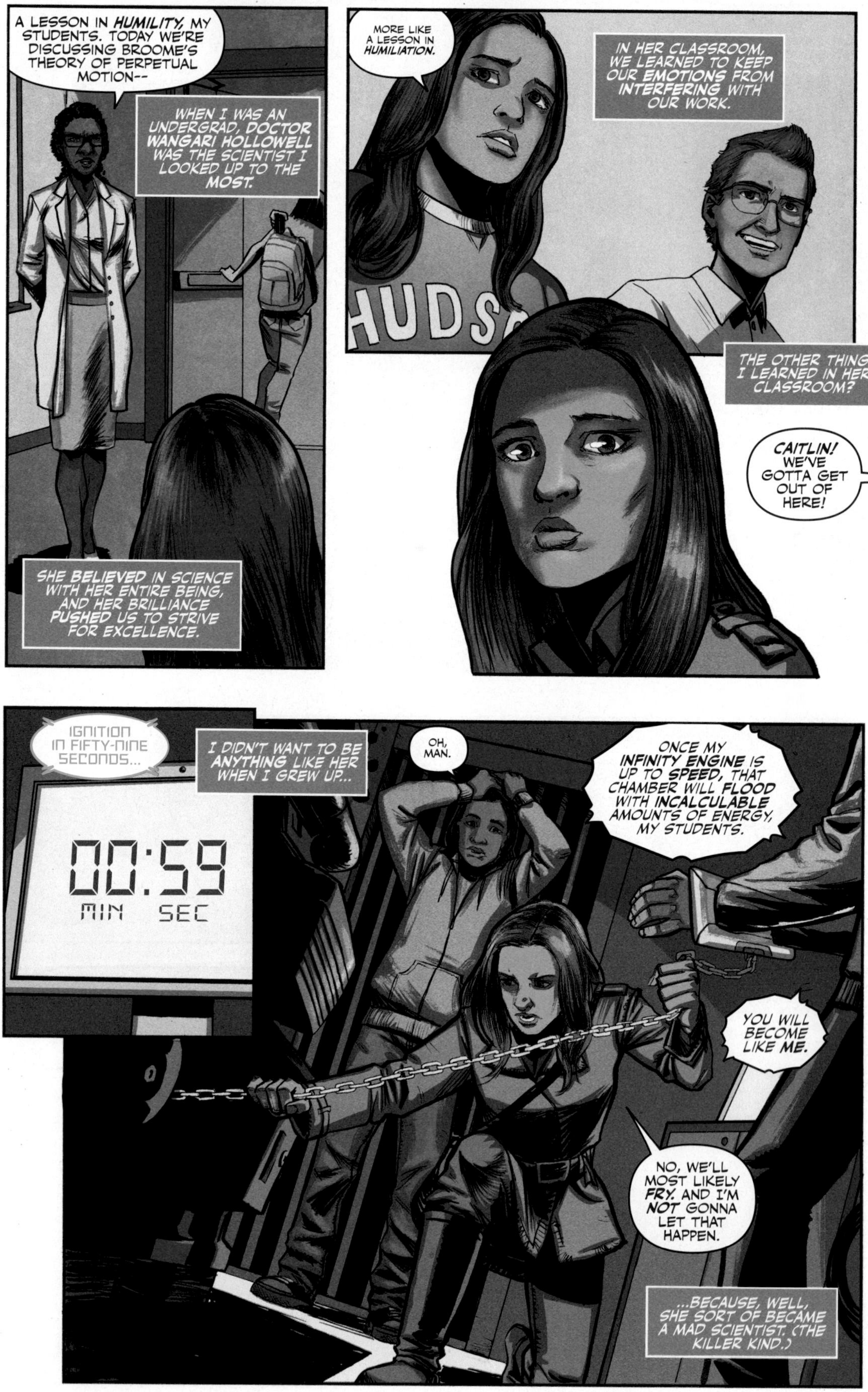
A LESSON IN HUMILITY, MY STUDENTS. TODAY WE'RE DISCUSSING BROOME'S THEORY OF PERPETUAL MOTION--
WHEN I WAS AN UNDERGRAD, DOCTOR WANGARI HOLLOWELL WAS THE SCIENTIST I LOOKED UP TO THE MOST.
SHE BELIEVED IN SCIENCE WITH HER ENTIRE BEING, AND HER BRILLIANCE PUSHED US TO STRIVE FOR EXCELLENCE.
MORE LIKE A LESSON IN HUMILIATION.
IN HER CLASSROOM, WE LEARNED TO KEEP OUR EMOTIONS FROM INTERFERING WITH OUR WORK.
HUDS
THE OTHER THING I LEARNED IN HER CLASSROOM?
CAITLIN! WE'VE GOTTA GET OUT OF HERE!
IGNITION IN FIFTY-NINE SECONDS...
I DIDN'T WANT TO BE ANYTHING LIKE HER WHEN I GREW UP...
OH, MAN.
ONCE MY INFINITY ENGINE IS UP TO SPEED, THAT CHAMBER WILL FLOOD WITH INCALCULABLE AMOUNTS OF ENERGY, MY STUDENTS.
00:59
MIN SEC
YOU WILL BECOME LIKE ME.
NO, WE'LL MOST LIKELY FRY. AND I'M NOT GONNA LET THAT HAPPEN.
...BECAUSE, WELL, SHE SORT OF BECAME A MAD SCIENTIST. (THE KILLER KIND.)

CISCO, YOU HAVE FIFTEEN SECONDS TO FIGURE OUT HOW THIS MACHINE *RUNS* AND TURN IT *OFF*.

ON IT.

00:49
MIN SEC

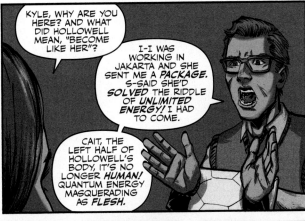

KYLE, WHY ARE YOU HERE? AND WHAT DID HOLLOWELL MEAN, "BECOME LIKE HER"?

I-I WAS WORKING IN JAKARTA AND SHE SENT ME A *PACKAGE*. S-SAID SHE'D *SOLVED* THE RIDDLE OF *UNLIMITED ENERGY!* I HAD TO COME.

CAIT, THE LEFT HALF OF HOLLOWELL'S BODY, IT'S NO LONGER *HUMAN!* QUANTUM ENERGY MASQUERADING AS *FLESH*.

CRAZED METAHUMAN? *NEW PLAN*.

YOU'RE NOT GONNA GET THROUGH TO THE *POLICE* DOWN HERE--

AFTER CAPTAIN COLD KIDNAPPED ME, CISCO *UPGRADED* OUR CELL PHONES. I CAN SEND A TEXT FROM *ANYWHERE*.

WHAT'S A "CAPTAIN COLD"?

SEND

HEY! JUST GOT YOUR TEXT.

SORRY IT TOOK ME SO LONG, *HUGE* BIKER GANG THING OVER ON WAID AVE.

WHAT'S THE SCOOP?

SSSSSS

IGNITION IN TEN SECONDS... NINE... EIGHT...

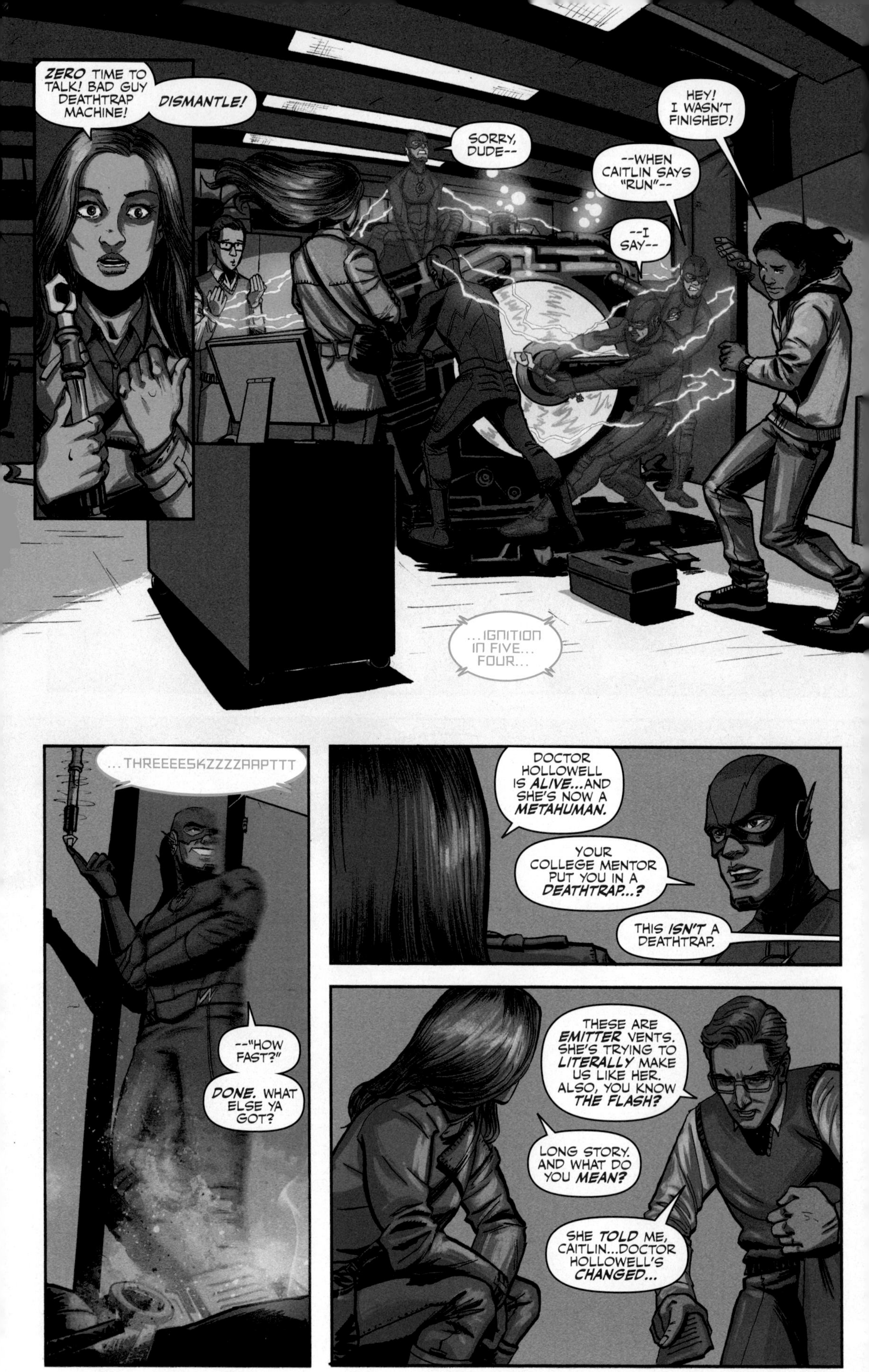
ZERO TIME TO TALK! BAD GUY DEATHTRAP MACHINE!
DISMANTLE!
SORRY, DUDE--
HEY! I WASN'T FINISHED!
--WHEN CAITLIN SAYS "RUN"--
--I SAY--
...IGNITION IN FIVE... FOUR...
...THREEEEESKZZZZAAPTTT
--"HOW FAST?"
DONE. WHAT ELSE YA GOT?
DOCTOR HOLLOWELL IS ALIVE...AND SHE'S NOW A METAHUMAN.
YOUR COLLEGE MENTOR PUT YOU IN A DEATHTRAP...?
THIS ISN'T A DEATHTRAP.
THESE ARE EMITTER VENTS. SHE'S TRYING TO LITERALLY MAKE US LIKE HER. ALSO, YOU KNOW THE FLASH?
LONG STORY. AND WHAT DO YOU MEAN?
SHE TOLD ME, CAITLIN...DOCTOR HOLLOWELL'S CHANGED...

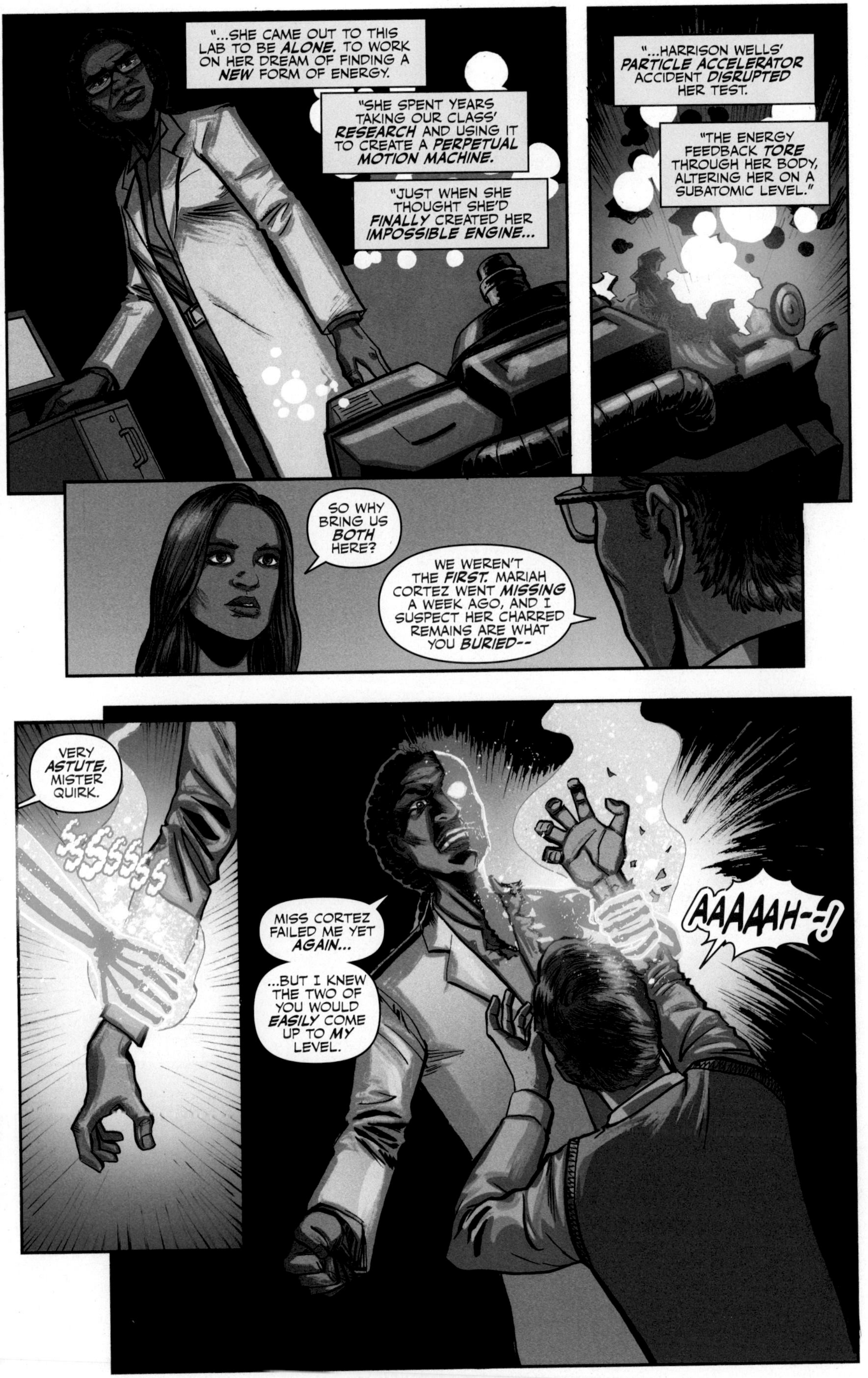
"...SHE CAME OUT TO THIS LAB TO BE ALONE. TO WORK ON HER DREAM OF FINDING A NEW FORM OF ENERGY.
"SHE SPENT YEARS TAKING OUR CLASS' RESEARCH AND USING IT TO CREATE A PERPETUAL MOTION MACHINE.
"JUST WHEN SHE THOUGHT SHE'D FINALLY CREATED HER IMPOSSIBLE ENGINE...
"...HARRISON WELLS' PARTICLE ACCELERATOR ACCIDENT DISRUPTED HER TEST.
"THE ENERGY FEEDBACK TORE THROUGH HER BODY, ALTERING HER ON A SUBATOMIC LEVEL."
SO WHY BRING US BOTH HERE?
WE WEREN'T THE FIRST. MARIAH CORTEZ WENT MISSING A WEEK AGO, AND I SUSPECT HER CHARRED REMAINS ARE WHAT YOU BURIED--
VERY ASTUTE, MISTER QUIRK.
SSSSSS
MISS CORTEZ FAILED ME YET AGAIN...
...BUT I KNEW THE TWO OF YOU WOULD EASILY COME UP TO MY LEVEL.
AAAAAH--!

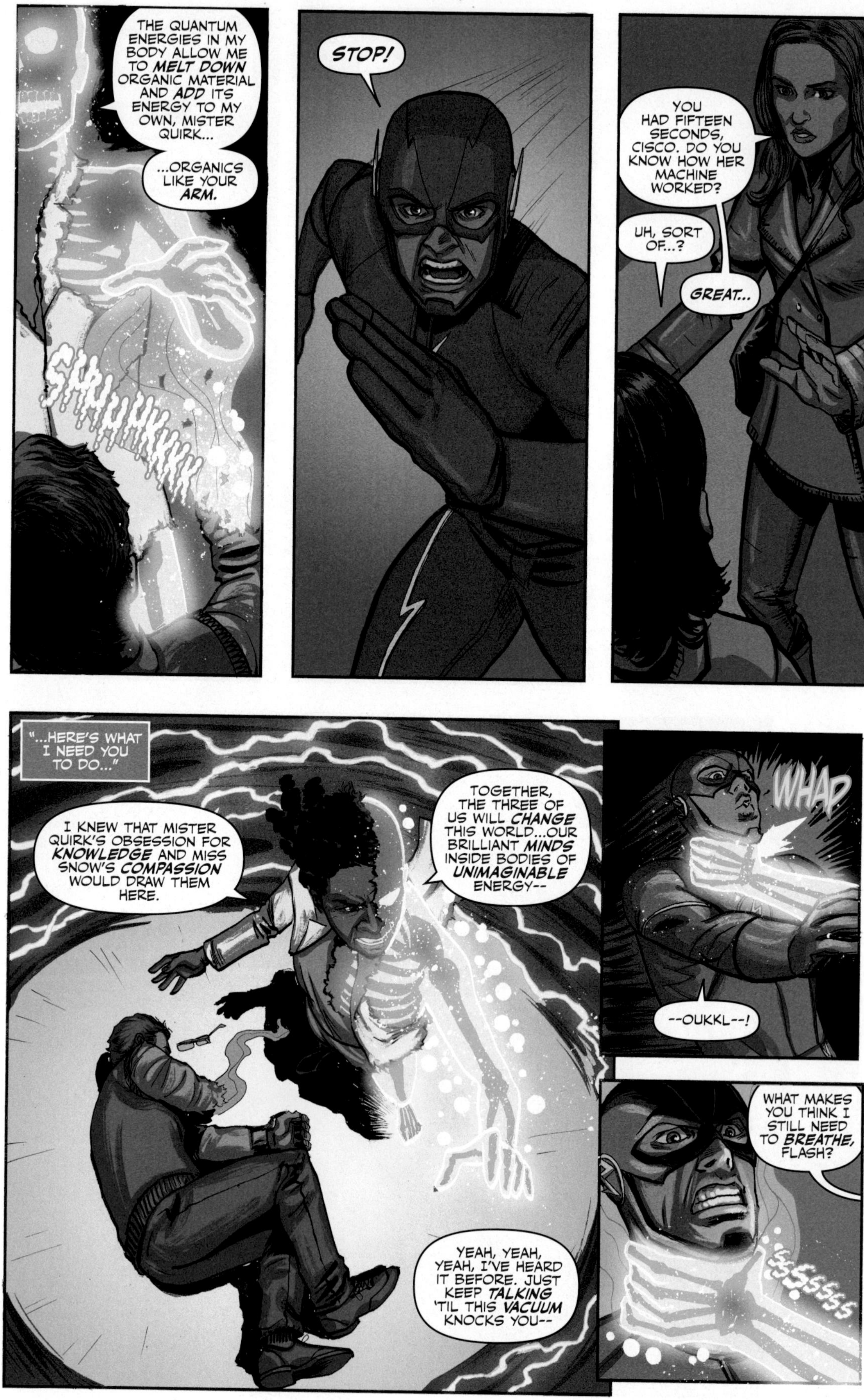
THE QUANTUM ENERGIES IN MY BODY ALLOW ME TO MELT DOWN ORGANIC MATERIAL AND ADD ITS ENERGY TO MY OWN, MISTER QUIRK...
...ORGANICS LIKE YOUR ARM.
SHHHHKKKK
STOP!
YOU HAD FIFTEEN SECONDS, CISCO. DO YOU KNOW HOW HER MACHINE WORKED?
UH, SORT OF...?
GREAT...
"...HERE'S WHAT I NEED YOU TO DO..."
I KNEW THAT MISTER QUIRK'S OBSESSION FOR KNOWLEDGE AND MISS SNOW'S COMPASSION WOULD DRAW THEM HERE.
TOGETHER, THE THREE OF US WILL CHANGE THIS WORLD...OUR BRILLIANT MINDS INSIDE BODIES OF UNIMAGINABLE ENERGY--
YEAH, YEAH, YEAH, I'VE HEARD IT BEFORE. JUST KEEP TALKING 'TIL THIS VACUUM KNOCKS YOU--
WHAP
--OUKKL--!
WHAT MAKES YOU THINK I STILL NEED TO BREATHE, FLASH?
SSSSSS

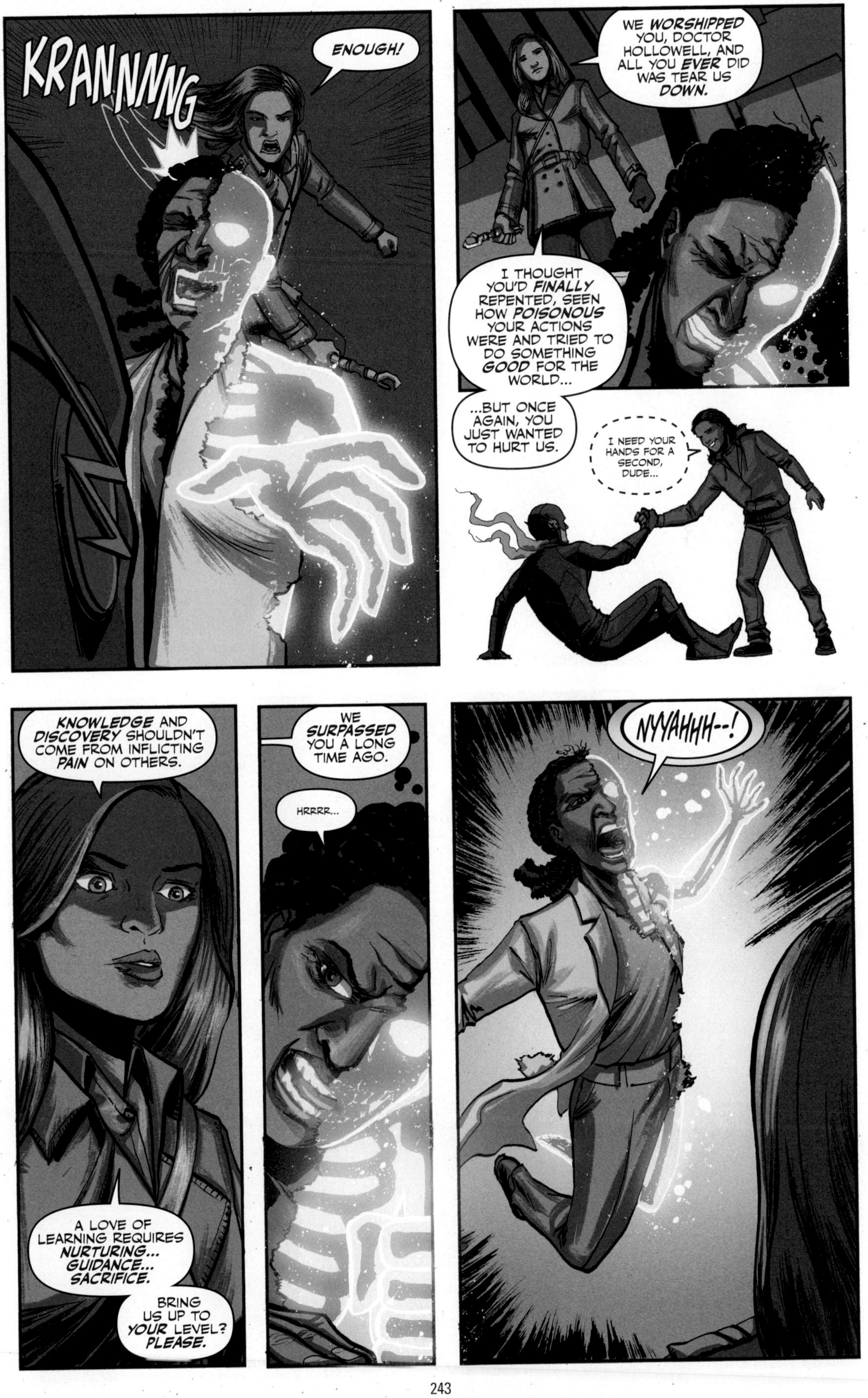
KRANNNNG
ENOUGH!
WE WORSHIPPED YOU, DOCTOR HOLLOWELL, AND ALL YOU EVER DID WAS TEAR US DOWN.
I THOUGHT YOU'D FINALLY REPENTED, SEEN HOW POISONOUS YOUR ACTIONS WERE AND TRIED TO DO SOMETHING GOOD FOR THE WORLD...
...BUT ONCE AGAIN, YOU JUST WANTED TO HURT US.
I NEED YOUR HANDS FOR A SECOND, DUDE...
KNOWLEDGE AND DISCOVERY SHOULDN'T COME FROM INFLICTING PAIN ON OTHERS.
A LOVE OF LEARNING REQUIRES NURTURING... GUIDANCE... SACRIFICE.
BRING US UP TO YOUR LEVEL? PLEASE.
WE SURPASSED YOU A LONG TIME AGO.
HRRRR...
NYYAHHH--!

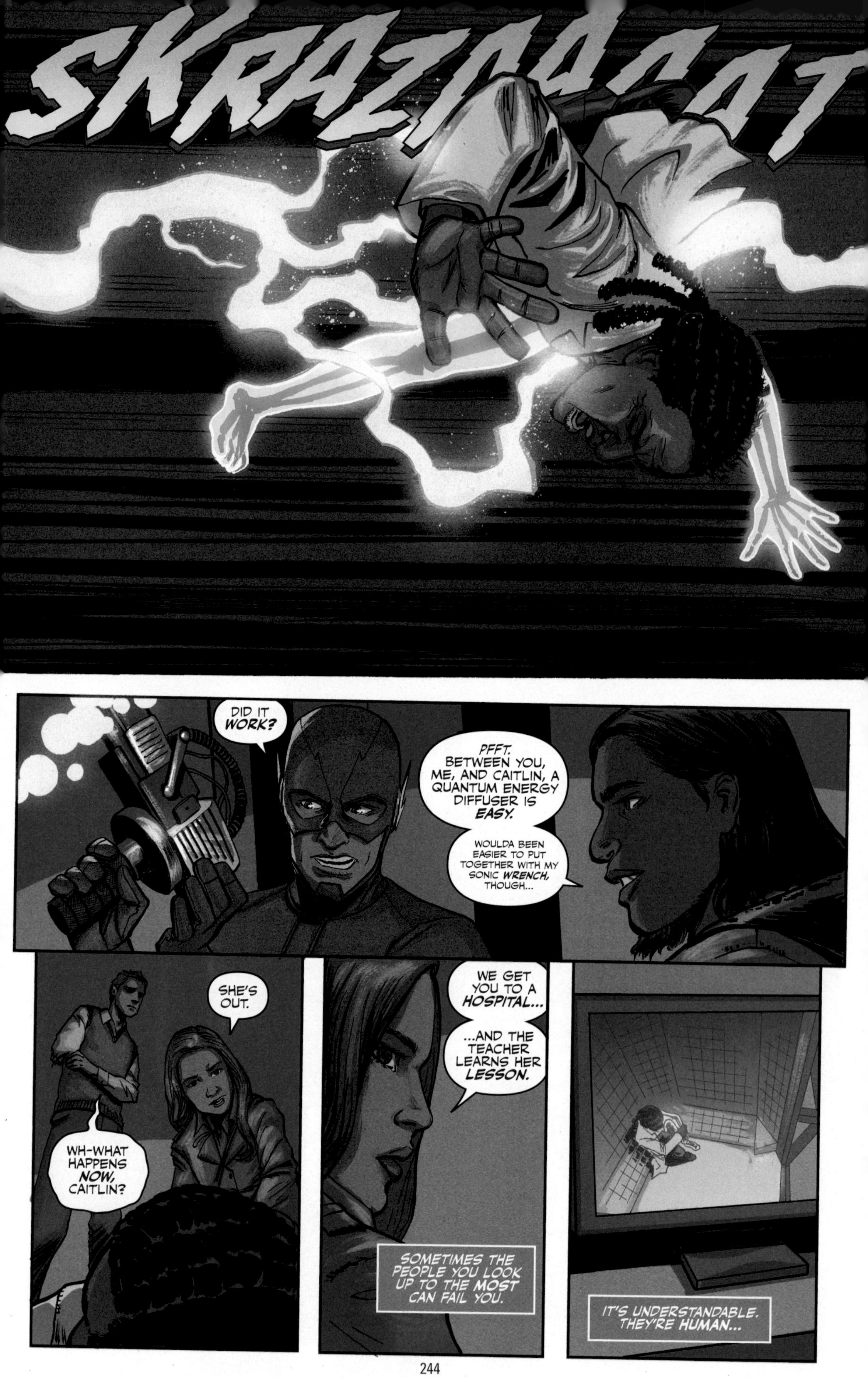
SKRAZAAAAT
DID IT WORK?
PFFT. BETWEEN YOU, ME, AND CAITLIN, A QUANTUM ENERGY DIFFUSER IS EASY.
WOULDA BEEN EASIER TO PUT TOGETHER WITH MY SONIC WRENCH, THOUGH...
SHE'S OUT.
WH-WHAT HAPPENS NOW, CAITLIN?
WE GET YOU TO A HOSPITAL...
...AND THE TEACHER LEARNS HER LESSON.
SOMETIMES THE PEOPLE YOU LOOK UP TO THE MOST CAN FAIL YOU.
IT'S UNDERSTANDABLE. THEY'RE HUMAN...

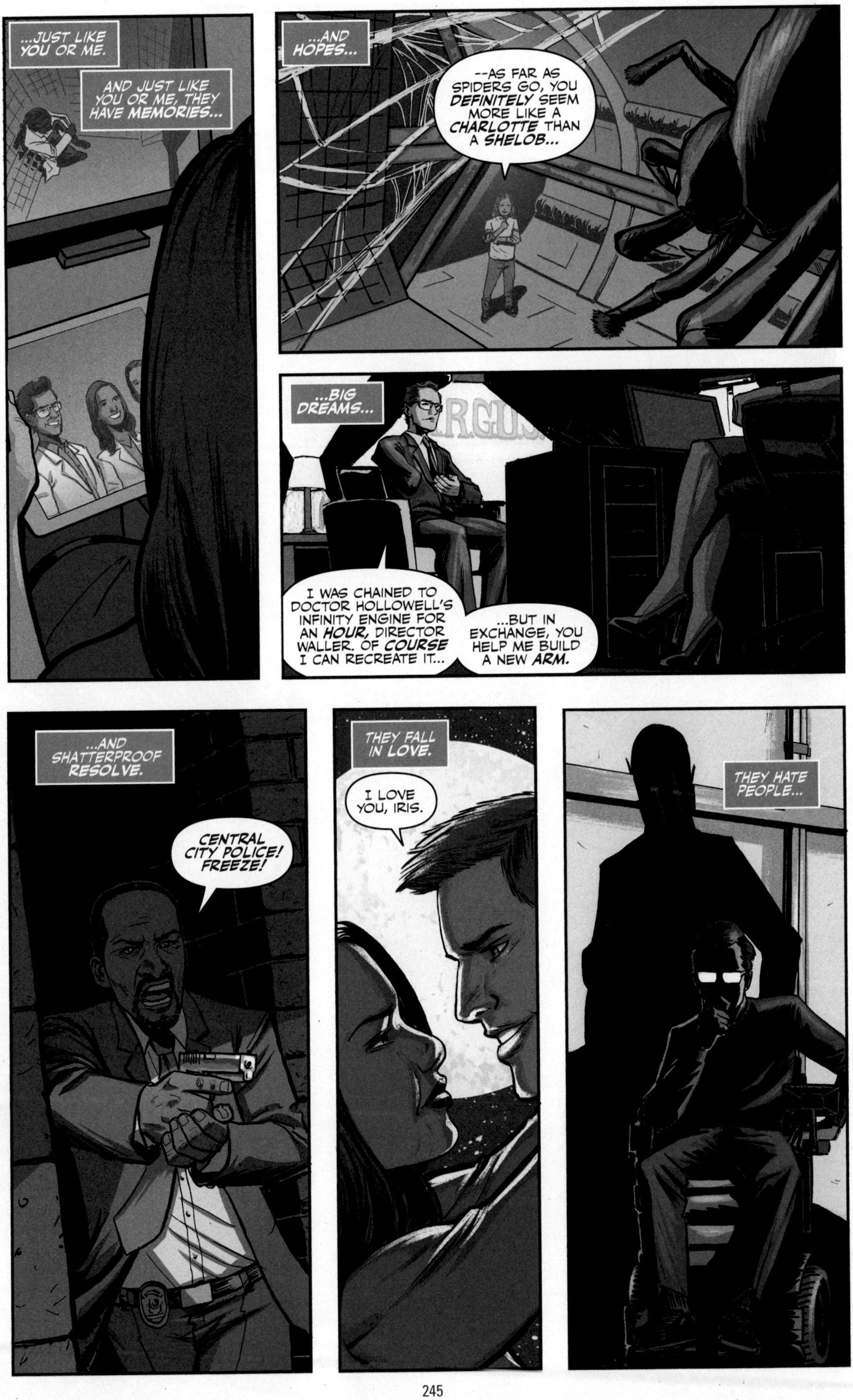
...JUST LIKE YOU OR ME.
AND JUST LIKE YOU OR ME, THEY HAVE MEMORIES...
...AND HOPES...
--AS FAR AS SPIDERS GO, YOU DEFINITELY SEEM MORE LIKE A CHARLOTTE THAN A SHELOB...
...BIG DREAMS...
I WAS CHAINED TO DOCTOR HOLLOWELL'S INFINITY ENGINE FOR AN HOUR, DIRECTOR WALLER. OF COURSE I CAN RECREATE IT...
...BUT IN EXCHANGE, YOU HELP ME BUILD A NEW ARM.
...AND SHATTERPROOF RESOLVE.
CENTRAL CITY POLICE! FREEZE!
THEY FALL IN LOVE.
I LOVE YOU, IRIS.
THEY HATE PEOPLE...

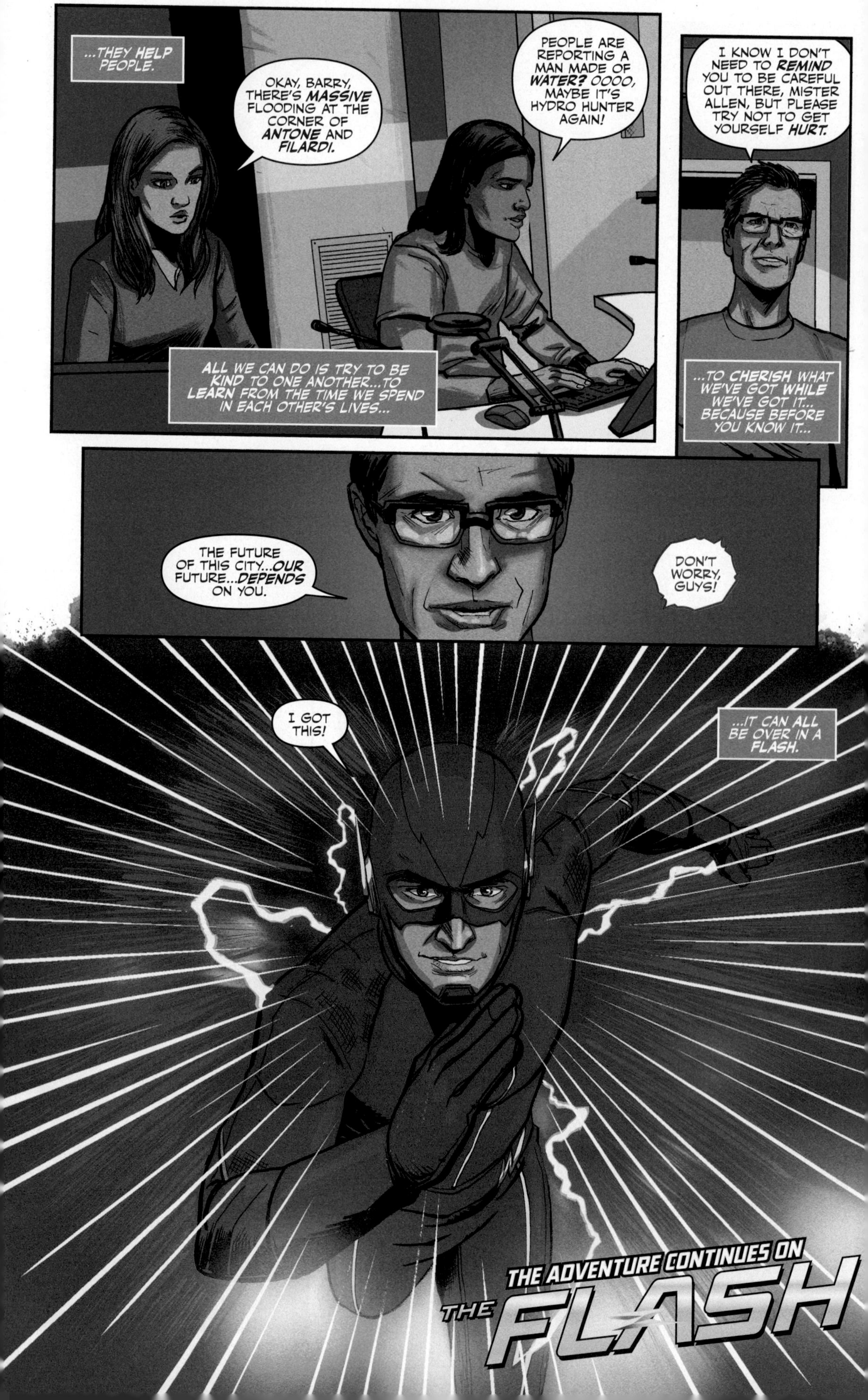

...THEY HELP PEOPLE.
OKAY, BARRY, THERE'S MASSIVE FLOODING AT THE CORNER OF ANTONE AND FILARDI.
PEOPLE ARE REPORTING A MAN MADE OF WATER? OOOO, MAYBE IT'S HYDRO HUNTER AGAIN!
ALL WE CAN DO IS TRY TO BE KIND TO ONE ANOTHER...TO LEARN FROM THE TIME WE SPEND IN EACH OTHER'S LIVES...
I KNOW I DON'T NEED TO REMIND YOU TO BE CAREFUL OUT THERE, MISTER ALLEN, BUT PLEASE TRY NOT TO GET YOURSELF HURT.
...TO CHERISH WHAT WE'VE GOT WHILE WE'VE GOT IT... BECAUSE BEFORE YOU KNOW IT...
THE FUTURE OF THIS CITY...OUR FUTURE...DEPENDS ON YOU.
DON'T WORRY, GUYS!
I GOT THIS!
...IT CAN ALL BE OVER IN A FLASH.
THE ADVENTURE CONTINUES ON
THE FLASH

THE FLASH SEASON ZERO COVER GALLERY

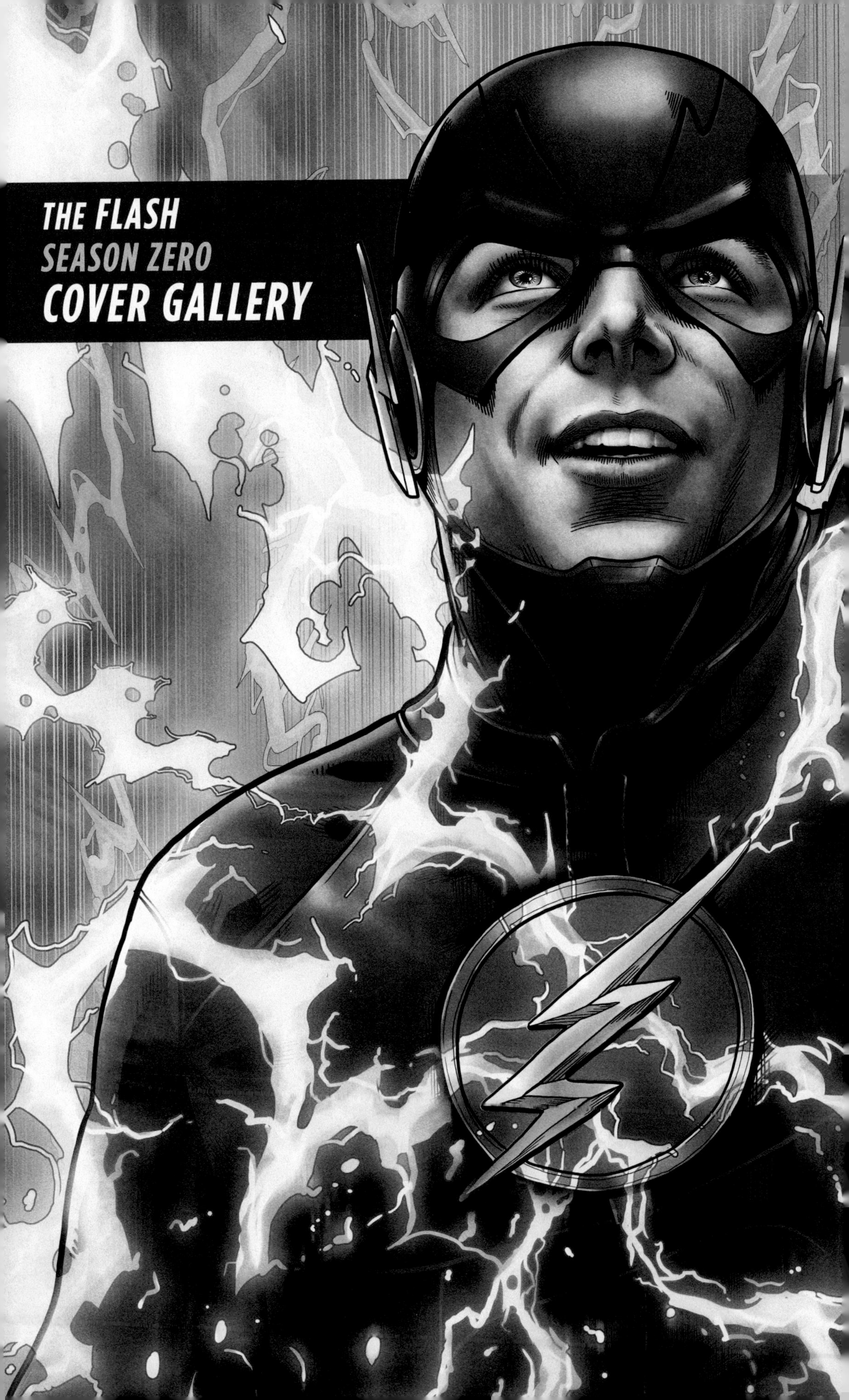

THE FLASH: SEASON ZERO #1 COVER

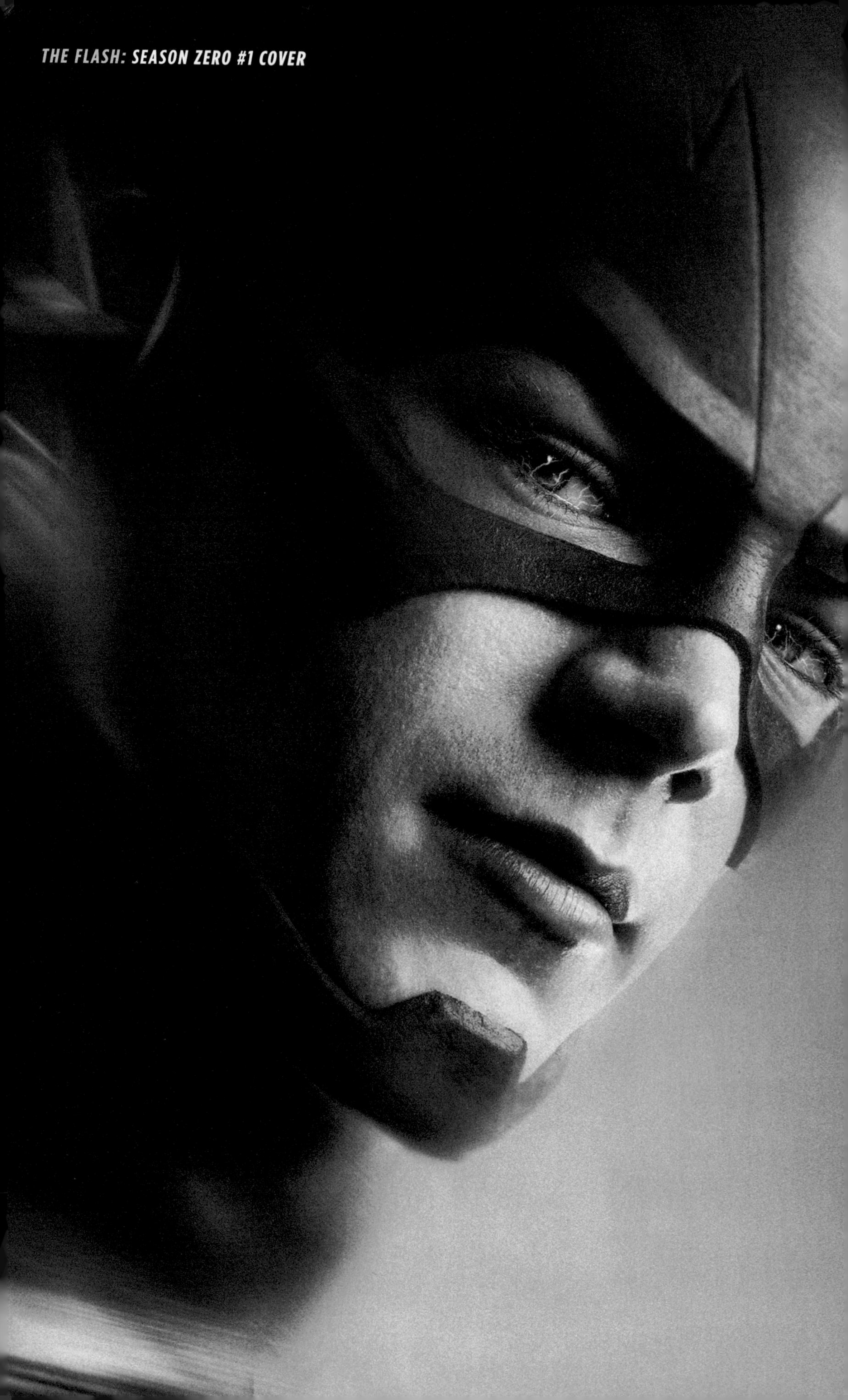

THE FLASH: SEASON ZERO #1
VARIANT COVER BY FRANCIS MANAPUL

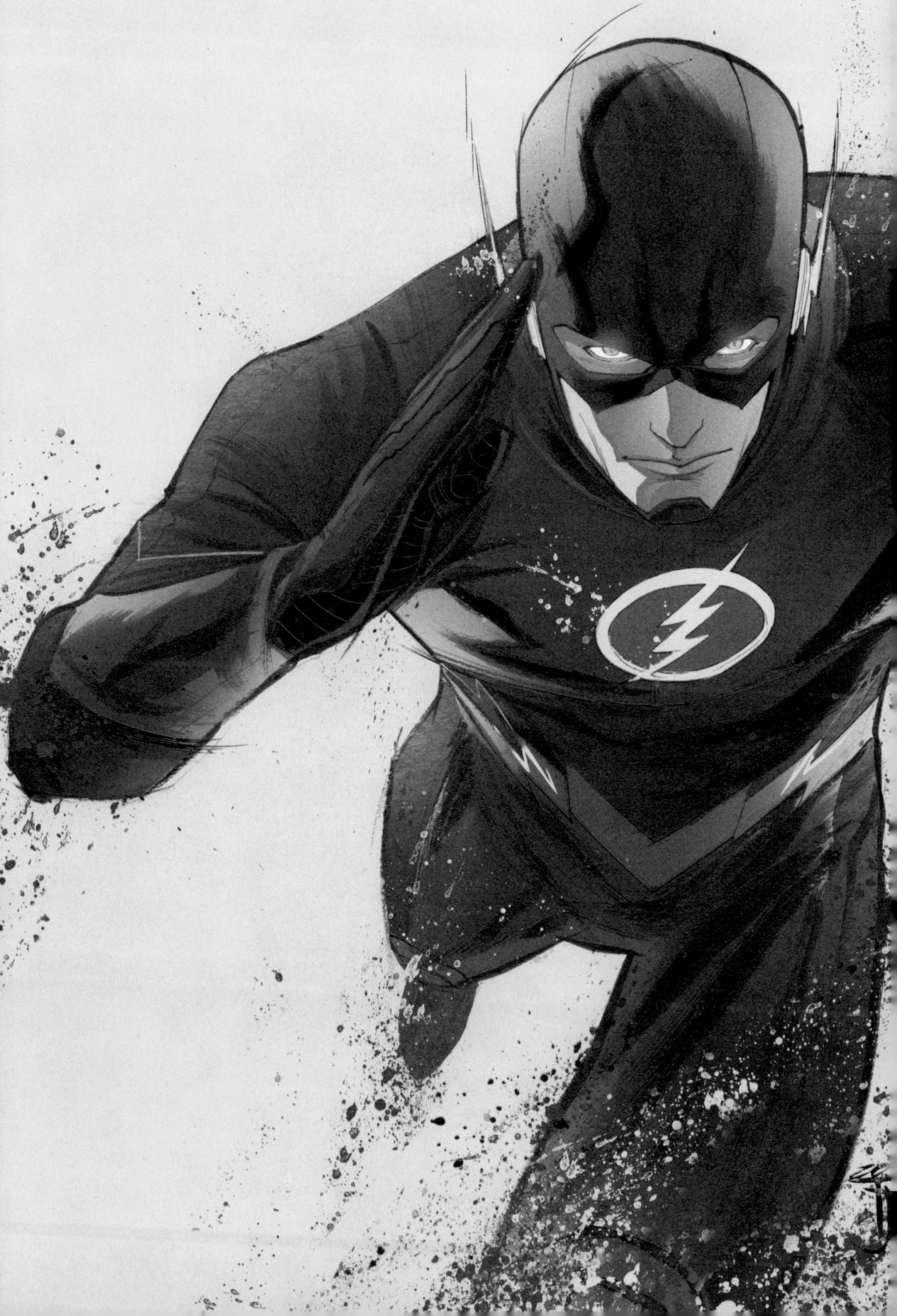

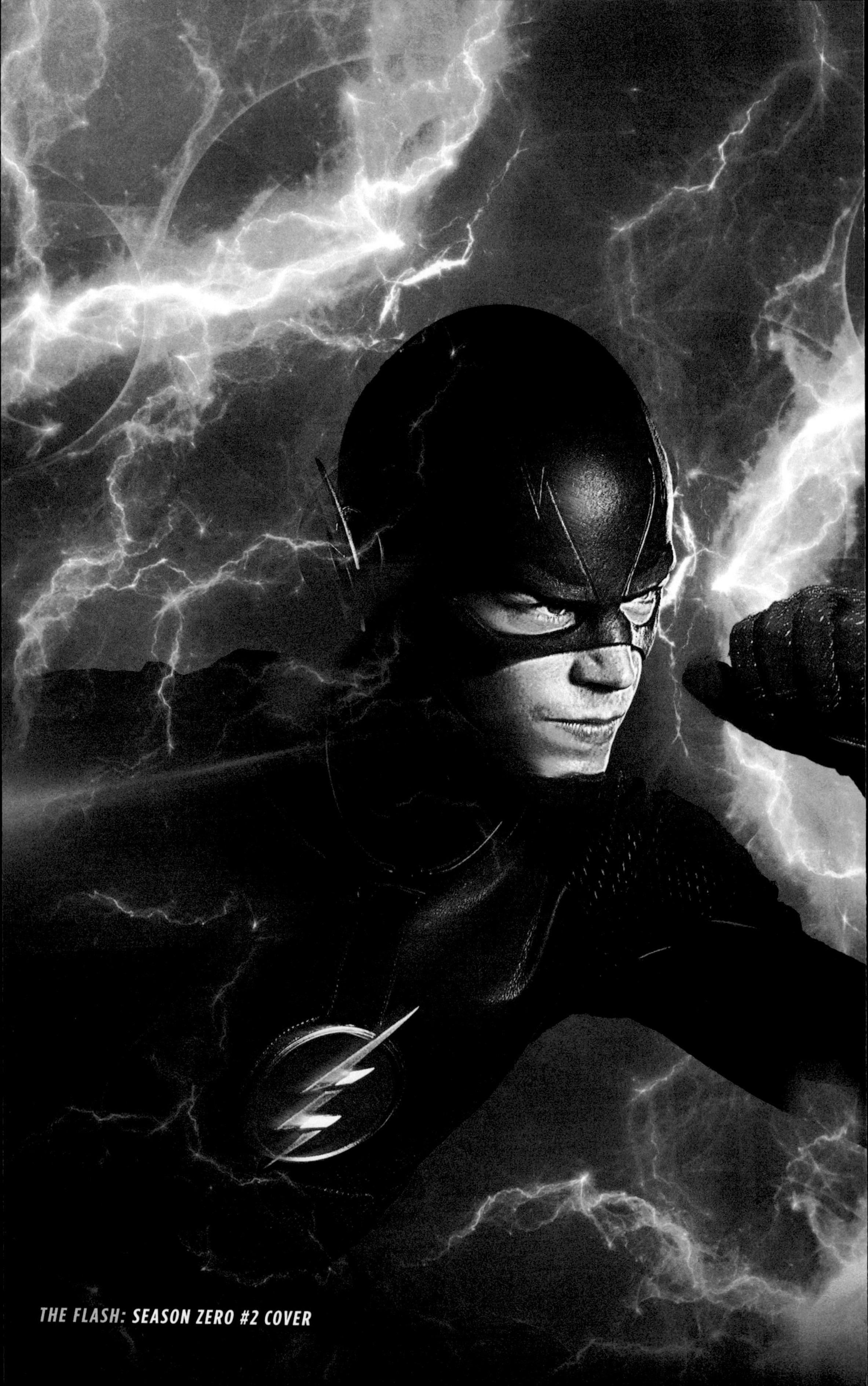

***THE FLASH:* SEASON ZERO #2 COVER**

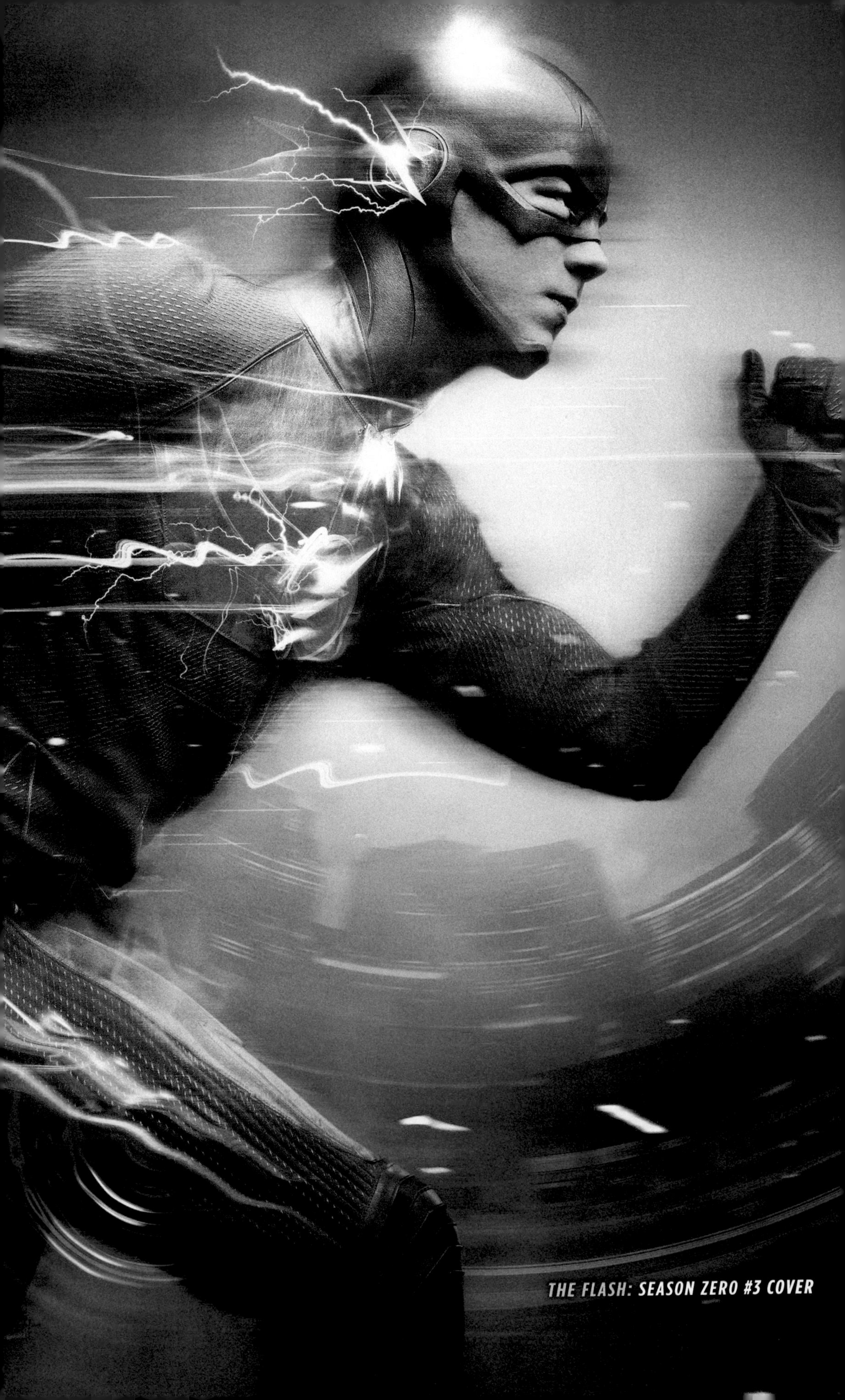

THE FLASH: SEASON ZERO #3 COVER

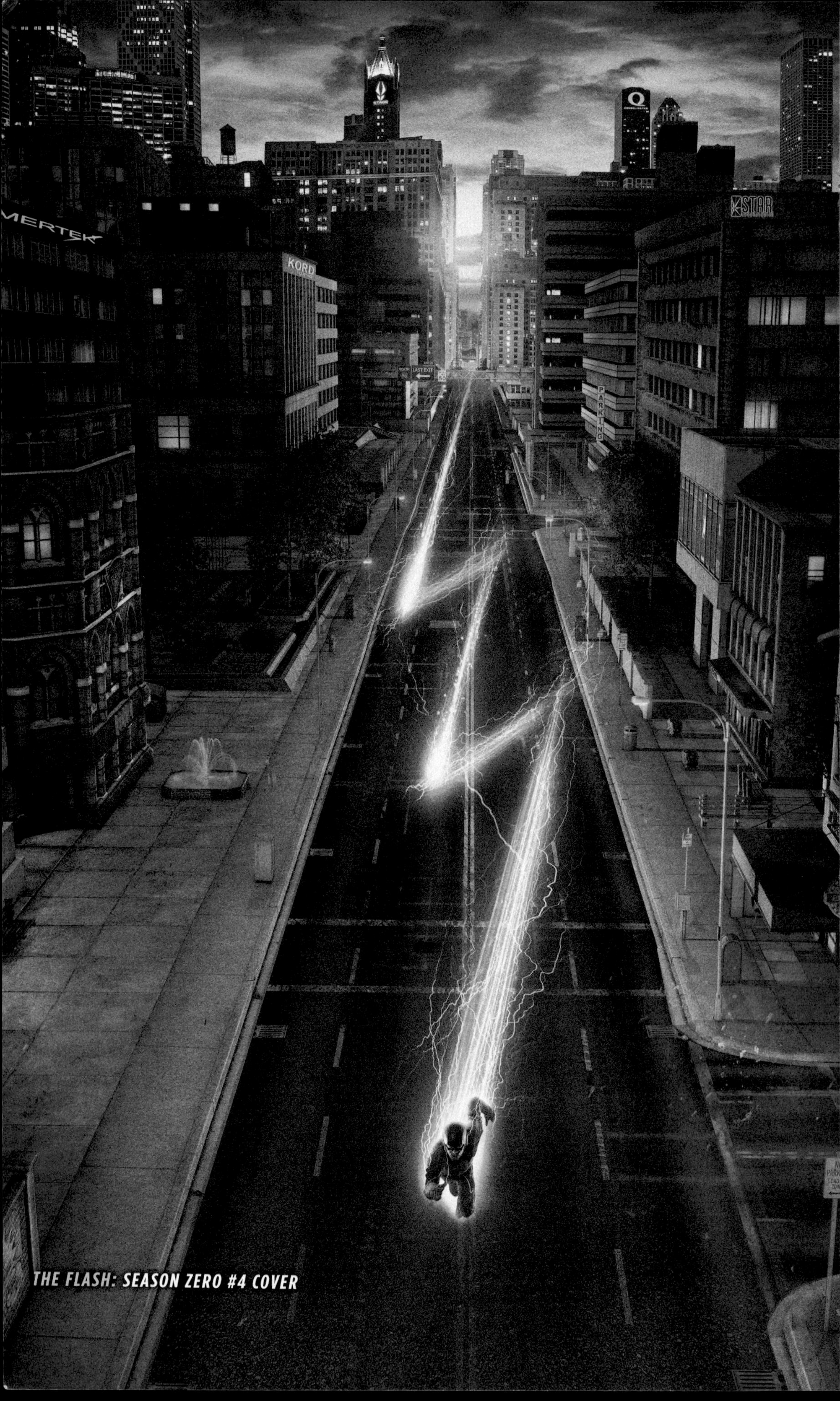
MERTEK
KORD
STAR
PARKING
LAST EXIT

THE FLASH: SEASON ZERO #4 COVER

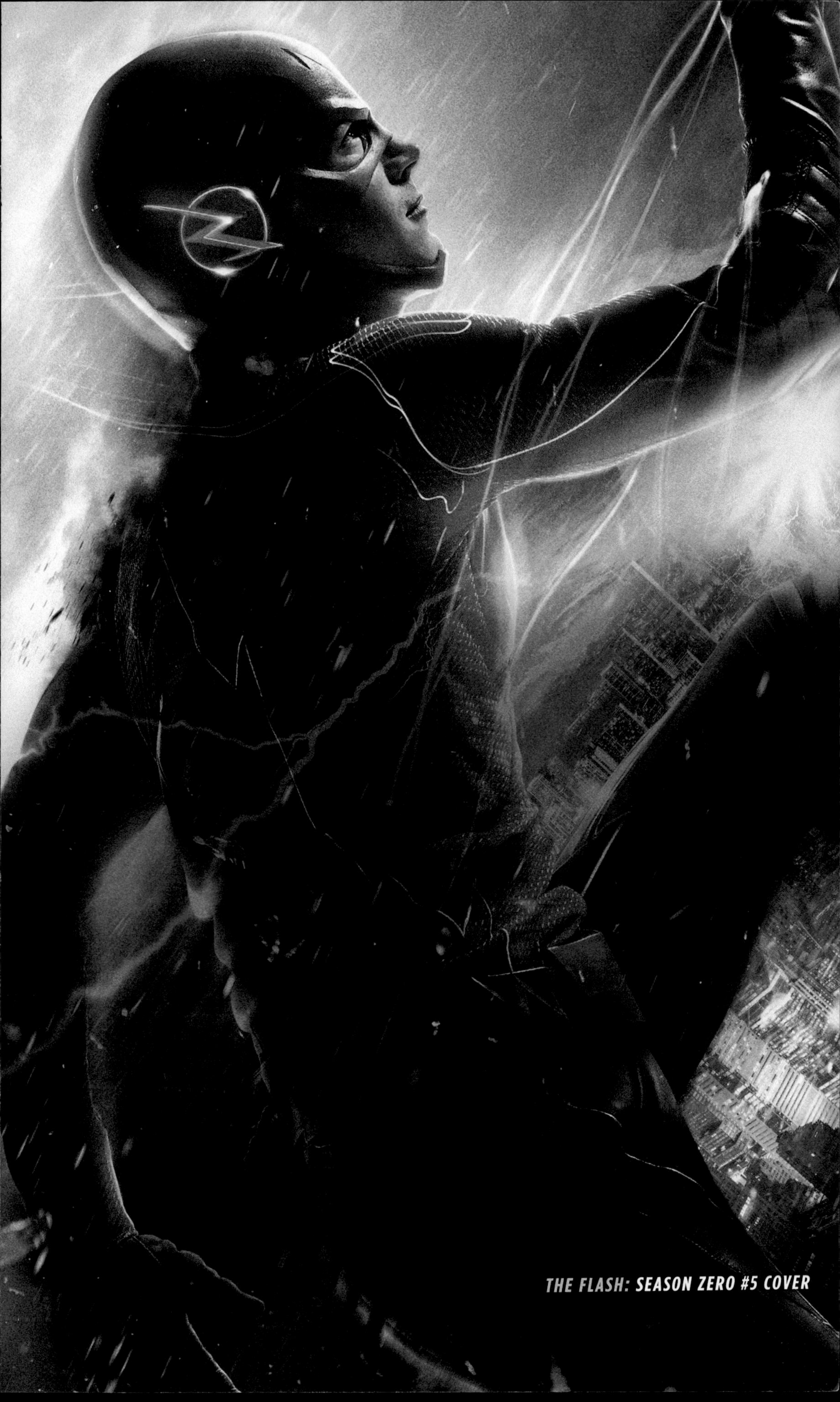

THE FLASH: **SEASON ZERO #5 COVER**

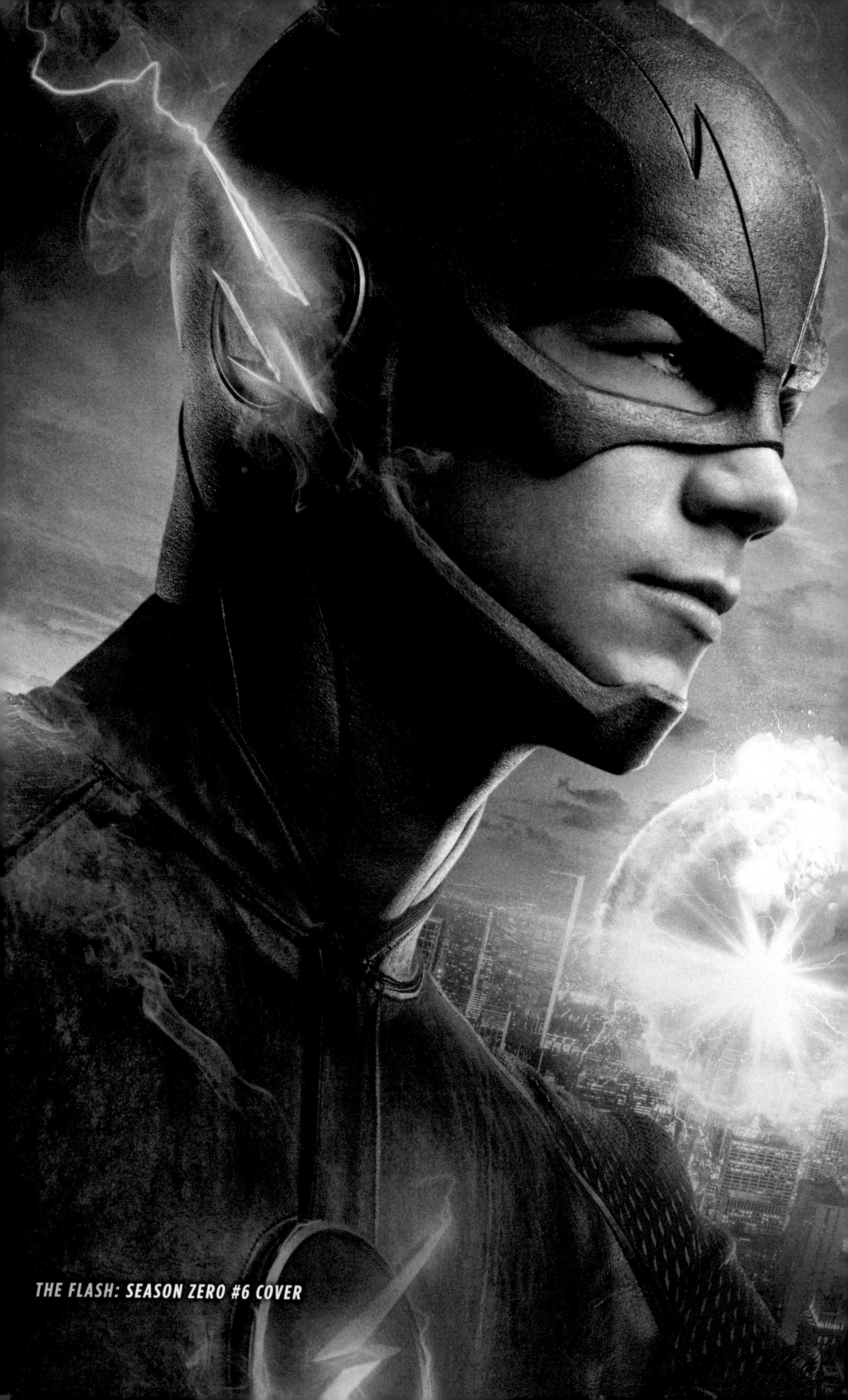

THE FLASH: **SEASON ZERO #6 COVER**

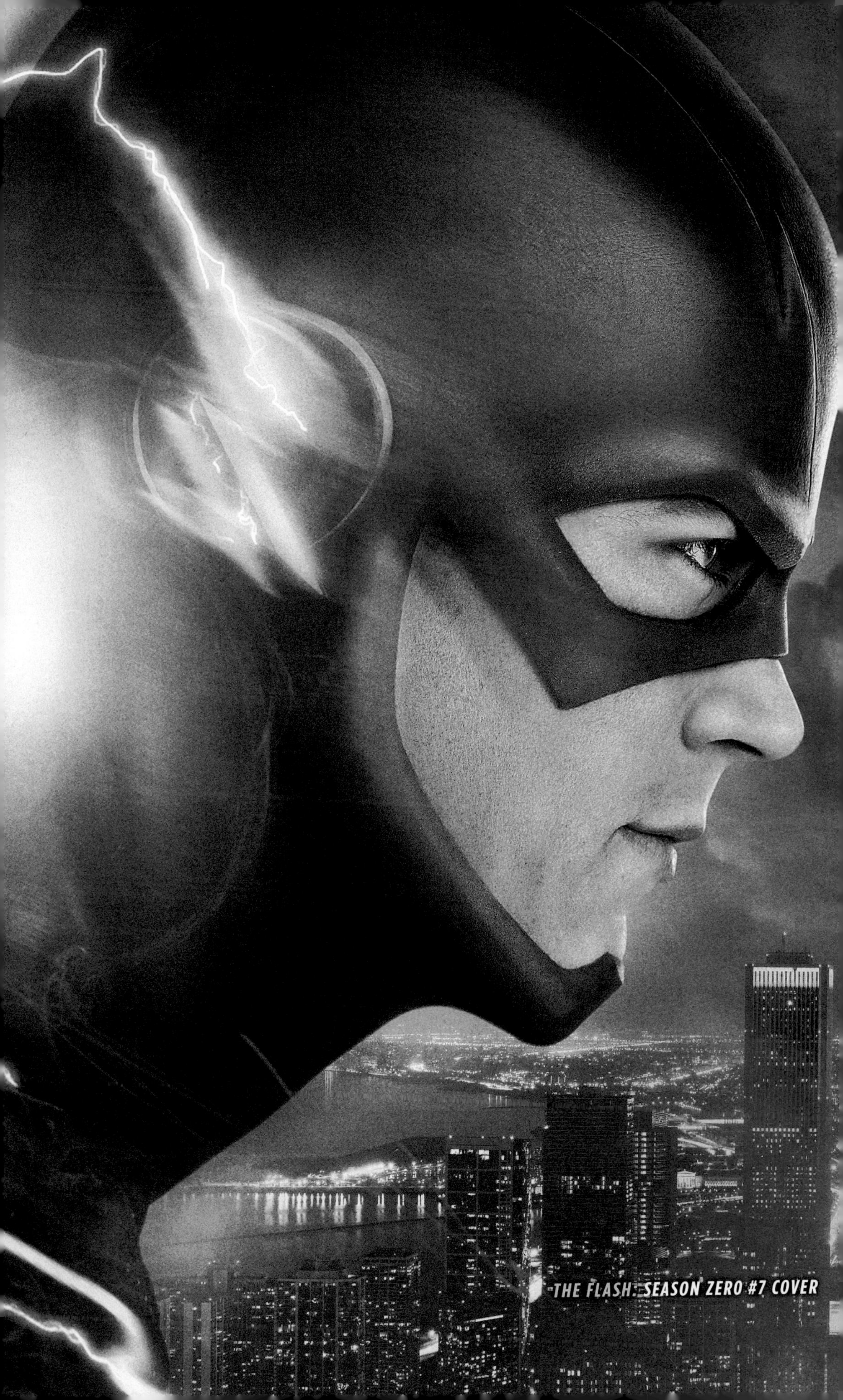

THE FLASH: SEASON ZERO #7 COVER

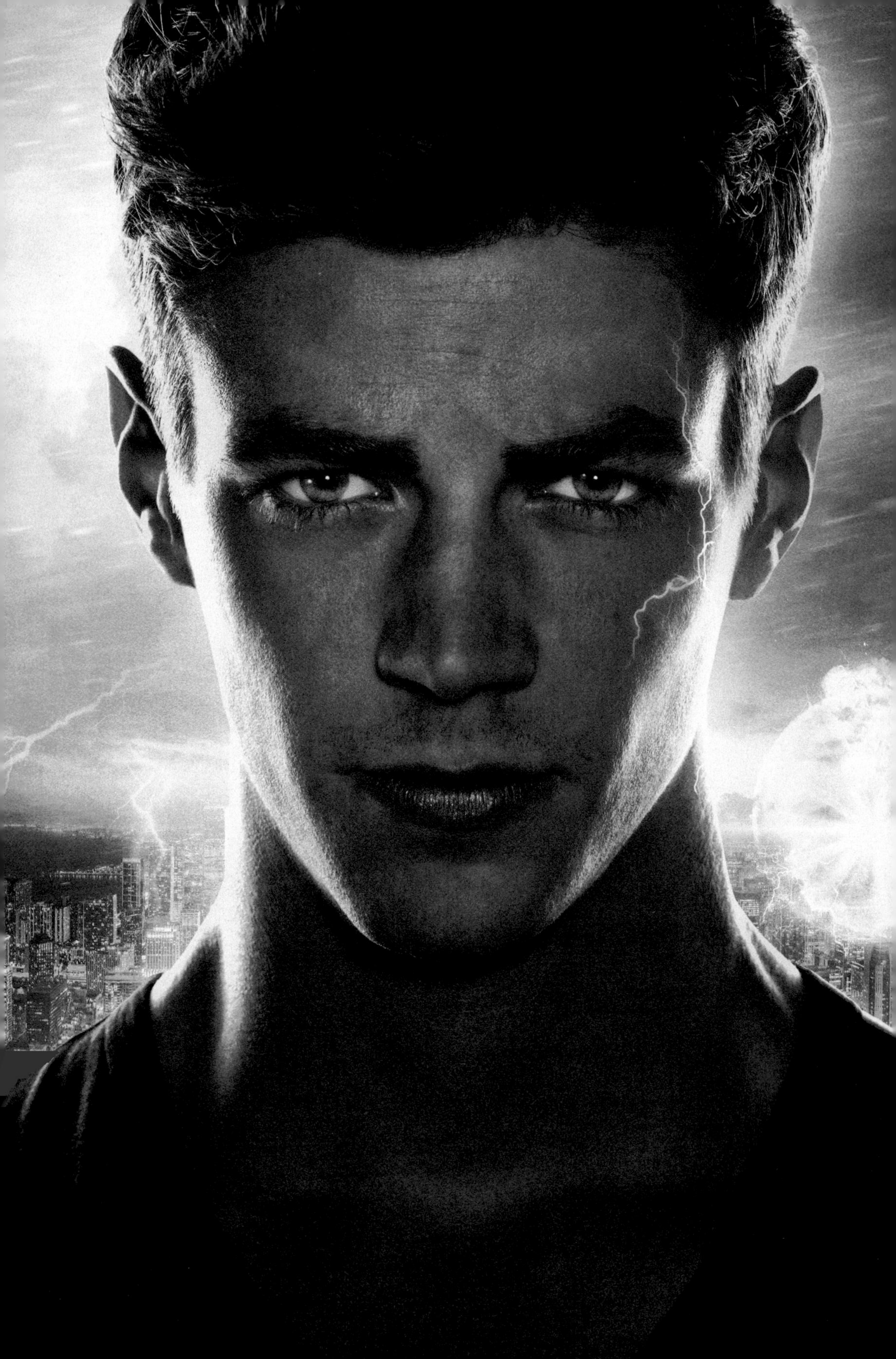

THE FLASH: SEASON ZERO #8 COVER

THE FLASH: SEASON ZERO #9
COVER BY JASON BADOWER & ANNETTE KWOK

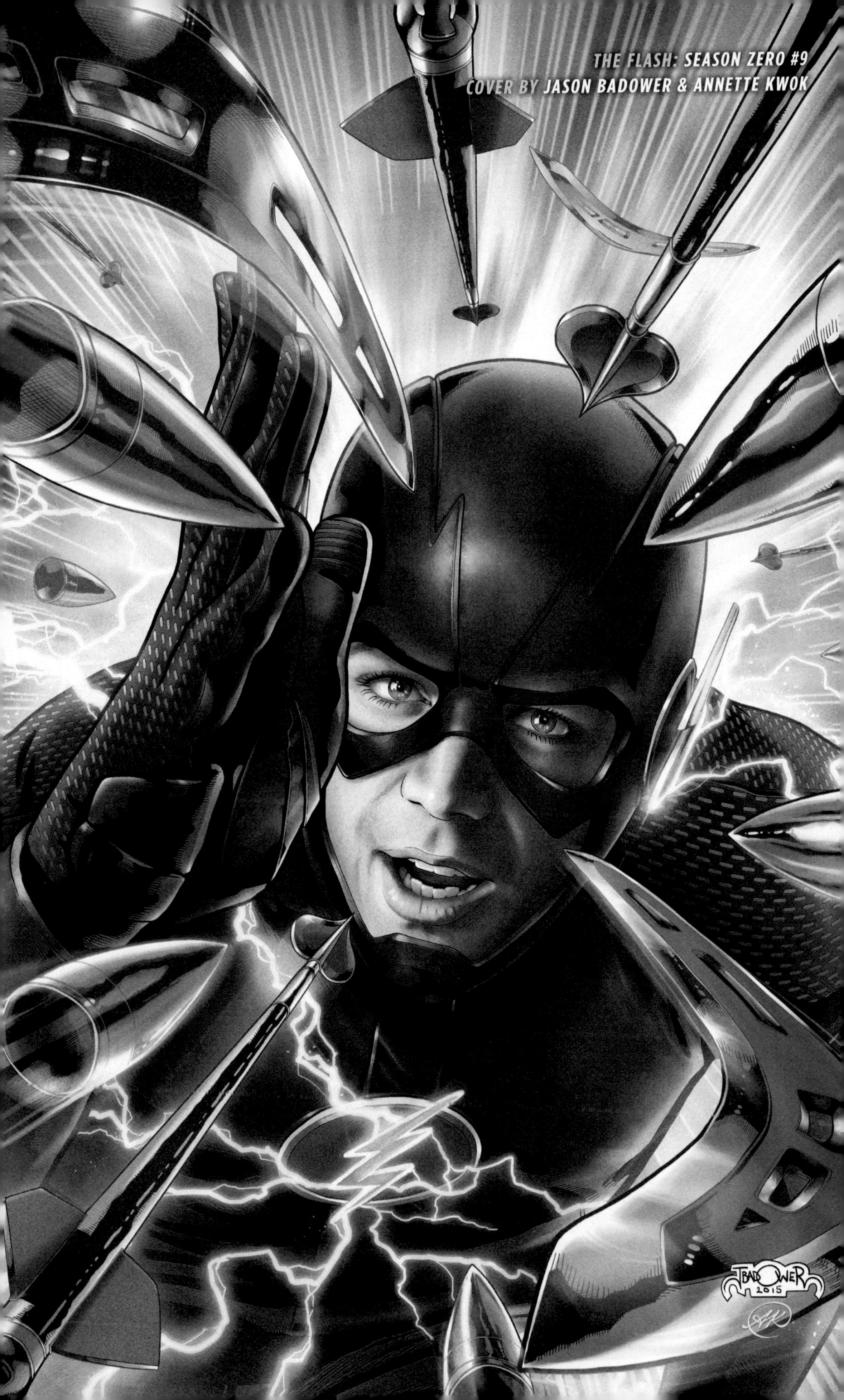
J.BADOWER
2015

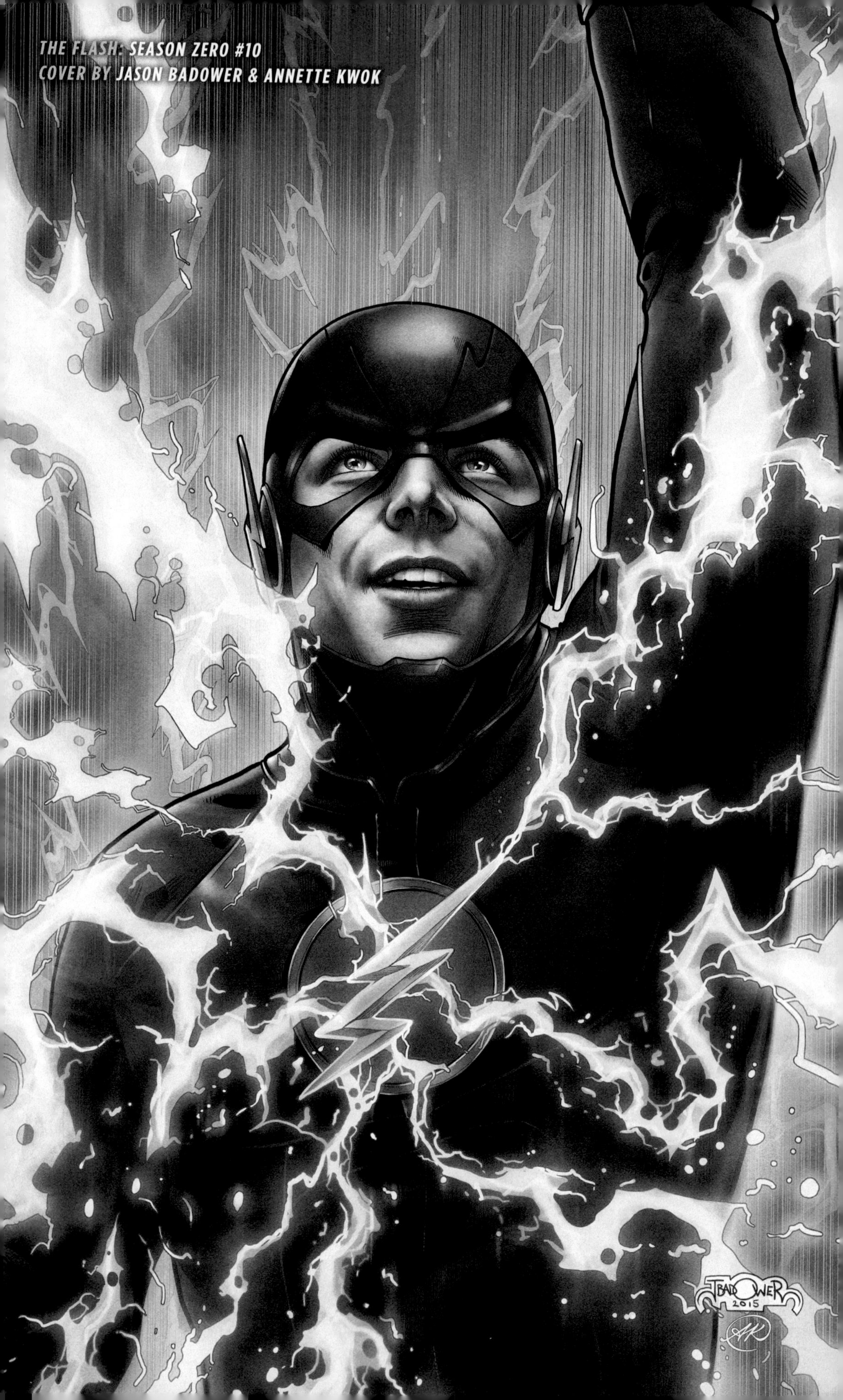
J BADOWER
2015

THE FLASH: SEASON ZERO #10
COVER BY JASON BADOWER & ANNETTE KWOK

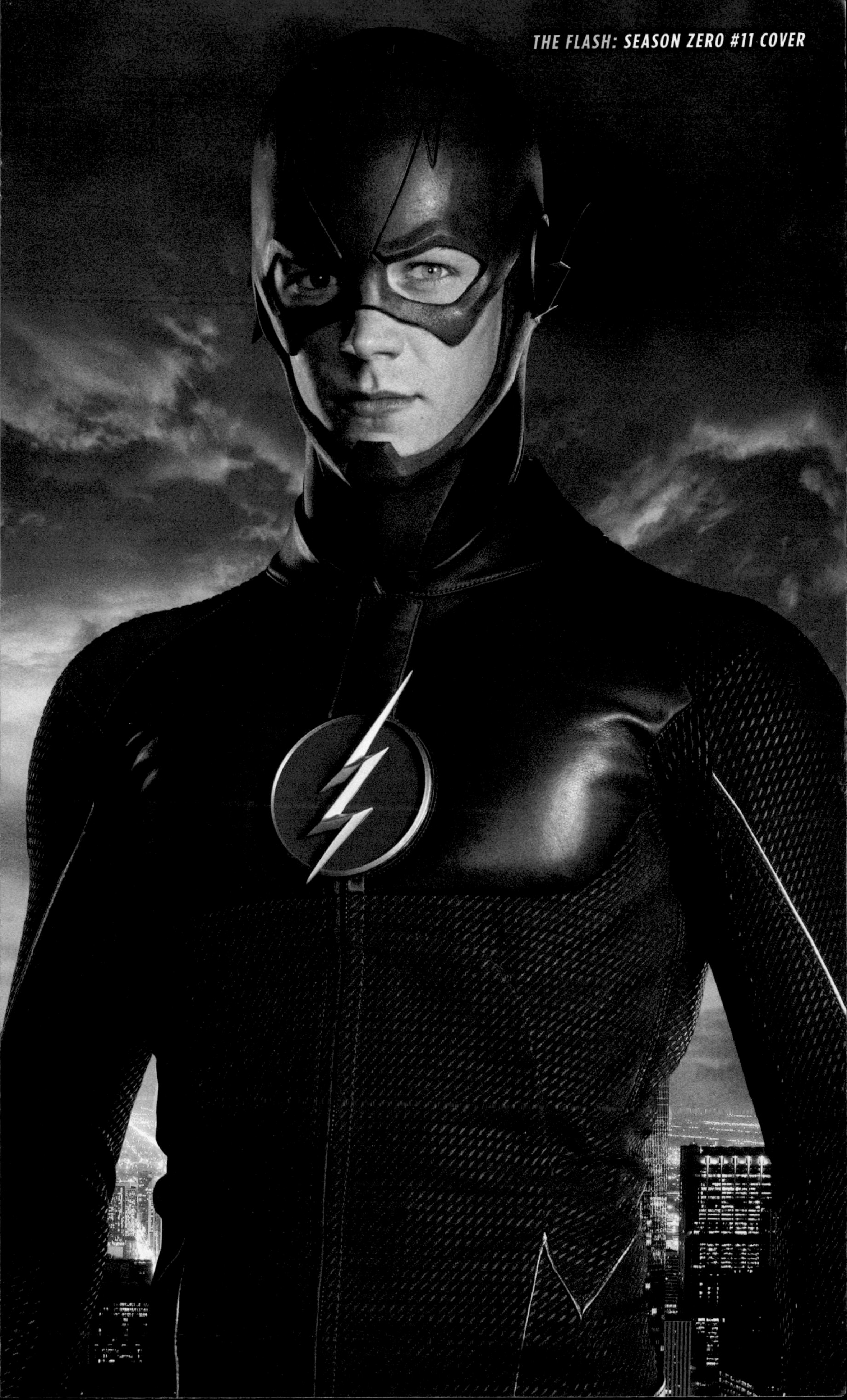

THE FLASH: SEASON ZERO #11 COVER

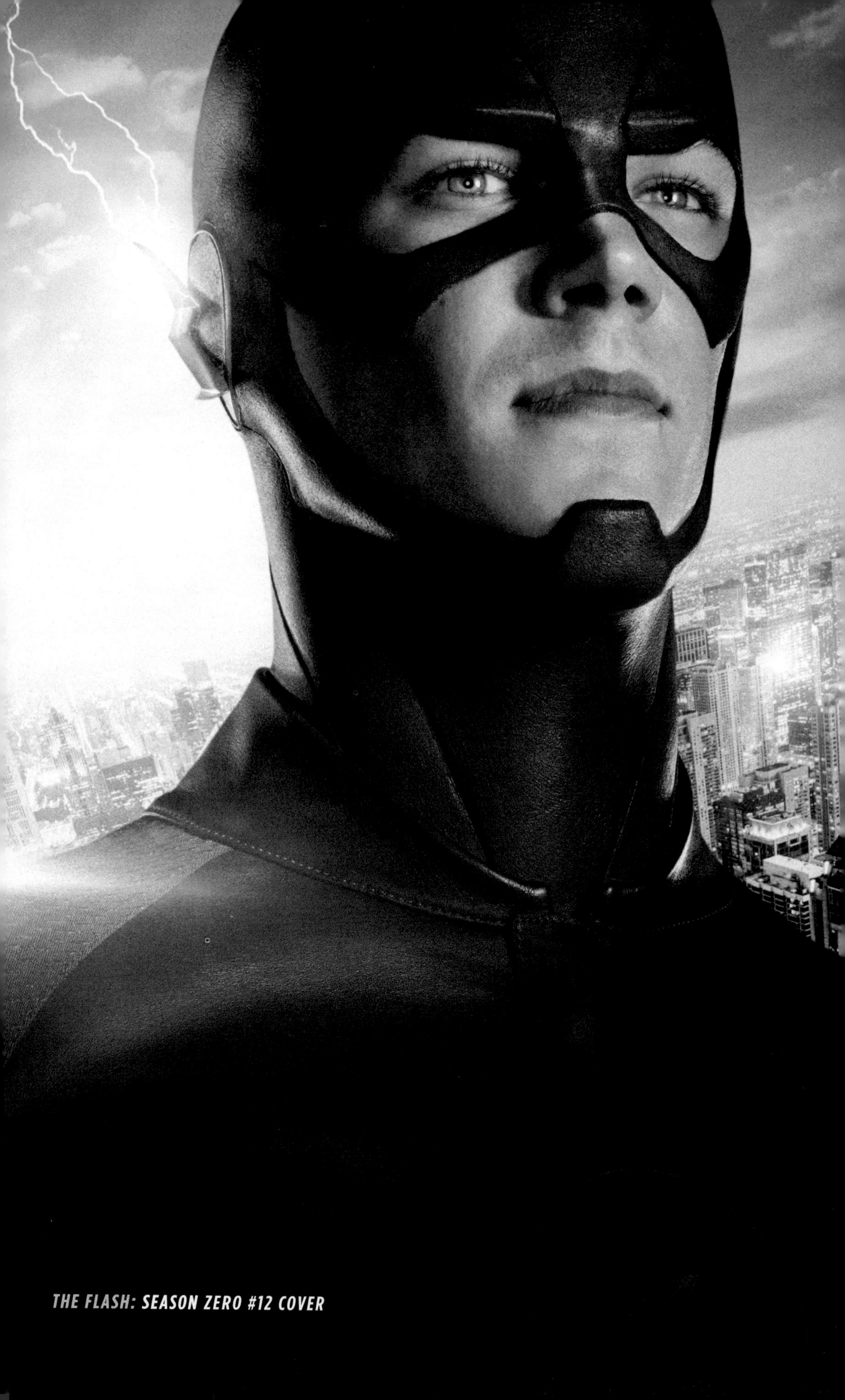

THE FLASH: SEASON ZERO #12 COVER

START AT THE BEGINNING!

THE FLASH
VOLUME 1: MOVE FORWARD

THE FLASH VOL. 2:
ROGUES REVOLUTION

THE FLASH VOL. 3:
GORILLA WARFARE

JUSTICE LEAGUE
VOL. 1: ORIGIN

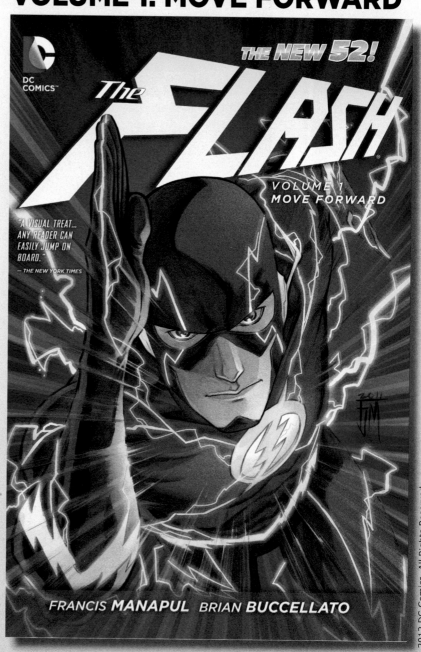

FRANCIS MANAPUL **BRIAN** BUCCELLATO

DC COMICS™

"Impressive."
—MTV SPLASH PAGE

"The Flash couldn't be in better hands."
—NEWSARAMA

"Geoff Johns on THE FLASH has been a true boon for the Scarlet Speedster, putting him right up there in popularity with the likes of Batman, Superman and Green Lantern."
—USA TODAY

FROM THE WRITER OF *JUSTICE LEAGUE* AND *GREEN LANTERN*

GEOFF JOHNS

with ETHAN VAN SCIVER

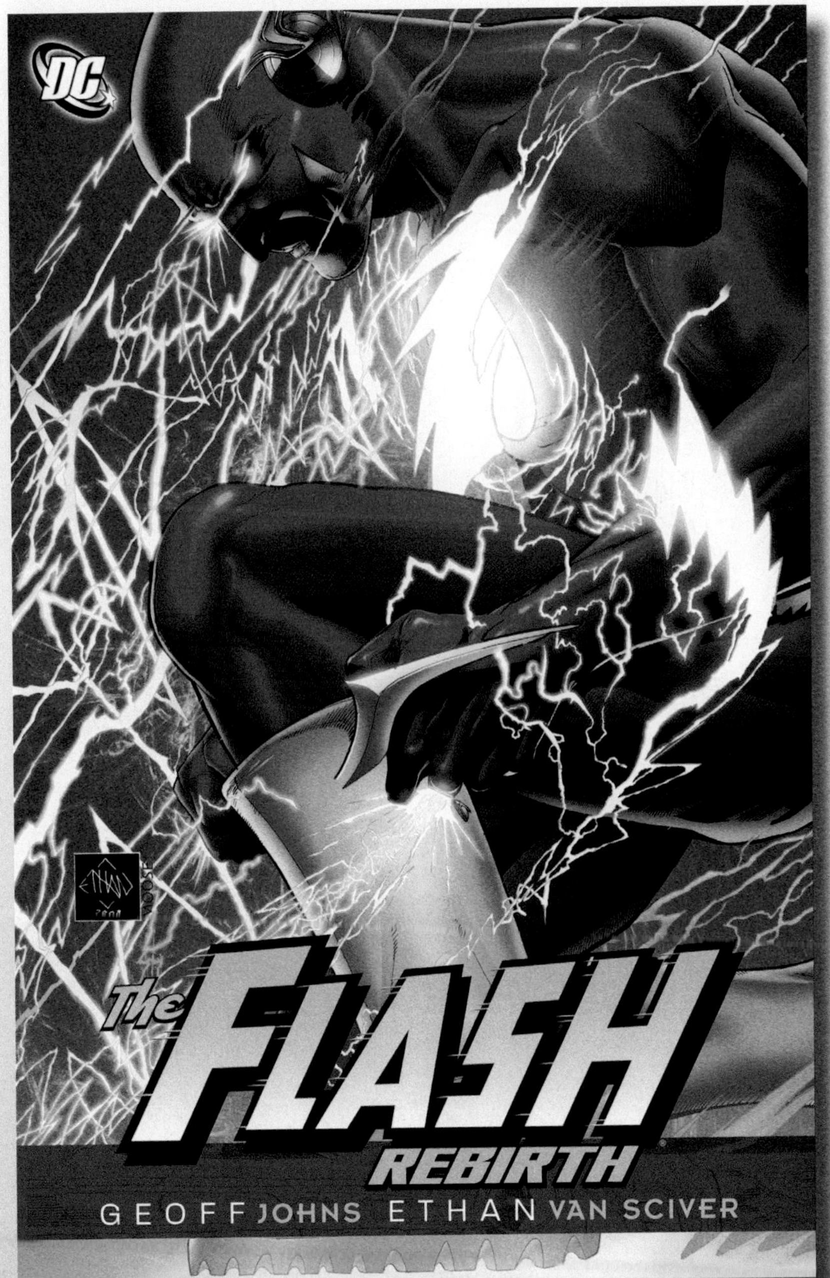

DC
The FLASH
REBIRTH
GEOFF JOHNS ETHAN VAN SCIVER

THE FLASH: THE DASTARDLY DEATH OF THE ROGUES!

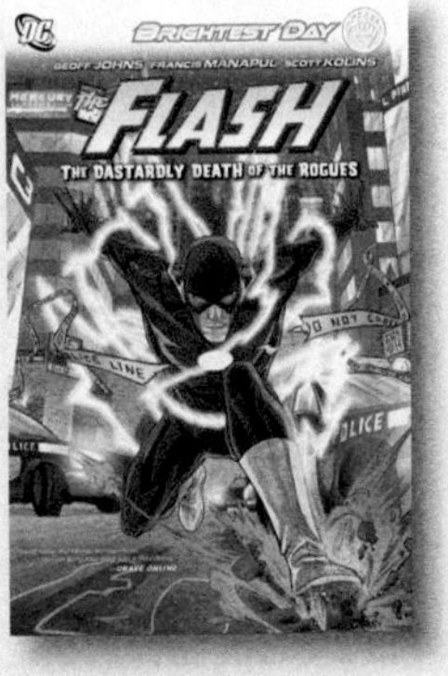

BRIGHTEST DAY
GEOFF JOHNS FRANCIS MANAPUL SCOTT KOLINS
THE FLASH
THE DASTARDLY DEATH OF THE ROGUES

with FRANCIS MANAPUL

THE FLASH: THE ROAD TO FLASHPOINT

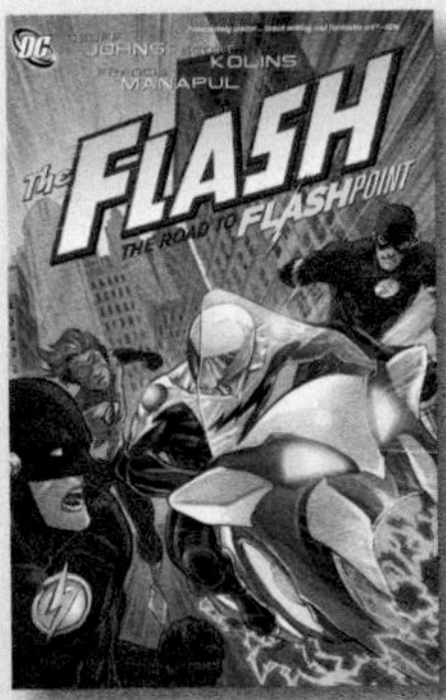

JOHNS
KOLINS
MANAPUL
The FLASH
THE ROAD TO FLASHPOINT

with FRANCIS MANAPUL and SCOTT KOLINS

FLASHPOINT

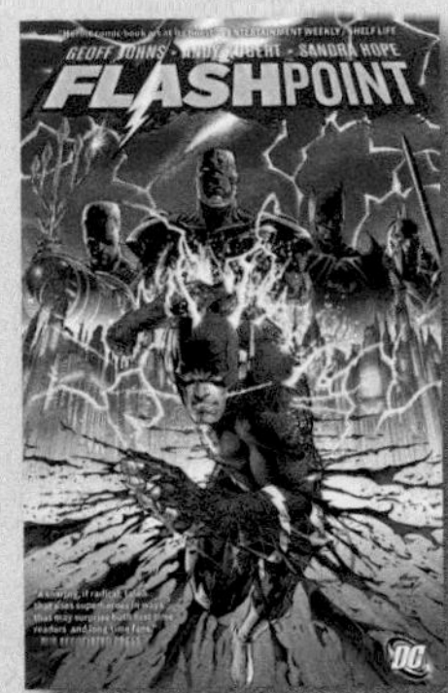

GEOFF JOHNS · ANDY KUBERT · SANDRA HOPE
FLASHPOINT

with ANDY KUBERT

"Dynamite."
—IGN

"Intriguing."
—AIN'T IT COOL NEWS

"Comic-book art at its finest."
—ENTERTAINMENT WEEKLY SHELF LIFE

"Ambitious."
—USA TODAY

FLASHPOINT
GEOFF JOHNS with ANDY KUBERT

FLASHPOINT: THE WORLD OF FLASHPOINT FEATURING BATMAN

FLASHPOINT: THE WORLD OF FLASHPOINT FEATURING GREEN LANTERN

READ THE ENTIRE EPIC!

FLASHPOINT

FLASHPOINT: THE WORLD OF FLASHPOINT FEATURING BATMAN

FLASHPOINT: THE WORLD OF FLASHPOINT FEATURING THE FLASH

FLASHPOINT: THE WORLD OF FLASHPOINT FEATURING GREEN LANTERN

FLASHPOINT: THE WORLD OF FLASHPOINT FEATURING SUPERMAN

FLASHPOINT: THE WORLD OF FLASHPOINT FEATURING WONDER WOMAN

"Heroic comic-book art at its finest" – ENTERTAINMENT WEEKLY / SHELF LIFE

GEOFF JOHNS · ANDY KUBERT · SANDRA HOPE

FLASHPOINT

"A soaring, if radical, tale that uses superheroes in ways that may surprise both first-time readers and long-time fans."
– THE ASSOCIATED PRESS

DC COMICS™